LAYTIME AND DEMURRAGE

FOURTH EDITION

LLOYD'S SHIPPING LAW LIBRARY

Series editors: M. T. Wilford and T. G. Coghlin

DATE DUE FOR RETURN

The loan period may be shortened if the item is requested.

LAYTIME AND DEMURRAGE

BY

JOHN SCHOFIELD, M.A.

of Gray's Inn, Barrister

FOURTH EDITION

LONDON   HONG KONG

2000

LLP Professional Publishing
(a trading division of Informa Publishing Group Ltd)
69–77 Paul Street
London EC2A 4LQ

EAST ASIA
LLP Asia
Sixth Floor, Hollywood Centre
233 Hollywood Road
Hong Kong

©

John Schofield
1986, 1990, 1996, 2000

First edition, 1986
Second edition, 1990
Third edition, 1996
Fourth edition, 2000

British Library Cataloguing in Publication Data
A catalogue record
for this book is available
from the British Library

I00204377X   ISBN 1–85978–558–1

Whilst every effort has been made to ensure that the
information contained in this book is correct neither the
author nor LLP Professional Publishing can accept any responsibility
for any errors or omissions or for any consequences
resulting therefrom.

Text set 10 on 12pt Times by
Interactive Sciences, Gloucester
Printed in Great Britain by
MPG Books

To

V.G.S.

L.J.S.   *C.G.S.*

Preface to the Fourth Edition

Since the last edition was published in April 1996, there has continued to be a steady stream of reported judicial and arbitral decisions.

A new edition has provided an opportunity to revise and update the text, particularly in relation to notices of readiness in relation to arrival; the nature of a charterer's duty to enable a vessel to become an arrived ship; always accessible and exclusion clauses; and multiple charterparties, especially in relation to the vegetable oil trade.

The law is stated as at 1 June 2000.

London   JOHN SCHOFIELD
June 2000

Contents

	PAGE
Preface to the Fourth Edition	vii
Table of Cases	xvii
Table of Statutes	xxxvii

CHAPTER 1.   GENERAL PRINCIPLES   1

CHAPTER 2.   LAYTIME CLAUSES—FIXED AND
             CUSTOMARY LAYTIME   9

FIXED LAYTIME   9

Calendar days	10
Conventional days	11
Running days	12
Working days	12
Weather working days	16
Calculation of weather interruptions in weather working days	20
Saturdays and other incomplete days	25
Voylayrules 1993	27
Working days, running hours, running days, weather permitting	27
Working hours, working days of 24 hours, weather permitting	31
Working hours per working day	33
Working days of 24 consecutive hours, working days of 24 running hours, weather permitting	34
Weather working day of 24 consecutive hours	35

LAYTIME BY REFERENCE TO RATES OF WORKING CARGO   36

Rate per working hatch (or available workable hatch)	36
Availability of holds	40
Rate per hatch	41
Rate per hook	42
Laytime expressed as a total daily rate	43
Laytime expressed as a total daily rate basis—a specified number of available workable hatches	47

CUSTOMARY LAYTIME   50

What is a reasonable time?   50
Effect of custom   53
Commencement of the obligation to load/discharge   55
Delays due to charterers/shippers/receivers   57
   Failure to provide a berth on arrival   57
   Failure to have a cargo in readiness   58
   Alternative methods of discharge   59
   Provision of defective cargo   60
Delays arising without the default of either shipowners or charterers   61
   Congestion   61
   Strikes   62
   Actions of port and other authorities   63
   Delay due to other third parties   63
   Weather and other natural phenomena   64
Other terms of the charterparty   65
Where customary laytime is exceeded   65

CHAPTER 3.   COMMENCEMENT OF LAYTIME   67

The specified destination   67
Berth charters   73
Dock charters   74
Port charters   76
   Arrival within the port   77
   At the immediate and effective disposition of the charterer 79

READINESS TO LOAD AND DISCHARGE   92

Physical readiness   93
   Overstowed cargo   99
   Equipment   99
   Other physical matters   102
Legal readiness   102
   Common law   104
   Free pratique and quarantine   105
   Additional requirements   108
   Implied requirements   111
      The Indian cases   111
Notice of Readiness   113
   When and how to be given   114
   Express provisions   115
   Notice in advance of arrival   119
   Time lapse between readiness and commencement of laytime   119
   Notice given before commencement date for laytime   120
   Correctness of notice of readiness   121
   Notice of Readiness and clause 6 of the Asbatankvoy form of charter   124

Acceptance of notice   126
Readiness and readiness   132
Work before laytime commences   134

CHANGES TO THE BEGINNING OF LAYTIME   135

Custom   136
Obstacles created by the charterer   137
    Failure to have cargo available or arrangements for discharge   137
    Congestion due to charterer's other commitments   138
Charterer's duty to act to enable a vessel to become an arrived ship   140
Whether in berth or not   142
Whether in port or not   147
Time lost in waiting for berth to count as laytime   148
How time lost should be counted   153
Time lost in waiting for berth to count in full   153
Norgrain charter—waiting for berth   154
Reachable on arrival/always accessible   154
    Baltic Code 2000   160
    Always accessible—for how long must the berth be accessible?   160
So near thereto as she may safely get   162
    A. Nature of the obstacle   164
    B. Length of time actually spent waiting   165
    C. Length of anticipated delay   166
    D. Degree of risk known to exist   166
    E. How close to the intended port the vessel can get   166
    F. Proportion of cargo to be loaded/discharged at the obstructed port   168
In regular turn/in usual turn   168
Limits of delay   171
Custom and practice   171
Loss of turn   172
Delay after berthing   172
Demurrage in respect of waiting time   172
Time to commence on being reported at the Custom House   173
To be loaded as per colliery guarantee   174

CHAPTER 4.   INTERRUPTIONS AND EXCEPTIONS TO LAYTIME   175

The *contra proferentem* rule   176
General principles   177
Fault of the shipowner   178
    Bunkering   181
    Ballasting and deballasting   182
Non-production of bills of lading   183
Communications with vessel   184
The *Altus*   184
Exclusion of fault   185

General exceptions clauses   186
   "Any other cause beyond the control of charterers"   189
     Cases relating to principle A   189
     Cases relating to principle B   192
     Cases relating to principle C   194
Overtime ordered by port authorities to count as laytime   196
Congestion   197

ADVERSE WEATHER   197

The limits of weather   199
Particular types of weather   200
  Frost   200
  Ice   202
  Surf   204
  Swell   205
  Bore tides   206
Causation and weather   207
Interruptions   207
Exceptions   209
Conoco weather clause   212

HOLIDAYS   213

What is a holiday?   213
  Regulations and law   214
  Custom and practice   216
Particular types of holidays   216
  "General or local holidays"   217
  "Legal holidays"   217
  "Official and local holidays"   217
  "Charterparty holidays"   218
  "Non-working holidays"   218
The BIMCO calendar   219
Holidays and working days   219
Part holidays   220
Saturdays   222
  Overtime   223
  Custom   223
  Local law   224
  Saturdays today   225
  Baltimore Form C Saturday clause   226
  Weekend clause   227
Working in excepted periods   227
  Where provided for   227
  Where not provided for   229

STRIKES 230

Meaning of "strike" 231
Causation 234
  A. Provision of cargo 235
  B. Congestion and consequential delays 235
    Where consequential delay allowed 235
    When consequential delay not allowed 236
  C. Duty to lessen effect 237
    Alternative action 237
    Alternative port 238
    Alternative cargo 239
    Alternative methods of loading/discharging and/or change of berth within the port 240
    Alternative labour 242
  D. Length of delay 243
Centrocon strike clause 244
  First part 245
    The specified causes 245
    Obstructions beyond the control of the charterers in the docks or other loading
      places 246
    Obstructions beyond the control of the charterers on the railways 246
    Stoppages 247
    Riots and civil commotion 248
    Strike or lock-out of any class of workmen essential to the loading/discharging 248
  Second part 249
  Third part 251
  Fourth part 252
Gencon strike clause 252
  First paragraph 253
  Second paragraph 255
  Third paragraph 256

SHIFTING AND LIGHTENING 259

Shifting 259
  From anchorage to berth 259
    Clauses providing for time not to count 260
    Custom 261
    Shifting from anchorages outside the port 261
    Reachable on arrival 262
    The limits of The *Laura Prima* decision 264
  From one berth to another 269
  Enforced shifting 270
  Shifting expenses 271
Warping 274
Lightening 275
  Time used in lightening 277

CHAPTER 5.   OTHER LAYTIME MATTERS   279

COMPLETION OF LAYTIME   279

Dry cargo   282
  Loading   282
  Discharge   286
Liquid cargo   288

AVERAGING AND REVERSING   292

Laytime "averaged"   293
"Reversible" laytime   294
Cases on averaging   294
Cases on reversing   297
Other similar clauses   300

MULTIPLE CHARTERS   300

Are the charters to be read separately or together?   301
Commencement and running of laytime   303
Time lost in waiting for berth   304
Demurrage   308
Carriage of edible vegetable oils   310
  Nomination of loading and discharging berths   310
  Commencement of laytime and waiting time   310
  Laytime and demurrage   310
  Squeegeeing and sweeping   314
  Transhipment   315

CHAPTER 6.   DEMURRAGE   317

Meaning and nature   317
Length of demurrage   319
Rate and payment of demurrage   321
  New Worldscale—Full title: New Worldscale Tanker Nominal Freight Scale   322
  Payment   323
Damages in addition to demurrage   323
Mitigation and proof of loss   331
Default of charterer   333
Default of shipowner   336
Exceptions clauses and demurrage   342
Shifting   346
Half rate demurrage   346
  Storm   348
Notices of readiness, periods of notice and commencement of demurrage   349
Tanker warranties   351
The effect of deviation on demurrage   357
The end of demurrage—permanent and temporary absence from the port   360

LIABILITY FOR DEMURRAGE   362

General principles   362
Incorporation of charterparty terms into bills of lading   364
Liability of shippers, consignees, indorsees and receivers   365
Liability of charterers as bill of lading holders   370
Nature of lien for demurrage   371
Cesser clauses   373
Construction of the charter   374
Effectiveness of the lien   376
Waiver of cesser clause   379
Liabilities before and after shipment   379
Master's rights to claim demurrage   380
Liability of bills of lading holders *inter se*   381
    One calculation or many calculations   381
    How much must each pay?   382
Demurrage time bars   384
Time of payment   386

CHAPTER 7.   DESPATCH   387

Some later cases   391
Notice provisions   392
Reversing and double despatch   393
The Centrocon strike clause   395
Delay after loading or discharging   396

CHAPTER 8.   DETENTION   397

Delay before the vessel reaches its specified destination   398
Delay after arrival at the specified destination and during the running of laytime   404
Delay during the running of demurrage   406
Delay after the end of laytime and/or demurrage   406
Delay by agreement   409
Exception clauses   410
Lien for damages for detention   411

CHAPTER 9.   FRUSTRATION   413

A. Destruction of ship or cargo   415
B. Inordinate delay   416
C. Illegality   422
Self-induced frustration   424
The Law Reform (Frustrated Contracts) Act 1943   424

APPENDIX 425

A. Laytime definitions 425
B. Charterparty Laytime Definitions 1980 427
C. Voyage Charterparty Laytime Interpretation Rules 1993 431
D. Baltic Code 2000 Charterparty and Laytime Terminology and Abbreviations 435

Index 439

Table of Cases

A/B Nordiska Lloyd v. J Brownlie & Co (Hull) Ltd (1925) 30 CC 307; (1925) 22 Ll L Rep 79
(CA) 3.217,
3.303
A/S Uglands Rederi v. The President of India (The Danita) [1976] 2 Lloyd's Rep 377 .... 2.41
A/S Westfal-Larsen & Co v. Russo-Norwegian Transport Co Ltd (1931) 40 Ll L Rep 259 .... 4.175, 4.181
Acatos v. Burns (1878) 3 Ex D 282 .... 2.251
Action SA v. Britannic Shipping Corporation Ltd (The Aegis Britannic), LMLN 148, 4 July 1985 ...... 6.103,
6.242
Adelfa, The (Adelfamar SA v. Mangimi & Martini SpA), LMLN 218, 12 March 1988; [1988] 2 Lloyd's
Rep 466 .... 6.44,
6.50
Adelfamar SA v. Mangimi & Martini SpA (The Adelfa), LMLN 218, 12 March 1988; [1988] 2 Lloyd's
Rep 466 .... 6.44, 6.50
Aden Refinery Co Ltd v. Ugland Management Co Ltd [1986] 2 Lloyd's Rep 336 .... 4.417
Admiral Shipping Co Ltd v. Weidner Hopkins & Co [1916] 1 KB 429 .... 9.19
Adolf Leonhardt, The (R Pagnan & Fratelli v. Finagrain Compagnie Commerciale Agricole et Financière
SA) [1986] 2 Lloyd's Rep 395 .... 3.226, 3.374, 4.100, 4.320
Aegis Britannic, The (Action SA v. Britannic Shipping Corporation Ltd), LMLN 148, 4 July 1985 .. 6.103, 6.242
Aegis Progress, The (Cargill Inc v. Marpro Ltd) [1983] 2 Lloyd's Rep 570 .... 2.154, 2.156, 2.163, 2.202
Aello, The (Agrimpex Hungarian Trading Co for Agricultural Products v. Sociedad Financiera de Bienes
Raices SA) [1957] 2 Lloyd's Rep 423; [1958] 2 Lloyd's Rep 65 (CA); [1961] AC 135; [1960] 1
Lloyd's Rep 623 (HL) 3.48, 3.86, 3.89, 3.92, 3.93, 3.95, 3.96, 3.100, 3.166, 3.168,
3.184, 3.267, 3.345, 3.382, 4.16, 5.121, 7.30
Agamemnon, The [1998] 1 Lloyd's Rep 675 .... 3.263, 3.264
Agios Stylianos, The (Agios Stylianos Compania Naviera SA v. Maritime Associates International Ltd
Lagos) [1975] 1 Lloyd's Rep 426 .... 3.148, 3.393, 5.120, 5.124, 5.125, 5.127, 5.134, 5.135
Agios Stylianos Compania Naviera SA v. Maritime Associates International Ltd Lagos (The Agios
Stylianos) [1975] 1 Lloyd's Rep 426 .... 3.148, 3.393, 5.120, 5.124, 5.125, 5.127, 5.134, 5.135
Agrimpex Hungarian Trading Co for Agricultural Products v. Sociedad Financiera de Bienes Raices SA
(The Aello) [1957] 2 Lloyd's Rep 423; [1958] 2 Lloyd's Rep 65 (CA); [1961] AC 135; [1960] 1
Lloyd's Rep 623 (HL) 3.48, 3.86, 3.89, 3.92, 3.93, 3.95, 3.96, 3.100, 3.166, 3.168,
3.184, 3.267, 3.345, 3.382, 4.16, 5.121, 7.30
Akties Adalands v. Whittaker (1913) 18 CC 229 .... 4.325
Akties Glittre v. Gabriel, Wade & English (1926) 24 Ll L Rep 372 .... 2.221, 2.224, 2.269
Akties Laboremus v. Steava Française (1925) 21 Ll L Rep 381 .... 3.223
Aktieselskabet Dampskibs Cleveland v. Horsley, Smith & Co Ltd (1923) 16 Ll L Rep 323 .... 2.272
Aktieselskabet Hekla v. Bryson, Jameson & Co (1908) 14 CC 1 .... 2.237
Aktieselskabet Inglewood v. Millar's Karri and Jarrah Forests Ltd (1903) 8 CC 196 .... 3.334
Aktieselskabet Olivebank v. Dansk Svovlsyre Fabrik Ltd [1919] 1 KB 388; [1919] 2 KB 162 .... 3.7, 3.12
Aktieselskabet Reidar v. Arcos Ltd (1926) 25 Ll L Rep 30; [1927] 1 KB 352; (1926) 25 Ll L Rep 513
(CA) 6.5, 6.16, 6.17, 6.28, 6.30, 6.31, 6.34, 6.36, 6.37, 6.38, 6.42, 6.43, 6.66
Alaska, The (Medtank Ltd v. Adam Maritime Corporation) (NV Arb), LMLN 452, 1 March 1997 ...... 4.168
Albion, The (President of India v. Davenport Marine Panama SA) [1987] 2 Lloyd's Rep 365 .... 3.203, 3.205
Aldebaran Compania Maritima SA v. Aussenhandel AG (The Darrah) [1974] 2 Lloyd's Rep 435; [1976]
1 Lloyd's Rep 285 (CA); [1977] AC 157; [1976] 2 Lloyd's Rep 359 (HL) 2.41, 2.55, 2.100,
2.102, 3.379, 3.381, 3.383, 3.384, 3.389, 3.390, 3.392, 3.399, 3.427, 4.156, 4.158,
4.159, 5.99, 5.136
Alhambra, The (1881) 6 PD 68 .... 4.456, 4.457
Allen v. Coltart (1883) 11 QBD 782 .... 6.206

Alma Shipping Co SA *v.* V M Salgaoncar E Irmaos Ltda [1954] 1 Lloyd's Rep 220 .... 5.77, 5.83, 5.85
Altus, The (Black Swan Inc *v.* Castle Supply and Marketing Inc) (NY Arb), LMLN 275, 19 May 1990 ..... 4.407
Altus, The (Total Transport Corporation of Panama *v.* Amoco Trading Co), LMLN 140, 14 March 1985;
    [1985] 1 Lloyd's Rep 423 .... 4.47, 5.66, 6.31, 6.32, 6.41, 6.42, 6.110, 6.127
Alvion Steamship Corporation Panama *v.* Galban Lobo Trading Co SA of Havana (The Rubystone)
    [1954] 2 Lloyd's Rep 309; [1955] 1 Lloyd's Rep 9 (CA) 2.27, 2.28, 2.31, 2.32, 2.46, 2.52,
                                                    2.61, 2.62, 2.63, 2.79, 2.90, 7.19
Amiral Fahri Engin, The (Sale Corporation of Monrovia *v.* Turkish Cargo Lines General Manager) [1993]
    1 Lloyd's Rep 75 .... 3.194, 3.417
Amstelmolen, The (NV Reederij Amsterdam *v.* President of India) [1960] 2 Lloyd's Rep 82; [1961] 2
    Lloyd's Rep 1 (CA) 3.362, 4.98, 4.320, 6.67
Anderson *v.* Anderson [1895] 1 Q3 749 .... 4.73
Angelos Lusis, The (Sociedad Carga Oceanica SA *v.* Idolinoele Vertriebsgesellschaft mbH) [1964] 2
    Lloyd's Rep 28 .... 3.403, 3.426, 4.395, 4.413, 8.20
Anglo-Danubian Transport Co Ltd *v.* Ministry of Food (1949) 83 Ll L Rep 137 .... 3.12
Anglo-Oriental Navigation Co Ltd *v.* T & J Brocklebank Ltd (1927) 27 Ll L Rep 359 .... 6.238
Anna Ch, The (Islamic Republic of Iran Shipping Lines *v.* The Royal Bank of Scotland plc) [1987] 1
    Lloyd's Rep 266 .... 6.95
Antalya, The (Oceansky Co Ltd *v.* Hugo New & Sons Inc) (NY Arb), LMLN 291, 29 December 1990 ..... 3.12,
                                                     6.50
Antclizo Shipping Corporation *v.* Food Corporation of India (The Antclizo) (No 2) [1991] 2 Lloyd's Rep
    485; [1992] 1 Lloyd's Rep 558 (CA) 3.205, 6.287
Ante Topic, The (Compania Naviera Termar SA *v.* Tradax Export SA) [1965] 1 Lloyd's Rep 198; [1965]
    2 Lloyd's Rep 79 (CA); [1966] 1 Lloyd's Rep 566 (HL) 4.392, 4.393, 4.429
Apollon, The (NZ Michalos *v.* The Food Corporation of India) [1983] 1 Lloyd's Rep 409 .... 3.202
Apostolis, The [1999] 2 Lloyd's Rep. 292 .... 2.179, 4.92
Arden Steamship Co *v.* Andrew Weir & Co (1905) 11 CC 26; [1905] AC 501 .... 2.240, 2.244, 4.274
Arden Steamship Co *v.* Mathwin & Son, 1912 SC 215 .... 4.275
Argobeam, The (J C Carras & Sons (Shipbrokers) Ltd *v.* President of India) [1970] 1 Lloyd's Rep
    282 .... 5.41, 8.55
Argonaut Navigation Co Ltd *v.* Ministry of Food (1948) 81 Ll L Rep 371; (1949) 82 Ll L Rep 223
    (CA) 5.22, 5.23, 5.25, 6.61, 6.66
Armada Lines Continent Mediterranean Service Ltd *v.* Naviera Murueta SA (The Elexalde) [1985] 2
    Lloyd's Rep 485 .... 4.355
Armement Adolf Deppe *v.* John Robinson & Co Ltd [1917] KB 204 .... 3.152, 3.153
Ashcroft *v.* Crow Orchard Colliery Co (1874) LR 9 QB 540 .... 2.208, 2.211
Associated Bulk Carriers Ltd *v.* Shell International Petroleum Co Ltd (The Nordic Navigator) [1984] 2
    Lloyd's Rep 182 .... 6.85
Athamas, The (Athamas (Owners), The *v.* Dig Vijay Cement Co Ltd) [1962] 2 Lloyd's Rep 120; [1963]
    1 Lloyd's Rep 287 (CA) 3.443, 3.444, 3.452, 3.456, 3.457, 3.460, 3.461, 3.462, 3.463
Athamas (Owners), The *v.* Dig Vijay Cement Co Ltd (The Athamas) [1962] 2 Lloyd's Rep 120; [1963]
    1 Lloyd's Rep 287 (CA) 3.443, 3.444, 3.452, 3.456, 3.457, 3.460, 3.461, 3.462, 3.463
Athinoula, The (Bravo Maritime (Chartering) Est *v.* Alsayed Abdullah Mohamed Baroom) [1980] 2
    Lloyd's Rep 481 .... 6.240
Atkinson *v.* Ritchie (1809) 10 East 530 .... 4.111
Atlantic Sun, The (Fury Shipping Co Ltd *v.* State Trading Corporation of India Ltd) [1972] 1 Lloyd's Rep
    509 .... 5.89, 5.95, 7.28
Atlantic Sunbeam, The (Sunbeam Shipping Co Ltd *v.* President of India) [1973] 1 Lloyd's Rep
    482 .... 3.166, 3.200, 3.277, 3.327, 3.339, 3.341, 3.342, 3.344, 3.345, 5.48, 6.48, 8.22, 8.51
Austin Friars, The (1894) 10 TLR 633 .... 3.174
Australian Wheat Board *v.* British India Steam Navigation Co Ltd and Associated Companies (1923) 14
    Ll L Rep 117 .... 7.17

BHP Petroleum Ltd *v.* British Steel plc and Dalmine SpA [1999] 2 Lloyd's Rep 583 .... 4.12
BTP Tioxide Ltd *v.* Pioneer Shipping Ltd. *See* Pioneer Shipping Ltd *v.* BTP Tioxide Ltd.
Balian *v.* Joly, Victoria & Co (1890) 6 TLR 345 .... 6.169
Bank Line Ltd *v.* Arthur Capel & Co [1919] AC 435 .... 9.9, 9.43, 9.48
Bargate Steam Shipping Co Ltd *v.* Penlee & St Ives Stone Quarries Ltd (1921) 6 Ll L Rep 71 .... 2.227,
                                                     2.232
Barque Quilpue Ltd *v.* Brown (1903) 9 CC 13 .... 2.239, 3.337, 3.479

Barrie v. Peruvian Corporation (1896) 2 CC 50 .... 4.8

Bastifell v. Lloyd (1862) 1 H & C 388 .... 3.457

Batis, The (Batis Maritime Corporation v. Petroleos Mediterraneo SA), LMLN 263, 2 December 1989;
[1990] 1 Lloyd's Rep 345 .... 3.13, 3.17

Bedford Steamship Co Ltd v. Navico AG (The Ionian Skipper) [1977] 2 Lloyd's Rep 273 .... 6.39

Bennetts & Co v. J & A Brown (1907) 13 CC 110 .... 2.48, 2.51, 4.132

Black Swan Inc v. Castle Supply and Marketing Inc (The Altus) (NY Arb), LMLN 275, 19 May 1990 ...... 4.407, 6.110

Blight v. Page (1801) 3 B & P 295n 4.7

Blue Anchor Line Ltd v. Alfred C Toepfer International GmbH (The Union Amsterdam) [1982] 2 Lloyd's
Rep 432 .... 4.20, 4.49, 4.52, 4.56, 6.88, 6.91

Bocimar NV v. Bayway Refining Co (The Permeke), LMLN 416, 14 October 1995 .... 3.191

Bonde, The (Richo International Ltd v. Alfred C Toepfer International GmbH) [1991] 1 Lloyd's Rep
136 .... 6.32, 6.43, 6.44

Boral Gas, The (Rashtriya Chemicals and Fertilizers Ltd v. Huddart Parker Industries Ltd) [1988] 1
Lloyd's Rep 342 .... 3.342, 6.223, 6.243, 8.1, 8.21

Boukadora, The (Boukadora Maritime Corporation v. Société Anonyme Marocaine de L'Industrie et du
Raffinage) [1989] 1 Lloyd's Rep 393 .... 5.60, 8.56

Bow Princess, The (NY Arb), LMLN 349, 20 March 1993 .... 6.158

Brandt v. Liverpool, Brazil and River Plate Steam Navigation Co Ltd (1923) 29 CC 57 (CA) ... 6.166, 6.206, 6.208

Brankelow Steamship Co Ltd v. Canton Insurance Office Ltd; sub nom. Williams & Co and the
Brankelow Steamship Co Ltd v. Canton Insurance Office Ltd [1899] 2 QB 178; [1901] AC 462
(HL) 6.246

Brankelow Steamship Co Ltd v. Lamport & Holt (The Highfield) [1897] 1 QB 570; (1897) 2 CC
89 .... 2.47, 2.50, 2.60, 4.252

Bravo Maritime (Chartering) Est v. Alsayed Abdullah Mohamed Baroom (The Athinoula) [1980] 2
Lloyd's Rep 481 .... 6.240

Brereton v. Chapman (1831) 7 Bing 559 .... 3.66

Brightman & Co v. Bunge y Born Ltda Sociedad. See H A Brightman & Co v. Bunge y Born Ltda
Sociedad.

British and Mexican Shipping Co Ltd v. Lockett Brothers & Co Ltd (1910) 16 CC 75; [1911] 1 KB 264
(CA) 2.26, 2.30, 2.51, 4.133, 4.174

British Steel Corporation v. National Dock Labour Board [1971] 2 Lloyd's Rep 439 (CA) 4.118

Brouncker v. Scott (1811) 4 Taunt 1 .... 6.260

Brown v. Johnson (1842) 10 M & W 331 .... 3.68

Brunner v. Webster (1900) 5 CC 167 .... 9.42

Brutus v. Cozens [1972] 3 WLR 521 .... 4.102

Bryden v. Niebuhr (1884) C & E 241 .... 6.216

Budgett & Co v. Binnington & Co [1891] 1 QB 35 .... 4.25, 4.32, 6.56, 6.70, 6.72, 6.78, 6.79, 6.83

Bulk Shipping AG v. Ipco Trading SA (The Jasmine B) [1992] 1 Lloyd's Rep 39 .... 3.14

Bulman & Dickson v. Fenwick & Co [1893] 1 QB 179 .... 4.286

Burmester v. Hodgson (1810) 2 Camp 488 .... 2.206, 2.207, 2.254

Burnett Steamship Co Ltd v. Joint Danube & Black Sea Shipping Agencies [1933] 2 KB 438; (1933) 46
Ll L Rep 231 (CA) 2.22, 2.53, 4.152

Burnett Steamship Co Ltd v. Olivier & Co Ltd (1934) 48 Ll L Rep 238 .... 3.220

C A Van Liewen v. Hollis Bros & Co Ltd (The Lizzie) (1918) 23 CC 332; (1918) 24 CC 117 (CA); (1919)
1 Ll L Rep 529; (1919) 25 CC 83 (HL) 2.208, 2.215, 2.222, 2.223, 2.237, 6.269, 6.270

California and Hawaiian Sugar Co v. The National Cereal and Produce Board of Kenya (The Sugar
Islander), (NY Arb), LMLN 318, 11 January 1992 .... 8.40

Caltex Oil (Australia) Pty Ltd v. Howard Smith Industries Pty Ltd (The Howard Smith) [1973] 1 Lloyd's
Rep 544 .... 4.80

Camelia, The and The Magnolia (Magnolia Shipping Co Ltd of Limassol v. Joint Venture of the
International Trading & Shipping Enterprises and Kinship Management Co Ltd of Brussels) [1978]
2 Lloyd's Rep 182 .... 2.98, 2.99, 2.102, 4.154, 4.156, 4.158, 4.160

Cantiere Navale Triestina v. Handelsvertretung der Russe Soviet Republik Naphtha Export (1925) 21
Ll L Rep 204 (CA) 4.432, 6.180

Capper & Co v. Wallace Brothers (1880) 5 QBD 163 .... 3.453

Carga del sur Compania Naviera SA *v.* Ross T Smyth & Co Ltd (The Seafort) [1962] 2 Lloyd's Rep 147 .. 3.348
Cargill Inc *v.* Marpro Ltd (The Aegis Progress) [1983] 2 Lloyd's Rep 570 .... 2.154, 2.156, 2.163, 2.202
Cargill Inc *v.* Rionda de Pass Ltd (The Giannis Xilas) [1982] 2 Lloyd's Rep 511 .... 2.158, 2.163, 2.196
Carlton Steamship Co Ltd *v.* Castle Mail Packets Co Ltd (1897) 2 CC 286; (1898) 3 CC 207 (CA); [1898]
   AC 486 (HL) 2.213, 2.270, 2.273, 2.274, 3.45, 3.337
Carron Park, The (1890) 15 PD 203 .... 4.54, 6.89
Castel and Latta *v.* Trechman (1884) 1 C & E 276 .... 3.452
Castlegate Steamship Co Ltd *v.* Dempsey [1892] 1 QB 854 (CA) 2.221, 2.257, 2.278
Cawthron *v.* Trickett (1864) 15 CB(NS) 754 .... 6.261
Cazalet *v.* Morris [1916] Sc 952 .... 6.57
Central Argentine Railway Ltd *v.* Marwood [1915] AC 981 (HL) 4.272, 4.308
Chadwick Weir & Co Ltd *v.* Louis Dreyfus & Co (1923) 14 Ll L Rep 108 .... 7.33
Chandra, The (Valla Giovanni & C SpA *v.* Gebr Van Weelde Scheepvaartkantoor BV) [1985] 1 Lloyd's
   Rep 563 .... 4.90, 4.325
Chandris *v.* Government of India [1955] 2 Lloyd's Rep 212; [1956] 1 Lloyd's Rep 11 (CA) 5.35, 5.38,
                                                           5.40, 8.55
Chandris *v.* Isbrandtsen-Moller Co Inc (1950) 83 Ll L Rep 385 .... 6.31, 6.33, 6.34
Charlton Steam Shipping Co *v.* T W Allen & Sons and Gabriel, Wade & English (1921) 9 Ll L Rep 148 ... 2.232
Chief Controller of Chartering of the Government of India *v.* Central Gulf Steamship Corporation (The
   Mosfield) [1968] 2 Lloyd's Rep 173 .... 4.175, 4.177, 4.178, 4.205, 4.218, 4.227, 4.233
Chios Faith, The (Sunward Overseas SA *v.* Cargill Inc) (NY Arb), LMLN 349, 20 March 1993 .... 4.166
Christensen *v.* Hindustan Steel Ltd [1971] 1 Lloyd's Rep 395 .... 3.149, 3.252, 3.253, 3.256
Christos, The (EG Cornelius & Co Ltd *v.* Christos Maritime Co Ltd) [1995] 1 Lloyd's Rep 106 5.166, 6.191
Chrysovalandov Dyo, The [1981] 1 Lloyd's Rep 159 .... 8.27
Cia Argentina de Pesca *v.* Eagle Oil & Shipping Co Ltd (1939) 65 Ll L Rep 168 .... 6.142
Clerco Compania Naviera SA *v.* The Food Corporation of India (The Savvas) [1981] 1 Lloyds Rep 155;
   [1982] 1 Lloyd's Rep 22 (CA) 2.178, 2.179, 4.467, 4.471
Clink *v.* Hickie, Borman & Co (No 2) (1899) 4 CC 292 .... 6.98
Clink *v.* Radford & Co [1891] 1 QB 625 (CA) 6.234, 6.249, 8.65, 8.66
Clydebank Engineering & Shipbuilding Co Ltd *v.* Don Jose Ramos Yzquierdo y Castoneda [1905]
   AC 6 .... 6.50
Cobelfret NV *v.* Cyclades Shipping Co Ltd (The Linardos) [1994] 1 Lloyd's Rep 28 .... 3.142, 3.145
Cochran *v.* Retberg (1800) 3 Esp 121 .... 2.13, 2.24, 4.200
Commercial Steamship Co *v.* Boulton (1875) LR 10 QB 346 .... 2.9, 6.22
Compagnie Chemin de Fer du Midi *v.* A Bromage & Co (1921) 6 Ll L Rep 178 .... 3.43
Compania Argentina de Navegación de Ultramar *v.* Tradax Export SA (The Puerto Rocca) [1978] 1
   Lloyd's Rep 252 .... 3.188, 3.492
Compania Crystal de Vapores *v.* Herman & Mohatta (India) Ltd (The Maria G) [1958] 1 Lloyd's Rep
   616 .... 2.56, 4.110, 4.114, 4.140, 4.149, 4.431, 4.435, 4.440
Compania de Naviera Nedelka SA *v.* Tradax International SA (The Tres Flores) [1973] 2 Lloyd's Rep
   247 (CA) 3.128, 3.131, 3.132, 3.141, 3.142, 3.169, 3.248, 3.286
Compania de Navigación Zita SA *v.* Louis Dreyfus & Cie (The Corfu Island) [1953] 2 Lloyd's Rep
   472 .... 1.33, 2.150, 2.151, 2.153, 2.163, 2.196, 2.202, 7.2
Compania Naviera Azuero SA *v.* British Oil & Cake Mills Ltd [1957] 2 QB 293; [1957] 1 Lloyd's Rep
   312 .... 2.41, 2.47, 2.53, 2.54, 2.181, 4.117, 4.150, 6.264, 6.267, 6.272, 7.5
Compania Naviera Termar SA *v.* Tradax Export SA (The Ante Topic) [1965] 1 Lloyd's Rep 198; [1965]
   2 Lloyd's Rep 79 (CA); [1966] 1 Lloyd's Rep 566 (HL) 4.392, 4.393, 4.429
Conrad Alfred Van Liewen *v.* Hollis Bros & Co Ltd. *See* C A Van Liewen *v.* Hollis Bros & Co Ltd.
Constantine Line *v.* Imperial Smelting Corporation [1942] AC 164 (HL) 9.49
Continental Grain Co *v.* Armour Fertiliser Works, Fed Supp 49 (1938) 6.67
Cordelia, The [1909] P 27 .... 3.470, 3.483
Corfu Island, The (Compania de Navegación Zita SA *v.* Louis Dreyfus & Cie) [1953] 2 Lloyd's Rep
   472 .... 1.33, 2.150, 2.151, 2.153, 2.163, 2.196, 2.202, 7.2
Corrado Società Anonima di Navigazione *v.* Expothleb (1932) 43 Ll L Rep 509 .... 4.219
Cosmar Compania Naviera SA *v.* Total Transport Corporation (The Isabelle) [1982] 2 Lloyd's Rep 81;
   [1984] 1 Lloyd's Rep 366 (CA) 4.134, 4.445
Crawford and Rowat *v.* Wilson, Sons & Co (1895) 1 CC 154 .... 4.66
Crossman *v.* Burrill, 179 US 100 (1900) 6.67
Cunard Carrier, Eleranta and Martha, The [1977] 2 Lloyd's Rep 261 .... 6.220, 6.231, 6.250
Curley (James) *v.* Barrellier & Francastel (1923) 16 Ll L Rep 42 .... 9.27

D A Stathatos Steamship Co Ltd *v.* Cordoba Central Railway Co Ltd (1931) 40 Ll L Rep 274 .... 4.304

D/S A/S Gulnes v. ICI Ltd (1937) 59 Ll L Rep 144 .... 9.15
Dahl v. Nelson. See Nelson v. Dahl.
Dahl (Robert H) v. Nelson, Donkin. See Nelson v. Dahl.
D'Amico Mediterranean Pacific Line Inc v. Procter and Gamble Manufacturing Co (The Giovanni
    D'Amico) [1975] 1 Lloyd's Rep 202 .... 6.58
Damodar General T J Park and King Theras, The (Mosvolds Rederi A/S v. Food Corporation of India)
    [1986] 2 Lloyd's Rep 68 .... 3.108
Dampskibsselskabet Botnia A/S v. C P Bell & Co [1932] 2 KB 569; (1931) 41 Ll L Rep 160 .... 2.53,
                                                                                                            4.129, 4.135
Dampskibsselskabet Svendborg v. Love & Stewart Ltd, 1915 SC 543 .... 4.333
Danita, The (A/S Uglands Rederi v. The President of India) [1976] 2 Lloyd's Rep 377 .... 2.41
Darrah, The (Aldebaran Compania Maritima SA v. Aussenhandel AG [1974] 2 Lloyd's Rep 435; [1976]
    1 Lloyd's Rep 285 (CA), [1977] AC 157; [1976] 2 Lloyd's Rep 359 (HL) 2.41, 2.55,
                        2.100, 2.102, 3.379, 3.381, 3.383, 3.384, 3.389, 3.390, 3.392, 3.399, 3.427, 4.156,
                                                                                     4.158, 4.159, 5.99, 5.136
Davies v. McVeagh (1879) 4 Ex D 265 .... 3.43, 3.70
Davies-Evans v. Ladoga Ltd (The Kingsland) (1910) 16 CC 18 .... 2.267
Davis v. Garrett (1830) 6 Bing 716 .... 6.169
Davis Contractors Ltd v. Fareham Urban District Council [1956] AC 696 .... 9.13, 9.33
Delian Leto, The (The Food Corporation of India v. Carras Shipping Co Ltd) [1983] 2 Lloyd's Rep
    496 .... 2.179, 3.202, 6.101
Delian Spirit, The (Shipping Developments Corporation SA v. V/O Sojuzneftexport) [1971] 1 Lloyd's
    Rep 64; [1971] 1 Lloyd's Rep 506 (CA) 3.98, 3.99, 3.176, 3.177, 3.340, 3.410,
                                               3.411, 3.427, 4.394, 5.4, 7.2, 8.19, 8.20, 8.30
Demosthenes v. The (Gerani Compania Naviera SA v. General Organization for Supply Goods) (No 1)
    [1982] 1 Lloyd's Rep 275 .... 3.160
Demosthenes v. The (Gerani Compania Naviera SA v. Alfred C Toepfer) (No 2) [1982] 1 Lloyd's Rep
    282 .... 6.251
Denniston & Co v. Zimmerman (1894) 11 TLR 113 .... 4.185
Denny, Mott & Dickson Ltd v. Jas B Fraser & Co [1944] AC 265 (HL) 9.3, 9.11
Dias, The (Dias Compania Naviera SA v. Louis Dreyfus Corporation) [1976] 2 Lloyd's Rep 395; [1977]
    1 Lloyd's Rep 485 (CA); [1978] 1 Lloyd's Rep 325; [1978] 1 WLR 261 (HL) 6.6, 6.18, 6.20, 6.101
Dias Compania Naviera SA v. Louis Dreyfus Corporation (The Dias) [1976] 2 Lloyd's Rep 395; [1977]
    1 Lloyd's Rep 485 (CA); [1978] 1 Lloyd's Rep 325; [1978] 1 WLR 261 (HL) 6.6, 6.18, 6.20, 6.101
Dickinson v. Martini & Co (1874) 1 R (Sess Cas) 1185 .... 4.461
Dimech v. Corlett (1858) 12 Moo PC 199 .... 6.11
Dow Chemical (Nederland) BV v. BP Tanker Co Ltd (The Vorras) [1983] 1 Lloyd's Rep 579
    (CA) ... 2.3, 2.45, 2.92, 2.96, 2.101, 2.103, 2.105, 2.108, 2.109, 2.139, 2.143, 4.146, 4.147, 4.153, 4.159
Dreyfus & Co v. Tempus Shipping Co [1931] AC 726 (HL) 4.55, 6.90
Dunlop & Sons v. Balfour, Williamson & Co [1892] 1 QB 507 (CA) 6.235, 8.65, 8.67

E B Aaby's Rederi A/S v. LEP Transport Ltd (1948) 81 Ll L Rep 465 .... 9.17
E G Cornelius & Co Ltd v. Christos Maritime Co Ltd (The Christos) [1995] 1 Lloyd's Rep 106 .... 5.166, 6.191
Eastern City, The (Leeds Shipping Co Ltd v. Société Française Bunge) [1958] 2 Lloyd's Rep 127 ...... 4.442
Eleni 2, The (Lemythou Compania Naviera SA v. Ahmed Bamaodah) [1985] 1 Lloyd's Rep 107 .... 6.207
Elevit, The (Hanjin Shipping Co Ltd v. R J International Inc) (NY Arb), LMLN 372, 5 February 1994 ...... 9.39
Elexalde, The (Armada Lines Continent Mediterranean Service Ltd v. Naviera Murueta SA) [1985]
    2 Lloyd's Rep 485 .... 4.355
Elli 2, The (Ilyssia Compania Naviera SA v. Ahmed Bamaodah) [1985] 1 Lloyd's Rep 107 .... 6.207
Ellis Shipping Corp v. Voest Alpine Intertrading (The Lefthero) [1991] 2 Lloyd's Rep 599; [1992]
    2 Lloyd's Rep 109 (CA) 4.62, 6.108
Embiricos v. Sydney Reid & Co (1914) 19 CC 263 .... 9.22
Epaphus, The (Eurico SpA v. Philipp Brothers) [1986] 2 Lloyd's Rep 387; [1987] 2 Lloyd's Rep 215
    (CA) 3.7, 3.9, 3.10, 3.132
Etabllissements Soules et Cie v. Intertradax SA (The Handy Mariner) [1991] 1 Lloyd's Rep 378; LMLN
    288, 17 November 1990 .... 3.36
Ethel Radcliffe Steamship Co v. W R Barnett Ltd (1926) 24 Ll L Rep 277 (CA) 6.17, 8.10
Eugenia, The [1964] 2 QB 226 .... 9.11
Eurico SpA v. Philipp Brothers (The Epaphus) [1986] 2 Lloyd's Rep 387; [1987] 2 Lloyd's Rep 215
    (CA) 3.7, 3.9, 3.10, 3.132
Eurus, The [1998] 1 Lloyd's Rep 351 .... 5.8
Evans v. Forster (1830) 1 B & Ad 118 .... 6.260

Evia, The (Kodros Shipping Corporation v. Empresa Cubana de Fletes) [1982] 3 WLR 637 (HL) 9.6

Fairbridge v. Pace (1844) 1 C & K 317 .... 3.216
Federal Commerce & Navigation Co Ltd v. Tradax Export SA (The Maratha Envoy) [1975] 2 Lloyd's
    Rep 223; [1977] 3 WLR 1372; [1977] 2 Lloyd's Rep 217 (CA); [1977] 2 Lloyd's Rep 301 (HL) 3.105,
                                                                3.106, 3.107, 3.267, 3.269, 3.352, 8.20
Fibrosa Spolka Akcyjna v. Fairbairn, Lawson [1943] AC 32 .... 9.10, 9.43
Fidelitas Shipping Co Ltd v. V/O Exportchleb [1963] 1 Lloyd's Rep 246; [1963] 2 Lloyd's Rep 113
    (CA) 6.193, 6.225, 6.229, 6.246, 6.252, 6.254, 6.257
Field v. Receiver of Metropolitan Police [1907] 2 KB 859 .... 4.329
Fina Supply Ltd v. Shell UK Ltd (The Poitou) [1991] 1 Lloyd's Rep 452 .... 4.165
Finix, The (Nea Tyhi Maritime Co v. Compagnie Grainière SA) [1975] 2 Lloyd's Rep 415 ...... 3.27, 3.389, 3.392
Fitzgerald v. Lona (Owners) (1932) 44 Ll L Rep 212 .... 2.247
Fjordaas, The (K/S Arnt J Moerland v. Kuwait Petroleum Corporation) [1988] 1 Lloyd's Rep 336 ...... 3.416,
                                                                                            3.426, 3.439, 4.419
Fontevivo, The (Gem Shipping Co of Monrovia v. Babanaft (Lebanon) SARL) [1975] 1 Lloyd's Rep
    339 .... 4.23, 4.437
Food Corporation of India, The v. Carras Shipping Co Ltd (The Delian Leto) [1983] 2 Lloyd's Rep
    496 .... 2.179, 3.202, 6.101
Ford v. Cotesworth (1868) LR 4 QB 127; (1870) LR 5 QB 544 .... 2.207, 2.210, 2.264, 4.8, 5.48
Forest Steamship Co Ltd v. Iberian Iron Ore Co Ltd; sub nom. Rhymney Steamship Co Ltd v. Iberian Iron
    Ore Co Ltd (1898) 3 CC 316 (CA); (1899) 5 CC 83 (HL) 2.117, 2.119, 2.121, 2.123, 2.126, 2.137, 2.138
Fornyade Rederiaktiebolaget Commercial v. Blake & Co (1931) 39 Ll L Rep 205 (CA) 3.331, 3.455
Forum Craftsman, The (Islamic Republic of Iran Shipping Lines v. Ierax Shipping Co), LMLN 276, 2
    June 1990; [1991] 1 Lloyd's Rep 81 .... 3.438, 4.62, 6.96, 6.107
France, Fenwick & Co Ltd v. Philip Spackman & Sons (1912) 18 CC 52 .... 4.87
Francesco v. Massey (1873) LR 8 Ex 101 .... 6.255
Franco-British Steamship Co Ltd v. Watson & Youell (1921) 9 Ll L Rep 282 .... 3.217, 3.218, 4.11
Freedom Maritime Corporation v. International Bulk Carriers SA (The Khian Captain) [1985] 2 Lloyd's
    Rep 212 .... 2.41, 4.59
Freijo, The (Logs & Timber Products (Singapore) Pte Ltd v. Keeley Granite (Pty) Ltd) [1978] 1 Lloyd's
    Rep 257; [1978] 2 Lloyd's Rep 1 (CA) 3.63, 3.183, 3.186, 3.187
Furness Bridge, The (Seabridge Shipping Ltd v. Antco Shipping Ltd) [1977] 2 Lloyd's Rep 367 .... 9.46
Fury Shipping Co Ltd v. State Trading Corporation of India Ltd (The Atlantic Sun) [1972] 1 Lloyd's Rep
    509 .... 5.89, 5.95, 7.28

Gardano & Giampieri v. Greek Petroleum George Mamidakis & Co [1961] 2 Lloyd's Rep 259 .... 6.203,
                                                                                                                            6.205
Gardiner v. Macfarlane, M'Crindell & Co (1889) 26 Sc LR 492 .... 6.234, 8.65
Gardner & Sons v. Trechmann (1884) 15 QBD 154 .... 6.193
Gatoil International Inc v. Tradax Petroleum Ltd (The Rio Sun), LMLN 127, 13 September 1984; [1985]
    1 Lloyd's Rep 350 .... 3.23, 6.137, 8.16
Gebr Broere BV v. Saras Chimica SpA [1982] 2 Lloyd's Rep 436 .... 2.55, 2.58, 2.92, 2.102, 2.104,
                                                                2.106, 2.107, 4.161, 4.162, 4.164, 4.431
Geipel v. Smith (1872) LR 7 QB 404 .... 4.111, 9.23
Gem Shipping Co of Monrovia v. Babanaft (Lebanon) SARL (The Fontevivo) [1975] 1 Lloyd's Rep
    339 .... 4.23, 4.437
General Capinpin, Proteus, Free Wave and Dinara, The (President of India v. Jebsens (UK) Ltd) [1987]
    2 Lloyd's Rep 354; [1989] 1 Lloyd's Rep 232 (CA); LMLN 287, 3 November 1990; [1991] 1
    Lloyd's Rep. 1 (HL) 2.192, 2.196, 2.197, 2.198, 2.199, 2.201, 2.203
General Guisan, The (Suisse Atlantique Société d'Armement Maritime SA v. NV Rotterdamsche Kolen
    (Centrale) [1961] 1 Lloyd's Rep 166; [1965] 1 Lloyd's Rep 533 (CA); [1966] 1 Lloyd's Rep 529
    (HL) 6.28, 6.31, 6.35, 6.36, 6.37, 6.38, 6.43, 6.44, 6.49, 6.175
George Mitchell (Chesterhall) Ltd v. Finney Lock Seeds Ltd [1983] 3 WLR 163 .... 4.53
Gerani Compania Naviera SA v. General Organization for Supply Goods (The Demosthenes V) (No 1)
    [1982] 1 Lloyd's Rep 275 .... 3.160
Gerani Compania Naviera SA v. Alfred C Toepfer (The Demosthenes V) (No 2) [1982] 1 Lloyd's Rep
    282 .... 6.251
Giannis Xilas, The (Cargill Inc v. Rionda de Pass Ltd) [1982] 2 Lloyd's Rep 511 .... 2.158, 2.163, 2.196
Gill & Duffus SA v. Rionda Futures Ltd [1994] 2 Lloyd's Rep 67 .... 3.115, 6.224
Giovanni D'Amico, The (D'Amico Mediterranean Pacific Line Inc v. Procter and Gamble Manufacturing
    Co) [1975] 1 Lloyd's Rep 202 .... 6.58

Glen & Co v. Royal Commission on the Sugar Supply (1922) 10 Ll L Rep 510 (CA) 2.239
Glendevon, The [1893] P 269 .... 7.7, 7.10, 7.11, 7.12, 7.15
Good & Co v. Isaacs [1892] 2 QB 555 (CA) 2.222, 2.228, 2.266
Goulandris Brothers Ltd v. B Goldman & Son [1958] 1 QB 74 .... 4.55, 6.90
Government of Ceylon v. Société Franco-Tunisienne d'Armement-Tunis (The Massalia) (No 2) [1960]
   2 Lloyd Rep 352 .... 3.117, 3.148, 3.149, 3.250, 3.260, 3.393, 3.395, 5.113, 5.120,
                                   5.121, 5.123, 5.125, 5.126, 5.127, 5.134, 5.135, 5.136
Graigwen (Owners) v. Anglo-Canadian Shipping Co Ltd [1955] 2 Lloyd's Rep 260 .... 3.248
Grampian Steamship Co Ltd v. Carver & Co (1893) 9 TLR 210 .... 3.159
Grant v. Coverdale (1884) 9 App Cas 470 .... 4.14, 4.15, 4.274
Granvias Oceanicas Armadora SA v. Jibsen Trading Co (The Kavo Peirantis) [1977] 2 Lloyd's Rep
   344 .... 6.241, 6.250
Gray v. Carr (1871) LR 6 QB 522 .... 6.193, 6.234, 8.65
Greenmast Shipping Co SA v. Jean Lion et Cie SA (The Saronikos) [1986] 2 Lloyd's Rep 277 .... 8.59, 8.62
Groves, Maclean & Co v. Volkart Brothers (1885) 1 TLR 454 .... 3.119
Gullischen v. Stewart Brothers (1884) 13 QBD 317 (CA) 6.193, 6.216, 6.218

H A Brightman & Co v. Bunge y Born Ltda Sociedad (1923) 16 Ll L Rep 200; [1924] 2 KB 619; (1924)
   19 Ll L Rep 384 (CA); (1925) 22 Ll L Rep 395 (HL) 4.276, 4.290, 4.291, 4.300, 4.323, 4.327
Hain Steamship Co Ltd v. Canadian Transport Co Ltd (1942) 73 Ll L Rep 80 .... 4.79
Hain Steamship Co Ltd v. Minister of Food (1949) 82 Ll L Rep 386 .... 2.177
Hain Steamship Co Ltd v. Sociedad Anonima Comercial de Exportación e Importación (Louis Dreyfus
   & Cia Ltda) (The Tregantle) (1932) 43 Ll L Rep 136 .... 4.176, 4.191, 4.204
Hain Steamship Co Ltd v. Sociedad Anonima Comercial de Exportación e Importación (Louis Dreyfus
   & Co Ltd) (The Trevarrack) (1934) 49 Ll L Rep 86 .... 2.15, 4.182, 4.229, 4.231, 4.232
Hain Steamship Co Ltd v. Tate and Lyle Ltd (1936) 41 CC 350 .... 6.173
Hall Steamship Co v. Paul (1914) 19 CC 384 .... 4.459
Hamburg Arbitration, LMLN 32, 22 January 1981 .... 4.137
Handy Mariner, The (Establissements Soules et Cie v. Intertradax SA) [1991] 1 Lloyd's Rep 378; LMLN
   288, 17 November 1990 .... 3.36
Hanjin Shipping Co Ltd v. R J International Inc (The Elevit) (NY Arb), LMLN 372, 5 February 1994 .... 9.39
Hans Maersk, The, 266 Fed 806 (1920) 6.67
Hanse Schiffahrtskontor GmbH v. Andre SA. See Heinrich Hanno Co BV v. Fairlight Shipping Co
   Ltd.
Hansen v. Harrold Brothers [1894] 1 QB 612 (CA) 6.236, 6.249, 6.253
Harman v. Clarke (1815) 4 Camp 159 .... 3.222
Harman v. Mant (1815) 4 Camp 161 .... 3.222
Harris v. Best, Ryley & Co (1892) 68 LT 76 (CA) 6.74, 6.80, 6.83
Harris v. Jacobs (1885) 15 QBD 247 .... 6.3
Harris and Dixon v. Marcus Jacobs & Co (1885) 15 QBD 247 .... 8.4
Harrowing v. Dupre (1902) 7 CC 157 .... 2.238, 3.336
Hayton v. Irwin (1879) 5 CPD 130 .... 3.453
Heinrich Hanno Co BV v. Fairlight Shipping Co Ltd; Hanse Schiffahrtskontor GmbH v. Andre SA (The
   Kostas K), LMLN 135, 3 January 1985; [1985] 1 Lloyd's Rep 231 .... 3.24, 8.16
Helle Skov, The (Sofial SA v. Ove Skou Rederi) [1976] 2 Lloyd's Rep 205 .... 3.285, 3.287, 3.288, 4.249
Henry & MacGregor Ltd v. Galbraith & Roy (1940) 66 Ll L Rep 71 .... 4.116, 4.118
Hermine, The (Unitramp v. Garnac Grain Co Inc) [1979] 1 Lloyd's Rep 212 (CA) 9.35
Heyman v. Darwins Ltd [1942] AC 356 .... 6.176
Hick v. Rodocanachi. See Pantland Hick v. Raymond & Reid.
Highfield, The (Brankelow Steamship Co Ltd v. Lamport & Holt [1897] 1 QB 570; (1897) 2 CC
   89 .... 2.47, 2.50, 2.60
Hirji Mulji v Cheong Yue Steamship Co [1926] AC 497 .... 9.50
Hirsley v. Price (1883) 11 QBD 244 .... 3.453
Hogarth (Samuel Crawford) v. Cory Brothers & Co Ltd (1926) 25 Ll L Rep 464 (PC) 3.330, 4.16, 8.13
Holman & Sons v. Peruvian Nitrate Co (1878) 15 SLR 349; (1878) 5 Ct of Sess Cas (4th series)
   657 .... 4.133, 4.252
Horsley Line Ltd v. Roechling Brothers, 1908 SC 866 .... 3.494
Houlder v. General Steam Navigation Co (1862) 3 F & F 170 .... 3.222
Houlder v. Weir (1905) 10 CC 228 .... 2.10, 4.36, 4.253, 4.254, 6.86
Howard Smith, The (Caltex Oil (Australia) Pty Ltd v. Howard Smith Industries Pty Ltd [1973] 1 Lloyd's
   Rep 544 .... 4.80

Hulthen v. Stewart & Co (1901) 6 CC 65; (1902) 7 CC 139 (CA); (1903) 8 CC 297 (HL) 2.230, 2.255,
2.276, 3.75, 3.77, 3.78, 3.79, 3.81
Huyton SA v. Inter Operators SA (The Stainless Emperor) [1994] 2 Lloyd's Rep 298 .... 4.16, 6.102

Ilyssia Compania Naviera SA v. Ahmed Bamaodah (The Elli 2); Kition Compania Naviera SA v. Ahmed
Bamaodah (The Toulla); Lemythou Compania Naviera SA v. Ahmed Bamaodah (The Eleni 2)
[1985] 1 Lloyd's Rep 107 .... 6.207
Imperial Smelting Corporation Ltd v. Joseph Constantine Steamship Line Ltd (1941) 70 Ll L Rep 1
(HL) 9.16
Inca Compania Naviera SA and Commercial and Maritime Enterprises Evanghelos P Nomikos SA v.
Mofinol Inc (The President Brand) [1967] 2 Lloyd's Rep 338 .... 3.390, 3.405, 3.411, 3.416, 3.422,
4.395, 4.402, 4.413, 4.414, 4.416, 4.418, 8.20, 8.30, 8.31
Internationale Guano-En Superphosphaatwerken v. Robert MacAndrew & Co (1909) 14 CC 194 .... 6.170
Inverkip Steamship Co Ltd v. Bunge & Co (1916) 22 CC 147; [1917] 2 KB 193; (1917) 22 CC 200
(CA) 1.14, 6.4, 6.14, 6.15, 6.29, 6.34, 7.2, 8.30, 8.31
Ionian Navigation Co Inc v. Atlantic Shipping Co SA (The Loucas N) [1970] 2 Lloyd's Rep 482; [1971]
1 Lloyd's Rep 215 (CA) 3.387, 3.389, 3.396, 4.320
Ioanian Skipper, The (Bedford Steamship Co Ltd v. Navico AG) [1977] 2 Lloyd's Rep 273 .... 6.39
Isabelle, The (Cosmar Compania Naviera SA v. Total Transport Corporation) [1982] 2 Lloyd's Rep 81;
[1984] 1 Lloyd's Rep 366 (CA) 4.134, 4.445
Islamic Republic of Iran Shipping Lines v. Ierax Shipping Co (The Forum Craftsman), LMLN 276, 2
June 1990; [1991] 1 Lloyd's Rep 81 .... 3.438, 4.62, 6.96, 6.107
Islamic Republic of Iran Shipping Lines v. The Royal Bank of Scotland Plc (The Anna Ch) [1987] 1
Lloyd's Rep 266 .... 6.95
Isles Steam Shipping Co Ltd v. Theodoridi & Co (1926) 24 Ll L Rep 362 .... 9.43

J C Carras & Sons (Shipbrokers) Ltd v. President of India (The Argobeam) [1970] 1 Lloyd's Rep 282 ...... 5.41,
8.55
J Glynn & Son Ltd v. Consorzio Approvvigionamenti Fra Meccanici Ed Affini (1920) 4 Ll L Rep 183 ...... 3.154
J Vermaas Scheepvaartbedriff NV v. Association Technique de L'Importation Charbonnière (The Laga)
[1966] 1 Lloyd's Rep 582 .... 4.270
Jackson v. Union Marine Insurance Co (1874) LR 10 CP 125 .... 6.14
Jag Leela, The (Union of India v. The Great Eastern Shipping Co Ltd), LMLN 242, 11 February 1989 ...... 3.204
Jasmine B, The (Bulk Shipping AG v. Ipco Trading SA) [1992] 1 Lloyd's Rep 39 .... 3.14
Jay Ganesh, The (United Nations Food and Agriculture Organisation World Food Programme v. Caspian
Navigation Inc) [1994] 2 Lloyd's Rep 358 .... 3.146
Jenneson, Taylor & Co v. Secretary of State for India in Council [1916] 2 KB 702 .... 6.237
Jesson v. Solly (1811) 4 Taunt 52 .... 6.260
Johanna Oldendorff, The (Oldendorff (EL) & Co GmbH v. Tradax Export SA [1972] 2 Lloyd's Rep 292
(CA); [1973] 2 Lloyd's Rep 285 (HL) 1.10, 1.18, 1.21, 1.24,
2.231, 3.2, 3.34, 3.47, 3.48, 3.61, 3.67, 3.69, 3.83, 3.86, 3.96, 3.97, 3.100, 3.101,
3.102, 3.104, 3.107, 3.108, 3.111, 3.267, 3.268, 3.269, 3.346, 3.349, 3.350, 3.351,
3.354, 3.357, 3.372, 3.377, 3.382, 3.388, 4.411, 8.20
John and James White v. The Steamship Winchester Co (1886) 23 SLR 342 .... 3.173
John Michalos, The (President of India v. N G Livanos Maritime Co) [1987] 2 Lloyd's Rep 188 .... 6.104,
6.105, 6.106, 6.109
John Sadd & Sons Ltd v. Bertrum Ratcliffe & Co (1929) 34 Ll L Rep 18 .... 3.242
John Stove, The (Sametiet M/T Johs Stove v. Istanbul Petrol Rafinerisi A/S) [1984] 1 Lloyd's Rep 38 ...... 4.59,
4.62, 4.272, 4.280, 6.91
Jones v. Adamson (1876) 1 Ex D 60 .... 3.482
Jones Ltd v. Green & Co (1903) 9 CC 20 .... 2.241
Joseph Thorley Ltd v. Orchis Steamship Co Ltd (1907) 12 CC 251 (CA) 6.169, 6.171

K/S Arnt J Moerland v. Kuwait Petroleum Corporation (The Fjordaas) [1988] 1 Lloyd's Rep 336 .... 3.416,
3.426, 3.439, 4.419
K/S A/S Seateam Co v. Iran National Oil Co (The Sevonia Team) [1983] 2 Lloyd's Rep 640 .... 6.203
Kalliopi A, The (Marc Rich & Co Ltd v. Tourloti Compania Naviera SA) [1988] 2 Lloyd's Rep 101 .... 4.62,
4.99, 6.105, 6.106
Katy, The [1895] P 56 (CA) 2.7, 3.311
Kavo Peirantis, The (Granvias Oceanicas Armadora SA v. Jibsen Trading Co) [1977] 2 Lloyd's Rep
344 .... 6.241, 6.250
Kawasaki Steel Corporation v. Sardoil SpA (The Zuitio Maru) [1977] 2 Lloyd's Rep 552 .... 6.42, 9.44

Kay v. Field (1882) 10 QBD 241 .... 4.14
Kell v. Anderson (1842) 10 M & W 331 .... 3.67, 3.68
Khian Captain, The (Freedom Maritime Corporation v. International Bulk Carriers SA) [1985] 2 Lloyd's
    Rep 212 .... 2.41, 4.59
Khios Breeze, The (Pteroti Compania Naviera SA v. National Coal Board) [1958] 1 Lloyd's Rep
    245 .... 3.314
King v. Hinde (1883) 12 LR Ir 113 .... 3.480
King v. Parker (1876) 34 LT 887 .... 4.262
King Line Ltd v. Moxey, Savon & Co Ltd (1939) 62 Ll L Rep 252 .... 4.295, 4.423
Kingsland, The (Davies-Evans v. Ladoga Ltd) (1910) 16 CC 18 .... 2.267
Kish v. Cory (1875) LR 10 QB 553 .... 6.256
Kish & Co v. Taylor (1910) 15 CC 268; (1910) 16 CC 59 (CA); (1912) 17 CC 355 (HL) 6.171
Kition Compania Naviera SA v. Ahmed Bamaodah (The Toulla) [1985] 1 Lloyd's Rep 107 ..... 6.207
Kodros Shipping Corporation v. Empresa Cubana de Fletes (The Evia) [1982] 3 WLR 637 (HL) 9.6
Kokusai Kisen Kabushiki Kaisha v. Flack & Son (1922) 10 Ll L Rep 635 .... 3.44
Kokusai Kisen Kabushiki Kaisha v. Wm H Muller & Co (Inc) (1925) 21 Ll L Rep 290 (CA) 6.63
Kostas K, The (Heinrich Hanno Co BV v. Fairlight Shipping Co Ltd; Hanse Schiffahrtskontor GmbH v.
    Andre SA), LMLN 135, 3 January 1985; [1985] 1 Lloyd's Rep 231 .... 3.24, 8.16
Kristiandsands Tankrederi A/S v. Standard Tankers (Bahamas) Ltd (The Polyglory) [1977] 2 Lloyd's Rep
    353 .... 4.442
Kurt A Becher GmbH & Co KG v. Roplak Enterprises SA (The World Navigator) [1991] 2 Lloyd's Rep
    23 .... 3.166, 3.339, 3.344, 8.32, 8.51
Kyzikos, The (Seacrystal Shipping Ltd v. Bulk Transport Group Shipping Co Ltd [1987] 1 Lloyd's Rep
    48; [1987] 2 Lloyd's Rep 122 (CA) [1989] 1 Lloyd's Rep 1 (HL) 1.22, 3.110, 3.111, 3.112,
                         3.347, 3.353, 3.354, 3.355, 3.357, 3.358, 3.364, 3.368, 3.402, 3.414, 3.424, 3.439,
                         4.418, 4.420
La Pintada, The [1983] 1 Lloyd's Rep 37 .... 6.287
Laga, The (J Vermaas Scheepvaartbedriff NV v. Association Technique de L'Importation Charbonnière)
    [1966] 1 Lloyd's Rep 582 .... 4.270
Laing v. Holloway (1878) 3 QBD 437 .... 7.7, 7.8, 7.12
Larrinaga Steamship Co v. Société Franco-Américaine (1923) 29 CC 1 .... 9.1
Larsen v. Sylvester & Co (1908) 13 CC 328 .... 4.86, 4.87
Latus, Linsley & Co v. J H Douglas & Co (1922) 12 Ll L Rep 63 .... 2.272
Laura Prima, The (Nereide SpA di Navigazione v. Bulk Oil International Ltd) [1980] 1 Lloyd's Rep 466;
    [1981] 2 Lloyd's Rep 24 (CA); [1982] 1 Lloyd's Rep 1 (HL) 3.5, 3.412, 3.416, 3.420, 3.421,
                         3.426, 4.170, 4.172, 4.396, 4.397, 4.399, 4.401, 4.402, 4.413, 4.415, 4.416, 4.417,
                         4.420, 4.422
Lavabre v. Wilson (1779) 1 Doug KB 284 .... 6.166
Lawson v. Burness (1862) 1 H & C 396 .... 3.469
Lee Frances, The (R & H Hall plc v. Vertom Scheepvaart en Handelsmaatschappij BV), LMLN 253, 15
    July 1989 (Com Ct) 6.44, 6.50
Leeds Shipping Co Ltd v. Duncan Fox & Co Ltd (1932) 37 CC 213; (1932) 42 Ll L Rep 123 ...... 4.27,
                         6.53, 6.56, 6.64
Leeds Shipping Co Ltd v. Société Francaise Bunge (The Eastern City) [1958] 2 Lloyd's Rep 127 .... 4.442
Leer v. Yates (1811) 3 Taunt 387 .... 6.269
Lefthero, The (Ellis Shipping Corp v. Voest Alpine Intertrading) [1991] 2 Lloyd's Rep 599; [1992] 2
    Lloyd's Rep 109 (CA) 4.62, 6.108
Leidemann v. Schultz (1853) 14 CB 38 .... 3.468
Lemythou Compania Naviera SA v. Ahmed Bamaodah (The Eleni 2) [1985] 1 Lloyd's Rep 107 .... 6.207
Leonidas D, The [1985] 2 Lloyd's Rep 18 .... 3.295
Leonis Steamship Co Ltd v. Joseph Rank Ltd (No 1) (1906) 12 CC 173; [1908] 1 KB 499; (1907) 13 CC
    136 (CA) 1.21, 2.231, 3.57, 3.71, 3.81, 3.82, 3.83, 3.86, 3.88, 3.89, 3.92, 3.93, 3.95, 3.100,
                         3.102, 3.153, 3.168, 3.267, 3.473
Leonis Steamship Co Ltd v. Joseph Rank Ltd (No 2) (1908) 13 CC 161; (1908) 13 CC 295 (CA) 2.14,
                         4.278, 4.283, 4.320
Lep Air Services Ltd v. Rolloswin Ltd; sub nom. Moschi v. Lep air Services Ltd [1972] 2 WLR
    1175 .... 6.175, 6.176
Leto, The (NV Maatschappij Zeevart v. Friesacher Soehne) [1962] 1 Lloyd's Rep 52 .... 2.64, 2.71
Lewis (T) v. Louis Dreyfus & Co (1926) 31 CC 239; (1926) 24 Ll L Rep 333 (CA) 4.127, 4.297, 4.298,
                         4.299, 4.300
Lilly v. Stevenson (1895) 22 Rett 278 .... 6.3, 6.5, 6.11, 6.14
Linardos, The (Coberfret NV v. Cyclades Shipping Co Ltd) [1994] 1 Lloyd's Rep 28 .... 3.142, 3.145

Lips, The (President of India v. Lips Maritime Corporation) [1987] 2 Lloyd's Rep 311 (HL) 6.6, 6.287
Liquid Bulk Tanker Services Inc v. The Embassy of Bangladesh (The Westport Clipper) (NY Arb),
   LMLN 360, 21 August 1993 .... 3.314, 4.241, 4.256
Little v. Stevenson [1896] AC 108 (HL) 2.240
Lizzie, The (CA Van Liewen v. Hollis Bros & Co Ltd) (1918) 23 CC 332; (1918) 24 CC 117 (CA); (1919)
   1 Ll L Rep 529; (1919) 25 CC 83 (HL) 2.208, 2.215, 2.222, 2.223, 2.237, 6.269, 6.270
Lockhart v. Falk (1875) LR 10 Ex 132 .... 6.2, 6.5, 6.234, 8.65
Lodza Compania de Navigacione SA v. Govt. of Ceylon (The Theraios) [1970] 2 Lloyd's Rep 142;
   [1971] 1 Lloyd's Rep 209 (CA) 2.165, 2.167, 2.196, 2.202
Logs & Timber Products (Singapore) Pte Ltd v. Keeley Granite (Pty) Ltd (The Freijo) [1978] 1 Lloyd's
   Rep 257; [1978] 2 Lloyd's Rep 1 (CA) 3.63, 3.183, 3.186, 3.187
London and Northern Steamship Co Ltd v. Central Argentine Railway Ltd (1913) 108 LT 527 .. 4.307, 4.310
London Arbitration, LMLN 1, 15 November 1979 .... 4.46
London Arbitration, LMLN 2, 29 November 1979 .... 2.252
London Arbitration, LMLN 10, 20 March 1980 .... 4.209
London Arbitration, LMLN 15, 29 May 1980 .... 3.228
London Arbitration, LMLN 18, 10 July 1980 .... 4.412
London Arbitration, LMLN 19, 24 July 1980 .... 6.46
London Arbitration, LMLN 35, 5 March 1981 .... 3.170
London Arbitration, LMLN 44, 9 July 1981 .... 3.229
London Arbitration, LMLN 62, 18 March 1982 .... 3.138
London Arbitration, LMLN 64, 15 April 1982 .... 4.134
London Arbitration, LMLN 71, 22 July 1982 .... 3.148, 5.115, 5.130, 5.134
London Arbitration, LMLN 72, 5 August 1982 .... 4.39, 5.65
London Arbitration, LMLN 74, 2 September 1982 .... 6.25
London Arbitration, LMLN 80, 25 November 1982 .... 6.182
London Arbitration, LMLN 90, 14 April 1983 .... 3.202
London Arbitration, LMLN 91, 28 April 1983 .... 4.365
London Arbitration, LMLN 102, 29 September 1983 .... 6.167
London Arbitration, LMLN 103, 13 October 1983 .... 3.246
London Arbitration, LMLN 114, 15 March 1984 .... 3.398
London Arbitration, LMLN 115, 29 March 1984 .... 4.114, 4.163
London Arbitration, LMLN 117, 26 April 1984 .... 4.394, 4.457
London Arbitration, LMLN 123, 19 July 1984 .... 4.383, 4.413, 4.417
London Arbitration, LMLN 127, 13 September 1984 .... 2.160
London Arbitration, LMLN 129, 11 October 1984 .... 2.172
London Arbitration 2/84, LMLN 113, 1 March 1984 .... 9.36
London Arbitration 6/84, LMLN 117, 26 April 1984 .... 3.189
London Arbitration 10/84, LMLN 121, 21 June 1984 .... 6.132, 6.152
London Arbitration 29/84, LMLN 134, 20 December 1984 .... 6.92
London Arbitration, LMLN 143, 25 April 1985 .... 3.371
London Arbitration, LMLN 151, 15 August 1985 .... 3.225, 4.417
London Arbitration 13/85, LMLN 160, 19 December 1985 .... 6.102, 6.111
London Arbitration 15/85, LMLN 160, 19 December 1985 .... 6.86, 6.111
London Arbitration 2/86, LMLN 166, 13 March 1986 .... 6.121
London Arbitration 14/86, LMLN 179, 11 September 1986 .... 3.179, 3.194
London Arbitration 15/86, LMLN 180, 25 September 1986 .... 3.141, 3.289
London Arbitration 16/86, LMLN 180, 25 September 1986 .... 2.142
London Arbitration 7/87, LMLN 197, 21 May 1987 .... 4.419
London Arbitratiion 12/87, LMLN 204, 29 August 1987 .... 8.52
London Arbitration 13/87, LMLN 205, 12 September 1987 .... 8.24
London Arbitration 14/87, LMLN 205, 12 September 1987 .... 3.208
London Arbitration 15/87, LMLN 206, 26 September 1987 .... 3.290
London Arbitration 18/87 and 22/87, LMLN 209, 7 November 1987 .... 4.186
Lodzon Arbitration 19/87, LMLN 209, 7 November 1987 .... 6.153
London Arbitration 21/87, LMLN 209, 7 November 1987 .... 4.240
Londson Arbitration 23/87, LMLN 212, 19 December 1987 .... 4.180
London Arbitration 5/88, LMLN 230, 27 August 1988 .... 3.401
London Arbitration 7/88, LMLN 239, 31 December 1988 .... 3.139
London Arbitration 10/89, LMLN 247, 22 April 1989 .... 6.110
London Arbitration 11/89, LMLN 248, 6 May 1989 .... 3.197
London Arbitration 13/89, LMLN 251, 17 June 1989 .... 6.112

London Arbitration 16/89, LMLN 253, 15 July 1989 .... 5.32
London Arbitration 18/89, LMLN 254, 29 July 1989 .... 6.126, 6.277, 6.284
London Arbitration 19/89, LMLN 256, 26 August 1989 .... 3.23
London Arbitration 26/89, LMLN 262, 18 November 1989 .... 3.291, 5.143, 5.152
London Arbitration 1/90, LMLN 266, 13 January 1990 .... 3.195
London Arbitration 2/90, LMLN 267, 27 January 1990 .... 4.407, 6.110
London Arbitration 4/90, LMLN 274, 5 May 1990 .... 3.195
London Arbitration 5/90, LMLN 274, 5 May 1990 .... 3.108
London Arbitration 6/90, LMLN 274, 5 May 1990 .... 3.295
London Arbitration 9/90, LMLN 285, 6 October 1990 .... 3.127, 3.247, 6.129
London Arbitration 10/90, LMLN 285, 6 October 1990 .... 6.153
London Arbitration 11/90, LMLN 285, 6 October 1990 .... 6.25, 6.126, 6.278
London Arbitration 12/90, LMLN 286, 20 October 1990 .... 3.13, 8.3, 8.58
London Arbitration 1/91, LMLN 299, 20 April 1991 .... 4.37
London Arbitration 6/91, LMLN 300, 4 May 1991 .... 4.242
London Arbitration 7/91, LMLN 303, 15 June 1991 .... 4.403
London Arbitration 8/91, LMLN 304, 29 June 1991 .... 3.49, 4.384
London Arbitration 9/91, LMLN 304, 29 June 1991 .... 4.40
London Arbitration 11/91, LMLN 304, 29 June 1991 .... 5.44
London Arbitration 12/91, LMLN 304, 29 June 1991 .... 8.28
London Arbitration 13/91, LMLN 304, 29 June 1994 .... 6.285, 6.287
London Arbitration 15/91, LMLN 305, 13 July 1991 .... 4.21
London Arbitration 17/91, LMLN 307, 10 August 1991 .... 3.246
London Arbitration 18/91, LMLN 308, 24 August 1991 .... 6.280
London Arbitration 27/91, LMLN 316, 14 December 1991 .... 4.385
London Arbitration 2/92, LMLN 319, 25 January 1992 .... 5.43
London Arbitration 4/92, LMLN 321, 22 February 1992 .... 4.18
London Arbitration 6/92, LMLN 321, 22 February 1992 .... 8.57
London Arbitration 7/92, LMLN 323, 21 March 1992 .... 2.58, 4.136, 4.163
London Arbitration 8/92, LMLN 324, 4 April 1992 .... 3.291, 3.314
London Arbitration 11/92, LMLN 324, 4 April 1992 .... 8.5
London Arbitration 17/92, LMLN 328, 30 May 1992 .... 3.146, 3.339
London Arbitration 20/92, LMLN 328, 30 May 1992 .... 8.30
London Arbitration 21/92, LMLN 329, 13 June 1992 .... 4.45, 6.187
London Arbitration 24/92, LMLN 336, 19 September 1992 .... 6.268
London Arbitration 25/92, LMLN 337, 3 October 1992 .... 6.281
London Arbitration 26/92, LMLN 337, 3 October 1992 .... 6.282
London Arbitration 27/92, LMLN 337, 3 October 1992 .... 3.130
London Arbitration 30/92, LMLN 338, 17 October 1992 .... 2.169
London Arbitration 31/92, LMLN 338, 17 October 1992 .... 3.275
London Arbitration 3/93, LMLN 351, 17 April 1993 .... 5.132
London Arbitration 4/93, LMLN 351, 17 April 1993 .... 3.161, 3.162, 4.29
London Arbitration 5/93, LMLN 351, 17 April 1993 .... 8.39
London Arbitration 11/93, LMLN 356, 26 June 1993 .... 3.423
London Arbitration 14/93, LMLN 358, 24 July 1993 .... 5.47
London Arbitration 19/93, LMLN 363, 2 October 1993 .... 6.154
London Arbitration 1/94, LMLN 383, 9 July 1994 .... 3.239
London Arbitration 2/94, LMLN 385, 6 August 1994 .... 4.81
London Arbitration 5/94, LMLN 386, 20 August 1994 .... 4.104, 6.107
London Arbitration 10/94, LMLN 387, 3 September 1994 .... 3.261
London Arbitration 4/95, LMLN 403, 15 April 1995 .... 4.30
London Arbitration 8/95, LMLN 408, 24 June 1995 .... 3.231, 4.214
London Arbitration 18/95, LMLN 417, 28 October 1995 .... 3.187
London Arbitration 21/95, 22/95 and 23/95, LMLN 421, 23 December 1995 .... 4.24
London Arbitration 24/95, LMLN 421, 23 December 1995 .... 5.19
London Arbitration 4/96, LMLN 426, 2 March 1996 .... 6.188
London Arbitration 8/96, LMLN 433, 8 June 1996 .... 2.185
London Arbitration 9/96, LMLN 434, 22 June 1996 .... 3.187, 3.277, 3.327
London Arbitratiion 10/96, LMLN 435, 6 July 1996 .... 3.138
London Arbitration 12/96, LMLN 445, 23 November 1996 .... 3.134
London Arbitration 14/96, LMLN 466, 7 December 1996 .... 3.196, 4.31
London Arbitration 1/97, LMLN 450, 1 February 1997 .... 3.315

London Arbitration 3/97, LMLN 450, 1 February 1997 .... 5.116
London Arbitration 7/97, LMLN 459, 7 June 1997 .... 4.243, 6.267
London Arbitration 11/97, LMLN 463, 2 August 1997 .... 3.433, 3.440, 3.441
London Arbitration 12/97, LMLN 464, 16 August 1997 .... 4.144
London Arbitration 15/97, LMLN 465, 30 August 1997 .... 4.217
London Arbitration 16/97, LMLN 466, 13 September 1997 .... 4.144
London Arbitration 17/97, LMLN 471, 22 November 1997 .... 3.109
London Arbitration 20/97, LMLN 473, 20 December 1997 .... 3.239
London Arbitration 4/98, LMLN 481, 14 April 1998 .... 4.16, 6.132, 6.284
London Arbitration 5/98, LMLN 481, 14 April 1998 .... 4.62
London Arbitration 9/98, LMLN 488, 21 July 1998 .... 3.182, 4.466
London Arbitration 11/98, LMLN 488, 21 July 1998 .... 5.33
London Arbitration 12/98, LMLN 488, 21 July 1998 .... 7.6
London Arbitration 16/98, LMLN 489, 4 August 1998 .... 3.418
London Arbitration 20/98, LMLN 491, 29 September 1998 .... 3.209
London Arbitration 21/98, LMLN 493, 29 September 1998 .... 6.276
London Arbitration 26/98, LMLN 499, 22 December 1998 .... 6.151
London Arbitration 3/99, LMLN 503, 18 February 1999 .... 2.186
London Arbitration 9/99, LMLN 510, 27 May 1999 .... 5.30, 5.114
London Arbitration 10/99, LMLN 510, 27 May 1999 .... 4.462
London Arbitration 11/99, LMLN 511, 10 June 1999 .... 3.139, 4.439, 6.156
London Arbitration 14/99, LMLN 511, 10 June 1999 .... 6.157
London Traders Shipping Co Ltd v. General Mercantile Shipping Co Ltd (1914) 30 TLR 493 .... 3.126
Loucas N, The (Ionian Navigation Co Inc v. Atlantic Shipping Co SA) [1970] 2 Lloyd's Rep 482; [1971]
    1 Lloyd's Rep 215 (CA) 3.387, 3.389, 3.396, 4.320
Louis Dreyfus & Cie v. Parnaso Cia Naviera SA [1959] 1 QB 498 .... 6.93
Love and Stewart Ltd v. Rowtor Steamship Co Ltd [1916] 2 AC 527 (HL) 4.189, 4.210, 4.211, 4.220,
    4.229, 4.230, 5.73, 5.86, 5.88, 6.215
Luctor, The (Protank Ltd v. Transatlantic Petroleum Ltd) (NY Arb), LMLN 349, 20 March 1993 .... 3.308,
    4.18, 4.419
Lyle Shipping Co Ltd v. Corporation of Cardiff; Churchill and Sim (1899) 5 CC 87; (1990) 5 CC 397
    (CA) 2.208, 2.214, 2.268, 6.222, 8.46
Lyndon v. Stanbridge (1857) 2 M & N 45 .... 4.65

Macbeth v. Wild & Co (1900) 16 TLR 497 .... 3.493
Machrihanish, The (1906), unreported (HL) 2.41
Mackay v. Dick (1881) 6 App Cas 251 .... 3.345
Mackay v. Spillers & Baker Ltd (1901) 6 CC 217 .... 2.220, 2.277
Magnolia Shipping Co Ltd of Limassol v. Joint Venture of the International Trading & Shipping
    Enterprises and Kinship Management Co Ltd of Brussels (The Camelia and the Magnolia) [1978]
    2 Lloyd's Rep 182 .... 2.98, 2.99. 2.102, 4.154, 4.156, 4.158, 4.160
Manchester Trust v. Furness [1895] 2 QB 539 .... 6.193
Maratha Envoy, The (Federal Commerce & Navigation Co Ltd v. Tradax Export SA) [1975] 2 Lloyd's
    Rep 223; [1977] 3 WLR 1372; [1977] 2 Lloyd's Rep 217 (CA); [1977] 2 Lloyd's Rep 301 (HL) 3.105,
    3.106, 3.107, 3.267, 3.269, 3.352, 8.20
March Rich & Co Ltd v. Tourloti Compania Naviera SA (The Kalliopi A) [1988] 2 Lloyd's Rep
    101 .... 4.62, 4.99, 6.105, 6.106
Mare del Nord, The (Misano Di Navigazione SpA v. United States of America), US Ct of App (2nd Cir),
    LMLN 335, 5 September 1992 .... 3.137
Margaronis Navigation Agency Ltd v. Henry W Peabody & Co of London Ltd [1964] 1 Lloyd's Rep 173;
    [1964] 2 Lloyd's Rep 153 (CA) 5.16, 5.17, 5.18, 5.35, 8.30
Maria G, The (Compania Crystal de Vapores v. Herman & Mohatta (India) Ltd) [1958] 1 Lloyd's Rep
    616 .... 2.56, 4.110, 4.114, 4.140, 4.149, 4.431, 4.435, 4.440
Maritime Transport Operators GmbH v. Louis Dreyfus et Cie (The Tropwave) [1981] 2 Lloyd's Rep
    159 .... 2.183, 2.196, 2.198, 2.202, 5.126, 5.140, 6.251
Marpesia, The, 292 Fed 957 (1923) 6.67
Massalia, The (Government of Ceylon v. Société Franco-Tunisienne d'Armement-Tunis) (No 2) [1960]
    2 Lloyd's Rep 352 .... 3.117, 3.148, 3.149, 3.250, 3.260, 3.393, 3.395, 5.113, 5.120, 5.121, 5.123,
    5.125, 5.126, 5.127, 5.134, 5.135, 5.136
Mastrogiorgis B, The (Orient Shipping Rotterdam BV v. Hugo Nev & Sons Inc), LMLN 451, 18
    February 1997 .... 4.92
Mawson Steamship Co v. Beyer (1913) 19 CC 59 .... 7.6, 7.9, 7.10, 7.12, 7.15

Medtank Ltd v. Adam Maritime Corporation (The Alaska) (NY Arb), LMLN 452, 1 March 1997 .... 4.168
Mein v. Ottman (1904) 41 SLR 144 .... 2.30
Mersey Steel Co v. Naylor, Benson & Co (1884) 9 App Cas 434 .... 6.14
Metalimex Foreign Trade Corporation v. Eugenie Maritime Co Ltd [1962] 1 Lloyd's Rep 378 .... 3.245
Metals & Ropes Co Ltd v. Filia Compania Limitada (The Vastric) [1966] 2 Lloyd's Rep 219 .... 3.386
Metcalfe v. Britannia Ironworks Co (1877) 2 QBD 423 .... 3.459
Metropolitan Water Board v. Dick, Kerr & Co [1917] 2 KB 1 .... 4.288
Mexico I, The (Transgrain Shipping BV v. Global Transporte Oceanico SA) [1988] 2 Lloyd's Rep 149;
    [1990] 1 Lloyd's Rep 507 (CA) 3.237, 3.257, 3.260, 3.288, 3.291, 3.293,
                                                           3.294, 3.296, 3.297, 5.108, 5.114, 5.144
Michalinos & Co v. Louis Dreyfus & Co (1925) 21 Ll L Rep 233 .... 4.124, 4.299
Miguel de Larrinaga Steamship Co Ltd v. D L Flack & Son (1924) 20 Ll L Rep 268; (1925) 21 Ll L Rep
    284 (CA) 3.471, 4.326
Mikkelsen v. Arcos Ltd (1925) 23 Ll L Rep 33 .... 8.9
Mira Oil Resources of Tortola v. Bocimar NV [1999] 2 Lloyd's Rep 101 .... 6.284
Miramar, The (Miramar Maritime Corporation) v. Holborn Oil Trading Ltd [1984] 1 Lloyd's Rep 142
    (CA); [1984] 2 Lloyd's Rep 129 (HL) 1.31, 6.190, 6.194, 6.195, 6.196, 6.220
Miramar Maritime Corporation v. Holborn Oil Trading Ltd (The Miramar) [1984] 1 Lloyd's Rep 142
    (CA); [1984] 2 Lloyd's Rep 129 (HL) 1.31, 6.190, 6.194, 6.195, 6.196, 6.220
Misano Di Navigazione SpA v. United States of America (The Mare del Nord), US Ct of App (2nd Cir),
    LMLN 335, 5 September 1992 .... 3.137
Mitchell Cotts & Co v. Steel Bros & Co Ltd (1916) 22 CC 63 .... 2.249, 2.252
Mobil Courage, The (Mobil Shipping and Transportation v. Shell Eastern Petroleum (Pte) Ltd), LMLN
    202, 1 August 1987 .... 6.95
Mobil Shipping and Transportation v. Shell Eastern Petroleum (Pte) Ltd (The Mobil Courage), LMLN
    202, 1 August 1987 .... 6.95
Molière Steamship Co Ltd v. Naylor, Benzon & Co (1897) 2 CC 92 .... 5.71, 5.77, 5.78
Monsen v. Macfarlane, McCrindell & Co (1895) 1 CC 51 .... 2.38, 3.495, 3.496
Moor Line Ltd v. Distillers Co Ltd, 1912 Sc 514 .... 4.279, 8.64
Moor Line Ltd v. Manganexport GmbH (1936) 55 Ll L Rep 114 .... 3.475, 3.477
Moschi v. Lep Air Services Ltd. See Lep Air Services Ltd v. Rolloswin Ltd.
Mosfield, The (Chief Controller of Chartering of the Government of India v. Central Gulf Steamship
    Corporation) [1968] 2 Lloyd's Rep 173 .... 4.175, 4.177, 4.178, 4.205, 4.218, 4.227, 4.233
Mosvolds Rederi A/S v. Food Corporation of India (The Damodar General T J Park and King Theras)
    [1986] 2 Lloyd's Rep 68 .... 3.108
Mozart, The [1985] 1 Lloyd's Rep 239 .... 4.88, 4.90
Mudie v. Strick & Co Ltd (1909) 14 CC 135; (1909) 14 CC 227 (CA) 4.74

NV Maatschappij Zeevart v. Friesacher Soehne (The Leto) [1962] 1 Lloyd's Rep 52 .... 2.64, 2.71
NV Reederij Amsterdam v. President of India (The Amstelmolen) [1960] 2 Lloyd's Rep 82; [1961] 2
    Lloyd's Rep 1 (CA) 3.362, 4.98, 4.320, 6.67
NZ Michalos v. The Food Corporation of India (The Apollon) [1983] 1 Lloyd's Rep 409 .... 3.202
Naamlooze Vennootschap AC Lensen's Stoomvaart Maatschappij v. Muller & Co (London) Ltd (1921)
    7 Ll L Rep 248 .... 4.264
National Carriers Ltd v. Panalpina (Northern) Ltd [1981] 2 WLR 45 (HL) 9.12, 9.14
Navico AG v. Vrontados Naftiki Etairia PE [1968] 1 Lloyd's Rep 379 .... 4.314, 7.30
Navrom v. Callitsis Ship Management SA (The Radauti) [1987] 2 Lloyd's Rep 276; [1988] 2 Lloyd's Rep
    416 (CA) 4.59, 4.99, 4.100, 4.320
Nea Tyhi Maritime Co v. Compagnie Grainière SA (The Finix) [1975] 2 Lloyd's Rep 415 .... 3.389, 3.392
Nelson v. Dahl; sub nom. Dahl v. Nelson (1879) 12 Ch D 568; (1879) 12 Ch D 580 (CA); (1880) 6 App
    Cas 38 (HL) 2.223, 2.229, 2.233, 2.238, 3.38, 3.42, 3.68, 3.72, 3.80, 3.221, 3.443, 3.445, 3.450,
                                                           3.454, 3.457, 3.460, 3.461
Nelson & Sons Ltd v. Nelson Line (Liverpool) Ltd (No 3) (1907) 12 CC 185; [1907] 2 KB 705 (CA);
    (1908) 13 CC 235 (HL) 2.26, 2.47, 3.312, 3.314, 4.202, 4.252,
                                                           4.254, 4.255, 4.256, 7.7, 7.10, 7.12, 7.14, 7.15
Nelson, Donkin and others v. Robert H Dahl. See Nelson v. Dahl.
Nema, The (Pioneer Shipping Ltd v. BTP Tioxide Ltd); sub nom. BTP Tioxide Ltd v. Pioneer Shipping
    Ltd (The Nema); [1980] QB 547; [1980] 2 Lloyd's Rep 339; [1980] 1 Lloyd's Rep 519n (CA);
    [1982] AC 724; [1981] 2 Lloyd's Rep 239; [1981] 3 WLR 292 (HL) 9.4, 9.14, 9.28, 9.31, 9.33

Nereide SpA di Navigazione v. Bulk Oil International Ltd (The Laura Prima) [1980] 1 Lloyd's Rep 466;
    [1981] 2 Lloyd's Rep 24 (CA); [1982] 1 Lloyd's Rep 1 (HL) 3.5, 3.412, 3.416, 3.420, 3.421,
                    3.426, 4.170, 4.172, 4.396, 4.397, 4.399, 4.401, 4.402, 4.413, 4.415, 4.416, 4.417,
                    4.420, 4.422
Nestor, The (President of India v. Diamantis Pateras (Hellas) Marine Enterprises Ltd) [1987] 2 Lloyd's
    Rep 649 .... 3.203, 3.205
New Horizon, The (Tramp Shipping Corporation v. Greenwich Marine Inc) [1974] 2 Lloyd's Rep 210;
    [1975] 2 Lloyd's Rep 314 (CA) 4.265, 4.266, 4.268, 4.326
New York Arbitration, SMA 1437, LMLN 24, 2 October 1980 .... 6.118
New York Arbitration, LMLN 25, 16 October 1980 .... 6.128
New York Arbitration, BIMCO Bulletin 2/90 .... 5.157
New York Arbitration (The Sea Wind) LMCN 531 .... 3.162, 3.427, 4.24, 6.26, 8.20
New York Arbitration (The Tai Ning) LMCN 532 .... 4.27
Newman and Dale Steamship Co Ltd v. The British and South American Steamship Co (1902) 8 CC 87 ... 4.9
Nicholas E Ambatielos v. Anton Jurgens' Margarine Works (1922) 13 Ll L Rep 357 .... 4.83
Nicholson v. Williams (1871) LR 6 QB 632 .... 3.56
Nielsen & Co v. Wait, James & Co (1885) 16 QBD 67 ...... 2.12, 2.17, 2.25, 2.29, 4.201, 4.390, 4.458, 4.460
Nippon Yusen Kaisha v. Société Anonyme Marocaine de L'Industrie du Raffinage (The Tsukuba Maru)
    [1979] 1 Lloyd's Rep 459 .... 6.102, 6.116, 6.121, 6.127
Nobel's Explosives Co Ltd v. Jenkins & Co [1896] 2 QB 326; (1896) 1 CC 436 .... 3.449, 4.111
Noemijulia Steamship Co Ltd v. Minister of Food (1950) 84 Ll L Rep 354 .... 3.121, 3.151, 3.155
Norden Steamship Co v. Dempsey (1876) 1 CPD 654 .... 3.324
Nordic Navigator, The (Associated Bulk Carriers Ltd v. Shell International Petroleum Co Ltd) [1984] 2
    Lloyd's Rep 182 .... 6.85
Norrkopings Rederiaktiebolag v. Wulfsberg & Co (1920) 3 Ll L Rep 256 .... 2.218, 3.323
North King, The (Pacific Carriers Corporation v. Tradax Export SA) [1971] 2 Lloyd's Rep 460 .... 3.212,
                    3.233, 3.244, 3.279
North River Freighters Ltd v. President of India (The Radnor) [1955] 2 Lloyd's Rep 73; [1955] 2 Lloyd's
    Rep 668 (CA) 3.27, 3.35, 3.384, 3.385, 5.123
Northfield Steamship Co Ltd v. Compagnie L'Union des Gaz (1911) 17 CC 74 (CA) 3.347
Notos, The (SAMIR v. Notos Maritime Corporation of Monrovia) [1985] 1 Lloyd's Rep 149; [1985] 2
    Lloyd's Rep 334 (CA); 1 Lloyd's Rep 503 (HL) 4.91, 4.389, 4.442, 6.113, 6.114
Novorossisk Shipping Co v. Neopetro Co Ltd (The Ulyanovsk) [1990] 1 Lloyd's Rep 425 .... 4.421, 5.6,
                    5.13, 5.14

Oakville Steamship Co Ltd v. Holmes (1899) 5 CC 48 .... 5.78
Ocean Trawlers Ltd v. Maritime National Fish Ltd (1935) 51 Ll L Rep 299 (PC) 9.49
Oceansky Co Ltd v. Hugo New & Sons Inc (The Antalya) (NY Arb), LMLN 291, 29 December 1990 .... 3.12,
                    6.50
Ogmore Steamship Co Ltd v. H Borner & Co Ltd (1901) 6 CC 104 .... 3.326, 3.332, 3.333
Olbena SA v. Psara Maritime Inc (The Thanassis A), LMLN 68, 10 June 1982 .... 6.115
Oldendorff (EL) & Co GmbH v. Tradax Export SA (The Johanna Oldendorff) [1972] 2 Lloyd's Rep 292
    (CA); [1973] 2 Lloyd's Rep 285 (HL) 1.10, 1.18, 1.21, 1.24, 2.231, 3.2, 3.34, 3.47, 3.48,
                    3.61, 3.67, 3.69, 3.83, 3.86, 3.96, 3.97, 3.100, 3.101, 3.102, 3.104, 3.107, 3.108,
                    3.111, 3.267, 3.268, 3.269, 3.346, 3.349, 3.350, 3.351, 3.354, 3.357, 3.372, 3.377,
                    3.382, 3.388, 4.411, 8.20
Oltenia, The [1982] 1 Lloyd's Rep 448 .... 6.276
Onisilos, The (Salamis Shipping (Panama) SA v. Edm Van Meerbeck SA) [1970] 2 Lloyd's Rep 405;
    [1971] 2 Lloyd's Rep 29 (CA) 4.285, 4.347, 4.348, 4.352, 4.353, 4.368, 4.370, 4.372, 4.374, 4.375
Orient Shipping Rotterdam BV v. Hugo Nev & Sons Inc (The Mastrogiorgis B), LMLN 451, 18 February
    1997 .... 4.92
Oriental Envoy, The (Transamerican Steamship Corporation v. Tradax Export SA) [1982] 2 Lloyd's Rep
    266 .... 3.148, 5.107, 5.131, 5.141, 6.60
Oriental Maritime Pte Ltd v. Ministry of Food, Government of the People's Republic of Bangladesh (The
    Silva Plana, Bahamastars and Magic Sky) [1989] 2 Lloyd's Rep 371 .... 2.198
Oriental Steamship Co v. Tylor [1893] 2 QB 518 .... 5.29
Orpheus Steamship Co v. Bovill & Sons (1916) 114 LT 750 .... 2.113, 2.124, 2.125
Overseas Transportation Co v. Mineralimportexport (The Sinoe) [1971] 1 Lloyd's Rep 514; [1972] 1
    Lloyd's Rep 201 (CA) 6.81, 6.82, 6.83, 6.228, 6.247, 6.248, 6.249, 6.250, 6.251
Owners of Borg v. Darwen Paper Co (1921) 8 Ll L Rep 49 .... 3.244
Owners of Panghis Vergottis v. William Corg & Son (1926) 25 Ll L Rep 64 .... 3.329, 8.12

Owners of SS Dimitrios N Rallias v. Lavarello, Brizzolesi, Galliano & Co Ltd (1922) 13 Ll L Rep 196 ..... 2.244
Owners of the Breynton v. Theodoridi & Co (1924) 20 Ll L Rep 314 .... 8.7
Owners of the Spanish Steamship Sebastian v. Sociedad Altos Hornos de Vizcaya (1919) 1 Ll L Rep
  500 .... 8.50
Owners of the Steamship Nolisement v. Bunge and Born (1916) 22 CC 135 (CA) 5.26, 5.28, 7.34, 8.47

Pacific Carriers Corporation v. Tradax Export SA (The North King) [1971] 2 Lloyd's Rep 460 .... 3.212,
  3.233, 3.279
Palm Shipping Inc v. Kuwait Petroleum Corporation (The Sea Queen) [1988] 1 Lloyd's Rep 500 .... 3.415,
  3.426, 3.439, 4.419, 4.421
Palm Shipping Inc v. Vitol SA (The Universal Monarch) [1988] 2 Lloyd's Rep 483 .... 4.444
Panagos Lyras (Owners) v. Joint Danube & Black Sea Shipping Agencies of Braila (1931) 40 Ll L Rep
  83 .... 4.197, 4.206
Pantland Hick v. Raymond & Reid; sub nom. Hick v. Rodocanachi [1891] 2 QB 626 (CA) [1893] AC 22
  (HL) 2.205, 2.208, 2.212, 2259, 2.261
Parcel Tankers Inc v. Lever Brothers Company (NY Arb) 5.152
Parker v. Winslow (1857) 7 E & B 942 .... 3.457
Pasadena, The, LMLN 266, 13 January 1990 (NY Arb), LMLN 266, 13 January 1990 .... 6.102
Pearl Merchant, The [1978] 2 Lloyd's Rep 193 .... 6.287
Penelope, The [1928] P 180 .... 9.27
Permeke, The (Bocimar NV v. Bayway Refining Co), LMLN 416, 14 October 1995 .... 3.191
Petersen v. Dunn & Co (1895) 1 CC 8 .... 3.411, 5.5, 5.17
Petr Schmidt, The [1997] 1 Lloyd's Rep 284 .... 3.182, 3.236, 3.237
Petrinovic & Co Ltd v. Mission Française des Transports Maritimes (1941) 71 Ll L Rep 208 ... 4.437, 4.441,
  6.180
Photo Production Ltd v. Securicor Transport Ltd [1980] AC 827; [1980] 2 WLR 283 (HL) 4.5, 4.62,
  6.38, 6.175, 6.176
Pinch & Simpson v. Harrison, Whitfield & Co (1948) 81 Ll L Rep 268 .... 4.119
Pioneer Shipping Ltd v. BTP Tioxide Ltd (The Nema); sub nom. BTP Tioxide Ltd v. Pioneer Shipping
  Ltd (The Nema) [1980] QB 547; [1980] 2 Lloyd's Rep 339; [1980] 1 Lloyd's Rep 519n (CA);
  [1982] AC 724; [1981] 2 Lloyd's Rep 239; [1981] 3 WLR 292 (HL) 9.4, 9.14, 9.28, 9.31, 9.33
Plakoura Maritime Corporation v. Shell International Petroleum Co Ltd (The Plakoura) [1987] 2 Lloyd's
  Rep 258 .... 3.37, 3.195
Point Clear, The (Primula Compania Naviera SA v. Finagrain Cie Commerciale Agricole et Financière
  SA) [1975] 2 Lloyd's Rep 243 .... 4.235
Poitou, The (Fina Supply Ltd v. Shell UK Ltd) [1991] 1 Lloyd's Rep 452 .... 4.165
Polyglory, The (Kristiandsands Tankrederi A/S v. Standard Tankers (Bahamas) Ltd) [1977] 2 Lloyd's Rep
  353 .... 4.442
Porteous v. Watney (1878) 3 QBD 227; (1878) 2 QBD 534 (CA) 5.144, 6.193, 6.269
Portofino (Owners) v. Berlin Derunaptha (1934) 49 Ll L Rep 62 .... 6.262
Postlethwaite v. Freeland (1880) 5 App Cas 599 (HL) 1.17, 2.1, 2.205, 2.208, 2.209,
  2.212, 2.216, 2.254, 3.321, 6.61
Postlethwaite v. Freeland (1884) 9 App Cas 470 .... 2.240
President Brand, The (Inca Compania Naviera SA and Commercial and Maritime Enterprises Evanghelos
  P Nomikos SA v. Mofinol Inc) [1967] 2 Lloyd's Rep 338 .... 3.390, 3.405, 3.411, 3.416, 3.422,
  4.395, 4.402, 4.413, 4.414, 4.416, 4.418, 8.20, 8.30, 8.31
President of India v. Davenport Marine Panama SA (The Albion) [1987] 2 Lloyd's Rep 365 ..... 3.203, 3.205
President of India v. Diamantis Pateras (Hellas) Marine Enterprises Ltd (The Nestor) [1987] 2 Lloyd's
  Rep 649 .... 3.203, 3.205
President of India v. Edina Compania Naviera SA (The Stamatios G Embiricos) [1965] 1 Lloyd's Rep
  574 .... 4.93
President of India v. Hariana Overseas Corp (The Takafa) [1990] 1 Lloyd's Rep 536 .... 1.13
President of India v. Jebsens (UK) Ltd (The General Capinpin, Proteus, Free Wave and Dinara) [1987]
  2 Lloyd's Rep 354; [1989] 1 Lloyd's Rep 232 (CA); LMLN 287, 3 November 1990; [1991] 1
  Lloyd's Rep 1 (HL) 2.192, 2.196, 2.197, 2.198, 2.199, 2.201, 2.203
President of India v. Lips Maritime Corporation (The Lips) [1987] 2 Lloyd's Rep 311 (HL) 6.6, 6.287
President of India v. Metcalfe Shipping Ltd [1969] 2 Lloyd's Rep 476 .... 6.213
President of India v. N G Livanos Maritime Co (The John Michalos) [1987] 2 Lloyd's Rep 188 .... 6.104,
  6.105, 6.106, 6.109
President of India v. Olympia Sauna Shipping Co SA (The Ypatia Halcoussi) [1984] 2 Lloyd's Rep 455 ... 3.63
Primula Compania Naviera SA v. Finagrain Cie Commerciale Agricole et Financière SA (The Point
  Clear) [1975] 2 Lloyd's Rep 243 .... 4.235

Proctor, Garratt, Marston Ltd *v.* Oakwin Steamship Co (1925) 22 Ll L Rep 518 .... 6.16

Prometheus, The (Venizelos ANE of Athens *v.* Société Commerciale de Céréales et Financière SA of Zurich) [1974] 1 Lloyd's Rep 350 .... 4.320, 4.322

Protank Ltd *v.* Transatlantic Petroleum Ltd (The Luctor) (NY Arb), LMLN 349, 20 March 1993 .... 3.308, 4.18, 4.419

Pteroti Compania Naviera SA *v.* National Coal Board (The Khios Breeze) [1958] 1 Lloyd's Rep 245 .... 3.314, 4.256

Puerto Rocca, The (Compania Argentina de Navegación de Ultramar *v.* Tradax Export SA) [1978] 1 Lloyd's Rep 252 .... 3.188, 3.492

Pyman Brothers *v.* Dreyfus Brothers & Co (1889) 24 QBD 152 .... 3.73

Pyrene Co Ltd *v.* Scindia Navigation Co Ltd [1954] 2 QB 402 .... 6.197

R Pagnan & Fratelli *v.* Finagrain Compagnie Commerciale Agricole et Financière SA (The Adolf Leonhardt) [1986] 2 Lloyd's Rep 395 .... 3.226, 3.374, 4.100, 4.320

R Pagnan & Fratelli *v.* Tradex Export SA [1969] 2 Lloyd's Rep 150 .... 6.126, 6.130

R & H Hall plc *v.* Vertom Scheepvaart en Handelsmaatschappij BV (The Lee Frances), LMLN 253, 15 July 1989 (Com Ct) 6.44, 6.50

Radauti, The (Navrom *v.* Callitsis Ship Management SA) [1987] 2 Lloyd's Rep 276; [1988] 2 Lloyd's Rep 416 (CA) 4.59, 4.99, 4.100, 4.320

Radnor, The (North River Freighters Ltd *v.* President of India) [1955] 2 Lloyd's Rep 73; [1955] 2 Lloyd's Rep 668 (CA) 3.27, 3.35, 3.384, 3.385, 5.123

Ralli Brothers *v.* Compania Naviera Sota y Aznar (1919) 25 CC 155; (1920) 25 CC 227 (CA) 2.263, 4.10, 4.16, 9.41

Randall *v.* Lynch (1810) 2 Camp 352 .... 3.66

Rashtriya Chemicals and Fertilizers Ltd *v.* Huddart Parker Industries Ltd (The Boral Gas) [1988] 1 Lloyd's Rep 342 .... 3.342, 6.223, 6.243, 8.1, 8.21

Rayner *v.* Rederiaktiebolaget Condor (1895) 1 CC 80 .... 6.21

Reardon Smith Line Ltd *v.* East Asiatic Co (1938) 62 Ll L Rep 23 .... 3.362, 4.320

Reardon Smith Line Ltd *v.* Ministry of Agriculture Fisheries and Food [1959] 2 Lloyd's Rep 229; [1961] 1 Lloyd's Rep 385 (CA); [1963] AC 691; [1963] 1 Lloyd's Rep 12 (HL) 2.8, 2.16, 2.26, 2.30, 2.31, 2.41, 2.43, 2.52, 2.54, 2.59, 2.62, 2.68, 2.69, 2.71, 2.79, 2.81, 2.88, 2.95, 2.97, 2.125, 2.128, 3.7, 4.12, 4.153, 4.203, 4.209, 4.210, 4.215, 4.222, 4.223, 4.272, 4.288, 4.289, 4.290, 4.291, 4.292, 4.300, 4.301, 5.90, 5.91

Rederi Aktiebolaget Transatlantic *v.* Board of Trade (1924) 20 Ll L Rep 241 .... 6.252

Rederi Aktiebolaget Transatlantic *v.* La Compagnie Française des Phosphates de L'Océanie (1926) 26 Ll L Rep 253 (CA) 5.97, 6.99

Rederiaktieselkabet Superior *v.* Dewar and Webb (1909) 14 CC 99; (1909) 14 CC 320 (CA) 6.226

Reynolds & Co *v.* Tomlinson [1896] 1 QB 586 .... 4.458

Rhymney Steamship Co Ltd *v.* Iberian Iron Ore Co Ltd. *See* Forest Steamship Co Ltd *v.* Iberian Iron Ore Co Ltd.

Ricargo Trading SA *v.* Spliethoff's Bevrachtingskantoor BV (The Tassos N) [1983] 1 Lloyd's Rep 648 .... 6.181

Richardson *v.* M Samuel & Co. *See* Richardson and M Samuel & Co, In the matter of an Arbitration between.

Richardson and M Samuel & Co, In the matter of an Arbitration between (1897) 3 CC 79 (CA) 4.68, 4.262

Richo International Ltd *v.* Alfred C Toepfer International GmbH (The Bonde) [1991] 1 Lloyd's Rep 136 .... 6.32, 6.43, 6.44

Rio Claro, The (Transworld Oil Ltd *v.* North Bay Shipping Corporation) [1987] 2 Lloyd's Rep 173 ... 4.59

Rio Sun, The (Gatoil International Inc *v.* Tradax Petroleum Ltd), LMLN 127, 13 September 1984; [1985] 1 Lloyd's Rep 350 .... 3.23, 6.137, 8.16

Robert Dollar Co, The *v.* Blood, Holman & Co Ltd (1920) 4 Ll L Rep 343 .... 3.453, 4.221, 5.34

Robertson *v.* Jackson (1845) 2 CB 412 .... 3.468

Rodenacker *v.* May & Hassell Ltd (1901) 6 CC 37 .... 2.246

Rodgers *v.* Forresters (1810) 2 Camp 483 .... 2.206

Rolan-Linie Schiffahrt GmbH *v.* Spillers Ltd (The Werrastein) [1956] 2 Lloyd's Rep 211 ...... 3.484, 3.490, 6.271

Ropner & Co *v.* Ronnebeck (1914) 20 CC 95 .... 9.24

Ropner & Co *v.* Stoate, Hosegood & Co (1905) 10 CC 73 .... 2.219

Ropner Shipping Co Ltd *v.* Cleeves Western Valleys Anthracite Collieries Ltd (1927) Ll L Rep 317 (CA) 4.32, 4.34, 4.35, 4.52, 5.115, 5.130, 6.87

Rowland and Marwood's Steamship Co Ltd *v.* Wilson, Sons & Co Ltd (1897) 2 CC 198 .... 7.25

Royal Mail Steam Packet Co and River Plate Steamship Co, Re (1910) 15 CC 124 .... 7.7, 7.9, 7.12, 7.13

Rubystone, The (Alvion Steamship Corporation Panama *v.* Galban Lobo Trading Co SA of Havana
[1954] 2 Lloyd's Rep 309; [1955] 1 Lloyd's Rep 9 (CA) 2.27, 2.28, 2.31, 2.32, 2.46, 2.52,
2.61, 2.62, 2.63, 2.79, 2.90, 7.19

S & M Hotels Ltd *v.* Legal and General Assurance Society Ltd [1972] 1 Lloyd's Rep 157 .... 6.122
SAMIR *v.* Notos Maritime Corporation of Monrovia (The Notos) [1985] 1 Lloyd's Rep 149; [1985] 2
Lloyd's Rep 334 (CA); [1987] 1 Lloyd's Rep 503 (HL) 4.91, 4.389, 4.442, 6.113, 6.114
SS Bassa (Owners of) *v.* Royal Commission on Wheat Supplies (1924) 20 Ll L Rep 243 .... 4.324
SS County of Lancaster Ltd *v.* Sharp & Co (1889) 24 QBD 158 .... 6.211
SS Magnhild (Owners of) *v.* McIntyre Brothers & Co (1920) 25 CC 347 .... 4.77, 4.78, 4.82
Sailing Ship Garston Co *v.* Hickie (1885) 15 QBD 580 .... 3.58, 3.104
Sailing Ship Lyderhorn Co *v.* Duncan, Fox & Co (1909) 14 CC 293 .... 3.123, 3.125
Salamis Shipping (Panama) SA *v.* Edm Van Meerbeck SA (The Onisilos) [1970] 2 Lloyd's Rep 405;
[1971] 2 Lloyd's Rep 29 (CA) 4.285, 4.347, 4.348, 4.352, 4.353, 4.368, 4.370, 4.372, 4.374, 4.375
Sale Corporation of Monrovia *v.* Turkish Cargo Lines General Manager (The Amiral Fahri Engin) [1993]
1 Lloyd's Rep 75 .... 3.194, 3.417
Sametiet M/T Johs Stove *v.* Istanbul Petrol Rafinerisi A/S (The Johs Stove) [1984] 1 Lloyd's Rep
38 .... 4.59, 4.62, 4.272, 4.280, 6.91
Sanders *v.* Vanzeller (1843) 4 QB 260 .... 6.210
Sandgate (Owners) *v.* W S Partridge & Co (The Sandgate) (1929) 35 Ll L Rep 9; [1930] P 30; (1929)
35 Ll L Rep 151 (CA) 2.149, 2.150, 2.153, 2.163, 2.167, 2.196, 2.198, 2.202
Sanguinetti *v.* Pacific Steam Navigation Co (1887) 2 QBD 238 (CA) 6.219
Sarma Navigation SA *v.* Sidermar SpA (The Sea Pioneer) [1979] 2 Lloyd's Rep 409; [1982] 1 Lloyd's
Rep 13 (CA) 5.105, 5.106, 5.107, 5.108
Saronikos, The (Greenmast Shipping Co SA *v.* Jean Lion et Cie SA) [1986] 2 Lloyd's Rep 277 ... 8.59, 8.62
Saturnia, The (Superfos Chartering A/S *v.* NBR (London) Ltd) [1984] 2 Lloyd's Rep 366; [1987] 2
Lloyd's Rep 43 (CA) 4.348, 4.350, 4.353, 4.354, 4.358, 4.359, 4.361, 4.375, 4.376, 4.377
Savona, The [1900] P 252 .... 9.23
Savvas, The (Clerco Compania Naviera SA *v.* The Food Corporation of India) [1981] 1 Lloyd's Rep 155;
[1982] 1 Lloyd's Rep 22 (CA) 2.178, 2.179, 4.467, 4.471
Saxon Ship Co Ltd *v.* Union Steamship Co Ltd (1900) 5 CC 381 (HL) 2.40, 6.98
Schilizzi *v.* Derry (1855) 4 E & B 873 .... 3.444, 3.460
Sea Pioneer, The (Sarma Navigation SA *v.* Sidermar SpA) [1979] 2 Lloyd's Rep 409; [1982] 1 Lloyd's
Rep 13 (CA) 5.105, 5.106, 5.107, 5.108
Sea Queen, The (Palm Shipping Inc *v.* Kuwait Petroleum Corporation) [1988] 1 Lloyd's Rep 500 ...... 3.415,
3.426, 3.439, 4.419, 4.421
Sea Steamship Co *v.* Price, Walker & Co Ltd (1903) 8 CC 292 .... 2.217, 2.224, 4.183
Sea Wind, The. *See* New York Arbitration
Seabridge Shipping Ltd *v.* Antco Shipping Ltd (The Furness Bridge) [1977] 2 Lloyd's Rep 367 .... 9.46
Seacrystal Shipping Ltd *v.* Bulk Transport Group Shipping Co Ltd (The Kyzikos) [1987] 1 Lloyd's Rep
48; [1987] 2 Lloyd's Rep 122 (CA); [1989] 1 Lloyd's Rep 1 (HL) 1.22, 3.110, 3.111, 3.112,
3.347, 3.353, 3.354, 3.355, 3.357, 3.358, 3.364, 3.368, 3.402, 3.414, 3.424, 3.439,
4.418, 4.420
Seafort, The (Carga del Sur Compania Naviera SA *v.* Ross T Smyth & Co Ltd) [1962] 2 Lloyd's Rep
147 .... 3.348
Seeberg *v.* Russian Wood Agency Ltd (1934) 50 Ll L Rep 146 .... 4.269, 4.336
Serraino & Sons *v.* Campbell [1891] 1 QB 283 .... 6.193
Sevonia Team, The (K/S A/S Seateam Co *v.* Iran National Oil Co [1983] 2 Lloyd's Rep 640 .... 6.203
Sewell *v.* Burdick (1884) 10 App Cas 74 (HL) 6.201, 6.208
Shackleford, The (Surrey Shipping Co Ltd *v.* Compagnie Continentale (France) SA) [1978] 1 Lloyd's
Rep 191; [1978] 2 Lloyd's Rep 154 (CA) 3.33, 3.280, 3.282, 3.283, 3.287, 3.290, 3.357, 4.426
Shamrock Steamship & Co Ltd *v.* Storey & Co (1898) 4 CC 80; (1899) 5 CC 21 (CA) 4.70, 4.72, 4.281
Sheila, The [1909] P 31n 3.483, 4.14
Shipping Developments Corporation SA *v.* V/O Sojuzneftexport (The Delian Spirit) [1971] 1 Lloyd's
Rep 64; [1971] 1 Lloyd's Rep 506 (CA) 3.98, 3.99, 3.176, 3.177, 3.340, 3.410, 3.411,
3.427, 4.394, 5.4, 7.2, 8.19, 8.20, 8.30
Siam Venture and Darfur, The [1987] 1 Lloyd's Rep 147 .... 2.180
Silva Plana, Bahamastars and Magic Sky, The (Oriental Maritime Pte Ltd *v.* Ministry of Food,
Government of the People's Republic of Bangladesh) [1989] 2 Lloyd's Rep 371 .... 2.198
Silver Coast Shipping Co Ltd *v.* Union Nationale des Co-opératives Agricoles des Céréales (The Silver
Sky) [1981] 2 Lloyd's Rep 95 .... 6.180

Silver Sky, The (Silver Coast Shipping Co Ltd v. Union Nationale des Co-opeÍatives Agricoles des
  Céréales) [1981] 2 Lloyd's Rep 95 .... 6.180
Sinoe, The (Overseas Transportation Co v. Mineralimportexport) [1971] 1 Lloyd's Rep 514; [1972] 1
  Lloyd's Rep 201 (CA) 6.81, 6.82, 6.83, 6.228, 6.247, 6.248, 6.249, 6.250, 6.251
Sir R Ropner & Co Ltd v. Bunge North American Grain Corporation (1938) 62 Ll L Rep 111 .. 4.320, 4.321
Sir R Ropner & Co Ltd v. W S Partridge & Co (1929) 33 Ll L Rep 86 .... 7.22
Sjoerds v. Luscombe (1812) 16 East 201 .... 4.7
Smith v. Dart & Son (1884) 14 QBD 105 (CA) 3.172, 3.175
Smurthwaite v. Wilkins (1862) 11 CB(NS) 842 .... 6.204
Sociedad Carga Oceanica SA v. Idolinoele Vertriebsgellschaft mbH (The Angelos Lusis) [1964] 2
  Lloyd's Rep 28 .... 3.403, 3.426, 4.395, 4.413, 8.20
Sociedad Financiera de Bienes Raices v. Agrimpex. See Agrimpex Hungarian Trading Co for
  Agricultural Products v. Sociedad Financiera de Bienes Raices SA.
Societa Ligure di Armamento v. Joint Danube & Black Sea Shipping Agencies of Braila (1931) 39 Ll L
  Rep 167 .... 8.15
Société Anonyme Marocaine de L'Industrie du Ruffinage v. Notos Maritime Corporation. See SAMIR v.
  Notos Maritime Corporation of Monrovia.
Sofial SA v. Ove Skou Rederi (The Helle Skou) [1976] 2 Lloyd's Rep 205 .... 3.285, 3.287, 3.288, 4.249
Solon, The, Case No 1999 Folio 736, judgment dated 11 January 2000; LMLN 529, 17 February 2000 ..... 4.61
Sormovskiy 3068, The (Sucre Export SA v. Northern River Shipping Ltd), LMLN 380, 28 May
  1994 .... 6.198
South Australian Voluntary Wheat Pool v. Owners of The Riol (1926) 24 Ll L Rep 363 .... 6.23
Spalmatori, The (Union of India v. Compania Naviera Aeolus SA [1960] 1 Lloyd's Rep 112; [1961] 1
  Lloyd's Rep 132 (CA); [1962] 2 Lloyd's Rep 175 (HL) 1.30, 4.13, 4.282, 4.284, 4.285, 4.315,
                          4.317, 4.318, 4.327, 4.335, 4.336, 4.337, 4.340, 4.342, 4.347, 4.376, 6.6, 6.97,
                                                                                                           6.100, 6.101
Stag Line Ltd v. Board of Trade (1950) 83 Ll L Rep 356; (1950) 84 Ll L Rep 1 (CA) 3.26, 3.28
Stainless Emperor, The (Huyton SA v. Inter Operators SA) [1994] 2 Lloyd's Rep 298 .... 4.16, 6.102
Stamatios G Embiricos, The (President of India v. Edina Compania Naviera SA) [1965] 1 Lloyd's Rep
  574 .... 4.93
Stanton v. Austin (1872) LR 7 CP 651 .... 3.217
Steamship. See also under SS.
Steamship Calcutta Ltd v. Andrew Weir & Co [1910] 1 KB 759 .... 6.216
Steamship Induna Co Ltd v. British Phosphate Commissioners (1949) 82 Ll L Rep 430 .... 4.436
Steel, Young & Co v. Grand Canary Coaling Co (1902) 7 CC 213 (CA) 6.4
Stephens v. Harris & Co (1887) 56 LJQB 516; (1887) 57 LJQB 203 (CA) 2.94, 2.95, 2.96, 2.97,
                                                                                                     2.99, 2.101, 4.153, 4.262
Steven v. Bromley & Son [1919] 2 KB 722 (CA) 8.62
Stewart Line (Belfast) v. Wallace Bros Ltd (Dublin) (1921) 7 Ll L Rep 98 .... 6.23
Stindt v. Roberts (1818) 5 D & L 460 .... 6.206
Straker v. Kidd (1878) 3 QBD 223 .... 6.269
Sucre Export SA v. Northern River Shipping Ltd (The Sormovskiy 3068), LMLN 380, 28 May
  1994 .... 6.198
Sugar Islander, The (California and Hawaiian Sugar Co v. The National Cereal and Produce Board of
  Kenya) (NY Arb), LMLN 318, 11 January 1992 .... 8.40
Suisse Atlantique Société d'Armement Maritime SA v. NV Rotterdamsche Kolen Centrale (The General
  Guisan) [1965] 1 Lloyd's Rep 166; [1965] 1 Lloyd's Rep 533 (CA); [1966] 1 Lloyd's Rep 529
  (HL) 6.28, 6.31, 6.35, 6.36, 6.37, 6.38, 6.43, 6.44, 6.49, 6.175
Sun Shipping Co Ltd v. Watson & Youell Shipping Agency Ltd (1926) 24 Ll L Rep 28 .... 2.224, 3.157
Sunbeam Shipping Co Ltd v. President of India (The Atlantic Sunbeam) [1973] 1 Lloyd's Rep 482 .... 3.166,
                          3.200, 3.277, 3.327, 3.339, 3.341, 3.342, 3.344, 3.345, 5.48, 6.48, 8.22, 8.51
Sunward Overseas SA v. Cargill Inc (The Chios Faith) (NY Arb), LMLN 349, 20 March 1993 .... 4.166
Superfos Chartering A/S v. NBR (London) Ltd (The Saturnia) [1984] 2 Lloyd's Rep 366; [1987] 2
  Lloyd's Rep 43 (CA) 4.348, 4.350, 4.353, 4.354, 4.358, 4.359, 4.361, 4.375, 4.376, 4.377
Surrey Shipping Co Ltd v. Compagnie Continentale (France) SA (The Shackleford) [1978] 1 Lloyd's Rep
  191; [1978] 2 Lloyd's Rep 154 (CA) 3.33, 3.280, 3.282, 3.283, 3.287, 3.290, 3.357, 4.426
Svenssons Travarvaktiebolag v. Cliffe Steamship Co Ltd (1931) 41 Ll L Rep 262 .... 5.20

Tabb & Burleston v. Briton Ferry Works Ltd (1921) 6 Ll L Rep 181 .... 4.264
Tai Ning, The. See New York Arbitration
Takafa, The (President of India) v. Hariana Overseas Corp [1990] 1 Lloyd's Rep 536 .... 1.13
Tamplin Steamship Co v. Anglo Mexican Petroleum Co [1916] 2 AC 397 .... 9.9, 9.25, 9.43

Tapscott v. Balfour (1872) LR 8 CP 46 .... 3.40, 3.70, 3.71
Tassos N, The (Ricargo Trading SA v. Spliethoff's Berrachtingskantoor BV) [1983] 1 Lloyd's Rep 648 ... 6.181
Taylor v. Caldwell (1863) 3 B & S 826 .... 9.15
Taylor v. Clay (1846) 9 QBD 713 .... 3.481
Taylor v. Great Northern Railway (1866) LR I CP 385 .... 2.211
Thanassis A, The (Olbena SA v. Psara Maritime Inc), LMLN 68, 10 June 1982 .... 6.115
Tharsis Sulphur & Copper Co Ltd v. Morel Brothers & Co [1891] 2 QB 647 .... 3.6
Themistocles (Owners) v. Compagnie Intercontinentale de L'Hyperphosphate of Tangier (1948) 82 Ll L
    Rep 232 .... 3.478, 7.16, 7.18, 7.29
Theraios, The (Lodza Compania de Navigacione SA v. Govt. of Ceylon) [1970] 2 Lloyd's Rep 142;
    [1971] 1 Lloyd's Rep 209 (CA) 2.165, 2.167, 2.196, 2.202
Thiis v. Byers (1876) 1 QBD 244 .... 2.46
Thomasson Shipping Co Ltd v. Henry W Peabody & Co of London Ltd [1959] 2 Lloyd's Rep 296 ....   7.8,
                                                                                                                          7.19, 7.20
Thorman v. Dowgate Steamship Co Ltd (1909) 15 CC 67 .... 3.46, 4.75, 4.79, 4.87
Tillmans & Co v. The Steamship Knutsford Ltd (1908) 13 CC 244 .... 4.73, 4.77
Timna, The (Zim Israel Navigation Co Ltd v. Tradax Export SA) [1970] 2 Lloyd's Rep 409; [1971] 2
    Lloyd's Rep 91 (CA) 3.22, 3.211, 3.273, 4.457, 8.16
Total Transport Corporation of Panama v. Amoco Trading Co (The Altus), LMLN 140, 14 March 1985;
    [1985] 1 Lloyd's Rep 423 .... 4.47, 5.66, 6.31, 6.32, 6.41, 6.42, 6.127
Toulla, The (Kition Compania Naviera SA v. Ahmed Bamaodah) [1985] 1 Lloyd's Rep 107 .... 6.207
Touteng v. Hubbard (1802) 3 B & P 291 .... 4.7
Trading Society Kwik-Hoo-Tong v. Royal Commission on Sugar Supply (1923) 15 Ll L Rep 24 .... 6.2
Trading Society Kwik-Hoo-Tong of Jarva v. The Royal Commission on Sugar Supply (1924) 19 Ll L Rep
    90 .... 6.2
Tramp Shipping Corporation v. Greenwich Marine Inc (The New Horizon) [1974] 2 Lloyd's Rep 210;
    [1975] 2 Lloyd's Rep 314 (CA) 4.265, 4.266, 4.268, 4.326
Transamerican Steamship Corporation v. Tradax Export SA (The Oriental Envoy) [1982] 2 Lloyd's Rep
    266 .... 3.148, 5.107, 5.131, 5.141, 6.60
Transgrain Shipping BV v. Global Transporte Oceanico SA (The Mexico I) [1988] 2 Lloyd's Rep 149;
    [1990] 1 Lloyd's Rep 507 (CA) 3.237, 3.257, 3.260, 3.288, 3.291, 3.293,
                                                                                       3.294, 3.296, 3.297, 5.108, 5.114, 5.144
Transoceanica Societa Italiana di Navigazione v. Shipton & Sons (1922) 28 CC 64 .... 2.251
Transworld Oil Ltd v. North Bay Shipping Corporation (The Rio Claro) [1987] 2 Lloyd's Rep 173 ....   4.59
Tregantle, The (Hain Steamship Co Ltd v. Sociedad Anonima Comercial de Exportación e Importación
    (Louis Dreyfus & Cia Ltda)) (1932) 43 Ll L Rep 136 .... 4.176, 4.191, 4.204
Tres Flores, The (Compania de Naviera Nedelka SA v. Tradax International SA) [1973] 2 Lloyd's Rep
    247 (CA) 3.128, 3.131, 3.132, 3.141, 3.142, 3.169, 3.248, 3.286
Trevarrack, The (Hain Steamship Co Ltd v. Sociedad Anonima Comercial de Exportación e Importación
    (Louis Dreyfus & Co Ltd) (1934) 49 Ll L Rep 86 .... 2.15, 4.182, 4.229, 4.231, 4.232
Tropwave, The (Maritime Transport Operators GmbH v. Louis Dreyfus et Cie) [1981] 2 Lloyd's Rep
    159 .... 2.183, 2.196, 2.198, 2.202, 5.126, 5.140, 6.251
Tsakiroglou & Co v. Noblee Thorl GmbH [1962] AC 93 (HL) 9.3
Tsukuba Maru, The (Nippon Yusen Kaisha v. Société Anonyme Marocaine de L'Industrie du Raffinage)
    [1979] 1 Lloyd's Rep 459 .... 6.102, 6.116, 6.121, 6.127
Turnbull, Scott & Co v. Cruickshank & Co (1904) 7 Fraser 265 (Ct of Sess) 2.135, 2.138
Tyne & Blyth Shipowning Co Ltd v. Leach (1900) 5 CC 155 .... 6.179

Ulyanovsk, The (Novorossisk Shipping Co v. Neopetro Co Ltd) [1990] 1 Lloyd's Rep 425 .... 4.421, 5.6,
                                                                                                                          5.13, 5.14
Unifert International SAL v. Panous Shipping Co Inc (The Virginia M) [1989] 1 Lloyd's Rep 603 ... 3.162, 3.163
Union Amersterdam, The (Blue Anchor Line Ltd v. Alfred C Toepfer International GmbH) [1982] 2
    Lloyd's Rep 432 .... 4.20, 4.49, 4.52, 4.56, 6.88, 6.91
Union of India v. Compania Naviera Aeolus SA (The Spalmatori) [1960] 1 Lloyd's Rep 112; [1961] 1
    Lloyd's Rep 132 (CA); [1962] 2 Lloyd's Rep 175 (HL) 1.30, 4.13, 4.282, 4.284,
                        4.285, 4.315, 4.317, 4.318, 4.327, 4.335, 4.336, 4.337, 4.340, 4.342, 4.347, 4.376,
                                                                                                          6.6, 6.97, 6.100, 6.101
Union of India v. The Great Eastern Shipping Co Ltd (The Jag Leela), LMLN 242, 11 February 1989 .... 3.204
United British Steamship Co Ltd v. Minister of Food [1951] 1 Lloyd's Rep 111 ... 2.181, 2.182, 6.266, 6.267, 7.5
United Nations Food and Agriculture Organisation World Food Programme v. Caspian Navigation Inc
    (The Jay Ganesh) [1994] 2 Lloyd's Rep 358 .... 3.146

TABLE OF CASES

United States Shipping Board v. Bunge y Born (1924) 18 Ll L Rep 422; (1924) 20 Ll L Rep 97 (CA); (1925) 23 Ll L Rep 257 (HL) 6.172, 6.176
United States Shipping Board v. Strick & Co Ltd (1926) 25 Ll L Rep 73 (HL) 2.226, 3.89, 3.470, 3.472, 3.476
Unitramp v. Garnac Grain Co Inc (The Hermaine) [1979] 1 Lloyd's Rep 212 (CA) 9.35
Universal Cargo Carriers Corporation v. Pedro Citati [1957] 1 Lloyd's Rep 174 .... 9.34, 9.35, 9.39
Universal Monarch, The (Palm Shipping Inc v. Vitol SA) [1988] 2 Lloyd's Rep 483 .... 4.444

V M Salgaoncar E Irmaos v. Goulandris Brothers Ltd [1954] 1 Lloyd's Rep 56 .... 2.188, 2.202
Valla Giovanni & C SpA v. Gebr Van Weelde Scheepvaartkantoor BV (The Chanda) [1985] 1 Lloyd's Rep 563 .... 4.90, 4.325
Van Liewen (CA) v. Hollis Bros & Co Ltd. See C A Van Liewen v. Hollis Bros & Co Ltd.
Van Nievelt Goudriaan Stoomvaart Maatschappij v. C A Forslind & Son Ltd (1925) 22 Ll L Rep 49 .... 2.23, 3.78, 3.88
Vancouver strike cases. See Reardon Smith Line Ltd v. Ministry of Agriculture, Fisheries and Food.
Vastric, The (Metals & Ropes Co Ltd v. Filia Compania Limitada) [1966] 2 Lloyd's Rep 219 .... 3.386
Vaughan v. Campbell, Heatley & Co (1885) 2 TLR 33 .... 3.158, 4.36
Venizelos A N E of Athens v. Société Commerciale de Céréales et Financière SA of Zurich (The Prometheus) [1974] 1 Lloyd's Rep 350 .... 4.320, 4.322
Venore, The (Venore Transportation Co v. President of India) [1973] 1 Lloyd's Rep 494 .... 3.338
Vergottis (Andreas) v. Robinson David & Co (1928) 31 Ll L Rep 23 .... 6.193
Verren v. Anglo-Dutch Brick (1927) Ltd (1929) 34 Ll L Rep 56; (1929) 34 Ll L Rep 210 (CA) .. 2.16, 5.87, 6.172
Virginia M, The (Unifert International SAL v. Panous Shipping Co Inc) [1989] 1 Lloyd's Rep 603 .. 3.162, 3.163
Voltaz, The [1997] 1 Lloyd's Rep 35 .... 6.284
Vorras, The (Dow Chemical (Nederland) BV v. BP Tanker Co Ltd) [1983] 1 Lloyd's Rep 579 (CA) ... 2.3, 2.45, 2.92, 2.96, 2.101, 2.103, 2.105, 2.108, 2.109, 2.139, 2.143, 4.146, 4.147, 4.153, 4.159

W I Radcliffe Steamship Co Ltd v. Exporthleb (1939) 64 Ll L Rep 250 .... 4.428
Watson v. H Borner & Co Ltd (1900) 5 CC 377 .... 3.333
Watson Brothers Shipping Co Ltd v. Mysore Manganese Co Ltd (1910) 15 CC 159 .... 2.122, 2.127, 5.73, 5.80, 5.82, 5.84, 5.85
Watts, Watts & Co Ltd v. Mitsui & Co Ltd (1917) 22 CC 242 .... 4.111
Weir v. Union Steamship Co Ltd [1900] AC 525 .... 3.120
Weir & Co v. Richardson (1897) 3 CC 20 .... 2.267
Werrastein, The (Roland-Linie Schiffahrt GmbH v. Spillers Ltd) [1956] 2 Lloyd's Rep 211 ... 3.484, 3.490, 6.271
Western Steamship Co Ltd v. Amaral Sutherland & Co Ltd (1913) 19 CC 1, (1914) 19 CC 272 (CA) ... 6.12, 6.14
Westoll v. Lindsay (1916) Sess Cas 782 .... 4.282
Westport Clipper, The (Liquid Bulk Tanker Services Inc v. The Embassy of Bangladesh) (NY Arb), LMLN 360, 21 August 1993 .... 3.314, 4.241, 4.256
Whittal & Co v. Rahtkens Shipping Co Ltd (1907) 12 CC 226 .... 4.254
William Alexander & Sons v. Aktieselskabet Dampskabet Hansa (1919) 25 CC (HL) 2.2, 4.3, 4.26, 6.78, 6.79
Williams & Co and the Brankelow Steamship Co Ltd v. Canton Insurance Office Ltd. See Brankelow Steamship Co Ltd v. Canton Insurance Office Ltd.
Williams Brothers (Hull) Ltd v. Naamlooze Venootschap W H Berghuys Kolenhandel (1915) 21 CC 253 .... 4.263, 4.303
Wilson and Coventry Ltd v. Otto Thoresen's Linie (1910) 15 CC 262 .... 6.12, 6.15
Wolff v. Horncastle (1798) 1 B & P 316 .... 6.200
World Navigator, The (Kurt A Becher GmbH & Co KG v. Roplak Enterprises SA) [1991] 2 Lloyd's Rep 23 (CA) 3.166, 3.339, 3.344, 8.32, 8.51
Wright v. New Zealand Shipping Co (1879) 4 Ex D 165 .... 2.208, 2.211

Yeoman v. Rex (1904) 9 CC 269 .... 2.6
Yewglen (Owners) v. Helical Bar and Engineering Co (1926) 25 Ll L Rep 170 .... 4.267
Young v. Moeller (1855) S E & B 755 .... 6.206
Ypatia Halcoussi, The (President of India v. Olympia Sauna Shipping Co SA) [1984] 2 Lloyd's Rep 455 .... 3.63

Z Steamship Co Ltd v. Amtorg, New York (1938) 61 Ll L Rep 97 .... 4.184, 4.192, 4.225, 4.233, 5.89, 6.239, 6.245, 7.26
Zim Israel Navigation Co Ltd v. Tradax Export SA (The Timna) [1970] 2 LLoyd's Rep 409; [1971] 2 Lloyd's Rep 91 (CA) 3.22, 3.211, 3.273, 4.457, 8.16
Zuiho Maru, The (Kawasaki Steel Corporation v. Sardoil SpA) [1977] 2 Lloyd's Rep 552 .... 6.42, 9.44

Table of Statutes

Act 210 of 1958 (Louisiana) 4.177
Arbitration Act 1979—
  s. 1 .... 5.13
Bills of Lading Act 1855 .... 6.203, 6.204,
               6.205, 6.206, 6.210, 6.211
  s. 1 .... 6.201, 6.203
  s. 2 .... 6.205
Carriage of Goods by Sea Act (COGSA)
  (US) 4.49, 4.50, 6.88
Contracts of Employment Act 1963 .... 4.261
  Sched. 1, para. 11 .... 4.261
Customs Act 1962 (India) 3.204
  s. 30 .... 3.203
  s. 31 .... 3.203, 3.204
Employment Act 1982—
  s. 20(1) 4.332
  Sched. 2, para. 7(1) 4.332
Employment Protection (Consollidation) Act
  1978—
  s. 151(1) 4.332
  Sched. 13, para. 24 .... 4.332
Employment Rights Act 1996—
  s. 235(5) 4.261

Hague Rules 6.91
  Art iv(3) 6.64
Law of Property Act 1925—
  s. 136 .... 6.201
Law Reform (Frustrated Contracts), Act
  1943 .... 1.36, 9.50
  s. 2(5) 9.50
Merchant Shipping Act 1894—
  Pt vii 6.189
National Recovery Act 1933 (US) 4.194
Negotiable Instruments Act 1881 (India) 4.180
  s. 25 .... 4.180
Sale and Supply of Goods Act 1994 .... 6.202
Sale of Goods Act 1893 .... 6.202
Sale of Goods Act 1979 .... 6.202
  s. 17 .... 6.202
  s. 18 .... 6.202
Sale of Goods (Amendment) Act 1995 .... 6.202
Trades Union and Labour Relations (Consolidation) Act 1992—
  s. 235(4) 4.332
  s. 246 .... 4.261

CHAPTER 1

General Principles

1.1 The present law relating to laytime and demurrage has for the most part been developed by judicial interpretation of commercial charterparties over the last one hundred and fifty years, although some of the basic principles were established around the time that Queen Victoria came to the throne.

1.2 The development of this branch of the law has been closely allied to the historical and social changes that took place as sail gave way to steam, and more recently as improved methods of communication have given greater central control to those controlling the commercial adventure, which a voyage charter still represents. It is perhaps one of the few remaining areas of English common law where there has been little statutory intervention.

1.3 The establishment of standard forms of charter, the meaning of almost each word of which has been the subject of judicial interpretation, might have resulted in a static law, but fortunately that has not been so and the law continues to develop to meet present and future needs. The increasing use of additional clauses to charterparties, some of which are not always accidentally ambiguous, will also no doubt continue to provide much material for future litigation.

1.4 It is perhaps important to remember that whilst judges, and increasingly arbitrators, lay down the interpretation to be given to particular clauses, these are often drafted by commercial men and the interpretation they are given in practice only rarely reaches arbitration, and still more rarely the higher courts.

1.5 Recent changes in arbitral law and practice have meant fewer appeals and this has reinforced the importance of publishing some arbitration awards of general importance in a form where the identity of the parties is not disclosed and the confidentiality of the award is perserved. *Lloyd's Maritime Law Newsletter* is now the accepted forum for this type of limited publication and many of the awards reported in it are quoted in this book.

1.6 An indication of the number of reported cases there have been over the years is given by the length of the Table of Cases.

1.7 There have been three attempts to introduce standardised laytime and demurrage clause definitions: the *Charterparty Laytime Definitions 1980*, the *Voyage Charterparty Laytime Interpretation Rules 1993* and the *Baltic Code 2000*. These are each reproduced in full in the Appendix to this book. Each definition is, in addition, dealt with under the relevant chapter heading. These definitions will, however, only apply where they are specifically incorporated into the relevant charterparty, although they are often quoted as being persuasive of the meaning of the term in question.

1.8 This first chapter is intended to set the scene on laytime and demurrage. It deals with the general principles involved and is intended to present an overview of the subject for anyone who is not familiar with it. All the topics covered in this first chapter are dealt with in greater detail elsewhere in the book.

1.9 It is important before considering the principles of laytime to see how laytime fits into the scheme of a voyage charter. The words "laytime" and "demurrage" are themselves defined in the following terms in the *Voylayrules 1993*.[1]

"LAYTIME" shall mean the period of time agreed between the parties during which the owner will make and keep the vessel available for loading or discharging without payment additional to the freight.

"DEMURRAGE" shall mean an agreed amount payable to the owner in respect of delay to the vessel beyond the laytime, for which the owner is not responsible. Demurrage shall not be subject to laytime exceptions.

Laytime is probably a shortened version of lying alongside time.

1.10 In *The Johanna Oldendorff*,[2] Lord Diplock divided the adventure contemplated by a voyage charter into four successive stages. These are:

    (1) The loading or approach voyage, viz. the voyage of the vessel from wherever she is at the date of the charterparty or the conclusion of her previous fixture, if that is later, to the place specified as the place of loading.

    (2) The loading operation, viz. the delivery of the cargo to the vessel at the place of loading and its stowage on board.

    (3) The carrying or loaded voyage, viz. the voyage of the vessel from the place of loading to the place specified in the charter as the place of delivery.

    (4) The discharging operation, viz. the delivery of the cargo from the vessel at the place of delivery and its receipt there by the charterer or other consignee.

1.11 The stages are consecutive and each must be completed before the next can begin. There cannot therefore be any gap between them, nor is there any overlap.

1.12 In its simplest form, a voyage charter therefore provides that:

The vessel shall proceed to (the specified place of loading) and there load (the designated cargo) and being so loaded shall proceed to (the specified place of discharge) and deliver the same.

1.13 The two voyage stages are in the hands of the shipowner, whilst loading and discharging are joint operations between the shipowner and the charterer, or those for whom he is responsible. The shipowner's aim is that all stages should be completed as economically as possible, whilst earning the maximum possible return on his capital investment. The charterer, on the other hand, wishes his cargo to be carried to its destination, at the least possible cost. Time may or may not be of importance to him compared with cost, but to the shipowner, time is money. The voyage stages, including proceeding to sea, are normally to be prosecuted with all reasonable or convenient despatch.[3] However, depending on bunker costs at the time, the shipowner may negotiate to perform the laden voyage at a reduced speed, usually referred to as slow steaming, taking slightly longer but resulting in a lower overall cost, because of the bunker savings achieved.

1.14 As far as the periods underway during the voyage stages are concerned, the adventure is normally entirely under the control of the shipowner and it is therefore logical

---

    1. See Appendix and the similar definition in *Baltic Code 2000*.
    2. *Oldendorff (EL) & Co GmbH* v. *Tradax Export SA (The Johanna Oldendorff)* [1973] 2 Lloyd's Rep 285, at p. 304. The wording given here differs slightly from that used by Lord Diplock.
    3. *President of India* v. *Hariana Overseas Corp (The Takafa)* [1990] 1 Lloyd's Rep 536.

that he should bear the risk of any delay occurring during this time. With regard to the periods not underway during the voyage stages and the time taken during the loading and discharging operations, it is open to the parties to decide which risks of delay each shall be responsible for, together with how long shall be allowed for the loading and discharging operations. As Scrutton LJ said in *Inverkip Steamship Co Ltd v. Bunge & Co*[4]:

The sum agreed for freight in a charter covers the use of the ship for an agreed period of time for loading and discharging, known as the lay days, and for the voyage.

The apportionment of risk will depend on the freight payable and the state of the freight market, i.e. the amount of commercial pressure that each can bring to bear against the other.

1.15 Voyage charters are divided into two principal types depending on the laytime provisions they contain. There are those with customary laytime and those with fixed laytime. Each will be considered in detail in subsequent chapters.

1.16 Under a customary laytime charter, the laytime allowed is that length of time which is reasonable in the circumstances appertaining in the particular port with the particular ship at the time of loading or discharging, as the case may be. Since the time will vary from ship to ship and time to time, the period allowed cannot be determined in advance. In the absence of default by the charterer, the normal risks of delay, e.g. congestion, weather, holidays, strikes, etc., usually lie with the shipowner. If the parties fail to specify how much laytime is allowed, then customary laytime will be implied by law.

1.17 The other type of laytime allowed is fixed laytime. As its name implies, it is of fixed duration. It may either be described in terms of days or hours, a particular type thereof or as a rate of working cargo. Examples of the former would be "to load in 3 running days" or "to discharge in 7 weather working days", and of the latter, "to load at an average of 2000 metric tons per day" or "to discharge at an average rate of 500 tons per working hatch per working day". The point about fixed laytime is that its duration can in theory be predicted in advance. The reason why it is only "in theory" is because the unit of time chosen by the parties, e.g. weather working days and other clauses in the charter, may cause time to be suspended during the running of laytime so that the actual time taken to expend a given number of days of that type may be more than originally thought. However, in the absence of modifying provisions, the incidence of risk in this type of charter as between the shipowner and the charterer lies entirely with the charterer. In other words, the situation is exactly the opposite to a customary laytime charter. As Lord Selborne LC said in *Postlethwaite v. Freeland* of the undertaking by the charterer to load within a fixed period of time,[5] that is

an absolute and unconditional engagement, for the non-performance of which he is answerable, whatever may be the nature of the impediments which prevent him from performing it and which cause the ship to be detained in his service beyond the time stipulated.

4. *Inverkip Steamship Co Ltd v. Bunge & Co* (1917) 22 CC 200, at p. 204.
5. *Postlethwaite v. Freeland* (1880) 5 App Cas 599, at p. 608.

1.18 The parties having decided that the charterer should bear the risk of delay, the reason why this should be an absolute liability was explained by Lord Diplock in *The Johanna Oldendorff* in the following terms[6]:

Charterparties originated at a period when contractual obligations were as a general rule treated as absolute. A party's obligation was to secure that anything that he warranted should be done, was done. If it was not, then, unless this was the result of some default of the other party, he was liable in damages, even though circumstances over which he himself had no control and could not even have foreseen made it impossible for it to be done.

1.19 Whilst the customary laytime charter was once an important form of commercial document, it has of late fallen into comparative disuse and nowadays is only rarely encountered. However, it is occasionally used and its development has played an important role in the law relating to laytime.

1.20 The reason why fixed laytime charters are preferred is probably because of their greater certainty when it comes to estimating the permitted length of a charter and because they offer more flexibility by the use of exception clauses in varying the apportionment of risk.

1.21 Whichever form of laytime is chosen, voyage charters are also divided up into berth, dock and port charters, depending on which of these three alternatives is chosen as the specified destination for loading or discharging as the case may be. There is no reason why a charter should not be, say, a berth charter for loading and a port charter for discharging. In general, however, laytime commences upon the vessel's arrival at the specified destination, having given notice of readiness (if required) and after any time provided for in the charter has elapsed. Upon laytime commencing, liability for delay may change from the shipowner to the charterer, depending on the terms of the charter. This is why it is important to be able to establish precisely when the specified destination is reached. Berth and dock charters on the whole create few problems in this respect, since it is comparatively easy to say whether a vessel has reached its berth or dock. The port charter is, however, more difficult. Until the decision of the Court of Appeal in *Leonis Steamship Co* v. *Rank*,[7] the law was in some confusion, but in that case the court held that in a port charter, the specified destination was reached when the vessel arrived in the commercial area of the port and not as some of the earlier cases had suggested when the vessel actually arrived in berth. Later, difficulties arose in deciding what the Court of Appeal had meant and what factors had to be taken into account before it could be decided whether the usual waiting place was within the commercial area of the port. These were resolved by the House of Lords in *The Johanna Oldendorff*, where Lord Reid laid down what has subsequently become known as "the Reid test"[8]:

Before a ship can be said to have arrived at a port she must, if she cannot proceed immediately to a berth, have reached a position within the port where she is at the immediate and effective disposition of the charterer.

The presumption is that if the vessel concerned is at a place where waiting ships of that type usually lie and this is within the port, then she is at the "immediate and effective disposition of the charterer".

---

6. *Oldendorff (EL) & Co GmbH* v. *Tradax Export SA (The Johanna Oldendorff)* [1973] 2 Lloyd's Rep 285, at p. 304.
7. *Leonis Steamship Co Ltd* v. *Joseph Rank Ltd (No 1)* [1908] 1 KB 499.
8. *Oldendorff (EL) & Co GmbH* v. *Tradax Export SA (The Johanna Oldendorff)* [1973] 2 Lloyd's Rep 285, at p. 291.

1.22 It is, however, open to the parties to advance the time when laytime commences or to provide in some other way for time to count earlier than would be the case under the normal rules. In the case of a berth charter, the parties may agree that time should count "whether in berth or not", thus advancing commencement of time when the delay is due to congestion.[9] Similarly, the parties may wish to allow time to start as soon as the vessel ceases to be underway, even if still outside the port limits.

1.23 Once laytime has commenced to run it may nevertheless be suspended either by an interruption or an exception to laytime. The difference between these terms, as used in this book, is that an interruption to laytime excludes periods outside the definition of laytime as expressed in the laytime clause. Excepted periods are within the definition, but expressly excluded. Adverse weather would be an interruption to laytime expressed in weather working days, but a clause excluding time lost by strikes, would be an exception. The principal difference lies in the fact that with an interruption, it is only necessary to show that the excluded state of affairs exists, but with an exception, it is necessary to show a causal connection between what is excluded and the failure to work cargo.

1.24 As Lord Diplock also pointed out in *The Johanna Oldendorff*[10]:

In the case of maritime carriage this rule (as to absolute liability) was subject to the exception that performance was excused if it were prevented by Act of God or of the King's enemies or by inherent vice in the goods carried.[11] At a very early date it became usual to incorporate in charterparties express exceptions for other maritime perils, and in modern charterparties these have been extended to strikes and other hindrances to performance which take place on land.

1.25 Once commenced, laytime will continue to run until loading (or discharging) has been completed, or until it expires, if these operations are not finished earlier. In the tanker trade, it is usual to define completion in terms of disconnection of hoses.

1.26 The laytime allowed may be a single period covering both loading and discharging, or the charter may provide for separate calculations for each. In the event of the latter, provision may be made for the transfer of unused laytime from loading to the time allowed for discharge, or vice versa. The different methods by which this can be achieved are referred to as averaging and reversing.

1.27 In certain trades, e.g. the parcel tanker trade, a vessel may be under a number of different charters at the same time, each covering part of the cargo.

1.28 If loading or discharging are not completed within the time allowed, then the shipowner is entitled to be compensated for the extra time taken. This may either take the form of liquidated damages, demurrage, or unliquidated damages, where the claim is one for detention. Demurrage is usually specified in the charter as a daily rate and the parties may either agree for a limited period on demurrage, or more commonly, for an unlimited period. It is now generally accepted that failure by the charterer to complete loading (or discharging) within the time allowed is a breach of contract.

1.29 The demurrage rate fixed by the parties will be intended to cover the vessel's daily running costs, plus the profit the shipowner would have been able to earn, had his vessel been released timeously. Clearly, from a commercial point of view, it makes sense for this figure to be agreed in advance and, like freight, it will be subject to market pressures.

---

9. *Seacrystal Shipping Ltd v. Bulk Transport Group Shipping Co Ltd (The Kyzikos)* [1989] 1 Lloyd's Rep 1.

10. *Ibid.*, at p. 305.

11. These were the defences open to a common carrier, whether by land or by sea.

1.30 A phrase much used with regard to demurrage is "once on demurrage, always on demurrage". What this is intended to signify is that demurrage is payable on a running day basis, and that laytime exceptions do not apply once demurrage commences. It will take very clear words to convince a court that the parties intended a particular exception to apply once the vessel is on demurrage. In *The Spalmatori*,[12] in discussing whether the Centrocon strike clause applied to strikes commencing after the vessel was on demurrage, Lord Reid said[13]:

> . . . if it occurs after demurrage has begun to accrue the owner might well say: "True your breach of contract in detaining my ship after the end of the laytime did not cause the strike, but if you had fulfilled your contract the strike would have caused no loss because my ship would have been on the high seas before it began: so it is more reasonable that you should bear the loss than that I should."

The same reasoning, of course, applies to any exception. Likewise, laytime exceptions and even demurrage exceptions do not normally apply to claims for detention.

1.31 *Prima facie*, liability for demurrage rests with the charterer and even if the terms of the charter are effectively incorporated into the bills of lading issued under the charter, this will not be sufficient in the absence of an express provision to make the receiver jointly liable for any demurrage that has accrued.[14] However, one way in which the receiver may be made liable for demurrage, particularly demurrage at the discharge port, is by the grant of an express lien on the cargo in favour of the shipowner. If this is combined with an effective cesser clause then the result will be to transfer all liability for demurrage to the receiver. However, a lien for demurrage is only a possessory lien so that if the shipowner loses control of the cargo, he loses his lien and the receiver can no longer be held liable for any demurrage that might otherwise be due. In these circumstances the shipowner will have lost his right to claim demurrage from either the charterer or the receiver.

1.32 If loading or discharging is completed within the laytime allowed, then if so provided for in the charter, despatch will be payable either in respect of all time saved or, less commonly, for all working time saved.

1.33 As Devlin J said in *Compania de Navigación Zita SA* v. *Louis Dreyfus & Cie*[15]:

> The shipowner's desire is to achieve a quick turn-round; time is money for him. The object of fixing lay days and providing for demurrage and despatch money is to penalize dilatoriness in loading and to reward promptitude.

Where despatch money is payable, it almost always is at half the demurrage rate.

1.34 A claim for detention will arise where a vessel is delayed by default of the charterer, or those for whom he is responsible, during the currency of a charter. Unliquidated damages are recoverable for such delay, except where it occurs after the vessel has reached its specified destination and loading or discharging, as the case may be, have not been completed, when any remaining laytime may be offset against the delay, or if the vessel is on demurrage then demurrage will be payable.

---

12. *Union of India* v. *Compania Naviera Aeolus SA (The Spalmatori)* [1962] 2 Lloyd's Rep 175.
13. *Ibid.*, at p. 180.
14. *Miramar Maritime Corporation* v. *Holborn Oil Trading Ltd (The Miramar)* [1984] 2 Lloyd's Rep 129 (HL).
15. *Compania de Navigación Zita SA* v. *Louis Dreyfus & Cie* [1953] 2 Lloyd's Rep 472, at p. 475.

1.35 Once laytime has expired, then if the charter contains a provision for demurrage this will become payable until loading or discharging is complete or the charter is brought to an end by its future performance becoming frustrated or by one of the parties evincing an intention to repudiate the charter, which repudiation is accepted by the other party. Thus if the charterer failed to provide a cargo and showed an intention never to so do, the shipowner would be entitled to claim that he had repudiated the charter and accept that repudiation. If, on the other hand, the shipowner did not accept that repudiation then demurrage would continue to be payable until the shipowner did so accept or until the charter became frustrated. The difference between these two ways in which the charter can come to an end is that frustration occurs upon the happening of an external event, whereas repudiation and acceptance thereof is by act of the parties.

1.36 Whether or not a charter is frustrated is a question of law, but the courts will not interfere with a finding to that effect by the appointed tribunal provided it is shown to have applied the right legal test. The date on which a charter becomes frustrated is a question of fact. The Law Reform (Frustrated Contracts) Act 1943 does not apply to voyage charters.

CHAPTER 2

Laytime clauses—
fixed and customary laytime

FIXED LAYTIME

2.1 If by the terms of the charterparty, the charterer has agreed to load or unload within a fixed period of time, that is "an absolute and unconditional engagement, for the non-performance of which he is answerable, whatever may be the nature of the impediments which prevent him from performing it and which cause the ship to be detained in his service beyond the time stipulated".[1]

2.2 As was said by Lord Hunter, the Lord Ordinary, in the Scottish case of *William Alexander & Sons* v. *Aktieselskabet Dampskabet Hansa and others*[2]:

It is well settled that where a merchant has undertaken to discharge a ship within a fixed number of days he is liable in demurrage for any delay of the ship beyond that period unless such delay is attributable to the fault of the shipowner or those for whom he is responsible. The risk of delay from causes for which neither of the contracting parties is responsible is with the merchant.

2.3 It is of course open to the parties to agree that certain periods or causes of delay should be excepted, and this may be done either by incorporating the exclusion in the way the fixed laytime is defined—e.g. by reference to "weather working days", thus excepting periods of adverse weather and holidays—or by an additional clause.[3]

2.4 The advantage to the shipowner of a charter providing for fixed laytime is that he can pre-determine the length of time that his vessel will be engaged in loading or discharging, if there are no exceptions, and if there are, then at least he will have some idea of the likelihood of delay because only certain causes of delay will be for his account. Any others not so specified will be for the charterer's account.

2.5 Fixed laytime may be expressed in one or other units of time, which will form the subject of most of this chapter, or as a rate of working cargo, which once the amount of cargo is known, will enable the amount of laytime to be calculated. Even if expressed as a rate of working cargo, there will still be a time element to which the following principles will apply, but there will also be specific rules for this form of laytime, which are dealt with towards the end of this chapter.[4]

---

1. *Postlethwaite* v. *Freeland* (1880) 5 App Cas 599, at p. 608 *per* Lord Selborne LC. See also *ante* at para. 1.17.
2. Quoted in the speech of Viscount Finlay in the judgment of the House of Lords, reported at (1919) 25 CC 13, at p. 15.
3. The significance between the two methods is that where the exception is in an additional clause then a causal connection must be shown—*Dow Chemical (Nederland) BV* v. *BP Tanker Co Ltd (The Vorras)* [1983] 1 Lloyd's Rep 579, at p. 584. See also *post* at para. 4.7.
4. See *post* at para. 2.144.

Calendar days

2.6 When steamships became more common in the second half of the nineteenth century new principles also emerged relating to the counting of time during loading and discharging. The importance of time to the steamship owner was stressed by Mathew LJ in *Yeoman* v. *Rex*, where he said[5]:

At 9 o'clock on Saturday morning the lay days were over, or rather the lay hours because in this charter, as is usual with reference to steamships, time is calculated by hours and not by days.

2.7 It was usual in the days of sail and the early days of steam for charters to provide for a specified number of lay days, but not to provide expressly when laytime was to commence after arrival. There was, however, no need for the charter to specify this, because it was customary for time to count from the day following the vessel's arrival, unless the merchant chose to commence cargo operations earlier.[6] The number of days allowed, which were calendar days from midnight to midnight, then ran consecutively, with part days counting as whole ones. It was not necessary for a pro-rata provision in the clause specifying the demurrage rate, since demurrage was bound to be a whole number of days.

2.8 Lord Devlin put it this way in *Reardon Smith Line Ltd* v. *Ministry of Agriculture*[7]:

In the beginning, a day was a day—a Monday, a Tuesday or a Wednesday, as the case might be. Work began, one may suppose, sometime in the morning and ended in the evening, the number of hours that were worked varying from port to port and in different trades. But whatever the number was, at the end of the Monday one lay day had gone and at the end of the Tuesday another; and if the work went into Wednesday, that counted as a whole day because of the rule that a part of a day was to be treated as a day. For this reason the charterer was not obliged to use a "broken" day. If notice of readiness was given during the day he could, if he chose, wait until the following day so that he could start with a whole day.

2.9 The working of these rules may be illustrated by the facts of *Commercial Steamship Co* v. *Boulton*,[8] where, all lay days having been used up at the port of loading, a vessel arrived in dock at the port of discharge at 5 p.m. on a Tuesday. Discharge commenced at 8 a.m. on the Wednesday and finished at 8 a.m. on the Thursday. In these circumstances, it was held that charterers were liable for two whole days' demurrage.

2.10 The same rules relating to broken periods apply to the calculation of laytime, where the charter provides for a rate of cargo working. Thus, in *Houlder* v. *Weir*,[9] the charterers were entitled to 29 days and a portion of a day for the discharge of the cargo and it was held that, in the absence of anything to the contrary, the charterers were entitled to 30 days.

2.11 Whilst lay days are to count consecutively, their continuity can be interrupted by the exclusion of Sundays and holidays, if there is an express provision to this effect or local custom so provides.

2.12 Speaking of how lay days should be calculated, Lord Esher MR said in *Nielsen* v. *Wait*[10]:

5. *Yeoman* v. *Rex* (1904) 9 CC 269, at p. 273.
6. *The Katy* [1895] P 56, at p. 63 *per* Lord Esher.
7. *Reardon Smith Line Ltd* v. *Ministry of Agriculture, Fisheries and Food* [1963] AC 691, at p. 738.
8. *Commercial Steamship Co* v. *Boulton* (1875) LR 10 QB 346.
9. *Houlder* v. *Weir* (1905) 10 CC 228.
10. *Nielsen & Co* v. *Wait, James & Co* (1885) 16 QBD 67, at p. 73.

They must begin from the time, when the ship is at her berth in the usual place of delivery, where she can deliver. They must begin then, and they are to be counted, unless something appears to the contrary, consecutively. That is not because the phraseology says that they are consecutive, but because it is taken as a necessary implication of the meaning of both parties, that the moment the ship begins to unload they are to go on consecutively each day to unload her and they must not either of them at their option take a holiday without the leave of the other.

2.13 An example of how a local custom could affect the consecutive running of days is provided by *Cochran v. Retberg*,[11] where it was found that the word "days" in a bill of lading providing for the carriage of goods from the River Elbe to London meant, by usage of the port of London, working days and thus Sundays and Customs House holidays were excluded.

Conventional days

2.14 The alternative to counting days from midnight to midnight (the calendar day) is the conventional day where time runs in periods of 24 hours, starting from the time when the notice of readiness expired. If, therefore, the parties agree a stipulation about the commencement of laytime which causes laytime to start at a specified hour then the general rules relating to broken days are displaced. At first instance, in a decision subsequently affirmed on appeal, Bingham J said[12]:

If the clause had stopped at the words "Cargo to be loaded at the rate of 200 tons per running day, Sundays and holidays excepted", I should have said that it meant that the cargo must be loaded at the rate of 200 tons per calendar day—that is, a day counting from midnight to midnight. But the clause continues:—"Time for loading shall commence to count 12 hours after written notice has been given by the master . . . on working days between 9 a.m. and 6 p.m. to the charterers or their agents that the vessel is in readiness to receive cargo". That, in my opinion, alters the construction that would otherwise have been put on the clause, and it makes the loading time commence at an hour during the twenty-four to be reckoned with reference to the notice given by the captain.

2.15 If Sundays and holidays are excepted, then any periods which fall under these headings have to be excluded from the, at least two, conventional days in which they fall.[13]

2.16 The question also arises as to whether the rule that a part of a day counts as a whole day applies equally to conventional days as it does to calendar days. In *Reardon Smith Line Ltd v. Ministry of Agriculture*, Lord Devlin, having posed the question, answered it thus[14]:

In *Verren v. Anglo-Dutch Brick (1927) Ltd* (1929) 34 Ll L Rep 56, at p. 58, Mr Justice Roche held that it did not. In the Court of Appeal (1929) 34 Ll L Rep 210, at p. 213, Lord Justice Scrutton reserved the point. Nevertheless, it is now the general practice, so your Lordships were told, to treat a part of an artificial day as a fraction.

11. *Cochran v. Retberg* (1800) 3 Esp 121.
12. *Leonis Steamship Co Ltd v. Joseph Rank Ltd (No 2)* (1908) 13 CC 161, at p. 163.
13. *Hain Steamship Co Ltd v. Sociedad Anonima Comercial de Exportación e Importación (Louis Dreyfus & Co Ltd) (The Trevarrack)* (1934) 49 Ll L Rep 86, at p. 88.
14. *Reardon Smith Line Ltd v. Ministry of Agriculture, Fisheries and Food* [1963] AC 691, at p. 738.

Running days

2.17 The term running days came into use towards the end of the last century as a means of distinguishing "days" from "working days". The leading case on its evolution is *Nielsen* v. *Wait* and in particular the judgment of Lord Esher MR, who said[15]:

> "Days" include every day. If the word "days" is put into the charterparty—so many days for loading and unloading—and nothing more, that includes Sundays and it includes holidays. "Working days" are distinguished from "days". But I suppose and take it, that there might be another dispute as to what "days" would mean. If "days" are put in, there is sure to come some discussion about what is the length of the day during which the charterer is to be obliged to be ready to take delivery or the shipowner to deliver, because the length of days may vary according to the custom of the port. In some countries, for anything that I know, the custom of the ports may be to work only four hours a day, and if "days" are put into the charterparty, there may be a dispute—although I do not say that it would be a valid contention according to English law—whether the day included more than four hours. And merchants and shipowners have invented this nautical term, about which there can be no dispute. They have invented the phrase "running days". It can be seen what it means. What is the run of the ship? how many days does it take a ship to run from the West Indies to England? that is the running of the ship. The run of a ship is a phrase well known . . .

2.18 And later in the same judgment:

> "Running days" therefore mean the whole of every day when a ship is running. What is that? That is every day, day and night. There it is as plain as possible. They are the days, during which, if the ship were at sea, she would be running. That means every day.

2.19 However, in the same case, Lord Esher did also go on to say[16] that the sequence of days could be interrupted, either by an express provision or by proof of a custom excluding certain days at the particular port.

2.20 The *Voylayrules 1993* provide[17]:

> "RUNNING DAYS" or "CONSECUTIVE DAYS" shall mean days which follow one immediately after the other.

2.21 Some charters provide for "running hours". In such a case, time runs continuously, by day and by night, both during and out of normal hours, except for those periods excluded expressly or by custom. The term "running hours" is used most commonly in the oil trade where it is used in conjunction with both exclusion clauses and warranties as to the vessel's performance.[18]

2.22 An illustration of an express provision interrupting running days is given by *Burnett Steamship Co Ltd* v. *Joint Danube & Black Sea Shipping Agencies*, where a laytime clause provided for a loading rate per running day, Sundays and non-working holidays excepted.[19]

Working days

2.23 A working day is a day in the normal sense, in that it has twenty-four hours, and is used to describe those days at the port in question when work can normally be expected

15. *Nielsen & Co* v. *Wait, James & Co* (1885) 16 QBD 67, at p. 72.
16. *Ibid.*, at p. 73.
17. See Appendix. The same definition appears in *Baltic Code 2000*.
18. See *post* at para. 6.132.
19. *Burnett Steamship Co Ltd* v. *Joint Danube & Black Sea Shipping Agencies* (1933) 46 Ll L Rep 231.

to take place. It is much older in usage than its variant, the weather working day, which will be considered later.[20]

2.24 Originally, it may have been used specifically to exclude Sundays and holidays. In *Cochran* v. *Retberg*, Lord Eldon held, with regard to what was then customary in the Port of London[21]:

... the fourteen days mentioned in the bill of lading means working days, that is a construction which excludes Sundays and holidays ...

2.25 A more elaborate description of how working days may vary from country to country was given in *Nielsen* v. *Wait* by Lord Esher MR, who said[22]:

... but working days in England are not the same as working days in foreign ports, because working days in England, by the custom and habits of the English, if not by their law, do not include Sundays. In a foreign port working days may not include saints' days. If it is the custom or the rule of the foreign port that no work is to be done on the saints' days, then working days do not include saints' days. If by the custom of the port certain days in the year are holidays, so that no work is done in that port on those days, then working days do not include those holidays. Working days in an English charterparty, if there is nothing to shew a contrary intention, do not include Christmas Day and some other days, which are well known to be holidays. Therefore "working days" mean days on which, at the port, according to the custom of the port, work is done in loading and unloading ships, and the phrase does not include Sundays.

2.26 In *Nelson & Sons Ltd* v. *Nelson Line (Liverpool) Ltd (No 3)*,[23] Channell J commented that where the charterparty said "working days", the mention of Sundays and holidays would be unnecessary as those days would not be working days. However, what "working days" does also exclude is the local equivalent of Sunday in non-Christian countries. Thus, in *Reardon Smith Line Ltd* v. *Ministry of Agriculture*, Lord Devlin said[24]:

But there may, of course, be days in some ports, such as the Mohammedan Friday, which are not working days and yet cannot well be described as Sundays or holidays.

Lord Devlin then went on to approve what he described as a comprehensive definition by Hamilton J in *British and Mexican Shipping Co Ltd* v. *Lockett Brothers & Co Ltd*, where the judge said[25]:

"working day" in this charterparty means something contradistinguished from days which are not working days, a day of work as distinguished from days for play or rest; and I think it is immaterial whether the days for play or rest are so for secular or religious reasons, and whether they are so by the ancient authority of the Church or by the present authority of the state ...

In the Court of Appeal, where the decision was reversed on another point, counsel for the plaintiffs said, somewhat succinctly, in his argument that the judge below had held "that a working day included every day except days appointed for prayer or play".[26]

2.27 There was, however, a stream of judicial thinking that went further than the definitions set out above. The argument thus put forward was that the term "working day"

---

20. See *post* at para. 2.41.
21. *Cochran* v. *Retberg* (1800) 3 Esp. 121, at p. 123.
22. *Nielsen & Co* v. *Wait, James & Co* (1885) 16 QBD 67, at p. 71.
23. *Nelson & Sons Ltd* v. *Nelson Line (Liverpool) Ltd (No 3)* (1907) 12 CC 185, at p. 193.
24. *Reardon Smith Line Ltd* v. *Ministry of Agriculture, Fisheries and Food* [1963] 1 Lloyd's Rep 12, at p. 39.
25. *British and Mexican Shipping Co Ltd* v. *Lockett Brothers & Co Ltd* [1911] 1 KB 264, at p. 273.
26. *British and Mexican Shipping Co Ltd* v. *Lockett Brothers & Co Ltd* (1910) 16 CC 75, at p. 83.

not only distinguished a working from a non-working day, but also had the effect of cutting down a day from 24 hours to whatever part of it was usually expended in work. This judicial rivulet reached its greatest force in *Alvion Steamship Corporation Panama v. Galban Lobo Trading Co SA of Havana (The Rubystone)*,[27] a decision of the Court of Appeal where the leading judgment was given by Lord Goddard, then Lord Chief Justice, who put the argument this way[28]:

> . . . I venture to think that if you say to a workman or to an employer of workmen: "What is your working day? How many hours is your working day?", they would not say: "Twenty-four hours". That is not the working day; you are asleep for a good part of the 24 hours. To say a working day is a period of 24 hours seems to me to ignore entirely the fact that the word "working" qualifies the word "day" and cuts it down . . .

2.28 In *The Rubystone*, the charterparty provided for cargo to be loaded at a specified rate per weather working day and the normal working day was established as eight hours. The Court of Appeal went on to uphold McNair J's finding that in construing the phrase "working day" regard should be paid, not to a calendar day of 24 hours, but to the normal working hours of a calendar day.[29]

2.29 Some support for this is to be found in the judgment of Lord Esher MR in *Nielsen v. Wait* where he said[30]:

> Now "working days" if that term is used in the charterparty, will vary in different ports; "working days" in the Port of London are not the same as working days in some other ports, even in England; . . .

2.30 The Scottish case of *Mein v. Ottman*[31] was also cited by Lord Goddard in support of his proposition, but commenting on this in *Reardon Smith Line Ltd v. Ministry of Agriculture*, Lord Devlin said[32]:

> In the Scottish case of *Mein v. Ottman*, it was held that a working day was a day of 12 hours, but it does not appear how the figure was calculated. This is the only case cited before *The Rubystone* in which "working day", unless qualified in some way in the charterparty, has been held to be a number of working hours. Mr Justice Hamilton, in his judgment . . . in *British and Mexican Shipping Co Ltd v. Lockett Brothers & Co Ltd* . . . contrasts a working day "as a term of hours" and a working day "in its ordinary English sense" . . . But no authority before *Mein v. Ottman* and *The Rubystone* has been cited for the proposition that the expression "working day" by itself means a number of working hours; Lord Goddard treats it as self-evident.

2.31 In *Reardon Smith Line v. Ministry of Agriculture*, the House of Lords firmly rejected Lord Goddard's views that a working day could relate only to that part of the day spent in working. Viscount Radcliffe put it this way[33]:

> I regard the decision of the Court of Appeal in *(The Rubystone)* as misconceived in so far as it treats a working day as a period of hours less than a calendar day or relates the idea of working day to an individual employee's hours of work at normal or basic rates of pay.

---

27. *Alvion Steamship Corporation Panama v. Galban Lobo Trading Co SA of Havana (The Rubystone)* [1955] 1 Lloyd's Rep 9 (CA).
   28. *Ibid.*, at p. 13.
   29. *The Rubystone* [1954] 2 Lloyd's Rep 309 (McNair J).
   30. *Nielsen & Co v. Wait, James & Co* (1885) 16 QBD 67, at p. 71.
   31. *Mein v. Ottman* (1904) 41 SLR 144.
   32. *Reardon Smith Line Ltd. v. Ministry of Agriculture, Fisheries and Food* [1963] 1 Lloyd's Rep 12, at p. 39.
   33. *Ibid.*, at p. 31.

2.32 Lord Devlin said[34]:

The truth is that the rights and obligations of the charterer as to the hours in which he can load or discharge have nothing to do with the computation of the lay days . . .

and summing up his speech[35]:

First, I conclude with respect that it is contrary to all authority before 1955[36] to say that a working day is a calendar day cut down. "Working" does not define a part of a day but describes the character of a day as a whole. Secondly, I conclude that the character of a day as a working day cannot be determined by inquiring whether on that day or on a part of it work was done at standard rates. There is no established authority for that view which I think stems from the misconception that the "working day" of the laytime clause has something to do with the hours of the day during which the ship can be compelled to work . . .

2.33 Applying these principles, the House of Lords held that Saturday in Vancouver was a working day for the whole day.[37] In so doing, they appear to have affirmed that the nature of a day will normally fall to be determined by how it is treated for the port as a whole, rather than for those involved in the particular vessel.[38]

2.34 Before leaving the meaning of working days, brief mention should be made of two variants:

Running working days
Colliery working days

2.35 "Running working days" was a phrase used in the Gencon charterparty until 1976. However, in their normally accepted meanings, running and working are inconsistent when used to describe lay days, since the former means every day, including Sundays and holidays, and the latter excludes these. Therefore, for the words to have a logical meaning, it was necessary to ignore the word "running" and simply calculate the laytime allowed in terms of working days.

2.36 Since 1976, however, laytime in the Gencon form of charter has been expressed in "running hours", thus removing the difficulty.

2.37 The term "Colliery working day" and its associated phrase, the colliery guarantee, arose in coal charters in this country in the days prior to the nationalization of the coalmines. Most of the reported cases arose in the last ten years of the last century, many from a general strike in the South Wales coalfield in 1898.

2.38 The usual practice was for a charterer to contract with a specific colliery on terms set out in a colliery guarantee for the colliery to supply coal to a named vessel. In *Monsen v. Macfarlane, McCrindell & Co*, Smith LJ said of the colliery guarantee[39]:

It is a document which the charterer who takes coal from a colliery wherewith to load a ship is anxious to have incorporated into the charterparty so that as regards the time to be occupied in loading the ship he may be under no more obligation to the shipowner than the colliery is under obligation to him . . .

---

34. *Ibid.*, at p. 40.
35. *Ibid.*, at p. 42.
36. 1955 was the date of *The Rubystone—Alvion Steamship Corporation Panama* v. *Galban Lobo Trading Co SA of Havana* [1955] 1 Lloyd's Rep 9.
37. For a more detailed description of "Saturdays", see *post* at para. 4.214.
38. For what constitutes a holiday, see *post* at para. 4.174.
39. *Monsen* v. *Macfarlane, McCrindell & Co* (1895) 1 CC 51, at p. 65.

2.39 The charterparty may, as in that case, be made earlier than the colliery guarantee but provide for its later incorporation. Most guarantees were given on fairly standard terms.

2.40 The colliery guarantee, and hence the charterparty, would provide for loading in a specified number of colliery working days. A colliery working day is a day which is an ordinary working day for the colliery in normal times and in normal circumstances. Sundays and holidays, including local ones such as Mabon's day in South Wales, are excluded. Days on which the colliery would normally work, but does not because of a strike, are included.[40]

Weather working days

2.41 A weather working day is a type of working day.[41] It is a working day on which the weather[42] allows the particular ship in question to load or discharge cargo of the type intended to be loaded or discharged, if she is then at a place or position where the parties intend her to so load or discharge.[43] If she is not in such a position but is still awaiting her turn to berth, then it will count as a weather working day if the weather would allow that type of cargo to be worked at the berth where the parties intend the vessel to go.[44] It is immaterial whether work is intended on the particular day.[45]

2.42 If there is or would have been a partial prevention of work due to weather then it is still a weather working day but part of the day must be excluded for the purpose of laytime calculations.[46]

2.43 It is possible for two ships to be at adjacent berths and for time to count as a weather working day in one case and not the other, depending on the type of cargo being worked.[47]

2.44 The *Charterparty Laytime Definitions 1980* provide[48]:

"WEATHER WORKING DAY" means a working day or part of a working day during which it is or, if the vessel is still waiting for her turn, it would be possible to load/discharge the cargo without interference due to the weather. If such interference occurs (or would have occurred if work had been in progress), there shall be excluded from the laytime a period calculated by reference to the ratio which the duration of the interference bears to the time which would have or could have been worked but for the interference.

---

40. *Saxon Ship Co Ltd* v. *Union Steamship Co Ltd* (1900) 5 CC 381 (HL).

41. *Reardon Smith Line Ltd* v. *Ministry of Agriculture, Fisheries and Food* [1963] 1 Lloyd's Rep 12, at p. 31 *per* Viscount Radcliffe.

42. For a consideration of what constitutes weather, see *post* at para. 4.102.

43. *Aldebaran Compania Maritima SA* v. *Aussenhandel AG (The Darrah)* [1977] AC 157 (HL). This must be subject to the vessel being an Arrived ship. See also *Freedom Maritime Corporation* v. *International Bulk Carriers SA and another (The Khian Captain)* [1985] 2 Lloyd's Rep 212.

44. See *The Machrihanish* (1906), an unreported decision of the House of Lords mentioned in *A/S Uglands Rederi* v. *The President of India (The Danita)* [1976] 2 Lloyd's Rep 377.

45. *Compania Naviera Azuero SA* v. *British Oil & Cake Mills Ltd and others* [1957] 1 Lloyd's Rep 312, at p. 329 *per* Pearson J.

46. For a more detailed exposition, see *post* at para. 2.59.

47. *Reardon Smith Line Ltd.* v. *Ministry of Agriculture, Fisheries and Food* [1963] 1 Lloyd's Rep 12. At least three of their Lordships make it clear that the criterion is not what happened in the port generally but on board the ship in question.

48. See Appendix and also at para. 2.91 in relation to the corresponding *Voylayrules 1993* definition. The 1980 definition, it is suggested, reflects the common law position whereas the 1993 definition does not. The same definition as appears in the 1980 definition is contained in the *Baltic Code 2000* definition which is also reproduced in the Appendix.

2.45 In English law, unlike American law on this point, there need be no causal connection between the weather and the failure to load or discharge the particular vessel. The reference to weather is therefore descriptive, rather than exceptive.[49]

2.46 Weather working days is a term that appears to have come into use in the last decade of the nineteenth century.[50] In those days delay in a fixed laytime charter usually fell on the charterer. Thus, in *Thiis* v. *Byers*,[51] a charterer unsuccessfully tried to avoid liability for demurrage where there was a delay in discharge due to bad weather, by claiming that the master was not ready or able to deliver. The judgment of the court, consisting of Blackburn and Lush JJ, was given by Lush J, who said[52]:

> We took time to look into the authorities, and are of the opinion that, where a given number of days is allowed to the charterer for unloading, a contract is implied on his part that, from the time when the ship is at the usual place of discharge, he will take the risk of any ordinary vicissitudes which may occur to prevent him releasing the ship at the expiration of the lay-days.

and towards the end of his judgment, he added:

> The obvious convenience of such a rule in preventing disputes about the state of the weather on particular days, or particular fractions of days, and the time thereby lost to the charterer in the course of discharge, makes it highly expedient that this construction should be adhered to, whatever may be the form of words used in the particular charterparty.

2.47 Despite this judicial disdain for such disputes, some twenty years later the first reported case concerning weather working days came before the courts.[53] In argument, it was stated that there had not to date been any judicial interpretation of the expression "weather working day". Despite this invitation, Lord Russell of Killowen CJ, who heard the case, did not consider it necessary to fill this vacuum, in deciding the points then in issue.[54] Indeed, 60 years later in *Compania Naviera Azuero SA* v. *British Oil & Cake Mills Ltd and others*,[55] Pearson J was still able to say:

> As there is no decisive authority . . . I must consider and decide the question as best I can, and the question is: What is the proper meaning of the expression "weather working days"?

In *Nelson & Sons Ltd* v. *Nelson Line (Liverpool) Ltd (No 3)*, Channell J said[56]:

> . . . the words used are "seven weather working days" which practically means seven fine days.

However, he then went on to suggest that it could be argued that seven weather working days might include a fine Sunday and that was why, in the particular case, a careful draftsman had expressly excepted Sundays and holidays. On the merits of such an argument, he made no comment and neither did the Court of Appeal and House of Lords

---

49. *Dow Chemical (Nederland) BV* v. *BP Tanker Co Ltd (The Vorras)* [1983] 1 Lloyd's Rep 579.
50. *Alvion Steamship Corporation Panama* v. *Galban Lobo Trading Co SA of Havana (The Rubystone)* [1955] 1 Lloyd's Rep 9, at p. 13 *per* Lord Goddard LCJ.
51. *Thiis* v. *Byers* (1876) 1 QBD 244.
52. *Ibid.*, at p. 249.
53. *Brankelow Steamship Co Ltd* v. *Lamport & Holt* (1897) 2 CC 89.
54. Two parts of Lord Russell's judgment in *Brankelow Steamship Co Ltd* v. *Lamport & Holt*, have been reported. The first at (1897) 2 CC 89 was a finding that where part of a day was affected by weather, this should count as a half weather working day. See *post* at para. 2.61. The second report of the case is as a note to Channell J's judgment in *Nelson & Sons Ltd* v. *Nelson Line (Liverpool) Ltd (No 3)* (1907) 12 CC 185, at p. 189, concerning whether work on a Sunday should count against laytime where Sunday was an excepted period. See *post* at para. 4.254.
55. *Naviera Azuero SA* v. *British Oil & Cake Mills Ltd and others* [1957] 1 Lloyd's Rep 312, at p. 329.
56. *Nelson & Sons Ltd* v. *Nelson Line (Liverpool) Ltd (No 3)* (1907) 12 CC 185, at p. 193.

when they in turn considered the case.[57] However, Sunday is not normally a working day.

2.48 The question of whether a custom of the port could affect the meaning to be given to weather working days was considered in *Bennetts & Co* v. *J & A Brown*,[58] a decision of Walton J. The facts were that a charter provided for discharge at "one or two good safe ports between Valparaiso and Pisagua" at a specified rate of discharge per weather working day. The charterers chose Valparaiso for discharge, which took place from an anchorage into lighters, which were then either discharged into other vessels or on to the beach. Evidence was given that, by a custom of the port, the port captain could declare days on which it was dangerous to discharge on to the beach as surf days, which were deemed not to be weather working days. On the days so declared, discharge into the lighters continued, but those lighters which were due to then discharge on to the beach were unable to do so.

2.49 Walton J held in these circumstances that as a custom of the port of Valparaiso gave a meaning to the words "weather working days" different from their plain and natural one, it was not competent for the charterers to adopt it under the terms of the charter. They could, however, rely on an exception relating to detention by surf to cover such delay.

2.50 In his judgment, Walton J said of the phrase "weather working days"[59]:

... I think it has a natural meaning—namely, a day on which the work, it may be of loading, but here it is of discharging, is not prevented by bad weather. Of course it might be a half a day. Half a day might not be a weather working day and the other half might be weather working, but I think that is the natural meaning of the words ... [60]

2.51 However, on similar facts involving the port of Iquique, the Court of Appeal, in a ruling on a preliminary point of law, in *British and Mexican Shipping Co* v. *Lockett Brothers*[61] refused to allow a submission by the plaintiffs that a defence to a claim for demurrage based on a similar custom could not in law be a valid defence. In that case the charter provided for discharge at a specified rate per working day (not weather working day) and was specifically for discharge at Iquique. At first instance,[62] Hamilton J had followed the earlier decision of Walton J[63] and held that the custom could not provide a defence. It is submitted however that the decision of the Court of Appeal does not really go any further than saying that if the parties to a charter wish to agree a special meaning to a type of laytime term, then there is nothing in law to prevent them from so doing. All three judges stressed that their ruling was only on a preliminary point of law with regard to the specific question they were asked.

2.52 Another attempt to explain the meaning of weather working days was that of Lord Goddard CJ in *Alvion Steamship Corporation Panama* v. *Galban Lobo Trading Co SA of Havana*. Although this case can no longer be considered authoritative on the question of

---

57. [1907] 2 KB 705 (CA), (1908) 13 CC 235 (HL).
58. *Bennetts & Co* v. *J & A Brown* (1907) 13 CC 110.
59. *Ibid.*, at p. 116.
60. In referring to half days, Walton J was following the decision in *Brankelow Steamship Co Ltd* v. *Lamport & Holt* (1897) 2 CC 89.
61. *British and Mexican Shipping Co Ltd* v. *Lockett Brothers & Co Ltd* (1910) 16 CC 75.
62. *British and Mexican Shipping Co Ltd* v. *Lockett Brothers & Co Ltd* [1911] 1 KB 264.
63. *Bennetts & Co* v. *J & A Brown* (1907) 13 CC 110.

how long a working day is and how interruptions due to weather should be calculated,[64] the following passage in Lord Goddard's judgment[65] remains valid:

There does not seem to be any doubt between the parties as to what the word "weather" means. It means that from the working day, whatever it may be, is to be deducted the time during which the men are stood off, or the loading is suspended, by reason of rain or other weather conditions. For example, there might be a hurricane, or something of that sort, to prevent work being done; but, at any rate, it simply means that the working day is to be reduced by the time in which working is suspended by reason of the weather . . .

2.53 This was followed by Pearson J's decision in *Compania Naviera Azuero SA* v. *British Oil & Cake Mills Ltd*[66] where the earlier cases relating to the meaning of weather working days were reviewed in some detail. In the particular case with which Pearson J was dealing, there had been rain on several occasions during discharge, but this had not delayed discharge because work was not actively in progress at the time. Having considered the alternative arguments that were before him as to whether the reference to weather was exceptive, i.e. a causal connection was necessary between the bad weather and the delay, or descriptive, Pearson J then went on to give his own definition of the phrase[67]:

In my view, a correct definition of a "weather working day" is a day on which the weather permits the relevant work to be done, whether or not any person avails himself of that permission; in other words, so far as the weather is concerned, it is a working day.
   In my view, also, the converse proposition must be on the same basis. A day is not a weather working day, it fails to be a weather working day, in so far as the weather on that day does not permit the relevant work to be done, and it is not material to inquire whether any person has intended or planned or prepared to do any relevant work on that day. The status of a day as being a weather working day, wholly or in part or not at all, is determined solely by its own weather, and not by extraneous factors, such as the actions, intentions and plans of any person.

The judgment continues by pointing out that such an interpretation avoids the obvious absurdity that a day where the weather consists of continual storms of rain, snow and sleet, would be counted as a weather working day if nobody had planned to do relevant work on that day.

2.54 In the *Reardon Smith* case,[68] Lord Devlin said:

It is well established that whether a day is a weather working day or not depends on the character of the day and not on whether work was actually interfered with. The authorities on this point have recently been reviewed by Mr Justice Pearson in *Compania Naviera Azuero SA* v. *British Oil &*

---

64. Since the judgment of the House of Lords in *Reardon Smith Line Ltd* v. *Ministry of Agriculture, Fisheries and Food* [1963] 1 Lloyd's Rep 12. For a consideration of the length of a working day see *ante* at para. 2.23 and for how weather interruptions are calculated with regard to w.w.d. see *post* at para. 2.59.

65. *Alvion Steamship Corporation Panama* v. *Galban Lobo Trading Co SA of Havana (The Rubystone)* [1955] 1 Lloyd's Rep 9.

66. *Compania Naviera Azuero SA* v. *British Oil & Cake Mills Ltd and others* [1957] 1 Lloyd's Rep 312. Apart from the cases mentioned above, the following were also considered: *Dampskibsselskabet Botnia A/S* v. *C P Bell & Co* [1932] 2 KB 569, where days on which loading could not commence because of ice were held not to be weather working days; *Burnett Steamship Co Ltd* v. *Joint Danube & Black Sea Shipping Agencies* [1933] 2 KB 438, where Scrutton LJ was prepared to hold that where laytime was expressed in weather working days once bad weather was established that would suffice to prevent a day being a weather working day. No causal connection was needed.

67. *Compania Naviera Azuero SA* v. *British Oil & Cake Mills Ltd and others* [1957] 1 Lloyd's Rep 312, at p. 329.

68. *Reardon Smith Line Ltd.* v. *Ministry of Agriculture, Fisheries and Food* [1963] 1 Lloyd's Rep 12, at p. 41.

Cake Mills Ltd and others [1957] 2 QB 293; [1957] 1 Lloyd's Rep 312, and neither side challenged the correctness of his decision.

2.55 It sometimes happens that weather may prevent a vessel getting into berth or when it is in berth may force it to leave. In the former case, provided the vessel has become an Arrived ship or is deemed to be so by an additional clause, then time will begin to run.[69] Under general principles applicable to any fixed laytime provision time will then run continuously in the absence of any provision to the contrary or default of the vessel.[70] Where the laytime allowed is measured in weather working days, then during the period the vessel is waiting for a berth (whether the delay is due to weather or congestion) time will count except for any periods during which loading or discharging would not have been possible due to weather had the particular vessel been in berth.[71]

2.56 The effect on laytime measured in weather working days of a vessel having to leave her berth because bad weather was expected was the question considered in *Compania Crystal de Vapores* v. *Herman & Mohatta (India) Ltd (The Maria G).*[72] The ship concerned, the *Maria G*, was ordered to move off the berth to buoys by the harbourmaster because a "bore tide" was expected and he feared possible damage to the jetty and the vessel.

2.57 In his judgment, Devlin J (as he then was) assumed, without deciding, that a "bore tide" was weather. He then went on to hold that the expression "weather working days" could not be construed so widely so as to cover the circumstances of this case, in that if the effect of weather was not to interfere with the operation of loading but to render the berth unsafe the time so lost was not what the parties contemplated when they referred to weather working days.

2.58 Where weather first stops loading and then forces a vessel to leave its berth, then time will not count against laytime measured in weather working days from the time weather stopped until the weather improved sufficiently so as to allow loading or discharging had the vessel been back in berth. It matters not that the weather does not actually allow the vessel to return to its berth—the question is simply would loading have been possible if the vessel was back in berth.[73]

Calculation of weather interruptions in weather working days

2.59 The leading case on how these are to be calculated is *Reardon Smith Line Ltd* v. *Ministry of Agriculture*.[74] However, before considering this, it may be useful to see how the law has developed.

---

69. See *post* at para. 4.1.
70. See *ante* at para. 1.25.
71. *Aldebaran Compania Maritima SA* v. *Aussenhandel AG (The Darrah)* [1977] AC 157. See also Parker J's comments on that case in *Gebr Broere BV* v. *Saras Chimica SpA* [1982] 2 Lloyd's Rep 436, at p. 438.
72. *Compania Crystal de Vapores* v. *Herman & Mohatta (India) Ltd (The Maria G)* [1958] 1 Lloyd's Rep 616.
73. This analysis of the effect of weather was put forward by Parker J in *Gebr Broere BV* v. *Saras Chimica SpA* [1982] 2 Lloyd's Rep 436, at p. 439, in relation to a clause providing for laytime expressed as "running hours weather permitting", which it is submitted applies equally to "weather working days". See also London Arbitration 7/92—LMLN 323, 21 March 1992, quoting the above passage.
74. *Reardon Smith Line Ltd* v. *Ministry of Agriculture, Fisheries and Food* [1963] 1 Lloyd's Rep 12 (HL).

2.60 The distinction between calendar and conventional days has already been considered.[75] However, even where the laytime was calculated in calendar days so that laytime ran from midnight to midnight, the courts were nevertheless prepared to count weather interruptions in terms of half days after 1897. This was the result of a decision of Lord Russell of Killowen CJ in *Brankelow Steamship Co Ltd* v. *Lamport & Holt*.[76]

2.61 The *Highfield*, the vessel concerned in this case, was fixed to load at two ports, the first being Rosario. Cargo was to be loaded at a rate of 175 tons per weather working day, giving a total time available for loading of 16.7 weather working days, which was as usual rounded up to 17 days. At Rosario rain interrupted loading on at least one day, although on the particular day the weather cleared up in the afternoon and a considerable quantity of cargo was loaded. The shipowners wanted to claim the day as a whole day but the charterers argued that only a portion should count. Supporting charterers' contentions, Lord Russell said[77]:

Suppose the weather on a particular day is at first such that there is a reasonable expectation that a day's work may be done, but after two or three hours' work it changes so that it becomes unreasonable or impossible to work at all. Are the charterers then to be charged with that day as a whole day because they worked in good faith while the weather permitted? Such a thing would, to my mind, be inequitable: . . . There might be a succession of days upon which work was begun. If they were counted as whole days the charterer might not have the benefit of half the number of days actually allowed him under his charter. It would be inequitable to reject such days from the calculation altogether, because the ship gains something from despatch. A still more equitable view is this. Do not cut the days into fine fragments, but, if a half-day, or thereabouts, is used, calculate it as a half day; and if twelve hours are occupied calculate it as a whole day.

2.62 In *Alvion Steamship Corporation Panama* v. *Galban Lobo Trading Co SA of Havana (The Rubystone)*,[78] Lord Goddard CJ objected to what he called this "rule of thumb" method of dealing with weather interruptions as being far too imprecise by limiting the fraction to be counted to half days. To this extent, the House of Lords in the *Reardon Smith* case[79] agreed with Lord Goddard, although they disagreed with him on the method of calculation to be followed.

2.63 Although now discredited, the method adopted by Lord Goddard is worthy of some consideration still, since it highlights the alternative meanings that could be given to the phrase "weather working days". Lord Goddard's view is summed up in the following extract from his judgment[80]:

. . . I think a working day is a length of time consisting of a number of hours which, according to the custom of the port, are usually worked at the port of discharge or loading, as the case may be, and the presence of the word "weather" seems to qualify it so that from the number of hours which would be the ordinary hours of the port is to be deducted the length of time during which the weather interferes with the work.

75. See *ante* at para. 2.6 and 2.14.
76. *Brankelow Steamship Co Ltd* v. *Lamport & Holt (The Highfield)* (1897) 2 CC 89.
77. *Ibid.*, at p. 91. The wording above from the report of the case in the Commercial Cases differs somewhat from the wording in the Law Reports ([1897] 1 QB 570) although the sense is much the same—see McNair J's comments on the difference between the two wordings in *Alvion Steamship Corporation Panama* v. *Galban Lobo Trading Co SA of Havana (The Rubystone)* [1954] 2 Lloyd's Rep 309, at p. 313 and Lord Goddard CJ's comments on the same point in the same case in the Court of Appeal ([1955] 1 Lloyd's Rep 9, at p. 13).
78. *Alvion Steamship Corporation Panama* v. *Galban Lobo Trading Co SA of Havana (The Rubystone)* [1955] 1 Lloyd's Rep 9 (CA).
79. *Reardon Smith Line Ltd* v. *Ministry of Agriculture, Fisheries and Food* [1963] 1 Lloyd's Rep 12 (HL).
80. *The Rubystone* [1955] 1 Lloyd's Rep 9, at p. 15.

2.64 What was meant by the "ordinary hours of the port" was the question that arose in *NV Maatschappij Zeevart* v. *Friesacher Soehne (The Leto)*[81]—did it include overtime? Elwes J held that it did not. The calculation should be based on the number of hours worked at standard rates.

2.65 In essence, therefore, under this method of calculation, working day means the working part of the day and the laytime statement is laid out showing for each calendar day the number of hours worked, up to a maximum of the ordinary hours of the port. The actual time of each stoppage is deducted, whether this is due to weather or some other excepted cause and the allowed laytime is used up when the total expended reaches a figure in hours arrived at by multiplying the ordinary hours of the port per day by the number of weather working days allowed.

2.66 In the following example showing such a calculation, three weather working days have been allowed as laytime; the ordinary hours of the port are 07 00–19 00; laytime commenced at 16 00 on 1 June, and there were two interruptions—one due to weather between 10 00–12 00 on 2 June and one due to a winch failure between 08 00–10 00 on 3 June.

	D	H M	
Tuesday, 1 June		3 00	
Wednesday, 2 June		10 00	rain 10 00–12 00
Thursday, 3 June		10 00	winch failure 08 00–10 00
Friday, 4 June		12 00	
Saturday, 5 June		1 00	
	3	00 00	i.e. 36 hours of actual work

2.67 On this basis, demurrage would have commenced one hour after work recommenced on 5 June, i.e. at 08 00.

2.68 However, as has been discussed earlier,[82] the House of Lords took the view in the *Reardon Smith* case that a working day was not a cut down calendar day,[83] and the description "working" was used to distinguish such a day from a non-working day such as a Sunday or holiday.[84] The method shown above therefore no longer applies.

2.69 In *Reardon Smith Line* v. *Ministry of Agriculture*,[85] Viscount Radcliffe, Lord Keith of Avonholm and Lord Devlin all gave some guidance on how time should be calculated where weather prevents, or would prevent if the vessel was in its loading/discharging place, the working of cargo for part of a day. The remaining Law Lords were content to agree with Lord Devlin. The views that were expressed were in fact *obiter*, but since they have now stood for over 30 years, they may be considered as authoritative.

2.70 All three of the speeches mentioned agreed that some fraction of the working day should be allowed and all said that the actual calculation was a question of fact.

2.71 Lord Devlin, having earlier pointed out the difficulties in ascertaining what are the normal hours of working, went on to reject the suggestion made in *NV Maatschappij*

81. *NV Maatschappij Zeevart* v. *Friesacher Soehne (The Leto)* [1962] 1 Lloyd's Rep 52.
82. See *ante* at para. 2.31.
83. *Reardon Smith Line Ltd* v. *Ministry of Agriculture, Fisheries and Food* [1963] 1 Lloyd's Rep 12, e.g. at p. 39 *per* Lord Devlin.
84. *Ibid.*, e.g. at p. 31 *per* Viscount Radcliffe.
85. *Ibid.*

Zeevart v. *Friesacher Soehne (The Leto)*[86] that these excluded overtime, which he held to be the rule rather than the exception in most ports.[87] Later on, having again referred to this, he continued[88]:

I think that the best that can be done by way of expansion of the phrase "weather working days" is to infer that it is intended by it that a reasonable apportionment should be made of the day—Lord Russell of Killowen CJ based his decision on an "equitable view" according to the incidence of the weather upon the length of the day that the parties either were working or might be expected to have been working at the time.

Viscount Radcliffe, however, was more specific[89]:

But in my opinion the basic calculation in such case should be determined by ascertaining what part of the calendar day was used, if loading was actually being done, or could reasonably have been used, if there was in fact no loading. The proportion which this bears to the working hours of the ship should be charged to the shipper. Thus, if those hours are decided by the arbitrator to have been 16 hours out of the 24, and, of those 16, four have been obstructed by bad weather, three-quarters of the whole day, that is 18 hours, are for the shipper's account.

2.72 He then went on to confirm that weather interruptions outside working hours did not affect the issue, a point also specifically made by Lord Keith, who put the main proposition thus[90]:

If the amount of interference, or interruption, by weather with work during working hours is applied proportionally to the period of 24 hours a reasonable and equitable result is, I consider, achieved.

2.73 In order to apply these principles, the following questions must first therefore be answered:
  1. Did the weather interruption occur on a working day[91]?
  2. What were the relevant hours of work?
  3. Did the interruption occur in working hours?
  4. What is the proportion that the interruption bore to the total daily hours of work?
  5. What is that fraction applied to 24 hours expressed in hours and minutes?

2.74 Clearly, if the weather interruption was not on a working day or outside the relevant working hours, then it is itself irrelevant and a full weather working day should be counted. However, this does not of course explain what were the relevant working hours and it would seem from the speeches quoted above that the criterion is not what hours were worked in the port generally or even in a particular trade, but what hours were worked on this ship with this cargo at this point at this time. It is clear that this includes overtime. Thus, if generally throughout the working week, the vessel loaded (or discharged) for 12 hours per day from 07 00–19 00 then these are the relevant hours.[92] The

86. *NV Maatschappij Zeevart* v. *Friesacher Soehne (The Leto)* [1962] 1 Lloyd's Rep 52.
87. *Reardon Smith Line Ltd* v. *Ministry of Agriculture, Fisheries and Food* [1963] 1 Lloyd's Rep 12, at p. 41.
88. *Ibid.*, at p. 43.
89. *Ibid.*, at p. 32.
90. *Ibid.*, at p. 33.
91. See *ante* at para. 2.23. It would seem that whilst to determine the relevant hours of work it is necessary to look at the particular vessel, to determine whether a day is a working day it is necessary to look at the port as a whole.
92. They would equally be the relevant hours for a Saturday, which was a working day, even if the only work normally done on Saturdays was overtime.

basic hours of any particular trade of workmen essential to cargo operations, e.g. grain elevator operators, longshoremen, etc., are irrelevant. Once the relevant hours are established, the answers to the remaining questions are largely a matter of mathematics. When the answer to Question 5 is arrived at, that is the allowance to be deducted from the day in question to find the laytime used.

2.75 If the laytime allowed is measured in conventional days,[93] as is normal these days, then it may still be permissible to make up the laytime statement on a calendar basis, with parts of a day at the beginning and end of laytime. Indeed Viscount Radcliffe appears to suggest that this is the correct method.[94] However, it is sometimes done strictly on a conventional day basis, with the laytime used debited against each weather working day, the first of which would thus start at whatever hour of the day laytime started to run. On this basis, a particular weather working day could start at 08 00 on Saturday and run until 08 00 on Monday, the intervening Sunday not counting.

2.76 Whichever method is used, the result will be the same. In the following example, the calendar day basis has been used and the following facts assumed: three weather working days have been allowed as laytime; the relevant hours of work are 07 00–19 00; laytime commenced at 16 00 on 1 June and there were two interruptions—one due to weather between 10 00–12 00 on 2 June and one due to a winch failure between 08 00– 10 00 on 3 June.

	D	H M	
Tuesday, 1 June		8 00	
Wednesday, 2 June		20 00	rain 10 00–12 00
Thursday, 3 June		22 00	winch failure 08 00–10 00
Friday, 4 June		22 00	
	3	00 00	i.e. 72 hours

2.77 In the statement above, the interruption due to rain was two hours, within working hours (the relevant hours) on a working day. The interruption therefore accounted for one-sixth of the total usual daily hours of work and applying this fraction to 24 hours produces an excepted period of four hours. Thus for that day, 20 hours count as used laytime.

2.78 It will be noted that this method of calculation produces a gearing effect, increasing the actual time work was interrupted by weather by a factor which is the same as the ratio between 24 hours and the total usual daily hours of work (the relevant hours). Thus where, as here, the vessel could work 12 hours per day, the uplift will be 24:12, i.e. twice. It will also be noted that this only applies to weather interruptions, not other excepted periods.

2.79 In this example, the vessel went on demurrage at 22 00 on 4 June, whereas when the same facts were applied to the *Rubystone* formula,[95] demurrage commenced at 08 00

---

93. See *ante* at para. 2.14.
94. See that part of his speech quoted in the text to fn. 89.
95. *Alvion Steamship Corporation Panama* v. *Galban Lobo Trading Co SA of Havana (The Rubystone)* 1 Lloyd's Rep 9 (CA). See *ante* at para. 2.27.

on 5 June, some 10 hours later.[96] However, the *Reardon Smith* formula will not always produce such a result and in certain circumstances the effect may be to defer the point at which laytime is used up. All that may be said with certainty is that where there are any interruptions due to weather, the two formulae will produce different results and that using the principles of the *Reardon Smith* case will be correct.

Saturdays and other incomplete days

2.80 Where a vessel is destined to load or discharge at a port where weekend work is not the norm, the charter may provide for time not to count from, say, 17 00 on Friday or after mid-day on Saturday until, say, 08 00 on Monday.[97] If the effect of such a clause is to make Friday, Saturday and possibly Monday, days where the working period is shorter than usual, then how weather interruptions should be calculated where laytime is in weather working days is a question of some complexity. No difficulty will normally arise with regard to Sunday,[98] since that is not a working day. Although what follows relates particularly to Saturdays, the same principles will apply to other days on which there is reduced working.

2.81 In the absence of a special clause, Saturday presents no problems since it is a normal working day and the method of calculating interruptions previously described will apply. As Viscount Radcliffe said in the *Reardon Smith* case[99]:

The only thing that matters in this case is, I think, that Saturday was not a holiday at the Port of Vancouver and the possibilities of working were not affected by bad weather. If so, Saturday counts among the lay days that are imputed to the charterers and it counts as a whole day, since the parties have made no stipulation for charging fine working days by any more meticulous scale.

2.82 It is therefore clear that in these circumstances, even if there is a reduced working period on Saturday, then unless the parties are held to have provided to the contrary, the full weekday period will be used against which to proportion any weather interruption.

2.83 There seem to be three possible ways in which weather interruptions on Saturdays can be dealt with where the charter provides for time not to count after a specified time.

Method A

2.84 This involves treating the Saturday exception clause literally so that, if for instance it provides for "time not to count after 12 00" then the maximum period that can be debited against charterers is the 12 hours up to 12 00. From this maximum must be deducted an appropriate allowance for any time lost by bad weather. This is calculated on the same basis as interruptions on weekdays so that if the full weekday working period is 12 hours and one hour is lost by adverse weather on Saturday morning then this is geared

---

96. One immediate artificiality is that in each case 12 hours was taken as the daily period of working, whereas in *The Rubystone* formula overtime is excluded but included in the *Reardon Smith* formula. For the same period to apply therefore it would have to be a most unusual port where overtime was unknown! If the number of working hours per day is increased in the present example to reflect overtime, the gearing effect is reduced and demurrage starts earlier.
97. Similar provisions often apply to the days preceding and following a holiday.
98. Friday in Islamic countries. See *ante* at para. 2.24.
99. *Reardon Smith Line Ltd* v. *Ministry of Agriculture, Fisheries and Food* [1963] 1 Lloyd's Rep. 12, at p. 32.

up to represent an interruption of two hours (the proportion that one hour bears to 12 hours applied to 24 hours). This is then credited to charterers so that instead of 12 hours counting only 10 hours are debited against the laytime allowed.

Method B

2.85 Using the same times as in Method A and assuming that Saturday working commences at 08 00, Method B involves interpreting the Saturday clause as meaning that the working period on Saturdays is between 08 00 and 12 00 when time ceases to count. On the basis if one hour is lost due to adverse weather then this represents $\frac{1}{4}$ of the hours available for work and therefore charterers should be debited with $\frac{3}{4}$ of a day against the laytime allowed, i.e. 18 hours.

Method C

2.86 This is in effect a cross between the other two methods. In this the Saturday clause is again given a literal meaning so that the maximum that can be debited against charterers is 12 hours. If one hour is lost due to adverse weather then since $\frac{1}{4}$ of the working period has been lost, this is then applied not to 24 hours, but to the 12 hours of the day that could count, reducing it by three hours to give nine hours debited against laytime.

2.87 Needless to say in each case it is only interruptions during working hours that can count.

2.88 Method A might be justified by reference to that part of Viscount Radcliffe's speech in the *Reardon Smith* case[100] where he says:

But in my opinion the basic calculation in such cases should be determined by ascertaining what part of the calendar day was used, if loading was actually being done, or could reasonably have been used, if there was in fact no loading. The proportion which this bears to the working hours of the ship while in the particular port is the proportion of the calendar day which should be charged to the shipper.

This seems to suggest that whatever is determined as the hours of work for the particular ship at that time should be applied to each day regardless of the actual hours worked.

2.89 Method B might be justified, again in the words of Viscount Radcliffe,[101] as a stipulation charging fine working days by a more meticulous scale, notwithstanding that the meaning given to the Saturday clause is perhaps not the most obvious one.

2.90 Method C is harder to justify as a matter of law. However, Methods A and B can and sometimes do produce somewhat illogical answers. For instance, applying Method A if all the Saturday working period is lost, charterers are still charged four hours against laytime. With Method B, if no time is lost then charterers are charged a full day and the Saturday clause is apparently given no effect. Method C avoids both these pitfalls giving answers of 12 hours laytime used where no time was lost and no time used where all the working period was lost. Despite its doubtful parentage, Method C would seem to give the right result but would have to be justified by saying that in providing a Saturday clause (or

100. *Ibid.*, at p. 32.
101. *Ibid.* See *ante* at para. 2.81.

other reduced period) the parties agreed to a special definition of a weather working day for that day. This comes perilously close to the *Rubystone* formula.[102]

Voylayrules 1993

2.91 The *Voylayrules 1993*[103] provide a common definition for a weather working day, a weather working day of 24 hours and a weather working day of 24 consecutive hours. They provide that these phrases:

> shall mean a working day of 24 consecutive hours except for any time when weather prevents the loading or discharging of the vessel or would have prevented it had work been in progress.

This definition is effectively the same as that provided for in the *Charterparty Laytime Definitions 1980* in relation to a weather working day of 24 consecutive hours.[104] What it purports to do therefore is define the working day as 24 hours and therefore the actual duration of any interruption due to weather, or deemed interruption if the vessel is not in berth, is to be discounted irrespective of the working practices at the port in question. Whilst this undoubtedly simplifies any calculation as to time lost, this definition will only apply where the *Voylayrules 1993* are specifically incorporated into the charter.

Working days, running hours, running days, weather permitting

2.92 At first sight, it might seem that the addition of the words "weather permitting" either before or after the laytime clauses set out above would simply exclude any periods when adverse weather actually prevented loading or discharging, or in other words that they are words of exception. That this is not so and that when they are attached directly to a laytime clause they become words of description and thus part of the clause itself (as does "weather" when added to "working day") is the effect of two decisions made within a few months of each other.[105]

2.93 The present position is therefore that, having become an Arrived ship, time will not run if the weather does not permit the ship concerned to load or discharge cargo of the type intended to be loaded or discharged if the vessel is then at a place or position where the parties intended her to work cargo. If she is not in such a position, but is still awaiting a berth, then time will not count if, had she been in such a position, the weather would have permitted working cargo. The situation is thus very similar to the effect of "weather" where laytime is measured in "weather working days". The only difference lies in the method of calculating interruptions—here the actual time lost is deducted and there is therefore no apportionment in relation to the length of the working day.

2.94 In *Stephens v. Harris*,[106] the laytime clause provided for loading at a rate of "400 tons per weather working day, weather permitting". The vessel concerned duly reached her loading berth and was lying under the spouts ready to receive her cargo of ore, which was to come from five miles away. However, bad weather delayed the cargo being brought to the vessel. There was also a strike, but in so far as the weather was concerned, the court

---

102. *The Rubystone* [1955] 1 Lloyd's Rep 9 (CA). See *ante* at para. 2.62.
103. See Appendix.
104. See *post* at para. 2.140 and Appendix.
105. *Gebr Broere BV* v. *Saras Chimica SpA* [1982] 2 Lloyd's Rep 436. *Dow Chemical (Nederland) BV* v. *BP Tanker Co Ltd (The Vorras)* [1983] 1 Lloyd's Rep 579.
106. *Stephens* v. *Harris & Co* (1887) 57 LJQB 203 (CA).

held that laytime was not interrupted, because the weather did not affect the loading of the vessel, it only affected the transportation of the cargo to the vessel.

2.95 Commenting on this decision in *Reardon Smith Line Ltd* v. *Ministry of Agriculture*, Lord Devlin said[107]:

... if the weather was to be treated as if it were an excepted peril excusing work only when it was actually operating, words could, of course, be found to do it. In *Stephens* v. *Harris & Co*, the Court of Appeal held that the phrase "weather permitting" in that laytime clause had that effect. I see no reason to doubt the authority of that decision although there has been some controversy about it.

Later in his speech, he added[108]:

If the parties want to keep closer to reality, they should use "weather permitting" or some other phrase of exception.

2.96 Explaining these passages, Sir John Donaldson MR said in *The Vorras*[109]:

Undoubtedly Lord Devlin was saying that "weather permitting" is a "phrase of exception" which requires regard to be had to the actual effect which weather is having on the loading process and he was basing himself on the Court of Appeal decision in *Stephens* v. *Harris*. But regard can be had to the actual effect of the weather in two different ways. You can look to see whether the loading process is in fact prevented by the weather or you can look to see whether it is the weather which is the actual cause of the particular vessel not being loaded.

2.97 Sir John then went on to point out that both in *Stephens* v. *Harris* and in the case that Lord Devlin was considering, the answers to each of these questions would have been the same. In neither case was the loading process affected by the weather. The particular vessel was prevented from loading in *Stephens* v. *Harris* because the cargo could not be brought to the ship and in the *Reardon Smith* case because of strikes preventing the elevators from being worked. Lord Devlin therefore did not have to consider a case where weather was the sole cause of the loading process being at a standstill for the vessel alongside and where there was an additional reason affecting the particular vessel he was considering, namely that she was not in berth.

2.98 In *The Camelia and the Magnolia*,[110] Brandon J, as he then was, had to consider a laytime clause providing for laytime defined as " ... 750 metric tons per day of 24 consecutive hours per weather permitting working day". There was also a "berth occupied" clause providing for time to count if there was any delay before berthing.

2.99 In his judgment, Brandon J asked himself what is the effect of the words "per weather permitting working day" in relation to actual laytime after the ship was in berth and also what was their effect on notional laytime before the ship berthed. The answer he gave to the first question based on *Stephens* v. *Harris*[111] was that whether "weather permitting" came before or after "working day", it meant[112]:

... a working day which counted unless work was actually prevented by the weather...

107. *Reardon Smith Line Ltd* v. *Ministry of Agriculture, Fisheries and Food* [1963] 1 Lloyd's Rep 12, at p. 41.
108. *Ibid.*, at p. 43.
109. *Dow Chemical (Nederland) BV* v. *BP Tanker Co Ltd (The Vorras)* [1983] 1 Lloyd's Rep 579, at p. 583.
110. *Magnolia Shipping Co Ltd of Limassol* v. *Joint Venture of the International Trading & Shipping Enterprises and Kinship Management Co Ltd of Brussels (The Camelia and the Magnolia)* [1978] 2 Lloyd's Rep 182.
111. *Stephens* v. *Harris & Co* (1887) 57 LJQB 203 (CA).
112. *The Camelia and the Magnolia* [1978] 2 Lloyd's Rep 182, at p. 184.

2.100 With regard to the second question, Brandon J held that whilst weather could not affect laytime under this particular clause unless the vessel was in berth, the effect of the berth occupied clause was to put both parties in the same position as if the vessel was in berth. This therefore meant that weather interruptions were excluded whilst the vessel was waiting for a berth, as if she had been in berth.[113]

2.101 The judge's answer to the first question was said, however, by Sir John Donaldson MR in *The Vorras* to be "based upon a misreading of *Stephens* v. *Harris*".[114]

2.102 The first of the two most recent decisions to consider this type of laytime clause was *Gebr Broere BV* v. *Saras Chimica SpA*,[115] a decision of Parker J, where the laytime clause was expressed in "running hours weather permitting". In the course of his judgment, the judge confirmed[116] that, from the point of view of the effect of weather, there was no material difference between a clause which fixed laytime by reference to "working days weather permitting", and a clause which did so by reference to "running days weather permitting" or as in the case with which he was then dealing "running hours weather permitting". He then went on to find that in a port charter there had to be excluded from the computation of laytime used up, any periods during which had the vessel berthed on arrival, weather would have prevented loading which would otherwise have taken place. Although pointing out that on the actual laytime clause, Brandon J had held that it was impossible for work actually to be prevented by weather because the vessel was not in berth,[117] Parker J then went on to cite Brandon J's decision in *The Camelia and the Magnolia* and the House of Lords' decision in *The Darrah*[118] as authority for this proposition.

2.103 It is difficult to see, however, how the former can support this statement and with regard to the latter, which was apparently the basis of the decision at first instance in *The Vorras*,[119] in that case in the Court of Appeal Sir John Donaldson MR said he did not see its relevance since it was a weather working day case.[120]

2.104 Whilst apparently agreeing with Parker J's conclusion, Sir John expressly refrained from commenting on the reasoning in the *Gebr Broere* case.[121]

2.105 In *The Vorras*, having reviewed the previous cases, Sir John Donaldson MR continued[122]:

I have to construe the words used in their natural meaning. The words are "72 hours weather permitting". The essence of the owners' argument is that this phrase means "72 hours unless the weather prevents the vessel from loading". There would be something to be said for this if the antonym for "permitting" was "preventing". But it is not. It is "prohibiting". If the phrase is to be inverted, it reads "72 hours unless the weather prohibits loading". In my judgment the weather prohibited any vessel of this general type from loading and it is nothing to the point that owing to the presence of another vessel in the berth, the prohibition was not the operative cause which

---

113. This was based on the House of Lords' decision, *The Darrah* [1977] AC 157—see *post* at para. 3.384.

114. *Dow Chemical (Nederland) BV* v. *BP Tanker Co Ltd (The Vorras)* [1983] 1 Lloyd's Rep 579, at p. 584.

115. *Gebr Broere BV* v. *Saras Chimica SpA* [1982] 2 Lloyd's Rep 436.

116. *Ibid.*, at p. 439.

117. *The Camelia and the Magnolia* [1978] 2 Lloyd's Rep 182.

118. *The Darrah* [1977] AC 157 (HL).

119. *The Vorras* [1983] 1 Lloyd's Rep 579.

120. *Ibid.*, at p. 584.

121. *Ibid.* Apparently this was because there was a possibility that the *Gebr Broere* case might eventually reach the Court of Appeal, the decision of Parker J having been made on a preliminary point of law.

122. *The Vorras* [1983] 1 Lloyd's Rep 579, at p. 584.

prevented the vessel from loading. I would construe "72 hours weather permitting" as meaning "72 hours when the weather was of such a nature as to permit loading".

2.106 It is suggested that in referring to the weather prohibiting "any vessel of this general type from loading" in this passage, the Master of the Rolls was simply saying that not only would weather have prevented the specific ship from loading but any similar type of ship as well. In the *Gebr Broere* case,[123] it was clearly the specific ship that the judge had in mind. It is submitted that that was correct and the reference to vessels of a general type, e.g. tanker or dry cargo, should not be taken as detracting from the principle that it is the particular ship with its type of cargo that should be considered.

2.107 In the *Gebr Broere* case, the judge also went on to consider the effect of weather on laytime when the vessel could not get into berth or had to leave the berth.[124] Having pointed out that it is well established that laytime will not in the absence of exceptions be interrupted if the safety of the vessel and her cargo justifies her removal from the berth, he then went on to hold that if weather first stopped loading and then forced the vessel to leave, it must follow that in each case laytime would be interrupted. Whilst the vessel was alongside it prevented loading and it did not cease to do so when it had the added effect of rendering it necessary for the vessel to leave her berth. He continued[125]:

If this be right, it must follow that if the vessel for her own safety, refrains from going into berth, laytime will be interrupted if the weather is such that it would both have prevented loading and required the vessel to leave her berth had she been in berth. It will not be interrupted, albeit she could not for safety reasons reach her berth if loading would not have been interrupted by weather had she been in berth.

2.108 It is submitted that these wider considerations fit in harmoniously with the arguments put forward by Sir John Donaldson MR in *The Vorras* and are therefore correct, notwithstanding any criticism that may be made of the earlier part of the judgment in the *Gebr Broere* case.[126]

2.109 At the end of his judgment in *The Vorras*, Sir John Donaldson MR added[127]:

Prima facie, any clause defining laytime is descriptive and any clause providing that time shall not count against laytime so defined . . . is exceptive. If it matters, I would classify the expression "72 running hours weather permitting" as descriptive.

The other two members of the Court of Appeal involved in this case gave shorter but concurring judgments.

2.110 In a descriptive laytime clause of this type when calculating interruptions, the emphasis must always be on what the weather permits. The intentions of the parties are therefore irrelevant and there is therefore no need to examine whether the weather interruption occurred at an hour at which it was either intended or even possible to work cargo—the one qualification to this, however, must be that if "weather permitting" is added to "working day" then of course it must not be on a Sunday or holiday. In setting out the laytime statement, all that is necessary is to deduct the actual time of the interruption.

---

123. *Gebr Broere BV* v. *Saras Chimica SpA* [1982] 2 Lloyd's Rep 436.
124. *Gebr Broere BV* v. *Saras Chimica SpA* [1982] 2 Lloyd's Rep 436, at pp. 439–440.
125. *Ibid.*, at p. 440.
126. See *ante* at the text to fn. 121.
127. *Dow Chemical (Nederland) BV* v. *BP Tanker Co Ltd (The Vorras)* [1983] 1 Lloyd's Rep 579, at p. 584.

2.111 It occasionally happens that "weather permitting" is added to "weather working day" with the laytime allowed being described as say, "five weather working days weather permitting". It is submitted, however, that in these circumstances the words "weather permitting" add nothing and the phrase should be construed as if it simply read "five weather working days".

Working hours, working days of 24 hours, weather permitting

2.112 It sometimes happens that the parties to a charterparty may wish to provide for allowed laytime in terms of a specified number of hours' work. Where this is done, it is perhaps more common for it also to be expressed as a rate of work. Thus the full phrase might be:

... and discharge to be at the rate of 350 tons per working day of 24 hours, weather permitting.

For the purpose of this section, however, it is only the unit of time that will be considered.[128] The rules relating to the phrase "weather permitting" have already been considered and similar principles will apply.[129]

2.113 As with other laytime clauses, the courts will look at all the relevant clauses of the charter before deciding what the parties intended. This may be why one of the three reported cases dealing specifically with this type of clause might be said to provide a somewhat different interpretation[130] to the other two. However, where the courts do conclude that the parties did intend to provide for a specified period of work and expressed it in terms of "working days of 24 hours" then all that is needed is to convert this into working hours by multiplying the number of days so provided by 24. This will then give the total number of working hours to be allowed to the charterers.

2.114 Clearly, a "working hour" must be part of a working day.[131] However, whether it is confined to those hours within normal working hours for the trade at the port in question or includes those hours on which overtime is usually worked is perhaps less clear.

2.115 On balance it is submitted that those hours on which overtime is normally worked (whether or not actually used) should count[132] and therefore similar principles will apply to those used in determining the length of the working day where laytime is expressed in terms of weather working days.[133] However, if greater, the actual "working hours" used must count.

2.116 If, therefore, a charter were to allow "two working days of 24 hours" and each working day was found to consist of 12 working hours, it would take four calendar days before the laytime was used up.

2.117 The leading case on this type of clause is *Forest Steamship Co Ltd* v. *Iberian Iron Ore Co Ltd*,[134] a case which eventually reached the House of Lords.

2.118 The facts were that the parties had agreed that the plaintiffs would supply ships for the carriage of iron ore from Seville to the United Kingdom and elsewhere over a

---

128. For the rules relating to laytime expressed as a rate of discharge, see *post* at para. 2.144.
129. For "weather permitting", see *ante* at para. 2.92.
130. *Orpheus Steamship Co* v. *Bovill & Sons* (1916) 114 LT 750. See also *post* at para. 2.124.
131. For "working day", see *ante* at para. 2.23.
132. See *post* at para. 2.126.
133. See *ante* at para. 2.74.
134. *Forest Steamship Co Ltd* v. *Iberian Iron Ore Co Ltd* (1899) 5 CC 83 (HL).

period of 12 months. An ordinary single voyage charter was used, appropriately adapted. The material provisions of the charter were as follows:

Charterers . . . to be allowed 350 tons per working day of twenty-four hours weather permitting (Sundays and holidays excepted), for loading and discharging . . . Steamer to work at night if required, also on Sundays and holidays, such time not to count as laydays unless used . . .

2.119 Rejecting an argument from the plaintiff shipowners that the charterers were only entitled to one working day for each 350 tons of ore, no matter of what number of hours such working day might happen to consist, Smith LJ said in the Court of Appeal[135]:

. . . the plaintiffs' contention appears to me to give the go-by to the words which presumably were inserted for some purpose in the charter—viz. "of twenty-four hours"—and reads the charterparty as if those words were not there. Why were these words inserted? It seems to me for the express purpose of giving to the charterers a fixed period of twenty-four working hours wherein to load or unload each 350 tons of ore, no matter what number of hours might constitute a working day at the port of loading or the ports of discharge.

Later he added:

But a "working day of twenty-four hours" is not the same as "a working day" . . .

He also found significant support for the defendant charterers' argument in the "unless used" clause which as far as the working at night part was concerned would have been unnecessary if the shipowners were right.

2.120 On the other hand, in a dissenting judgment, Rigby LJ argued that the charterers' view totally ignored the established meaning of "working day" by converting it into 24 working hours. The third judgment by Vaughan Williams LJ supported the charterers and thus, by a majority, the Court of Appeal held that the laytime clause meant that charterers were to be allowed 24 working hours for discharging each 350 tons.

2.121 This conclusion was upheld, although not without some doubt, by the House of Lords, where the only speech of any length was given by the Earl of Halsbury LC, who concluded that the parties intended to manufacture a conventional or artificial day out of a certain number of hours.[136]

2.122 The next case to consider the problem was *Watson Brothers Shipping Co Ltd* v. *Mysore Manganese Co Ltd*[137] where the laytime specified was "500 tons per clear working day of 24 hours (weather permitting) Sundays and holidays excepted". If work was carried out on these excepted periods then half was to count as laytime. There was also a provision requiring the ship to work day and night if requested to do so.

2.123 Having concluded that the charter that he was then considering could not be successfully distinguished from that in the *Forest Steamship* case,[138] Hamilton J added:

. . . apart from authority the natural construction of the clause would be that the defendants (the charterers) . . . are to have, not a day by the calendar or a day which is a working day as distinguished from a calendar day which is a holiday, but a certain number of hours upon which work in the ordinary course may be done.

---

135. *Sub nom. Rhymney Steamship Co Ltd* v. *Iberian Iron Ore Co Ltd, Forest Steamship Co Ltd* v. *Iberian Iron Ore Co Ltd* (1898) 3 CC 316, at p. 318.
136. *Forest Steamship Co Ltd* v. *Iberian Iron Ore Co Ltd* (1899) 5 CC 83, at p. 85.
137. *Watson Brothers Shipping Co Ltd* v. *Mysore Manganese Co Ltd* (1910) 15 CC 159.
138. *Forest Steamship Co Ltd* v. *Iberian Iron Ore Co Ltd* (1899) 5 CC 83 (HL).

2.124 These cases were, however, distinguished in *Orpheus Steamship Co* v. *Bovill & Sons*,[139] a decision of Scrutton J, who had been the unsuccessful counsel for the plaintiff shipowners in the previous case considered above. The dispute arose out of the carriage of a cargo of grain to Avonmouth, where discharge was to be "in accordance with the rules of the Bristol Channel and West of England Corn Trade Association", under which eight "working days of twenty-four hours each", Sundays excluded, were allowed for the particular discharge. Under these rules time counted from arrival off Avonmouth, whether berthed or not. There was no allowance for interruptions by bad weather and Scrutton J therefore held that in these circumstances effectively what was allowed was eight working days. He relied on the fact that the charter did not mention any time outside working hours to show that there was none, saying[140]:

There is no provision as there was in the other cases about what you are to do with the period after the working hours . . . In this case there is no provision either authorising you to exclude it or saying what will happen if it is worked. In these circumstances it seems to me that it is part of the working day. It is a day on which work can be done between the parties and the parties can require work to be done during that time. I see no reason to exclude it.

It may be therefore that this case should simply be considered as an illustration of a particular number of working hours, viz. 24, being agreed between the parties as being the usual number to be worked each day in the port and trade in question. On this basis there would be no discord with the earlier cases.

2.125 Commenting on this type of laytime clause in *Reardon Smith Line Ltd* v. *Ministry of Agriculture*, Lord Devlin said[141]:

It is, of course, possible, and it is sometimes done, for the lay days to be defined as a number of working hours. Or they may be defined as working days of 24 or some other number of hours, though the authorities are not entirely agreed on what that means.

The reference in the last part of this quotation is presumably to Scrutton J's decision in *Orpheus Steamship Co* v. *Bovill & Sons*.[142]

Working hours per working day

2.126 As mentioned at the start of the last section, one of the questions to be determined is which hours during the working day are to count. As Smith LJ pointed out in the Court of Appeal in the *Forest Steamship Co* case,[143] the number of hours which constitute a working day may vary at different ports. It also seems to be an inference of his judgment that where more than the normal hours of the port are used then the actual time should count. However, in that case there was an "unless used" provision relating to, *inter alia*, night time work. In the House of Lords, the Earl of Halsbury commented[144]:

nobody supposes people work for twenty-four hours.

However, he did not say what period should be considered.

139. *Orpheus Steamship Co* v. *Bovill & Sons* (1916) 114 LT 750.
140. *Ibid.*, at p. 752.
141. *Reardon Smith Line Ltd* v. *Ministry of Agriculture, Fisheries and Food* [1963] 1 Lloyd's Rep 12, at p. 39.
142. *Orpheus Steamship Co* v. *Bovill & Sons* (1916) 114 LT 750.
143. *Sub nom. Rhymney Steamship Co Ltd* v. *Iberian Iron Ore Co Ltd, Forest Steamship Co Ltd* v. *Iberian Iron Ore Co Ltd* (1898) 3 CC 316, at p. 318.
144. *Forest Steamship Co Ltd* v. *Iberian Iron Ore Co Ltd* (1899) 5 CC 83, at p. 86.

2.127 In *Watson Brothers Shipping Co Ltd* v. *Mysore Manganese Co Ltd*, Hamilton J referred to the "usual hours of working at the port",[145] and later on to the "hours upon which work in the ordinary course may be done". Dealing with work done at an unusual hour (even without an "unless used" clause), he added[146]:

I take it that if he (the shipper) does require the ship to work in hours not usually worked on, and the ship complies with its obligation, the shipper could not deny that such hours having been used were part of the working day of 24 hours.

2.128 In *Reardon Smith Line Ltd* v. *Ministry of Agriculture*, Lord Devlin pointed out that[147]:

The number of hours of a day or working day . . . which a charterer can use will depend on how he can mobilize the resources of the port and what rights he has got to exact co-operation from the ship.

Later on, he added[148]:

Overtime in ports is the rule rather than the exception.

2.129 It is submitted, therefore, that the usual working hours will include regular overtime and will fall to be determined for the particular trade at the port in question. Furthermore the hours to count for a particular day will be the greater between the total normal hours (including regular overtime) and the hours actually worked.

2.130 If either of these laytime clauses are used without the addition of the words "weather permitting" then under general principles relating to interruptions in fixed laytime already considered,[149] there will be no effect due to adverse weather.

2.131 When "weather permitting" is added the words become part of the clause itself, rather than an exception to it and are thus descriptive rather than exceptive.[150] As before, the emphasis must always be on what the weather permits. The intentions of the parties are therefore irrelevant, provided the weather interruption occurred on a working day and within the hours actually worked or the hours in which work is usually carried out as defined above. Adverse weather outside these periods has no effect on laytime and may be ignored. An alternative way of putting the same point is to say that the laytime clock must be running, apart from the weather, before weather can have any effect.

2.132 Where it does have an effect, the actual period of the interruption is subtracted from the laytime used.

Working days of 24 consecutive hours, working days of 24 running hours, weather permitting

2.133 Although at first sight these may seem very similar to one of the laytime clauses considered in the previous section, as will be seen, the one word that is different makes a considerable change, although there is no difference between the two alternatives.

2.134 A working day of 24 consecutive or running hours is a conventional day of 24 hours which follow one after the other throughout the day and night and which is a

---

145. *Watson Brothers Shipping Co Ltd* v. *Mysore Manganese Co Ltd* (1910) 15 CC 159, at pp. 165, 166.
146. *Ibid.*, at p. 166.
147. *Reardon Smith Line Ltd* v. *Ministry of Agriculture, Fisheries and Food* [1963] 1 Lloyd's Rep 12, at p. 40.
148. *Ibid.*, at p. 41.
149. See *ante* at para. 2.3.
150. See *ante* at para. 2.92.

working day as opposed to a Sunday or holiday. The full period of 24 hours therefore counts against laytime and not merely the hours usually or actually worked where the words "consecutive" or "running" are omitted.[151]

2.135 The leading case where one of the clauses was considered was a Scottish case, *Turnbull, Scott & Co* v. *Cruickshank & Co.*[152]

2.136 The case arose out of the carriage of a cargo of iron ore from Spain to Ardrossan on the Clyde. Loading and discharging were to be "at the rate of 500 tons per working day of 24 consecutive hours, weather permitting, Sundays and holidays always excepted".

2.137 Relying on *Forest Steamship Co Ltd* v. *Iberian Iron Ore Co Ltd*,[153] the charterers claimed they were entitled to an artificial period of 24 hours in each of which work was usually performed to load or discharge each 500 tons. On the other hand, the shipowners contended that what they were allowed was a day of 24 actually consecutive hours for loading/discharging each 500 tons so that apart from weather interruptions and Sundays/holidays, time would run and count continuously.

2.138 In the court below, the Sheriff-substitute commented that he could not read consecutive hours "as meaning anything else than hours following one another immediately and without interval of time".[154] The Court of Session upheld the shipowner's argument. Lord Trayner pointed out that in the *Forest Steamship* case, the laytime clause was held to mean 24 working hours rather than 24 consecutive hours, adding[155]:

In the clause before us there is the exception that hours when the weather did not permit of loading or discharging were not to be reckoned against the charterers, nor were holidays nor Sundays. But in every twenty-four consecutive hours from the commencement of the loading or discharging, 500 tons were to be loaded or discharged if the weather did not hinder it or a holiday or Sunday intervene. And in my opinion the words "working day" in the clause before us are used only in antithesis to the days which were Sundays or holidays.

2.139 The effect of the "weather permitting" part of the clause will be similar to other laytime clauses where this phrase is used.[156] Where weather does not permit cargo working or would not if any had been intended or the vessel in a position so to do, then the actual period so affected must be deducted. This applies even if the period concerned is in the middle of the night, whether or not working was possible at such an hour. This follows from the decision of the Court of Appeal in *The Vorras*,[157] where the addition of "weather permitting" was said to make the whole clause descriptive, rather than exceptive.[158]

Weather working day of 24 consecutive hours

2.140 In the *Charterparty Laytime Definitions 1980*, this is defined as follows[159]:

"WEATHER WORKING DAY OF 24 CONSECUTIVE HOURS" means a working day or part of a working day of 24 hours during which it is or, if the ship is still waiting for her turn, it would be possible to load/

---

151. See *ante* at para. 2.112.
152. *Turnbull, Scott & Co* v. *Cruickshank & Co* (1904) 7 Fraser 265 (Ct of Sess).
153. *Forest Steamship Co Ltd* v. *Iberian Iron Ore Co Ltd* (1899) 5 CC 83.
154. *Turnbull, Scott & Co* v. *Cruickshank & Co* (1904) 7 Sess Cas, 5th Series 265, at p. 269 (note).
155. *Ibid.*, at p. 273.
156. See *ante* at para. 2.92.
157. *Dow Chemical (Nederland) BV* v. *BP Tanker Co Ltd (The Vorras)* [1983] 1 Lloyd's Rep 579.
158. *Ibid.*, at p. 584 *per* Sir John Donaldson MR.
159. See Appendix. A similar definition appears in *Baltic Code 2000*.

discharge the cargo without interference due to the weather. If such interference occurs (or would have occurred if work had been in progress) there shall be excluded from the laytime the period during which the weather interfered or would have interfered with the work.

2.141 The *Voylayrules 1993* contain a similar definition[160]:

" . . . WEATHER WORKING DAY OF 24 CONSECUTIVE HOURS" shall mean a working day of 24 consecutive hours except for any time when weather prevents the loading or discharging of the vessel or would have prevented it had work been in progress.

2.142 It will be noted that it is the actual period of interruption or deemed interruption that is discounted, regardless of what proportion this might bear to the daily period of work and that furthermore it does not matter whether the weather interruption occurs within or without the daily period of work.[161]

2.143 In comparison with "weather working day" *simpliciter*, the effect of the additional words is therefore to fix the length of the daily working period at 24 hours, no matter what the actual period is. If "weather permitting" be added as well then it is submitted that the meaning remains the same, the additional words being mere surplusage.[162]

LAYTIME BY REFERENCE TO RATES OF WORKING CARGO

2.144 Such laytime clauses may provide for a total rate of loading/discharging or alternatively for a rate per hatch or per hook. In the case of the latter this may be so many tons per hatch or so many tons "per working (or available workable) hatch". In each alternative the time element may be "per day", "per working day", "per weather working day" or any other of the time units previously considered.

Rate per working hatch (or available workable hatch)

2.145 A typical clause would be:

At the average rate of . . . tons per working hatch per day.

2.146 A working hatch is one from which on a particular day, cargo is being worked and therefore once the hold served by that hatch is empty or full, as the case may be, the hatch ceases to be a working hatch. Since the total amount of cargo to be worked on a particular day is the sum of the rates for those hatches still working, this will, if all hatches are being worked equally, decrease steadily during loading/discharge until only one hatch remains working. The laytime allowed may therefore be calculated by ascertaining which hold is to have or had the most cargo, which will be the last one to continue working, and dividing the quantity it now contains or contained by the agreed working rate.

2.147 The *Voylayrules 1993* provide[163]:

---

160. See Appendix. A Similar definition also appears in Baltic Code 2000.
161. See London Arbitration 16/86—LMLN 180, 25 September 1986 where the tribunal so held.
162. This must follow from the meaning given to "weather permitting" in a laytime clause since *Dow Chemical (Nederland) BV* v. *BP Tanker Co Ltd (The Vorras)* [1983] 1 Lloyd's Rep. 579. See also *ante* at para. 2.105.
163. See Appendix. A similar definition appears in *Baltic Code 2000*.

"PER WORKING HATCH PER DAY (WHD)" or "PER WORKABLE HATCH PER DAY (WHD)" shall mean that the laytime is to be calculated by dividing (A), the quantity of cargo in the hold with the largest quantity, by (B), the result of multiplying the agreed daily rate per working or workable hatch by the number of hatches serving that hold. Thus:

$$\text{Laytime} = \frac{\text{Largest Quantity in One Hold}}{\text{Daily Rate per Hatch} \times \text{Number of Hatches Serving that Hold}} = \text{Days}$$

Each pair of parallel twin hatches shall count as one hatch. Nevertheless, a hatch that is capable of being worked by two gangs simultaneously shall be counted as two hatches.

2.148 It is only after the completion of loading when the precise quantities loaded into each hold are known that the exact amount of laytime can be determined.

2.149 The leading case in which this type of clause was considered is *The Sandgate*,[164] in which a charter on the Welsh Coal Charter 1896 form provided for the carriage of a cargo of coal from Cardiff to San Rosario. The charter provided for an "average rate of discharge of 125 tons per working hatch per day . . . ". The ship had four hatches and the shipowners argued that this meant a discharge rate of 500 tons per day. The charterers said, however, that this ignored the fact that once a hold became empty, it could no longer be described as a working hatch and they contended that the total discharging rate should be proportionately reduced as each hold became empty, without affecting the rate per hatch. Both before Hill J and on appeal the charterers' view was preferred. In the course of his judgment, Hill J said[165]:

I suppose worked out most accurately you would take these several quantities (that is the quantity in each hold) and start with 500 and go on reducing to 375, reducing to 250 and finally 125; but you get exactly the same result, and the shipowner would have no difficulty in doing the arithmetic if he took the quantity in the hold which contains the largest quantity and divided that by 125, then that would give you the period in which the discharge had to be carried out, and you would then take into account Sundays and holidays.

On appeal, Scrutton LJ said, rejecting the shipowners' argument[166]:

. . . the phrase cannot be read as a roundabout way of saying what might have been said quite simply: "I will discharge 500 tons per day out of four cargo hatches, 125 tons for each hatch". What it does mean is to assume that the amount may vary per day, according as there is a working hatch—a hatch which can be worked because there is coal in it. Whether it was a reasonable agreement to make or not, it is not for me to say.

2.150 A similar provision was considered by Devlin J in *Compania de Navigación Zita SA* v. *Louis Dreyfus & Cie*.[167] In this case, clause 5 of the charter provided for the cargo to be loaded "at an average rate of not less than 150 metric tons per available workable hatch per . . . ", In argument, neither party suggested that there was any relevant difference in meaning between the phrase "working hatch" in *The Sandgate*[168] and "available workable hatch" as in the present case, at least as far as the basic calculation of laytime was concerned.

2.151 The shipowners, however, contended that laytime for loading should be calculated by reference to the number of available and workable hatches at a given time. As long as there were five available workable hatches, loading should have proceeded at

164. *The Sandgate* [1930] P 30 (CA).
165. *Sandgate (Owners)* v. *W S Partridge & Co* (1929) 35 Ll L Rep 9, at p. 13.
166. *The Sandgate* [1930] P 30, at p. 34.
167. *Compania de Navigación Zita SA* v. *Louis Dreyfus & Cie* [1953] 2 Lloyd's Rep 472.
168. *The Sandgate* [1930] P 30.

an average daily rate of 750 tons. When this was reduced to three at the second load port, loading should have been 450 tons and when the last parcel of cargo was loaded at the same port with only two hatches available, the average rate should have been 300 tons. The charterers, on the other hand, argued however that loading should be calculated by dividing by 150 the largest quantity of cargo loaded in any one of the vessel's holds.

2.152 In upholding the charterers' contentions, Devlin J said[169]:

There is, I think, an overwhelming objection to the owners' construction of the clause. It is that on that construction the number of lay days depends upon the way in which the charterers choose to load the vessel. There may possibly be good reasons why they should load one hold after the other, but there may also be bad ones; and on the owners' construction there is no way of distinguishing between excusable delay and wanton delay . . .

. . . the fundamental error in them [the owners' submissions] is that they treat clause 5[170] as if it were laying down a method of loading. If it were, it would be appropriate to suggest that it should not be construed as requiring the charterers to load each hold each day at exactly the same rate and for exactly the same time. Clause 5 in my opinion is not prescribing a method, but setting a standard; it is drawing a notional line above which there will be a bonus and below a penalty . . .

. . . But is reasonable to think that the standard set will be one which assumes that as far as possible work will go on simultaneously on all the holds, because that is the way that is most economical of the ship's time.

2.153 In *The Sandgate*[171] there was only one discharge port and although in *Compania de Navigación Zita SA* v. *Louis Dreyfus & Cie*[172] there were two load ports, it does not appear to have been suggested that the number of load or discharge ports, as the case may be, made any difference.

2.154 This point, however, was considered by Hobhouse J in *Cargill Incorporated* v. *Marpro Ltd*[173] (*The Aegis Progress*). Cargill were the sellers of two parcels of sugar, f.o.b., with Antwerp and Dunkirk nominated as loading ports. The contract of sale provided for a rate of loading of 150 metric tons per workable hatch. Prior to calling at Antwerp, the *Aegis Progress* had called at Rouen and loaded a part cargo with which Cargill were unconcerned.

2.155 The buyers of the cargo argued that as four of the vessel's seven holds were available at each load port, the total quantity of cargo loaded at both ports should be divided by four and the loading rate applied to this, notwithstanding that the available holds were not the same at each port. The sellers, on the other hand, said they were entitled to make separate calculations for each load port based on the largest quantity loaded in any one hold at that port. Although stressing that the clause should be construed as requiring a single calculation, nevertheless Hobhouse J held that in this case the calculation should be based on, not the hold with the greatest quantity from both ports, but the sum of the hold with the greatest quantity loaded at Antwerp and the corresponding one at Dunkirk. He concluded[174]:

In most cases the required calculation can be done by identifying the critical hatch or hold and then calculating the laytime for that hatch; in exceptional cases and this is one, more than one hatch is critical and therefore more than one hatch has to be taken into account in calculating the laytime.

169. *Compania de Navigación Zita SA* v. *Louis Dreyfus & Cie* [1953] 2 Lloyd's Rep 472, at p. 474.
170. *Ibid.*, at p. 475.
171. *The Sandgate* [1930] P 30.
172. *Compania de Navigación Zita SA* v. *Louis Dreyfus & Cie* [1953] 2 Lloyd's Rep 472.
173. *Cargill Inc* v. *Marpro Ltd* (*The Aegis Progress*) [1983] 2 Lloyd's Rep 570.
174. *Ibid.*, at p. 577.

2.156 Furthermore, said Hobhouse J, earlier in his judgment,[175]

When one is considering workability one must disregard uneven loading (or discharge) which arises from the shippers' choice as opposed to reasons which disable them from working the hatches evenly.

It may therefore, as it did in this case, also become necessary to correct the quantities actually loaded in each hatch to produce a theoretical figure which would have been loaded in each hold, had loading been done evenly. It is the biggest of the corrected figures for each port that then goes into the calculation.

2.157 This correction is necessary because the earlier cases construed such clauses as setting a standard and, furthermore, one based on even loading.[176] However, the problem can only arise with a part cargo.

2.158 A further aspect was considered by Bingham J in *Cargill Inc* v. *Rionda de Pass Ltd (The Giannis Xilas)*.[177] This case concerned the shipment of a parcel of bagged sugar from Antwerp in a vessel with an unconventional layout, in that one of the hatches gave, via a common 'tween deck access, to two of the lower holds. In his judgment, Bingham J rejected a submission by the buyers that where a hatch gave access to two different cargo spaces, one of which was served by another hatch, then the quantity of cargo in the hold served by two hatches could be halved or otherwise split. He said[178]:

I find no warrant in the language used for thinking in terms of notional hatches or notional metal bars, nor do I think it legitimate to pay attention to cargo spaces, which are not mentioned, in preference to hatches which are.

2.159 Although Bingham J's attention was drawn to the *Charterparty Laytime Definitions 1980*[179] which provide for a hatch which is capable of being worked by two gangs simultaneously to be counted as two hatches, as do the *Voylayrules 1993*, he also found on the evidence that for it to have been done in this case, whilst theoretically possible and occasionally adopted, would have been contrary to what was considered good and accepted practice at Antwerp.

2.160 The meaning of "available workable hatch" was also considered in a London Arbitration.[180] In that case, the vessel had four holds and five hatches at upper deck level, hold No 4 being served by two hatches. Each hatch was served by two pairs of winches, except for No 2 hatch which was served by two pairs of winches at the forward end and two more at the after end. Each end of No 2 hatch could therefore be worked simultaneously.

2.161 The charterers submitted that the correct method of calculating the laytime allowed was to identify the hatch/hold with the most cargo, which they said in this case was hatch/hold No 2 and divide the quantity loaded by the rate of loading provided in the charter. The owners, however, contended that as hatches Nos 4 and 5, which both served No 4 hold were the same size, then the same quantity would be loaded through each hatch, i.e. half the quantity stowed in hold No 4 which was actually greater than that stowed in hold No 2. Furthermore, as hatch No 2 was double rigged, the owners argued that it should

175. *The Aegis Progress* [1983] 2 Lloyd's Rep 570, at p. 574.
176. See *ante*, at para. 2.149.
177. *Cargill Inc* v. *Rionda de Pass Ltd (The Giannis Xilas)* [1982] 2 Lloyd's Rep 511.
178. *Ibid.*, at p. 514.
179. See Appendix.
180. London Arbitration—LMLN 127, 13 September 1984.

count as two hatches and in support of this they pointed to the *Charterparty Laytime Definitions*.[181] On this basis the cargo loaded through hatches Nos 4 and 5 would still be being loaded when all the cargo loaded through hatch No 2 had been finished.

2.162 The arbitrators, however, rejected the owners' arguments, saying that the focal point of the dispute turned upon the construction of the words "per available workable hatch" and applying the principles laid down in the cases, the charterers were right. The *Charterparty Laytime Definitions* were intended for voluntary adoption to avoid arguments over the construction of words and phrases but the parties had not in this case chosen to adopt them. What was relevant was that the largest quantity of cargo had passed through hatch No 2. Large as that hatch was, no notional argument could make it into two. The same, of course, applies to the *Voylayrules 1993*.

Availability of holds

2.163 The insertion of "available" in the phrase "per available working hatch" does not affect the initial calculation of laytime allowed, but acts as a built-in exceptions clause. In *Compania de Navigación Zita SA* v. *Louis Dreyfus & Cie*, Devlin J put it this way[182]:

Unavailability is therefore outside the formula and a matter for a separate calculation. You take the formula figure just as you would take a specified number of lay days and make the appropriate deductions, where necessary, for Sundays and holidays and bad weather and unavailability of hatches. It is not irrelevant to observe that the unavailability must be something that matters, that is, it must interfere with the work. If, for example, a hatch broke down after a hold had been completely loaded, it clearly would not matter. If . . . (one of the smaller holds) broke down at the beginning for, say, four days, equally it would not matter, for it would not be long enough to prevent the loading of the hold within the standard time.

Thus, unlike the inclusion of weather in "weather working day",[183] for unavailability to be excluded, there must be a causal connection. Where availability is not added to the laytime phrase, then the situation as to unavailability may be governed by whatever exception clauses are contained in the charterparty. However, in *Cargill Inc* v. *Marpro Ltd (The Aegis Progress)*,[184] Hobhouse J suggested that even if "available" is not added to the laytime phrase, then the word "workable" of itself might exclude periods of non-availability. He commented[185]:

Availability may overlap with workability. The relevant clause in the *Zita* case specifically used the word "available" as well as workable. Mr Justice Devlin treated unavailability as an exception from laytime as opposed to part of the description of laytime. Obviously, as contemplated by Mr Justice Bingham (in *The Giannis Xilas*), events such as winch breakdowns may interrupt loading or discharging and may conveniently be treated as periods of unavailability in the way he suggests. For myself I am unpersuaded that to introduce the word "available" either into the clause or the judicial discussion adds anything of substance . . . Lest it be thought that the word "available" has to be introduced to cover the situation where a hatch cannot be worked for reasons other than that the hold is full or empty, this is neither correct as a matter of English language—the word "workable" is subject to no such limitation—nor was it the view of Mr Justice Bingham who expressly included in his definition of "workable" the words—

---

181. See Appendix.
182. *Compania de Navigación Zita SA* v. *Louis Dreyfus & Cie* [1953] 2 Lloyd's Rep 472, at p. 477.
183. See *ante* at para. 2.41.
184. *Cargill Inc* v. *Marpro Ltd* [1983] 2 Lloyd's Rep 570.
185. *Ibid.*, at p. 576.

. . . being a hatch the party responsible for loading or discharging is not for any reason disabled from working . . . (p. 513).

Fullness and emptiness are the commonest reasons and therefore feature most prominently in the cases. But *The Sandgate* clearly contemplates that there may be other reasons and in my opinion Mr Justice Bingham was clearly right to formulate the definition as he did.

Rate per hatch

2.164 The usual sort of clause might be:

At the average rate of . . . tons per hatch per working day.

2.165 The question of whether this should be construed the same as clauses referring to a rate per working hatch fell to be considered by the Court of Appeal in *Lodza Compania de Navigacione SA* v. *Government of Ceylon (The Theraios).*[186]

2.166 In the original arbitration proceedings out of which the appeal arose, the arbitrators held that an average rate per hatch per day meant simply what it said and that to find the total daily rate all that was necessary was to multiply the rate by the number of hatches. If the total quantity loaded was then divided by this figure, this produced the allowed laytime.

2.167 In the High Court, Mocatta J held[187] that this was not so and the way to determine the laytime allowed was to use the *Sandgate*[188] formula as with rates per working hatch, where the laytime allowed was calculated by dividing the largest quantity loaded in any one hold by the agreed rate. This view was unanimously rejected by the Court of Appeal who reinstated the judgment of the arbitrators. Salmon LJ said[189]:

All that matters to the owners is the actual time occupied by those (loading and discharging) operations. . . . Since this vessel has five hatches, the clause seems to me to be a roundabout way of saying that the vessel shall be loaded and discharged at an average rate of 600 tons per day, that is to say five hatches at 120 tons per hatch. This meaning could certainly have been more clearly expressed by saying simply that "the cargo is to be loaded and discharged at the average rate of 600 tons a day". But charterparties are hardly renowned for the invariable clarity and simplicity of their language.

And Widgery LJ commented[190]:

In the absence of any express reference to "working" hatches and of any compelling need to imply that adjective in order to give business efficacy to the contract, I am unable to say that the arbitrators erred in law in adopting the owners' construction of the charterparty.

2.168 The *Charterparty Laytime Definitions 1980* provide[191]:

"PER HATCH PER DAY"—means that laytime is to be calculated by multiplying the agreed daily rate per hatch of loading/discharging the cargo by the number of the ship's hatches and dividing the quantity of the cargo by the resulting sum. Thus

$$\text{Laytime} = \frac{\text{Quantity of Cargo}}{\text{Daily Rate} \times \text{Number of Hatches}} = \text{Days}$$

---

186. *Lodza Compania de Navigacione SA* v. *Govt. of Ceylon (The Theraios)* [1971] 1 Lloyd's Rep 209.
187. *Lodza Compania de Navigacione SA* v. *Govt. of Ceylon (The Theraios)* [1970] 2 Lloyd's Rep 142.
188. *The Sandgate* [1930] P 30.
189. *The Theraios* [1971] 1 Lloyd's Rep 209, at p. 211.
190. *Ibid.*, at p. 213.
191. See Appendix.

A hatch that is capable of being worked by two gangs simultaneously shall be counted as two hatches.

2.169 The laytime provision considered in London Arbitration 30/92[192] provided for a loading rate of: "500 metric tons per hatch . . . two hatches . . . Basis two hatches". The ship had four holds and seven hatches. She had twin hatches serving No 2 hold and it was that hold in which it was intended to load the cargo. The charterers said that the laytime calculation should be worked out as if only one hatch had been provided because it was not possible to work each hatch with a double gang as they had intended, i.e. a total of four. The tribunal cast doubt whether this would have been feasible even if two hatches each serving a single hold had been designated for the cargo. However, they decided the case in favour of the owners on the basis that the charter simply referred to two hatches and that was what the charterers got.

2.170 This case should be contrasted with the definition of "per hatch per day" in the *Voylayrules 1993*[193] which state:

"PER HATCH PER DAY" shall mean that the laytime is to be calculated by dividing (A), the quantity of cargo, by (B), the result of multiplying the agreed daily rate per hatch by the number of the vessel's hatches. Thus:

$$\text{Laytime} = \frac{\text{Quantity of Cargo}}{\text{Daily Rate} \times \text{Number of Hatches}} = \text{Days}$$

Each pair of parallel twin hatches shall count as one hatch. Nevertheless, a hatch that is capable of being worked by two gangs simultaneously shall be counted as two hatches.

These rules of course only apply if specifically incorporated. The provision that, *prima facie*, a twin hatch shall count as one hatch is an addition to the corresponding definition in the *Charterparty Laytime Definitions 1980*.

2.171 Had these definitions been included in the arbitration case considered above, the end result would, however, have been the same. The *prima facie* presumption that a twin hatch should count as one hatch would have been rebutted by the fact that it was capable of being worked by two gangs, although not four as contended for in that case. From a commercial point of view it makes sense to say that a twin hatch should only count as two hatches if it is capable of being worked by two gangs simultaneously.

Rate per hook

2.172 The meaning of a laytime provision which provided for the laytime allowed to be calculated on the basis of "150 m.t. per Hook PWWD of 24 Consec. hrs. . . . " has been considered in a London Arbitration.[194]

2.173 The vessel concerned had three holds to which access was obtained by three hatches. The configuration of the cargo compartments was such that a maximum of four gangs could work at the same time. The hatches were served by six derricks and two cranes. When loading a cargo such as bagged copra, the derricks would usually be coupled in union purchase with one "hook" operated by each pair of derricks. Given the availability of the cranes and limited by the maximum working space within the holds for

---

192. London Arbitration 30/92—LMLN 338, 17 October 1992.
193. See Appendix and the similar definition that appears in *Baltic Code 2000*.
194. London Arbitration—LMLN 129, 11 October 1984.

the loading/discharging gangs, the vessel was properly to be regarded as a "four-hook ship".

2.174 The owners argued that as the vessel was a four-gang ship, the rate of cargo operations ought to be 600 tons per day. The charterers contended that the permitted period of laytime ought to be calculated by reference to the number of hooks actually used, which at the load ports was a maximum of two at any one time, whilst at the discharge ports three hooks were utilized.

2.175 The arbitrators held that describing a ship by reference to "hooks" gave a more accurate picture of the vessel's cargo working capabilities than by reference merely to the number of hatches/holds. Physically, there might be any number of extra hooks available, by ship's gear working singly or by shore cranes, but "hooks" in the sense used here went to the heart of the matter, namely how many gangs at maximum could be worked on board the ship. Given a description of a vessel by reference to its "hooks", a reliable estimate could be made of the vessel's prospects of completing cargo work by a simple calculation, which took the vessel's characteristics into account as well as local factors. Whereas some holds could only be worked by one gang, others were of sufficient size and with adequate hatchway access to enable the efficient use of two gangs simultaneously. Thus the expression a "four-hook" ship was the same as saying a "four-gang" ship, providing the vessel was to be worked with conventional loading gear whether on shore or on the ship. The arbitrators therefore held that the laytime allowed was to be based on loading/ discharging 600 tons per day. It did not relate to the maximum number of "hooks" that might be dangled over the hatches, even though some could not be serviced by a gang, and neither did it import the concept of being based on the number of hooks actually used as contended for by the charterers.

Laytime expressed as a total daily rate

2.176 A common provision might be:

The steamer shall be loaded at the rate of . . . tons per running day and at destination cargo to be received at . . . tons per weather working day.

Whilst it might be imagined that this type of clause could not give rise to any disputes over the calculation of laytime allowed, nevertheless a number of cases have come before the courts.

2.177 In *Hain Steamship Co Ltd* v. *Minister of Food*,[195] one of the questions that arose concerned whether, as the shipowners contended, the lay days should be calculated upon the actual quantities loaded and discharged, or as the charterers argued, on a formula based on the freight provision. In the event on this point, the umpire, Sellers J, and the Court of Appeal were all agreed that the lay day provisions were wholly independent of the clauses which provided for the calculation and payment of freight. The shipowners were therefore awarded demurrage based on laytime being calculated on the *actual* quantities loaded and discharged—there was a slight difference between the two based on shrinkage in transit of the cargo, which was mainly bagged wheat.

---

195. *Hain Steamship Co Ltd* v. *Minister of Food* (1949) 82 Ll L Rep 386.

2.178 In *Clerco Compania Naviera SA* v. *The Food Corporation of India (The Savvas)*[196] one of the questions that was considered was whether discharge laytime should be calculated on the full cargo carried or on the reduced amount remaining after lightening. By additional clauses, the charterparty provided:

18. Cargo is to be discharged by consignee's stevedores free of risk and expense to vessel at the average rate of 1500 tons . . .
22. Lightening, if any, at discharging port to be at Owners' risk and expense and time used not to count as laytime.

The other question was whether the time used in lightening was simply the time taken to remove that portion of the cargo from the ship or whether it included the period the vessel had to wait for lighters to become available.

2.179 Having first determined that time used in lightening had the more restricted meaning and only covered the actual discharge time,[197] all three tribunals that considered the point, the umpire, the High Court and the Court of Appeal, then went on to find that laytime should be calculated on the full cargo carried. Parker J put it this way in the High Court[198]:

With regard to the other matter, whether the laytime is to be calculated on the full amount of the cargo or only on the reduced amount, the argument centred upon the use of the words "Cargo is to be discharged by consignee's stevedores free of risk and expense" and it was submitted that the result of those words was that the clause could only be applicable to the cargo remaining at the end of the lightening process. To give that significance to those words appears to me to be unwarranted. As a matter of commercial sense if a charterer is to have time running against him as from the moment that the fully laden vessel arrives at the port he should have available for dealing with the cargo on board that number of laydays appropriate to the cargo then on board.

2.180 In *The Siam Venture and Darfur*,[199] the parties agreed a discharge rate of 2,500/3,000 tons per day, and the question arose as to whether this was too vague to create an obligation at a rate which was certain or a rate by which laytime could be calculated. Rejecting this argument, Sheen J held that owners could only enforce the contract in the way least burdensome on the defendants and that under their agreement, the defendants would have avoided liability for demurrage if they had discharged at a rate of 2,500 tons per day. The laytime allowed should therefore be calculated on this basis.

2.181 Another area of conflict that has come before the courts is whether, where a charterparty provides for more than one load port or discharge port, the laytime allowed should be calculated separately for each port. In *United British Steamship Co Ltd* v. *Minister of Food*[200] there was one receiver but two discharge ports and in *Compania Naviera Azuero SA* v. *British Oil and Cake Mills Ltd and others*,[201] there were also two discharge ports, but a total of 14 receivers. In the latter case Pearson J considered a third alternative, that there might be 14 separate calculations, one for each bill of lading, at least

196. *Clerco Compania Naviera SA* v. *The Food Corporation of India (The Savvas)* [1982] 1 Lloyd's Rep 22.
197. See also *The Food Corporation of India* v. *Carras Shipping Co Ltd (The Delian Leto)* [1983] 2 Lloyd's Rep 496, where time spent in lightening was held to count because the vessel was on demurrage.
198. *Clerco Compania Naviera SA* v. *The Food Corporation of India (The Savvas)* [1981] 1 Lloyd's Rep 155, at p. 158. In *The Apostolis* [1999] 2 Lloyd's Rep. 292, Longmore J. held that where some cargo had been discharged at the load port following a fire and not reloaded, only the cargo loaded and intended to be carried was relevant for the purpose of calculating loading laytime.
199. *The Siam Venture and Darfur* [1987] 1 Lloyd's Rep 147.
200. *United British Steamship Co Ltd* v. *Minister of Food* [1951] 1 Lloyd's Rep 111.
201. *Compania Naviera Azuero SA* v. *British Oil and Cake Mills Ltd and others* [1957] 1 Lloyd's Rep 312.

where the receivers and not the charterers were liable for demurrage. However, this last alternative he quickly rejected.

2.182 In each case the laytime clause provided for an average rate (in the singular) of discharge. Commenting on this Pearson J said[202]:

> Then the clause has the words "an average rate" suggesting one calculation, whereas "average rates" in the plural, or "average rate at each discharging port", or some similar phrase, could have been used to suggest two separate calculations if that had been the intention.

Pearson J later went on to endorse what Croom-Johnson J said in *United British Steamship Co Ltd* v. *Minister of Food*[203]:

> This is, I think, after all is said and done, a perfectly simple situation. This is one adventure and one enterprise. If the parties wanted to make an agreement under which they were going to pay demurrage for delay at one point and only get one-third of the demurrage . . . for any time they saved at the other port, they could no doubt have framed an appropriate clause which would have produced that result.
>
> It is quite plain that they have not done it, and it seems to me that, looking at this charterparty as a whole, when I see "cargo to be discharged at the average rate of" so-and-so, I think those words really mean what they say. It looks to me as if it would have been so simple to say, "cargo to be discharged at the average rate of so-and-so at each port". But they never did it.

In both cases, therefore, it was held that there should be a single laytime calculation.

2.183 In *The Tropwave*,[204] the laytime provision was:

> . . . 1000 metric tonnes provided minimum 5 hatches or pro rata, if less than 5 hatches available, per weather working day.

2.184 At the commencement of discharge only four hatches were available and the arbitrator decided that the discharge rate was 800 tonnes per day. The buyers of the cargo contended that this could possibly necessitate in circumstances which they suggested that the largest hatch would have to be discharged at 500 tonnes per day to meet this overall rate and therefore this conclusion was wrong because the clause contemplated a discharge rate of 200 tonnes per hatch per day. Dismissing this argument, Parker J said[205]:

> The argument is highly ingenious but it involves reading the clause as if it said 200 tonnes per hatch per day and it does not. It is an overall rate and the charterer or receiver is free to discharge in what order and at what rate he chooses. Since one hatch will very often if not always be longer than the others, the buyers' construction would involve the result that the specified rate was seldom if ever 1000 tonnes even if five hatches were available at the outset. This is wholly inconsistent with the wording.

2.185 In London Arbitration 8/96,[206] the relevant charter provided for discharge at a rate of 2,000 mt per WWD of 24 consecutive hours. The charterers argued this should be reduced to 1,600 mt because one of the vessel's six holds was occupied by other cargo. As the owners pointed out, 1,600 was not five-sixths of 2,000. The ship was described as having "minimum five holds/hatches" and there was no representation or warranty that all the ship's hatches would be made available for this cargo. The tribunal therefore held that as there was no express provision altering the basis for calculating laytime and there was

---

202. *Ibid.*, at p. 324.
203. *United British Steamship Co Ltd* v. *Minister of Food* [1951] 1 Lloyd's Rep 111, at p. 115.
204. *Maritime Transport Operators GmbH* v. *Louis Dreyfus et Cie* (*The Tropwave*) [1981] 2 Lloyd's Rep 159.
205. *Ibid.*, at p. 168.
206. London Arbitration 8/96—LMLN 433, 8 June 1996.

no obligation of which the owners were in breach, there was no basis for a claim for damages that could conveniently be calculated by an adjustment to the laytime allowed.

2.186 London Arbitration 3/99[207] concerned a vessel which had been fixed to carry two separate cargoes under different charters, although with the same shippers and both cargoes were loaded by the same stevedores who were to work under the direction and control of the master who was also to supervise and be responsible for stowage. Most of the vessel's holds were to contain both cargoes. The original intention was that the cargoes be loaded consecutively but the owners agreed to allow both cargoes to be loaded simultaneously which meant there were a number of occasions when loading of the first cargo was prevented in one or more of the four holds allocated for it. The charterers argued successfully that time should be reduced pro rata for those periods when less than four hatches were made available.

2.187 Similar problems often occur due to cargo gear breakdowns which mean that one or more hatches cannot be worked. The normal practice in such circumstances is either to reduce the loading rate, thus allowing more time or to reduce the time used by pro rating the number of hatches available against the number that should be available. The end result is the same.

2.188 A different disagreement was resolved by Devlin J in *V M Salgaoncar E Irmaos* v. *Goulandris Brothers Ltd*.[208] The crucial clause here was clause 5, the laytime clause, which provided as follows:

> The cargo to be shipped at the rate of 600 tons when vessel is in berth and 350 tons whilst in stream . . .

2.189 The *Granford*, the vessel concerned, was chartered to proceed to Mormugao and there load "at one or two safe berths in charterers' option" a full and complete cargo, which after loading was ascertained at 9,600 tons. The owners argued that laytime at Mormugao should be calculated by dividing the quantity actually loaded in berth by 600 and that in stream by 350. The charterers, on the other hand, said that the calculation fell to be made by applying the notional daily rates to the time the vessel was actually in berth or stream, the laytime being exhausted when the total reached 9,600 tons, the quantity loaded. The advantage to the charterers of this method was that, for the waiting period in the stream when no loading took place, they were charged at the lower rate.

2.190 The respective arguments were summarized by Devlin J as follows[209]:

> The charterers submit that you must count the waiting days because that is what clause 5 requires: "The cargo to be shipped at the rate of 600 tons when a vessel is in a berth and 350 tons whilst in stream". The fallacy in the owners' calculation, they submit, is that it counts only the days on which loading takes place and treats the clause as if it read: "The cargo to be loaded (shipped) at the rate of 600 tons when vessel is *loading* in berth and 350 tons whilst *loading* in stream".

Upholding the owners' contentions, the judge continued[210]:

> Clause 5 is not really prescribing what the ship has actually got to do. It is setting a standard by reference to which the lay days can be calculated. The lay days are not intended to be made more or less according to the directions which may be given to the ship. The only thing in this type of

---

207. London Arbitration 3/99—LMLN 503, 18 February 1999.
208. *V M Salgaoncar E Irmaos* v. *Goulandris Brothers Ltd* [1954] 1 Lloyd's Rep 56.
209. *Ibid.*, at p. 59.
210. *Ibid.*, at p. 60.

clause that depends on actuality is the exact quantity of the cargo loaded in each place; if that were known in advance, the exact period for loading could be specified in the charterparty.

Laytime expressed as a total daily rate basis—a specified number of available workable hatches

2.191 This type of laytime provision has been in common use in Governmental charters to the Indian sub-continent for a number of years. A typical provision provides:

Cargo to be discharged[211] ... at the average rate of 1000 metric tonnes basis 5 or more available workable hatches, pro rata, if less number of hatches per weather working day.

2.192 The meaning of this type of clause fell to be considered in a series of arbitrations,[212] which gave rise to a consolidated appeal which eventually reached the House of Lords. The case is usually known as *The General Capinpin* after the first named vessel.

2.193 Each case concerned the method of calculating laytime at the port of discharge. The precise wording of the relevant clause in each charter differed slightly but it was common ground that the differences were immaterial.

2.194 The first and major issue was whether this provision invoked the "available workable hatch" approach to calculating the laytime allowed or whether it simply provided for an overall rate.[213]

2.195 In each arbitration, charterers argued that the effect of the clause was that the contractual rate of discharge would diminish from time to time as holds became empty, and that in consequence the time permitted for discharge was governed by the quantity of cargo in the hold into which the greatest quantity of cargo had been loaded, dividing that cargo by 200 tonnes per day for a vessel with five hatches. In all four awards that contention was rejected.

2.196 In support of their argument, charterers relied on passages from the judgment of Bingham J in *The Giannis Xilas*[214] and he in turn on the earlier cases of the *Sandgate* and *Compania De Navigación Zita S A* v. *Louis Dreyfus & Cie (The Corfu Island).*[215] In the High Court the owners adopted the reasoning of the Arbitrators in the *General Capinpin* who in their award said[216]:

The passage (from *The Giannis Xilas*) upon which the charterers relied made it quite clear that the judge was addressing himself to the question of clauses where the cargo is to be loaded or discharged at a quantity per workable hatch per day. Where, as in this case, a figure for the entire vessel is used, it seems to us that one arrives at the total permitted laytime by dividing the total cargo tonnage by the daily rate of the vessel. The words "available workable" are not thereby ignored, because they are relevant for how laytime is to be adjusted if a hatch is unworkable for any reason

---

211. There were similar provisions in relation to loading where the corresponding rate was usually 8,000 tonnes per day.

212. *President of India* v. *Jebsens (UK) Ltd and others (The General Capinpin, Proteus, Free Wave and Dinara)* [1987] 2 Lloyd's Rep 354.

213. With certain types of 'tween deckers lifting about 14,000 tonnes, the difference between these two methods of calculating the allowed laytime could double the laytime allowed, significantly reducing the amount of discharge demurrage, since delay even beyond the extended laytime is quite common at many ports in the Indian sub-continent. With a much larger loading rate and quicker methods of loading, the different approaches are much less significant at load ports.

214. *Cargill Inc* v. *Rionda De Pass Ltd (The Giannis Xilas)* [1982] 2 Lloyd's Rep 511, at p. 513.

215. *The Sandgate* (1930) 35 Ll L Rep 151. *Compania de Navigación Zita S A* v. *Louis Dreyfus & Cie (The Corfu Island)* [1953] 2 Lloyd's Rep 472.

216. Quoted in *The General Capinpin* [1987] 2 Lloyd's Rep 354, at p. 356.

other than merely the fact that it is empty. The difference of emphasis in the two different formulae, one based on a rate for the vessel and the other based on a rate for a hatch, seem to us to make a crucial difference.

Commenting on this, Webster J said[217]:

There are, unhappily, conflicting *dicta* on the question whether there is any difference between a formula based on a rate for the vessel and one based on a rate for a hatch. According to two *dicta* of Lord Justice Scrutton (in *The Sandgate*[218]) and Mr Justice Parker (as he then was) (in *The Tropwave*[219]) there is a difference, but according to two other *dicta* of Lords Justices Salmon and Megaw (in *The Theraios*[220]), there is not.

Having cited the *dicta*, the judge said that he preferred the views of Scrutton LJ and Parker J at least to the extent that whilst 200 tonnes per hatch per day given five hatches might be the same as 1,000 tonnes per day for the vessel, 1,000 tonnes per day might not be the same as 200 tonnes per hatch for five hatches because, for a variety of reasons, discharge might have to take place at more than 200 tonnes per day through one or more hatches to achieve the specified rate for the vessel. The judge therefore accepted that the effect of the laytime provision in this case was different to those in the cases he had previously considered. In his view the question was whether the difference gave a different meaning to the word "workable" and his conclusion was that it did not. On that he concluded that following the cases starting with *The Sandgate*,[221] a hatch over an empty hold was not a workable hatch. He continued[222]:

If the answer were otherwise, and if the arbitrators and the umpire were right in their conclusion on this point, it would mean that the expression "available workable hatches" has one meaning for the purpose of a discharge clause expressed as an average rate for the vessel and a different meaning in a discharge clause expressed as a daily rate per hatch, . . . for the reasons I have given, I see no reason for making any such differentiation.

He therefore held in favour of charterers on that point.

2.197 When the case came before the Court of Appeal, the judgment of the court was given by Neill LJ, who commented that Webster J had approached the construction of the relevant clauses on the basis that the question for his decision was whether the word "workable" had the same meaning in these clauses as it had in clauses where a rate per hatch was prescribed. However the Court of Appeal disagreed saying[223]:

We see the force of the argument that a daily rate which is expressed to be based on "available workable hatches" is only apt to describe a daily rate which reduces as the holds beneath the hatches are filled or emptied and the available workable hatches become fewer in number. In our view, however, this argument fails to give proper weight to the fact that the obligation to discharge in the present case is expressed to be at the average rate of 1000 metric tonnes per weather working day. The obligation to discharge is qualified, it is true, but the obligation is imposed by reference to rate for the vessel and not to a rate per hatch. In the opinion of this Court this is a fundamental distinction.

217. *The General Capinpin* [1987] 2 Lloyd's Rep 354, at p. 356.
218. *The Sandgate* (1930) 35 Ll L Rep 151, at p. 153.
219. *The Tropwave* [1981] 2 Lloyd's Rep 159, at p. 168.
220. *The Theraios* [1971] 1 Lloyd's Rep 209, at pp. 211 and 214.
221. *The Sandgate* (1930) 35 Ll L Rep 151.
222. *The General Capinpin* [1987] 2 Lloyd's Rep 354, at p. 358.
223. *The General Capinpin* [1989] 1 Lloyd's Rep 232, at p. 237.

2.198 The court went on to say that they found support for this in the judgments in *The Sandgate* and *The Tropwave*,[224] even though in the latter, no reference was made to cases such as *The Sandgate*. Concluding their judgment on this point, the court said[225]:

We would therefore answer the first question in favour of the owners. We have reached this conclusion with some diffidence as we are differing from the opinion of a distinguished commercial Judge.[226] On the other hand, it is satisfactory to observe that the construction which we prefer is that which appealed to a number of the most experienced arbitrators in this branch of the law.

2.199 In the House of Lords,[227] the view of the majority in favour of the owners was expressed by Lord Goff, who also clearly was impressed by the fact that in the original arbitrations from which the appeals lay, the construction favoured by the owners was unanimously adopted by the arbitrators. On this he said:

It is plain that what really struck the arbitrators was that the clause did indeed provide for an overall rate of discharge, and did not expressly provide for a rate per hatch, despite the existence of well-known authorities dealing with clauses which so provided. They were simply not prepared to ignore the express provision for the overall rate; they preferred to treat the reference to "available workable hatches" not as substituting a rate per hatch for the expressly provided overall rate for the ship, but rather as imposing a qualification upon it.

2.200 The second point considered by the courts arose only from the arbitrations in respect of *The Proteus* and *Dinara*. Those vessels were ordered to small ports in India where discharging had to take place in the stream where discharge was effected using the ships' gear. Although each vessel had five hatches, each only carried four cranes. In these circumstances, charterers contended that the contractual average rate of discharge should be limited to 800 tonnes on the basis of four available workable hatches. In both arbitrations, that argument was also rejected.

2.201 Agreeing with this conclusion in the High Court Webster J said[228]:

I agree with this conclusion which seems to me to follow inevitably from the hypothetical example of a gearless vessel sent by charterers to discharge at a port where discharge has to take place in the stream and where there are no floating cranes. In such a case, if the charterers' contention were correct and if owners and charterers were to stand on their rights, laytime would continue indefinitely until the contract was terminated by frustration. This would seem to me to be an absurd result.

2.202 The judge also reached the same conclusion by pointing out that a hatch was not the same as a piece of cargo gear by which cargo could be loaded or discharged and he found no authority in any of the five cases that were relevant[229] to show that laytime by

---

224. *The Sandgate* (1929) 35 Ll L Rep 9, at p. 12; *The Tropwave* [1981] 2 Lloyd's Rep 159, at p. 168.
225. *The General Capinpin* [1989] 1 Lloyd's Rep 232, at p. 238.
226. In *The Silva Plana* [1989] 2 Lloyd's Rep 371, at p. 375, Steyn J allowed an appeal following the Court of Appeal decision in *The General Capinpin* which had become available since the original arbitration where the arbitrators had followed the High Court ruling in the same case. *Oriental Maritime Pte Ltd* v. *Ministry of Food, Government of the People's Republic of Bangladesh (The Silva Plana, Bahamastars* and *Magic Sky).*
227. *President of India* v. *Jebsens (UK) Ltd (The General Capinpin)*, LMLN 287, 3 November 1990; [1991] 1 Lloyd's Rep 1.
228. *The General Capinpin* [1987] 2 Lloyd's Rep 354, at p. 359.
229. *The Sandgate* (1929) 35 Ll L Rep 9, at p. 12—see *ante* at para. 2.149; (1930) 35 Ll L Rep 151, at p. 152. *Compania de Navegación Zita S.A.* v. *Louis Dreyfus & Cie (The Corfu Island)* [1953] 2 Lloyd's Rep 472, at p. 475 and p. 477)—see *ante* at para. 2.150. *The Theraios* [1971] 1 Lloyd's Rep 209—see *ante* at para. 2.165. *The Tropwave* [1981] 2 Lloyd's Rep 159—see *ante* at para. 2.183. *Cargill Inc* v. *Marpro Ltd (The Aegis Progress)* [1983] 2 Lloyd's Rep 570, at p. 576—see *ante* at para. 2.163. See also *V M Salgaoncar E Irmaos* v. *Goulandris Brothers Ltd* [1954] 1 Lloyd's Rep 56—see *ante* at para. 2.188.

reference to a "hatch" relates to the availability of loading or discharging gear. He also suggested that when Hobhouse J mentioned "winch" breakdowns discussing the earlier cases, this was an error since they did not.[230]

2.203 In the Court of Appeal, the court agreed with both the High Court and the arbitrators saying[231]:

> ... the charterer was given an option as to the safe port or anchorage which he could choose ... the charterer was given the right to use ships' gear but was not obliged to do so.
>
> In these circumstances it seems to us that the laytime provisions cannot be affected by the fact that the charterer ordered the vessels to be discharged by small ports in India where shore cranes could not be used, so that only the four cranes on board each vessel could be employed to unload the five hatches.

2.204 The court agreed the position might have been different had one or more of the hatches been unworkable by reason of a defect in the hatch or hold itself, but they were not and they therefore concluded[232]:

> ... the calculation of laytime cannot be affected by the fact that only four cranes were available for the five loaded hatches.

This point was not considered by the House of Lords.

CUSTOMARY LAYTIME

2.205 If the parties to a contract of affreightment do not in their agreement provide for the period in which the vessel is to be allowed to load or discharge her cargo, then a reasonable time for these operations will be allowed by implication of law.[233] It may be that the contract is wholly silent as to the time within which these tasks are to be carried out[234] or the contract may contain some such phrase as "with all dispatch according to the custom of the port".[235] In either case the period allowed will be dependent on the circumstances encountered at the particular port and may therefore vary from ship to ship and from time to time. It will thus be noted that unlike fixed laytime, the period allowed cannot be determined in advance of loading or discharging as the case may be.

What is a reasonable time?

2.206 The obligation, where no time was fixed, to do the work of discharging (and by implication loading) in a reasonable time arose in two early cases decided within a few days of each other. The facts in each case were similar. Both cases concerned the discharge of cargoes into bond, where delay was caused by congestion in the docks. In *Rodgers* v. *Forresters*[236] the charterparty expressly stated that "the said freighter should be allowed the usual and customary time to unload the ship or vessel at her port of discharge", and Lord Ellenborough ruled that the usual and customary time was that which would be taken

---

230. *Cargill Inc* v. *Marpro Ltd (The Aegis Progress)* [1983] 2 Lloyd's Rep 570, at p. 576.
231. *The General Capinpin* [1989] 1 Lloyd's Rep 232, at p. 238.
232. *Ibid.*, at p. 239.
233. *Postlethwaite* v. *Freeland* (1880) 5 App Cas 599, at p. 608 *per* Lord Selbourne LC. See *post* at para. 2.210.
234. E.g. *Pantland Hick* v. *Raymond & Reid* [1893] AC 22 (HL).
235. *Postlethwaite* v. *Freeland* (1880) 5 App Cas 599 (HL).
236. *Rodgers* v. *Forresters* (1810) 2 Camp 483.

to discharge into a bonded warehouse in the then state of the docks. In *Burmester* v. *Hodgson*,[237] which came before Mansfield CJ three days later, there was no charterparty, but the question arose on a bill of lading. The bill was silent as to the period of discharge and it took some 63 days before the discharge was completed. In his judgment, the learned Chief Justice said:

Here the law could only raise an implied promise to do what was in *Rodgers* v. *Forresters* stipulated for by an express covenant; viz. to discharge the ship in the usual and customary time for unloading such a cargo. That has been rightly held to be the time within which a vessel can be unloaded in turn, into the bonded warehouses. Such time has not been exceeded by the defendant. If the brandies were to be bonded they could not be unloaded sooner, and the defendant seems to have been as anxious to receive, as the plaintiff was to deliver them.

2.207 In *Ford and others* v. *Cotesworth and another*,[238] based on *Burmester* v. *Hodgson*[239] it was argued that what was usual and customary for each port should be determined objectively, based on the normal state of affairs at that port, rather than the actual circumstances encountered. If accepted, such an argument would have meant that the charterparty should be construed as if a specified number of lay days had been inserted, the only point being that instead of the parties fixing the number of days, they left that to be ascertained by subsequent inquiry as to what was usual and customary in the port for such a vessel. However, this argument was vigorously rejected by Blackburn J, who held that where a charterparty provides that a ship shall proceed to a certain port and there, or as near thereto as she can safely get, deliver the cargo in the usual and customary manner, but is silent as to the time to be occupied in the discharge, the contract implied by law is that each party will use reasonable diligence in performing that part of the delivery which by the custom of the port falls upon him. He also held that there is no implied contract that the discharge shall be performed in the time usually taken at the port.

2.208 However, a different judicial attitude on this latter point was taken in *Ashcroft* v. *Crow Orchard Colliery Co*[240] and *Wright* v. *New Zealand Shipping Co*,[241] where some of the judgments suggest that performance should be measured against the time usually taken. Much judicial and academic effort seems to have been expended in reconciling these two cases with later decisions of the House of Lords,[242] but the simpler view is that they were wrongly decided.[243]

2.209 Shortly after these two cases, the whole question was considered by the House of Lords in *Postlethwaite* v. *Freeland*.[244] The facts of the case were that a vessel, the *Cumberland Lassie*, was chartered for the carriage of a cargo of steel rails and fastenings from Barrow-in-Furness to East London, South Africa. The charterparty provided for the "cargo to be discharged with all dispatch according to the custom of the port". At East London, it was customary for such vessels to anchor some distance outside the harbour

---

237. *Burmester* v. *Hodgson* (1810) 2 Camp 488.
238. *Ford and others* v. *Cotesworth and another* (1868) LR 4 QB 127.
239. *Burmester* v. *Hodgson* (1810) 2 Camp 488.
240. *Ashcroft* v. *Crow Orchard Colliery Co* (1874) LR 9 QB 540.
241. *Wright* v. *New Zealand Shipping Co* (1879) 4 Ex D 165.
242. *Postlethwaite* v. *Freeland* (1880) 5 App Cas 599. *Pantland Hick* v. *Raymond & Reid* [1893] AC 22. *C A Van Liewen* v. *Hollis Bros & Co Ltd (The Lizzie)* (1919) 25 CC 83.
243. "As regards the case of *Wright* v. *New Zealand Shipping Co*, in my judgment it is not law . . . ", *per* Smith LJ in *Lyle Shipping Co Ltd* v. *Corporation of Cardiff* (1990) 5 CC 397, at p. 405. See also *The Lizzie*, *supra*, at p. 89 *per* Lord Dunedin.
244. *Postlethwaite* v. *Freeland* (1880) 5 App Cas 599.

and for their cargo to be discharged into lighters, which were then manually warped into the harbour. The whole operation was under the control of a private company, which discharged each ship in turn, except that mail steamers were given priority. Due to a shortage of suitable lighters and congestion at the port, the *Cumberland Lassie* had to wait some 31 working days before discharge was commenced.

2.210 The House of Lords held that the claim for demurrage failed. The Lord Chancellor, Lord Selborne, put it this way[245]:

There is no doubt that the duty of providing and making proper use of sufficient means for the discharge of cargo, when a ship which has been chartered arrives at its destination and is ready to discharge, lies (generally) upon the charterer. If, by the terms of the charterparty, he has agreed to discharge it within a fixed period of time, that is an absolute and unconditional engagement, for the non-performance of which he is answerable, whatever may be the nature of the impediments which prevent him from performing it and which cause the ship to be detained in his service beyond the time stipulated. If, on the other hand, there is no fixed time, the law implies an agreement on his part to discharge the cargo within a reasonable time; that is (as was said by Mr Justice Blackburn in *Ford* v. *Cotesworth*[246] "a reasonable time under the circumstances"). Difficult questions may sometimes arise as to the circumstances which ought to be taken into consideration in determining what time is reasonable. If (as in the present case) an obligation, indefinite as to time, is qualified or partially defined by express or implied reference to the custom or practice of a particular port, every impediment arising from or out of that custom or practice, which the charterer could not have overcome by the use of any reasonable diligence, ought (I think) to be taken into consideration.

2.211 Blackburn J, who had by now become Lord Blackburn, was also a member of the court and, perhaps not surprisingly, he reiterated his earlier views basing himself in part on a railway case, *Taylor* v. *Great Northern Railway*,[247] where it was held that "a reasonable time" meant what was reasonable under the circumstances. He also distinguished *Ashcroft* v. *Crow Orchard Colliery Co*[248] and suggested a way around *Wright* v. *New Zealand Shipping Co*.[249]

2.212 In *Pantland Hick* v. *Raymond & Reid*,[250] the House of Lords again had a chance to consider whether reasonable meant reasonable under ordinary or actual circumstances. In this case, a cargo was shipped under bills of lading which did not specify any discharge time. Upon arrival, the dock company began to unload the cargo, but work was held up by a strike of dock labourers. It was not possible for the consignees to provide their own or any other labour, and the court therefore held that the consignees were not liable for the delay. Attempts to distinguish *Postlethwaite* v. *Freeland*,[251] as applying only where a custom of the port was referred to, were rejected. In the course of his speech, Lord Herschell said[252]:

. . . I would observe, in the first place, that there is of course no such thing as a reasonable time in the abstract. It must always depend upon circumstances. Upon "the ordinary circumstances" say the learned counsel for the appellant. But what may without impropriety be termed the ordinary circumstances differ in particular ports at different times of the year . . . It appears to me that the appellant's contention would involve constant difficulty and dispute and that the only sound

245. *Ibid.*, at p. 608.
246. *Ford and others* v. *Cotesworth and another* (1868) 4 LR QB 127.
247. *Taylor* v. *Great Northern Railway* (1866) LR 1 CP 385.
248. *Ashcroft* v. *Crow Orchard Colliery Co* (1874) LR 9 QB 540.
249. *Wright* v. *New Zealand Shipping Co* (1879) 4 Ex D 165.
250. *Pantland Hick* v. *Raymond & Reid* [1893] AC 22 (reported in the Court of Appeal as *Hick* v. *Rodocanachi* [1891] 2 QB 626).
251. *Postlethwaite* v. *Freeland* (1880) 5 App Cas 599.
252. *Pantland Hick* v. *Raymond & Reid, supra*, at p. 48.

principle is that the "reasonable time" should depend on the circumstances that actually exist. If the cargo has been taken with all reasonable despatch under those circumstances I think the obligation of the consignee has been fulfilled.

2.213 A similar view was expressed by Lord Herschell in *Carlton SS Co Ltd* v. *Castle Mail Packets Co,* again in the House of Lords, where he said[253]:

There is no such thing as reasonable time in the abstract. The question is whether, having regard to all the obligations of the contract, to its conditions, to its restrictions and to its limitations, more than a reasonable time has been taken in the performance of any one of these obligations in respect of which the parties have not, by their contract, expressed any limit of time for its performance.

2.214 In *Lyle Shipping Co Ltd* v. *Corporation of Cardiff*, Romer LJ said[254]:

The first question we have to consider is as to the meaning of the not uncommon provision in a charterparty as to the ship being discharged "with all dispatch as customary". I think it is now settled that such a provision means that the discharge shall take place with all reasonable dispatch, and that in considering what is reasonable you must have regard, not to a hypothetical state of things (that is, to what would be reasonable in an ordinary state of circumstances), but to the actual state of things at the time of discharge and in particular to the customs of the port of discharge.

2.215 Later authorities only confirmed that "reasonable must be reasonable under all the circumstances of the case".[255]

Effect of custom

2.216 The words "custom" and "as customary" may be expressly referred to in this type of laytime clause. Whether they are or are not is to a certain extent irrelevant since the law implies an obligation to follow the customs of the port in question for the particular trade.[256] What was meant by custom was discussed by Lord Blackburn in *Postlethwaite* v. *Freeland*,[257] where he said:

"custom" in the charterparty did not mean custom in the sense in which the word is sometimes used by lawyers, but meant a settled and established practice of the port . . .

2.217 The question of for how long a practice must exist before it becomes a custom was considered by Kennedy J in *Sea Steamship Co Ltd* v. *Price, Walker and Co Ltd*.[258] In that case, it was suggested that some 14 years before, the resident merchants, the owners of lighters and the local stevedores had come to an agreement concerning the rate at which certain vessels should be discharged and that this therefore constituted a custom. Rejecting this, Kennedy J said[259]:

In my opinion, in order to establish a mercantile custom it is necessary, not only to show that a large number of influential people at the place have agreed that it would be a good thing . . . but also that the agreement was acted upon, because, unless it is acted on, no one will challenge it . . . A custom cannot be established merely by three or four important classes of persons in a community of a port agreeing that it is desirable. It must be enforced . . .

253. *Carlton Steamship Co Ltd* v. *Castle Mail Packets Co Ltd* [1898] AC 486, at p. 491.
254. *Lyle Shipping Co Ltd* v. *Corporation of Cardiff* (1900) 5 CC 397, at p. 407.
255. *C A Van Liewen* v. *Hollis Bros (The Lizzie)* (1919) 25 CC 83, at p. 87 *per* Lord Dunedin.
256. *Postlethwaite* v. *Freeland* (1880) 5 App Cas 599, at p. 613 *per* Lord Blackburn.
257. *Ibid.,* at p. 616.
258. *Sea Steamship Co* v. *Price, Walker & Co Ltd* (1903) 8 CC 292.
259. *Ibid.,* at p. 295. It would however appear that Kennedy J thought that if the practice could be shown to have operated for this period, it would be very strong evidence of a custom.

2.218 There is, however, no objection to the custom being reduced to writing. In *Norrkopings Rederiaktiebolag* v. *Wulfsberg & Co*,[260] Greer J declared:

The custom of the port, for the convenience of shipowners and merchants, has been reduced to writing, and though one does not necessarily interpret the document in exactly the same wording as one would a document which was written out for the purpose of containing the terms of a particular contract, still effect has got to be given to the words used, because people going to the port of Hull must be presumed to know, and probably do know, that the custom of the port has been put into the document, and can be found there just as readily as the Rule for Preventing Collisions at Sea.

2.219. Once a custom is established, the fact that people may contract themselves out of the custom does not of itself destroy the custom, but the practice of contracting out may become so general as to destroy the custom. When once the custom becomes the exception and not the rule, there is no longer a custom.[261]

2.220 An example of contracting out of a custom arose in *Maclay and others* v. *Spillers & Baker Ltd*,[262] where the bill of lading provided for the goods to be received by the consignee "immediately the vessel is ready to discharge and continuously . . . , any custom of the port to the contrary notwithstanding". The Court of Appeal, reversing the judge below, held that the express provision excluded the custom of the port.

2.221 Where the words "custom" or "customary" are used, they relate to the way in which cargo is loaded or discharged, rather than the time the operation should take.[263] In *Castlegate Steamship Co* v. *Dempsey*,[264] Fry LJ had put this slightly differently and, with respect, more accurately, saying:

They, therefore, primarily refer to manner of discharge, and secondarily only to time. They are not entirely disconnected with time, because the dispatch is to be in the customary manner, and that manner may be one which expedites or delays the discharge of the cargo.

2.222 As Lord Dunedin said in *The Lizzie*,[265] "a custom consists in a method of doing something". However, as was pointed out in *Good & Co* v. *Isaacs*[266] discharge by the customary method may not be the quickest way and thus cause delay. In the same case, it was also held that "as customary" related directly to the discharge and delivery by the ship, rather than to taking delivery by a consignee.

2.223 Having established a custom, there remains a further hurdle to be overcome, namely whether the custom is reasonable. Describing what a custom is, Jessel MR in the Court of Appeal said in *Nelson* v. *Dahl*[267]:

It must be so notorious that everybody in the trade enters into a contract with that usage as an implied term. It must be uniform as well as reasonable and it must have quite as much certainty as the written contract itself.

---

260. *Norrkopings Rederiaktiebolag* v. *Wulfsberg & Co* (1920) 3 Ll L Rep 256.
261. *Ropner & Co* v. *Stoate, Hosegood & Co* (1905) 10 CC 73, at p. 85 *per* Channell J.
262. *Maclay and others* v. *Spillers & Baker Ltd* (1901) 6 CC 217.
263. In *Akties Glittre* v. *Gabriel, Wade & English* (1926) 24 Ll L Rep 372, Roche J said: "The words in the charterparty 'as customary' refer, in my opinion, exclusively to the method of loading and not to the time of loading."
264. *Castlegate Steamship Co* v. *Dempsey and others* [1892] 1 QB 854, at p. 861.
265. *C A Van Liewen* v. *Hollis Bros & Co Ltd (The Lizzie)* (1919) 25 CC 83, at p. 90.
266. *Good & Co* v. *Isaacs* [1892] 2 QB 555.
267. *Nelson* v. *Dahl* (1879) 12 Ch 568, at p. 575. See also *The Lizzie, supra*, at p. 127 *per* Swinfen Eady MR.

2.224 In *Sea Steamship Co Ltd* v. *Price Walker & Co Ltd*,[268] a custom relating to the wood trade at Sharpness was held to be unreasonable on two counts—first because it purported to give a preference to similar vessels arriving from Baltic ports as opposed to those with the same type of cargo coming from the other side of the Atlantic, and secondly because it envisaged the same daily rate of discharge, irrespective of the size of the ship. As was pointed out, this would effectively mean a larger vessel "would practically be converted into a warehouse".

Commencement of the obligation to load/discharge

2.225 In a charter providing for customary laytime, it may still be necessary to determine when the approach and carrying voyages come to an end. As will be seen shortly, however, the question of when the vessel concerned becomes an Arrived ship may be of less significance in this type of charter than in one providing for fixed laytime.

2.226 Whilst similar general principles have been established to those applying to fixed laytime, they may be varied by the parties to the charter. As was said by Viscount Cave in *United States Shipping Board* v. *Strick & Co Ltd*[269]:

... these rules like all other rules of construction, must yield to the express terms of the contract entered into between the parties; and if the contract contains terms which are inconsistent with the application of the general rules of construction, the contract and not the rules must prevail.

2.227 Thus, in *Bargate Steam Shipping Co Ltd* v. *Penlee & St Ives Stone Quarries Ltd*,[270] the charter provided that time for discharging was to count from high water at or after arrival at or off the discharging berth. However, such an express provision is comparatively unusual. What is more common is for the charter to specify a berth, dock or port.

2.228 As with a fixed laytime charter, in the case of a berth charter, the vessel must reach her loading or discharging berth before she can be said to have arrived at her specified destination. In *Good & Co* v. *Isaacs*,[271] the Court of Appeal went further and said that a vessel cannot properly be said to be in her berth unless she occupies it by the direction of, or with the assent of, the appropriate harbour authority. If, though she has arrived there, she is not permitted to remain for the purpose of loading or unloading, but is directed by the port authorities to another place, she cannot be said to have arrived so as to impose an obligation upon the charterer.

2.229 In *Nelson* v. *Dahl* in the Court of Appeal,[272] Brett LJ made a detailed analysis of the earlier cases relating to when the voyage ends, both under fixed and customary laytime charters. He concluded that under both types of charter, the specified destination was reached when the vessel concerned entered the dock. It was not, however, necessary for the vessel to berth within the dock for this to happen.[273]

268. *Sea Steamship Co Ltd* v. *Price, Walker & Co Ltd* (1903) 8 CC 292, at p. 296. See also on unreasonability *Akties Glittre* v. *Gabriel, Wade & English* (1926) 24 Ll L Rep 372, and *Sun Shipping Co Ltd* v. *Watson & Youell Shipping Agency Ltd* (1926) 24 Ll L Rep 28.
269. *United States Shipping Board* v. *Strick & Co Ltd* (1926) 25 Ll L Rep 73, at p. 75.
270. *Bargate Steam Shipping Co Ltd* v. *Penlee & St Ives Stone Quarries Ltd* (1921) 6 Ll L Rep 71.
271. *Good & Co* v. *Isaacs* [1892] 2 QB 555, at p. 560.
272. *Nelson* v. *Dahl* (1879) 12 Ch D commencing at p. 580. The case subsequently went to the House of Lords as *Dahl* v. *Nelson* (1880) 6 App Cas 38.
273. For a more detailed analysis of when the specified destination is reached in berth, dock and port charters, see *post* at para. 3.2.

2.230 The question of the commencement of the charterer's obligation to discharge was one of the issues raised in *Hulthen* v. *Stewart & Co*,[274] although the main issue was whether because the usual time for discharging a timber ship could be quantified in terms of so many days, this meant that the charter was effectively a fixed laytime one, a contention rejected by all the courts that considered the case.

2.231 The facts were that the *Anton*, the ship concerned, arrived at Gravesend, having been ordered to Surrey Commercial Docks. Owing to congestion there was a delay before the ship could enter the docks and a further delay before she berthed. The cargo was timber and the customary method of discharge of such cargo was into lighters or on to the quay. All the courts agreed that although Gravesend was within the Port of London, the *Anton* was not an Arrived ship on arrival there. At first instance, Phillimore J held that "she was an arrived ship only when she reached a place at which she could discharge". In a later case, it was suggested that this meant that the *Anton* did not reach her specified destination until she arrived in berth,[275] although discharge into lighters was a method often used and it would therefore seem that Phillimore J's criterion would have been met on arrival in dock. However, at the time of this case, the question of when the specified destination was reached in a port charter was one that had still not been finally settled. That happened in *Leonis Steamship Co* v. *Rank (No 1)*,[276] which is usually taken as the start point of most modern considerations on the question of the commencement of laytime in a port charter. The case concerned a fixed laytime charter, although many of the earlier authorities considered were customary laytime charters. Neither the *Leonis* case nor *The Johanna Oldendorff*,[277] a more recent decision of the House of Lords, drew any distinction between customary and fixed laytime charters on the question of when a vessel becomes an Arrived ship, and if there ever was any difference, it is unlikely that it still remains. In a customary laytime charter, which is a port charter, the specified destination will be reached when, if she cannot proceed direct to a berth, she anchors within the port limits at the usual anchorage for ships of that sort, so that she is at the immediate and effective disposition of the charterer.[278]

2.232 However, reaching the specified destination in a customary laytime charter does not mean necessarily that the charterer is under an obligation to load or discharge the vessel forthwith or that any delay will count against him. This is well illustrated by *Bargate Steam Shipping Co Ltd* v. *Penlee & St Ives Stone Quarries Ltd*,[279] a case which has already been mentioned and where laytime was expressly stated to commence from high water at or after arrival at or off the discharging berth. However, the vessel was unable to berth due to congestion, and since it was beyond the charterers' control, the delay was held to be excused. A provision relating to when the vessel was an Arrived ship was irrelevant to what happened thereafter. However, there is nothing to stop the parties from expressly excepting delay due to congestion for the benefit of the shipowner if they wish, so that the charterer is liable for the delay and cannot claim to be excused because

274. *Hulthen* v. *Stewart & Co* (1901) 6 CC 65, (1902) 7 CC 139 (CA), (1903) 8 CC 297 (HL).
275. *Van Nievelt Goudriaan Stoomvaart Maatschappij* v. *C A Forslind & Son Ltd* (1925) 22 Ll L Rep 49, at p. 52 *per* Atkin LJ.
276. *Leonis Steamship Co* v. *Rank (No 1)* (1907) 13 CC 136.
277. *Oldendorff (EL) & Co GmbH* v. *Tradax Export SA (The Johanna Oldendorff)* [1973] 2 Lloyd's Rep 285.
278. This is usually known as the Reid test as it was put forward by Lord Reid in *The Johanna Oldendorff* [1973] 2 Lloyd's Rep 285, at p. 291—see also *post* at para. 3.102.
279. *Bargate Steam Shipping Co Ltd* v. *Penlee & St Ives Stone Quarries Ltd* (1921) 6 Ll L Rep 71.

of the exercise of due diligence, which is what happened in *Charlton Steam Shipping Co v. T W Allen & Sons and Gabriel, Wade & English.*[280]

2.233 Alternatively, whilst the charter may have a specific destination so that normally the vessel concerned would not be an Arrived ship until it reached the named destination, it may also provide for the vessel to proceed "as near thereto as she may safely get". Such a provision was included in the charter considered by the House of Lords in *Robert H Dahl v. Nelson, Donkin and others.*[281] In this case a vessel arrived at the Surrey Commercial Docks, which were the named destination in the charterparty. On arrival at the dock gates, she was refused admittance because of congestion. The charterer declined to name an alternative discharging place and the master therefore took the vessel to the Deptford Buoys (the nearest place where the vessel could lie in safety) and discharged the cargo by lighters into the Surrey Commercial Docks. In holding that the master was warranted in so doing, the House of Lords held that the shipowner was not bound to wait for an unreasonable period until the dock authorities were able to allocate a berth in the docks.

2.234 In these circumstances, it is submitted that the vessel becomes an Arrived ship when she reaches the place which is as near to the named place as she can get and at which the cargo is discharged.

Delays due to charterers/shippers/receivers

2.235 All parties to the voyage must act with reasonable diligence in the circumstances prevailing to enable the vessel concerned to be loaded and discharged in a reasonable time. The cases that follow are instances when it has been suggested that cargo interests, which will be the collective term used for parties in the heading above, have failed to meet this standard.

Failure to provide a berth on arrival

2.236 In some cases it has been suggested that a custom of the port requires a berth to be provided on arrival and, in others, it has been said that other commitments of cargo interests have prevented a berth being available.

2.237 In the former category, it was held in *Aktieselskabet Hekla v. Bryson, Jameson & Co*[282] that in 1908 by the custom and practice of the port of Hull, there was an absolute obligation on the receiver of a wood cargo to have ready on the arrival in dock of a vessel with such cargo, a suitable berth for her and a clear quay space or a sufficient number of railway bogies whereon or wherein her cargo could be discharged. However, some 10 years later in *The Lizzie*,[283] it was held by the House of Lords that notwithstanding the

280. *Charlton Steam Shipping Co v. T W Allen & Sons and Gabriel, Wade & English* (1921) 9 Ll L Rep 148.
281. *Robert H Dahl v. Nelson, Donkin and others* (1880) 6 App Cas 38.
282. *Aktieselskabet Hekla v. Bryson, Jameson & Co* (1908) 14 CC 1.
283. *Conrad Alfred Van Liewen v. Hollis Bros & Co Ltd and others (The Lizzie)* (1918) 24 CC 117 (CA), (1919) 1 Ll L Rep 529 (HL).

existence of such a custom, any delay was excusable where the failure to comply was not due to a lack of reasonable diligence.[284]

2.238 The question of other commitments of cargo interests was considered in *Harrowing and others* v. *Dupre*,[285] one of a series of cases arising out of the port regulations at Maryport which provided that when other vessels were waiting to berth, each receiver might only have one vessel alongside at a time. In this case, four other vessels for the same receivers were ahead of the *Ethelreda*, the vessel concerned, in the queue of vessels waiting to berth. The charterers, against whom the action was brought, were also the shippers, but were not the receivers. In giving judgment, Bigham J held that the delay was not the fault of the charterers, and that where under a charterparty the delay complained of is such as ought to have been in the contemplation of both parties at the time of the contract, the shipowner has no cause of action against the charterer. The shipowner must therefore accept as reasonable any delay resulting from the normal business of cargo interests.

2.239 A similar situation arose in *Barque Quilpue Ltd* v. *Brown*,[286] where a sailing vessel was chartered by a colliery. To be able to berth, the ship had to produce a loading order from the colliery and this was not forthcoming for some time because of the number of other vessels on charter to the same colliery, although it was not proved that they had chartered an unreasonable amount of tonnage in relation to the ordinary course of their business. The Court of Appeal had no doubt that the charterparty was entered into on the footing that the charterers would carry on their business in the normal course, which might involve detention of the ship; they had not acted unreasonably and therefore were not liable for the delay.[287]

Failure to have a cargo in readiness

2.240 In a charterparty, in the absence of any qualification to the contrary, the undertaking of the charterer to furnish a cargo is absolute.[288] This principle was affirmed by the House of Lords in the Scottish case of *Arden Steamship Co* v. *Andrew Weir & Co*,[289] where it was held that the mere existence of circumstances beyond the control of the shipper, which make it impractical for him to have his cargo ready, will not relieve him from paying damages for breach of his obligation. However, this does not mean that if a berth becomes available unexpectedly, or would if cargo had been available, that the charterer or shipper as the case may be must have his cargo ready. This is the effect of a somewhat misunderstood decision of the House of Lords in *Little* v. *Stevenson*,[290] where it was held that the shipper's or charterer's obligation is only to have his cargo ready when the ship

284. In a similar vein, in *Robert H Dahl* v. *Nelson, Donkin and others* (1880) 6 App Cas 38 the House of Lords held there was no custom at London requiring charterers of timber ships to secure permission for such vessels to enter on their arrival off the named or nominated dock. Had such a custom been found, it is submitted that charterers would still be excused if they exercised due diligence.
285. *Harrowing and others* v. *Dupre* (1902) 7 CC 157.
286. *Barque Quilpue Ltd* v. *Brown* (1903) 9 CC 13.
287. In *Glen & Co* v. *Royal Commission on the Sugar Supply* (1922) 10 Ll L Rep 510, the Court of Appeal affirmed an earlier judgment of Horridge J in which he held that the shipowners concerned could not rely on the presence of other vessels under charter to the Commission as showing that the Commission had prevented the shipowners' vessel, which was also under charter to them, from berthing.
288. *Postlethwaite* v. *Freeland* (1884) 9 App Cas 470 *per* Lord Blackburn.
289. *Arden Steamship Co* v. *Andrew Weir & Co* (1905) 11 CC 26, [1905] AC 501.
290. *Little* v. *Stevenson* [1896] AC 108.

is ready to receive it in ordinary course, and that he is not bound to be prepared for a contingency or fortuitous circumstance not contemplated by either of the parties.

2.241 An illustration of what may be taken to be within the contemplation of the parties is provided by the case of *Jones Ltd* v. *Green & Co*,[291] where a ship was chartered to load coal at Newcastle, New South Wales, from a colliery to be nominated by the charterers. By custom of the port, the vessel concerned could not berth until it received a coaling order advising that a cargo was available. The colliery nominated had a limited output and, as was known to all parties, its coal was in great demand. A delay was therefore inevitable.

2.242 In these circumstances, the Court of Appeal held that the charterers were not bound to have a cargo ready against the chance of the ship's arrival by a certain date, but that their obligation was discharged if the ship got her due turn in the rotation of ships booked to load from the particular colliery; and that, if this was done, the cargo was provided within a reasonable time having regard to the facts as the parties were found to have contemplated them at the date of the charterparty.

2.243 It therefore follows that where the cargo is to come from a definite source known to both parties, and no time is fixed for loading, there is no absolute obligation on the charterer to have a cargo ready immediately on the ship's arrival at the port of loading.

2.244 As was pointed out in *Arden Steamship Co* v. *Weir*,[292] there is a considerable difference between a failure to provide a cargo and a delay in loading. In that case, the failure of the charterers to perform their primary duty of providing a cargo was the cause of the delay.[293]

Alternative methods of discharge

2.245 It may sometimes happen that a custom of the port provides for more than one method of discharge, although one of these may be the more common. In these circumstances if the usual method cannot be followed then the alternative should be used.

2.246 In *Rodenacker* v. *May and Hassell Ltd*,[294] a charterparty provided that a cargo of Danzig oak logs should be discharged at Milwall Dock "with all dispatch as fast as steamer can deliver, as customary". The more usual method was to discharge such a cargo into railway trucks, but it was possible to discharge into lighters. When therefore railway trucks could not be obtained, it was held that it was the duty of the receivers to discharge into lighters.

2.247 In *Fitzgerald* v. *Lona (Owners)*,[295] this was taken a stage further. There the charter provided for discharge on to the quay or into lighters at the consignees' option. However, a strike of lightermen interfered with discharge and, notwithstanding the consignees' wish for discharge into lighters, the shipowners discharged on to the quay. In these circumstances, it was held that the shipowners were bound to land the cargo on to the quay and need not give notice or offer an alternative to the consignees. It also followed

291. *Jones Ltd* v. *Green & Co* (1903) 9 CC 20.
292. *Arden Steamship Co* v. *Andrew Weir & Co* (1905) 11 CC 26, at p. 33 *per* Lord Davey.
293. See also *Owners of SS Dimitrios N Rallias* v. *Lavarello, Brizzolesi, Galliano & Co Ltd* (1922) 13 Ll L Rep 196.
294. *Rodenacker* v. *May & Hassell Ltd* (1901) 6 CC 37.
295. *Fitzgerald* v. *Lona (Owners)* (1932) 44 Ll L Rep 212.

that the selection by consignees of the method of discharge was not irrevocable, but depended upon the availability of that method at the time of discharge.

Provision of defective cargo

2.248 Where delay is caused by the condition of the cargo, whether the shipowners will succeed in recovering for the delay will depend on whether the owners did or could have known of the defect which caused the delay. This is an extension of the common law duty of a shipper of dangerous goods towards any person who is injured by the shipment of such goods without notice of their nature to the shipowner.

2.249 The leading case on this extended doctrine is *Mitchell Cotts & Co* v. *Steel Bros & Co Ltd*,[296] where a vessel carrying rice was detained for 22 days whilst transiting the Suez Canal because the vessel did not have permission to proceed to the nominated destination. The charterers, who were held liable, knew that such permission was necessary, had not obtained it and had not advised the owners that it was needed. In his judgment, Atkin J said[297]:

Whatever may be the full extent of the shipper's obligations, it appears to me that it amounts at least to this; he stipulates that he will not ship goods likely to involve unusual danger or delay to the ship without communicating to the owner facts which are within his knowledge indicating that there is such risk, which facts the owner does not and could not reasonably know of. I think that is putting the obligations of the shipper within very moderate limits, and it may be considerably wider.

2.250 This principle applies equally to fixed and customary laytime charterparties, but its working may be illustrated by the following cases.

2.251 In *Transoceanica Societa Italiana di Navigazione* v. *Shipton & Sons*,[298] a vessel carried a cargo of barley under a customary laytime charter. Discharge, which was by suction, was delayed because of the presence of stones and other foreign matter in the cargo. With regard to a claim for delay, the court held that the receivers had in fact taken the barley as fast as the ship could deliver, as required by the charterparty and that the case did not come within the principle stated above. Similarly, in *Acatos* v. *Burns*[299] a claim by a shipowner failed where difficulties were caused when a cargo of maize sprouted, because, said the Court of Appeal, the owner had an opportunity to examine the cargo.

2.252 On the other hand, in a London Arbitration,[300] shipowners succeeded in a claim for failure to use reasonable diligence in loading a cargo of wheat which was defective because it had not been inspected by the US Department of Agriculture before loading. The arbitrators found that it was very unusual for wheat not to be inspected before loading and the risk of rejection by the US Department of Agriculture after it had been loaded was not one which the owners should reasonably have known about. The case therefore came within the *Mitchell Cotts*[301] principle and the charterers were liable for the delay arising

---

296. *Mitchell Cotts & Co* v. *Steel Bros & Co Ltd* (1916) 22 CC 63.
297. *Ibid.*, at p. 66.
298. *Transoceanica Societa Italiana di Navigazione* v. *Shipton & Sons* (1922) 28 CC 64.
299. *Acatos* v. *Burns* (1878) 3 Ex D 282.
300. London Arbitration—LMLN 2, 29 November 1979.
301. *Mitchell Cotts & Co* v. *Steel Bros & Co Ltd* (1916) 22 CC 63.

from loading defective cargo, since it must have amounted to a breach of their duty to use reasonable diligence in performing their part of the loading operation.

Delays arising without the default of either shipowners or charterers

2.253 In general where delay is caused by the actions or omissions of third parties or natural phenomena, then the shipowner will have no cause of action and any loss will lie where it falls, unless there be an express provision providing to the contrary. However, what follows is a more detailed consideration of certain common causes of delay.

Congestion

2.254 In *Postlethwaite* v. *Freeland*,[302] the facts of which were given earlier,[303] the delay to the vessel was caused by a combination of congestion and a shortage of lighters. As Lord Blackburn said[304]:

But if there had been either fewer ships waiting, or more lighters available, this ship would not have been kept so long. There was evidence that the number of ships was unusually great, owing to the fact that the railway material was then being discharged.

And later in his speech he said[305]:

... the point for which the ruling in *Burmester* v. *Hodgson*[306] is in this case valuable—that in considering what is reasonable dispatch under the circumstances, the number of ships there, though unusually large, is one of the circumstances to be taken into account.

The House of Lords then unanimously held that there had been no unreasonable delay and therefore the delay fell to the account of the shipowner.

2.255 In *Hulthen* v. *Stewart*,[307] the details of which have also been considered earlier,[308] one of the periods of delay was after the vessel had entered the docks, where the delay in berthing was due to congestion. Dismissing the appeal to the House of Lords, the Lord Chancellor, the Earl of Halsbury, said[309]:

The master has shown all possible diligence, and this is an attempt to impose an unconditional term on the respondents (the charterers) for which there is no foundation in the charterparty.

2.256 It is therefore clear that delay due to congestion will not normally fall to the charterer's account in a customary laytime charterparty, whether the delay occurs before the vessel concerned becomes an Arrived ship or after. In the former case the delay will

---

302. *Postlethwaite* v. *Freeland* (1880) 5 App Cas 599 (HL).
303. At para. 2.209.
304. *Postlethwaite* v. *Freeland* (1880) 5 App Cas 599, at p. 615.
305. *Ibid.*, at p. 621.
306. *Burmester* v. *Hodgson* (1810) 2 Camp 488.
307. *Hulthen* v. *Stewart & Co* (1903) 8 CC 297 (HL).
308. At para. 2.231.
309. *Hulthen* v. *Stewart* (1903) 8 CC 297, at p. 300.

be on the approach or carrying voyage as the case may be, and in the latter, it will be one of the facts to be taken into account in establishing a reasonable time.

Strikes

2.257 The effect of a strike delaying loading or discharge has been considered in a number of cases. In *Castlegate Steamship Co Ltd* v. *Dempsey and others*[310] the facts were that by a custom of the port of discharge, the dock company undertook all the work of discharging cargo, which would otherwise have been undertaken in part by the shipowners and in part by the charterers. Because of a strike by dock labourers, discharge was delayed by four days.

2.258 In the Court of Appeal, Lord Esher MR said[311]:

By reason of the very same cause, viz. the strike of the dock labourers, the share of the work for which the shipowners would originally be responsible was prevented from being done, as well as the share of the work for which the charterers would be responsible. It seems to be impossible, under these circumstances, in the case of a charterparty which fixes no definite time, to say that the charterers are to bear the whole burden of what happened.

2.259 Lord Esher then went on to comment that the result might have been the same even where the strike affected only the charterers' part of discharge, which broadly speaking is what happened in *Pantland Hick* v. *Raymond & Reid*.[312]

2.260 By the time this case reached the House of Lords, it had been agreed that the cesser clause was effective and the action lay against the consignees, rather than the charterers, who were therefore liable to discharge the cargo and also would have been responsible for any culpable delay. Again, unloading was delayed by a strike of dock labourers, but in this case the only part of unloading which had to be performed by the shipowner was the trimming of the cargo and this the ship's crew was able and willing to do, notwithstanding the strike. It was thus clear that the dock company were only the agents of the consignees and not of the shipowners. Nevertheless, the consignees were absolved from blame for the delay, since they could neither find others to effect the discharge nor do it themselves.

2.261 In both cases referred to above, the strike was by the servants of a third party and the question therefore arises as to whether it would make a difference if the strike had been by the servants of the charterers or consignees as the case may be. It is submitted that the answer is "No", provided that it is shown that no alternative source of labour was available. However, in his speech in *Hick* v. *Raymond & Reid*,[313] Lord Ashbourne does seem to suggest that a relevant factor might be whether "the happening of the strike was entirely beyond and outside the control of either" party.

2.262 If by this is simply meant that in the event of a strike, alternative sources of labour must, if possible, be found, then no problem arises. However, if it was intended to suggest that the causes of a strike might be relevant, then considerable difficulty might arise in deciding culpability or otherwise for the delay.

310. *Castlegate Steamship Co* v. *Dempsey and others* [1892] 1 QB 854.
311. *Ibid.*, at p. 860.
312. *Pantland Hick* v. *Raymond & Reid* [1893] AC 22.
313. *Ibid.*, at p. 33.

Actions of port and other authorities

2.263 Where the actions or omissions of port and other authorities, whether *de facto* or *de jure*, delay or impede loading or discharge, the resultant loss suffered by the shipowner will not be recoverable from the charterers.[314]

2.264 Thus, in *Ford and others* v. *Cotesworth and another*,[315] a vessel was discharging at Callao when news arrived of the approach of a Spanish fleet. The local Customs authorities, apprehending a bombardment of the port, refused to allow any more goods to be discharged into the Custom House since they wished it to be cleared of goods already landed before the arrival of the Spanish fleet. The vessel consequently lay part discharged for seven days, when she was ordered away to be out of the danger of bombardment, after which she returned and discharge was finally completed.

2.265 In these circumstances it was held at first instance by the trial judge that there was no claim for the period whilst the vessel was away from Callao and by the full court that there could also be no recovery for the time whilst discharge was suspended by order of the Customs authorities.

2.266 Similarly, in *Good & Co* v. *Isaacs*,[316] a ship was chartered to carry oranges to Hamburg, discharging at a usual fruit berth. When she arrived, the usual fruit berths were occupied and the fruit warehouses full. The warehouses and the cranes used for discharging were under the control of government officials, who did not give permission for the vessel to berth for five days. The Court of Appeal rejected the shipowner's claim for this delay. Kay LJ said[317]:

I think the true result of the evidence is that there was no delay except what was occasioned by the custom of the port, and for this the charterers are not responsible.

2.267 In *Weir & Co* v. *Richardson*,[318] it was held that the principles set out above applied even where the dock authority, the River Wear Commissioners, were negligent in discharging the ship.[319]

Delay due to other third parties

2.268 This also will be excused, provided it has not been caused or contributed to by the relevant cargo interest. In *Lyle Shipping Co Ltd* v. *Corporation of Cardiff*[320] a charterparty provided for customary dispatch. By custom of the port of discharge, cargo was discharged into railway wagons. Any wagons could be used, but it was normal for consignees to contract with one railway company for their supply. Owing to a press of work, however, the railway company concerned failed to supply sufficient wagons and

---

314. This will apply equally where performance of the contract would be illegal by the law of the country where loading or discharge was to take place. Apart from being beyond the control of either party, in *Ralli Brothers* v. *Compania Naviera Sota y Aznar* (1920) 25 CC 227, the Court of Appeal held that in the absence of very special circumstances, the English courts will not enforce an English contract which provides for performance in a foreign country, if at the time fixed for performance, the law of that country made performance there illegal.

315. *Ford and others* v. *Cotesworth and another* (1868) LR 4 QB 127.

316. *Good & Co* v. *Isaacs* [1892] 2 QB 555.

317. *Ibid.*, at p. 565.

318. *Weir & Co* v. *Richardson* (1897) 3 CC 20.

319. Approved and adopted on similar facts in *Davies-Evans* v. *Ladoga Ltd (The Kingsland)* (1910) 16 CC 18.

320. *Lyle Shipping Co Ltd* v. *Corporation of Cardiff* (1900) 5 CC 397 (CA).

discharge was delayed. Nevertheless, both Bigham J and the Court of Appeal ruled that the consignees were not liable to pay damages for the detention of the ship.

2.269 In *Akties Glittre* v. *Gabriel, Wade & English*,[321] a shortage of labour at the loading port was similarly excused.

Weather and other natural phenomena

2.270 The leading case on this aspect is *Carlton Steamship Co Ltd* v. *Castle Mail Packets Co Ltd*,[322] a decision of the House of Lords. In that case the difficulty encountered concerned the depth of water at the loading berth during neap tides. The *Carlton*, the vessel concerned, was ordered to load a cargo at Senhouse Dock, Maryport, "always afloat" with customary laytime. Prior to arrival, the *Carlton* bunkered, increasing her arrival draught aft. After about a fifth of her cargo was loaded, it became apparent that the remainder would not be able to be loaded before the onset of neap tides and that at low water neaps she would not be "always afloat". The *Carlton* therefore sailed but, by agreement between the parties, returned a fortnight or so later to complete loading, which she did during the next spring tides. The question was who was responsible for the delay and additional expenses incurred.

2.271 It was unsuccessfully argued on behalf of the shipowner that the stipulation "always afloat" should be ignored in determining what was a reasonable time. Rejecting this argument, Lord Herschell said[323]:

It is admitted, my Lords, that the vessel could not by any human being have been loaded, whatever the diligence employed, an hour sooner than she was loaded, if she was to be loaded always afloat. Under these circumstances it seems to me impossible to hold that where the obligation has been performed as soon as it could, owing to the natural circumstances of the port, the person performing it has taken more than a reasonable time to do so.

In a similar vein, Lord Macnaghten said[324]:

I cannot understand how it can be unreasonable when it is the period required by the character of the harbour, the laws of nature, and the regular recurrence of spring tides.

2.272 In *Latus, Linsley & Co* v. *J H Douglas & Co*[325] and in *Aktieselskabet Dampskibs Cleveland* v. *Horsley, Smith & Co Ltd*,[326] loading was impeded by ice, which was held to be one of the circumstances to be taken into account in determining whether a reasonable time to load had been exceeded.

2.273 Whilst the sentiments expressed in the *Carlton Steamship* case[327] clearly apply to such surface phenomena as tides and ice, it is submitted they go beyond and apply to all natural phenomena, including weather. It should be noted, however, that for it to be excusable, the phenomenon must be the cause of the delay.

---

321. *Akties Glittre* v. *Gabriel, Wade & English* (1926) 24 Ll L Rep 372.
322. *Carlton Steamship Co Ltd* v. *Castle Mail Packets Co Ltd* (1898) 3 CC 207.
323. *Ibid.*, at p. 212.
324. *Ibid.*, at p. 216.
325. *Latus, Linsley & Co* v. *J H Douglas & Co* (1922) 12 Ll L Rep 63.
326. *Aktieselskabet Dampskibs Cleveland* v. *Horsley, Smith & Co Ltd* (1923) 16 Ll L Rep 323.
327. *Carlton Steamship Co Ltd* v. *Castle Mail Packets Co Ltd* (1898) 3 CC 207.

Other terms of the charterparty

2.274 The question of what effect the other express terms of the charter have on determining a reasonable time in the circumstances was one of the questions raised in *Carlton Steamship Co Ltd* v. *Castle Mail Packets Co Ltd*, where Lord Herschell said[328]:

Therefore it seems to me quite inadmissible to shut out any of the provisions of the charterparty which would render the time in certain circumstances longer, when you are inquiring whether more than a reasonable time has been taken.

2.275 He then went on to give an example of a restriction limiting loading to daylight, and asked whether that was to be ignored in determining a reasonable time, which clearly he felt it would not.

2.276 However, it is not all limiting clauses that will have this effect. Thus, in *Hulthen* v. *Stewart*[329] in the Court of Appeal, it was held that a strike clause was unnecessary because the consignees had the necessary protection without it. In general, therefore, an exclusion clause will be unnecessary and ineffective in so far as it seeks to exclude something outside the control of the party for whose benefit it was inserted.

2.277 On the other hand, a clause adding to the burden imposed by law will be upheld. An example of this is provided by *Maclay and others* v. *Spillers & Baker Ltd*,[330] where a bill of lading provided that the goods were to be received by the consignee "immediately the vessel is ready to discharge and continuously at all such hours as the Custom House authorities may give permission for the ship to work, any custom of the port to the contrary notwithstanding". This, said the Court of Appeal, meant that immediately the ship was ready to discharge, there was an absolute obligation on the consignee to receive the cargo continuously, even though sufficient labour and dock appliances were not then available.

Where customary laytime is exceeded

2.278 Where the parties agree that loading and/or discharge shall be by customary laytime, they may also provide for demurrage to be payable for any period in excess. At one stage it was thought that a demurrage clause might provide evidence of an intention by the parties to fix laytime. In *Castlegate Steamship Co* v. *Dempsey*,[331] after dismissing such an argument, Lord Esher MR then went on to say:

It has often been held that there cannot be demurrage days in the proper sense of the term, unless there is a fixed number of preceding lay days. In this charterparty there are no lay days properly so called; there is no fixed number of lay days. So we must construe the charterparty as meaning that the demurrage specified is to commence after the time when the cargo ought to be discharged as customary if all dispatch were used.

2.279 If the agreement between the parties does not mention demurrage, or no provision is made for laytime or there is no express agreement between the parties at all, so that customary laytime is implied by law, then any excess period will form the basis of a claim for damages for detention.

328. *Ibid.*, at p. 211.
329. *Hulthen* v. *Stewart & Co* (1902) 7 CC 139, at p. 147.
330. *Maclay and others* v. *Spillers & Baker Ltd* (1901) 6 CC 217.
331. *Castlegate Steamship Co Ltd* v. *Dempsey and others* [1892] 1 QB 854, at p. 858.

CHAPTER 3

Commencement of Laytime

3.1 Normally three conditions must be satisfied before the charterer can be required to start loading or discharging, as the case may be, and therefore before the laytime allowed starts to run. These are that—

1. The ship must have arrived at the destination specified in the charter.
2. The ship must be ready and in a fit condition to receive or discharge her cargo.
3. Where required, notice of her readiness must have been given to the charterer. In the absence of an express provision to the contrary, however, this last requirement only applies at the first load port.

When these conditions have been met the vessel is an Arrived ship and subject to the expiry of any period prescribed in the charter laytime begins to run.

The specified destination

3.2 In *The Johanna Oldendorff*,[1] Lord Diplock analysed the essential characteristics of a voyage charter and divided the adventure into four successive stages:

(1) The loading voyage, viz. the voyage of the chartered vessel from wherever she is at the date of the charterparty to the place specified in it as the place of loading.
(2) The loading operation, viz. the delivery of the cargo to the vessel at the place of loading and its stowage on board.
(3) The carrying voyage, viz. the voyage of the vessel to the place specified in the charterparty as the place of delivery.
(4) The discharging operation, viz. the delivery of the cargo from the vessel at the place specified in the charterparty as the place of discharge and its receipt there by the charterer or other consignee.

3.3 Arrival at the specified destination is the point both geographically and in time when the voyage stages end and the loading/discharging operations begin. Fixed laytime charters are traditionally divided into berth, dock and port charters depending on where the voyage stages end and these will be considered in more detail later.[2] Although the same divisions apply to customary laytime charters and there still therefore comes a point at which laytime begins, it is generally a less significant event in such charters because most of the risk of delay thereafter remains with the shipowner. However, the same principles apply.

---

1. *Oldendorff (EL) & Co GmbH* v. *Tradax Export SA (The Johanna Oldendorff)* [1973] 2 Lloyd's Rep 285, at p. 304.
2. See *post* at paras 3.30 (berth charters); 3.38 (dock charters); 3.48 (port charters).

3.4 Sometimes instead of naming a specific berth, dock or port, a charter will specify that the vessel concerned is to proceed to one or more berths, docks or ports within a stated geographical area, e.g.,

> "one or two safe berths Mississippi River"
> "one dock London River"
> "one port German North Sea"

3.5 Where such a formula is used, the effect is as if the berths, docks or ports, as the case may be, which are subsequently nominated by the charterer, were written into the original fixture. The ship therefore reaches her specified destination, not when she reaches the geographical area named in the charter, but when she reaches the first berth, dock or port named by the charterer and the charter is accordingly a berth, dock or port charter.[3]

3.6 The option that is thus given is one given by the shipowner for the benefit of the charterer and is a true option. In *Tharsis Sulphur & Copper Co Ltd* v. *Morel Brothers & Co and others*,[4] a vessel was chartered to proceed to the Mersey and deliver her cargo at any safe berth as ordered on arrival in the dock at Garston. On arrival a berth was ordered by the harbour-master as customary but there was a delay in unloading due to the crowded state of the dock which prevented the vessel being berthed for some time and the shipowners claimed demurrage. The principal point at issue was when the vessel became an Arrived ship and on this the Court of Appeal held that the charter was a berth charter so that time did not begin to run until the vessel berthed. In the course of his judgment, however, Bowen LJ dealt with the exercise of an option by a charterer to nominate a berth, dock or port saying[5]:

Then we were told that an option was given to the charterer, and that it was not properly exercised unless a berth was chosen that was empty. But I think there was a confusion in this argument also. The option is given for the benefit of the person who was to exercise it. He is bound to exercise it in a reasonable time, but is not bound in exercising it to consider the benefit or otherwise of the other party. The option is to choose a port or berth or dock, that is one that is reasonably fit for the purpose of delivery. It will not do, for instance, to choose a dock the entrance to which is blocked—that would be practically no exercise at all of the option. . . . To limit the option of the charterer by saying that, in the choice of a berth, he is to consider the convenience of the shipowner, is to deprive him of the benefit of his option. The most that can be said is that the charterer does not exercise his option at all unless he chooses a berth that is free or is likely to be so in a reasonable time.

3.7 In the absence of a reachable on arrival provision,[6] the shipowner has no right to complain if he cannot get into the nominated berth or dock, or indeed port, on arrival, because of some temporary obstruction, whether natural or man induced, such as lack of water or congestion. *Dicta* in the *Reardon Smith* case suggest that the only limitation to the charterers' right to nominate is where the delay caused by the "temporary" obstruction would be so unreasonable as to frustrate the commercial adventure.[7] However, in *The*

---

3. In *The Laura Prima* [1980] 1 Lloyd's Rep 466 in the High Court, however, Mocatta J held at p. 468 that in an Exxonvoy 69 or Asbatankvoy form of charter, even where the loading port was declared as "one safe berth . . . ", the charter remained a port charter.
4. *Tharsis Sulphur & Copper Co Ltd* v. *Morel Brothers & Co and others* [1891] 2 QB 647.
5. *Ibid.*, at p. 652.
6. See *post* at para. 3.402.
7. *Reardon Smith Line Ltd* v. *Ministry of Agriculture, Fisheries and Food* [1959] 2 Lloyd's Rep 229, at p. 248.

Epaphus,[8] a commodity sale and purchase case, Staughton J in the High Court and a majority of the Court of Appeal, led by Sir John Donaldson MR, held that the nomination of a port which the vessel was too deep to enter was a good one. In that case a named ship (although the position would apparently have been the same under that contract if it had been unnamed) was to discharge at "one main Italian port" nominated by the buyers of the cargo. They nominated Ravenna, which the ship was unable to enter. There was no requirement that the port nominated be a safe one. In the Court of Appeal, Sir John Donaldson distinguished the *Reardon Smith* case[9] and a case he called the *Olivebank* case,[10] where charterers had nominated a Danish port which the ship concerned was unable to enter owing to a prohibition by the British Government applied during the First World War, saying[11]:

Any implication that orders could never be given to go to Vancouver (in the *Vancouver Strikes* case) or to Aalborg (in the *Olivebank* case) would have contradicted the express terms of the contract. But it would be quite otherwise if the term to be implied was that the vessel could be ordered to Vancouver/Aalborg, unless that port should have become impossible subsequently to the making of the contract.

3.8 He continued that in the cases he had mentioned, the "impossibility" arose after the date of the contract and he concluded that it would have been quite different in the instant case, where a sudden storm had silted the harbour at Ravenna and reduced the maximum permissible draught.

3.9 In the High Court, Staughton J took a view apparently largely shared by the majority in the Court of Appeal[12]:

In my judgment, if a shipowner contracts to go to one out of a number of named ports, such as the charterer shall nominate, and does not qualify that choice with the word "safe", there is a good deal to be said for the view that he takes upon himself the task of ascertaining that his ship is of a size that can enter all those ports.

3.10 In the Court of Appeal, Sir John Donaldson did however admit[13] that had the contract provided for delivery "at one Italian port" rather than "at one main Italian port" there would have been scope for considering whether the parties intended to restrict the choice to one suited to the vessel, which he said would have involved no contradiction of the express terms, only their construction.

3.11 It would therefore seem that the more restrictive or qualified the range of ports, the less the courts are likely to interfere with the nomination made by the party having the choice. The distinction between a dock that is blocked on more than a transient basis and a port that is too shallow to enter seems somewhat fine, unless of course one is due to a supervening event, as suggested by Sir John Donaldson. It therefore seems likely that this subject will again come before the courts before very long.

3.12 Once the charterer has made his nomination without reservation, then in the absence of a provision to the contrary in the charter, he has no right to change the

---

8. *Eurico SpA* v. *Philipp Brothers (The Epaphus)* [1986] 2 Lloyd's Rep 387; [1987] 2 Lloyd's Rep 215.
9. *Reardon Smith Line Ltd* v. *Ministry of Agriculture, Fisheries and Food* [1961] 1 Lloyd's Rep 385.
10. *Aktieselskabet Olivebank* v. *Dansk Svovlsyre Fabrik Ltd* [1919] 2 KB 162.
11. *Eurico SpA* v. *Philipp Brothers (The Epaphus)* [1987] 2 Lloyd's Rep 215, at p. 220.
12. *Eurico SpA* v. *Philipp Brothers (The Epaphus)* [1986] 2 Lloyd's Rep 387, at p. 392.
13. *Eurico SpA* v. *Philipp Brothers (The Epaphus)* [1987] 2 Lloyd's Rep 215, at p. 219.

nomination,[14] unless for some reason the original nomination can be shown to be invalid.[15]

3.13 Most tanker charters, however, allow the charterer to nominate alternative ports after a first nomination or to order the vessel to proceed to a holding destination for further instructions to be passed by radio. Thus the Asbatankvoy form specifies Gibraltar or Land's End for orders and the STB Voy form also adds Quoin Island, Suez and Aruba. Moreover there may become a point after which the right to change the nomination becomes spent. In *The Batis*,[16] charterers sought to change the load port after arrival at the original nominated port. The charter was on an ASBA II form and provided for 1/2 load ports. Owners complied with the change under protest and reserved their rights to claim additional renumeration. In arbitration, the arbitrators held that the right to change the nominated load port had been lost but compliance with the charterers' orders deprived the owners from the full remedy sought. Leave to appeal from the finding that the changed orders were illegitimate was refused by the High Court who held that it was not an order that the charterers were entitled to give. They did however hold that the owners were not to be denied their remedy because they had complied with the orders.

3.14 The case may be contrasted with *The Jasmine B*,[17] where the charter provided at special provision 2 for discharge at 1/2 safe ports in three ranges with a maximum of three ports total. A further clause, M1, provided for charterers to have the right to change at any time its nomination of the loading and/or discharging ports subject to special provision 2. The charterers ordered the vessel to discharge at Porto Torres in Sardinia and after arrival at that port, ordered her in succession to proceed to Houston for orders, which the owners challenged, to wait outside Porto Torres for instructions, to proceed to New York for orders and finally to discharge at Genoa.

3.15 The High Court affirmed the general principle that in the absence of any special provision in a charterparty, the effect of the nomination of a loading or discharging port by the charterer was that the charterparty was thereafter to be treated as if the nominated port had originally been written in the charter and the charterer had neither the right nor the obligation to change that nomination.

3.16 The nominations for orders were outside the terms of the charter. The court held that clause M1 was in wide terms and entitled the charterers to change at any time their nomination and there was no reason to imply the words "so long as Notice of Readiness had not been given" or "so long as the vessel is not already on demurrage" into the clause. It was further held that the general principle set out above should not be extended so as to hold that a representation that the nominated port was to be the sole discharging port constituted the exercise of a right of election or selection and that even if that was wrong, the charterers were entitled to change their nomination under clause M1 of Porto Torres as sole discharge port to Genoa as sole discharge port. If Porto Torres had become an effective port of discharge since the vessel had tendered Notice of Readiness, then the

---

14. *Anglo-Danubian Transport Co Ltd* v. *Ministry of Food* (1949) 83 Ll L Rep 137, at p. 139 *per* Devlin J and cases cited therein. See also *The Antalya* (NY Arb), LMLN 291, 29 December 1990.

15. *Aktieselskabet Olivebank* v. *Dansk Svovlsyre Fabrik Ltd* [1919] 1 KB 388, where the nomination of a Danish port to which a British ship could not lawfully proceed was held to be nugatory, obliging the charterers to give a fresh nomination.

16. *Batis Maritime Corporation* v. *Petroleos Mediterraneo SA (The Batis)*, LMLN 263, 2 December 1989; [1990] 1 Lloyd's Rep 345. See also London Arbitration 12/90—LMLN 286, 20 October 1990.

17. *Bulk Shipping AG* v. *Ipco Trading SA (The Jasmine B)* [1992] 1 Lloyd's Rep 39.

effect of the order was that the charterers changed their nomination so that Porto Torres became the first port of discharge and Genoa the second.

3.17 In *The Batis*, the High Court only considered whether the charterers were entitled to change their nomination under the change of load/discharge ports provision, not under any other term of the charter, such as that allowing loading at more than one port, although that argument was rejected in arbitration.

3.18 It is suggested that the following principles apply:

A. A charter may provide for change of load or discharge ports by the charterer even after arrival at the port concerned but very clear words will be needed to achieve this effect.

B. Normally the right to change load or discharge ports under a provision allowing such changes will be lost after Notice of Readiness is presented.

C. Even if the right to change load or discharge ports is lost, the charterer may still have the right to nominate additional load or discharge ports provided this is within the total number/range of such ports allowed, notwithstanding his original nomination even if that was declared as the sole port.

3.19 An example of a particularly widely drafted change in a nomination clause is clause 9(*b*) of the Exxonvoy 84 form, which provides:

CHANGE OF DESTINATION. After nominating loading and/or discharging port(s) or place(s) pursuant to Paragraph (a) of this Clause, Charterer may nominate new port(s) or place(s), whether or not they are within the range of the previously nominated port(s) or place(s) and/or vary the rotation of any nominated port(s) or place(s) . . .

3.20 The clause goes on to make it clear that the right to nominate a different loading/discharging port in a different range is lost once Notice of Readiness is tendered at a nominated loading/discharging port. This leaves open the question as to whether a different port may be nominated within the same range. Probably the answer is that by implication it can.

3.21 Under the Worldscale system of freight calculation used in virtually all tanker charters, the freight payable depends on the actual load and discharge ports and, furthermore, clause 9(*b*) goes on to provide a formula for compensating the shipowner for any time wasted by the change so the clause is by no means as one-sided as it might at first appear. It does, however, allow the charterer to totally change the agreed voyage at any stage en route.

3.22 What happens if the charterer fails to nominate a discharge port timeously was the question that arose in *The Timna*, where the vessel concerned was ordered to the River Weser but the charterers failed to specify which of the Weser ports they intended to discharge at in sufficient time to avoid delay. In the High Court Donaldson J held[18] there was no implied term, as had been suggested, that if the charterers failed to nominate the port of discharge within the time limited by the charter or within some further period thereafter, the master could himself make the nomination. As the vessel never became an Arrived ship during the period of delay, the shipowner's claim for demurrage therefore failed but he was entitled to claim damages for detention for the delay until the charterers did in fact give orders as to which port to proceed to. This finding was upheld by the Court

---

18. *Zim Israel Navigation Co Ltd v. Tradax Export SA (The Timna)* [1970] 2 Lloyd's Rep 409.

of Appeal, who also held that to constitute a valid order to proceed to a port of discharge, the order must be a firm one.[19]

3.23 A failure to nominate the discharge port in sufficient time to avoid delay was one of the many issues that were considered in *The Rio Sun*,[20] which was a dispute not under a charter but under a c.i.f. contract of sale. In that case, Bingham J held that it was implicit in the sale contract that the buyer should nominate the discharge port in sufficient time to enable the vessel to sail to that port without interruption or delay, and that failure to do so was a breach of contract. A different sort of problem arose out of late nomination of discharge ports in London Arbitration 19/89[21] where a failure to nominate the second discharge port before completion of loading meant that the master did not have a chance to load the cargo in such a way so as to avoid lightening at the first port after discharge of the cargo destined for that port in order to reach the second. The charterers' failure to give timeous orders had caused the loss they had suffered by having to discharge additional cargo at the first port where the price was lower.

3.24 The late nomination of a discharge port may result in the voyage being extended and/or in a delay on arrival at the discharge port,[22] e.g. because of local requirements to give notice for tugs, etc.[23] The loss that flows from the former is usually quantified by calculating the time lost and multiplying it by the demurrage rate with the addition of the cost of bunkers wasted.

3.25 If there is a delay at the discharge port, on the other hand, then the type of claim will, it is suggested, depend on whether the vessel concerned is an Arrived ship, i.e. it will depend on whether the relevant charter is a berth or port charter. If the vessel is not an Arrived ship then there will be a claim for detention for the period of delay, quantified at the demurrage rate. If the vessel is an Arrived ship then laytime will run and any remaining laytime may be used to offset the delay.

3.26 It is important to distinguish between the express right of a charterer to select the loading berth given in the charterparty and his implied right to do so. As already mentioned, the effect of the express right given by such expressions as "one or two safe berths Mississippi River" is to prevent a vessel from becoming an Arrived ship until she gets into the designated berth. However, even if the charter does not expressly give the charterer this right, he still has the implied right to select the berth. In that case, however, the vessel becomes an Arrived ship when she gets within the larger area named in the charter, i.e. the port or dock.[24]

3.27 Sometimes difficult questions of construction can arise as to whether the parties intended the charterer to have an express or an implied right to nominate the berth. In *North River Freighters Ltd* v. *President of India*[25] Parker LJ decided that the words "one safe berth Dairen" expressly gave the charterer the right to name the loading berth, but went on to suggest that if the charter had said that the vessel was "to proceed to Dairen

19. *Zim Israel Navigation Co Ltd* v. *Tradax Export SA (The Timna)* [1971] 2 Lloyd's Rep 91 (CA).

20. *Gatoil International Inc* v. *Tradax Petroleum Ltd (The Rio Sun)*, LMLN 127, 13 September 1984; [1985] 1 Lloyd's Rep 350.

21. London Arbitration 19/89—LMLN 256, 26 August 1989.

22. See also *Heinrich Hanno Co BV* v. *Fairlight Shipping Co Ltd; Hanse Schiffahrtskontor GmbH* v. *Andre SA (The Kostas K)*, LMLN 135, 3 January 1985; [1985] 1 Lloyd's Rep 231.

23. For instance at Milford Haven, 48 hours' notice is required for the provision of tugs for a VLCC.

24. *Stag Line Ltd* v. *Board of Trade* (1950) 83 Ll L Rep 356, at p. 358 *per* Devlin J. This general principle was specifically endorsed on appeal by Lord Oaksey in the Court of Appeal (1950) 84 Ll L Rep 1, at p. 3.

25. *North River Freighters Ltd* v. *President of India* [1955] 2 Lloyd's Rep 668. *See also The Finix* [1975] 2 Lloyd's Rep. 415 at p. 442 *per* Donaldson J.

and then load at one safe berth", without adding "as ordered by the charterer" the right would have been implied so that the vessel would become an Arrived ship when she got within the port.

3.28 Similarly, in *Stag Line Ltd* v. *Board of Trade*,[26] the Court of Appeal upheld the decision of the lower court that a clause providing that the vessel should "proceed to one or two safe ports East Canada or Newfoundland, place or places as ordered by charterers" was an express right to nominate the berth so that the charter was a berth charter.

3.29 There are three exceptions to the general rule that a vessel is not an Arrived ship until she reaches the destination named in the charter or that subsequently selected by the charterer under an express right. These are (a) custom, (b) obstacles created by the charterer and (c) special provisions in the charter, and these will be considered later.[27]

Berth charters

3.30 Berth charters are probably the oldest form of charter, arrival in berth being the natural completion point of the voyage. The *Voylayrules 1993*[28] define berth in the following terms:

"BERTH" shall mean the specific place within a port where the vessel is to load or discharge. If the word "BERTH" is not used, but the specific place is (or is to be) identified by its name, this definition shall still apply.

3.31 The principal change from the *Charterparty Laytime Definitions 1980* is the addition of the words "within a port" in the first line.

3.32 A berth is an individual loading point on a jetty, wharf or in a dock system. Individual berths are not usually given names but numbers, being referred to as No 1 berth, No 2 berth, etc. In most berth charters, the designation is "one safe berth X port" leaving the charterer free to nominate any berth in that port or more commonly to inform the shipowner which berth he has been allocated by the port authority. Occasionally, however, a charter specifies a particular wharf or jetty, which may have, say, two or three berths on it, but such a charter is usually held to be of the same character as a berth charter.

3.33 The original concept of a berth charter was one where a particular berth was named in the charter but, as has already been discussed,[29] this has been extended to include situations where the vessel is to proceed to a berth at the charterer's express (as opposed to implied) option within the port.[30]

3.34 In a berth charter, the specified destination is reached when the vessel is in that berth and does not need to move further to load or discharge. In *E L Oldendorff & Co GmbH* v. *Tradax Export SA*, Lord Diplock said[31]:

Where a single berth was specified in the charterparty as being the place of loading or of discharge, the loading voyage or the carrying voyage did not end until the vessel was at that very berth. Until then no obligation could lie upon the charterer to load the cargo, or to receive it, as the case might

26. *Stag Line Ltd* v. *Board of Trade* (1950) 84 Ll L Rep 1 (CA).
27. See *post* at para. 3.317.
28. See Appendix and the similar definition in *Baltic Code 2000*.
29. See *ante* at para. 3.4.
30. *Surrey Shipping Co Ltd* v. *Compagnie Continentale (France) SA (The Shackleford)* [1978] 2 Lloyd's Rep 154, at p. 161 *per* Sir David Cairns.
31. *Oldendorff (EL) & Co GmbH* v. *Tradax Export SA (The Johanna Oldendorff)* [1973] 2 Lloyd's Rep 285, at p. 305.

be. If the specified berth were occupied by other shipping, the vessel was still at the voyage stage while waiting in the vicinity of the berth until it became available, and time so spent was at the shipowner's expense.

3.35 In a similar vein, in *North River Freighters Ltd* v. *President of India*, Jenkins LJ drew a distinction between port and berth charters, saying about the latter[32]:

whereas in the case of a berth charter (that is to say, a charter which requires the vessel to proceed for loading to a particular berth either specified in the charter or by the express terms of the charter to be specified by the charterer) lay days do not begin to run until the vessel has arrived at the particular berth, is ready to load, and has given notice to the charterer in manner prescribed by the charter of her readiness to load.

3.36 In *The Handy Mariner*,[33] the Court of Appeal held on appeal from a GAFTA tribunal that a sale contract providing for c.i.f. free out Lorient with a discharging rate should be construed as a berth charter provision notwithstanding that had the contract been construed as a charter, it would have been held to be a port charter.

3.37 Occasionally disputes arise as to when a vessel arrived at a particular berth, usually when there has been some delay between the first line being passed and completion of the mooring process. Clause 14 of the Shellvoy 3 form of charter (which unlike most tanker charterparties is a berth charter) requires the vessel to be securely moored before laytime can commence and this, it is suggested, would be the position in any event.[34] Taking the point one stage further, however, what this means is that the vessel must be secured by sufficient mooring lines to enable the safe working of cargo. In some ports at certain times of the year or when adverse weather is expected, additional heavier lines are added a little while after the vessel's arrival. These are sometimes referred to as "hurricane hawsers" but normally these are an additional precaution and not part of the usual mooring process. The vessel therefore arrives in berth when the normal mooring lines are secured.

Dock charters

3.38 The *Oxford English Dictionary* defines a dock as "an artificial basin excavated, built round with masonry and fitted with flood gates, into which ships are received for purposes of loading and unloading or for repair". Often there are a series of inter-linked basins with a range of berths and wharves. In one sense, therefore, a dock charter is a hybrid between a berth and a port charter, and like a port charter, it covers a geographical area. In *Nelson* v. *Dahl*[35] in 1879 in the Court of Appeal, dock charters were said to be "a comparatively recent introduction".

3.39 Dock systems may be either tidal or non-tidal but since they usually have a clearly defined entrance, there is usually little dispute as to when a vessel arrives in dock, and that will be when she reaches her specified destination.

3.40 In *Tapscott* v. *Balfour*[36] the charterparty concerned specified that the ship should load a cargo of coal at "any Liverpool or Birkenhead dock as ordered by charterers", and

32. *North River Freighters Ltd* v. *President of India* [1955] 2 Lloyd's Rep 668, at p. 679.
33. *Etablissements Soules et Cie* v. *Intertradax SA (The Handy Mariner)* [1991] 1 Lloyd's Rep 378; LMLN 288, 17 November 1990.
34. *Plakoura Maritime Corporation* v. *Shell International Petroleum Co Ltd (The Plakoura)* [1987] 2 Lloyd's Rep 258.
35. *Nelson, Donkin and others* v. *Robert H Dahl* (1879) 12 Ch D 568, at p. 575.
36. *Tapscott* v. *Balfour* (1872) LR 8 CP 46.

the charterers ordered the vessel to Wellington Dock. However, on arrival, the vessel was unable to enter the dock and when she did so some days later, there was a further delay before she was able to get into a position where she could commence loading. The charterers argued that they were not responsible for these delays.

3.41 Rejecting this argument, Denman J commented[37]:

... on the day when the ship arrived in the dock the shipowner had done all that [he] was bound to do.

Of the nomination of the specific dock by the charterers, Bovill CJ said[38]:

It seems to me that the effect of such selection was precisely as if that dock had been expressly named in the charterparty originally and the agreement had been that the vessel should proceed direct to the Wellington Dock . . .

3.42 Some eight years later the courts again had to consider the question of responsibility for delay because of congestion in relation to dock charters when the House of Lords held in *Dahl* v. *Nelson, Donkin and others*[39] that "the ship did not fulfil the engagement in the charterparty to proceed to the Surrey Commercial Docks by merely going to the gates of the docks". What had happened was that on arrival in the Thames, the *Euxine*, the vessel concerned, proceeded to the Surrey Commercial Docks with her cargo of timber, but the dock manager refused it entrance into the docks as they were full and the ship could not be given a discharging berth.[40]

3.43 However, if a vessel does gain admittance to the docks, for whatever reason, she has nevertheless arrived at the specified destination. This was the result in *Compagnie Chemin de Fer du Midi* v. *A Bromage & Co*[41] where a vessel called the *Smut* was ordered to discharge her cargo of pit props at Barry Dock. On arrival, although no berth was available, she was allowed to enter the dock as she was short of bunkers. On completion of bunkering, she gave Notice of Readiness although not in berth. Charterers therefore argued that laytime should not start to run because she was not in berth and/or because the vessel had only been admitted because of her unseaworthiness by reason of being short of bunkers. Both these arguments were rejected by Greer J, who said[42]:

It seems to me there are many reasons which may expedite or delay the arrival of a ship in the place from which her time was to count. The fact that the arrival was expedited in this case by the good nature of the dock authorities in letting her in in order to prevent her from lying in the roads without sufficient coal, is one of the circumstances that have in fact resulted in her being an arrived ship before she would otherwise have been.

3.44 A somewhat unusual set of circumstances arose in *Kokusai Kisen Kabushiki Kaisha* v. *Flack & Son*[43] where a ship was ordered to load "in such dock as may be ordered" by the charterers at Delagoa Bay, but there were no docks at Delagoa Bay! The reference to "such dock", etc., should therefore be ignored, said the Court of Appeal, so

---

37. *Ibid.*, at p. 55.
38. *Ibid.*, at p. 52.
39. *Robert H Dahl* v. *Nelson, Donkin and others* (1880) 6 App Cas 38.
40. The charter also had an "as near thereto as she may safely get" provision and this was satisfied by the cargo being discharged at buoys a short distance downstream.
41. *Compagnie Chemin de Fer du Midi* v. *A Bromage & Co* (1921) 6 Ll L Rep 178. A similar view was taken by the Court of Appeal in *Davies* v. *McVeagh* (1879) 4 Ex D '265 where the vessel was allowed into the dock because, being empty, she was in danger outside.
42. *Compagnie Chemin de Fer du Midi* v. *A Bromage & Co* (1921) 6 Ll L Rep 178, at p. 179.
43. *Kokusai Kisen Kabushiki Kaisha* v. *Flack & Son* (1922) 10 Ll L Rep 635.

that although the charter was a dock charter in form, it took effect as though it were a port charter.

3.45 In *Carlton Steamship Co Ltd* v. *Castle Mail Packets Co Ltd*,[44] a customary laytime charter provided for a vessel to load at a named dock "always afloat". The vessel proceeded to the dock, which was tidal, but was forced to leave during loading because of steadily falling tides, returning later as the spring tides approached. The main issue was the question of liability for the delay which arose after the vessel became an Arrived ship and on this a majority of the Court of Appeal held, reversing the lower court, that the delay was not unreasonable and therefore, under the normal rules for customary laytime charters, fell to the shipowner's account. On the question of when the vessel became an Arrived ship, Smith LJ (who dissented on the main issue) said[45]:

... here the ship was an arrived ship when she got to Senhouse Dock, Maryport ... The owners had done their part in bringing her to Senhouse Dock, Maryport.

3.46 Similar sentiments were expressed by Hamilton J in *Thorman* v. *Dowgate Steamship Co Ltd*, where he said[46]:

The charterparty itself is a charter to proceed to a named dock in a named port and ... under the ordinary rule applicable to charterparties she would be arrived at her destination when she was in the dock.

3.47 There is, however, one further exception to the general principle that the specified destination is reached on arrival in dock and not in berth and this exception applies equally to port charters. This is that where a berth is available immediately on arrival so that the vessel is able to go straight into berth, then the end of the voyage is on arrival in berth. Lord Diplock explained the reasoning behind this in *The Johanna Oldendorff*, saying[47]:

Since the business purpose of the voyage stages is to bring the vessel to a berth at which the cargo can be loaded or discharged, the shipowner does not complete the loading or the carrying voyage until the vessel has come to a stop at a place within the larger area whence her proceeding further would serve no business purpose. If on her arrival within the dock or port there is a berth available at which the charterer is willing and able to load or discharge the cargo, the vessel must proceed straight there and her loading or carrying voyage will not be completed until she reaches it. But if no berth is available, the voyage stage ends when she is moored at any convenient place from which she can get to a berth as soon as one is vacant. The subsequent delay while waiting for a berth does not fall within the voyage stage under a dock charter or port charter, but in the loading or discharging stage.

Port charters

3.48 Under a port charter, a vessel reaches its specified destination when it arrives within the port and is in such a position as to be at the immediate and effective disposition of the charterer. The current state of the law is succinctly summarized in the following passage from Lord Reid's speech in *The Johanna Oldendorff*[48]:

Before a ship can be said to have arrived at a port she must, if she cannot proceed immediately to a berth, have reached a position within the port where she is at the immediate and effective

44. *Carlton Steamship Co Ltd* v. *Castle Mail Packets Co Ltd* (1897) 2 CC 286.
45. *Ibid.*, at p. 291.
46. *Thorman* v. *Dowgate Steamship Co Ltd* (1909) 15 CC 67.
47. *Oldendorff (EL) & Co GmbH* v. *Tradax Export SA (The Johanna Oldendorff)* [1973] 2 Lloyd's Rep 285, at p. 305 (HL).
48. *Ibid.*, at p. 291.

disposition of the charterer. If she is at a place where waiting ships lie, she will be in such a position unless in some extraordinary circumstances proof of which would lie on the charterer...

If the ship is waiting at some other place in the port then it will be for the owner to prove that she is as fully at the disposition of the charterer as she would have been if in the vicinity of the berth for loading or discharge.

This criterion has become known as "the Reid test", replacing the earlier "Parker test", put forward by Parker LJ in *The Aello*.[49]

3.49 It will be noted that this test only applies where there is a delay between the vessel's arrival in the port and its moving to a berth. Where the vessel can proceed direct to its berth then, as with a dock charter,[50] it does not reach its specified destination until arrival in berth.[51]

3.50 These two requirements, that the vessel must have arrived within the port and be in such a position as to be at the immediate and effective disposition of the charterer, will now be considered in more detail.

Arrival within the port

3.51 What constitutes a port is the first of the definitions given in the *Charterparty Laytime Definitions 1980* and is in the following terms[52]:

"PORT" means an area within which ships are loaded with and/or discharged of cargo and includes the usual places where ships wait for their turn or are ordered or obliged to wait for their turn no matter the distance from that area. If the word "PORT" is not used, but the port is (or is to be) identified by its name, this definition shall still apply.

3.52 The *Voylayrules 1993* give a similar definition in the following terms:

"PORT" shall mean an area, within which vessels load or discharge cargo whether at berths, anchorages, buoys or the like, and shall also include the usual places where vessels wait for their turn or are ordered or obliged to wait for their turn no matter the distance from that area. If the word "PORT" is not used, but the port is (or is to be) identified by its name, this definition shall still apply.

3.53 Whilst the courts and arbitrators have tended of late to accept that some anchorages a considerable distance from the areas where cargo operations are carried out are within port limits, as will be seen, there are, at common law, rules which provide for a more restrictive definition of port limits. It by no means follows, in the absence of these definitions being specifically incorporated into the relevant charter, that all anchorages where vessels may have to wait will be deemed to be within port limits.[53]

3.54 There are some ports, e.g. Hull, Glasgow and the Weser ports, where the usual waiting area is not within the port. In such cases, these definitions are therefore inaccurate.

3.55 The limits of a particular port may vary according to the purpose for which the limits are being defined. Thus port limits may be defined by law or by custom and the

---

49. *Agrimpex Hungarian Trading Co for Agricultural Products* v. *Sociedad Financiera de Bienes Raices SA (The Aello)* [1958] 2 Lloyd's Rep 65, at p. 76. See *post* at para. 3.93.
50. See *ante* at para. 3.47.
51. See also London Arbitration 8/91—LMLN 304, 29 June 1991.
52. See Appendix and the similar definition in *Baltic Code 2000*.
53. See *post* at paras 3.102 *et seq*.

extent of the port may be different for administrative, fiscal, geographical and commercial purposes.

3.56 An early explanation of why ports must have limits was given by Lush J in *Nicholson* v. *Williams*, where he said[54]:

Ports and havens are not merely geographical expressions; they are places appointed by the Crown "for persons and merchandises to pass into and out of the realm" and at such places only is it lawful for ships to load and discharge cargo. The assignment of such places to be "the inlets and gates" of the realm is, and always has been, a branch of the prerogative resting, as Blackstone remarks, partly upon a fiscal foundation in order to secure the King's marine revenue. Their limits and bounds are necessarily defined by the authority which creates them, and the area embraced within those limits constitutes the port.

3.57 In *Leonis Steamship Co* v. *Rank (No 1)*, Kennedy LJ observed[55]:

The limits of a port established by law or ancient custom may be very wide, or again in the case of a newly established place of shipping traffic the limits may be uncertain because not yet defined by any competent authority for any purpose . . . Just as a port may have one set of limits, if viewed geographically, and another set of limits for fiscal or pilotage purposes, so when it is named in a commercial document, and for commercial purposes, the term is to be construed in a commercial sense in relation to the objects of the particular commercial transaction.

3.58 As it was put by Brett MR in the *Sailing Ship Garston Co* v. *Hickie*[56]:

The word "port" in a charterparty does not necessarily mean an Act of Parliament pilotage port, or, which is the better word, "pilotage district". Therefore, when you are trying to define the port with regard to which persons who enter into a charterparty are contracting, you endeavour to find words which will shut out those things which you know they do not intend.

3.59 Later in his judgment, having said: "There will never be a port, in the ordinary business sense of the word, unless there is some element of safety in it for the ship and goods", he went on to say[57]:

Now sometimes you have only a place of comparative safety, a place in which neither the natural configuration of the land with regard to the sea, nor the artificial walls make a perfectly safe port, but only a place of comparative safety. Then you have not such easy means of ascertaining what the parties to a charterparty must have meant by "the port", and you must find out where, in fact, people have had their ships loaded and unloaded. The moment you can find that the loading and unloading of ships takes place at a particular spot, you may safely infer that the parties understood that spot to be within "the port", because as a general rule people do not load or unload goods outside the port . . . But the port may extend beyond the place of loading and unloading . . .
Then, if you want to find out how far the port extends beyond the place of loading and unloading, what is the next test you would apply? If you find that the authorities, who are known in commercial business language as "the port authorities", are exercising authority over ships within a certain space of water, and that the shipowners and shippers who have ships within that space of water are submitting to the jurisdiction which is claimed by those authorities, whether legally or not, whether according to Act of Parliament or not, if you find what are called "the port authorities" exercising port discipline, and the ships which frequent that water submitting to the port discipline so exercised, that seems to be the strongest possible evidence that the shipowners, the shippers and the port authorities . . . have all come to the conclusion to accept that space of water in which the authority is so exercised as "the port" of the place.

---

54. *Nicholson* v. *Williams* (1871) LR 6 QB 632, at p. 641.
55. *Leonis Steamship Co Ltd* v. *Joseph Rank (No 1)* (1907) 13 CC 136, at p. 152.
56. *Sailing Ship Garston Co* v. *Hickie* (1885) 15 QBD 580, at p. 587.
57. *Ibid.*, at p. 589.

3.60 This question of control was also taken up by Bowen LJ in his judgment in the same case, where he said[58]:

Another matter which ought to be considered is the authority exercised, and the limits within which that authority is exercised, not for fiscal purposes, but for purposes connected with the loading and unloading, the arrival and departure of ships; the mode in which the business of loading and unloading is done, and the general usage of the place. Taking all these things together, you must make up your mind in each particular case as to the sense in which shipowners and charterers would be likely to intend to employ the term "port".

3.61 In *The Johanna Oldendorff*, both Lord Reid and Lord Diplock stressed that in practice it was usually relatively simple to decide whether the normal waiting area was within the port or outside it. Lord Reid put it this way[59]:

Then it was argued that the limits of many ports are so indefinite that it would introduce confusion to hold that a ship is an arrived ship on anchoring at a usual waiting place within the port. But I find it difficult to believe that there would, except perhaps in rare cases, be any real difficulty in deciding whether at any particular port the usual waiting place was or was not within the port. The area within which a port authority exercises its various powers can hardly be difficult to ascertain. Some powers with regard to pilotage and other matters may extend far beyond the limits of the port. But those which regulate the movements and conduct of ships would seem to afford a good indication. And in many cases the limits of the port are defined by law. In the present case the umpire has found as a fact (par. 19) that the ship was "at the Bar anchorage, within the legal, administrative and fiscal areas of Liverpool/Birkenhead".

3.62 Comparing the relative areas occupied by a dock and a port, Lord Diplock said[60]:

The area of a port, however, may be much larger. It may sometimes be less easily determinable, because of absence of definition of its legal limits or variations between these and the limits within which the port authority in actual practice exercises control of the movement of shipping; but I do not believe that in practice it is difficult to discover whether a place where ships usually wait their turn for a berth is within the limits of a named port; or is outside those limits as is the case with Glasgow and with Hull.

3.63 That the reported cases contain so few references to disputes as to whether a waiting area is within the limits of a particular port probably bears out what Lords Reid and Diplock say. Even in a case such as *Logs & Timber Products (Singapore) Pte Ltd* v. *Keeley Granite (Pty) Ltd (The Freijo)*,[61] which concerned the port of Lourenço Marques which apparently has no specified fiscal or commercial limits, it would appear that the arbitrator had no difficulty in deciding that the waiting area was within the port.

At the immediate and effective disposition of the charterer

3.64 As already indicated, to be an Arrived ship a vessel must not only be within the limits of the nominated port but must be in a part of the port where she is at the immediate

---

58. *Ibid.*, at p. 595.
59. *Oldendorff (EL) & Co GmbH* v. *Tradax Export SA (The Johanna Oldendorff)* [1973] 2 Lloyd's Rep 285, at p. 291.
60. *Ibid.*, at p. 306.
61. *Logs & Timber Products (Singapore) Pte Ltd* v. *Keeley Granite (Pty) Ltd (The Freijo)* [1978] 1 Lloyd's Rep 257, [1978] 2 Lloyd's Rep 1 (CA). See also *President of India* v. *Olympia Sauna Shipping Co SA (The Ypatia Halcoussi)* [1984] 2 Lloyd's Rep 455, where the dispute was whether a number of grain elevator berths were in the same or different ports.

and effective disposition of the charterer. Just which part of the port comes within this description has been the subject of some judicial controversy from time to time as developments in the law have taken place.

3.65 The law has changed because shipping itself has changed, as sail gave way to steam, as ports developed and as communication became easier with the introduction of, first, telephones and, later, radio. Each of these developments has had an effect on when a ship can be considered "at the immediate and effective disposition of the charterer". It should also be remembered that during the early part of the nineteenth century, customary rather than fixed laytime was the rule, and whereas under the latter, the risk of delay after the vessel concerned becomes an Arrived ship is for the charterer's account unless specifically excluded, under the former most of the usual delays encountered, e.g. congestion, are borne by the shipowner. In a customary laytime charter, therefore, the question of when the specified destination is reached is much less important.

3.66 In the nineteenth century, particularly the first half thereof, custom played a much more important role in deciding cases than it does today. Many of the early cases were decided on the basis of custom. Thus, in *Brereton* v. *Chapman*[62] it was proved that it was the custom of the port of Wells, then a large port, that a vessel was not an Arrived ship until she reached the quay. In the absence of any such custom, the specified destination was reached when the vessel arrived at a usual place of loading or discharging within the port for that particular trade. Dependent upon the practice of the particular trade this could be at a berth, in a dock or by lighters whilst the vessel was anchored off the berth. However, proof had to be adduced that loading or discharging at that place and in that way was the usual practice. In *Randall* v. *Lynch*[63] the description of the carrying voyage was as to the ending of it "to proceed direct to the said port of London, and upon arrival there, that is to say at the London Docks, to make discharge and faithful delivery of the said homeward cargo, &c, and there end and complete both out and homeward voyages". The ship arrived in the London Docks but was delayed in discharging by the crowded state of the docks. On the question of when laytime commenced, Lord Ellenborough said "when she was brought into the docks, all had been done which depended on the plaintiff", the shipowner.

3.67 In *Kell* v. *Anderson*,[64] the Court of Exchequer held that in the case of a sailing ship chartered to carry coals to the Port of London where the usual discharging place for coals was in the Pool of London, laytime did not start to run when, on the orders of the harbour master, owing to congestion in the Pool she moored off Gravesend to wait her turn until room became available for her in the Pool for her to discharge her cargo. Gravesend was within the legal limits of the Port of London and was the usual place for colliers to wait their turn if the Pool was congested, but it was some 22 miles downriver from the Pool. Commenting on this case in *The Johanna Oldendorff*, Lord Diplock said[65]:

A sailing ship's journey upriver from Gravesend would be dependent upon favourable wind and weather. There was no knowing how long it would take her to reach the Pool after she had notice that there was room to discharge her cargo there. So she was not, while at her moorings, at the disposal of the charterer for discharging her cargo.

62. *Brereton* v. *Chapman* (1831) 7 Bing. 559.
63. *Randall* v. *Lynch* (1810) 2 Camp. 352.
64. *Kell* v. *Anderson* (1842) 10 M & W 331.
65. *Oldendorff (EL) & Co GmbH* v. *Tradax Export SA (The Johanna Oldendorff)* [1973] 2 Lloyd's Rep 285, at p. 306.

3.68 This case may be contrasted with *Brown* v. *Johnson*,[66] decided in the same year as *Kell* v. *Anderson*. In this case, a sailing ship was chartered to proceed to a port in the United Kingdom and Hull was subsequently nominated. Fifteen days laytime were allowed for discharging in the charter. The ship arrived within the port limits on 1 February, in dock on 2 February but did not get into a place of unloading in the dock until 4 February because of congestion. On these facts, Alderson B ruled in the Court of Exchequer that laytime commenced on the day she arrived in dock and not when she arrived in berth in the dock. In a later case,[67] Brett LJ commented that: "It must have been assumed or proved that the usual place of unloading all ships in the port of Hull was in a dock."

3.69 In *The Johanna Oldendorff*, Lord Diplock said[68] that the distinction between the two cases was that in the latter the waiting area was inside the dock and therefore close to the discharging berths. This meant that as soon as a berth fell vacant, the ship could be warped to it from her moorings without any significant delay and she was therefore at the immediate disposal of the charterer.

3.70 As already mentioned,[69] dock charters came into common use as a separate class of charter during the third quarter of the nineteenth century, following the general expansion of trade about that time which had led to the development of extensive dock systems at many of the major ports. By 1872, it had become accepted[70] that in the case of a dock charter, the specified destination had been reached when the ship concerned entered the dock regardless of whether it had reached a point where it could load or discharge cargo.

3.71 In *Tapscott* v. *Balfour*,[71] Bovill CJ was also prepared to hold that the same principle applied to a port charter, although it took a further 37 years, until the decision of the Court of Appeal in *Leonis Steamship Co* v. *Rank (No 1)*,[72] before the point was finally settled. Bovill CJ said that the rule was that where a port was named in the charterparty as the port to which the vessel was to proceed then lay days did not commence upon her arrival in the port, but upon her arrival at the usual place of loading in the port, not the actual berth at which she loaded but the dock or roadstead where loading usually took place.

3.72 In *Nelson* v. *Dahl*,[73] in the Court of Appeal, Brett LJ carried out a comprehensive review of the earlier authorities dealing with the question of when a ship becomes an Arrived ship under berth, dock and port charters. On dock and port charters, he said[74]:

If it describes a larger place, as a port or dock, the shipowner may place his ship at the disposition of the charterer when the ship arrives at that named place, and, so far as she is concerned, is ready to load, though she is not then in the particular part of the port or dock in which the particular cargo is to be loaded.

66. *Brown* v. *Johnson* (1842) 10 M & W 331. Subsequently upheld by Lord Abinger.
67. *Nelson* v. *Dahl* (1879) 12 Ch D 568, at p. 586.
68. *Oldendorff (EL) & Co GmbH* v. *Tradax Export SA (The Johanna Oldendorff)* [1973] 2 Lloyd's Rep 285, at p. 307.
69. See *ante* at para. 3.38.
70. *Tapscott* v. *Balfour* (1872) LR 8 CP 46. See also *Davies* v. *McVeagh* (1879) 4 Ex D 265.
71. *Tapscott* v. *Balfour* (1872) LR 8 CP 46.
72. *Leonis Steamship Co Ltd* v. *Joseph Rank (No 1)* (1907) 13 CC 136 (CA).
73. *Nelson* v. *Dahl* (1879) 12 Ch D 568. The case later went to the House of Lords and is reported under *Dahl* v. *Nelson, Donkin and others* (1880) 6 App Cas 38.
74. *Nelson* v. *Dahl* (1879) 12 Ch D 568, at p. 580.

3.73 Another slightly later case dealing with when the specified destination was reached in a port charter was *Pyman Brothers* v. *Dreyfus Brothers & Co.*[75] In that case, a ship was chartered to proceed to Odessa "or as near thereunto as she might safely get". At Odessa, there was an outer and inner harbour with quays in both harbours. The quays were the only places at which it was practicable to load cargo. The cargo for the *Lizzie English*, the ship concerned, was stored at a quay in the inner harbour and charterers' agents were unwilling to load it elsewhere. On arrival, the *Lizzie English* anchored in the outer harbour to await a berth in the inner harbour. Because of congestion, a berth did not become available until 17 days after her arrival when she was able to proceed into the inner harbour. Because of the crowded condition of the port, she could not have obtained a quay berth in either harbour earlier. Interestingly enough, there was also a finding that there was no custom of the port that a ship did not become an Arrived ship until moored alongside a quay.

3.74 On these facts, both the High Court and the arbitrator, before whom the matter was originally argued, held that the *Lizzie English* became an Arrived ship on arrival in the outer harbour. In his judgment, Mathew J said[76]:

Here the vessel arrived on December 22 at a point she was at the disposition of the charterers. They had only to indicate the place to which she was to go for her cargo, and she would have been there immediately.

3.75 In *Hulthen* v. *Stewart & Co*, a case which eventually reached the House of Lords,[77] the principal issue was whether the charter being considered was a customary or fixed laytime charter and on this all the courts were agreed that it was the former. However, both the judge at first instance and the Court of Appeal referred to when the vessel became an Arrived ship. The case concerned a steamship called the *Anton* which was to carry a cargo of timber to London. The ship arrived at Gravesend and was ordered to discharge in the Surrey Commercial Docks. Owing to congestion there was some delay before the ship could enter the docks, and, after entering, before she could obtain a berth alongside the quay. Evidence was given that about 98 per cent of the type of cargoes carried by the *Anton* were discharged in Surrey Commercial Docks with a small quantity of the remainder being discharged at different tiers in the river and the rest at other docks within the port. Discharge was either onto the quay or into lighters and it was proved that there was at the time of discharge nowhere else where the *Anton* could have been sent within the port where the cargo could have been unloaded quicker.

3.76 At first instance, Phillimore J asked[78]:

When was the *Anton* an arrived ship?

And answered:

In my opinion she was an arrived ship only when she reached a place at which she could discharge. Therefore when the vessel was at Gravesend, she had not arrived in London within the meaning of the charterparty, because it is not usual to discharge ships at Gravesend.

3.77 In the Court of Appeal, Collins MR said[79]:

---

75. *Pyman Brothers* v. *Dreyfus Brothers & Co* (1889) 24 QBD 152.
76. *Ibid.*, at p. 157.
77. *Hulthen* v. *Stewart & Co* (1903) 8 CC 297 (HL).
78. *Hulthen* v. *Stewart & Co* (1901) 6 CC 65, at p. 70.
79. *Hulthen* v. *Stewart & Co* (1902) 7 CC 139, at p. 147.

... this vessel got, we will assume, to the Surrey Commercial Docks gate, the place where 98 per cent of the timber cargoes are discharged. If there had been an absolute obligation to discharge, with named days, I think she would then have been in a position to say that she was an arrived ship and that her lay days must begin to count. But here we are not tied to a specific number of days: so that she is an arrived ship on the day after she got into the Port of London, then we have to consider whether, in these circumstances, she has been detained beyond a reasonable time.

3.78 In the later case of *Van Nievelt Goudriaan Stoomvaart Maatschappij* v. *C A Forslind & Son Ltd*, Atkin LJ commented[80] that in *Hulthen* v. *Stewart*, Phillimore J had found that the obligation upon the charterer to discharge[81] did not arise until the *Anton* had in fact got to her berth. However, arrival at the specified destination and arrival at the place where the charterer's obligation to load or discharge would not necessarily coincide in a charter with customary laytime since the risk of delay between arrival at the specified destination and reaching a point where loading and discharging could commence would in ordinary circumstances remain with the shipowner.

3.79 The evidence in *Hulthen* v. *Stewart*[82] was that the usual place of discharge for a vessel such as the *Anton* was in the Surrey Commercial Docks, either alongside a quay or into lighters. Therefore, it would seem that Phillimore J's definition of when she was an Arrived ship would have been met when she entered the dock.

3.80 Collins MR's statement as to when the *Anton* was an Arrived ship is more difficult to understand since he appears to be saying that there is a difference between when this happens in a customary laytime as opposed to a fixed laytime charter. Interestingly enough, neither point he selects appears to coincide with that chosen by Phillimore J. It may be that by getting to the dock gate, Collins MR meant after entering the dock gate, or it may be that he had in mind an argument which found favour with the Court of Appeal in *Nelson* v. *Dahl* where a distinction was drawn between entry into a privately controlled dock, such as the Surrey Commercial Docks, and arrival in the general area of a port. In that case, James LJ said[83]:

There is, in my mind, a marked and broad distinction between the port of discharge, the usual public place of discharge in that port, which it is the shipowner's business at all events and at his own risk to reach and the private quay, wharf or warehouse, or private dock, adjoining or near the port, on which or in which he is to co-operate with the merchant in the delivery of the cargo.

A little earlier in his judgment, he also said[84]:

In my opinion it is more reasonable to hold that the voyage, qua voyage, ends where the public highway ends, and that everything afterwards is part of the mutual and correlative obligations of the shipowner and merchant ...

3.81 It must be remembered that when the *Anton* was an Arrived ship was not directly in issue in *Hulthen* v. *Stewart*, but what the case does show is that even in the first part of the first decade of this century it was by no means decided when the specified destination was reached in a port charter. This question, however, arose for direct decision

---

80. *Van Nievelt Goudriaan Stoomvaart Maatschappij* v. *C A Forslind & Son Ltd* (1925) 22 Ll L Rep 49, at p. 52.
81. Atkin LJ actually referred to the obligation to load, but this was presumably a misstatement since the dispute only concerned discharge.
82. *Hulthen* v. *Stewart & Co* (1901) 6 CC 65.
83. *Nelson* v. *Dahl* (1879) 12 Ch D 568, at pp. 603–604.
84. *Ibid.*, at p. 603.

in *Leonis Steamship Co* v. *Rank (No 1)*[85] where the controversy as to whether a vessel under port charter had to reach a place where it could load or discharge before reaching its specified destination was finally settled. The answer given by the Court of Appeal, that it was not so necessary, is also the start point of further disagreement as to where within the port limits a vessel must be to have arrived at its specified destination.

3.82 The facts of the case were straightforward and not in dispute. Under a voyage charter, the steamship *Leonis* was ordered to Bahia Blanca in the River Parana to load. On arrival, she was unable to go alongside the railway pier, the designated loading place, as all berths were full. She therefore anchored some three ship lengths off the pier to await a berth, which did not become available for a month. The charter provided for specified laytime to commence 12 hours after written notice was given that she had reached her destination. At first instance,[86] Channell J held that the place where she anchored was a possible loading place, but not the usual one and on that basis found that laytime did not commence until arrival in berth. This was unanimously reversed by the Court of Appeal[87] who decided laytime commenced 12 hours after notice of readiness had been given by the master on anchoring off the pier on arrival within the port.

3.83 In the Court of Appeal, judgments were given by Buckley and Kennedy LJJ. Lord Alverstone CJ, who presided, concurred in both. In *The Johanna Oldendorff*, Lord Reid said of the judgments given in *The Leonis* case[88]:

It has always been held that the Court of Appeal in *Leonis* laid down general principles which must be followed: The difficulty has been to find out what those principles are. Buckley and Kennedy LJJ each delivered long judgments and Lord Alverstone CJ agreed with both. So he must have thought that there was no substantial difference between them. And that has been the view of almost all the many judges who have since then had to consider the matter. The judgment of Kennedy LJ has generally been regarded as the leading judgment, perhaps because it is rather less obscure than that of Buckley LJ. The charterers in this case invited us to concentrate on the judgment of Buckley LJ. I would agree that it is capable of being read as being more favourable to the charterers than that of Kennedy LJ. But I am far from being satisfied that it ought to be so read, and I would adopt the general view hitherto held that there is no substantial difference between them.

Both judges reviewed the existing authorities in detail. In the course of his judgment, Buckley LJ said[89]:

The true proposition, I think, is that, where the charter is to discharge in a named place which is a large area in some part or in several parts of which the ship can discharge, the laydays commence so soon as the shipowner has placed the ship at the disposal of the charterer in that named place as a ship ready, so far as she is concerned, to discharge, notwithstanding that the charterer has not named, or has been unable owing to the crowded state of the port to name, a berth at which, in fact, the discharge can take place.

3.84 He then explained that in the term "berth" he included "a berth or a wharf or a quay, or a place where by the use of lighters or other means a vessel can load or discharge". Later in his judgment,[90] Buckley LJ referred to the commercial ambit of the port, as distinguished from the whole port in a geographical or maritime sense, and said

85. *Leonis Steamship Co Ltd* v. *Joseph Rank (No 1)* (1906) 12 CC 173, (1907) 13 CC 136 (CA).
86. *Leonis Steamship Co Ltd* v. *Joseph Rank (No 1)* (1906) 12 CC 173.
87. *Leonis Steamship Co Ltd* v. *Joseph Rank (No 1)* (1907) 13 CC 136 (CA).
88. *Oldendorff (EL) & Co GmbH* v. *Tradax Export SA (The Johanna Oldendorff)* [1973] 2 Lloyd's Rep 285, at p. 288.
89. *Leonis Steamship Co Ltd* v. *Joseph Rank (No 1)* (1907) 13 CC 136, at p. 144.
90. *Ibid.*, at p. 146.

that this covered "such part of the port as is a proper place for discharging". He emphasized that this was an area of the port and not just a berth. Arrival in the commercial ambit of the port meant the end of the voyage.

3.85 Earlier, Buckley LJ pointed out that in a dock charter, arrival in the dock meant the commencement of lay days. He continued[91]:

If this is so it is difficult to grasp any ground of principle differentiating a dock from that part of a port at which the ship would be as closely proximate to a berth as she would be in a dock. What logical difference can exist? The ship either is not or is an arrived ship when she has not reached a berth. If she is when the named place is a dock, why is she not when the named place is [a] port, and she is at a place as closely proximate to a berth as she would be in a dock?

3.86 It was these suggestions of geographical proximity between the berth and the point where the vessel can become an Arrived ship that were later to cause some difficulty.[92] It must be remembered, however, that in the case that was being considered, the *Leonis* had anchored very close to the pier and the court did not have to consider how far from the pier she could be and still be an Arrived ship—only whether she had to reach it.

3.87 In his judgment, Kennedy LJ also stressed the importance of establishing which part of a port could be considered to be the commercial area when he said[93]:

If, then, we find a charterparty naming a port simply and without further particularity or qualification, as the destination for the purpose of loading or unloading, we must construe it in regard to the arrival of the ship at that destination as meaning that port in its commercial sense—that is to say, as it would be understood by the persons engaged in shipping business and entering into the charterparty in regard to the arrival of the ship there for the purposes of the charterparty. In the case of a small port it may or may not mean the whole of the geographical port. In the case of a widely extended area, such as London, Liverpool, or Hull, it certainly means some area which is less than the geographical port, and which may, I think, not unfitly be called the commercial area.

Taking up the same theme later on, he said[94]:

. . . the commercial area of a port, arrival within which makes the ship an arrived ship, and as such entitled to give notice of readiness to load, and at the expiration of the notice to begin to count lay days, ought, I think, to be that area of the named port of destination on arrival within which the master can effectively place his ship at the disposal of the charterer, the vessel herself being then, so far as she is concerned, ready to load, and as near as circumstances permit to the actual loading spot.

At the end of his judgment, he commented[95]:

If as she then lay [off the pier] she was an arrived ship and at the charterers' disposal and ready to load it is, under such a charterparty as the charterparty of the *Leonis*, quite immaterial whether she was in a place in which the physical act of loading was possible or impossible.

3.88 In the *Leonis* case, the charter under consideration was a fixed laytime one and there is no mention in any of the judgments whether similar principles applied to customary laytime charters, although many of the cases cited were of this type. However,

---

91. *Ibid.*, at p. 145.
92. In *Agrimpex Hungarian Trading Co for Agricultural Products* v. *Sociedad Financiera de Bienes Raices SA (The Aello)* [1960] 1 Lloyd's Rep 623, reversed some 13 years later in *The Johanna Oldendorff* [1973] 2 Lloyd's Rep 285.
93. *Leonis Steamship Co Ltd* v. *Joseph Rank (No 1)* (1907) 13 CC 136, at p. 153.
94. *Ibid.*, at p. 155.
95. *Ibid.*, at p. 160.

in *Van Nievelt Goudriaan Stoomvaart Maatschappij* v. *C A Forslind & Son Ltd*, Bankes LJ said that in a claim for demurrage there were two questions to be answered[96]:

The first question is this: when did the vessel become an arrived ship?; and the second: having fixed the date when she became an arrived ship, does the charterparty provide for a discharge within a fixed number of days after the date of arrival, or for a discharge within a reasonable time after the date of arrival?

The order in which these questions are posed strongly suggests that, at least as far as Bankes LJ is concerned, there is no difference between when a vessel reaches its specified destination under a fixed laytime port charter and when it does under a customary laytime charter. Logically there would seem no reason why there should be any difference.

3.89 In *United States Shipping Board* v. *Strick & Co Ltd*,[97] the House of Lords approved the decision *Leonis Steamship Co* v. *Rank (No 1)*.[98] However, some 34 years later, the House again considered the *Leonis* decision in a case called *Agrimpex Hungarian Trading Co for Agricultural Products* v. *Sociedad Financiera de Bienes Raices SA (The Aello)*.[99] The facts of the case were somewhat unusual.

3.90 The *Aello*, the ship concerned, was under charter on a Centrocon form to carry maize to Hamburg. After loading a part cargo at Rosario, the vessel was ordered to complete at Buenos Aires. The usual waiting place for vessels arriving at that port was close to the loading berths, but owing to temporary congestion, the port authority decided a few weeks before the *Aello* arrived that ships waiting for a berth and cargo must in future wait near Intersection, some 22 miles or three hours' steaming from the loading berths. The decree introducing this restriction was intended to be a temporary one whilst the port was heavily congested, but it was still in force on the *Aello*'s arrival. The anchorage at Intersection was, however, within the limits of the port of Buenos Aires.

3.91 On these facts, Ashworth J, the Court of Appeal and a majority in the House of Lords decided that the *Aello* was not an Arrived ship whilst she was at the anchorage.

3.92 In the Court of Appeal, the judgment of the court was given by Parker LJ, who took as his start point the judgment of Kennedy LJ in the *Leonis* case. Having said that Kennedy LJ had held that, to be an Arrived ship, a vessel must have reached the commercial area of the port and how that had been defined in the *Leonis* case, Parker LJ went on to say[100]:

In *Leonis Steamship Co Ltd* v. *Rank Ltd, supra*, the ship in question was not 22 miles away from the dock area—she was anchored but a few ship lengths off the pier alongside which loading took place. I agree, of course, that distance is not a conclusive factor, but what Kennedy LJ was, I think, contrasting throughout his judgment was an area where loading takes place as opposed to the actual loading spot. The commercial area was intended to be that part of the port where a ship can be loaded when a berth is available.

3.93 This requirement that to be an Arrived ship the vessel must be in an area where loading or discharging takes place became known as "the Parker test". When the case

---

96. *Van Nievelt Goudriaan Stoomvaart Maatschappij* v. *C A Forslind & Son Ltd* (1925) 22 Ll L Rep 49, at p. 50.
97. *United States Shipping Board* v. *Strick & Co Ltd* (1926) 25 Ll L Rep 73.
98. *Leonis Steamship Co Ltd* v. *Joseph Rank (No 1)* (1907) 13 CC 136.
99. *Agrimpex Hungarian Trading Co for Agricultural Products* v. *Sociedad Financiera de Bienes Raices SA (The Aello)* [1957] 2 Lloyd's Rep 423, [1958] 2 Lloyd's Rep 65 (CA), [1960] 1 Lloyd's Rep 623 (HL).
100. *The Aello* [1958] 2 Lloyd's Rep 65, at p. 77.

came before the House of Lords, the majority accepted the interpretation Parker LJ had put on the *Leonis* test. Lord Jenkins also added[101]:

The judgments (in the *Leonis* case), as I think, clearly postulate as the "commercial area" a physical area capable (though no doubt only within broad limits) of identification on a map. When the given ship enters that area and positions herself within it in accordance with the requirements just stated she is (in point of geographical position) an arrived ship.

3.94 Lord Morris apparently envisaged that the limits of the commercial area should be in close geographical proximity to the cargo berths, for he said that a ship may become an Arrived ship[102]:

. . . even if she is at anchor at a place where the charterer does not intend to load her, or even could not load her provided that the place bears a relationship to the actual or probable loading spot comparable with that which would exist between presence in a dock and presence at a particular berth in a dock . . .

3.95 Lords Radcliffe and Cohen dissented. Lord Radcliffe said he regarded the Parker test as[103]:

. . . altogether too imprecise as a general guide for identifying the relevant area: it is also in my opinion a misunderstanding of the true significance of the *Leonis* v. *Rank* decision to seek to treat "the commercial area" for the purposes of any particular charterparty as if it were a fixed area of defined geographical limits which the ship must be treated as reaching or failing to reach without regard to the actual circumstances that prevailed at the time when the obligations of the particular voyage matured.

Presumably by this Lord Radcliffe had in mind that the limits of the commercial area might vary from time to time, for instance where, as with *The Aello*, a temporary limitation was introduced by the port authorities against proceeding further.

3.96 The difficulties of implementing the Parker test became apparent in the years that followed the decision, about which Roskill LJ said in the Court of Appeal in *The Johanna Oldendorff*[104]:

. . . It is now over 12 years since *The Aello* was finally decided. It is widely known that it was not a popular decision either in St Mary Axe or in the Temple. It is also widely known that its application has from time to time caused difficulty not only to brokers but also to arbitrators and umpires and indeed to judges . . .

3.97 In the same case, of the Parker test itself, Lord Reid said[105]:

Although Kennedy LJ clearly based his judgment on what he thought was commercial good sense, I do not find the judgment of Parker LJ any consideration of that matter.

3.98 An interesting illustration of the sort of difficulties that could arise from the Parker test is provided by *Shipping Developments Corporation SA* v. *V/O Sojuzneftexport (The Delian Spirit)*.[106] In this case, the *Delian Spirit* was ordered to load a cargo of crude oil

---

101. *Agrimpex Hungarian Trading Co for Agricultural Products* v. *Sociedad Financiera de Bienes Raices SA (The Aello)* [1960] 1 Lloyd's Rep 623, at p. 660.
102. *Ibid.*, at p. 664.
103. *Ibid.*, at p. 638.
104. *The Johanna Oldendorff* [1972] 2 Lloyd's Rep 292, at p. 311.
105. *The Johanna Oldendorff* [1973] 2 Lloyd's Rep 285, at p. 289.
106. *Shipping Developments Corporation SA* v. *V/O Sojuzneftexport (The Delian Spirit)* [1971] 1 Lloyd's Rep 64 (Donaldson J), [1971] 1 Lloyd's Rep 506 (CA).

at the Soviet Black Sea port of Tuapse. The charter was a port charter[107] and as all four berths in the harbour were occupied, she anchored in the roads outside the harbour some $1\frac{1}{4}$ miles from the berth. The anchorage was within the administrative, pilotage and fiscal limits of the port of Tuapse and the *Delian Spirit* lay at the anchorage for some five days before a berth became available. One of the issues raised was whether she was an Arrived ship at the anchorage. Donaldson J opened his judgment in the High Court to which the case had been referred from arbitration upon a case stated by saying[108]:

The argument upon this award in the form of a special case has a looking-glass quality which would have delighted Lewis Carroll, for the claimant shipowners have been busily contending that the motor tanker *Delian Spirit* was not an arrived ship before she berthed at Tuapse, whereas the charterers contend that she became an arrived ship several days earlier when she anchored in the roads. Alas, this is not a practical expression of the spirit of Christmas but a belief on the part of the shipowners that they will recover more by way of damages for the detention of the vessel than by way of demurrage . . .

3.99 On the question of whether the *Delian Spirit* was an Arrived ship, the judge carefully avoided the Parker test, saying[109]:

Here, say the owners, the berth was in the harbour, whereas the vessel lay in the roads, which is manifestly a different part of the port. I agree that physically this is so. Nevertheless, I do not think that either Lord Parker or the House of Lords had in mind a small port such as Tuapse. What they had in mind was a large port, such as London, in which there are many ports each bigger than Tuapse, and the port in effect consists of separate ports within a larger port. In my judgment, the vessel when in the roads lay within the commercial area of the port of Tuapse.

3.100 The Court of Appeal agreed (on this point).[110] However, in *The Johanna Oldendorff*, Viscount Dilhorne described the decision as "bold"[111] and said that the interpretation put on the *Leonis* case[112] by the majority of the House of Lords in *The Aello*[113] was not applied. Therefore, by the Parker test, the case was wrongly decided. However, from a commercial as opposed to a strictly legal point of view, the decision was clearly right.

3.101 In view of the sustained criticism of the Parker test, the House of Lords agreed to reconsider the matter, which they did in *The Johanna Oldendorff*.[114] The question in that case was whether the *Johanna Oldendorff* was an Arrived ship on anchoring at the Mersey Bar, having been ordered to Liverpool/Birkenhead with a cargo of grain. The Mersey Bar anchorage was the usual waiting place for grain ships wishing to proceed upriver and was within the port limits. However, it was some 17 miles from the nearest discharging berth.

3.102 Nevertheless the House of Lords had no doubt that she was an Arrived ship and, furthermore, that the Parker test was wrong, having put an unjustifiable gloss on the

---

107. Although it also contained a "reachable on arrival" provision. On this aspect see *post* at para. 3.402.
108. *The Delian Spirit* [1971] 1 Lloyd's Rep 64, at p. 65.
109. *Ibid.*, at p. 69.
110. *The Delian Spirit* [1971] 1 Lloyd's Rep 506.
111. *The Johanna Oldendorff* [1973] 2 Lloyd's Rep 285, at p. 301.
112. *Leonis Steamship Co Ltd* v. *Joseph Rank (No 1)* (1907) 13 CC 136.
113. *Agrimpex Hungarian Trading Co for Agricultural Products* v. *Sociedad Financiera de Bienes Raices SA (The Aello)* [1960] 1 Lloyd's Rep 623.
114. *Oldendorff (EL) & Co GmbH* v. *Tradax Export SA (The Johanna Oldendorff)* [1973] 2 Lloyd's Rep 285.

Leonis case.[115] They therefore substituted what has become known as the "Reid test", summarized in this passage from Lord Reid's speech[116]:

Before a ship can be said to have arrived at a port she must, if she cannot proceed immediately to a berth, have reached a position within the port where she is at the immediate and effective disposition of the charterer. If she is at a place where waiting ships usually lie, she will be in such a position unless in some extraordinary circumstances, proof of which would lie in the charterer. For as Mr Justice Donaldson [1971] 2 Lloyd's Rep 96, at p. 100, points out:

> " . . . In this context a delay of two or three hours between the nomination of a berth and the ship reaching it is wholly immaterial because there will be at least this much notice before the berth becomes free . . . "

If the ship is waiting at some other place in the port then it will be for the owner to prove that she is as fully at the disposition of the charterer as she would have been if in the vicinity of the berth for loading or discharge.

3.103 The reason why the area of a port where a vessel can be considered to be an Arrived ship is so much larger today than it was at the turn of the century was discussed by Lord Diplock. Having said that the requirements of a waiting area within the port are that the ships there should count for a berth in order of arrival, that the charterer should be able to communicate with them, and that there should be no significant delay in their moving into berth when one becomes free, his Lordship continued[117]:

The waiting places within the limits of an extensive port which have these characteristics alter as ships become more manoeuvrable, faster or larger, and communications between ship and shore improve . . .

In days of sailing ships close proximity to berths likely to become vacant may have been necessary in order that a place should possess those characteristics, but distance from the actual berth becomes of less importance as steam and diesel power replaces sail and instantaneous radio communication is available between ship and shore.

3.104 In his speech, Viscount Dilhorne summarized the state of the law as follows[118]:

(1) That under a port charterparty to be an arrived ship, that is to say a ship at a place where a valid notice of readiness to load or discharge can be given, she must have ended her voyage at the port named.

(2) The port named in the charterparty must be given the meaning which those persons using it as a port, shippers of goods, charterers of vessels and shipowners, would give it.

(3) The physical limits of a port afford no reliable guide, for the physical limits, as indeed the pilotage limits, may extend far beyond the limits of what those using it would regard as the port.

(4) The area of some ports may be defined by law . . .

(5) A vessel has not reached her port of destination until it has ended its voyage within the port, either in its legal, or, if it differs, in its commercial sense. If it is refused permission and ordered to wait outside the port by the port authority it is not an "arrived ship".

(6) If it is within the port in its legal sense it does not follow that it is within the port in its commercial sense.

(7) Brett MR's definition in *Steamship Garston Co* v. *Hickie & Co (supra)*[119] and his reference to port discipline may be useful in determining what are the limits of the port in its legal sense but

---

115. *Leonis Steamship Co Ltd* v. *Joseph Rank (No 1)* (1907) 13 CC 136.

116. *The Johanna Oldendorff* [1973] 2 Lloyd's Rep 285, at p. 291.

117. *Ibid.*, at p. 307.

118. *Oldendorff (EL) & Co GmbH* v. *Tradax Export SA (The Johanna Oldendorff)* [1973] 2 Lloyd's Rep 285, at p. 302.

119. *The Sailing* (not *Steamship* as stated by Viscount Dilhorne) *Ship Garston Co* v. *Hickie & Co* (1885) 15 QBD 580, at p. 590.

port disciplining may be exercised and submitted to over a wider area than the port in its commercial sense.

(8) Under a port charterparty a vessel has arrived when
    (i) if it can proceed directly to a berth or dock, it has arrived there and
    (ii) if it cannot do so, it has reached that part of the port in which vessels waiting to load or discharge cargo usually lie before moving directly to a dock or berth. At that part of the port she can be effectively placed at the charterer's disposal for loading or unloading and that part of the port is to be regarded as part of the port in its commercial sense.

(9) If within the port though not for some reason at the usual waiting place, a ship may still be an "arrived ship" if, at the place where she is, she can be effectively placed at the disposal of the charterers.

(10) The "usual place" may be changed by a port authority or by a regulation. If, for some reason due to the conditions of the port and not of the ship, a vessel wishing to wait at the usual waiting place is ordered to lie elsewhere by the port authority, I think, though the question does not arise for decision in this case, that she ought to be regarded as an arrived ship.

3.105 In *Federal Commerce & Navigation Co Ltd* v. *Tradax Export SA (The Maratha Envoy)*,[120] an attempt was made unsuccessfully to widen the guidelines set out above so that a vessel anchored at the usual waiting place would always be considered an Arrived ship under a port charter, whether the waiting place was inside or outside the port limits. This approach was firmly rejected by the House of Lords.

3.106 In that case, the *Maratha Envoy* was ordered to Bremen after lightening at Brake on the River Weser. The dispute concerned whether she was an Arrived ship for Brake when she anchored at the Weser lightship, which was the usual waiting area for the four Weser ports but outside the port limits of Brake. Whilst waiting at the anchorage, she moved upriver to Brake on the flood tide, turned in the river off the port of Brake and went back to the anchorage, as anchoring in the river in or near the area of the port was forbidden. The manoeuvre was said by Lord Diplock to have been variously described as "showing her chimney", "a charade" and "a voyage of convenience".[121] The reason given by Donaldson J[122] at first instance why a voyage of convenience did not serve to make the *Maratha Envoy* an Arrived ship at the port of Brake was that the essential feature of an Arrived ship was that the voyage should have ended and the vessel be waiting. This never happened in the case of the *Maratha Envoy*.

3.107 In the Court of Appeal,[123] it was suggested for the first time that arrival at the Weser lightship was itself arrival at the port of Brake, although some 25 miles separated them and the lightship anchorage was outside the legal, fiscal and administrative limits of the port. This suggestion found favour with a majority of the court,[124] who were prepared to regard the rationale of the test laid down in *The Johanna Oldendorff*[125] as based exclusively upon the vessel being "as effectively at the disposal of the charterer for loading or discharging while at that waiting place as she would have been if waiting in the immediate vicinity of the berth". Whilst conceding that this approach might have much to be said for it if the chartering of ships was a recent innovation instead of one of the earliest forms of commercial contract, nevertheless the House of Lords rejected it. The

120. *Federal Commerce & Navigation Co Ltd* v. *Tradax Export SA (The Maratha Envoy)* [1977] 2 Lloyd's Rep 301.
121. *Ibid.*, at p. 306.
122. *The Maratha Envoy* [1975] 2 Lloyd's Rep 223.
123. *The Maratha Envoy* [1977] 1 Lloyd's Rep 217 (CA).
124. Lord Denning MR and Shaw LJ.
125. *The Johanna Oldendorff* [1973] 2 Lloyd's Rep 285, at p. 291.

views of the House were given by Lord Diplock, who said[126] that whilst, until *The Johanna Oldendorff*, there might have been uncertainty under a port charter as to where within the named port a ship must be in order to complete the voyage stage, there was legal certainty that neither in port nor berth charter was the voyage stage brought to an end by the arrival of the ship at any waiting place short of the limits of the named port. He continued[127]:

Where charterers and shipowners as part of their bargain have desired to alter the allocation of the risk of delay from congestion at the named port which would otherwise follow from the basic nature of their contract, they have not sought to do so by undermining whatever legal certainty had been attained as to when a voyage stage ends. Instead they have achieved the same result without altering the basic nature of the contract, by inserting additional clauses to provide that time should begin to run for the purposes of laytime or demurrage if, although the voyage stage is not yet ended, the ship is compelled to wait at some place outside the named port of destination until a berth falls vacant in that port.

3.108 An interesting illustration of some of the criteria set by Viscount Dilhorne in *The Johanna Oldendorff*[128] is provided by London Arbitration 5/90.[129] Here, the ship in question was ordered to Haldia in India which, although a separate port, came under the aegis of the Calcutta Port Trust. Notice of Readiness was given by the vessel on arrival at the Sandheads anchorage, some two hours' steaming from Haldia, in accordance with commercial practice. Sandheads[130] was, however, outside the legal limits of the jurisdiction of the Calcutta Port Trust, although they exercised *de facto* control of the anchorage, giving orders as to anchoring and arranging pilots. This, the arbitrator held, was sufficient and she was an Arrived ship.

3.109 A slightly different question arose in London Arbitration 17/97.[131] The vessel concerned was chartered on a berth charter and was carrying a number of different parcels of cargo for different shippers/charterers. On arrival at the discharge port, she berthed at a berth where the cargo could have been discharged. On berthing, notice of readiness was given. However the following morning the ship shifted to another berth where the cargo was actually discharged. The charterers submitted that the shift had been arranged by or on behalf of the owners to suit the convenience of other cargo and therefore claimed the vessel was not effectively at their disposal until arrival in the second berth. Whilst the tribunal had some sympathy with the charterers, they pointed out that the charter had a WIBON provision and that shifting time was expressly excluded, which clearly envisaged that notice could be tendered before the vessel reached the discharging berth. Although the charter made no provision for shifting berths, the tribunal held that there was no basis upon which the shifting of the vessel could invalidate a previously valid Notice of Readiness.

126. *The Maratha Envoy* [1977] 2 Lloyd's Rep 301, at p. 308.
127. *Ibid.*
128. *Oldendorff (EL) & Co GmbH* v. *Tradax Export SA (The Johanna Oldendorff)* [1973] 2 Lloyd's Rep 285 at p. 291. See *ante* at para. 3.104.
129. London Arbitration 5/90—LMLN 274, 5 May 1990.
130. Charters with the Indian Government where discharge at Calcutta is a possibility often contain a so-called "Sandheads" clause covering tendering of NOR on arrival at Sandheads. In *Mosvolds Rederi A/S* v. *Food Corporation of India (The Damodar General T J Park and King Theras)* [1986] 2 Lloyd's Rep 68, Steyn J was prepared to imply a provision into a Sandheads clause allowing NOR to be given at Saugor, some 40 miles closer to Calcutta.
131. London Arbitration 17/97—LMLN 471, 22 November 1997.

3.110 A different sort of challenge as to what was meant by "at the immediate and effective disposition of the charterer" was made in *The Kyzikos*,[132] based not on the geographical position of the vessel, but on its inability to get into berth because of weather.

3.111 On arrival at Houston the vessel anchored because of fog. She made a second attempt to get into berth, but was again forced to anchor. In the High Court, having held that a WIBON provision did not protect owners against delay due to weather, Webster J said[133]:

Finally, even if contrary to my conclusion the "Wibon" provision has the effect of converting a berth charter to a port charter, I would conclude that the vessel was an arrived ship at the port within the meaning of Lord Reid's test in *The Johanna Oldendorff*, until she left her second anchorage there, because she was not until that time "at the immediate and effective disposition of the charterers", even though, as the arbitrator found, she was not being used for the owners' purpose.

3.112 Commenting on this in the Court of Appeal, Lloyd LJ said[134]:

I do not believe that the Reid test was intended to introduce a new factor into the equation. It is true that Lord Reid speaks of a vessel's geographical position being of secondary importance. But it is still a position which he has in mind. If she is in the place where waiting ships usually lie, then she will normally be in that position. In exceptional or extraordinary cases, the proof of which would lie on the charterers, she may be required to be at some other place. But nothing in Lord Reid's speech suggests that if she is where waiting ships usually lie she may, nevertheless, not be at the immediate and effective disposition of the charterers because of the weather.

3.113 The case subsequently went to the House of Lords, which restored the judgment of the High Court on the WIBON point, which had been reversed by the Court of Appeal, but the House of Lords did not consider it necessary to consider the point of whether weather could affect whether the vessel was "at the immediate and effective disposition of the charterers". The law as it stands is that therefore declared by the Court of Appeal, namely that weather does not affect the readiness of the vessel.

READINESS TO LOAD AND DISCHARGE

3.114 When the vessel has arrived at the specified destination, whether in order to load or to discharge, she must then meet the second requirement necessary for the commencement of laytime. She must, so far as she is concerned, be in all respects ready for loading or discharge.

3.115 Whilst the vessel must be ready in all respects, nevertheless in, *Gill & Duffus SA v. Rionda Futures Ltd*,[135] Clarke J held that the shipowners' exercise of a lien, in that case for general average, provided it was both lawful and reasonable, did not prevent the vessel being ready and a valid Notice of Readiness (NOR) could be tendered.

In the case of loading, this means that she must be ready in all her holds so as to give the charterers complete control of every part of the ship in which cargo is to be loaded and

---

132. *Seacrystal Shipping Ltd v. Bulk Transport Group Shipping Co Ltd (The Kyzikos)* [1987] 1 Lloyd's Rep 48; [1987] 2 Lloyd's Rep 122; [1989] 1 Lloyd's Rep 1.
133. *The Kyzikos* [1987] 1 Lloyd's Rep 48, at p. 57.
134. *The Kyzikos* [1987] 2 Lloyd's Rep 122, at p. 127.
135. *Gill & Duffus SA v. Rionda Futures Ltd* [1994] 2 Lloyd's Rep 67.

must also be properly equipped and ready for the reception of cargo. Similarly, the ship must have obtained all papers and permits necessary for loading.

3.116 It is not, however, necessary that the ship should be in all respects ready to sail before Notice of Readiness to load can be given. It will suffice if she is in a condition in which the cargo can be safely received and expects to be ready to sail on completion of loading. For example, some repairs to the engines may be needed and provided these would not interrupt loading and are expected to be completed during loading, then the ship may still be in a state of readiness to load.

3.117 At the port of discharge, the vessel must be ready to discharge before laytime can commence. As Diplock J said in *The Massalia (No 2)*[136]:

It seems to me common sense that the same principle as regards availability of holds would apply to discharging as to loading . . .

Equally the same principles on legal readiness apply to discharging as they do to loading.

3.118 It is usual to consider the physical and legal aspects of readiness separately and this approach will also be followed here.

Physical readiness

3.119 In *Groves, Maclean & Co* v. *Volkart Brothers*, Lopes J said[137]:

A ship to be ready to load must be completely ready in all her holds . . . so as to afford the merchant/charterer complete control of every portion of the ship available for cargo.

3.120 In a similar vein, in *Weir* v. *Union SS Co Ltd*, Lord Davey commented[138]:

. . . you must read such expressions as "with clear holds" or "the whole reach or burthen of the vessel" as meaning the full space of the vessel proper to be filled with cargo . . .

3.121 Which parts of the ship can be considered to be those which should be available for cargo was one of the issues raised in *Noemijulia Steamship Co Ltd* v. *Minister of Food*.[139]

3.122 On arrival at Buenos Aires to load a cargo of grain, the charterers found that No 3 hold (both 'tween deck and lower holds) contained bunker coal. The charter, which was on the Centrocon form, provided, *inter alia*, for the charterers "to have the full reach and burthen of the steamer including 'tween and shelter decks, bridges, poop, etc. (provided same are not occupied by bunker coals and/or stores)". The charterers rejected the Notice of Readiness tendered by the vessel on four different grounds and purported to cancel the charter. One of their arguments was that they were entitled to do so because of the presence of bunker coal in No 3 lower hold, the proviso they said applying only to No 3 'tween deck. This argument was rejected by the Court of Appeal, who pointed out that both No 3 'tween deck and lower hold were designated as reserve bunker spaces. Furthermore, both spaces would reasonably have been needed for bunkers for the voyage.

---

136. *Government of Ceylon* v. *Société Franco-Tunisienne d'Armement-Tunis (The Massalia (No 2))* [1960] 2 Lloyd's Rep 352, at p. 357.
137. *Groves, Maclean & Co* v. *Volkart Brothers* (1885) 1 TLR 454.
138. *Weir* v. *Union Steamship Co Ltd* [1900] AC 525, at p. 532.
139. *Noemijulia Steamship Co Ltd* v. *Minister of Food* (1950) 84 Ll L Rep 354.

The presence of coal did not therefore mean that the "full reach and burthen" of the steamer had not been made available to the charterers.

3.123 One exception that certainly used to exist to the rule that all inward cargo must have been discharged before a ship could be considered ready to load outward cargo arose because sailing ships empty of both cargo and ballast were relatively unstable. Thus, it was normal for sailing ships, as they discharged, to take on board sufficient new cargo or ballast to keep the vessel upright and stable on completion of discharge. This new cargo or ballast could only be stowed in the holds since there was nowhere else. In *Sailing Ship Lyderhorn Co.* v. *Duncan, Fox & Co*, Cozens Hardy MR said[140]:

I think that the authorities really decide that a vessel is not ready to load unless she is discharged and ready in all her holds so as to give the charterers complete control of every portion of the ship available for cargo, except so much as is reasonably required to keep her upright.

3.124 Although most modern tankers have segregated ballast tanks, it was not uncommon until comparatively recently for tankers to use their cargo tanks to carry ballast on the non-carrying voyage. However, the presence of ballast in the cargo tanks did not prevent Notice of Readiness being tendered at the load port, although it was and is common for most tanker charters to exclude from laytime time spent in deballasting.

3.125 This exception apart, the holds must be clear and available. The reason why was explained by Kennedy LJ in the *Sailing Ship Lyderhorn* case as follows[141]:

... it is impossible to say that a ship is at the disposal of the shipper who is to load her when there is still in the ship's holds a quantity of cargo for a consignee who is engaged in discharging. It is impossible to suppose that the thing can be done without friction and without arrangement between two persons who have no connexion with one another, the receiver of the inward cargo and the loader of the outward cargo.

3.126 It may have been the possibility of a special arrangement being made that Phillimore LJ had in mind when in *London Traders Shipping Co Ltd* v. *General Mercantile Shipping Co Ltd*, he said[142]:

... the decision of the court must not be deemed to whittle down the general duty of the shipowner to have all outward cargo discharged when he presented his vessel to receive the homeward cargo, unless in special circumstances, or when dealing with a particular cargo the loading and unloading could continue simultaneously.

3.127 In that case, a large quantity of coal from the previous voyage was stored on deck because the shipowner had purchased it as bunkers for the homeward voyage. This did not, held the Court of Appeal, prevent the vessel from being ready to load maize, for although it had been cargo it was not at the relevant time.[143]

3.128 The importance of the holds being ready at the time Notice of Readiness is presented was stressed by the Court of Appeal in *The Tres Flores*, where Roskill LJ said[144]:

---

140. *Sailing Ship Lyderhorn Co* v. *Duncan, Fox & Co* (1909) 14 CC 293, at p. 297.
141. *Ibid.*, at p. 300.
142. *London Traders Shipping Co Ltd* v. *General Mercantile Shipping Co Ltd* (1914) 30 TLR 493, at p. 494.
143. In London Arbitration 9/90—LMLN 285, 6 October 1990, the arbitrators held that NOR could be given whilst the vessel was being used as floating storage for the same cargo for the same charterer.
144. *Compania de Naviera Nedelka SA* v. *Tradax International SA (The Tres Flores)* [1973] 2 Lloyd's Rep 247, at p. 251.

... it has long been accepted in this branch of the law that a vessel which presents herself at a loading port must be in a position to give the charterer unrestricted access to all her cargo spaces before she can give a valid notice of readiness. This state of readiness must be unqualified. It is not open to the shipowner to say: "Here is my ship; she is not quite ready yet but I confidently expect to be able to make her ready by such time as I consider it likely that you will in fact need her." The charterer has contracted for the exclusive and unrestricted use of the whole of the vessel's available cargo space, and he is entitled to expect that that space will be placed at his disposal before he can be called upon to accept the vessel as having arrived and thereafter being at his risk and expense as regards time.

3.129 In the same case, Lord Denning put forward a similar view[145]:

One thing is clear. In order for a notice of readiness to be good, the vessel must be ready at the time that the notice is given, and not at a time in the future. Readiness is a preliminary existing fact which must exist before you can give a notice of readiness ...

and a little later on, he continued[146]:

In order to be a good notice of readiness, the master must be in a position to say: "I am ready at the moment you want me, whenever that may be, and any necessary preliminaries on my part to the loading will not be such as to delay you." Applying this test it is apparent that notice of readiness can be given even though there are some further preliminaries to be done, or routine matters to be carried on, or formalities observed. If those things are not such as to give any reason to suppose that they will cause any delay, and it is apparent that the ship will be ready when the appropriate time arrives, then notice of readiness can be given.

3.130 However it was held in London Arbitration 27/92[147] that a valid Notice of Readiness might be given where the vessel had slops of previous cargo on board where the charterers had previously evinced an intention to load at a second load port and the tank in which the slops were held was not originally required but only required after the charterers changed their minds and wished to load two parcels at the first load port.

3.131 The dispute in *The Tres Flores* arose because when the vessel's holds were inspected by the port authorities prior to loading a cargo of maize, they were found to be infested. As a result, the port authorities ordered the fumigation of the vessel and it was not until this was completed that the courts held that she was ready.

3.132 In the *Tres Flores* case, there was an additional clause which provided that: "Before tendering notice Master has to take necessary measures for holds to be clean, dry, without smell and in every way suitable to receive grain to Shippers'/Charterers' satisfaction." This was said by the Court of Appeal[148] to provide a condition precedent to the validity of a Notice of Readiness to load. The presence of pests requiring the holds to be fumigated was a breach of both this specific clause and the shipowners' common law duty with regard to the condition of the holds. However, a distinction must be drawn between infestation prior to loading and infestation discovered after loading, but prior to discharge. In the absence of evidence to the contrary, such infestation is likely to have been brought on board with the cargo and would affect only the readiness of the cargo to be discharged, not the readiness of the vessel to discharge that cargo.[149]

---

145. *Ibid.*, at p. 249.
146. *Ibid.*
147. London Arbitration 27/92—LMLN 337, 3 October 1992.
148. [1973] 2 Lloyd's Rep 247, at p. 249 *per* Lord Denning MR.
149. *Eurico SpA* v. *Philipp Brothers* (*The Epaphus*) [1986] 2 Lloyd's Rep 387, at p. 393; [1987] 2 Lloyd's Rep 215, at p. 220.

3.133 If there is no such specific clause relating to the condition of the holds, then the degree of cleanliness necessary will be a question of fact to be determined according to the practice of the particular trade and the degree of particularity of cargo agreed between the parties. In other words, the wider the range of cargoes which could lawfully be carried under a particular charter, the more general becomes the shipowner's responsibility as to the degree of cleanliness required. If the holds are damp after being cleaned and the cargo is likely to be damaged by being put into those holds in their then condition then the ship is not ready to load.

3.134 However if the commodity to be carried is not described in detail, then it would seem the shipowner has to prepare the vessel to carry any cargo which comes within that description. This is illustrated by London Arbitration 12/96.[150] Here a charter was concluded by an exchange of telexes. In the first, which was described as a "Recap Agreement", the cargo was described as "full and complete bulk rice". The last two lines of the recap provided that the fixture was to be based on a stated earlier charter "logically amended". The response lifting subjects referred to the mainterms previously agreed and Charterparty details to be based on the earlier charter, logically amended.

3.135 The actual dispute was as to whether the charterers were entitled to cancel the charter because the ship was not ready to load edible milled rice by the cancelling date.

3.136 Whilst most of the case centred on the meaning of the broking terms involved and whether a reference to edible milled rice in the earlier charter should be removed, the end result was that the tribunal held that the standard of cleanliness required was to load any rice cargo and not, as the owners argued, to a lower standard which they equated to grain standard.

3.137 In one American case,[151] where the charter emphasised that the holds were to be cleaned to the satisfaction of the charterers (the US Government), it was held that the only limitation that should be imposed was that they should act in good faith. It was not appropriate to impose an objective reasonable standard.

3.138 One factor that may be taken into account in determining the amount of cleaning that could reasonably be expected is the time scale known to both parties between discharge of one cargo and loading the next. An illustration of this is provided by a London Arbitration Award described in *Lloyd's Maritime Law Newsletter*,[152] where the relevant charter stated that there was expected to be some three days "all going well" between completion of discharge at one port and arrival at the next ready to load. It also provided that the owners should "instruct the Master to thoroughly wash the holds and hatches during the ballast voyage to loadport so as to be clean on arrival". This the crew did. The charter was to load a cargo of heavy grain, sorghum or soyas and on arrival the vessel was inspected, *inter alia*, by a USDA surveyor who rejected the vessel on account of paint and rust scale. After further cleaning by shore contractors the vessel was accepted. The charterers claimed that had the vessel met the required standard on arrival then she would have berthed without delay and they calculated a balance of despatch on this basis. However, this was rejected by the arbitrators, who said they could not interpret the charter

---

150. London Arbitration 12/96—LMLN 445, 23 November 1996.
151. *Misano Di Navigazione SpA* v. *United States of America (The Mare del Nord)* US Ct of App (2nd Cir), LMLN 335, 5 September 1992.
152. LMLN 62, 18 March 1982 but see London Arbitration 10/96—LMLN 435, 6 July 1996, where only the owners were aware of the scale of the cleaning problem.

as requiring the owners to have all paint and rust scale removed from the holds in the short period known to be available. The owners had simply undertaken to make the holds clean, which they had done.

3.139 London Arbitration 7/88[153] concerned a vessel which had purported to give Notice of Readiness whilst still Butterworthing her tanks. The arbitrators, however, found that the ship was not ready to load for the purposes of giving a valid Notice of Readiness until her tanks had been cleaned and the water and crude slops collected into separate tanks.

3.140 In the parcel tanker trade, where the risk of contamination is clearly much greater, it is common for the parties to agree in more detail what standard of cleanliness is required. Thus, Part II of the Bimchemvoy charter[154] contains the following clauses relating to the condition of the tanks on loading:

1. Condition of Vessel

. . . The Owners shall
(a) before and at the beginning of the loaded voyage exercise due diligence to make the Vessel seaworthy and in every way fit for the voyage, with her tanks, valves, pumps and pipelines tight, staunch, strong and in good order and condition . . .

2. Last Cargo

Last cargo(es) as stated in Box 11 but the last cargo carried shall, to the best of Owners' knowledge, not be harmful to the carriage of the contracted cargo.

8. Inspection of Cargo Tanks

Charterers' inspection of tanks, pipes and pumps nominated for the contracted cargo as specified in Box 21 to take place as soon as possible after Vessel tenders notice but latest on Vessel's arrival at loading berth, otherwise any time lost shall count as laytime.

9. Cleaning

Owners shall clean Vessel's tanks pipes and pumps at their expense and in their time and unless the Master certifies that Vessel's coils have been tested and found tight, shall test tightness of coils at their expense and in their time to the satisfaction of Charterers' inspector.

If, in Owners' opinion, acceptance of the tanks and/or coils is unreasonably withheld, then an independent inspector shall be appointed whose decision shall be final. If the independent inspector considers that the tanks are insufficiently clean to receive the cargo, then they shall be further cleaned at Owners' expense and time to the satisfaction of the independent inspector whose fees and expenses shall be paid by the Owners. If the independent inspector considers that the tanks are sufficiently clean to receive the cargo his fees and expenses plus any loss of time and expense incurred by Owners shall be borne by Charterers.

Upon acceptance of tanks, the inspector shall provide the Vessel with a "Clean Tank" Certificate.

In addition to the inspection mentioned above, it is common practice to take a "first foot" sample from each tank at the start of loading.

3.141 It would seem that the strict rule that all the vessel's holds must be ready before Notice of Readiness can be given applies not only where the place of arrival is the place

153. London Arbitration 7/88—LMLN 239, 31 December 1988. See also London Arbitration 11/99—LMLN 511, 10 June 1999.
154. The Baltic and International Maritime Conference Standard Voyage Charterparty for the Transportation of Chemicals in Tank Vessels. Code name: "Bimchemvoy".

where loading is to be effected but also where the vessel can become an Arrived ship before moving into berth.[155]

3.142 Despite the strict requirements of the common law in relation to the physical condition of the holds or tanks prior to presentation of Notice of Readiness, it is always open to the parties to agree some other criteria. As was stated by Colman J in *The Linardos*[156]:

... one must not lose sight of the fact that, although in general a valid notice of readiness cannot be given unless and until the vessel is in truth ready to load, it is always open to the parties to ameliorate the black or white effect of this principle by express provisions to the contrary, as recognised by Roskill LJ in *The Tres Flores*.[157]

3.143 This case concerned a standard form of Richards Bay coal charter, clause 4 of which provided as follows:

Time commencing ... 18 hours after Notice of Readiness has been given by the Master, certifying that the vessel has arrived and is in all respects ready to load whether in berth or not ...

Any time lost subsequently by vessel not fulfilling requirements for ... readiness to load in all respects, including Marine Surveyor's Certificate ... or for any other reason for which the vessel is responsible, shall not count as notice time or as time allowed for loading ...

The charter also incorporated the Richards Bay Coal Terminal Regulations.

3.144 The problem arose because the vessel gave Notice of Readiness and three days later, when she berthed, a local marine surveyor failed her because of water and rust in her hatches. Just under a day later, she was accepted for loading.

3.145 The arbitrator concerned found in favour of the owners, holding that the assumed intention of the parties must have been that if congestion prevented the ship from berthing, Notice of Readiness might be tendered if given in good faith, even if she subsequently failed inspection. As Colman J pointed out on appeal in relation to lines 75/78, which provided for any time lost subsequent to tendering Notice of Readiness by the vessel not fulfilling requirements for free pratique or readiness to load in all respects, including marine surveyor's certificate not to count as notice time or as time allowed for loading[158]:

If it were not for lines 75/78, owners whose vessel having given notice of readiness at the anchorage, then had to wait for a period of several days or even weeks because no berth was available, was found on getting into berth to need one final washing of one or more of her cargo spaces, perhaps only a few hours work, could lose the benefit of all time lost at the anchorage. The printed form of this charterparty avoids that very commercially unbalanced result.

3.146 A similar result was reached in *The Jay Ganesh*,[159] also a decision of Colman J in relation to a Worldfood charter, and in London Arbitration 17/92,[160] a decision relating to a sugar charterparty. In this latter case, the clause concerned required the holds to be washed and dried if a cargo injurious to sugar had previously been carried but, if not,

---

155. *Compania de Naviera Nedelka SA* v. *Tradax International SA (The Tres Flores)* [1973] 2 Lloyd's Rep 247, at p. 250 *per* Cairns LJ. See also London Arbitration 15/86—LMLN 180, 25 September 1986.

156. *Cobelfret NV* v. *Cyclades Shipping Co Ltd (The Linardos)* [1994] 1 Lloyd's Rep 28, at p. 31.

157. *Compania de Naviera Nedelka SA* v. *Tradax International SA (The Tres Flores)* [1973] 2 Lloyd's Rep 247, at p. 253.

158. *The Linardos* [1994] 1 Lloyd's Rep 28, at p. 32.

159. *United Nations Food and Agriculture Organisation World Food Programme* v. *Caspian Navigation Inc (The Jay Ganesh)* [1994] 2 Lloyd's Rep 358.

160. London Arbitration 17/92—LMLN 328, 30 May 1992.

the holds only to be cleaned prior to loading, i.e. it could by implication be done after presenting Notice of Readiness. Any time thus lost would of course be for the owners' account.

Overstowed cargo

3.147 It sometimes happens that different parcels of cargo are carried on the same voyage in the same vessel, but under different contractual arrangements entered into directly by the owner. This may either be under multiple charters or under a charter which also contains a liberty to the shipowner to complete with other cargo. A typical clause of the latter type is the Centrocon completion clause, the gist of which reads:

Owners have the liberty to complete with other . . . merchandise from port to ports en route for owners' risk and benefit, but . . . same not to hinder the . . . discharging of this cargo.

3.148 In either of these circumstances, a valid Notice of Readiness cannot be given in respect of the cargo which has been overstowed until all that cargo is accessible. However, it need only be accessible, it is not necessary that all the cargo that has been stowed on top be discharged before a valid notice can be tendered.[161]

3.149 In *The Massalia (No 2)*[162] Diplock J held that in the circumstances of that particular case, as notice had already been given, although premature, and as the charterers were already discharging the vessel from those hatches where their cargo was accessible, it was not necessary for a further notice, or to allow the period of time that would normally have had to elapse after a valid notice, before laytime could begin. This view has, however, been doubted in a later case.[163]

Equipment

3.150 Although the holds must be ready to receive cargo on reaching the specified destination before the vessel can be considered in a state of readiness, the loading and discharging gear or other equipment need not be rigged and absolutely ready but only in such a state that they can be made ready and available for use when actually required.

3.151 In *Noemijulia Steamship Co Ltd* v. *Minister of Food*, Tucker LJ explained the point this way[164]:

It seems to me that there is a real distinction to be drawn between the cargo space and the gear. The charterer is entitled to the control of the whole of the cargo space from the outset of the voyage . . .

The loading gear had not got to be placed at his disposal and he had no rights with regard thereto save in so far as it was necessary to enable the shipowner to perform his contractual obligations under the charterparty. Providing the shipowner was able, when required, to load any cargo which the charterer was entitled to tender to him alongside, it was a matter for him to decide by what means he would carry out his contractual obligations.

---

161. *Government of Ceylon* v. *Société Franco-Tunisienne d'Armement-Tunis (The Massalia (No 2))* [1960] 2 Lloyd's Rep 352; *Agios Stylianos Compania Naviera SA* v. *Maritime Associates International Ltd Lagos (The Agios Stylianos)* [1975] 1 Lloyd's Rep 426; *Transamerican Steamship Corporation* v. *Tradax Export SA (The Oriental Envoy)* [1982] 2 Lloyd's Rep 266; London Arbitration—LMLN 71, 22 July 1982.
162. *Government of Ceylon* v. *Société Franco-Tunisienne d'Armement-Tunis (The Massalia (No 2))* [1960] 2 Lloyd's Rep 352, at p. 358.
163. *Christensen* v. *Hindustan Steel Ltd* [1971] 1 Lloyd's Rep 395, at p. 399 *per* Donaldson J. See also *post* at para. 3.248.
164. *Noemijulia Steamship Co Ltd* v. *Minister of Food* (1950) 84 Ll L Rep 354, at p. 362.

3.152 In that case, responsibility for loading and discharge lay with the shipowner. It often happens that the charter makes the charterer responsible for these tasks. However, even then, it is suggested, the equipment need only be ready when required provided it is clear that it will be so ready when the ship reaches the specified destination. Similar considerations apply to the opening of the hatches. This was one of the issues raised in *Armement Adolf Deppe* v. *John Robinson & Co Ltd*, where Swinfen Eady LJ said[165]:

The ship was lying at a waiting berth, her voyage being ended; it would have been an idle form to take on board men and open hatches and make other preparations at the buoys when there was no desire or intention of the merchants to receive cargo until the ship was berthed at the quay.

The ship was ready to discharge in a business and mercantile sense, and the idle formality of incurring useless expense was not necessary as a condition precedent to the commencement of the lay days.

3.153 In the same case, Scrutton LJ explained[166] that it was only after it had become settled in *Leonis Steamship Co* v. *Rank (No 1)*[167] that laytime under a port charter could commence at the waiting berth that the question of opening hatches and rigging equipment before arrival in berth arose. He concluded[168]:

And I cannot bring myself to hold that it was necessary for such a ship before her time would begin . . . to make preparations for discharging at a place where on the hypothesis discharging will not take place.

3.154 Similar sentiments were expressed by Greer J in *J Glynn & Son Ltd* v. *Consorzio Approvvigionamenti Fra Meccanici Ed Affini*, where he said[169]:

With reference to the question whether she was ready, it is clear that those words do not mean that she is to be when she gives notice in a position to start the discharge immediately the minute after the notice has been given.

What it means is ready in a commercial sense to discharge, that is to say, in such a position that the tackle can be got ready for use as soon as the receivers are in the ordinary course to do their part of the discharge . . . The hatches were not off, but matters of that sort do not prevent a vessel being ready to discharge, providing that she is in such a condition that her tackle and apparatus can be readily put in order to commence her discharge . . . "Ready to discharge" means having the tackle ready to be put into operation.

3.155 What equipment must be ready will depend on the terms of the charter and the instructions given by the charterer. In *Noemijulia Steamship Co Ltd* v. *Minister of Food*,[170] one of the issues raised was the ability of the *San George*, the vessel concerned, to load the cargo required by the charterer. The charterparty provided for her to load a full and a complete cargo of wheat and/or maize and/or rye in bags and/or bulk. Charterers were also given the option of shipping other lawful merchandise. Whilst the previous cargo was being discharged, a fire occurred and shortly after this was extinguished the main mast collapsed, breaking two wooden derricks. Temporary repairs were effected and an interim certificate of class was issued for the prospective voyage. Charterers, however, claimed that the vessel was not ready because she had no mainmast or after derricks.

---

165. *Armement Adolf Deppe* v. *John Robinson & Co Ltd* [1917] KB 204, at p. 208.
166. *Ibid.*, at p. 212.
167. *Leonis Steamship Co Ltd* v. *Joseph Rank (No 1)* [1908] 1 KB 499.
168. *Armement Adolf Deppe* v. *John Robinson & Co Ltd* [1917] KB 204, at p. 213.
169. *J Glynn & Son Ltd* v. *Consorzio Approvvigionamenti Fra Meccanici Ed Affini* (1920) 4 Ll L Rep 183, at p. 184.
170. *Noemijulia Steamship Co Ltd* v. *Minister of Food* (1950) 84 Ll L Rep 354.

3.156 In the subsequent arbitration proceedings, the umpire found that two of the holds could not have been loaded by ship's gear but that since the charterer intended to load bulk grain the derricks would not have been necessary and although for safety reasons some of the cargo had to be in bags, these could have been loaded by other means. In the High Court, Devlin J held that the rule as to readiness to load applicable to cargo space ought not to be so stringently applied in the case of gear required for loading and that, on the facts found by the umpire, the ship was not proved to be unready in a business sense. The Court of Appeal agreed.[171] It would seem from this case that the onus is on the charterer and that so far as the ship's equipment is concerned, if he wishes to contend that the ship is unready, he must show that the ship would be unable to load some cargo which the charterer was entitled to load.

3.157 In *Sun Shipping Co Ltd* v. *Watson & Youell Shipping Agency Ltd*,[172] Rowlatt J held that a vessel chartered to load grain was not ready on arrival at a loading position when only some of the shifting boards required in the holds had been fitted.

3.158 In *Vaughan and others* v. *Campbell, Heatley & Co*,[173] the charterparty provided for shipment of a full and complete cargo of wheat and/or flour in bags or other lawful merchandise. The ship was not at the cancelling date lined in the manner usual and necessary for the protection of a wheat or flour cargo. The charterers cancelled the charter because they said the ship was not in a state of readiness at the cancelling date. However, the Court of Appeal held that they were not entitled to do so. The case is very briefly reported, but it appears that Lord Esher MR based his judgment on the ground that the charter required the ship to be ready to load, not fit to load. Cotton and Lindley LJJ, however, added that the charter left it open to the charterers to load any kind of cargo and that many kinds of cargo would not require the ship to be lined. There was no evidence as to what kind of cargo it was intended to load, but the additional ground on which the Lords Justices based their decision negatives the idea that, so far as equipment is concerned, the shipowner has got to be ready from the outset to deal with any kind of cargo which the charterer is entitled under the charter to call upon him to take on board.

3.159 In *Grampian Steamship Co Ltd* v. *Carver & Co*,[174] the charter required the shipowner to provide the necessary mats for a cargo of cottonseed, wheat, beans, maize or other grain. Laurence J decided that it was not obligatory on the shipowners to have the mats laid down in order to be ready to load, but it was sufficient if they had the mats ready to lay if required.

3.160 In *The Demosthenes V (No 1)*,[175] Staughton J drew a distinction between the ship being ready and equipment which was to be brought from shore being ready and available. The facts were that the *Demosthenes V* was to discharge a cargo of grain at Alexandria. An additional clause in the charter required owners to guarantee a minimum of six vacuators at the discharge port. On arrival her Notice of Readiness was rejected because at that time she had no vacuators on board. Three days later three vacuators were put on board which were capable of discharging at a rate greater than that specified in the charter.

171. *Ibid.*, at p. 362.
172. *Sun Shipping Co Ltd* v. *Watson & Youell Shipping Agency Ltd* (1926) 24 Ll L Rep 28.
173. *Vaughan & others* v. *Campbell, Heatley & Co* (1885) 2 TLR 33.
174. *Grampian Steamship Co Ltd* v. *Carver & Co* (1893) 9 TLR 210.
175. *Gerani Compania Naviera SA* v. *General Organization for Supply Goods (The Demosthenes V) (No 1)* [1982] 1 Lloyd's Rep 275.

Later three more were supplied. By the time she was able to berth, she had the six vacuators required by the charter. In finding that the absence of vacuators on arrival did not prevent the ship being ready on arrival the judge said[176]:

> The vacuators were essentially, as I see it, equipment which was to emerge from the shore when the operation of discharge was to commence. The ship, as a ship, was ready. All that had not been done was to supply the equipment which the owners were to supply for the purposes of discharge.

He therefore held that the requirement as to vacuators was not a condition precedent to giving notice and that even if they were an essential part of the vessel's readiness, the vessel would have been ready when three were supplied and the remaining three could have been obtained at short notice.

3.161 In London Arbitration 4/93,[177] the tribunal held that the fact that a windlass motor failed due to a latent defect subsequent to the vessel's arrival, delaying her shifting from the anchorage to her loading berth, did not invalidate the Notice of Readiness presented by the vessel on her arrival.

Other physical matters

3.162 In *The Virginia M*,[178] Hobhouse J had to consider the validity of a Notice of Readiness tendered at Lagos where the vessel was due to discharge. The problem was that the vessel had steam winches and arrived with only about 15 tons of fresh water, but a daily consumption of 20 tons. The laytime allowed for discharge was in excess of 15 weather working days and therefore the vessel would have been unable to discharge all her cargo.

3.163 In arbitration, the arbitrators held that the notice was valid. However, the judge disagreed, saying[179]:

> If the vessel having proceeded into berth and having discharged some cargo has to stop and take on fresh water or bunkers either at that berth or another berth, that is not consistent with the vessel having been ready to discharge . . .

Nevertheless, he also added[180]:

> In some ports, maybe even in most ports in the world, the taking on board of further fresh water at a discharging berth may be a mere formality which will in no way impede or hold up the discharge of the cargo and will not prevent the vessel from being ready to discharge the whole cargo as soon as the charterers may wish and at the rate at which they may wish.

3.164 Presumably, the same would apply to bunkers. It would therefore seem that whether insufficient supplies of water or bunkers will invalidate a Notice of Readiness will very much depend on what facilities may be available at the particular port.

---

176. *Ibid.*, at p. 279.

177. London Arbitration 4/93—LMLN 351, 17 April 1993.

178. *Unifert International SAL* v. *Panous Shipping Co Inc (The Virginia M)* [1989] 1 Lloyd's Rep 603. See also London Arbitration 4/93—LMLN 351, 17 April 1993. In *The Sea Wind* LMLN 531 16 March 2000, New York Arbitrators refused to reduce the rate of discharge where the Charterers had *chosen* to use only three out of five hatches. It is suggested that had the Charterers been able to use only three hatches when five should have been available, they would have been entitled to the reduction sought.

179. *Unifert International SAL* v. *Panous Shipping Co Inc (The Virginia M)* [1989] 1 Lloyd's Rep 603, at p. 607.

180. *Ibid.*

Legal readiness

3.165 Just as a ship must be physically ready to load or discharge, so must it also be legally ready. At common law, by this is meant that the ship must have all her papers in order, there must be no infection on board and all permits or consents which it is customary for the ship to obtain must have been received so that there is likely to be no legal impediment to the commencement of loading or discharge when the charterers or those concerned are ready so to do. If any such permit is normally obtained by the charterers or those for whom they are responsible, then, if this is necessary for the ship to proceed from an anchorage where she would not have been deemed to have reached her specified destination to such a point, the charterers, etc., are bound to act with reasonable diligence to ensure it is received as timeously as possible. Where the vessel concerned has already reached her specified destination and the permit is needed for her to proceed further, then its absence does not, unless there is a clause to the contrary, normally prevent her from becoming an Arrived ship. This is the effect of the two decisions which are now discussed.

3.166 The first of these is *The Atlantic Sunbeam*,[181] a decision of Kerr J. Here the *Atlantic Sunbeam* was due to complete the discharge of her cargo at Calcutta. However, she could not proceed beyond the anchorage off Sandheads, which was outside the port until a document called a "jetty challan" had been obtained from the port authorities. This enabled her to then proceed up the River Hooghly to Calcutta. The procedure was described by Kerr J as follows[182]:

The first step which is required has to be taken by the owners. This is the lodgment with the Calcutta Customs of the lodging of the ship's manifest. Once that has been done, certain steps have to be taken, first by the consignees or receivers, secondly by the port authority, and thirdly by the Customs authorities. . . . Once the port authority and the Customs have gone through all the documentary procedures which are required in any particular case, the consignees obtain a document called a "jetty challan" from the port commissioners. Once that document has been obtained and presumably passed over to the owners' agents, the vessel is free to come up the River Hooghly . . .

However, having arrived at Sandheads, there was a delay of some days before a "jetty challan" was issued and the owners pointed out that the charterers could only be responsible for their own or consignee's delay (in this case they were effectively both) and not delay by the port or Customs authorities. The judge said of the level of diligence required from the charterers[183]:

A requirement of a high standard of initiative, let alone any excessive zeal, cannot be implied in a situation of this nature, however much one would like to see it used. Something of that kind would require an express term. If, for instance, there were two procedures in a certain port whereby a vessel's documentation can be dealt with, one on paying an expedition fee or taking some special steps, and the other one the ordinary procedure, then it seems to me that the charterers would be under no implied obligation to use the speedier and unusual procedure.

It therefore follows that in my view the term to be implied in this case is to the effect that the charterers were bound to act with reasonable dispatch and in accordance with the practice of the Port of Calcutta in doing those acts which had to be done by them as consignees to enable the ship to become an arrived ship.

181. *Sunbeam Shipping Co Ltd* v. *President of India (The Atlantic Sunbeam)* [1973] 1 Lloyd's Rep 482.
182. *Ibid.*, at p. 484.
183. *Ibid.*, at p. 488, but see the comments of Staughton LJ in *The World Navigator* [1991] 2 Lloyd's Rep 23 at p. 30, quoted at para. 3.345, as to whether the obligation on the charterers is an absolute one, as suggested in *The Aello* [1960] 1 Lloyd's Rep 623, or one of reasonable diligence/best endeavours, as suggested in this case.

3.167 The judge continued that the onus of proof in this case rested with the shipowner but that the arbitrators would, of course, be entitled to draw an inference adverse to the charterers if there were unexplained periods of delay or inactivity. However, as he was unable to see whether the arbitrators had taken the approach he had set out or how they had arrived at the period of undue delay they had found, the case was remitted back to them for further consideration. In such a case, the shipowner will, of course, only be able to recover for any excess period beyond what is reasonable, not for the whole of the delay.

3.168 The second decision is *The Aello*,[184] which has already been considered in some detail,[185] and the basic facts of which need not be repeated. One of the peripheral issues considered was the effect of a Customs permit known as a "giro", which at the material time was required for a vessel to proceed beyond Intersection, the temporary waiting area some 22 miles from Buenos Aires. The practice was for the shipper to obtain a certificate from the Grain Board to the effect that a cargo was available and a giro would then be issued when that cargo was ready to be loaded. Until this happened the vessel was held at Intersection. In the House of Lords, Lord Radcliffe, who dissented from the majority on the main issue as to whether the *Aello* had reached her specified destination on arrival at Intersection, commented[186]:

It is, of course, possible to take the view that until the giro was granted the *Aello* had not arrived because she had not got into the required area of the port. That is one thing. But, if you do not take that view and think that she was in the port within the meaning of the charterparty, the giro became, under the prevailing conditions, nothing but official permission to enter a loading berth. If the absence of such permission prevents an arrived ship from claiming that its lay days have begun, the distinction between port charters and berth charters established by *Leonis Steamship Co Ltd* v. *Rank Ltd* [1908] 1 KB 499 disappears again and every ship waiting for a berth, however correct its standard of propinquity, must also be waiting for its lay days to begin. In my opinion this point is unmaintainable.

Common law

3.169 The usual clearances that a vessel must receive are from the Customs, Immigration and Health authorities. The documentation that they will wish to inspect may include the ship's certificate of registry, the cargo manifest, the official log book, list of dutiable stores, crew list and ship's articles. Individual ports or countries may add considerably to this, according to local requirements established by custom and local or national law. It is the ship's duty to have on board whatever documentation is required at the port in question. Provided that the master has no reason to believe that such clearances will be withheld, he may proceed at common law to declare his vessel ready on reaching the specified destination even though clearance has not yet been given. Such clearances may usually therefore be considered to be one of the preliminaries, etc., Lord Denning had in mind in *The Tres Flores* when he said[187]:

... notice of readiness can be given even though there are some further preliminaries to be done, or routine matters to be carried on, or formalities observed. If those things are not such as to give any reason to suppose that they will cause any delay, and it is apparent that the ship will be ready when the appropriate time arrives, then notice of readiness can be given.

184. *Agrimpex Hungarian Trading Co for Agricultural Products* v. *Sociedad Financiera de Bienes Raices SA (The Aello)* [1957] 2 Lloyd's Rep 423; [1958] 2 Lloyd's Rep 65 (CA); [1960] 1 Lloyd's Rep 623 (HL).
185. See *ante* at para. 3.90.
186. *The Aello* [1960] 1 Lloyd's Rep 623, at p. 642.
187. *Compania de Naviera Nedelka SA* v. *Tradax International SA (The Tres Flores)* [1973] 2 Lloyd's Rep 247, at p. 249.

3.170 In addition to the clearances mentioned above, other local authorities may have their own requirements. An instance of this is provided by the London Arbitration Award described in *Lloyd's Maritime Law Newsletter* No 35.[188] This concerned a routine inspection of a vessel by the local harbour authorities on her arrival at a Chinese port. The dispute concerned whether clearance by the harbour authorities was required before laytime could commence. The inspection itself took 40 minutes and there was no evidence to show that this was other than the approximate time usual for this operation. The inspection did not find anything untoward with the vessel and was not causative of any delay to the ship; after the inspection the vessel waited for a discharge berth for about a week. The arbitrator decided the case in favour of the owners: he considered that a fairly broad approach should be taken to preliminaries which have to be carried out when vessels arrive at a port and such preliminaries cannot be carried out for some time after the vessel has arrived, assuming no failure by those on board the vessel in presenting the vessel for the preliminaries. He accepted the owners' plea that a routine inspection is a mere formality which can be ignored for the purpose of commencement of laytime and that it is not a condition precedent or something of such substance that it prevents the triggering off of the laytime clock.

Free pratique and quarantine

3.171 These two terms are in one sense opposites in that a ship which is refused free pratique may have quarantine restrictions imposed upon her. Pratique is a permission or licence granted by the port medical authorities to a vessel upon arrival from a foreign port for her crew to go ashore and for local people to go on board. If a ship fails to get pratique, either because of serious infectious illness on board or because she has arrived from a place where such illness is known to be rampant, then she may have quarantine restrictions imposed upon her. At most ports there is a quarantine anchorage to which the ship may be sent, usually in a more isolated part of the port. Traditionally, a ship in quarantine signifies this fact by flying a yellow flag (flag Q in the international alphabet of signal flags). Originally, quarantine was for 40 days, although nowadays some other period may be specified in the quarantine order.

3.172 Where a quarantine restriction is placed upon a ship, she cannot be considered ready because the result of the restriction is that work is prevented and the charterers do not have unrestricted access. In *Smith* v. *Dart & Son*,[189] a ship was chartered to carry oranges from Spain to England. She was, however, delayed on her approach voyage by very rough weather so that she was not ready to load, free of pratique, at the first load port by the cancelling date as required by the charter, with the result that the charterers cancelled the charter. The main argument before the court was whether the delay was excused by an exceptions clause in the charter relating to heavy weather. This argument was rejected, the court deciding that the requirement to arrive and be ready before the cancelling date was an absolute one. The charterers were therefore entitled to cancel. In that case, the ship was physically ready at the appropriate time but not free of pratique. It should, however, be noted that this was a specific requirement of the charter.

188. London Arbitration—LMLN 35, 5 March 1981.
189. *Smith* v. *Dart & Son* (1884) 14 QBD 105 (CA).

3.173 In the Scottish case of *John and James White* v. *The Steamship Winchester Co*,[190] the *Winchester* arrived to load a cargo, her previous port of call being Port Said. As a result, quarantine restrictions were placed upon her so that access to the ship was prevented. In the Court of Session, Lord Shand said:

The vessel would be an arrived ship in name only, but not in reality, so far as regarded the charterer, whose duty and obligation—the loading or unloading—should begin on arrival. The charterer might be quite ready to unload, or ready with a cargo waiting to load the vessel, but the disqualification of the ship would prevent this, and indeed, would lead to the ship being sent away from the place of loading or discharge. She would thus never be at the disposal of the charterer so as to enable him to fulfil his obligation.

3.174 The third of the early cases dealing with quarantine restrictions and the granting of free pratique, and perhaps the most difficult and unusual, is *The Austin Friars*.[191] The case came before the High Court as part of a collision action. The facts were as follows. The *Austin Friars* had sailed from Constantinople in ballast on an approach voyage to Galatz and en route she collided with another steamship, causing her to put back to Constantinople for temporary repairs. After these were completed, she sailed again and arrived at Galatz at 11 p.m. on 10 October 1893. However, on arrival no one could board or leave until pratique was given after the ship had been visited by the port doctor and pronounced clear of infection. This occurred the following morning but unfortunately the charter provided that the charterers could cancel the charter if the vessel was not ready by midnight on 10 October, which they did. In the collision action therefore, the owners of the *Austin Friars* claimed, *inter alia*, damages from the other vessel for their losses arising out of the cancellation of the charter. The main issue in the case was whether the charterers were entitled to cancel, which in turn depended on whether the vessel was ready in time.

3.175 The case was decided by Sir Francis Jeune, the President of the PDA Division of the High Court. Having reviewed the two earlier cases, he said[192]:

It was argued before me that the present is not a case of quarantine, nor in strictness is it. But there seems to me no distinction for this purpose between a medical officer in authority ordering a ship into quarantine, and his prohibiting access to her till he can examine into her conditions. In both cases a superior authority, in pursuance of sanitary regulations, disqualifies a ship from taking cargo on board. It was also argued that some charterparties (for example that in *Smith* v. *Dart*) add "free of pratique" to the words "ready to load". This, of course, shows that those who framed the charterparty doubted if it were sufficiently clear that readiness to load included the absence of sanitary disqualifications, but I do not think that the practice of adding these words has been so usual or so authoritative as to show such a doubt is well founded. I think, therefore, that the damages in this case must include damages by reason of the loss of the charterparty.

3.176 Although it does not appear to have influenced the decision, one factor why the *Austin Friars* was not ready to load was that, because of the port health restrictions, the master was unable to proceed ashore to give Notice of Readiness until after the charterers' option to cancel had arisen. In *The Delian Spirit*,[193] Lord Denning said of the *Austin Friars* decision that "It was a very special case" and did not warrant the proposition that Notice of Readiness was not valid without free pratique.

190. *John and James White* v. *The Steamship Winchester Co* (1886) 23 SLR 342.
191. *The Austin Friars* (1894) 10 TLR 633.
192. *Ibid.*, at p. 634.
193. *Shipping Developments Corporation SA* v. *V/O Sojuzneftexport (The Delian Spirit)* [1971] 1 Lloyd's Rep 506, at p. 510.

3.177 There is, however, a distinction between a vessel which has not yet obtained free pratique and one which has been refused clearance. In *The Delian Spirit*, Lord Denning also said[194]:

> I can understand that, if a ship is known to be infected by a disease such as to prevent her getting her pratique, she would not be ready to load or discharge. But if she has apparently a clean bill of health such that there is no reason to fear delay, then even though she has not been given her pratique, she is entitled to give notice of readiness, and laytime will begin to run.

At first instance in the same case, Donaldson J said[195]:

> It is an idle exercise to obtain free pratique before the time for loading unless it be required for ship's purposes, and if it is a fact that it can be obtained at any time and without the possibility of delaying the loading, the mere fact that it has not been obtained does not prevent the ship from becoming an arrived ship.

3.178 In British ports, clearance is usually obtained in the form of a certificate issued by the Medical Officer of Health for the port upon a declaration being made by the master or medical officer, if one is carried, that no member of the crew or passenger is suffering from any notifiable disease. In the United States, a practice exists whereby certain ships, such as cruise liners, may obtain radio pratique by giving similar information by radio shortly before arrival.

3.179 As will be apparent from the above, the actual obtaining of free pratique is not now a requirement at common law before a ship can be considered ready.[196] Nevertheless, it is common for charters to still contain the phrase "whether in free pratique or not" in conjunction with a readiness clause. Since this is not a requirement, the phrase is probably surplusage, at least where there is no impediment to free pratique being granted. It is doubtful whether the phrase would extend to allowing time to commence where pratique was actually refused or where there were grounds for believing that it would be at a later date.

3.180 The *Voylayrules 1993* provide[197]:

> "VESSEL BEING IN FREE PRATIQUE" and/or "HAVING BEEN ENTERED AT THE CUSTOM HOUSE" shall mean that the completion of these formalities shall not be a condition precedent to tendering notice of readiness, but any time lost by reason of the delay in the vessel's completion of either of these formalities shall not count as laytime or time on demurrage.

3.181 In so far as the free pratique part of this definition is concerned, whilst it is true that obtaining free pratique is usually a formality and that the phrase "whether in free pratique or not" does not add anything, nevertheless where the parties have expressly required free pratique to be obtained prior to tendering Notice of Readiness, it must mean something. It is therefore suggested that unless the Voylayrules are specifically incorporated into the charter, an express requirement of free pratique would normally be a condition precedent.

3.182 However it should be stressed that any such requirement must be clearly expressed. Thus in London Arbitration 9/98,[198] the clause in question merely required the

---

194. *Ibid.*
195. *Shipping Developments Corporation SA v. V/O Sojuzneftexport (The Delian Spirit)* [1971] 1 Lloyd's Rep 64, at p. 70.
196. It can, however, be a specific requirement of the charter, when it will be a condition precedent to the vessel's readiness. See, for example, London Arbitration 14/86—LMLN 179, 11 September 1986.
197. See Appendix and the similar definition in *Baltic Code 2000.*
198. London Arbitration 9/98—LMLN 488, 21 July 1998.

master to immediately protest in writing if free pratique was not granted promptly and that such protest be attached to any claim for demurrage. Rejecting the suggestion that the granting of free pratique was a condition precedent to a valid notice of readiness being given, the tribunal held it was merely a formality. They also relied on a *dictum* of Longmore J in *The Petr Schmidt*, where the judge said[199]:

... in the absence of express wording, courts generally lean against constraint clauses as conditions precedent to liability.

3.183 Whilst the grant of free pratique usually refers to medical clearance, at some ports it does have a wider meaning. Thus, in *The Freijo*, the arbitrator found[200]:

At Lourenço Marques free pratique is granted only when a vessel has reached the limits of the inner anchorage, at which time Health, Customs and Immigration Authorities are brought on board by launch by the local agent. According to local ruling, free pratique covers clearance by all Authorities including immigration. A vessel is adjudged in free pratique only after compliance with the usual inward formalities by the Authorities concerned. This is at variance with custom in other parts of the world but it was the custom in the former territories of Mozambique and Angola.

3.184 In *The Aello*, another subsidiary matter considered related to the issue of a police permit which was required before people from shore could come on board. However, this was held to be a mere formality, especially as the *Aello* had arrived from another Argentinian port.[201]

Additional requirements

3.185 There is, of course, nothing to prevent the parties to a charter from agreeing additional requirements that must be met before the ship concerned can be considered legally ready. The difficulty in such cases usually comes from the fact that the additional requirement can only be met in one part of the port. The cases that follow illustrate this point.

3.186 In *The Freijo*[202] the principal clause dealing with the commencement of laytime contained a requirement that the vessel be in free pratique, which as already mentioned, could only be obtained at inner anchorage. An additional clause, however, provided that, if through congestion, the vessel was kept waiting off the port then lay days were to commence as per the principal clause but not until 36 hours from arrival. Owing to congestion, the vessel was so delayed and a dispute arose as to whether the granting of free pratique was a condition precedent to the commencement of laytime under the additional clause.

3.187 However, the arbitrator, the High Court[203] and the Court of Appeal were all agreed that it was not. What the charter contemplated was one of two things. Either the vessel was able to proceed at least as far as the inner anchorage, when free pratique would be a condition precedent or it would be held up off the port, in which case the additional

199. *The Petr Schmidt* [1997] 1 Lloyd's Rep 284 at p. 286.
200. *Logs & Timber Products (Singapore) Pte Ltd* v. *Keeley Granite (Pty) Ltd (The Freijo)* [1978] 2 Lloyd's Rep 1, at p. 3, quoted by Roskill LJ.
201. *Agrimpex Hungarian Trading Co for Agricultural Products* v. *Sociedad Financiera de Bienes Raices SA (The Aello)* [1960] 1 Lloyd's Rep 623, at p. 642 *per* Lord Radcliffe.
202. *Logs & Timber Products (Singapore) Pte Ltd* v. *Keeley Granite (Pty) Ltd (The Freijo)* [1978] 2 Lloyd's Rep 1 (CA).
203. *The Freijo* [1978] 1 Lloyd's Rep 257 (Donaldson J).

clause operated so that the only requirement was that 36 hours should elapse before laytime commenced. The reference to the principal clause in the additional clause was not intended to refer to the commencement of laytime.[204]

3.188 A similar situation arose in *The Puerto Rocca*,[205] this time concerning Customs clearance. Here the *Puerto Rocca* was inward bound to Liverpool with a cargo of grain on a berth charter, with a clause providing for time to count "whether in berth or not". On arrival at the Mersey Bar anchorage, no grain berth was available and initially she did not proceed further. Time was to count a specified period after Customs clearance but this could not be obtained at the anchorage. An additional clause, however, provided that if the vessel was unable to berth immediately upon arrival because of congestion, she was to present Notice of Readiness at the Mersey Bar anchorage in accordance with the principal clause dealing with the commencement of laytime. Notice of Readiness at the anchorage having been rejected by the charterers, the owners ordered her to a lay-by berth in the dock where she was to berth when one became available. Here a second Notice of Readiness was presented and this time accepted. The argument between the parties was as to whether the first notice was valid or just the second. Mocatta J was in no doubt that the first notice was a good notice. The reference to "berth" in the additional clause was to the discharging berth and to require a vessel to go additionally to a lay-by berth just to give notice seemed unreasonable and uncommercial in the context of a berth charter.

3.189 An interesting illustration of the relationship between an additional requirement relating to the commencement of laytime and a reachable on arrival clause is provided by London Arbitration 6/84.[206] Here an additional clause provided that " ... At ... discharging before tendering notice of readiness the vessel to comply with all port formalities including Gas Free Certificate ... ". Although not stated in the brief report available, the vessel was presumably a combination carrier and at the time carrying dry cargo. On arrival at the discharge port, there was a three and a half day delay before an Inspector could get out to the vessel at the anchorage because of bad weather (which prevented small boats coming out but would not have prevented the vessel from berthing, had a berth been available). In fact, the ship concerned did not berth until 13 days after arrival owing to congestion. The charterers argued that laytime could not commence until after the Gas Free Certificate was obtained, whereas the owners argued that time should run from six hours after her arrival, there being also a provision to that effect.

3.190 On those facts, the arbitrators held the charterers to be in breach of the reachable on arrival clause. Had a berth been available on the vessel's arrival, she would probably have berthed a few hours after arrival and the Gas Free Inspection would have been completed and a certificate issued two hours after that. That, then, said the arbitrators, would have been the point in time from which the six hours before laytime commenced would have run and the owners were entitled to claim demurrage based on this notional timescale.

3.191 Had it not been for the specific provision requiring a Gas Free Certificate, it is likely that such an inspection of a vessel carrying other than a liquid cargo or whose

---

204. See also London Arbitration 18/95—LMLN 417, 28 October 1995 and London Arbitration 9/96—LMLN 434, 22 June 1996.

205. *Compania Argentina de Navegación de Ultramar* v. *Tradax Export SA (The Puerto Rocca)* [1978] 1 Lloyd's Rep 252.

206. London Arbitration—LMLN 117, 26 April 1984.

previous cargo had been other than a liquid cargo (if she arrived in ballast) would have been considered a routine matter or formality, such as not to delay the giving of Notice of Readiness. The case may be contrasted with one that came before New York arbitrators, *The Permeke*.[207] The vessel was again an OBO (ore/bulk/oil carrier) but this time carrying a cargo of crude oil.

3.192 The vessel arrived off New York and tendered a Notice of Readiness. US law prohibited foreign flag vessels from off loading oil in US waters unless they held a Tank Vessel Examination Letter (TVEL). This could only be obtained on first arrival in the US following an inspection by the US Coast Guard (USCG), which in this case took some three and a half hours from when the USCG boarded until issue of the letter. No deficiencies in the vessel were found.

3.193 The charter did not specifically refer to the vessel having a TVEL but did have a provision requiring the vessel to have on board all necessary certificates and furthermore, at the time of fixing, the owners warranted the vessel was eligible to trade to the US. In fact no time was lost to the charterers by the failure to have this certificate and the owners argued its provision was a mere formality. This was rejected by the tribunal who held that time did not begin to run until six hours after the TVEL was issued. It is likely that the decision would have been the same had this been London Arbitration.

3.194 In *The Amiral Fahri Engin*,[208] time charterers sought to claim against head owners because they said the master failed to obtain free pratique from the customs, sanitary and port authorities at Tuapse upon arrival or protest against the failure to grant free pratique or if this was to be given by radio by the port medical officer or sanitary authority as was required by the subcharter. A further clause in the subcharter provided that if free pratique was not granted promptly upon arrival the master should protest and in the absence of protest, laytime should commence at the earliest "upon receipt of free pratique". The sanitary authority gave free pratique by radio on 1 January 1989 on the vessel's arrival but she was delayed in berthing until 8 January. It was argued that laytime did not therefore commence until 8 January. This argument was rejected by Saville J who held that as is customary the only authority to grant free pratique was the medical authority which they did on the vessel's arrival.[209]

3.195 Other examples of conditions precedent include a certificate of compliance with US Coast Guard regulations relating to the transfer of oil,[210] a requirement that formalities for entering port had been passed by the port authorities[211] and a requirement that the vessel be securely moored at the loading or discharging place.[212]

3.196 In London Arbitration 14/96,[213] provision of a stowage plan was held not to be an additional requirement.

---

207. *Bocimar NV* v. *Bayway Refining Co (The Permeke)*, LMLN 416, 14 October 1995.
208. *Sale Corporation of Monrovia* v. *Turkish Cargo Lines General Manager (The Amiral Fahri Engin)* [1993] 1 Lloyd's Rep 75.
209. See also London Arbitration 14/86—LMLN 179, 11 September 1986.
210. London Arbitration 1/90—LMLN 266, 13 January 1990.
211. London Arbitration 4/90—LMLN 274, 5 May 1990.
212. *Plakoura Maritime Corporation* v. *Shell International Petroleum Co Ltd (The Plakoura)* [1987] 2 Lloyd's Rep 258—the main issue in this case was actually whether the reference to place meant the port or the specific part of the port, the court holding it meant the latter.
213. London Arbitration 14/96—LMLN 446, 7 December 1996.

Implied requirements

3.197 In London Arbitration 11/89,[214] charterers sought unsuccessfully to argue that the charter, an Asbatankvoy form, contained an implied term that the master should ensure that everything necessary or customary is done on arrival at the discharge port to facilitate the prompt berthing of the vessel. Given the type of charter, this was probably an attempt to avoid the effect of the reachable on arrival provision.[215]

3.198 The vessel arrived off the port late in the evening and the master cabled Notice of Readiness to the charterers' agents. The cable took a little under nine hours to arrive. In the meantime another vessel arrived and registered her arrival with the Port Control by VHF, which the first vessel had not, resulting in the second ship gaining priority in berthing. Charterers argued there was an implied term to the charter that "the master and/ or crew would do as soon as practically possible any and all things necessary or customary to facilitate the prompt berthing of the ship and the discharge of her cargo" and this meant she should have registered with the port authority.

3.199 The arbitrators disagreed. No such term should be implied. Furthermore, it was the charterers' duty to designate and procure a berth reachable on arrival. The charterers had provided detailed voyage orders, but had not instructed the master to register with the port authority.

THE INDIAN CASES

3.200 The reports contain a number of cases arising out of particular requirements imposed by Indian Customs law in relation to commencement of laytime. The case of *The Atlantic Sunbeam*[216] has already been considered. That case related to a requirement for ships to obtain a document called a "jetty challan" before proceeding up the River Hooghly to Calcutta and although this is issued by the port commissioners, there is a Customs input.

3.201 At Indian ports there are a number of stages to be followed in order to gain Customs clearance. The usual practice is for the owners or their agents to lodge with the Customs a "prior entry" document or documents before the ship's arrival. This consists principally of the ship's manifest and once filed enables the receivers to process the documents required for receiving and clearing the goods. On arrival at an inner anchorage, if the vessel is to discharge at an anchorage, or at a berth, if the vessel is to discharge alongside, then the final Customs procedures are followed. This involves the representation of the manifest, together with such documents as the ship's register, port clearance from the last port of call, list of vessel's stores and list of crew's private property. Upon receipt of these, which may be tendered at any time, "inward entry" will be granted, usually on the following business day. "Inward entry" is sometimes referred to in the cases as "final entry" and, *inter alia*, grants to the vessel permission from the Customs to break bulk.

214. London Arbitration 11/89—LMLN 248, 6 May 1989.
215. See *post* at para. 3.402.
216. *Sunbeam Shipping Co Ltd* v. *President of India (The Atlantic Sunbeam)* [1973] 1 Lloyd's Rep 482. See *ante* at para. 3.166.

3.202 In a London Arbitration referred to in *Lloyd's Maritime Law Newsletter* No 90,[217] in *The Apollon*,[218] and in *The Delian Leto*,[219] each of the laytime clauses contained a requirement as a condition precedent that the vessel concerned should have been entered at the Custom House before laytime could commence. In each of these cases, one of the issues raised was whether it was necessary for the full Customs procedure to be followed or whether it would suffice for the first or "prior to entry" stage to have been completed. In each case the decision was that the initial stage would suffice. In *The Apollon*, Bingham J said[220]:

Although the language of the charterparty did not expressly refer to entry under the "prior to entry" rules, it was in my judgment both the correct and commercial construction of this contract that the vessel was indeed entered at the time when entry was necessary and required in order to permit discharge.

3.203 However, in *The Albion*[221] and *The Nestor*,[222] Webster J and Leggatt J were each persuaded that entry at the Customs House meant final rather than prior entry. It seems that each of the judges accepted a finding by the respective arbitrators that discharge of cargo prior to final entry was illegal under sections 30, 31 of the Indian Customs Act 1962. The practical effect of these decisions in most cases is to turn such charters into berth charters, putting the risk of delay due to congestion on to owners.

3.204 Interestingly enough, the Indian High Court at Bombay decided in a case called *The Jag Leela*[223] that prior, rather than final, entry should be the criterion. The court therefore declined to follow what at that time were the most recent English High Court cases and pointed out that the words "entered at the Customs House" did not appear in the Indian Act. The words "entry inwards" in section 31 of the Act was nothing to do with the relations between the parties as governed by the charter. The ship's agents had to take the steps leading to prior entry, but thereafter the rest of the procedure was for the proper officer of the Customs and was nothing to do with the obligations of the parties under the charter.

3.205 In *The Antclizo (No 2)*,[224] Hirst J considered all four previous English cases at length and concluded that he should not follow the decisions in *The Albion* and *The Nestor*[225] and that completion of prior entry satisfied requirements in the charter with which he was concerned as to Customs clearance which required the vessel to have been entered at the Custom House and in free pratique. That decision was upheld by the Court of Appeal[226] aand therefore as both Indian and English law now stand, completion of prior entry will suffice. It should be noted, however, that this latest English decision did not decide that prior entry was a mere formality or did not form a condition precedent to

217. London Arbitration—LMLN 90, 14 April 1983.
218. *NZ Michalos v. The Food Corporation of India (The Apollon)* [1983] 1 Lloyd's Rep 409.
219. *Food Corporation of India v. Carras Shipping Co Ltd (The Delian Leto)* [1983] 2 Lloyd's Rep 496.
220. *The Apollon* [1983] 1 Lloyd's Rep 409, at p. 412.
221. *President of India v. Davenport Marine Panama SA (The Albion)* [1987] 2 Lloyd's Rep 365.
222. *President of India v. Diamantis Pateras (Hellas) Marine Enterprises Ltd (The Nestor)* [1987] 2 Lloyd's Rep 649.
223. *Union of India and others v. The Great Eastern Shipping Co Ltd (The Jag Leela)*, LMLN 242, 11 February 1989.
224. *Antclizo Shipping Corporation v. Food Corporation of India (The Antclizo (No 2))* [1991] 2 Lloyd's Rep 485.
225. *The Albion* [1987] 2 Lloyd's Rep 365; *The Nestor* [1987] 2 Lloyd's Rep 649.
226. *Antclizo Shipping Corporation v. Food Corporation of India (The Antclizo (No 2))* [1992] 1 Lloyd's Rep 558.

tendering Notice of Readiness. In this respect it should be contrasted with the *Voylayrules 1993* definition[227] of entry at the Custom House which reads as follows:

"VESSEL BEING IN FREE PRATIQUE" and/or "HAVING BEEN ENTERED AT THE CUSTOM HOUSE" shall mean that the completion of these formalities shall not be a condition precedent to tendering notice of readiness, but any time lost by reason of delay in the vessel's completion of either of these formalities shall not count as laytime or time on demurrage.

3.206 This definition will therefore only apply if the rules are specifically incorporated into the charter.

Notice of Readiness

3.207 The *Voylayrules 1993* provide[228]:

"NOTICE OF READINESS" (NOR) shall mean the notice to the charterer, shipper, receiver or other person as required by the charterparty that the vessel has arrived at the port or berth as the case may be and is ready to load or discharge.

A slightly different definition appears in *Baltic Code 2000*[229]:

NOTICE OF READINESS (NOR)—the notice to charterer, shipper, receiver or other person as required by the charter-party that the vessel has arrived at the port or berth, as the case may be, and is ready to load or discharge. (Alternatively: the notice may be specified to relate to the vessel arriving at/off the port or berth.)

The alternative definition is perhaps more accurately described as a Notice of Arrival rather than Readiness and is something an owner might wish to give in relation to a claim for detention rather than to commence laytime.

3.208 An unusual dispute was resolved in London Arbitration 14/87.[230] In this case, charterers relied upon clause 4 of the Vegoil form of charter which provided for notice to be given "to the charterer or its agent". Notice was not given to the charterers, but was given to the shippers, consignees or forwarding agents, who in each case were the relevant party for arranging loading and discharge. The charterers appointed no agents as such. At the time no complaint was made by the charterers and the arbitrators held that in the circumstances the parties, to whom notices were given, had to be considered as "agents" for the purpose of clause 4. The notices were therefore valid.

3.209 A similar challenge was mounted in London Arbitration 20/98[231] in relation to clause 6 of an Asbatankvoy form which required notice to be given to the charterer. What happened was that notice was given to the shippers and the local agents. On the facts, it was shown that the local agents were the only agents at the port and acted as agents for both the ship and the shippers. The tribunal therefore held that the shippers and their agents were to be treated as if they were "charterers'" agents for the purpose of tendering Notice of Readiness unless the charterparty specifically designated other agents, which it had not done.

3.210 If notice is tendered to agents, they must therefore be those of the shippers or charterers, not just of the owners.

---

227. See Appendix.
228. *Ibid.*
229. *Ibid.*
230. London Arbitration 14/87—LMLN 205, 12 September 1987.
231. London Arbitration 20/98—LMLN 491, 29 September 1998.

When and how to be given

3.211 The practical answer to this question to be given to any master is as follows[232]:

It is a good working rule . . . to give notice of readiness and to go on giving such notices in order that, when later the lawyers are brought in, no one shall be able to say: "If only the master had given notice of readiness, laytime would have begun and the owners would now be able to claim demurrage".

and for those to whom these notice are tendered[233]:

Just as it is a good working rule for a master, when in doubt, to give notices of readiness, it is an equally good working rule for charterers' agents to reject them if there is any conceivable doubt as to their validity.

3.212 At common law, Notice of Readiness may be given either orally or in writing,[234] or if no notice is given, the shipowner must show that the charterer was aware that the vessel was ready to load, having reached her specified destination at the first load port. Notice need not be given, in the absence of specific requirements to the contrary, at subsequent load ports or at discharge ports.

3.213 The logic behind this is quite simple. When a vessel arrives at the first load port, she may well have on board a cargo from the previous charter for discharge at that port. Whilst the new charterers, through their agents, may well be aware of her arrival, they will not know until they are so informed that she has completed discharge of that cargo and is now at their disposal. The situation is thus analogous to a vessel going on-hire under a time charter.

3.214 Once the charterers know that the vessel is available, they can order her to load and then proceed to subsequent load and discharge ports. Their agents at these, knowing that the vessel is proceeding under charterers' orders, may be expected to watch for her arrival and upon this event take action accordingly.

3.215 Needless to say, in practice this does not happen so simply and additional notice requirements are invariably included in charterparties.

3.216 In *Fairbridge* v. *Pace*, where the owners complained of a failure by the charterers to supply a cargo, Rolfe B said[235]:

Of the arrival of the ship the agents of the defendant may have been bound to take notice; but of the time at which the cargo discharged they could know nothing, and they were, therefore, entitled to notice of that fact from the captain.

3.217 A similar situation arose in *Stanton* v. *Austin*,[236] which concerned a charter for the carriage of a cargo of coal from Sunderland to India. On arrival at the load port, no notice was given and this, the court said, meant that the owners could not claim that the shippers had failed to provide a cargo. However, in *A/B Nordiska Lloyd* v. *J Brownlie & Co (Hull) Ltd*, Scrutton LJ said[237]:

232. *Zim Israel Navigation Co Ltd* v. *Tradax Export SA (The Timna)* [1970] 2 Lloyd's Rep 409, at p. 411 *per* Donaldson J.
233. *Ibid.*
234. Unless the charter provides to the contrary or it is unlawful to tender or accept Notice of Readiness at the port in question, notice may be given on a Sunday or a holiday or other excepted period. *The North King* [1971] 2 Lloyd's Rep 460. See *post* at para. 3.233.
235. *Fairbridge* v. *Pace* (1844) 1 C & K 317, at p. 318.
236. *Stanton* v. *Austin* (1872) LR 7 CP 651.
237. *A/B Nordiska Lloyd* v. *Brownlie & Co (Hull) Ltd* (1925) 30 CC 307, at p. 313.

... whether it is enough that the charterer knows of the presence of the ship from other circumstances, although he has no notice from the shipowner . . . is not decided by *Stanton* v. *Austin* and remains open for decision in some other case . . .

3.218 In *Franco-British Steamship Co* v. *Watson & Youell, the City of Amiens*, the vessel concerned, completed discharging inward cargo at Braila and then gave Notice of Readiness to load to the new charterers, who had an office at Braila. The charter provided for loading at Braila and/or Galatz. After a few days, as there was no cargo for her at Braila, the charterers ordered her to Galatz where they also had an office, and where they also acted as ship's agents for the *City of Amiens*. No Notice of Readiness in writing was submitted by the master on arrival at Galatz. However, said Horridge J[238]:

There is no request that notice in writing should be given and, therefore, verbal notice would be sufficient . . . One of the two houses of the charterers, the one at Braila, had notice that the ship was ready to load. When she came to Galatz, the captain would have to see the charterers, as the ship's agents, with reference to passing her through the Custom House and other matters, and under these circumstances it seems to me impossible to say there was no material on which the umpire could find that the charterers had notice of readiness of the ship to load . . . I cannot say time did not run because the master did not go up into the office and say formally: "I give you notice my ship is ready to load."

3.219 It seems probable that where no written notice is given or required by the charterparty, the shipowner must show either that the charterer (or shipper) was aware of the vessel's readiness to load or if he cannot show actual knowledge, that the charterer, etc., should have been so aware from facts actually known to him. Clearly, it would be easier to show this with regard to a vessel arriving in ballast at a very small port than one arriving to discharge a previous cargo at a large and complex one.

3.220 The question of whether additional notices are necessary at subsequent loading ports was considered in *Burnett Steamship Co Ltd* v. *Olivier & Co Ltd*. In this case, the steamship *Burnhope* was chartered to load cargo at a number of ports in Crete and at Alexandria. The charter provided for "lay days to commence on the day following notice of readiness to load . . . ". In his judgment, Branson J said[239]:

On the other hand, it is said that though the charterparty only speaks of one notice, as you find that the ship is chartered to go from port to port and not as an empty ship at the disposal of the charterers, the business of the contract makes it necessary to imply an obligation to give notice of readiness at each port to which the charterers are entitled to order the ship . . .
... it seems to me, if I have to assume what is the business of the matter, that the charterers should know near enough without a fresh notice of readiness at what time they are to have their cargo ready at the port to which they have ordered the ship to go.

He therefore concluded that additional notices were not necessary.

3.221 Whilst it is usual for the charterer to be responsible for loading, it is not uncommon for charters to contain a cesser clause[240] making the receivers liable for what happens at the discharge port(s). However, whether the receiver or charterer is liable for discharge port demurrage, in either case Notice of Readiness need not be given at the discharge port unless expressly provided in the bill of lading or charter or there is a custom to that effect at that port. With regard to charterers, Brett LJ said in *Nelson* v. *Dahl*[241]:

238. *Franco-British Steamship Co Ltd* v. *Watson & Youell* (1921) 9 Ll L Rep 282, at p. 284. See also *post* at para. 3.299.
239. *Burnett Steamship Co Ltd* v. *Olivier & Co Ltd* (1934) 48 Ll L Rep 238, at p. 240.
240. For a discussion on cesser clauses, see *post* at para. 6.227.
241. *Nelson, Donkin and others* v. *Robert H Dahl* (1879) 12 Ch D 568, at p. 583.

... the ship is ready so far as she is concerned to unload. The shipowner, however, is not bound to give notice that this ship is so arrived and is ready.

3.222 In a series of early cases,[242] it was held that similar principles apply as between shipowners and bills of lading holders.

3.223 In *Akties Laboremus* v. *Steaua Française* one of the arguments raised was that the Notice of Readiness was invalid because it did not purport to be signed by the master. Dismissing that argument, Roche J said[243]:

I am not prepared to dispose of the case on that ground either. I do not decide it, but unless something emerges to the contrary my impression is that that which the captain is required to do he may do by an agent as well as by himself. There would seem to be good reason for that. When a captain is in a foreign port—a Norwegian in a Romanian port—he may require to give notice in a foreign language, and there is good reason why he should do it by means of an agent. It must be a notice given while the ship is there, and given on behalf of the captain.

Express provisions

3.224 A typical charter provision relating to the giving of Notice of Readiness is that contained in clause 11 of the Exxonvoy 84 form of charter, which reads as follows:

NOTICE OF READINESS. Upon arrival at customary anchorage or waiting place at each loading and discharging port or place, Master or Vessel's agent shall give Charterer or its representative notice by letter, telegraph, telex, radio or telephone (if radio or telephone, subsequently confirmed promptly in writing) that Vessel is in all respects ready to load or discharge cargo, berth or no berth.

3.225 The *Voylayrules 1993* also provide[244]:

"IN WRITING" shall mean any visibly expressed form of reproducing words; the medium of transmission shall include electronic communications such as radiocommunications and tele-communications.[245]

3.226 In *The Adolf Leonhardt*,[246] Staughton J held that a notice initiated by radio, but reaching the charterers' agents in written form, qualified as written notice within clause 13 of the Centrocon charter.

3.227 A common provision is a requirement that notice be given within office hours. An indication of how such a clause might be interpreted is given by two decisions of London arbitrators, both relating to whether Saturday morning could be considered as within ordinary office hours, when the office to which notice was given was in fact closed.

3.228 In the first case,[247] the owners tendered Notice of Readiness at 08 50 hours one Saturday morning in Lisbon. The arbitrator said it was necessary to consider local circumstances and other provisions in the charter relating to laytime. The evidence on the former showed that the port was open on Saturday mornings and all port authorities

242. *Harman* v. *Clarke* (1815) 4 Camp. 159. *Harman* v. *Mant* (1815) 4 Camp. 161. *Houlder* v. *General Steam Navigation Co* (1862) 3 F & F 170.
243. *Akties Laboremus* v. *Steaua Française* (1925) 21 Ll L Rep 381, at p. 382.
244. See Appendix. The same definition appears in *Baltic Code 2000*.
245. See also London Arbitration—LMLN 151, 15 August 1985, or Notice of Readiness by cable. The majority of the panel then held that in that case three hours' transmission time should be allowed.
246. *R Pagnan & Fratelli* v. *Finagrain Compagnie Commerciale Agricole et Financière SA* (*The Adolf Leonhardt*) [1986] 2 Lloyd's Rep 395, at p. 403.
247. London Arbitration—LMLN 15, 29 May 1980.

available, stevedoring was charged at premium rates, all shipping agents were closed, except for those attending vessels, and the majority of, if not all, importers/exporters were closed. Other provisions in the charter included the exclusion of Saturday afternoon and Sunday from laytime. More weight, said the arbitrator, had to be given to the evidence relating to business offices, rather than to the hours which the port authorities and stevedores had to work. Therefore, written Notice of Readiness could not be received until Monday morning as the receivers' office was closed on Saturday.

3.229 The second case[248] concerns a vessel which arrived at the Mersey Bar at 03 09 one Saturday. Notice of Readiness was given by telex to the charterers' agents at 09 55 and to the charterers themselves at 10 00. However, neither the charterers' nor their agents' offices were open. The charter contained two provisions relating to giving notice. The first allowed for notice to be given on Saturday mornings before 12 00 if the vessel had been entered at the Custom House. The second said simply that notice was to be given during ordinary office hours, whether the vessel had been entered at the Custom House or not. The issue between the parties was whether the two clauses were linked, so that the times specified in the first indicated what was meant by ordinary office hours, or whether they were completely separate, providing different criteria depending on whether the vessel had been entered at the Custom House or not. There was also a clause in the charter relating to the vessel giving notice when approaching Land's End and the charterers thereupon giving orders for discharge.

3.230 On these facts, the arbitrators held that the notice given on Saturday morning was a good notice. It was clear from the clause relating to giving notice when the vessel had been entered at the Custom House and the clause dealing with giving notice off Land's End that the charterers looked upon Saturday morning as being good for the tendering of notices.

3.231 In a slightly different set of circumstances, the tribunal held in London Arbitration 8/95[249] that a provision that referred to Notice of Readiness being given between business hours of 00 01 and 24 00, meant literally that and notice could validly be given at any time even on Saturday 26 December which was not an official holiday at the port in question.

3.232 If a vessel does pass a written notice to charterers or their agents outside office hours where there is a provision requiring it to be given in office hours then such notice will, it seems, be deemed to have been given at the commencement of office hours on the next working day.

3.233 In *Pacific Carriers Corporation* v. *Tradax Export SA (The North King)*,[250] the *North King* was chartered for a voyage from one safe US port, for which the charterers subsequently nominated Baton Rouge, Louisiana, as the load port. The notice clause of the charter required notification of the vessel's readiness to be delivered at the office of the charterers or their agents "at or before 4 p.m. (or at or before 12 noon if on Saturday)".[251] The owners' agents therefore tendered Notice of Readiness at 09 00 on Saturday 1 November. However, that Saturday was All Saints' Day and a public holiday and the

248. London Arbitration—LMLN 44, 9 July 1981.
249. London Arbitration 8/95—LMLN 408, 24 June 95.
250. *Pacific Carriers Corporation* v. *Tradax Export SA (The North King)* [1971] 2 Lloyd's Rep 460.
251. The second sentence of the clause also required the vessel to have been entered at the Custom House and to have had her loading compartments passed for grain by the appropriate authorities, whereupon laytime was to commence at 7 a.m. on the next business day, whether in berth or not.

charterers contended that the notice was only deemed to be effectively tendered on the following Monday.

3.234 The umpire[252] in the arbitration proceedings and Mocatta J in the High Court both side-stepped the issue as to whether the notice provision allowed notification to be given on a public holiday, an excepted period, by finding that the parties had separately agreed that notice on behalf of the vessel should be accepted on the Saturday morning.[253] However, the umpire also pointed out that no evidence had been adduced to the effect that it was unlawful by the laws of the State of Louisiana to carry on business on All Saints' Day or any other public holiday and he found that it was not unlawful for the Notice of Readiness to be tendered or accepted on that day. It presumably follows from this that, apart from the notice clause in the charter, it would have been perfectly valid for notice to be given on a holiday or other excepted period.

3.235 On the meaning of the specific provision relating to notice in the charter, the umpire said he was inclined to think that by necessary implication from the express words of the clause, a valid Notice of Readiness could not ordinarily be given on a Sunday or a holiday or any other day which is not a business day. The judge contented himself with saying that if it was not for the question of the agreement between the parties, the decision would have turned upon interesting points in relation to the construction of the clauses of the charterparty.

3.236 A case where the question of notices being tendered outside the hours stipulated in the charterparty was the principal issue is *The Petr Schmidt*.[254] The clause in question required notices to be tendered "within 06 00 and 17 00 local time".

3.237 After referring to *The Mexico I*,[255] Longmore J continued[256]:

Mr Hamblen's submission requires as its foundation that the notices of readiness in the present case were invalid and a nullity in the sense used in the decided cases. I do not think that they were. In the present case the ship was ready when the notices of readiness were given. They were notices which stated the truth viz. that the vessel was ready to load or discharge as the case might be. The only thing wrong about the notices was the time that they were tendered, which was outside the contractual hours as specified in the contract. To say that such notices were invalid and must therefore be nullities begs the question. They were accurate but non-contractual in the sense that they were tendered outside the contractual hours. To my mind that does not make them invalid notices in the sense of being nullities; timing provisions have nothing to do with whether notices are nullities. It is only if a notice is untrue that it makes sense to say that it is invalid in the sense of being a nullity.

An "invalid" notice of readiness is a phrase of ambiguous meaning. It makes sense to say that an untruthful or inaccurate notice is invalid. It is not surprising that the courts have held that such a notice has no legal effect and is to be treated as a nullity. It may in a sense be correct to say that a notice given outside the contractual hours is invalid but only in the sense that it does not comply with the contract. It does not follow that the courts should hold that a premature notice of readiness is a nullity and of no effect. The fact that there are good reasons for holding an inaccurate notice to be of no effect (viz. the charterer cannot know when it will become accurate) does not of itself mean that there are similarly good reasons for holding an untimely notice to be of no effect. There is in my view no good reason why the notice should not be effective as at the time which the contract fixes for it to be tendered.

---

252. The late Mr Michael Summerskill, the learned and distinguished author of *Laytime*.
253. For a further discussion on this aspect, see *post* at para. 4.214.
254. *The Petr Schmidt* [1997] 1 Lloyd's Rep 284.
255. *The Mexico I* [1990] 1 Lloyd's Rep 507.
256. *The Petr Schmidt* [1997] 1 Lloyd's Rep 284 at p. 287.

Notice in advance of arrival

3.238 It sometimes happens that a charter provides for one or more notices to be given in advance of arrival. Thus, a vessel may be required to signal her ETA at the discharge port on sailing from the load port and, say, 72, 48 and 24 hours before arrival. Failure to give any of these will not prevent the vessel from giving Notice of Readiness on arrival, but if any delay is caused thereafter which can be shown to arise from the failure to give notice then the charterer will be able to claim damages for breach of the notice provision of an amount equal to that which would otherwise have been claimed by the shipowner as demurrage.

3.239 An interesting illustration of these principles, where there was an express provision relating to the consequences that would ensue in the event of a breach, is provided by London Arbitration 1/94.[257]

3.240 Here the charter required a total of seven notices at specified periods between 15 days and 24 hours to be given to both the discharging port agents and the charterers. In the event of the owners or master "failing to give the aforementioned notices", 24 hours' extra laytime was to be allowed. In the event, the discharging port agents received all but one of the required notices (the 15 days' notice) and the charterers three (the closest to the vessel's arrival being 72 hours' notice). Nevertheless the charterers claimed an additional 24 hours' laytime. In their finding, the tribunal held that the charterers were kept very adequately informed of the ship's ETA from a practical point of view and therefore they refused to hold that the notice provision should be read as a failure to give any notices at all. For the charterers to have succeeded, there would have had to have been a substantial failure which arguably might have had some effect on the operations of the vessel at the discharging port.

3.241 The practical effect of the clause was therefore that if there was a substantial breach, it provided its own remedy by way of increased laytime rather than damages at large which would have been the position had it not.

Time lapse between readiness and commencement of laytime

3.242 It is commonplace for a charter to provide for there to be a delay before laytime commences, either from when the vessel is actually ready to load or discharge, as the case may be, having reached the specified destination or from when the Notice of Readiness is given. This delay, which is intended to give time to prepare for the loading/discharging of the cargo, may either be a straight period of time or be fixed by reference to a point in time or to an external event. An example of the last of these is provided by *John Sadd & Sons Ltd* v. *Bertram Ratcliffe & Co*,[258] where the formula was: "Time for discharging to count from first high water on or after arrival providing sufficient water at the berth."

3.243 Most tanker charters contain a provision to the effect that laytime shall commence six hours after laytime has been given or upon the vessel's arrival in berth, whichever is earlier.

3.244 In a case called *Owners of Borg* v. *Darwen Paper Co*, the relevant charter provided for time to commence 24 hours after arrival at or off the port. One of the

257. London Arbitration 1/94—LMLN 383, 9 July 1994. See also London Arbitration 20/97—LMLN 473, 20 December 1997.
258. *John Sadd & Sons Ltd* v. *Bertram Ratcliffe & Co* (1929) 34 Ll L Rep 18.

questions before the court was how was the 24 hours to be reckoned. Of the argument that was raised, Rowlatt J said[259]:

It is not contended that if the hours began to run they are not interrupted because a non-working day intervenes. It is not contended that they are not to be interrupted if wet weather intervenes, or that if the non-working hours at night intervene, but it is said the 24 hours must begin upon a working day.

Having pointed out that the time that has to elapse before laytime commences is totally different from the time which has to count after discharge has begun, the judge continued[260]:

I think the plain course for me is to say that what is meant is that the consignee shall have 24 hours of ordinary time, from Monday to Tuesday, or Tuesday to Wednesday, or whatever it may be before his time for discharge begins.

   If at the moment discharge begins you find yourself in the middle of the night or a holiday, the work does not naturally begin until the ordinary working hours come round.

If, therefore, the charter provides for a period of time to elapse and the end of that period occurs in what would be an excepted period during the running of laytime then laytime will begin at the end of that excepted period.[261]

   3.245 In *Metalimex Foreign Trade Corporation* v. *Eugenie Maritime Co Ltd*,[262] the question that arose for consideration was the meaning of the following clause:

6. Time for loading to count from 8 a.m. 48 hours after the ship is reported and ready . . . and for discharging from 8 a.m. 24 hours after ship is reported . . .

At both the loading and discharging ports, notice was given at 09 00. The shipowners claimed that time ran from 09 00 two days later at load port and one day later at discharge port. The charterers, on the other hand, said that time counted from 08 00 three days later at load port and two days later at discharge port, i.e. that time should commence from the next 08 00 after the requisite period had elapsed. McNair J said the shipowners were right[263]:

It seems to me that proper business effect is given to the position of the respective parties if one says that the purpose of this is quite clearly to secure that the charterers get the dual protection suggested by the shipowners, namely 48 hours clear before the loading time shall start and that the expiry of the 48 hours shall not start at some inconvenient time, and one should accordingly, read: "from 8 a.m." as "not earlier than 8 a.m.". Well, on the whole, that seems to me to be a reasonable construction which does not do undue violence to any of the language or figures used in the clause.

Notice given before commencement date for laytime

3.246 It is usual for a charter to specify two dates, the period between sometimes being called the laycan spread. The effect of these is that it is agreed that laytime cannot commence before the earlier date and, if the ship is not ready by the later date, the charterers have the option to cancel the charterparty. However, the date when laytime can

   259. *Owners of Borg* v. *Darwen Paper Co* (1921) 8 Ll L Rep 49, at p. 50.
   260. *Ibid.*
   261. Unless the charter provides to the contrary or it would be unlawful, notice may, however, be given on a holiday or other excepted period. See *The North King* [1971] 2 Lloyd's Rep 460 and *ante* at para. 3.233.
   262. *Metalimex Foreign Trade Corporation* v. *Eugenie Maritime Co Ltd* [1962] 1 Lloyd's Rep 378.
   263. *Ibid.*, at p. 384.

commence and when notice can be given are totally different things. As was said in one London Arbitration[264]:

It was often thought that a notice of readiness could not be given before the commencement of lay days under a charter, but that was incorrect unless there was an express provision to that effect. In the absence of such a provision, a valid notice might be given at any time, but the laytime could not commence before the date given in the charter.

But this does not mean that any provision in the charter, such as notice to be given in office hours, can be ignored—it must still be complied with. If the charter provides for laytime to commence at a specified time, it will commence at that time after the opening of the laycan spread, provided of course any other restriction, e.g. that it is a working day, has also been met.[265]

3.247 In an analogous situation, in London Arbitration 9/90[266] the tribunal held that in a charter where the charterers were entitled to use the vessel for floating storage between loading and discharging, nevertheless the owners were entitled to present Notice of Readiness for discharge whilst the vessel was still performing storage services.

Correctness of notice of readiness

3.248 Where a Notice of Readiness is required either at common law (at first load port) or by the terms of the charter, then when it is given the vessel concerned must have arrived at her specified destination[267] (or have met the requirements of any clause advancing commencement of laytime), must then be in a state of readiness to load or discharge[268] and must have fulfilled any additional requirements e.g. entry at Custom House.

3.249 In relation to a laytime clause which read:

Lay days at first loading port to commence twenty-hours, Sundays and holidays excepted, after receipt by charterers or their agents of master's written notice during ordinary working hours, that steamer is entered at the Custom House and in all respects ready to load.

as McNair J said succinctly in *Graigwen (Owners) v Anglo-Canadian Shipping Co Ltd*[269]:

Clearly, although the clause only relates the commencement of the lay days to the giving of notice, the facts stated in the notice, namely the entry at the Custom House and readiness, must also be true at the time the notice is given.

It is also worth mentioning that the vessel must be where she purports to be and as already said, where she is required to be before notice can be given.

3.250 In *Government of Ceylon* v. *Société Franco-Tunisienne d'Armement-Tunis (The Massalia (No 2))*,[270] however, Diplock J was prepared to hold that a Notice of Readiness given before it was possible to discharge the cargo to which it related should take effect when the vessel was ready to discharge that cargo. Furthermore, he held that a provision in the notice clause that time should commence at a specified time need not be followed since charterers were already unloading at other hatches.

264. London Arbitration—LMLN 103, 13 October 1983.
265. London Arbitration 17/91—LMLN 307, 10 August 1991.
266. London Arbitration 9/90—LMLN 285, 6 October 1990.
267. See *ante* at para. 3.2.
268. Subject only to non-delaying preliminaries, routine matters or formalities—*The Tres Flores* [1973] 2 Lloyd's Rep 247, at p. 249 *per* Lord Denning. See *ante* at para. 3.114.
269. *Graigwen (Owners)* v. *Anglo-Canadian Shipping Co Ltd* [1955] 2 Lloyd's Rep 260, at p. 266.
270. *Government of Ceylon* v. *Société Franco-Tunisienne d'Armement-Tunis (The Massalia (No 2))* [1960] 2 Lloyd's Rep 352.

3.251 The facts of the case were that a vessel was chartered with a part cargo of flour from Antwerp and Bordeaux to Colombo. The owners were given liberty to complete with other cargo which they did, overstowing the flour in most of the holds. The laytime commencement clause at the discharge port provided for: "Time to commence at 2 p.m. if Notice of Readiness to discharge is given before noon, and at 8 a.m. next working day if notice given during office hours after noon." At 9 a.m. on the day of her arrival, the *Massalia* gave notice. Six days later, discharge of the flour and overstowed cargo began and all the flour cargo was accessible three days after that. It was only then, said Diplock J, that laytime commenced since the notice referred to in the laytime commencement clause was a Notice of Readiness to discharge flour.[271]

3.252 Of this case, Donaldson J said in *Christensen* v. *Hindustan Steel Ltd*[272]:

In reaching this decision that learned judge relied upon an unidentified authority which no one has been able to trace. He was also much influenced by the fact that the charterers were apparently the consignees of the overstowed cargo and so needed no notice of readiness. In my judgment, this decision turned upon very special facts and does not cast doubt upon the general rule that a notice of readiness is wholly ineffective if, subject to minimal qualifications, the vessel is not ready to discharge at the time at which it is given.

3.253 *Christensen* v. *Hindustan Steel Ltd*[273] was itself perhaps a slightly unexpected decision, although clearly commercially correct. The dispute concerned commencement of laytime at Vizagapatam, the loading port. The notice provision in the charter provided in respect of the load port for: "Time to commence at 24 hours after 1 p.m. if Notice of Readiness to load is given before noon and at 24 hours after 8 a.m. next working day if notice given during office hours after noon." Further clauses provided that notice could only be given in office hours and that the master was to give three days' and 24 hours' Notice of Readiness to load. Not surprisingly perhaps, the charterers argued that this meant that three notices were to be tendered—three days before, one day before and upon readiness to load.

3.254 Notice of Readiness to load was actually given on a Saturday morning. However, this did not say that the vessel was then ready but that it would be ready at 00 00 on Sunday. The ship had previously been discharging an inward cargo. The arbitrators found that at the material time the ship was ready to load and Donaldson J said that, on the balance of probabilities, this meant that she was ready to load at the time notice was given. Despite this actual readiness, the judge nevertheless said[274]:

In the present case the notice was on its face one of anticipated readiness and impliedly reported to the charterers that the vessel was not ready at the time at which it was given. Accordingly, it cannot be relied upon as a notice of actual readiness, even if in fact the vessel was ready.

3.255 Therefore it seems that not only must a Notice of Readiness be correct when it says that a vessel is ready but it cannot understate the case either, by saying it will be ready.

3.256 On the facts of the case, Donaldson J, however, went on to hold that the owners were right in claiming that the charter did not require notice of actual readiness so that only two notices were needed, and even if that given on Saturday morning purported to give 15 and not 24 hours' notice of anticipated readiness to load, the charterers suffered

271. The case also concerned how the period waiting for a berth should be dealt with and that aspect is considered *post*, at para. 5.120.
272. *Christensen* v. *Hindustan Steel Ltd* [1971] 1 Lloyd's Rep 395, at p. 399.
273. *Christensen* v. *Hindustan Steel Ltd* [1971] 1 Lloyd's Rep 395.
274. *Ibid.*, at p. 400.

no detriment since laytime could not in any case commence until Monday morning. His reasoning is summed up in the following passage from his judgment[275]:

Which is right? The charterers can suggest no business reason for the curious arrangement which they suggest was agreed. The owners, on the other hand, can point with force to the fact that when the charterparty was concluded . . . the vessel was already at Vitzagapatam to the knowledge of the charterers and that accordingly one would expect less rather than more notice than usual. In these circumstances, I have no real doubt that the owners' construction is to be preferred.

3.257 The whole question of what effect, if any, an incorrect Notice of Readiness has was considered by the Court of Appeal in *Transgrain Shipping BV* v. *Global Transporte Oceanico SA (The Mexico I)*[276] where the only reasoned judgment was that of Mustill LJ.

3.258 In so far as this issue is concerned, the facts of the case were relatively straightforward. *The Mexico I* arrived off Luanda with a part cargo of bagged maize which was overstowed by a completion cargo. Although the maize was not accessible on arrival, the master gave Notice of Readiness in respect of it. The maize did not become accessible for approximately two weeks and it was not until a further two weeks that discharge began. No further Notice of Readiness was given.

3.259 At arbitration, the arbitrators decided that the original Notice of Readiness became effective when the maize became accessible, a conclusion shared by the High Court. However, the Court of Appeal disagreed, holding that laytime began on discharge, counsel for the charterers having conceded that that was the latest point in time it could have begun. The court did not have to consider, therefore, whether it ever began at all in the absence of a second valid notice, a possibility hinted at in the judgment.[277]

3.260 In reviewing the earlier cases, Mustill LJ also cast doubt on the decision in *The Massalia (No 2)*,[278] saying the status of the premature Notice of Readiness was not fully argued in that case.[279] He also drew a distinction between the idea of an inchoate Notice of Readiness in its purest form and a modified form put forward in the present case. In the pure form, the notice automatically takes effect when the ship becomes ready. The main practical objection to this is that the charterer would not know when this was. The alternative or modified version is that it takes effect when the charterers know, or have the means of knowing, when the ship is actually ready, which the judge described as a fertile source of dispute.[280] He therefore concluded that the original notice was without any effect and went on to consider whether there had been any findings by the arbitrators that would have justified an inference of waiver, estoppel or agreement.[281] Having concluded that there were not, he then commented that had he upheld the "inchoate" concept, he would have said that notice time should be allowed, but that if time began by waiver, estoppel or agreement, the precise moment when this happened would depend on the facts leading to it.

---

275. *Christensen* v. *Hindustan Steel Ltd* [1971] 1 Lloyd's Rep 395.
276. *Transgrain Shipping BV* v. *Global Transporte Oceanico SA (The Mexico I)* [1990] 1 Lloyd's Rep 507.
277. *Ibid.*, at p. 510.
278. *Government of Ceylon* v. *Société Franco-Tunisienne d'Armement-Tunis (The Massalia) (No 2)* [1960] 2 Lloyd's Rep 352.
279. *The Mexico I* [1990] 1 Lloyd's Rep 507, at p. 512.
280. *Ibid.*, at p. 513.
281. *Ibid.*, at p. 515.

3.261 In London Arbitration 10/94,[282] two written Notices of Readiness were prepared both stating that they had been tendered at the same date and time, but both recording the times of events which occurred subsequent to the time when the notice was said to have been tendered. A copy of the second notice was returned to the vessel at a time when a valid notice could have been given. In these circumstances, the tribunal held that the notice should be treated as if it had been given again or a fresh one had been given at that time. The second notice was therefore valid despite what it said about the date and time of its tendering.

3.262 As was stated at the start of this section, where a Notice of Readiness is required, then when it is given, the vessel must first have arrived at her specified destination.

3.263 In *The Agamemnon*,[283] the vessel was fixed to load at Baton Rouge in the Mississippi but gave notice prematurely at the South West Pass, which is an anchorage at which ships lie whilst waiting to enter the Mississippi and must transit to enter the river. The vessel had been anchored at the South West Pass but had been forced to proceed out to sea because of the onset of Hurricane Opal; but when the weather abated and she returned, the master gave Notice of Readiness which was subsequently held to be premature and invalid.

3.264 It looks from the report of the case as though the master may have given notice whilst underway,[284] but no point was taken about that. The judge did, however, refer to a finding of fact made by the arbitral tribunal who first dealt with the case that the vessel had not "reached a point as close to the loading berth as she might be permitted to approach".[285] He continued[286]:

... when considering the condition as to the geographical position the vessel has reached, the statement in the notice of readiness may or may not be true as to the geographical position of the vessel or whether she has reached the point that is nearest to the port or berth (as the case may be); what matters however, is whether the condition in the charter-party for the giving of notice has been met and the vessel is, at the time the notice is given, at the point stipulated in the charter-party where notice can be given. That is the test for validity ...

Notice of Readiness and clause 6 of the Asbatankvoy form of charter

3.265 The Asbatankvoy form of charter (formerly Exxonvoy 69) is one of the most commonly used forms of tanker charterparty. Clause 6 of Part II of the charter deals with Notices of Readiness and provides:

NOTICE OF READINESS. Upon arrival at customary anchorage at each port of loading or discharge, the Master or his agent shall give the Charterer or his agent notice by letter, telegraph, wireless or telephone that the Vessel is ready to load or discharge cargo, berth or no berth and laytime, as hereinafter provided, shall commence upon the expiration of six (6) hours after receipt of such notice, or upon the Vessel's arrival in berth (i.e. finished mooring when at a sealoading or discharging terminal and all fast when loading or discharging alongside a wharf), whichever first occurs.

This presents a number of problems. If "arrival" in the opening line means anchoring, what is the position if the vessel proceeds directly into berth? The second part of the clause

---

282. London Arbitration 10/94—LMLN 387, 3 September 1994.
283. *The Agamemnon* [1998] 1 Lloyd's Rep 675.
284. See *post* at paras 3.266 *et seq.* for a discussion on Notices of Readiness being given under way.
285. *The Agamemnon* [1998] 1 Lloyd's Rep 675 at p. 677.
286. *Ibid.*, at p. 678.

provides for time to commence upon arrival in berth but that is after notice has been given at the customary anchorage.

3.266 This has led some masters and owners to believe that they can give Notice of Readiness underway—either passing through a customary anchorage or whilst pausing briefly underway, for example to pick up a pilot.

3.267 There have been a number of major decisions over the last 100 years relating to the point at which Notice of Readiness may be tendered under a port charterparty.[287] In most of these, the vessel concerned had anchored when notice was given. The exception is the case of *The Maratha Envoy*, where the vessel concerned first anchored at the Weser lightship at the mouth of the river Weser then moved up river to Brake on the flood tide, gave Notice of Readiness, turned in the river and went back to the anchorage. This manoeuvre was described by Lord Diplock in the House of Lords as "showing the chimney", "a charade" and "a voyage of convenience" and, perhaps not unsurprisingly, it was held that the notice given upriver was invalid.

3.268 In *The Johanna Oldendorff*, Viscount Dilhorne said[288]:

. . . that under a port charterparty [, for a ship] to be an arrived ship, that is to say a ship at a place where a valid notice of readiness to load or discharge can be given, she must have ended her voyage at the port named.

3.269 The point is made even more clearly in the speech of Lord Diplock[289] where he analysed the adventure contemplated by a voyage charterparty into four stages. These were the approach voyage (which he referred to as the loading voyage), the loading operation, the carrying voyage and the discharge of the cargo. As he made clear, these stages are consecutive and cannot overlap. Arrival at the specified destination is the point both geographically and in time when the voyage stages end and the loading/discharging operations begin. Lord Diplock continued[290]:

Since the business purpose of the voyage stages is to bring the vessel to a berth at which the cargo can be loaded or discharged, the shipowner does not complete the loading or the carrying voyage until the vessel has come to a stop at a place within the larger area whence her proceeding further would serve no business purpose. If on her arrival within the dock or port, there is a berth available at which the charterer is willing and able to load or discharge the cargo, the vessel must proceed straight there and her loading or carrying voyage will not be completed until she reaches it. But if no berth is available the voyage stage ends when she is moored at any convenient place from which she can get to a berth as soon as one is vacant.

This last sentence makes it clear what Lord Reid meant[291] when he refers to the vessel having "reached a position within the port where she is at the immediate and effective disposition of the charterer" and Viscount Dilhorne when he said "she must have ended her voyage at the port named" if no berth is immediately available. There is also support for this proposition in *The Maratha Envoy*, where Lord Diplock quoted with approval from the judgment of Donaldson J at first instance[292]:

---

287. *Leonis Steamship Co v. Rank (No 1)* (1907) 13 CC 136; *The Aello* [1960] 1 Lloyd's Rep 623; *The Johanna Oldendorff* [1973] 2 Lloyd's Rep 285; *The Maratha Envoy* [1977] 2 Lloyd's Rep 301.
288. *The Johanna Oldendorff* [1973] 2 Lloyd's Rep 285 at p. 302.
289. *Ibid.*, at p. 304. See *ante* at para. 1.110.
290. *Ibid.*, at p. 305.
291. *Ibid.*, at p. 291. See *ante* at para. 3.102.
292. *The Maratha Envoy* [1977] 3 WLR 1372 at p. 1378.

He applied the Reid test from *The Johanna Oldendorff*. "The essential feature," he said [1975] 1 WLR 1372, 1378 is that the voyage shall have ended and the vessel be waiting.

3.270 It is an essential feature of the division of the charterparty into the four stages that there is a clear division between the voyage stages and the loading/discharging operations. The voyage stages do not come to an end until the vessel is moored, i.e. anchored, or if the vessel can proceed directly, is alongside in the designated berth.

3.271 It follows that at common law, Notice of Readiness cannot normally be given whilst the vessel is underway whether the vessel be making way or temporarily stopped in the water.

3.272 However does the wording of clause 6 supersede what the position would be at common law? There appear to be two possible approaches to what meaning should be given to this clause. The first is to say that there should be an implied term in the opening line of the clause so that it reads:

Upon arrival at customary anchorage or in berth (as hereinafter defined) if proceeding direct to berth . . . "

and then apply the common law principles that the vessel does not reach her specified destination and therefore arrive until she either reaches a place "whence proceeding further would serve no business purpose", i.e. she anchors, or she arrives in berth.

3.273 The alternative, and, it is suggested, less satisfactory, solution is to give a wider meaning to the words "upon arrival" and allow Notice of Readiness to be given at some point before the vessel comes to a stop by anchoring or berthing. However this of itself would raise all sorts of practical problems. Must the ship pause, e.g. to pick up a pilot?; would an investigation have to be undertaken as to the anchorage limits?; what if there is more than one anchorage?; what if the vessel does not pass through any of the anchorages but proceeds directly to berth?[293]

Acceptance of notice

3.274 Where a notice is tendered in writing as a letter, it is usual for the master or agent presenting it to do so in at least two copies, getting the charterers (or the shippers/receivers as the case may be) or their agents to acknowledge receipt on one copy with the time of receipt clearly marked.

3.275 As was remarked in London Arbitration 31/92[294]:

Commonly notices of readiness were (i) tendered, (ii) received, and (iii) accepted, all at different times but in that order. Tendering and receipt were often simultaneous. Receipt and acceptance were frequently not. The latter activities should not be confused. Where a charter referred to receipt of a notice, regard had to be had to that and not to the time of its acceptance.

3.276 Some charterparties specifically require Notice of Readiness to be accepted and not merely tendered or received. What then is the position if the recipient delays acceptance?

3.277 That was the issue in London Arbitration 9/96[295] where clause 6 of the C(Ore) 7 Mediterranean Iron Ore form as amended required acceptance of Notice of Readiness

---

293. See the advice of Donaldson J (as he then was) given in *The Timna* [1970] 2 Lloyd's Rep 409 at p. 411, quoted *ante* at para. 3.211.
294. London Arbitration 31/92—LMLN 338, 17 October 1992.
295. London Arbitration 9/96—LMLN 434, 22 June 1996.

before the laytime clock was triggered. The notice was validly served on 15 June but not accepted by the shippers until 20 June. No explanation for the delay was given to the tribunal, who held that in the absence of authority they would have had no doubt that there was to be implied into clause 6 a term obliging the shippers to accept Notice of Readiness reasonably promptly, if not immediately. "Otherwise" said the tribunal, "the owners would be in an impossible situation, being entirely at the mercy of the shippers . . . ". They went on to hold on the basis of *The Atlantic Sunbeam*,[296] which they held applied in this case, that the shippers were bound to act with reasonable dispatch and in accordance with the ordinary practice of the port.

3.278 On the facts of the case, they upheld the owners' submission that, notice having been given on 15 June, it should have been accepted at 08 00 on 16 June at the latest.

3.279 In *Pacific Carriers Corporation* v. *Tradax Export SA (The North King)*,[297] the facts of which have already been given,[298] the judge and the umpire both decided the case on the basis that the charterers' agents, acting with the authority of their principals, had accepted the vessel's Notice of Readiness on a Saturday which was a holiday, when arguably under the charter they should not have done, in pursuance of an agreement with the owners' agents. The umpire was also prepared to hold that the charterers were estopped by acceptance of the notice from denying its validity and effectiveness. On this aspect, Mocatta J said[299]:

. . . it is not strictly necessary for me to consider whether the owners can also support the conclusion at which the umpire arrived on the basis of estoppel as distinct from that of agreement. I have no doubt that the proper inference of fact is that a representation was made to the effect that if a proper notice, in the sense that the ship was then ready physically, was given on Nov. 1, before noon, it would be treated as having the same effect as a similar notice given on any other Saturday. The question, however, whether the owners acted upon that representation in a way in which they would not otherwise have acted, is, perhaps more difficult. Accordingly, although it may be that on the point of estoppel, if it had stood alone, I would have reached the conclusion that the owners were entitled to succeed, I think it best not to base my judgment in the alternative upon that, but to restrict it to the firm ground with which I have already dealt, namely, that there was an agreement between the parties, the effect of which was to treat Saturday Nov. 1 in the same way as any other Saturday for the purposes of the giving of a Notice of Readiness.

3.280 The question of whether there was an estoppel when receivers' agents accepted a Notice of Readiness incorrectly was one of the main issues raised in *Surrey Shipping Co Ltd* v. *Compagnie Continentale (France) SA (The Shackleford)*.[300] Under the relevant charter, Notice of Readiness was required to be given to receivers or their agents at or before 4 p.m. on official working days, the vessel also having been entered at the Custom House. This latter requirement was therefore a condition precedent to the giving of notice, but unfortunately for the owners, the vessel could only be entered at the Custom House having berthed. However, it did not matter what sort of berth she arrived at, provided she was alongside, i.e. it did not have to be a discharging berth and could, for instance, be a bunkering berth.

296. *Sunbeam Shipping Co Ltd* v. *President of India (The Atlantic Sunbeam)* [1973] 1 Lloyd's Rep 482.
297. *Pacific Carriers Corporation* v. *Tradax Export SA (The North King)* [1971] 2 Lloyd's Rep 460.
298. See *ante* at para. 3.233.
299. *The North King* [1971] 2 Lloyd's Rep 460, at p. 468.
300. *Surrey Shipping Co Ltd* v. *Compagnie Continentale (France) SA (The Shackleford)* [1978] 2 Lloyd's Rep 154.

3.281 On arrival at the usual anchorage, the *Shackleford* tendered Notice of Readiness, although she had not been entered at the Custom House. Nevertheless, this was accepted by the receivers' agents, who also advised the owners that time would count from arrival in the roads off the port. As there was congestion in the port, there was some delay before the vessel could berth and the first berth she proceeded to was a bunkering berth. Customs entry was effected whilst she was in the bunkering berth and she then proceeded to a lay-by berth and eventually to a discharging berth. The owners argued that in reliance upon acceptance of Notice of Readiness by the receivers' agents and the message they subsequently received, they did not attempt to procure an earlier berth to effect Customs entry.

3.282 In the High Court,[301] Donaldson J held that the Notice of Readiness given on arrival was a good notice in that the vessel had arrived at Constantza, the discharging port, and was ready to discharge, but it was premature in that no Customs entry had been obtained; under the terms of the charter, the receivers could have rejected or ignored the notice but they had accepted it and this created an estoppel by conduct so that the charterers could not now allege that the notice was premature.

3.283 In the Court of Appeal one of the main points raised was whether the receivers were acting within their authority in accepting premature Notice of Readiness and on this the court were prepared to accept that it was open to the arbitrator to find from his own experience, in the absence of any evidence either way, that this was within their usual authority.[302]

3.284 On the estoppel issue, Sir David Cairns said[303]:

An important issue at the arbitration and before the judge was whether the acceptance was relied on by the shipowners. The arbitrator found that it was. The judge held that he was bound by that finding and charterers have not challenged that part of the judge's decision in this court.

3.285 Another case concerning acceptance of a Notice of Readiness was *Sofial SA* v. *Ove Skou Rederi (The Helle Skou)*.[304] Here the vessel concerned was chartered for the carriage of skimmed milk in bags, the previous cargo being fishmeal in bags. A clause in the charter required the vessel to be presented with holds clean and dry and free from smell. On presentation, the charterers accepted the vessel without verifying the state of the holds and commenced loading. In fact, the vessel was not free from smell and eventually it was decided that the cargo that had been loaded must be discharged so that the vessel might be cleaned. As a result some four days were lost. The owners admitted that Notice of Readiness should not have been given, but denied that the charterers were entitled, as they contended, to reject the Notice of Readiness since they had begun loading. It was, of course, not in dispute that damages were payable.

3.286 In upholding the owners' argument, Donaldson J said[305]:

There have been many cases of notice of readiness being rejected as premature and subsequently accepted: see, for example, *Compania de Naviera Nedelka SA* v. *Tradax International SA (The Tres Flores)* [1973] 2 Lloyd's Rep 247, but I think that this is the first case in which charterers have accepted such a notice and later claimed to reject it. I do not think that they can do so. As Mr

---

301. *Surrey Shipping Co Ltd* v. *Compagnie Continentale (France) SA (The Shackleford)* [1978] 1 Lloyd's Rep 191.
302. *The Shackleford* [1978] 2 Lloyd's Rep 154, at p. 160.
303. *Ibid.*
304. *Sofial SA* v. *Ove Skou Rederi (The Helle Skou)* [1976] 2 Lloyd's Rep 205.
305. *Ibid.*, at p. 214.

Hallgarten pointed out, the contrary view would enable a charterer to reject a notice of readiness and to start laytime all over again if he discovered some lack of readiness in the ship at a late stage in loading. And this would be the case even if the cargo did not have to be discharged.

A notice of readiness which is rightly rejected is a nullity, save to the extent that with the express or implied agreement of the charterers, it may be left with them instead of being re-served and will then take effect when it truly represents the facts. But this notice was far from being a nullity. It was the key which unlocked the holds of the vessel and allowed loading to begin. And it was the charterers' act which created this position. Whether it is labelled as waiver or estoppel or something else, I do not consider that the charterers can resile from this position, save upon grounds of fraud.

3.287 In *The Shackleford*, the Court of Appeal[306] mentioned that in that case, Donaldson J had in part relied upon his own earlier decision in *The Helle Skou*, but did not find it necessary to consider it further.

3.288 The following cases illustrate the attitude taken by various panels of arbitrators to the question of acceptance of defective notices. As Donaldson J pointed out in *The Helle Skou*,[307] it is a common commercial practice for defective Notices of Readiness to be left with those upon whom they have been served in the expectation that they will take effect when the vessel eventually meets all the requirements of readiness. The danger of so doing will be obvious from the judgment of the Court of Appeal in *The Mexico I*.[308]

3.289 In London Arbitration 15/86,[309] the tanker concerned tendered notice before berthing which was accepted by the refinery at about 20 15 on the day the vessel came alongside. The tanks were inspected some eight hours later and found unsuitable for loading the intended cargo of kerosene, the specification of which was included in the charter. The charterers then rejected the notice and owners claimed they were estopped from denying its validity. However, the tribunal rejected this, saying an estoppel could not be established where a mere acceptance was followed by a rejection of the vessel not many hours later. There was no reliance by owners upon the acceptance of the notice and neither did they suffer any detriment by it.

3.290 In London Arbitration 15/87,[310] a vessel was to load grain in the US Gulf. The charter required notice to be accompanied by a pass from the USDA. This was not in fact issued until a day after notice was accepted by the charterers' agents. Notice was accepted some two hours after it was tendered and owners argued that as a result of its acceptance and/or the fact that the vessel was subsequently prepared for loading, the charterers had waived or were estopped from relying upon any defects in it. This was rejected by the arbitrators, who compared the factual scenario with that in *The Shackleford*,[311] pointing out that two of the main factors favouring owners in that case were the difficulty they faced in establishing the true position and the closely connected identity of the charterers and their agents. In this case there was no reason to assume the agents could be identified more closely with their principals than any other independent port agent. The tribunal did,

---

306. *Surrey Shipping Co Ltd* v. *Compagnie Continentale (France) SA (The Shackleford)* [1978] 2 Lloyd's Rep 154, at p. 160.
307. *Sofial SA* v. *Ove Skou Rederi (The Helle Skou)* [1976] 2 Lloyd's Rep 205, at p. 214.
308. *Transgrain Shipping BV* v. *Global Transporte Oceanico SA (The Mexico I)* [1990] 1 Lloyd's Rep 507.
309. London Arbitration 15/86—LMLN 180, 25 September 1986.
310. London Arbitration 15/87—LMLN 206, 26 September 1987.
311. *Surrey Shipping Co Ltd* v. *Compagnie Continentale (France) SA (The Shackleford)* [1978] 2 Lloyd's Rep 154.

however, hold that laytime commenced after the requisite period specified in the charter after the pass had been issued.

3.291 A case where owners succeeded was London Arbitration 26/89.[312] However, it should be noted that this case was decided before *The Mexico I*[313] reached the Court of Appeal, the High Court having taken a more flexible view to questions of waiver, estoppel, etc. However, it is included for the sake of completeness.[314]

3.292 At the time when Notice of Readiness was tendered, the vessel was still outside the commercial limits of the port and therefore not an Arrived ship. No new notice was tendered when the vessel came within the limits of the port. On this the tribunal said:

... there was no general rule that premature notice of readiness became automatically effective when a vessel became ready. The general rule was that a notice had to be valid when tendered and if it was invalid it was ineffective. Once the conditions for a valid notice had been met, a fresh notice had to be tendered. If it was not, the original notice could only be considered to have become effective in the event of the charterers having waived their contractual entitlement to a valid notice (which would in fact be a second or further notice).

3.293 That statement probably represents the law at the time of writing with the possible exception that instead of waiver, it would be better to say "a bilateral agreement to vary the charter, or the existence of what has come to be called 'estoppel by convention' ".[315]

3.294 The arbitrators then went on to find that the charterers treated the notice as being effective because in reliance upon it they had the cargo available for immediate loading when the vessel berthed and the owners' agents were given no reason to suspect anything amiss. They found that laytime began on arrival within the port. Following the Court of Appeal decision in *The Mexico I*,[316] the tribunal might not have reached this conclusion. Whether preparing the cargo for loading is evidence of a bilateral agreement is open to question and estoppel in the absence of any positive act by owners except their failure to present a new notice would be difficult to prove.

3.295 This last point was, however, taken up in London Arbitration 6/90.[317] In that case the arbitrator held the original notice to be valid, but one of the arguments put forward by owners was that if it was not, charterers were estopped from challenging its validity by reason of their conduct in making no comment for a month and a half after they had received the notice. On this, the arbitrator accepted the evidence of the owners' broker that if there was any irregularity in a Notice of Readiness, the agents, charterers or receivers would be quick to draw attention to it. Had the owners in any way been alerted to a problem, they would have done something about it. The charterers countered that silence and inaction are equivocal and relied upon *The Leonidas D*.[318] The arbitrator accepted this was true on occasions, but in the circumstances of the present case said it was highly improbable that an experienced ship's agent would not reject a notice immediately if it was invalid or unacceptable. A reasonable man, especially one experienced in chartering and shipping, would expect an immediate objection to a faulty notice. There would

312. London Arbitration 26/89—LMLN 262, 18 November 1989.
313. *Transgrain Shipping BV* v. *Global Transporte Oceanico SA (The Mexico I)* [1988] 2 Lloyd's Rep 149; [1990] 1 Lloyd's Rep 507.
314. See also London Arbitration 8/92—LMLN 324, 4 April 1992.
315. *The Mexico I* [1990] 1 Lloyd's Rep 507, at p. 514.
316. *The Mexico I* [1990] 1 Lloyd's Rep 507.
317. London Arbitration 6/90—LMLN 274, 5 May 1990.
318. *The Leonidas D* [1985] 2 Lloyd's Rep 18.

inevitably be a reliance by owners on the actions or inactions of the agents and accordingly the charterers would be estopped from denying the validity of the notice.

3.296 Whilst what the arbitrator said was true and justified from a commercial point of view, whether the courts will accept that these facts would give rise to an estoppel is more open to question. It would seem that in *The Mexico I*,[319] the notice tendered was accepted and not rejected and a substantial period elapsed before discharge commenced without anything being said by the charterers. On those facts, the Court of Appeal was in no doubt there was insufficient to infer waiver, estoppel or agreement.

3.297 The leading case on defective notices must now be considered to be the Court of Appeal decision in *The Mexico I*.[320] An outline of the facts has already been given. Having rejected the inchoate theory relating to defective notices, either in its pure or modified form,[321] Mustill LJ turned to the questions of waiver, estoppel and agreements to vary the charter, saying[322]:

For my part I am sceptical about the deployment of the elusive concept of waiver, and would prefer to look for conduct from which one could infer either a bilateral agreement to vary the charter, or the existence of what has come to be called "estoppel by convention": namely, a situation in which the parties, having conducted themselves on the mutual assumption that their legal relations take a certain shape, cannot afterwards be heard to assert the contrary. I do not for a moment doubt that such a state of affairs, if proved to exist, could justify the conclusion that laytime began, after the giving of an invalid notice, but before the moment of actual discharge.

3.298 Turning to the case in question to see whether these principles had been met, Mustill LJ continued[323]:

First as to the facts. Whatever precisely the doctrine, one would be looking for some kind of bilateral representation and action, on the basis that the contractual arrangement about laytime had been replaced by something new. What do we find here? A notice invalidly given. The arbitrators have found, via the statement of facts, that it was "accepted". (Often this would be by countersignature of a document. Since the notice here was rendered by telex, we do not know the form of the acceptance.) However, since, as the arbitrators point out, the acceptance must have been given in reliance upon the master's implied assurance that the ship was ready for discharge, it cannot have any value. What else? Nothing, so far as the award is concerned. When the ship was ready to discharge the contractual cargo, there was no notification to the charterers or their agents. Nor is anything found in the award by way of an intimation on the part of the charterers they accepted that the laytime could now begin. It seems that the moment when the ship became ready for discharge passed in complete silence.

3.299 He therefore concluded that these were thin materials indeed to infer any waiver, estoppel or agreement and found that there was none. The court therefore found that laytime did not begin before the commencement of discharge, although it would seem that had the parties not agreed that that was the latest it could begin, the court would have been prepared to consider an argument to the effect that it never began in the absence of a valid Notice of Readiness or bilateral agreement, etc.[324] As was pointed out, this might have resulted in owners having to pay despatch on the full amount of laytime allowed.

3.300 To summarize the law as it now stands:

---

319. *The Mexico I* [1988] 2 Lloyd's Rep 149; [1990] 1 Lloyd's Rep 507.
320. *The Mexico I* [1990] 1 Lloyd's Rep 507.
321. *Ibid.*, at p. 512.
322. *Ibid.*, at p. 514.
323. *Ibid.*
324. *Ibid.*, at p. 510. See also *ante* at para. 3.219.

    A. A defective notice is invalid for all purposes.

    B. There is no doctrine of inchoate notice, although there may be an agreement with the recipient of the notice that it will be left with him, although then invalid, and will take effect when the vessel is ready but this will require some overt act on the part of the ship to signify when this is.

    C. Agents may or may not have implied or express authority to reach a bilateral agreement to vary the charter in respect of provisions relating to the submission of a valid Notice of Readiness.

    D. Charterers by their acts or conduct may be taken to have reached such an agreement.

    E. Failure to submit a valid Notice of Readiness may be cured by estoppel by convention.

    F. If no valid notice is ever submitted and there is no waiver, estoppel or agreement to vary the charter, there is no assurance that commencement of cargo operations will automatically trigger the running of laytime.

3.301 Although probably not strictly necessary, since time lost by default of the owner would not normally count as laytime, to avoid doubt, the charterers might well be prudent to include some such clause as the following, which is part of clause 7 of Part II of the Bimchemvoy charter:

> If after berthing the Vessel is found not to be ready in all respects to load or discharge, the actual time lost from the discovery thereof until she is in fact ready to load or discharge, shall not count as laytime.

Readiness and readiness

3.302 Many of the cases previously considered, particularly those relating to physical readiness, arose in relation to a cancellation clause rather than Notice of Readiness to load. In both cases, similar considerations arise. The principal distinction, however, appears to be that unless the charter provides to the contrary, no Notice of Readiness need be given at the first load port to prevent the charterer from cancelling the charter. All that is required is that the vessel has arrived at her specified destination and is in all respects ready to load, whereas for laytime to commence, notice must normally be given as well.

3.303 The leading case on the distinction is *A/B Nordiska Lloyd* v. *J Brownlie & Co (Hull) Ltd*,[325] a decision of the Court of Appeal. This concerned a ship called the *Gevalia*, which was ordered to Hull to load on a berth charter. Time was to count when written Notice of Readiness was received in business hours.

3.304 Other clauses of the charter provided:

> 7. If steamer be prevented from entering . . . docks or from arriving at or off loading place by reason of congestion . . . she is to be treated as a ready steamer from first high water on or after arrival . . . and entitled there-upon to give written Notice of Readiness . . .
>
> 11. . . . charterers to have the option of cancelling this charter . . . if she is not ready from any cause on or before Apr. 3 at 6 am.

3.305 The *Gevalia* arrived off Hull on Easter Saturday, which was 31 March, but owing to congestion was unable to enter the docks. The earliest she could have given notice under clause 7 was the start of business on 3 April since the previous day was Easter

---

325. *A/B Nordiska Lloyd* v. *J Brownlie & Co (Hull) Ltd* (1925) 22 Ll L Rep 79.

Monday and therefore a bank holiday. That was after the charterers' right to cancel had arisen, a right they sought to exercise. However, the Court of Appeal held they were wrong; the test was the actual readiness of the ship. Under this charter Notice of Readiness was irrelevant to cancellation. As Scrutton LJ said[326]:

In my view, if the charterers wished to put an additional provision into the (cancellation) clause as to giving notice they must say so.

Atkin LJ put it this way[327]:

It is necessary to distinguish between the obligation on the charterers and the right of the charterers to cancel the contract.

I see no reason to assume that the giving of a Notice of Readiness is a condition precedent to the charterers' right to put the contract at an end. In the cancelling clause there is no express provision that Notice of Readiness must be given. All that is provided is that if the ship is not ready from any cause on or before Apr. 3 the charterers have the option to cancel. In clause 7 it is said that the ship is to be treated as ready even if she is prevented from entering the harbour by congestion or other cause and Notice of Readiness may then be given, but that does not apply to the cancelling clause.

3.306 Most modern charters do, however, link cancellation with the giving of Notice of Readiness, rather than with just being ready. Thus, clause 12 of Part II of the Exxonvoy 84 form of charter provides:

CANCELLATION OF CHARTER. If Vessel has not tendered a valid Notice of Readiness by 16 00 hours local time on the Cancelling Date specified in Part I(B), Charterer shall have the right to cancel this Charter by notifying Owner or Owner's Agent by telegraph, telex or radio (if radio, subsequently confirmed promptly in writing) of such cancellation within forty-eight (48) hours local time after expiration of the said Cancelling Date, failing which this Charter shall remain in full force and effect. Charterer's said option shall continue to apply even if Vessel tenders Notice of Readiness within the just mentioned forty-eight hour period . . .

Similarly, clause 4 of Part II of the Bimchemvoy charter states:

Charterers' Option of Cancelling

If the Vessel has not given a valid Notice of Readiness as provided in Clause 7 by 12 midnight (24 00 hours) local time on the cancelling date specified in Box 16 Charterers shall have the option of cancelling this Charter Party . . .

3.307 Clearly, if a charter does allow a charterer to cancel unless notice is given then the question of whether the charterer's right has arisen is more clear cut. If no such notice is required for cancellation and the ship has reached her specified destination but not yet given Notice of Readiness to load, the charterer cannot be sure whether he has the right to cancel without first ascertaining the position from the shipowner. The only time he can be certain is when the vessel has not reached its specified destination by the cancelling date.

3.308 In an American case involving a vessel called the *Luctor*,[328] the charterers sought to argue that where a vessel arrived later than the cancelling date, but they failed to cancel, her late arrival would disentitle the owners from claiming demurrage. This contention was rejected by the arbitration tribunal concerned who held that the charterers could not

---

326. *Ibid.*, at p. 80.
327. *Ibid.*
328. *Protank Ltd* v. *Transatlantic Petroleum Ltd (The Luctor)*, LMLN 349, 20 March 1993.

unilaterally rewrite the charter and therefore the laytime provisions remained in force. The position would have been the same had this been an English case.

Work before laytime commences

3.309 Charters often specify that laytime should begin after the expiry of a given period after Notice of Readiness has been presented and it sometimes happens that work begins before the end of this time. It may even happen that work begins before the commencing date stated in the charter for laytime to begin.

3.310 Whilst notice may be given before the start of the laycan spread,[329] the courts will only hold that the parties have agreed to vary the time at which the charter says that laytime should begin upon very clear evidence of such an agreement, whether this be to advance the laytime commencement date or shorten the period after Notice of Readiness has been given. The principles that apply are similar to those that appertain to working on holidays or other excepted periods.[330]

3.311 The mere fact that work proceeds is not enough to evidence a variation of the charter. In at least one early case, however, this was not so, although in this case, *The Katy*,[331] the actual issue was whether work on part of a day should count as a whole day. Fourteen running days were allowed for loading and discharging but there was no provision as to when laytime should begin. However, it was usual for laytime to count only from the first full day and, in *The Katy*, the question was whether a full day should be counted as the ship berthed at 10 a.m. and cargo operations continued during the afternoon. On these facts, the Court of Appeal held that, by working the ship, the charterers had agreed to count a whole day against laytime. As Lord Esher said[332]:

The captain said "Come—agree with me to take delivery"; and they did agree to take delivery, and they did it. Is that, or is that not, agreeing to treat Saturday as one of the lay days?

3.312 However, in *Nelson & Sons* v. *Nelson Line Liverpool Ltd (No 3)*[333] the House of Lords refused to accept that working in an excepted period meant that both sides had agreed to count such time. Lord Loreburn LC, giving his reasons, said[334]:

In my view it is a question, not of law, but of fact, whether or not there was an agreement varying the terms of the charterparty and providing that the holidays in question should count as lay days. I am unable to see any evidence of such an agreement.

3.313 The most recent and germane case, however, on this issue is *Pteroti Compania Naviera SA* v. *National Coal Board (The Khios Breeze)*[335] where the charter provided for laytime to commence 24 hours after written notice was given. In fact, discharge commenced half an hour after the vessel's arrival—before notice was given and therefore before the 24-hour period had even started.

3.314 In refusing to accept that there had been any agreement to vary the terms of the charter, Diplock J drew attention to the House of Lords' decision in *Nelson & Sons* v.

---

329. See *ante* at para. 3.246.
330. See *post* at para. 4.244.
331. *The Katy* [1895] P 56.
332. *Ibid.*, at p. 63.
333. *Nelson & Sons Ltd* v. *Nelson Line (Liverpool) Ltd (No 3)* (1908) 13 CC 235 (HL).
334. *Ibid.*, at p. 240.
335. *Pteroti Compania Naviera SA* v. *National Coal Board (The Khios Breeze)* [1958] 1 Lloyd's Rep 245.

Nelson Line Liverpool Ltd (No 3)[336] and also to the dissenting judgment of Fletcher Moulton LJ in the Court of Appeal[337] in the same case, which pointed out the principles on which the court should be prepared to infer agreements of that kind between the parties and also contained a warning against an easy inference of such agreements. The judge continued[338]:

I can see no ground whatever on which I could infer an agreement here that, because the charterers started to unload, and the shipowners' servants assisted in doing so, at 2.30 in the morning, there was an agreement between the parties that laytime should start then . . . Equally, I can see no ground upon which I should be entitled to hold that it had been waived by the charterers.[339]

He also added that the clause relating to time commencing and the clause relating to notice were not ones put in solely for the benefit of the charterers, and were not ones to which waiver would apply in any event.[340]

3.315 In London Arbitration 1/97,[341] the laycan clause of a Baltimore berth form C charter had been amended by the addition of the following:

Owners option to tender prior to Laydays
but time to commence as per charterparty.
Prior time used to count as laytime.

The vessel arrived after the opening of the laycan spread and tendered Notice of Readiness at 09 50. Loading started at 17 00 on the same day. The charterers contended that laytime started at 08 00 the following day as provided for elsewhere in the charter but the owners successfully argued that time should count from when loading started on the basis that "prior time" meant time before laytime would otherwise commence and not time before the laydays/cancelling period started.

3.316 The *Voylayrules 1993* provide[342]:

"UNLESS SOONER COMMENCED" shall mean that if laytime has not commenced but loading or discharging is carried out, time used shall count against laytime.

It would be usual to expect this phrase to be added to the provision providing for the commencement or recommencement of laytime. It will therefore act to foreshorten any period of notice which must elapse after presentation of Notice of Readiness.

CHANGES TO THE BEGINNING OF LAYTIME

3.317 As discussed in the previous sections, the usual requirements for the beginning of laytime are that the vessel must have arrived at the specified destination, she must be ready to load or discharge and, in certain cases, she must have given notice of her readiness. Once these conditions have been met and any period prescribed in the charter has elapsed, time begins to run.

336. *Nelson & Sons Ltd* v. *Nelson Line (Liverpool) Ltd (No 3)* (1908) 13 CC 235 (HL).
337. *Nelson & Sons Ltd* v. *Nelson Line (Liverpool) Ltd (No 3)* [1907] 2 KB 705 (CA).
338. *Pteroti Compania Naviera SA* v. *National Coal Board (The Khios Breeze)* [1958] 1 Lloyd's Rep 245, at p. 249.
339. See also London Arbitration 8/92—LMLN 324, 4 April 1992.
340. See also *Liquid Bulk Tanker Services Inc* v. *The Embassy of Bangladesh (The Westport Clipper)* (NY Arb), LMLN 360, 21 August 1993.
341. London Arbitration 1/97—LMLN 450, 1 February 1997.
342. See Appendix. The same definition appears in *Baltic Code 2000*.

135

3.318 However, these basic conditions may be varied by express or implied terms, which may have the effect of advancing or delaying the commencement of laytime. In this section a number of general points will first be considered and then the effect of certain well-known clauses.

3.319 The clauses and phrases to be discussed are:

"Whether in berth or not"

"Whether in port or not"

"Time lost in waiting for berth to count as laytime"

"Time lost in waiting for berth to count in full"

"Reachable on Arrival"

"Always accessible"

"So near thereto as she may safely get"

"In regular turn"/"in usual turn"

"Demurrage in respect of waiting time"

"Time to commence on being reported at the Custom House"

"To be loaded as per colliery guarantee"

Custom

3.320 The effect of custom in modern charters is likely to be minimal, since for a custom to have any effect, it must be shown to be not inconsistent with any express terms of the charter and, of course, most charters provide expressly when laytime is to commence.

3.321 In *Postlethwaite* v. *Freeland*, Lord Blackburn said[343]:

The jurors were told, and I think quite correctly, that "custom" in the charterparty did not mean custom in the sense in which the word is sometimes used by lawyers, but meant a settled and established practice of the port . . . [344]

3.322 To prove any custom is difficult because it involves establishing that it is not only reasonable and certain, but invariably accepted by ships and merchants using the port concerned.

3.323 The effect of a custom may be either to advance or delay when laytime commences for the vessel concerned. In *Norrkopings Rederiaktiebolag* v. *Wulfsberg & Co*, a vessel was chartered to carry a cargo of pitprops to Hull under a fixed laytime port charter and the question arose as to when laytime commenced. Having said that a custom of the port might be reduced to writing for the convenience of shipowners and merchants, Greer J continued[345]:

Looking at the statement of the custom and practice of the port there are the words: "When a wood laden ship is chartered for the port of Hull simply and without prescribing any particular dock for discharge the receiver has the right to order her on or before arrival to any available dock, which she can forthwith enter and deliver her cargo." In my judgment that means that the vessel is not an arrived vessel until she enters the dock to which she has been ordered for the purpose of discharge by the receiver of the cargo. I think that extends her carrying voyage up to the time she gets into the dock to which she is ordered for the purpose of discharge.

---

343. *William Postlethwaite* v. *John Freeland and Alexander Freeland* (1880) 5 App Cas 599, at p. 616.
344. For a consideration of how customs are established and fall into abeyance, see *ante* at para. 2.217.
345. *Norrkopings Rederiaktiebolag* v. *Wulfsberg & Co* (1920) 3 Ll L Rep 256.

3.324 *Norden Steamship Co* v. *Dempsey*[346] is another illustration to similar effect. Here a charter provided for the cargo to be discharged at a certain dock. The shipowners claimed that the vessel was entitled to give Notice of Readiness and commence laytime on arrival in dock. However, a custom at that port to the effect that in such circumstances time did not start until the vessel was in berth was held to prevail.

3.325 In addition to local custom taking effect as an implied term, as in the above examples, a charter may expressly refer to custom. Thus, in one case where by charter a ship was to "deliver according to the custom of the port" this was held to refer not only to the manner of delivery, but included a custom whereby laytime did not start until the ship was berthed under the superintendence of the harbour master.[347]

Obstacles created by the charterer

3.326 If a vessel is prevented or delayed from becoming an Arrived ship by obstacles created by the charterer or those for whom he is responsible, the general principle is that the charterer becomes liable for the delay. Similar principles apply where the charterer, although not causing the obstacles, fails to remove them when it is his duty so to do. The point was put succinctly by Gorell Barnes J in *Ogmore* v. *Borner*, when he said[348]:

It is the ordinary and natural implication that neither party should prevent the other from performing that part of the contract which falls to be performed by that other; and if the charterers by themselves, or by their agents acting within the scope of their authority, have placed impediments in the way of shipowners bringing their vessel into dock, the charterers ought to be responsible for the delay so caused, as if the vessel had in fact arrived in dock.

3.327 There is an implied term that a charterer must act with reasonable dispatch and in accordance with the ordinary practice of the port to enable a vessel to become an Arrived ship, but the burden of proving that the charterer is in breach of such a term lies on the shipowner.[349] Where a breach of these principles occurs, however, it is not entirely certain whether the remedy lies in damages or whether the commencement of laytime is brought forward, although where the obstacle was a delay in acceptance of Notice of Readiness, one London arbitral tribunal,[350] at least, was prepared to hold that the commencement of laytime should be brought forward.

3.328 The cases relating to the creation of obstacles by the charterer appear to fall into two categories—those relating to a failure to have cargo available for loading or railway wagons available for discharge, where such is a requirement by the port authority before a berth is allocated; and secondly, those where a berth is refused because of the number of other ships under charter to the same charterer.

Failure to have cargo available or arrangements for discharge

3.329 In *Owners of Panaghis Vergottis* v. *William Cory & Son*,[351] the owners of the ship concerned complained that their vessel had been delayed in getting into dock at Barry to

---

346. *Norden Steamship Co* v. *Dempsey* (1876) 1 CPD 654.
347. Referred to in *The Handy Book for Shipowners and Masters*, at p. 287.
348. *Ogmore Steamship Co Ltd* v. *H Borner & Co Ltd* (1901) 6 CC 104, at p. 110.
349. *Sunbeam Shipping Co Ltd* v. *President of India (The Atlantic Sunbeam)* [1973] 1 Lloyd's Rep 482. See *ante* at para. 3.166.
350. London Arbitration 9/96—LMLN 434, 22 June 1996. See also *ante* at para. 3.277.
351. *Owners of Panaghis Vergottis* v. *William Cory & Son* (1926) 25 Ll L Rep 64.

load under a dock charter because the charterers had failed to comply with a dock company requirement that approximately one third of the cargo must be ready to load before the ship would be admitted to the dock. In holding that the charterers were liable for the delay, Greer J said[352]:

> But I think that shipowners and shippers of coal doing business at the South Wales ports would regard it as reasonable in times of congestion that the dock authority should require at least one-third of the vessel's cargo to be ready before she was admitted to the dock; and I think, in refusing to assist the plaintiff's ship to get into the dock by complying with the requirements of the dock authority, that the charterers broke their contract, and are liable to pay the agreed damages.

3.330 A similar failure by the charterers to have sufficient coal available, this time at Calcutta, to enable a berth to be obtained was considered by the Privy Council in *Samuel Crawford Hogarth* v. *Cory Brothers & Co Ltd*. The judgment of the court was given by Lord Phillimore, who, having repeated the general principle set out earlier, continued[353]:

> Whether the latter's [i.e. charterer's] measure of liability is arrived at by giving to the shipowner damages for the delay, or whether the lay days are ante-dated to that date when they ought to have begun, and the charterer pays for them at the agreed rate of demurrage, does not seem to have been determined. But no point as to which of these two measures of payment should prevail has been made by the parties in this case.

3.331 The point was therefore left open. However, in *Fornyade Rederiaktiebolaget Commercial* v. *Blake & Co and others*, where the dispute was about what sort of railway wagons were to be provided for discharge and the dock company refused to allow the vessel to dock until it was resolved, the Court of Appeal held that damages were the appropriate measure. Scrutton LJ said[354]:

> She is not entitled to demurrage properly so called, because after she got to the place of discharge she was discharged within the contract time. But what she is entitled to is damages for detention during the four days in which she was prevented, by the wrongful attitude taken up by the receivers, from getting to the place of discharge.

Congestion due to charterer's other commitments

3.332 The principle was stated by Gorell Barnes J in *Ogmore* v. *Borner* in the following terms[355]:

> ... if the charterers have other vessels which they have to discharge, and have arranged to discharge, in the dock before the vessel which by the charter is to proceed to the dock and by the practice of the port will not be admitted into the dock while the charterers have the other vessels in the way, the charterers do prevent the shipowners from performing their contract until the charterers have cleared away the impediments.

3.333 However, this is subject to two limitations which much reduce its importance. The first of these is that it only applies where the other vessels are under charter to the same charterer. It does not apply where the shipowner is claiming from a charterer who has sold the cargo to a consignee and the available berths are all occupied by vessels under

---

352. *Ibid.*, at p. 68.
353. *Samuel Crawford Hogarth and others* v. *Cory Brothers & Co Ltd* (1926) 25 Ll L Rep 464, at p. 468.
354. *Fornyade Rederiaktiebolaget Commercial* v. *Blake & Co and others* (1931) 39 Ll L Rep 205, at p. 211.
355. *Ogmore Steamship Co Ltd* v. *H Borner & Co Ltd* (1901) 6 CC 104, at p. 110.

charter to different charterers, but which are discharging cargo for the same consignee.[356] In the same vein, it does not apply where the cargo has been sold to a consignee, who for his own business purposes chooses to give a berth first to vessels arriving later, where the claim is against the charterer, notwithstanding that the charterer could have pressed for an earlier berth under the contract of sale with the consignee.[357]

3.334 It does, however, apply where the limitation is not that of the port authority but of the charterers themselves. Thus, in *Aktieselskabet Inglewood* v. *Millar's Karri and Jarrah Forests Ltd*,[358] a vessel was ordered to Fremantle to load. On arrival, the vessel was unable to proceed to the jetty to which she was ordered by the charterers because all the four practicable berths were occupied, three of them by ships, which the charterers were loading. The loading of these ships could apparently have been completed at an anchorage and, indeed, this was the normal practice, presumably because the depth of water alongside was restricted. In the circumstances, Kennedy J held that it was the charterer's own obligations which prevented the ship with which he was concerned from becoming an Arrived ship. He put the point this way[359]:

If a ship is prevented from going to the loading place, which the charterer has the right to name, by obstacles caused by the charterer or in consequence of the engagements of the charterer, the lay days commence to count as soon as the ship is ready to load, and would, but for such obstacles or engagements, begin to load at that place.

3.335 That, however, is subject to the second limitation that the principle does not apply where the delay complained of was such that it should have been within the contemplation of both shipowner and the charterer at the time the charter was made.

3.336 Thus, in *Harrowing* v. *Dupre*,[360] a vessel had to wait for 20 days before getting a berth. Had it not been for four ships under charter to the same charterer who were ahead of her, she would have berthed seven days earlier. Nevertheless, Bigham J held that the delay was not the fault of the charterer and that where, under such a berth charter, the delay was such as ought to have been in the contemplation of both parties at the time of making the charter, no cause of action arose.

3.337 The Court of Appeal reached a similar conclusion on another coal charter in *Barque Quilpue Ltd* v. *Brown*, where Vaughan Williams LJ cited with approval[361] a *dictum* of Rigby LJ in *Carlton Steamship Co* v. *Castle Mail Packets Co*, where he said[362]:

I do not think that a delay which arose from a contingency, the probability of which must have been perfectly well known to and contemplated by the shipowners when they entered into the charterparty, can be considered unreasonable.

Vaughan Williams LJ also added[363]:

In the present case I think it is clear that when the shipowners entered into the charterparty to load in regular turn, that is, regular colliery turn, they must have known that the charterers would have prior engagements which would delay the colliery turn of this particular ship, and they must also

---

356. *Ogmore Steamship Co Ltd* v. *H Borner & Co Ltd* (1901) 6 CC 104.
357. *Watson* v. *H Borner & Co Ltd* (1900) 5 CC 377.
358. *Aktieselskabet Inglewood* v. *Millar's Karri and Jarrah Forests Ltd* (1903) 8 CC 196.
359. *Ibid.*, at p. 201.
360. *Harrowing and others* v. *Dupre* (1902) 7 CC 157.
361. *Barque Quilpue Ltd* v. *Brown* (1903) 9 CC 13, at p. 18.
362. *Carlton Steamship Co Ltd* v. *Castle Mail Packets Co Ltd* (1897) 2 CC 286, at p. 293. The wording of this report is slightly different from the words quoted by Vaughan Williams LJ.
363. *Barque Quilpue Ltd* v. *Brown* (1903) 9 CC 13, at p. 18.

have known that a delay of the ship for loading for a number of days—certainly between 40 and 50 days—was not an impossible or even an unusual thing under the conditions of this port.

3.338 In the American case of *The Venore*,[364] it was held that even if the shipowner had been able to provide that other engagements of the charterer were a serious cause of delay, the evidence showed that when the contract was executed, the shipowner either knew or should have known of the charterer's other grain fixtures. Furthermore, the court held that where delay was caused by something taken into account in fixing the freight rate, the shipowner could not afterwards complain. It is likely that in this country such a factor will also be taken into consideration, at least by commercial arbitrators.

Charterer's duty to act to enable a vessel to become an arrived ship

3.339 The leading case on this aspect is *Sunbeam Shipping Co Ltd* v. *President of India (The Atlantic Sunbeam)*, which has already been considered in some detail.[365] In that case there was a delay of some four days in connection with part of the documentary procedures required in securing Customs clearance for the discharge of her cargo. One of the steps necessary for this had to be undertaken by the charterer and the question arose as to the level of diligence required from the charterer in getting this done. Having considered the various possibilities, Kerr J concluded[366]:

A requirement of a high standard of initiative, let alone any excessive zeal, cannot be implied in a situation of this nature, however much one would like to see it used. Something of that kind would require an express term. If, for instance, there were two procedures in a certain port whereby a vessel's documentation can be dealt with, one on paying an expedition fee or taking some special steps, and the other one the ordinary procedure, then it seems to me that the charterers would be under no implied obligation to use the speedier and unusual procedure.[367]

3.340 In the original arbitration proceedings from which the case arose, the arbitrators had held that there was a breach of duty for which they said damages were payable. Kerr J did not deal expressly with the question as to what remedy was appropriate where there was a breach, but presumably in not doing so agreed that they were right. However, in *The Delian Spirit*, which concerned a "reasonable on arrival" provision, Sir Gordon Willmer said[368]:

. . . I prefer to say no more upon the difficult question which might have arisen if the vessel had not been found to be an arrived ship at the time when she was lying in the roads. But I certainly do not wish to be taken as accepting that, even in that situation, the owners would necessarily be entitled to prosecute an independent claim for damages, without giving credit for the laytime to which the charterers were entitled, and for which, as we have been reminded, they paid when they paid the freight.

3.341 If that is so in a "reachable upon arrival" situation, then it may still be an open point in a situation such as that which arose in *The Atlantic Sunbeam*,[369] although it is

---

364. *Venore Transportation Co* v. *President of India (The Venore)* [1973] 1 Lloyd's Rep 494.

365. *Sunbeam Shipping Co Ltd* v. *President of India (The Atlantic Sunbeam)* [1973] 1 Lloyd's Rep 482. See *ante* at para. 3.166.

366. *Ibid.*, at p. 488.

367. See also *Kurt A Becher GmbH & Co KG* v. *Roplak Enterprises SA (The World Navigator)* [1991] 2 Lloyd's Rep 23, and London Arbitration 17/92—LMLN 328, 30 May 1992.

368. *Shipping Developments Corporation SA* v. *V/O Sojuzneftexport (The Delian Spirit)* [1971] 1 Lloyd's Rep 506, at p. 512.

369. *Sunbeam Shipping Co Ltd* v. *President of India (The Atlantic Sunbeam)* [1973] 1 Lloyd's Rep 482.

submitted that in both cases damages for detention should be payable and charterers should not be entitled to advance the running of laytime.[370]

3.342 One of the disputes that arose in *The Boral Gas*[371] concerned responsibility for the supply of pre-coolant preparatory to the carriage of a cargo of liquid ammonia. Under the terms of the charter, shippers were to supply the pre-coolant. The vessel could not tender a valid Notice of Readiness until the tanks were pre-cooled. It later transpired that charterers only instructed the shippers to provide the pre-coolant some time after the vessel's arrival. Charterers argued that the reference to shippers providing the pre-coolant imposed no obligation on them, and it was up to owners to make their own arrangements with shippers. This argument was rejected by Evans J, who held that on the express terms of the charter the obligation fell on the charterers. At the end of this part of his judgment, he commented[372]:

The majority of arbitrators referred to *The Atlantic Sunbeam* [1973] 1 Lloyd's Rep 482, as authority for an alternative approach leading to the same conclusion by reference to an implied duty upon the charterers to co-operate in enabling the vessel to become an arrived ship.

3.343 However, in view of his previous finding, he declined to comment further on this aspect.

3.344 *The Atlantic Sunbeam* was also considered in *The World Navigator.*[373] That case concerned a f.o.b. sale of maize. Under the terms of the contract, laytime only commenced when the vessel arrived in berth, although Notice of Readiness was given earlier. For the vessel to be allowed to berth, the sellers' documentation had to be in order. In this case, therefore, the lack of documentation affected not the giving of Notice of Readiness but laytime commencing, although it appears to have been accepted that in both cases, the same principles apply.

3.345 What term should be implied in these circumstances was considered by Staughton LJ in the Court of Appeal where he said[374]:

It seems a fair inference from the award that the ship nominated by the buyers could not proceed to a berth until some documentation required by the sellers was in order. In those circumstances there was to my mind plainly an implied obligation of some kind upon the sellers. The general nature of such an obligation was described by Lord Blackburn in *Mackay* v. *Dick* (1881) 6 App Cas 251 at p. 263:

"I think I may safely say, as a general rule, that where in a written contract it appears that both parties have agreed that something shall be done, which cannot effectively be done unless both concur in doing it, the construction of the contract is that each agrees to do all that is necessary to be done on his part for the carrying out of that thing, though there may be no express words to that effect."

That seems to me to be exactly applicable to this case. The buyers cannot arrange for their ship to be available for loading until the sellers' documentation is in order. It is therefore implied that the sellers will do all that is necessary to secure that it is in order.

As to the time for performance of the obligation, I can see no difficulty. By the Centro terms the buyers were to give at least 15 days' pre-advice of the vessel's readiness to load. That was evidentially considered a reasonable time for the sellers to make the necessary arrangements. Having

---

370. See also *post* at para. 8.6.
371. *Rashtriya Chemicals and Fertilizers Ltd* v. *Huddart Parker Industries Ltd (The Boral Gas)* [1988] 1 Lloyd's Rep 342.
372. *Ibid.*, at p. 346.
373. *The World Navigator* [1991] 2 Lloyd's Rep 23—for the facts of the case, see *post* at para. 8.32.
374. *Ibid.*, at p. 30.

received such a notice, they were obliged to do so within such time as would enable the vessel to be ready to load after fifteen days.

What does give rise to difficulty is the question whether the implied obligation is to use reasonable diligence (or best endeavours), or is absolute. There is ostensibly some conflict here between the decision of the House of Lords in *Sociedad Financiera de Bienes Raices* v. *Agrimpex (The Aello)* [1960] 1 Lloyd's Rep 623 . . . and that of Mr Justice Kerr in *Sunbeam Shipping Co Ltd* v. *President of India (The Atlantic Sunbeam)*, [1973] 1 Lloyd's Rep 482. In the first case it was held in terms by the majority, that the obligation was absolute. But in the second Mr Justice Kerr held (at p. 488) that—

> "The term to be implied in this case is to the effect that the charterers were bound to act with reasonable despatch and in accordance with the ordinary practice of the Port of Calcutta in doing those acts which had to be done by them as consignees to enable the ship to become an arrived ship."

It may well be that the cases can be reconciled if one has regard to the precise task which remained unperformed in each. In *The Aello* the charterers had not obtained a giro permit, because they did not have cargo available ready to be loaded. That was held to be solely their concern and they must bear the responsibility for lack of a cargo, even though their best endeavours had failed to find one. In *The Atlantic Sunbeam*, on the other hand, the obstacle was delay in obtaining a jetty challan, which required the co-operation not only of the consignees or receivers but also of the port authority and the customs. It was at least possible that the port authority or the customs had caused the delay.

Having explored the problem thus far, I agree with Lord Justice Parker that it need not be decided in this case, having regard to our conclusion as to damages if there was any breach of an implied term.

The precise nature of the implied term thus awaits further judicial consideration.

Whether in berth or not

3.346 This is perhaps the most common of the special clauses which have the effect of advancing the commencement of laytime from when it would otherwise start. In the case of a charter that names a berth as the specified destination or expressly gives the charterer the right to select the berth, this expression means that, if a berth is not available, laytime starts to run once any notice period has elapsed after the vessel arrives at "a position within the port where she is at the immediate and effective disposition of the charterer".[375] As the cases which follow show, the point of arrival must be inside and not outside the port limits. It is thus not necessary for the vessel to have reached her designated berth before laytime can commence, provided the berth is not available. As will become clear, the word "available" does not equate with accessible.

3.347 Although also frequently included in port charters, it there has little effect. The definitive decision on the meaning of the phrase is that of the House of Lords in *The Kyzikos*,[376] but before considering that case it may be convenient to consider the earlier cases in which it has been considered. The earliest judicial consideration of the phrase appears to be *Northfield Steamship Co Ltd* v. *Compagnie L'Union des Gaz*,[377] a decision of the Court of Appeal. That case concerned a berth charter which also contained a clause

---

375. *Oldendorff (EL) & Co GmbH* v. *Tradax Export SA (The Johanna Oldendorff)* [1973] 2 Lloyd's Rep 285, at p. 291, *per* Lord Reid. See *ante* at para. 3.48.

376. *Seacrystal Shipping Ltd* v. *Bulk Transport Group Shipping Co Ltd (The Kyzikos)* [1989] 1 Lloyd's Rep 1.

377. *Northfield Steamship Co Ltd* v. *Compagnie L'Union des Gaz* (1911) 17 CC 74 (CA).

which read: "Time to commence when steamer is ready to unload and written notice given, whether in berth or not." Of this, Farwell LJ said[378]:

Want of space to berth is of very frequent occurrence, and the parties appear to me to have expressly provided for it, and this disposes also of the contention that the ship was not ready to unload. She was ready so far as she was concerned, and the fact that she was not in a berth is rendered immaterial by this clause.

3.348 A more recent consideration is *Carga del Sur Compania Naviera SA* v. *Ross T Smyth & Co Ltd (The Seafort)*,[379] a decision of McNair J. Here the *Seafort* was chartered for the carriage of grain from Vancouver to London and Hull under a Baltimore berth grain charter. Under clause 9, "Time at second port to count from arrival of vessel at second port, whether in berth or not", Hull was the second port and it was usual for vessels of the *Seafort*'s size to wait for a berth to become available at Spurn Head Anchorage, some 22 miles from the port. The anchorage was outside the legal, administrative and fiscal limits of Hull. Rejecting the owners' claim that time started to run at Spurn Head, McNair J said[380]:

By using the words "arrival ... at second port" in this charterparty the parties must, I think, be presumed to have intended that the normal conditions which determine whether a ship has "arrived" at or in a port should apply.
    In my judgment, the true effect of the last sentence of clause 9 is to provide that time which has started to run at the first discharge port shall start to run again after the passage between the first and second discharging ports has been completed by arrival at the second discharging port ...

3.349 The meaning of the phrase was also considered by the Court of Appeal in *The Johanna Oldendorff*[381] on that case's way to the House of Lords.[382]

3.350 Having reviewed the authorities, Roskill LJ concluded[383]:

... upon the true construction of this phrase its application is, and the phrase has for 50 years always been regarded as, limited to a case where the ship is already an arrived ship[384] and that its use does not dispense with the necessity for the ship being an arrived ship before Notice of Readiness can be given and time start to count. Only when the ship has arrived does the clause operate to make laytime commence even though the vessel is not in berth.

He also pointed out that in that case the same result would have followed even though the phrase had not been used, since it was a port charter.

3.351 The other judgment to consider the matter was that of Buckley LJ, who said[385]:

In the case of a berth charter the ship does not reach her destination until she is berthed. In the case of such a charter the insertion of the words "whether in berth or not" makes lay days run from a time when the ship has not yet berthed. Whether it is right to say that the effect of the insertion in such a case is to make the operation of the charter the same as a port charter, so that the ship should

---

378. *Ibid.*, at p. 79.
379. *Carga del Sur Compania Naviera SA* v. *Ross T Smyth & Co Ltd (The Seafort)* [1962] 2 Lloyd's Rep 147.
380. *Ibid.*, at p. 154.
381. *Oldendorff (EL) & Co GmbH* v. *Tradax Export SA (The Johanna Oldendorff)* [1972] 2 Lloyd's Rep 292.
382. *The Johanna Oldendorff* [1973] 2 Lloyd's Rep 285. In the House of Lords, Viscount Dilhorne endorsed the reasoning of Buckley LJ, at p. 302.
383. *The Johanna Oldendorff* [1972] 2 Lloyd's Rep 292, at p. 314.
384. I.e. arrived within the port rather than in berth.
385. *The Johanna Oldendorff* [1972] 2 Lloyd's Rep 292, at p. 302.

be treated as "arrived" although she has not berthed, or whether the insertion merely advances the time from which lay days run notwithstanding that the ship may not technically have arrived, perhaps does not much matter. The latter seems to me to be probably the more correct view. The purpose of inserting the same words in a port charter is likely to be more obscure, because in such a case the commencement of lay days will not normally depend on whether the ship has berthed or not.

3.352 Lord Diplock also took a similar view in *The Maratha Envoy*, where he said[386]:

The effect of this well-known phrase in berth charters has been settled for more than half a century. Under it time starts to run when the vessel is waiting within the named port of destination for a berth there to become vacant. In effect it makes the Reid test[387] applicable to a berth charter. It has no effect in a port charter; the Reid test is applicable anyway.

3.353 In none of the previous cases was a berth available when Notice of Readiness was given. In *The Kyzikos*,[388] however, the berth was available but she could not reach it because of bad weather. What happened was that the vessel arrived off Houston to discharge but anchored because of fog. She made an abortive attempt to get into berth, but had to reanchor until the fog lifted. Apart from considering this phrase, the lower courts also considered whether in these circumstances the vessel was at the immediate and effective disposition of the charterers[389] and the meaning of an "always accessible provision", which was said to be the same as one providing for a berth "reachable on arrival".[390]

3.354 In arbitration, the arbitrator held in favour of owners that there was no limitation on the meaning of the phrase. Webster J in the High Court disagreed, saying[391] that such a provision did not have the effect of changing the primary obligation of the owners from being one to carry the cargo to a berth, to carry the cargo to a named port. He therefore disagreed with Roskill LJ when he said in *The Johanna Oldendorff*[392]:

The phrase "whether in berth or not" was designed to convert a berth charterparty into a port charterparty and to ensure that under a berth charterparty Notice of Readiness could be given as soon as the ship had arrived within the commercial area of the port concerned so that laytime would start to run on its expiry.

3.355 Having reviewed the authorities to see whether they supported the proposition that a WIBON provision has the effect of converting a berth to a port charter, Webster J concluded[393]:

I recognise that, when the vessel is unable to come alongside because no berth is available, the "Wibon" provision in the ordinary case has, in practice, that effect; but in my view it cannot be said without doubt that the authorities which I have considered, read as a whole, support the proposition that it has that effect in law, still less that it actually converts a berth charter into a port charter.

---

386. *Federal Commerce & Navigation Co Ltd v. Tradax Export SA (The Maratha Envoy)* [1977] 2 Lloyd's Rep 301, at p. 308.
387. See *ante* at para. 3.48.
388. *Seacrystal Shipping Ltd v. Bulk Transport Group Shipping Co Ltd (The Kyzikos)* [1987] 1 Lloyd's Rep 48; [1987] 2 Lloyd's Rep 122; [1989] 1 Lloyd's Rep 1.
389. See *ante* at para. 3.110.
390. See *post* at para. 3.402 and para. 4.394.
391. *The Kyzikos* [1987] 1 Lloyd's Rep 48, at p. 50.
392. *The Johanna Oldendorff* [1972] 2 Lloyd's Rep 292, at p. 312, quoted in *The Kyzikos* [1987] 1 Lloyd's Rep 48, at p. 55.
393. *The Kyzikos* [1987] 1 Lloyd's Rep 48, at p. 56.

3.356 He therefore held[394]:

... in the present case, time did not begin to run until the vessel was berthed, because it was not, before that time, waiting for a berth to become available, ready (so far as it was concerned) to unload.

3.357 In the Court of Appeal, the principal judgment, with which both other members of the court agreed, was given by Lloyd LJ, who, in addition to the other cases mentioned, also cited *The Shackleford*[395] where Buckley LJ had said[396] that there was no difference between himself and Roskill LJ in the views they had expressed in *The Johanna Oldendorff*,[397] as had previously been suggested in that case and again by Webster J in the present case. Reversing the decision of the High Court, Lloyd LJ said[398]:

I do not doubt that the reason why the provision was originally included in berth charters was to cater for the case where the port is congested and a berth unavailable. But there is nothing in the wording of the provision which limits its operation to such a case. The wording is quite general. Notice of Readiness may be given whether in berth or not. *Ex hypothesi*, therefore, Notice of Readiness may be given before the vessel has reached its contractual destination.

3.358 The principal speech in the House of Lords was that of Lord Brandon, who summarised the issues thus[399]:

The views have been advanced, at each stage of the proceedings, with regard to the meaning of the phrase "whether in berth or not" in a berth charterparty. One view, put forward by the charterers and accepted by Mr Justice Webster, is that the phrase covers cases where the reason for the ship not being in berth is that no berth is available but does not cover cases where a berth is available and the only reason why the ship cannot proceed to it is that she is prevented by bad weather such as fog. The other view, put forward by the owners and accepted by the arbitrator and the Court of Appeal, is that the phrase covers cases where a ship is unable to proceed to a berth either because none is available or because, although a berth is available, the ship is prevented by bad weather, such as fog, from proceeding to it.

3.359 Having reviewed the previous cases and pointed out that the effect of the phrase in the present circumstances had never previously arisen, Lord Brandon concluded in favour of charterers, saying[400]:

... I am of opinion, having regard to the authorities to which I referred earlier and the context in which the acronym "wibon" is to be found in the charterparty here concerned, that the phrase "whether in berth or not" should be interpreted as applying only to cases where a berth is not available and not also to cases where a berth is available but is unreachable by reason of bad weather.

3.360 On this basis, the same conclusion would have been reached had the reason for non-accessibility been lack of water or possibly some prohibition on navigation to the berth by the port authority, although the latter might give rise to some complicated questions on availability and how much more this means than simply that there is no other vessel currently occupying the designated berth.

---

394. *Ibid.*
395. *Surrey Shipping Co Ltd* v. *Compagnie Continentale (France) SA (The Shackleford)* [1978] 2 Lloyd's Rep 154.
396. Quoted in *The Kyzikos* [1987] 2 Lloyd's Rep 122, at p. 125.
397. *The Johanna Oldendorff* [1972] 2 Lloyd's Rep 292.
398. *The Kyzikos* [1987] 2 Lloyd's Rep 122, at p. 124.
399. *The Kyzikos* [1989] 1 Lloyd's Rep 1, at p. 5.
400. *Ibid.*, at p. 8.

3.361 Although the effect of the expression in a dock charter is not expressly discussed in any of the cases, it probably normally has no effect so that time runs from arrival in dock as usual.

3.362 Even in a berth charter, the effect of the phrase may be largely neutralized by a suitable exception clause, such as the Centrocon strike clause. Thus, in *The Amstelmolen*,[401] where the vessel concerned was unable to berth because of congestion, the Court of Appeal held that although laytime ran by virtue of the phrase "whether in berth or not", nevertheless there was an obstruction within the meaning of the Centrocon strike clause and time did not therefore count during the continuance of the obstruction.[402]

3.363 The *Voylayrules 1993* provide[403]:

22. "whether in berth or not" (WIBON) or "BERTH OR NO BERTH" shall mean that if no loading or discharging berth is available on her arrival the vessel, on reaching any usual waiting-place at or off the port, shall be entitled to tender Notice of Readiness from it and laytime shall commence in accordance with the charterparty. Laytime or time on demurrage shall cease to count once the berth becomes available and shall resume when the vessel is ready to load or discharge at the berth.

This differs somewhat from the definition in the *Charterparty Laytime Definitions 1980* which reads[404]:

26. "WHETHER IN BERTH OR NOT" or "BERTH NO BERTH"—means that if the location named for loading/discharging is a berth and if the berth is not immediately accessible to the ship, a Notice of Readiness can be given when the ship has arrived at the port in which the berth is situated.

A not dissimilar definition appears in *Baltic Code 2000*[405]:

WHETHER IN BERTH OR NOT (WIBON) or BERTH OR NO BERTH—if the designated loading or discharging berth is not available on her arrival, the vessel on reaching any usual waiting place within the port, shall be entitled to tender notice of readiness from it and laytime shall commence as provided under the charterparty.

It should be emphasised that these definitions will only apply if they are specifically incorporated into the charterparty.

3.364 As will be apparent, there are a number of differences between the first two definitions and between them and the meaning given to the phrase by judicial precedent. The Voylayrules definition refers to notice being given "on reaching any usual waiting-place at or off the port". This apparently is intended to allow notice to be given outside the port limits if that is where the usual waiting place is. It is clear, however, from the cases cited at paras 3.102 *et seq.* above that that is not the position at common law and the phrase only accelerates the commencement of laytime after arrival within the port limits. The second and probably most important change is that the Voylayrules definition refers to the berth being available whereas the previous one referred to it being accessible. This is clearly intended to reflect the House of Lords decision in *The Kyzikos*.[406]

3.365 There is, however, a third and more controversial change which is the suggestion in the last sentence of the Voylayrules definition that laytime or time on demurrage ceases once the berth becomes available, even though it may not have become accessible.

---

401. *NV Reederij Amsterdam* v. *President of India (The Amstelmolen)* [1961] 2 Lloyd's Rep 1 (CA).
402. See also *Reardon Smith Line Ltd* v. *East Asiatic Co* (1938) 62 Ll L Rep 23.
403. See Appendix.
404. *Ibid.*
405. *Ibid.*
406. *The Kyzikos* [1989] 1 Lloyd's Rep 1.

3.366 It is suggested that, whilst this obviously must apply if the Voylayrules are specifically incorporated, it should not apply where they are not, for sound legal and commercial reasons.

3.367 To take the commercial reasons first: an owner would ask for the clause in a berth charter to protect himself from delay due to congestion. It is therefore somewhat unfair to say to him that when his vessel arrives, time counts in his favour but ceases to count when the berth becomes free although by then, for other reasons, his vessel is unable to reach it. The situation is somewhat analogous to the discussion as to whether a laytime strike clause should protect the charterer after the vessel has gone on demurrage.[407]

3.368 The legal reasons are perhaps more complex. The phrase WIBON usually appears in a clause dealing solely with the commencement of laytime. Although in his speech in *The Kyzikos*[408] Lord Brandon referred to the availability of the berth in the present tense, there is no reason to suppose that by so doing he was intending to imply into it an ongoing meaning extending its effect from purely the commencement of laytime to the running of laytime and even demurrage. It may be that the authors of this definition were influenced by the meaning of the phrase "Time lost waiting for berth" which also relates to the availability of the berth in question. However, that phrase usually appears in a separate clause, or at least a separate sentence, to that dealing with the commencement of laytime and, by its reference to "time lost", the words themselves imply an ongoing situation.

3.369 Furthermore there is a general principle that once laytime or time on demurrage[409] commences, time runs continuously in the absence of a specific exception or interruption within the meaning of that term used in Chapter 4. It therefore follows, it is suggested, that at common law, the meaning of WIBON is confined to the commencement of laytime and thereafter time runs continuously until cargo operations are complete whether the berth becomes subsequently accessible or not, unless of course some other clause comes into play.

Whether in port or not

3.370 This phrase is frequently used in conjunction with the words "whether in berth or not" and the criteria for its use are broadly the same, of course, substituting port for berth.

3.371 A slightly unusual set of circumstances arose for consideration before London arbitrators[410] arising out of delays caused by the convoy system in force at the time for vessels carrying cargo to Iranian ports. Under the particular charter, the vessel concerned was ordered to Bandar Bushire. To get there, she had to join a convoy at Bandar Abbas, where she arrived in September 1981. The master cabled Notice of Readiness and eventually the vessel joined a convoy in late November, arriving at her destination in early December. She berthed a few days later and completed discharge towards the end of December.

3.372 The owners argued that their ship was an Arrived ship for Bandar Bushire, when she arrived at Bandar Abbas, although that was some 400 miles away. The owners

407. See *post* at para. 4.338.
408. *The Kyzikos* [1989] 1 Lloyd's Rep 1, at p. 8.
409. *Ibid.*, at p. 5.
410. London Arbitration—LMLN 143, 25 April 1985.

submitted that although their vessel was not then at the nominated discharge port, she was ready to discharge and fully at the disposal of the charterers. Thus, two out of three tests derived from *The Johanna Oldendorff*[411] were satisfied. The third test, namely physical arrival, was, argued the owners, displaced by clause 22 of the charter, which stipulated that a Notice of Readiness could be tendered "whether in port or not". The owners argued that the WIPON stipulation operated in the very special circumstances extant at Iranian ports at that time to make valid cabled notices given by the master in September.

3.373 The arbitrators, however, rejected these arguments, holding that the wait at Bandar Abbas could be regarded as an interruption to the voyage on which the vessel was engaged, a voyage which was only completed when the vessel arrived at the roads off Bandar Bushire. A place which was almost 400 miles distant from the port of destination could not possibly be held to be within the ambit of WIPON. If it were to be the only place at which a valid notice could be given, that could only be achieved by very clear and special wording in the charter. The convoy system was as much a hazard of the voyage falling to the owners' account as any other navigational impediment that might arise. Furthermore, Bandar Abbas could not be considered the "usual waiting place" for Bandar Bushire.

3.374 In *The Adolf Leonhardt*,[412] Staughton J had to consider whether it was effective to allow Notice of Readiness for the port of Rosario to be given at Intersection some 200 miles down river. As to its meaning, the judge said[413] that the use of the words might have been directed at ports with no waiting area within their limits; the vessel must reach *a* usual waiting area for the port in question and must be at the immediate and effective disposition of the charterers. On this he concluded[414]:

It seems to me that a vessel is as effectively at the disposition of the charterer at Intersection as modern conditions demand, given that she is not required to be in the port of Rosario by reason of the use of the words "whether in port or not". Accordingly I would have upheld the conclusion of the Board of Appeal that notice of readiness could be given there.

3.375 However, the judge also held that again the effect of the phrase could be largely cancelled out by a suitable exception clause such as the Centrocon strike clause.

3.376 These cases illustrate the point that, whilst a WIPON clause may operate to activate the commencement of laytime when the vessel concerned is a significant distance away from the port in question, nevertheless, the other criteria applicable to a WIBON provision must also be met and the anchorage that the ship has reached must be a recognised waiting place for that particular port.

Time lost in waiting for berth to count as laytime

3.377 The effect of this clause is that any time spent waiting for a berth counts against laytime. To that extent it is similar to a WIBON provision, but the major difference is that the place where the vessel waits need not necessarily be within the port limits. However, it must be sufficiently close to the port for the vessel to be able to say "we have gone as

411. *Oldendorff (EL) & Co GmbH* v. *Tradax Export SA (The Johanna Oldendorff)* [1973] 2 Lloyd's Rep 285.

412. *R Pagnan & Fratelli* v. *Finagrain Compagnie Commerciale Agricole et Financière SA (The Adolf Leonhardt)* [1986] 2 Lloyd's Rep 395.

413. *Ibid.*, at p. 403.

414. *Ibid.*

far as we can" and we are now waiting for a berth. It is suggested that the Reid test in *The Johanna Oldendorff* [415] might be suitably modified to answer the question whether the vessel has gone far enough where she is waiting outside the port limits—if she is at a place where waiting ships usually lie, she will be in such a position, but if she is waiting at some other point then it will be for the shipowner to show his availability to move into berth when one becomes available.

3.378 If the waiting place is within the port limits then the clause will have little effect in a port charter, but will advance the running of laytime in the case of a berth charter.

3.379 The expression originated in the Gencon charterparty. In the original 1922 version it appeared in separate clauses, the first reading "to count as loading time" and the second "to count as discharging time". The 1976 update of the charter combined the two to read "Time lost in waiting for berth to count as loading or discharging time, as the case may be". The variation used in the heading of this section appeared in *The Darrah*.[416] For practical purposes, all the variations now have the same effect.

3.380 The *Charterparty Laytime Definitions 1980* provide[417]:

25. "TIME LOST WAITING FOR BERTH TO COUNT AS LOADING/DISCHARGING TIME OR AS LAYTIME" means that if the main reason why a notice of readiness cannot be given is that there is no loading/discharging berth available to the ship the laytime will commence to run when the ship starts to wait for a berth and will continue to run, unless previously exhausted, until the ship stops waiting. The laytime exceptions apply to the waiting time as if the ship was at the loading/discharging berth provided the ship is not already on demurrage. When the waiting time ends time ceases to count and restarts when the ship reaches the loading/discharging berth subject to the giving of a notice of readiness if one is required by the charterparty and to any notice time if provided for in the charterparty, unless the ship is by then on demurrage.

And the *Voylayrules 1993* similarly provide[418]:

21. "TIME LOST WAITING FOR BERTH TO COUNT AS LOADING OR DISCHARGING TIME" or "AS LAYTIME" shall mean that if no loading or discharging berth is available and the vessel is unable to tender notice of readiness at the waiting-place then any time lost to the vessel shall count as if laytime were running, or as time on demurrage if laytime has expired. Such time shall cease to count once the berth becomes available. When the vessel reaches a place where she is able to tender notice of readiness, laytime or time on demurrage shall resume after such tender and, in respect of laytime, on expiry of any notice time provided in the charterparty.

3.381 It would seem that the emphasis lies on the availability or otherwise of a berth and therefore that the clause only takes effect where the vessel concerned is unable to move into berth due to congestion, and not where she is forced to wait by weather or other causes. Support for this proposition is contained in Lord Diplock's speech in *The Darrah* where he said[419]:

"Time lost in waiting for berth" in the context of the adventure contemplated by a voyage charter, as it seems to me, must mean the period during which the vessel would have been in berth and at the disposition of the charterer for carrying out the loading or discharging operation, if she had not been prevented by congestion at the port from reaching a berth at which the operation could be carried out.

---

415. *Oldendorff (EL) & Co GmbH* v. *Tradax Export SA (The Johanna Oldendorff)* [1973] 2 Lloyd's Rep 285, at p. 291. See *ante* at para. 3.48.
416. *Aldebaran Compania Maritima SA* v. *Aussenhandel AG (The Darrah)* [1976] 2 Lloyd's Rep 359 (HL).
417. See Appendix.
418. *Ibid.*
419. *The Darrah* [1976] 2 Lloyd's Rep 359, at p. 364.

3.382 In the case of a port charter, the clause was of more importance prior to the decision of the House of Lords in *The Johanna Oldendorff* [420] when their Lordships' earlier ruling in *The Aello* [421] held sway. This was because under the latter the vessel did not reach its specified destination unless it had arrived at a more proximate point to the place of discharge. However, the major judicial consideration of the clause has not been directed to the geographical point which a vessel must reach before the clause becomes applicable, but to the question as to whether laytime exceptions are applicable to waiting time.

3.383 Before considering the various decisions relating to the clause, it may be helpful to remember the commercial reasoning behind its introduction. This was said by Lord Diplock to be as follows [422]:

In a berth charter the effect of the clause is to put the shipowner in the same position financially as he would have been if, instead of being compelled to wait, his vessel had been able to go straight to her berth and the obligations of the charterer to carry out the loading or discharging operation had started then. In a port charter the clauses are superfluous so far as concerns time spent in waiting in turn within the limits of the port. This counts as laytime anyway; it is laytime. The clauses would, however, have the same effect as in a berth charter in respect of ports like Hull or Glasgow where the usual waiting place is outside the limits of the port.

3.384 The judicial history of this type of clause starts with *North River Freighters Ltd* v. *President of India (The Radnor)*. [423] This involved a berth charter. It had been contended by the charterer that time for loading did not start to run under the Gencon "time lost" clause until Notice of Readiness to load had been given. The only question of law for the decision of the court was whether this was so. The Court of Appeal held, reversing McNair J, [424] that it was not. On this Singleton LJ said [425]:

The time lost is to count as, or to be added to, loading time in order to ascertain the position between the parties. I am unable to accept the view that under the words in line 67 time is not lost until notice has been given under clause 17.

Commenting on this in *The Darrah*, Lord Diplock said [426]:

The correctness of the actual decision in *The Radnor* is not in doubt. It cannot have been intended that notice of readiness is required to start time running under the "time lost" clause, for if it were the clause could have no application in a berth charter, for which it is primarily designed, since notice of readiness under such a charter could never be given until the period of waiting was over and the vessel was already in berth.

3.385 In the course of their judgments in *The Radnor*, both Singleton and Parker LJJ referred to the "time lost" provision being independent of the laytime clause [427] and although the court never expressed any opinion on the way demurrage had been calculated

---

420. *Oldendorff (EL) & Co GmbH* v. *Tradax Export SA (The Johanna Oldendorff)* [1973] 2 Lloyd's Rep 285.
421. *Sociedad Financiera de Bienes Raices SA* v. *Agrimpex Hungarian Trading Co for Agricultural Products (The Aello)* [1961] AC 135. See *ante* at para. 3.89.
422. *Aldebaran Compania Maritima SA* v. *Aussenhandel AG (The Darrah)* [1976] 2 Lloyd's Rep 359, at p. 364.
423. *North River Freighters Ltd* v. *President of India (The Radnor)* [1955] 2 Lloyd's Rep 668 (CA).
424. *The Radnor* [1955] 2 Lloyd's Rep 73.
425. *The Radnor* [1955] 2 Lloyd's Rep 668, at p. 675.
426. *The Darrah* [1976] 2 Lloyd's Rep 359, at p. 364.
427. *The Radnor* [1955] 2 Lloyd's Rep 668, at p. 674 *per* Singleton LJ, and at p. 680 *per* Parker LJ.

in the original arbitration award, it had nevertheless been done on the basis that the laytime exceptions did not apply.

3.386 The next case to consider the matter was *Metals & Ropes Co Ltd* v. *Filia Compania Limitada (The Vastric)*,[428] again a decision of McNair J. The dispute concerned whether periods of time which would have counted as laytime if a berth had been available should nevertheless count under the waiting time provision. It is clear that the judge would have liked to have approached the matter by determining how much worse off the shipowners were because a berth was not available to them and on that basis he concluded that only a small period of time had been lost because the remainder would not have counted for laytime had the vessel been in berth. Of that approach and conclusion, he said[429]:

It seems to me that there is a very great commercial sense in that result.

However, he felt bound by the earlier Court of Appeal decision to hold that the period which would have been excluded from laytime if the vessel had been in berth must be allowed to count under the waiting time provision.

3.387 In *Ionian Navigation Co Inc* v. *Atlantic Shipping Co SA (The Loucas N)*,[430] the Court of Appeal had to consider the applicability of a Centrocon strike clause to waiting time. The *Loucas N*, the ship concerned, was chartered for a voyage from Caen and Antwerp to Houston, New Orleans and Tampa. She was delayed off Caen for a little over a day by congestion and off Houston by a combination of a strike and congestion following the strike. On these facts, the Court of Appeal held, dismissing an appeal by the charterers, that time had been lost at both ports waiting for a berth and that the time lost clauses which the charter contained were independent of the Centrocon strike clause under which, had the vessel been in berth, both the time lost due to the strike and due to congestion would have been excused. Of the relationship between the clauses Lord Denning said[431]:

On this point Mr Rokison stressed the words "lost in waiting", which show, he said, that you had to look for the damage which the owners had suffered by the vessel being delayed outside. I cannot accept this contention. If anyone had asked the master of this vessel, when she was waiting outside Houston, "What are you waiting for?", he would say: "I am waiting for a berth." No matter what was the cause of the waiting; no matter whether it was a strike or congestion or anything else at the port, he would say that he was waiting for a berth. That simple illustration shows that the time lost was lost in waiting for a berth.

3.388 Of this type of provision, Roskill LJ said in *The Johanna Oldendorff* in the Court of Appeal[432]:

. . . the sole question would be what the length of time was during which the vessel was waiting for berth and that (on the authorities) would be determined by reference to the calendar time so occupied. The exceptions in the laytime clause would not exclude from such calendar time Sundays, holidays and other periods excepted from laytime.

---

428. *Metals & Ropes Co Ltd* v. *Filia Compania Limitada (The Vastric)* [1966] 2 Lloyd's Rep 219.
429. *Ibid.*, at p. 225.
430. *Ionian Navigation Co Inc* v. *Atlantic Shipping Co SA (The Loucas N)* [1971] 1 Lloyd's Rep 215 (CA).
431. *Ibid.*, at p. 218.
432. *Oldendorff (EL) GmbH* v. *Tradax Export SA (The Johanna Oldendorff)* [1972] 2 Lloyd's Rep 292, at p. 312.

3.389 In the course of his judgment in the court below in *The Loucas N*, Donaldson J had also expressed the opinion[433] that under a port charter, notwithstanding that the time spent by the vessel in waiting for a berth would fall within the period in which laytime was actually running, the "time lost" code would override the laytime provisions so that periods which would have been excluded from laytime under the latter were not excepted. A similar result was held to apply by Donaldson J at first instance in *The Finix*.[434] However, these cases were followed by *The Darrah*, which eventually reached the House of Lords.[435]

3.390 In *The Darrah*, the relevant charter was a port charter under which the ship had been engaged to carry a cargo of cement from Novorossisk to Tripoli. The dispute concerned the time the vessel spent waiting for a berth at Tripoli within the port limits. Under the normal rules time had therefore commenced to run and the question was whether periods of adverse weather and holidays/weekends, which would normally be excluded from laytime, should be excluded from waiting time. At first instance, Ackner J held,[436] following the earlier cases, that no time was excluded from waiting time. This was reversed by the Court of Appeal,[437] who drew a distinction between waiting where the vessel was an Arrived ship and where she was not. In the former situation, the laytime exceptions applied, but in the latter they did not.[438] When the case came before the House of Lords, their Lordships decided that the laytime exceptions always applied whether the ship had reached her specified destination or not. The leading speeches were by Lord Diplock and Viscount Dilhorne, both of whom reviewed the earlier cases. Lord Diplock then explained why the law needed to be changed. One of the reasons he gave was that[439]:

. . . the results of ascribing to the clauses the meaning accepted since 1966 do not make commercial sense; it gives to the shipowner the chance of receiving a bonus dependent upon whether (a) his ship is lucky enough to be kept waiting for a berth and (b) is so kept waiting during a period which includes time which would not have counted against permitted laytime if the ship had been in berth.

3.391 Viscount Dilhorne took a similar view, saying[440]:

So in the present case it does not look right that there should be deducted from the permitted discharging time by virtue of the time lost provision periods of time which would not be counted under the discharging provision . . .

If my conclusion is correct, the fact that there is an overlap of the time lost and the discharging or loading provisions will not matter, for the time will be counted in the same way and a shipowner will not gain a greater advantage from his ship being kept waiting for a berth from her being kept at her berth.

3.392 After their Lordships' decision in *The Darrah* had been given, the Court of Appeal considered an appeal from the decision of Donaldson J in *The Finix*.[441] This aspect

433. *Ionian Navigation Co Inc v. Atlantic Shipping SA (The Loucas N)* [1970] 2 Lloyd's Rep 482.
434. *Nea Tyhi Maritime Co v. Compagnie Grainière SA (The Finix)* [1975] 2 Lloyd's Rep 415.
435. *Aldebaran Compania Maritima SA v. Aussenhandel AG (The Darrah)* [1976] 2 Lloyd's Rep 359 (HL).
436. *The Darrah* [1974] 2 Lloyd's Rep 435.
437. *The Darrah* [1976] 1 Lloyd's Rep 285 (CA).
438. A similar conclusion was reached by Roskill J in *Inca Compania Naviera SA v. Mofinol Inc (The President Brand)* [1967] 2 Lloyd's Rep 338.
439. *The Darrah* [1976] 2 Lloyd's Rep 359, at p. 366.
440. *Ibid.*, at p. 369.
441. *The Finix* [1975] 2 Lloyd's Rep 415.

took little of the court's time, Lord Denning saying simply that the decision of the umpire and the judge was wrong.[442]

3.393 Where there is more than one charter or the shipowner has been allowed to complete with other cargo, then with this sort of clause the waiting must be in respect of the cargo to which the charter relates and not some other cargo.[443]

How time lost should be counted

3.394 The question that arises is whether time lost in waiting should be counted at the beginning of lay days or added at the end. The two cases that discuss the problem give different answers, but it is suggested that the better answer is the second and later decision to the effect that it should be counted as it occurs.

3.395 The first case was *Government of Ceylon* v. *Société Franco-Tunisienne d'Armement-Tunis (The Massalia (No 2))* where Diplock J said[444]:

The last matter which I have to decide is whether one adds the time lost in waiting for a berth at the beginning or at the end of the lay days. That sounds to an arithmetician as if the sum must come to the same, but in this particular case I understand that it makes a difference of a day, because, if one adds it at the beginning, the Sunday, Oct 28, is excluded from the laytime and therefore counts as demurrage. If, on the other hand, one adds it at the end, then the Sunday comes during laytime, and does not count. So it does make a difference of 24 hours. Without giving any reason, I hold that it should be added at the end.

3.396 The other case was *Ionian Navigation Co Inc* v. *Atlantic Shipping Company SA (The Loucas N)*, where at first instance Donaldson J said[445]:

... I consider that it should be brought into account as and when the delay occurs. It is, of course, quite separate from the time allowed for loading and discharging but the extent of the delay in waiting for a berth affects the yardstick which has to be applied in determining how much chronological time remains available for the completion of these processes.

3.397 It must be remembered that at the time this judgment was given it was held that laytime exceptions did not apply to waiting time, whereas now they do and that was why the judge said that waiting time was quite separate. However, the fact that laytime exceptions do apply makes it even more appropriate that waiting time should be brought into account as it occurs.

Time lost in waiting for berth to count in full

3.398 This variation on the previous phrase has been considered in London arbitration.[446] The owners argued that the words "time lost in waiting for berth whether in free pratique or not to count in full" had the effect of ensuring that all time spent by the vessels in waiting for a berth at the discharge port should count without the application of any charterparty exceptions. They placed heavy reliance on the words "in full". On the other hand, the charterers contended that "time" meant laytime and therefore any exceptions applied just as they would had the vessel been in berth.

---

442. *The Finix* [1978] 1 Lloyd's Rep 16, at p. 18.
443. *The Massalia (No 2)* [1960] 2 Lloyd's Rep 352; *The Agios Stylianos* [1975] 1 Lloyd's Rep 426.
444. *The Massalia (No 2)* [1960] 2 Lloyd's Rep 352, at p. 359.
445. *The Loucas N* [1970] 2 Lloyd's Rep 482, at p. 487. The point was not pursued on appeal.
446. London Arbitration—LMLN 114, 15 March 1984.

3.399 The arbitrators held that the charterers were right and that following *The Darrah*[447] "any time lost" meant any laytime lost. If the intention had been to derogate from the opening words of the sentence so as to strike at the core of established laytime computations, sufficiently cogent language should have been used. The arbitrators suggested as an example of such wording, "Any time lost in waiting for berth to count in full, with all exceptions excluded". The owners' claim for a balance of demurrage therefore failed.

Norgrain charter—waiting for berth

3.400 The Norgrain charter has a provision at clause 17 covering the situation where a vessel is prevented from entering the commercial limits of the port. The clause provides for time so used in the circumstances specified to count against laytime and to be added to laytime or demurrage.

3.401 In London Arbitration 5/88,[448] the arbitrators concluded that, unlike the previous clause, the waiting time should be added after the main laytime calculation had been made. The reference to it counting as laytime meant it was to be calculated in that way. Thus, if some allowed laytime remained after computing the laytime used within the port, it could be set against the time spent in waiting. If there was no allowed laytime left, the waiting time was calculated in the same way as demurrage. If it was insufficient it counted part as laytime and part as demurrage.

Reachable on arrival/always accessible

3.402 Strictly speaking, a reachable on arrival or always accessible clause, which in the High Court in *The Kyzikos*[449] were said to be the same (at least as far as getting into berth is concerned), have no effect on when laytime commences and therefore in a charter containing such a clause laytime will commence on arrival at the specified destination after the elapse of any prescribed period. What they may do, however, is give rise to a claim for detention for any delay preventing the vessel from reaching its specified destination and may also affect the meaning to be given to any provision such as that contained in clause 6 of the Exxonvoy 69/Asbatankvoy form of charter, by which charterers are excused from responsibility for delay in the vessel getting into berth after Notice of Readiness has been given. The judicial history of the clause will now be considered, together with the first of these considerations. The second will be considered in a later chapter.[450]

3.403 The principal cases in which these phrases have been considered involve tankers. The phrase "reachable on arrival" is more often encountered in tanker charters and "always accessible" in dry cargo charters. The first to consider "reachable on arrival" was *Sociedad Carga Oceanica SA* v. *Idolinoele Vertriebsgesellschaft mbH (The Angelos*

447. *Aldebaran Compania Maritima SA* v. *Aussenhandel AG (The Darrah)* [1976] 2 Lloyd's Rep 359 (HL).
    448. London Arbitration 5/88—LMLN 230, 27 August 1988.
    449. *Seacrystal Shipping Ltd* v. *Bulk Transport Group Shipping Co Ltd (The Kyzikos)* [1987] 1 Lloyd's Rep 48.
    450. See *post* at para. 4.394.

Lusis),[451] a decision of Megaw J, as he then was. This concerned the motor tanker *Angelos Lusis* which had been fixed to load a cargo at Constantza. On arrival at the load port she was forced to anchor in the roads, where she was not an Arrived ship, since the port authorities would not allow her to proceed until a berth became available. The owners claimed there was an absolute obligation on the charterers to provide a place for loading reachable on the vessel's arrival. The charterers, on the other hand, claimed that this was a port charter and therefore the risk of delay prior to arrival in the port at a point where the vessel became an Arrived ship lay with the owners. Furthermore, they said "arrival" in the phrase reachable on arrival meant arrival in the port and it was only on her arrival in the port that they became under a duty to provide a berth.

3.404 The shipowners were right, said the judge. The phrase was intended to impose upon the charterers a contractual obligation of value to the shipowners. The charterers' obligation was to nominate a reachable place where she could load (i.e. a berth which the vessel, proceeding normally on her arrival, would be able to reach and occupy), whether within or outside the fiscal or commercial limits of the port, without being held up. As the charterers had failed to do this, the judge upheld an award of damages in respect of the delay in the roads.

3.405 A couple of years later, the phrase again came before the courts in a case called *Inca Compania Naviera SA and Commercial and Maritime Enterprises Evanghelos P Nomikos SA* v. *Mofinol Inc (The President Brand).*[452] Here the port in question was Lourenço Marques, which was the discharge port. On arrival there, the *President Brand* was unable to cross the bar to enter the port for four days because of her draught. When there was sufficient water for her to cross the bar she did so, anchoring again within the port to await a berth, which became available later the same day but to which she was unable to shift until the following day on the afternoon high tide. On arrival at the second anchorage she gave a valid Notice of Readiness, an earlier notice being held to be invalid since it was given on arrival off the port before she became an Arrived ship.

3.406 As Roskill J, before whom the case came, said[453]:

The central issue in the case is this: Who bears the risk of the time between Apr. 19 and Apr. 23 . . . when the vessel was unable to cross the bar owing to lack of sufficiency of water? . . .

3.407 Charterers, as in the previous case, sought to argue that arrival meant that the vessel had to be an Arrived ship, but again this contention was rejected, the judge finding that arrival was used in the popular sense of that word as opposed to the technical meaning it had in connection with when a vessel became an Arrived ship. Commenting on this aspect, Roskill J said[454]:

I think as a matter of ordinary common sense if one asked two businessmen if a ship had arrived at Lourenço Marques when she reported at the pilot station in that way and in those circumstances they would answer: "Yes, she has arrived there", notwithstanding that she had not yet got within the commercial limits of the port.

On the meaning of "reachable", he said[455]:

---

451. *Sociedad Carga Oceanica SA* v. *Idolinoele Vertriebsgellschaft mbH (The Angelos Lusis)* [1964] 2 Lloyd's Rep 28.
452. *Inca Compania Naviera SA and Commercial and Maritime Enterprises Evanghelos P Nomikos SA* v. *Mofinol Inc (The President Brand)* [1967] 2 Lloyd's Rep 338.
453. *Ibid.,* at p. 346.
454. *Ibid.,* at p. 348.
455. *Ibid.*

"Reachable" as a matter of grammar means "able to be reached". There may be many reasons why a particular berth or discharging place cannot be reached. It may be because another ship is occupying it; it may be because there is an obstruction between where the ship is and where she wishes to go; it may be because there is not a sufficiency of water to enable her to get there. The existence of any of those obstacles can prevent a particular berth or dock being reachable and in my judgment a particular berth or dock is just as much not reachable if there is not enough water to enable the vessel to traverse the distance from where she is to that place as if there were a ship occupying that place at the material time. Accordingly, in my judgment, the charterers' obligation was to nominate a berth which the vessel could reach on arrival and they are in breach of that obligation if they are unable so to do.

3.408 The judge also pointed out that in some cases, of which the present one was an example, a breach might arise without the fault of either party, but nevertheless even in those circumstances, as a matter of construction, the clause provided that loss of time should fall on the charterers and not the owners.

3.409 Later in his judgment, he went on to consider when the charterers' liability ended. On the day when the ship was able to cross the bar, she began to move at 01 30, anchored again at 04 00 within the port and gave Notice of Readiness at 11 00. The charterers argued that even if the judge was against them on the principal issue, nevertheless their liability should not extend beyond 04 00, when the vessel re-anchored to await a berth. However, on this point the judge also ruled against them holding that the owners had not unreasonably delayed before giving notice, but, he continued[456]:

I am not saying that if in another case it could be shown that the owners or the master has wrongly delayed giving notice of readiness the position might not be otherwise. That does not arise in the present case.

Roskill J therefore concluded that the *President Brand* had been delayed from her arrival at the Pilot Station at 08 00 on 19 April until 11 00[457] on 23 April by the charterers' failure to procure a berth, reachable on arrival, for which damages for detention calculated at the demurrage rate were payable. From that period, however, there was to be deducted the $2\frac{1}{2}$ hours between 01 30 and 04 00 on 23 April, during which the ship crossed the bar and moved into port. This was not, said the judge, time which was lost by the charterers' breach, but time which would have been occupied in any event coming into port had the vessel not been held up at the bar.

3.410 The Court of Appeal were given a chance to consider this type of provision in *Shipping Developments Corporation SA* v. *V/O Sojuzneftexport (The Delian Spirit)*.[458] In this case, the *Delian Spirit* arrived off the port of Tuapse to load a cargo of crude oil, but as, due to congestion, no berth was available she anchored in the roads and gave Notice of Readiness. She lay in the roads for five days before a berth became available.

3.411 In the subsequent arbitration proceedings, the umpire held that on arrival in the roads she was not an Arrived ship, but in the High Court[459] Donaldson J was in no doubt that she was an Arrived ship in the technical sense, a conclusion shared by the Court of Appeal. Despite his decision on this point, Donaldson J held that time ran under the laytime provisions but that the owners were nevertheless also entitled to claim damages

456. *Ibid.*, at p. 351.
457. The notice clause also contained a provision that time should run six hours after notice was given and therefore laytime did not commence until 17 00. That provision was unaffected by the previous delay.
458. *Shipping Developments Corporation SA* v. *V/O Sojuzneftexport (The Delian Spirit)* [1971] 1 Lloyd's Rep 506 (CA).
459. *The Delian Spirit* [1971] 1 Lloyd's Rep 64.

for detention during the same period by virtue of a breach of the "reachable on arrival" provision. The Court of Appeal disagreed, preferring the reasoning of Roskill J in *The President Brand*.[460] Lord Denning put it this way[461]:

So it is said the charterers are liable in damages . . . and are also liable to demurrage after the laytime expired. The judge accepted that submission, but I cannot agree with it. It would be most unjust that the charterers should be made liable twice over. The answer is given by a long line of cases which establish that where the charterers have been guilty of a breach causing delay, they are entitled to apply their laytime so as to diminish or extinguish any claim for the delay, leaving the shipowners to claim for demurrage at the agreed rate for any extra delay over and above the laytime.

The remainder of the court agreed, Fenton Atkinson LJ saying[462]:

While in certain circumstances which I do not think it is necessary to attempt to define on the facts of this case you can have an arrival of a ship . . . before that ship becomes technically an arrived ship for laytime purposes, and therefore the charterer who has failed to provide a berth at the time of such arrival will become liable for damages for detention, once the ship becomes an arrived ship in the technical sense the position is different, and in my judgment the charterer gets the advantage of the laytime provided by the charterparty . . .

3.412 In *Nereide SpA di Navigazione* v. *Bulk Oil International Ltd (The Laura Prima)*, the House of Lords considered the inter-relationship of a "reachable on arrival" clause and one excluding delay beyond the charterers' control in a vessel getting into berth after giving Notice of Readiness, but that raises a separate problem which will be considered in detail later.[463] In the same case, however, the lower courts[464] reviewed the earlier cases without significant comment on the meaning of the "reachable on arrival" provision on its own.

3.413 Since the previous case was decided, there have been a number of attempts by commercial arbitrators to restrict the ambit of "reachable on arrival" provisions to situations where vessels are unable to berth due to congestion or to physical obstructions including congestion and lack of water, but excluding weather. There have also been three judicial decisions at first instance where the same issues have been raised and these will be briefly considered now and in detail later.[465]

3.414 The first decision in time was *The Kyzikos*,[466] which eventually reached the House of Lords: but not on this point, which was considered only at first instance. In that case the requirement was that the discharging berth be "always accessible", a phrase which the court dealt with on the basis it meant "reachable on arrival". The reason *The Kyzikos* could not berth on arrival was because of fog, the berth itself being unoccupied. Having cited the *dictum* of Roskill J quoted above,[467] where he explained the meaning of "reachable", Webster J continued[468]:

460. *The Delian Spirit* [1971] 1 Lloyd's Rep 506, at p. 509.
461. Lord Denning said the long line of cases to which he referred started with *Petersen* v. *Dunn & Co* (1895) 1 CC 8 and finished with Roskill J's decision in *The President Brand* [1967] 2 Lloyd's Rep 338.
462. *The Delian Spirit* [1971] 1 Lloyd's Rep 506, at p. 510.
463. *Nereide SpA di Navigazione* v. *Bulk Oil International Ltd (The Laura Prima)* [1982] 1 Lloyd's Rep 1 (HL). For consideration of this point, see *post* at para. 4.396.
464. *The Laura Prima* [1980] 1 Lloyd's Rep 466 (Mocatta J) [1981] 2 Lloyd's Rep 24 (CA).
465. See *post* at para. 4.418.
466. *Seacrystal Shipping Ltd* v. *Bulk Transport Group Shipping Co Ltd (The Kyzikos)* [1987] 1 Lloyd's Rep 48.
467. See *ante* at para. 3.411.
468. *Seacrystal Shipping Ltd* v. *Bulk Transport Group Shipping Co Ltd (The Kyzikos)* [1987] 1 Lloyd's Rep 48, at p. 58.

I note that all the examples of circumstances preventing a berth being reachable, given by Mr Justice Roskill, are examples of physical obstruction preventing access to the berth, and I have no doubt that that decision is authority for the general proposition that a berth is not accessible or reachable if there is something which physically obstructs access to it. But fog, or any other bad weather, is not in my view to be regarded as a physical obstruction and, even if it is to be so regarded, it is certainly not an obstruction *sui generis* with the obstacles of which examples are given in that *dictum*.

He, therefore, held that charterers were not in breach of their obligation to provide an always accessible berth.

3.415 The second case was *The Sea Queen*,[469] a decision of Saville J. Here the delay was due to non-availability of tugs and bad weather. The same argument as in the previous case was put forward together with a suggestion that the word "reachable" was descriptive of the berth in the sense that the berth remained reachable albeit the vessel cannot for the time being reach it and finally that the charterers' duty was to procure a berth which the vessel proceeding normally would be able to reach. By "proceeding normally" was meant, it was suggested, in good weather and with tugs. None of these arguments, however, found favour with the judge, who was not prepared to restrict the meaning of reachable in any of the ways suggested.

3.416 The third and last case to be decided was *The Fjordaas*[470] where again there was an absence of tugs and bad weather, this time together with a prohibition on night navigation. The arguments put forward were the same and again rejected, this time by Steyn J, who said in relation to the physical obstruction argument[471]:

In my judgment the distinction between physical causes of obstruction and non physical causes rendering a designated place unreachable is not supported by the language of the contract or common sense; it is in conflict with the reasoning in *The Laura Prima*; and it is insupportable on the interpretation given to that provision in *The President Brand*. Quite independently of authority I believe it to be wrong.

3.417 In *The Amiral Fahri Engin*,[472] Saville J repeated that delay due to bad weather or congestion or a combination of both was a breach of a "reachable on arrival" provision.

3.418 In London Arbitration 16/98,[473] the facts were that the charterers had chartered two vessels to discharge at the same berth. When the second vessel arrived, the berth was empty but the first vessel, which the charterers wished to discharge first, had arrived the previous day and was waiting to berth but unable to do so—first because of weather and then because the tugs needed to berth her were unavailable due to New Year holidays.

3.419 After the holidays, the first vessel berthed and discharged her cargo and, when that was completed, the second vessel took her place on the berth.

3.420 The charterers argued that the berth was available when the second vessel arrived. Therefore, they said, *The Laura Prima*[474] did not apply, and they were also protected by an additional clause which provided for time not to count "on an inward passage moving from anchorage to first berth, including awaiting tugs, pilot . . .".

---

469. *Palm Shipping Inc* v. *Kuwait Petroleum Corporation* (*The Sea Queen*) [1988] 1 Lloyd's Rep 500.
470. *K/S Arnt J Moerland* v. *Kuwait Petroleum Corporation* (*The Fjordaas*) [1988] 1 Lloyd's Rep 336.
471. *Ibid.*, at p. 342.
472. *Sale Corporation of Monrovia* v. *Turkish Cargo Lines General Manager* (*The Amiral Fahri Engin*) [1993] 1 Lloyd's Rep 75.
473. London Arbitration 16/98—LMLN 489, 4 August 1998.
474. *The Laura Prima* [1982] 1 Lloyd's Rep 1.

3.421 On the basis of the cases cited above, the tribunal held that *The Laura Prima* did apply and then moved on to consider the effect of the additional clause. On that they said that the first few hours of delay were due to weather, but even after that it was not the second vessel that was delayed awaiting tugs but the first vessel.

3.422 With the case law as it now stands, it would seem where there is a breach of a "reachable on arrival" provision which gives rise to a claim for detention, i.e. where the vessel is delayed at a point before reaching her specified destination and thus becoming an Arrived ship, then the owners will be able to recover at the demurrage rate without any of the laytime exceptions or interruptions applying. This appears to follow from *The President Brand*,[475] where the vessel arrived off the port on a Sunday and the time on Sunday was allowed to count, although had it been laytime, time would not have commenced until Monday, since Sunday was an excepted period. Where she is delayed after becoming an Arrived ship, the exceptions, etc., apply.

3.423 A problem that sometimes arises in relation to whether the shipowner's claim is for damages for detention in a berth charter is where a "reachable on arrival/always accessible" provision is combined with another phrase accelerating the commencement of laytime, such as a WIBON provision. In these circumstances it is suggested that the correct approach is to first apply the second phrase. If the effect of this is to allow laytime to commence at the point the vessel has then reached, the effect of the "reachable on arrival" provision is probably confined to the question whether laytime exceptions, such as that in clause 6 of the Asbatankvoy charter, apply prior to the vessel reaching her berth.[476]

3.424 On the facts of *The Kyzikos*,[477] where the vessel was unable to berth because of fog, the WIBON provision was ineffective to accelerate the commencement of laytime prior to arrival in berth, and therefore the owners should have had a valid claim for damages for detention for the period prior to berthing because of the "always accessible" clause. Had the cause of delay been congestion, the WIBON provision would have been effective, laytime would have commenced on arrival at the port and the effect of the "always accessible" provision would have been minimal.

3.425 The *Voylayrules 1993* provide as follows[478]:

"REACHABLE ON HER ARRIVAL" or "ALWAYS ACCESSIBLE" shall mean that the charterer undertakes that an available loading or discharging berth be provided to the vessel on her arrival at the port which she can reach safely without delay in the absence of an abnormal occurrence.

This definition, which will only apply if the Voylayrules are specifically incorporated into the charter, differs in two significant ways from the position at common law. The first is the reference to "available" in the second line rather than "accessible", and the second is the reference to "an abnormal occurrence" in the last line.

3.426 It is clear from cases such as *The Fjordaas* and *The Sea Queen*[479] that the berth must not only be available but must also be accessible. On the second point, it is not clear what sort of circumstances would be considered an abnormal occurrence nor at what point in time they must arise to neutralise the charterers' undertaking to procure a berth "reachable on arrival/always accessible". The owners' argument that succeeded in *The*

475. *The President Brand* [1967] 2 Lloyd's Rep 338.
476. See *post* at para. 4.396. See also London Arbitration 11/93—LMLN 356, 26 June 1993.
477. *The Kyzikos* [1987] 1 Lloyd's Rep 48. See *ante* at para. 3.353.
478. See Appendix.
479. *The Fjordaas* [1988] 1 Lloyd's Rep 336; *The Sea Queen* [1988] 1 Lloyd's Rep 500.

Angelos Lusis[480] was that the obligation on the charterers was an absolute one. It is correct however that in *The Laura Prima* in the High Court[481] in a *dictum* expressly approved by the House of Lords,[482] Mocatta J referred to the charterers being protected where they had procured a berth reachable on arrival in the likelihood of some intervening event over which they had no control, e.g. an embargo or insufficiency of water, but that was by virtue of the exception in clause 6 of the charter, not by virtue of the definition of the phrase itself.

3.427 With a "reachable on arrival" or "always accessible" provision in his charter, the shipowner may therefore receive a bonus if he is delayed before reaching the specified destination (port or berth according to the charter). This, however, is precisely why, in *The Darrah*, Lord Diplock said[483] that the distinction between waiting and discharging (or loading) time was wrong. That case, of course, relates to provisions providing that time lost in waiting for a berth should count as laytime, and in a sense such a clause provides its own measure of damages, i.e. to count as laytime. A "reachable on arrival" provision is different, since damages fall to be determined separately. Nevertheless, what was thought unfair in that type of clause must logically be unfair in the type of clause now under consideration. It may be that this is what Sir Gordon Willmer had in mind when in *The Delian Spirit* he said[484]:

> . . . I prefer to say no more upon the difficult question which might have arisen if the vessel had not been found to be an arrived ship at the time when she was lying in the roads. But I certainly do not wish to be taken as accepting that, even in that situation, the owners would necessarily be entitled to prosecute an independent claim for damages, without giving credit for the laytime to which the charterers were entitled, and for which, as we have been reminded, they paid when they paid the freight.

Baltic Code 2000

3.428 A combined definition for "reachable on arrival and always accessible" appears in *Baltic Code 2000*[485]:

REACHABLE ON HER ARRIVAL or ALWAYS ACCESSIBLE—means that the charterer undertakes that an available and accessible loading or discharging berth will be provided to the vessel on her arrival at or off the port which she can reach safely without delay proceeding normally. Where the charterer undertakes the berth will be ALWAYS ACCESSIBLE, he additionally undertakes that the vessel will be able to depart safely from the berth without delay at any time during or on completion of loading or discharging.

Always accessible—for how long must the berth be accessible?

3.429 With a "reachable on arrival" provision, it is clear that whether the berth is reachable falls to be determined on the arrival of the vessel concerned and any effect of the warranty comes to an end, at the latest, when the vessel berths. The question now under consideration is whether the same applies to an "always accessible" provision.

480. *The Angelos Lusis* [1964] 2 Lloyd's Rep 28.
481. *The Laura Prima* [1980] 1 Lloyd's Rep 466, at p. 468.
482. *The Laura Prima* [1982] 1 Lloyd's Rep 1, at p. 5.
483. *The Darrah* [1976] 2 Lloyd's Rep 359, at p. 366. See also *ante* at para. 3.410.
484. *The Delian Spirit* [1971] 1 Lloyd's Rep 506, at p. 512. In *The Sea Wind* LMLN 531 16 March 2000 where the relevant charter had an "always accessible" provision, New York Arbitrators awarded Owners demurrage for the first two days delay after laytime expired then damages for detention where a vessel was delayed because the Shippers allowed other vessels to berth ahead of her. It is unlikely that the London Arbitrators would follow this decision.
485. See Appendix.

3.430 As already mentioned, "always accessible" provisions most commonly appear in dry cargo charters and "reachable on arrival" provisions in tanker charters. That of itself is probably of no significance in this context.

3.431 Whilst an "always accessible" provision may be attached to any charter, it frequently appears in Gencon charters in Part I of the charter in the boxes where the specified destination is stated. It commonly appears with a similar provision, namely that the vessel may lie "always afloat" at the berth in question. The abbreviation "AAAA" is often used for "always afloat, always accessible".

3.432 Arguably these phrases, when used in conjunction with the loading/discharging berth(s), are descriptive of the berth—it is one where the vessel may lie, always afloat, and which is always accessible.

3.433 Whether the berth must be accessible throughout cargo operations, i.e. after the vessel has berthed, was in issue in London Arbitration 11/97.[486]

3.434 What happened in this case was that the vessel had to wait over nine hours for the next high tide after completion of loading before she could unberth.

3.435 In the words of *Lloyd's Maritime Law Newsletter*, the owners submitted that:

... the berth was not "always accessible" and that in accordance with common law and the principles of equity and commonsense the charterers were in breach. They submitted that "always accessible" could only mean what was understood by a layman, and that there was no other meaning to those words than that the charterers should order the ship to a berth where there would be access to and from the berth at all times. In other words access to the berth for the vessel to reach it and access from the berth to the open sea.

3.436 Having said that, the textbooks were of little assistance on this occasion, seeming to concentrate on "always accessible" being synonymous with "reachable on arrival", ignoring its possible application to departure from the berth, as did the *Voylayrules 1993* (but see the definition in *Baltic Code 2000* quoted above). The tribunal inferred that this meant that the charterers, by agreeing "always accessible" terms, were under an obligation to provide a berth which was available immediately on arrival but that that particular regime did not apply after the ship was actually in berth, when the normal charterparty provisions as to laytime would apply.

3.437 That there had been no academic discussion of the point, or that it had not been considered by the authors of the Voylayrules, seems a rather weak basis to draw the inference the tribunal did. However, the tribunal then went on to consider dictionary meanings of "accessible" and concluded that none had made any mention of "access from" as opposed to "access to". They did not consider what effect the addition of the word "always" might have.

3.438 In *The Forum Craftsman*,[487] Hobhouse J said:

The word "always" imports an absence of qualification and is often used for that purpose in the drafting of exceptions clauses.

Applying this to the phrase "always accessible", the question becomes: does it mean the berth itself should be able to be approached by any vessel of the size of the vessel in question during the period of loading/discharging (or could be but for the presence of the berthed vessel); or is it more restricted in meaning, as the arbitral tribunal held, and means only that the particular vessel must be able to get to the berth when it wishes to do so?

---

486. London Arbitration 11/97—LMLN 463, 2 August 1997.
487. *The Forum Craftsman* [1991] 1 Lloyd's Rep 81.

3.439 The tribunal had a further reason for finding as they did based on the High Court decision in *The Kyzikos*,[488] where Webster J held that the expression "always accessible" did not mean that because fog or other weather conditions prevented the vessel from safely approaching the berth it was not accessible. However, on that point the subsequent decisions in *The Fjordaas*[489] and *The Sea Queen*[490] went the other way and, in relation to a "reachable on arrival" provision, held that bad weather was within the protection afforded by the phrase. On this point there is no logical reason why different considerations should apply between the two phrases and it is suggested that the *Fjordaas* and *Sea Queen* decisions are the ones that should be followed in relation to "always accessible".

3.440 This therefore leaves the question whether the arbitrators in London Arbitration 11/97[491] were right in their conclusion, based on "accessible" being limited to meaning "able to get into" but not extending to "able to get out of" the berth, and being confined to the vessel herself. If they were, then what does "always" add? The answer will perhaps have to await further arbitral and judicial decisions.

3.441 A further issue arose in London Arbitration 11/97[492] relating to a period of delay after the vessel had left the berth and anchored in the inner port, but was unable to leave the port until the next high tide. On that point, the tribunal were clearly right in holding that the phrase "always accessible" gave no protection to the owners since it clearly describes the berth and not the port.

3.442 If the warranty does extend to departure from the berth, any claim will be one for detention, since laytime or time on demurrage comes to an end on completion of loading or discharging as the case may be.

So near thereto as she may safely get

3.443 Unlike the previous three phrases, this clause acts by providing an alternative specified destination, which may take effect if certain conditions are met if the vessel concerned is unable to proceed to its primary destination. The two leading cases on the clause are *Dahl* v. *Nelson, Donkin & Co*[493] and *The Athamas (Owners)* v. *Dig Vijay Cement Co Ltd*,[494] the former being a decision of the House of Lords and the latter of the Court of Appeal.

3.444 In *The Athamas*, Sellers LJ said of this phrase[495]:

The words in that clause vitally affecting this case, "or so near thereto as she may safely get", go back possibly some 150 years to the days of sailing ships and have been in current use in relation to the carriage of goods by sea throughout the era of steamships and their modern successors.

Despite this, the judicial history of the phrase starts in 1855 with a case which was still giving trouble in 1963 and which will be considered later.[496]

---

488. *The Kyzikos* [1987] 1 Lloyd's Rep 48 at 57.
489. *The Fjordaas* [1988] 1 Lloyd's Rep 336.
490. *The Sea Queen* [1988] 1 Lloyd's Rep 500.
491. London Arbitration 11/97—LMLN 463, 2 August 1997.
492. *Ibid.*
493. *Dahl* v. *Nelson, Donkin and others* (1880) 6 App Cas 38, *sub nom.*, *Nelson* v. *Dahl* (1879) 12 Ch D 568.
494. *The Athamas (Owners)* v. *Dig Vijay Cement Co Ltd* [1963] 1 Lloyd's Rep 287 (CA).
495. *Ibid.*, at p. 292.
496. *Schilizzi* v. *Derry* (1855) 4 E & B 873. See *post* at para. 3.460.

3.445 The governing principle behind these words was said by Brett LJ in *Nelson v. Dahl* to be[497]:

... lay days do not begin to run, either for the purpose of loading or unloading, until the shipowner has brought his ship to the primary destination named in the charterparty, so as to be ready, so far as the ship is concerned, to receive or deliver there, unless he is prevented from getting his ship to that destination by some obstruction or disability of such a character that it cannot be overcome by the shipowner by any reasonable means, except within such a time as, having regard to the object of the adventure of both the shipowner and charterer, is as a matter of business wholly unreasonable.

3.446 The essence of the test, therefore, is whether it would be reasonable to expect the shipowner to wait until the disability or obstruction is removed and then proceed to the primary destination, or whether a point both geographically and in time has been reached at which it would be reasonable for him to load or discharge the cargo at an alternative place. What is reasonable is usually a question of fact and although certain broad propositions may be drawn from the decided cases, at the end of the day each case must be decided on its own facts.

3.447 In deciding what is reasonable, the following factors are amongst those to be taken into consideration:

A. Nature of obstacle.

B. Length of time actually spent waiting.

C. Length of anticipated delay.

D. Degree of risk known to exist at the time of making the charter.

E. How close to the intended port the vessel can get, not just in miles but as a proportion of the voyage.

F. Proportion of cargo to be loaded/discharged at the obstructed port.

3.448 Another way of putting it would be to say that what is reasonable will depend both upon the nature of the obstacle and the nature of the adventure. Whilst all of the factors are interrelated and must be considered, the weight to be given to each will vary from case to case. Before considering them in more detail, however, there are a number of general points which can be made.

3.449 The first of these is that it must be the vessel that is prevented from reaching the primary destination. The point is illustrated by *Nobel's Explosives Co Ltd v. Jenkins & Co*,[498] which concerned a shipment of explosives for delivery at Yokohama. When the ship arrived at Hong Kong en route, war had been declared between China and Japan. Explosives being contraband of war, the master, reasonably believing that the ship would be seized if he proceeded further with explosives on board, landed them at Hong Kong and then safely proceeded to Yokohama with the remainder of his cargo. Whilst finding that the master was protected by a "restraint of princes" clause and by an additional clause allowing him to land the goods at the nearest safe and convenient port in such circumstances, Mathew J held that the clause now under consideration did not apply, saying[499]:

For the defendant reliance was placed on the terms of the bill of lading that the steamer should proceed to Yokohama, "or so near thereunto as she might safely get". It was argued that at Hong Kong she was as near to Yokohama as she could safely get within the meaning of the bill of lading.

497. *Nelson v. Dahl* (1879) 12 Ch D 568, at p. 593.
498. *Nobel's Explosives Co Ltd v. Jenkins & Co* (1896) 1 CC 436.
499. *Ibid.*, at p. 438.

But the contract was not to carry the goods to the nearest place to which the goods could safely get, but to deliver the goods at Yokohama or as near thereto as the vessel could safely get. She did get to Yokohama and the obligation to deliver the goods under the clause in question thereupon became complete. This ground of defence seems to me untenable.

3.450 There is clearly a link between the doctrine of frustration and this type of clause. In *Dahl* v. *Nelson*, having considered a number of cases where the charterers had been commercially frustrated, Lord Watson continued[500]:

No doubt in these cases the contract had not passed the executory stage; but seeing that unreasonable delay in reaching the place of loading, when occasioned by no fault of either of the parties, is effectual to discharge such a contract altogether, I conceive that, *a fortiori*, a similar delay in reaching the primary place of discharge ought to have the effect of enabling the vessel to complete her voyage by proceeding to the alternative destination.

In the same case, Lord Blackburn also considered what the word "safely" added to the phrase. Without it, he said[501]:

. . . it would have been open to a charterer to contend that the ship must get as far as it was possible, however, dangerous it might be. I do not think it could have been successfully so contended, but those who originally framed this clause prevented the possibility of such a contention by inserting the word "safely".

Turning now to the factors to be considered:

A. Nature of the obstacle

3.451 This may be political, legal or physical. In the case of the last of these, this may be further divided into natural obstacles and congestion.

3.452 *Castel and Latta* v. *Trechman*[502] is an example of a political obstacle. That case concerned a blockade by the Turkish Government of all Russian ports in the Black Sea, although, on the facts, the vessel concerned was held not to be justified in going to Constantinople instead of the two remaining Russian ports which were the primary destination. However, in *The Athamas*[503] the owners were held to be justified in not proceeding to the primary destination because of a legal obstacle, namely the refusal of the pilotage authority to allow the vessel to proceed in an area of compulsory pilotage.

3.453 On the question of natural obstacles in relation to this clause. McCardie J said in *The Robert Dollar Co* v. *Blood, Holman & Co. Ltd*[504]:

I conceive that all vessels must take the risks of wind or storm or tide ere reaching the appointed port. These risks may, of course, be greater with a sailing ship than a steamer, but they are risks which fall on the shipowners and not on the charterer. As to tides, e.g., it was concisely put by a learned judge as follows[505]:

"If the cause of the detention be the arrival of the vessel during low tides, her having to wait for the tide to increase is one of the ordinary incidents of navigation, and the shipowner must submit to the delay so occasioned."

---

500. *Dahl (Robert H)* v. *Nelson, Donkin and others* (1880) 6 App Cas 38, at p. 62.
501. *Ibid.*, at p. 50.
502. *Castel and Latta* v. *Trechman* (1884) 1 C & E 276.
503. *The Athamas (Owners)* v. *Dig Vijay Cement Co Ltd* [1963] 1 Lloyd's Rep 287.
504. *The Robert Dollar Co* v. *Blood, Holman & Co Ltd* (1920) 4 Ll L Rep 343, at p. 348.
505. *Hirsley* v. *Price* (1883) 11 QBD 244, at p. 247.

If a natural obstacle prevents a vessel from reaching its specified destination then usually the shipowner is less likely to be able to invoke the clause now under consideration, unless he can show that the other factors outweigh the nature of the obstacle, e.g. unless he can show substantial delay (since that arising from most natural obstacles will be short-lived). Two examples where a natural obstacle was held sufficient are *Capper & Co* v. *Wallace Brothers*[506] and *Hayton* v. *Irwin*.[507] In both cases the vessel's draught was too great to allow it to proceed to the specified destination. In neither case, however, was it simply a question of waiting for spring tides to approach.

3.454 *Dahl* v. *Nelson*[508] is itself an example of congestion being held of sufficient magnitude to permit the vessel concerned to discharge at an alternative place. In that case it was congestion in the Surrey Commercial Docks, which were the usual discharging point for timber cargoes.

B. Length of time actually spent waiting

3.455 Scrutton LJ put the point this way in *Fornyade Rederiaktiebolaget Commercial* v. *Blake & Co and others*[509]:

When you are chartered to go to a discharging place and cannot get there, first of all you are bound to wait a reasonable time before having recourse to the clause "or so near thereunto as she may safely get". You cannot arrive, and when you find you cannot get in at the exact minute, or on the exact day you desire, you immediately go off to a place which you describe as "so near thereunto as she may safely get". When a reasonable time has elapsed, and when there is no chance of your getting in to your discharging place within a reasonable time, the ship is at liberty to go to a reasonable discharging place . . .

3.456 However, if during the course of the voyage it is known that the vessel will be unable to reach its primary destination for an indefinite period, then commonsense dictates that the vessel should immediately divert to an alternative port, particularly during the carrying voyage. To be justified in so doing, however, the obstacle must be one which very definitely will not be removed before the commercial purpose of the voyage becomes lost. Some support for this proposition can be gained from the *Athamas* case,[510] which involved a two-port discharge. On arrival at the first, it became apparent that the vessel concerned would be unable to proceed to the second port, whereupon she gave notice of an intention to treat the first discharge port also as the second under this clause. In one sense, therefore, she could be said to have diverted straight to the alternative discharge port. In the *Athamas* case the reason why she could not proceed as planned was because of a refusal by the pilotage authority of the area surrounding the second port to allow her to proceed, since the *Athamas* would have been unable to maintain a minimum speed of 10 knots which they maintained was the least that was required for a safe passage during the low water season.

---

506. *Capper & Co* v. *Wallace Brothers* (1880) 5 QBD 163.
507. *Hayton* v. *Irwin* (1879) 5 CPD 130.
508. *Dahl (Robert H)* v. *Nelson, Donkin and others* (1880) 6 App Cas 38.
509. *Fornyade Rederiaktiebolaget Commercial* v. *Blake & Co* (1931) 39 Ll L Rep 205, at p. 207.
510. *The Athamas (Owners)* v. *Dig Vijay Cement Co Ltd* [1963] 1 Lloyd's Rep 287.

C. Length of anticipated delay

3.457 This is obviously closely connected with the point considered above. Where the anticipated delay is short or uncertain then the owners must wait to see what happens. However, if it is clear from the outset that the delay will be prolonged, then the shipowner will be more justified in giving notice of his intention to proceed elsewhere earlier. In *Dahl* v. *Nelson*[511] the delay due to congestion was expected to last at least a month and possibly many months. In *The Athamas*,[512] the delay was expected to be five months. In both of these cases, the anticipated delay was held to be sufficient to justify the shipowner's actions. In *Parker* v. *Winslow*[513] and *Bastifell* v. *Lloyd*,[514] where the delay was for about a fortnight, this was said to be insufficient. However, in both cases the delay was due to having to wait for the approach of spring tides and, as mentioned earlier, incidents of navigation such as these are viewed less sympathetically by the courts as being part of the normal risks assumed by the shipowner. Whilst it is difficult to lay down any hard and fast rules, it would seem that a delay of about a month would be the sort of time that would be necessary to justify going to another port.

D. Degree of risk known to exist

3.458 If both parties are aware of circumstances existing at the time of making the charter, or likely to exist at the time of performance of the charter, then the courts will be less willing to hold that the vessel was justified in proceeding elsewhere.

3.459 In *Metcalfe* v. *Britannia Ironworks Co*,[515] a cargo of railway bars was shipped from England to Tagranog in the Sea of Azov or so near thereto as the ship could safely get. On the arrival of the ship at Kertch, in the straits leading from the Black Sea into the Sea of Azov, it was found that the Sea of Azov was blocked with ice and likely to remain so until the following spring. The cargo was therefore unloaded at Kertch. Upholding the lower court's finding against the shipowner, Lord Coleridge said[516]:

It is not necessary to say more than that the obstruction was only temporary, and is such as must be incident to every contract for a voyage to a frozen sea, and it cannot be said that in all these contracts the words "at that time," or "then and there", are to be inserted after the words "as near thereto as the ship can safely get".

E. How close to the intended port the vessel can get

3.460 This was one of the major issues in the *Athamas* case.[517] The difficulty lay in the early case of *Schilizzi* v. *Derry*.[518] In that case, a ship was chartered to proceed from London to Galatz or Ibrail or so near thereto as she might safely get and there load. Galatz and Ibrail are respectively 95 and 115 miles upriver from the mouth of the River Danube at Sulina. On 5 November she arrived at Sulina, but could not go upriver because there was not enough water over the bar. After remaining at Sulina until 11 December, she then

511. *Dahl (Robert H)* v. *Nelson, Donkin and others* (1880) 6 App Cas 38.
512. *The Athamas* [1963] 1 Lloyd's Rep 287.
513. *Parker* v. *Winslow* (1857) 7 E & B 942.
514. *Bastifell* v. *Lloyd* (1862) 1 H & C 388.
515. *Metcalfe* v. *Britannia Ironworks Co* (1877) 2 QBD 423.
516. *Ibid.*, at p. 426.
517. *The Athamas (Owners)* v. *Dig Vijay Cement Co Ltd* [1963] 1 Lloyd's Rep 287.
518. *Schilizzi* v. *Derry* (1855) 4 E & B 873.

proceeded to Odessa, 100 miles away, and loaded a cargo there. Had she remained at Sulina until 7 January she would have been able to cross the bar. It was held that, in these circumstances, she had not completed her voyage and that she was not prevented from doing so as the obstruction was only temporary. On the question of how close to the intended destination the ship must get, Lord Campbell CJ said[519]:

... the meaning of the charterparty must be that the vessel is to get within the ambit of the port, though she may not reach the actual harbour. Nor could it be said that the vessel, if she was obstructed in entering the Dardanelles, had completed her voyage. There can therefore be no doubt as to the first issue.

Of this phrase, "the ambit of the port", Lord Blackburn said in *Dahl* v. *Nelson*[520]:

Whether the language which Lord Campbell uses is quite the most accurate to express his idea may be doubted ...

3.461 In *The Athamas*, in the High Court, McNair J said[521]:

... The limit of the word "ambit" clearly did not arise for consideration or discussion in *Dahl* v. *Nelson, Donkin and others, supra*. The use of the word "near" clearly connotes some idea of proximity. But, just as Lord Blackburn (at p. 52) and Lord Watson (at pp. 58 and 59), when considering the question whether an obstacle is temporary or permanent, import the element of reasonableness in relation to time, so here it seems to me that, in considering whether a substitute discharging place or port is within the phrase "so near thereto as she may safely get", the court should apply the conception of reasonableness in relation to distance. There clearly will come a point at which the substituted port cannot properly be said to be near or within the ambit of the primary port, but is to be held to be at such a distance that it cannot be assumed to be within the contemplation of the parties as fair and reasonable men. What is a reasonable distance clearly has to be determined in the light of all the circumstances and of the particular adventure.

The Court of Appeal agreed. Pearson LJ said, having reviewed the earlier decisions[522]:

This examination of the authorities has not yielded any precise definition of the range of proximity or vicinity within which the substitute destination must lie in order to be, in relation to the named destination for the ship, "as near thereto as she may safely get". I do, however, derive from these authorities an impression that the range is fairly narrow, and that in an ordinary case a substitute destination 250 miles by water from the named destination would be outside the range of proximity. This, however, is an extraordinary case in that Saigon, though 250 miles by water away from Phnom-Penh, is nevertheless the nearest port to Phnom-Penh, at any rate for the purpose of unloading the cargo concerned.

It is clear that the longer the principal voyage, the greater will be the ambit of the port.[523]

---

519. *Ibid.*, at p. 886.
520. *Dahl (Robert H)* v. *Nelson, Donkin and others* (1880) 6 App Cas 38, at p. 51.
521. *The Athamas (Owners)* v. *Dig Vijay Cement Co Ltd* [1962] 2 Lloyd's Rep 120, at p. 130.
522. *The Athamas (Owners)* v. *Dig Vijay Cement Co Ltd* [1963] 1 Lloyd's Rep 287, at p. 302.
523. In *The Athamas*, Sellers LJ pointed out that the distance already travelled to the first discharge port was some 3,500 miles and Phnom Penh was only another 250 miles further on (at p. 95). He also mentioned (at p. 94) that an analysis of the decided cases showed that in those cases where it had been held that the ship had fulfilled the requirements of the charter to proceed "so near thereto as she may safely get" the distance ranged from under half-a-mile to 30 miles, and in four cases where the contrary had been held the distance ranged from 95 to 600 miles. The *Athamas* case is thus the furthest (250 miles) where the terms of the clause has been held to be met.

F Proportion of cargo to be loaded/discharged at the obstructed port

3.462 In *The Athamas*, the arbitrators said the following in their special case[524]:

We find (if this be a matter of fact) that it would be wholly unreasonable to expect that the *Athamas* should, with 2,100 tons (or any quantity) of cargo for Phnom Penh on board, wait from 21 March to mid-August in order to proceed to Phnom Penh and there discharge it.

The higher courts agreed. Presumably it follows that if the proportion of cargo to be delivered is small then the period of waiting which would be reasonable is less, and conversely if it is the whole of the cargo that is to be discharged, then a longer period of delay might be justified.

3.463 It is clear that the factors which have been considered above are not exhaustive. Others that might be considered were mentioned by Sellers LJ at the end of his judgment in *The Athamas*, where he said[525]:

In the present case the arbitrators were clearly of the opinion that the *Athamas* could not get to Phnom-Penh within a reasonable time. This was based on the arbitrators' knowledge of the nature of the adventure and of all the factors involved, the period of time, the carrying and earning capacity of the ship and the expense of the delay to both the charterers, who presumably wanted their cargo, and the shipowners, who would lose if their ship were idle.

In regular turn/in usual turn

3.464 These and similar phrases using the expression "turn" have the practical effect of changing what would otherwise be a port charter into a berth charter, as far as the commencement of laytime is concerned. The words "in regular turn" appear in the Chamber of Shipping Welsh Coal Charter and it is perhaps therefore not surprising that many of the decided cases arise in relation to the carriage of coal.

3.465 The turn referred to is the vessel's turn for a berth on arrival at either the port of loading or the port of discharge. It is customary at most ports for vessels to be dealt with in order of their arrival at the port. Depending on the facilities and customs of the port there may either be one list of vessels waiting or there may be separate lists for particular trades. A vessel's position on the list may depend on the time of its arrival at the pilot station or of it being reported at the Custom House or in accordance with some other local custom.

3.466 Since it is such a standard practice for ships to be dealt with in turn, it is perhaps somewhat unexpected that a reference to it in some such clause as one providing that the ship should "proceed to AB and there load . . . The cargo to be loaded in regular turn at the rate of . . . per day" should have the effect of delaying the commencement of laytime until the ship's turn to load arrives, i.e. until it arrives in berth. Whilst this may be something of an historical anachronism, it is one that is sufficiently well founded in authority to ensure that it remains.

3.467 The converse of regular or usual turn is free of turn. Where this is used it means that time counts whilst the vessel is waiting for her turn and laytime therefore begins on arrival at the specified destination, when she is ready to load and when any provisions relating to notice have been complied with.

---

524. *The Athamas (Owners)* v. *Dig Vijay Cement Co Ltd* [1963] 1 Lloyd's Rep 287, at p. 291.
525. *Ibid.*, at p. 296.

3.468 An early authority relating to turn was *Robertson* v. *Jackson*,[526] where the charter provided for a rate of discharge "to reckon from the time of the vessel being ready to unload and in turn to deliver" and it was held that the words "in turn to deliver" must be interpreted in accordance with the regulations in force at the port of discharge. In *Leidemann* v. *Schultz*[527] the charter provided that the ship was to proceed to Newcastle "and on arrival there be ready forthwith in regular turns of loading to take on board by spout or keel as directed" a cargo of coal and coke. The ship arrived in Newcastle and was able to load the coal at once, but had to wait more than a month for her turn to be loaded with coke. In an action for detention, it was held that the expression "in regular turns of loading" pointed to a course of dealing and that evidence should have been admitted as to the practice of the port.

3.469 In *Lawson* v. *Burness*[528] the relevant charter provided for the ship to proceed to a named dock and there to load a cargo of coke "to be loaded in regular turn". It was held that these words referred to the order of readiness to load and not to the order of entry in a book kept by the colliery company, but it was assumed throughout that if the vessel had been loaded in her order of readiness, though not immediately on her being ready, no demurrage would have been payable.

3.470 In *The Cordelia*[529] it was provided that a vessel should proceed to the Nob (on the River Exe) and deliver her cargo "in regular turn with other seagoing vessels at an average rate of 30 tons per weather working day". On arrival she was delayed because another ship consigned to the same charterers was ahead of her, being discharged by lighters, and she therefore had to wait her turn. In giving judgment against the shipowner's claim for demurrage, Gorell Barnes P said[530]:

It looks to me as [if] the plaintiff (the shipowner) expected that his vessel would find a string of barges when she got to the Nob. I am afraid the plaintiff could not reasonably expect more than that he should have his vessel discharged in regular turn with other seagoing vessels which were being discharged in turn with the usual dispatch. The terms of the charterparty do not justify the plaintiff in expecting more than that.

3.471 In *Miguel de Larrinaga Steamship Co* v. *Flack*,[531] a case primarily involving the cancellation of a charter, Roche J drew a distinction between when the vessel concerned became an Arrived ship and when the charterers' obligation to load began, saying[532]:

In the ordinary case she would not be an arrived ship until she got into dock, but having regard to the particular provision of the charterparty the contention was open to the charterers, and was availed of by them and accepted by the umpire, that, though an arrival might have been fixed and stipulated . . . the obligation to load at a certain specified rate per day did not arise until the vessel was "in turn", that is to say, was at the pier . . .

---

526. *Robertson* v. *Jackson* (1845) 2 CB 412.
527. *Leidemann* v. *Schultz* (1853) 14 CB 38.
528. *Lawson* v. *Burness* (1862) 1 H & C 396.
529. *The Cordelia* [1909] P 27. What the significance of this case is was the subject of some disagreement between the Court of Appeal and the House of Lords in *United States Shipping Board* v. *Strick & Co Ltd*—see in particular Lord Sumner's dissenting speech in the House of Lords—(1926) 25 Ll L Rep 73, at p. 82.
530. *The Cordelia* [1909] P 27, at p. 31.
531. *Miguel de Larrinaga Steamship Co Ltd* v. *D L Flack & Son* (1924) 20 Ll L Rep 268.
532. *Ibid.*, at p. 270.

3.472 The same distinction was drawn by the majority of the House of Lords in *United States Shipping Board* v. *Strick & Co Ltd.*[533] Having reviewed the earlier cases, Viscount Cave, the Lord Chancellor, said[534]:

... our courts have uniformly given effect to those expressions (i.e. "in turn" or "in regular turn") as having a bearing on the question of lay days. In most, if not all, of the cases the ship in question was an arrived ship and ready to load, but it was nevertheless held or assumed that the commencement of the loading or unloading days was by the terms of the contract postponed until the ship's "turn" arrived.

3.473 Lords Atkinson and Shaw agreed. However, in a lengthy dissenting speech, Lord Sumner,[535] with whom Viscount Haldane agreed, argued that in a fixed laytime charter the basic obligations of fixed laytime, i.e. that loading/discharging should be carried out in a specified period, meant that there was no room for such uncertainties as "regular turn or ready berths". Furthermore, the minority argued such provisions were inconsistent with the rules relating to commencement of laytime in port charters as settled in *Leonis Steamship Co* v. *Rank*. The majority disagreed, Viscount Cave saying[536]:

In other words, to the three conditions for the commencement of the lay days enumerated by Kennedy LJ, in *Leonis* v. *Rank* ... viz., arrival of the ship, readiness to load and notice of such readiness, there is added by the terms of the charterparty a fourth condition, namely the arrival of the turn. If the loading berth had been empty when the ship arrived in port, the time would not have commenced to run until notice of readiness had been given; and if notice of readiness is given before the berth is empty and ready to receive the ship, then the time does not run until the regular turn for loading arrives.

3.474 The inclusion of one of these phrases in a charter does not affect when the vessel becomes an Arrived ship, but rather acts in a similar manner to a clause providing for laytime to commence a given time after Notice of Readiness has been tendered. The difference is that with the latter the time scale is fixed, whereas with the former it is dependent upon the number of vessels waiting.

3.475 An exception to the general principles set out above is contained in *Moor Line Ltd* v. *Manganexport GmbH*,[537] a decision of Branson J. Here the charter contained two apparently inconsistent clauses—clause 2 referred to loading "in usual turn with other steamers loading ore for account of same charterers" and clause 6 provided for "Time for loading to count from 6 a.m. after the ship is reported and ready and in free pratique (whether in berth or not) in accordance with clause 2".

3.476 Apart from the reference to "whether in berth or not", there was another distinction between this case and the decision of the House of Lords in *United States Shipping Board* v. *Strick & Co Ltd*[538] and that was that in the latter the provision relating to turn and that relating to the commencement of time were in the same clause.

3.477 Finding in favour of the shipowner that clause 6 was the controlling clause, Branson J said[539] that if the parties had intended the words "in usual turn" to govern the time at which the time for loading was to commence, the words could have been expected

533. *United States Shipping Board* v. *Strick & Co Ltd* (1926) 25 Ll L Rep 73 (HL).
534. *Ibid.,* at p. 76.
535. *Ibid.,* starting at p. 80 and especially at p. 81.
536. *Ibid.,* at p. 77.
537. *Moor Line Ltd* v. *Manganexport GmbH* (1936) 55 Ll L Rep 114.
538. *United States Shipping Board* v. *Strick & Co Ltd* (1926) 25 Ll L Rep 73.
539. *Moor Line Ltd* v. *Manganexport GmbH* (1936) 55 Ll L Rep 114, at p. 117.

to be found in clause 6. Whether the case goes further than its own facts is perhaps doubtful.

Limits of delay

3.478 There is, of course, no reason why the shipowner and charterer should not agree that any delay whilst the vessel is waiting for her turn should not exceed a specified period. That was the outcome in a case called *Themistocles (Owners)* v. *Compagnie Intercontinentale de L'Hyperphosphate of Tangier*,[540] where the relevant clause read: "The vessel to be loaded . . . in the customary manner alongside the wharf reserved to shippers, at the berth they indicate and according to their orders, in turn not exceeding 48 running hours not including (Sundays and holidays)." The meaning of this, said Morris J, was that[541]:

> . . . the vessel must not be kept waiting from more than 48 hours for her turn to be at the particular loading berth indicated to the vessel by the shippers. Such period of 48 hours may, however, be extended on account of holidays or Sundays.
> . . . One example, merely by way of illustration, may be given of the manner in which the clause may operate. The vessel might arrive at the wharf reserved to shippers, might be admitted in free pratique and give notice that she is ready to load, and might then have to wait to be told at which precise berth she is to load. The vessel would then be in turn.

Custom and practice

3.479 As mentioned earlier, how a ship's turn is reckoned may vary from port to port or between trades at the same port. In *Barque Quilpue* v. *Brown*,[542] the relevant clause provided for the ship to proceed to "Newcastle and there in the usual and customary manner, load in regular turn from Brown's Duckenfield Colliery or any of the collieries that the freighters may name . . . ". Of the meaning to be given to this, Vaughan Williams LJ said[543]:

> . . . Mr Carver has contended that "regular turn" means "in the order of arrival of the ships". I do not agree with him. The authorities he has cited show that "in regular turn" *prima facie*, and unless there is something to lead to a different conclusion, does mean "in regular port turn", but not that the words cannot refer to colliery turn as distinguished from port turn; and here, I think, the words used do refer to colliery turn as distinguished from port turn.

3.480 In *King* v. *Hinde*,[544] a sailing ship was fixed to load coal at Whitehaven, but by a custom of the port, steam ships were given preference which led to the ship concerned being delayed. The owners' claim for demurrage failed, the relevant charter referred to "regular turn" and the meaning of this had to be decided in relation to the custom of the particular port.

---

540. *Themistocles (Owners)* v. *Compagnie Intercontinentale de L'Hyperphosphate of Tangier* (1948) 82 Ll L Rep 232.
541. *Ibid.*, at p. 237.
542. *Barque Quilpue Ltd* v. *Brown* (1903) 9 CC 13.
543. *Ibid.*, at p. 17.
544. *King* v. *Hinde* (1883) 12 LR Ir 113.

Loss of turn

3.481 If a ship, having arrived, loses her turn because she is not ready or through some other fault attributable to the vessel, then she cannot claim that her turn has come and the subsequent further delay must be borne by the shipowner.[545]

3.482 However, if the delay is caused by the charterer then he must bear the responsibility. Once the ship has been allocated her turn, or would have been had it not been for whatever omission there may have been by the charterer, then the effect of the turn clause is spent, so that under the normal rules relating to fixed laytime provisions, time runs thereafter continuously in the absence of any further exception. In *Jones* v. *Adamson*[546] the charter required a ship to load in regular turn, but when her turn came she was unable to load through default of the charterer and was thereafter delayed, first for 11 days until she was given another turn by which time all was ready, and then for a further three days because of an adverse wind. The charterer was held liable for all the delay.

Delay after berthing

3.483 The term "turn" or any of its variations has no effect on what happens after the ship berths, her turn having come. Thus, in *The Sheila*[547] a ship was chartered to load at the Great Western Railway jetties at Fowey. The loading was to be "in the customary manner (of) a full and complete cargo of china clay and china stone in bulk . . . customary turn by Great Western Railway as for steamers at Fowey to be allowed . . . ". A delay occurred because the railway failed to forward enough trucks to the jetties. The charterers, resisting a demurrage claim, argued that "customary turn by Great Western Railway" not only meant that the ship was to take its turn to get to the loading jetty, but the phrase was also to apply to the way in which she was loaded thereafter. Rejecting this contention, Bucknill J said[548]:

The word "customary" does not seem to me to apply at all to the mode of loading which they choose to adopt in loading ships which come to their jetty, but in my opinion it applies only to the ships getting to the loading place—the customary turn for loading.

Demurrage in respect of waiting time

3.484 The Australian Grain Charters 1928 and 1972 contain an express provision allowing demurrage for waiting time in specified circumstances before the vessel becomes an Arrived ship. The leading case on the application of this clause is *Roland-Linie Schiffahrt GmbH* v. *Spillers Ltd and others*,[549] a decision of Sellers J.

3.485 The relevant clause was clause 2, which provided:

2. Being so loaded, the vessel shall proceed . . . to discharge at one safe port . . . or so near thereunto as the vessel can safely get, always afloat, and there deliver the cargo . . . at any customary dock, wharf or pier as ordered by the charterers or their agents . . .
. . . Provided always that if such discharging place is not immediately available, demurrage in respect of all time waiting thereafter shall be paid at the rate . . .

---

545. *Taylor* v. *Clay* (1846) 9 QBD 713.
546. *Jones* v. *Adamson* (1876) 1 Ex D 60.
547. *The Sheila* [1909] P 31n (the report consists of a note after the report of *The Cordelia*, at p. 27).
548. *Ibid.*, at p. 34.
549. *Roland-Linie Schiffahrt GmbH* v. *Spillers Ltd and others (The Werrastein)* [1956] 2 Lloyd's Rep 211.

3.486 The *Werrastein*, the ship concerned, arrived off the port of Hull with a cargo of grain from Australia, but due to congestion she was unable to proceed to the King George Dock at Hull, which was the only dock then in use for discharge of bulk grain. She was therefore ordered to wait at the customary anchorage for such vessels off Spurn Head, some 22 miles from the port and outside the port limits. She waited there for a week before being allowed to enter the dock.

3.487 The receivers argued that the vessel had not arrived within the port limits when she was delayed and that the proviso only applied after they had nominated a discharging place, which they were not bound to do until she arrived.

3.488 Rejecting these arguments, Sellers J said[550]:

In my view the proviso deals with waiting time (due to the discharging place being unavailable) before lay days commence to run, and provides for just such an occasion as has arisen here. The loss due to waiting for discharge has to fall on one of the parties to the adventure and, of course depends on the terms of their bargain; but, provided the vessel has reached the recognized waiting place for the port, she can do no more than be ready and available to discharge. The cargo owner has the selection (within the terms of the contract) of the place of discharge. It does not seem wholly inappropriate that if loss by waiting for a berth is incurred it should fall on the charterers or consignees. The ship has to face the hazards of the voyage whereby she may be delayed by storm, fog, tides and many other events. But for clause 2, the waiting at the anchorage would likewise have fallen on the ship . . .

3.489 A little earlier in his judgment, the judge made it clear that it was only where a vessel is delayed due to congestion that the proviso applies, saying[551]:

An incoming vessel may go to one of the anchorages for various reasons. She may go to await the tide or a tug or because of damage or breakdown, illness of crew, etc. In any such case it could not be said that she had completed her voyage to Hull when she was still 22 miles away.

3.490 The judge also made it clear that he considered it would have been an idle and wasteful formality for the vessel to have proceeded within the port limits and then return to the anchorage, just to establish her rights.[552] The essence of the matter was that she had got as far as she could and being at the recognized waiting place the voyage was over for the purposes of the proviso, although she was not an Arrived ship.

Time to commence on being reported at the Custom House

3.491 Although it is usual in everyday speech to refer to people or vessels getting Customs clearance on arrival at a port, this is not strictly speaking correct. Strictly speaking, a vessel reports to the Customs on arrival and secures clearance on her departure.

3.492 A clause such as that in the heading may either take effect as an additional requirement to the usual conditions required before laytime can commence,[553] or if the wording is sufficiently clear it may replace them so as to advance the commencement of laytime.

---

550. *Ibid.*, at p. 217.
551. *Ibid.*, at p. 216.
552. *Roland-Linie Schiffahrt GmbH* v. *Spillers Ltd and others (The Werrastein)* [1956] 2 Lloyd's Rep 211.
553. See, for example, *Compania Argentina de Navegación de Ultramar* v. *Tradax Export SA (The Puerto Rocca)* [1978] 1 Lloyd's Rep 252, and *ante* at para. 3.188.

3.493 In *Macbeth* v. *Wild*,[554] a ship was to proceed "to a safe berth at Middlesbrough-on-Tees as directed", but a further clause provided that: "Lay days shall commence when the steamer is reported at the Custom House, and in free pratique—unless the loading or delivery has sooner commenced . . . " Bigham J held this meant that time began when the vessel had arrived in port, was in free pratique and had reported at the Custom House, even if this was before she got a berth.

3.494 Another example is the Scottish case of *Horsley Line Ltd* v. *Roechling Brothers*,[555] where the charter provided that the ship should "proceed to Savona or Genoa, as ordered . . . and there deliver the same . . . Time for discharging to commence on being reported at the Custom House". On arrival at Savona, the ship anchored in the roads due to congestion and was reported at the Custom House on the same day. The roads were outside the limits of the port and the vessel would not normally be expected to discharge there. Nevertheless, the Court of Session held that time began when the ship was reported, although the reasons given were not entirely consistent.

To be loaded as per colliery guarantee

3.495 The effect of this phrase in a charterparty is to incorporate the terms of the relevant colliery guarantee relating to the commencement of laytime. The function of a colliery guarantee was described thus in *Monsen* v. *Macfarlane, McCrindell & Co* by Smith LJ[556]:

It is a document which is obtained by a charterer who is about to load a ship under a charterparty with coals from a colliery, in order that the charterer may obtain from the colliery a guarantee that it will load the ship with coal within a given time, that is within a given time of lay days.

The judge continued that the charterer would be anxious for its incorporation into the charter so that he would be under no more liability to the shipowner than he could recover from the colliery.

3.496 The charter in this case required the ship to "proceed to a customary loading place in Royal Dock Grimsby" and there load a cargo of coals "as customary at Grimsby as per colliery guarantee in 15 colliery working days". It was not in dispute that if the guarantee was not incorporated then this was a berth charter and lay days would only commence when the vessel arrived in berth under the spout ready to load. The Court of Appeal, however, by a majority[557] found that the guarantee was incorporated and therefore, under its terms, laytime was advanced to arrival in dock. A factor of some influence in the decision appears to be that the actual loading took only three days whereas 15 days were allowed, which must have been intended to cover delays getting into position. On this Lord Esher MR said[558]:

It is ridiculous to suppose that, as a matter of business, the harbour master would put a ship under the spout if the cargo was not ready, because he would be keeping other ships from loading.

---

554. *Macbeth* v. *Wild & Co* (1900) 16 TLR 497.
555. *Horsley Line Ltd* v. *Roechling Brothers*, 1908 SC 866.
556. *Monsen* v. *Macfarlane, McCrindell & Co* (1895) 1 CC 51, at p. 65.
557. Lord Esher MR and Smith LJ, Kay LJ dissenting.
558. *Monsen* v. *Macfarlane, McCrindell & Co* (1895) 1 CC 51, at p. 57.

CHAPTER 4

Interruptions and Exceptions to Laytime

4.1 In this book, the term "interruptions to laytime" is used to cover those periods when laytime does not run because they are outside the definition of laytime as expressed in the laytime clause. Excepted periods, on the other hand, are those periods which are within the definition of laytime, but nevertheless excluded by an exceptions clause. The principal difference between the two is that with the latter it is necessary to show a causal connection between what is excepted and the failure to work cargo, whereas with the former all that need be shown for causation is that the excluded state of affairs exists at the place where cargo would have been worked.

4.2 The same phenomenon may be either an interruption or an exception to laytime, depending on the terms of the charter concerned. Thus, adverse weather would be an interruption to laytime where this was defined in terms of weather working days because these are not words of exception but a definition of the only kind of time that may count. On the other hand, an additional clause providing that "any time lost through bad weather is not to count as laytime" is an exception, so a causal connection must be shown to prove that time was actually lost due to weather. Clearly, time could only be lost if the vessel concerned was in a berth or position where loading could take place, whereas time may be interrupted whether the vessel was in berth or not once adverse weather is shown to exist.

4.3 As has already been mentioned,[1] if a charterer has agreed to load or discharge within a fixed period of time, and therefore the charter is a fixed laytime one, the charterer is answerable for the non-performance of this agreement after laytime commences whatever may be the nature of the impediments, unless they are covered by provisions in the charter interrupting laytime or excepting the particular impediment or they arose through the culpable fault of the shipowner or those for whom he is responsible.[2]

4.4 In a customary laytime situation[3] the position is usually reversed with the risk of delay after laytime has commenced normally falling to the shipowner. In this type of charter the charterer's obligation is merely to perform his part in the operations of loading and discharging within a reasonable time in the circumstances prevailing in the particular port at the time in question. In this type of charter, there can only therefore be exceptions and not interruptions to laytime.

---

1. See *ante* at para. 2.1.
2. *William Alexander & Sons* v. *Aktieselskabet Dampskabet Hansa and others* (1919) 25 CC 13 (HL).
3. See *ante* at para. 2.205.

The contra proferentem rule

4.5 In a fixed laytime charter, the interruptions and exceptions will normally be in favour of the charterer, whereas in a customary laytime charter, where they are usually much less frequent, exceptions will be intended to increase the burden on the charterer and protect the shipowner. Exceptions clauses are construed against the party for whose benefit they are included in the charter. As was said by Lord Wilberforce in *Photo Production Ltd* v. *Securicor Transport Ltd*,[4] after setting out a particular exclusion clause:

These words have to be approached with the aid of the cardinal rules of construction that they must be read *contra proferentem* and that in order to escape from the consequences of one's wrongdoing, or that of one's servant, clear words are necessary.

4.6 It is thus first necessary to decide for whose benefit the clause was intended, since if the clause is ambiguous or it is doubtful whether the given circumstances are covered by it, the issue will be decided in favour of the other party.

4.7 In some early charterparties it was customary to set out the duties of each of the parties in separate parts of the charter and not merely in separate clauses. This led to the view that exceptions in that part dealing with the shipowner's duties only relieved the shipowner and not the charterer. This was so in *Sjoerds* v. *Luscombe*,[5] in *Touteng* v. *Hubbard*,[6] and in *Blight* v. *Page*.[7] In charterparties so framed it was inevitable that the exceptions should be construed as enuring for the benefit of the owner only. In the latter half of the nineteenth century, the form of charterparties changed with the various duties of the owner and charterer being set out in separate clauses (rather than parts of the charter).

4.8 With this change of form, the attitude to exceptions clauses also changed so that where they are general and may, or some parts of them may, equally refer to either owner or charterer, they are held to do so. One of the earlier cases where this occurred was *Ford* v. *Cotesworth*,[8] where Martin B was inclined to take this view with regard to a "restraint of princes" exception which formed part of a clause setting out the master's duties, but the clause was followed by the words "throughout this charterparty". In *Barrie* v. *The Peruvian Corporation*,[9] Mathew J held that the general exceptions clause he was there considering was intended for the protection of the charterers as well as the shipowner.

4.9 This was followed with some hesitation by Bigham J in *Newman and Dale Steamship Co Ltd* v. *The British and South American Steamship Co*,[10] where an exception of fire was held to protect the charterers, although the general exceptions clause concerned did not contain the words "mutually excepted", which were sometimes added to avoid doubt.

4.10 In *Ralli Brothers* v. *Compania Naviera Sota y Aznar*, Bailhache J reviewed the earlier cases and concluded[11]:

4. *Photo Production Ltd* v. *Securicor Transport Ltd* [1980] 2 WLR 283, at p. 292.
5. *Sjoerds* v. *Luscombe* (1812) 16 East 201.
6. *Touteng* v. *Hubbard* (1802) 3 B & P 291.
7. *Blight* v. *Page* (1801) 3 B & P 295n.
8. *Ford and others* v. *Cotesworth and another* (1870) LR 5 QB 544.
9. *Barrie* v. *Peruvian Corporation* (1896) 2 CC 50.
10. *Newman and Dale Steamship Co Ltd* v. *The British and South American Steamship Co* (1902) 8 CC 87.
11. *Ralli Brothers* v. *Compania Naviera Sota y Aznar* (1919) 25 CC 155, at p. 165. This case went on to the Court of Appeal, the report of which is at (1920) 25 CC 227, although not on this part of the case.

I take it that the law now stands that, unless a contrary intention is expressed or is to be gathered from the form of the charterparty, exceptions are mutual where they are contained, as is the modern practice, in one of the numerous separate clauses of a charterparty and do not form part of a clause dealing solely with the obligations of the shipowner or charterer as the case may be. Especially is that the case where, as here, there is only one set of exceptions and not, as in many modern charterparties two sets—one appropriate to the charterers' and one to the owners' obligations.

4.11 Whilst not dissenting from this, in *Franco-British Steamship Co Ltd* v. *Watson & Youell*, Horridge J quoted some words of Scrutton LJ. Apparently the eminent Lord Justice had recently said[12]:

Ever since I was at the Bar it has been argued with considerable heat by counsel concerned whether or not certain exceptions of the charterparty apply for the protection of the charterer or only for the protection of the shipowners. In my view, it is quite impossible to lay down any general rule which will enable the question to be answered.

It is perhaps for this reason that two recent charters brought into use[13] perpetuate the trend that has continued for many years now and expressly state which party is to have the benefit of which exceptions.

4.12 Even if it is held that an exceptions clause was intended to benefit one of the parties, it must still be shown that the circumstances concerned are covered by it. To overcome this difficulty, exceptions clauses have been developed so as to include omnibus phrases like "and any other causes beyond the charterer's control" and words of general purpose like "hindrances and obstructions".[14] The scope of such general terminology will be considered later.[15]

General principles

4.13 An exceptions clause will normally be construed as only applying to the period covered by laytime. It will not protect the charterer after the vessel has come on demurrage, unless it explicitly so provides, although it may of course affect the time at which demurrage commences by suspending the laytime clock prior to this point.[16]

4.14 Furthermore, exceptions clauses will be limited to the loading and discharging operations and periods whilst these are going on unless they clearly indicate that they are also to apply to the operation of bringing the cargo down to the loading place or removing it after discharge.[17]

4.15 The charterer's duty to have the cargo at the loading place ready for shipment at the right time is an absolute one. No matter what difficulties there may be in procuring the cargo and getting it despatched to the loading place, the charterer will be liable if it is not ready in time, unless the exceptions clause clearly covers not only the actual loading but also the preliminary operation. In *Grant* v. *Coverdale*, Lord Selborne said[18]:

12. *Franco-British Steamship Co Ltd* v. *Watson & Youell* (1921) 9 Ll L Rep 282, at p. 285.
13. Bulk Unicharter 1982; Exxonvoy 84.
14. See, for instance, *Reardon Smith Line Ltd* v. *Ministry of Agriculture, Fisheries and Food* [1963] 1 Lloyd's Rep 12, at p. 27 *per* Viscount Radcliffe.
15. See *post* at para. 4.57. For a discussion on exemption and limitation clauses, see *BHP Petroleum Ltd and others* v. *British Steel plc and Dalmine SpA* [1999] 2 Lloyd's Rep 583.
16. *Union of India* v. *Compania Naviera Aeolus SA (The Spalmatori)* [1962] 2 Lloyd's Rep 175, at p. 180 *per* Lord Reid. See also *post* at para. 6.97.
17. *Grant* v. *Coverdale* (1884) 9 App Cas 470; *Kay* v. *Field* (1882) 10 QBD 241; *The Sheila* [1909] P 31n.
18. *Grant* v. *Coverdale* (1884) 9 App Cas 470.

It would appear to me to be unreasonable to suppose that the shipowner has contracted that his ship may be detained for an unlimited time on account of impediments, whatever their nature may be, to those things with which he has nothing whatever to do, which precede the operation of loading and which belong to that which is exclusively the charterer's business.

4.16 However, the charterer fulfils his duty to have the cargo ready for shipment in time if he has sufficient at the loading point to allow loading to start when the ship arrives and is ready to load, and suitable arrangements had been made for the rest to be available at such time and in such quantities as will enable loading to continue without interruption.[19] In *The Stainless Emperor*,[20] the charterers warranted that the cargo to be loaded (and this was construed as the full cargo) would be available upon arrival of the vessel and that any delay resulting from a breach of this warranty should count as "used laytime". There was also a holiday exception clause. The charterers argued unsuccessfully both in arbitration and in the High Court that the holiday exception should apply to reduce the used laytime that counted as a result of their failure to have a full cargo available. If local regulations require a percentage of the cargo to be on the quay ready for shipment, before the ship is allowed to enter the port or berth as the case may be, then the charterer must have the right proportion ready by the time the vessel is ready to enter the port (or berth). Putting this another way, the charterer cannot prevent the vessel becoming an Arrived ship and time starting to count against him by his own inactivity, or fault. However, it is always open to the parties to agree specifically that the vessel concerned should be kept at a port at the owners' risk of delay until a cargo can be provided.[21] A charterer may also be excused from his duty to provide a cargo by illegality if it is illegal to ship cargo of the contract description from the loading port for export to the country where it is to be discharged[22] and also where the contract of carriage is frustrated.

Fault of the shipowner[23]

4.17 It is well established that whilst a charterer's obligation to complete loading or discharging within the prescribed lay days is unconditional, nevertheless laytime will not run whilst there is a delay caused by the fault of the shipowners or those for whom they are responsible. In other words, the delay and the cause of the delay must be contemporaneous. This principle applies even in the absence of a specific clause saying that laytime is not to count.

4.18 Thus in London Arbitration 4/92,[24] where a vessel suffered engine problems which extended the voyage which in turn, the charterers alleged, resulted in reinfestation of the vessel's cargo causing delay whilst it was refumigated, the tribunal held that time should run during the delay at the discharge port.[25]

19. *Samuel Crawford Hogarth and others* v. *Cory Brothers & Co Ltd* (1926) 25 Ll L Rep 464 (PC), *per* Lord Phillimore. See also London Arbitration 4/98—LMLN 481, 14 April 1998.

20. *Huyton SA* v. *Inter Operators SA (The Stainless Emperor)* [1994] 2 Lloyd's Rep 298.

21. *Agrimpex Hungarian Trading Co for Agricultural Products* v. *Sociedad Financiera de Bienes Raices SA (The Aello)* [1960] 1 Lloyd's Rep 623, at p. 643 *per* Lord Reid.

22. *Ralli Brothers* v. *Compania Naviera Sota y Aznar* (1920) 25 CC 227 (CA).

23. See also paras 6.70 *et seq.*

24. London Arbitration 4/92—LMLN 321, 22 February 1992.

25. See also for instance *The Luctor* (NY Arb), LMLN 349, 20 March 1993, also *ante* at para. 3.308.

4.19 The principles that apply are similar to those that appertain in similar circumstances after the vessel has gone on demurrage and many of the cases relate to events occurring whilst the vessel concerned was on demurrage.

4.20 In both cases, the defence of "fault" of the owners appears to be a simple defence rather than a cross-claim by the charterers of an equal amount giving rise to a defence of circuity of action.[26] The defence is an example of the more general principle that a plaintiff cannot claim damages if the claim is based on his own fault or default.

4.21 Whilst the default of the shipowner must relate to something which happens whilst laytime and demurrage are running to come within the principle now under discussion, nevertheless if the default alleged caused delay at some other point in time, e.g. during the approach or carrying voyages, which in turn results in a delay at the next loading/discharging port, the charterer may be able to show a breach of a separate clause in the charter, other than the provisions relating to laytime and demurrage, and claim damages for that breach, namely the loss of time subsequently suffered. That would of course be a cross-claim and the charterer would have as usual to show that the loss he has suffered was a foreseeable consequence of the breach. The case reported as London Arbitration 15/91[27] is best seen as an illustration of this principle, although the way it is reported suggests that it was argued on the basis that the alleged default was a straight defence to the claim for demurrage.

4.22 What happened was that the charterers sought to add an additional load port for topping off, for which the parties agreed an addendum to the charter in which the owners gave an estimate of the date of arrival of the vessel at the topping off port but which was said to be dependent on how loading went at the second load port. On the facts, the tribunal held that the estimate was honestly and reasonably given. However, had they found to the contrary, it is suggested that this should not have affected the running of time at the topping off port, and therefore owners' claim for demurrage, but would have entitled the charterers to claim a breach of the ETA provision in the addendum, the damages payable for which would have been some or all of the demurrage payable to the owners.

4.23 On the question of what amounts to default on the part of the shipowner in relation to the running of laytime or demurrage, in *The Fontevivo* Donaldson J, as he then was, said[28]:

... the mere fact that the shipowner by some act of his prevents the continuous loading or discharging of the vessel is not enough to interrupt the running of the lay days; it is necessary to show also that there was some fault on the part of the shipowner ...

4.24 Once a vessel has reached her destination and given Notice of Readiness, she ought thereafter to be at the entire disposal of the charterers to enable them to complete their work within the agreed lay days and clearly any periods when the ship is effectively taken out of their disposal, whether physically or by the owners failing to perform some

---

26. *Blue Anchor Line Ltd v. Alfred C Toepfer International GmbH (The Union Amsterdam)* [1982] 2 Lloyd's Rep 432, at p. 436 *per* Parker J.
27. London Arbitration 15/91—LMLN 305, 13 July 1991.
28. *Gem Shipping Co of Monrovia v. Babanaft (Lebanon) SARL (The Fontevivo)* [1975] 1 Lloyd's Rep 339, at p. 342.

essential function, should not count against laytime.[29] This does not, however, explain what is meant by fault.

4.25 An early case to consider what constituted "fault" was *Budgett & Co* v. *Binnington & Co*,[30] which concerned a strike during discharge which was interrupted as a result. Some of those on strike had been engaged by the shipowners to perform their part of the discharge and some by the consignees to do their part. There was no strike exception.

4.26 The consignees argued that since part of discharge had to be undertaken by those employed by the shipowners, there was a default on the part of the vessel. This the Court of Appeal rejected, holding that the shipowner had no control over those on strike and was therefore not responsible. A similar answer was given by the House of Lords in the Scottish case of *William Alexander & Sons* v. *Aktieselskabet Dampskabet Hansa and others*,[31] where the delay arose from a general shortage of labour at the port of discharge.

4.27 Explaining these cases, MacKinnon J said in *Leeds Shipping Co Ltd* v. *Duncan Fox & Co Ltd*[32]:

> ... the charterer is liable to pay the agreed demurrage unless the failure to have the ship discharged in the agreed time is due to the fault of the shipowner, in that the shipowner has not done his part in regard to something which it was within his power to do. The result is that supposing there is a strike or an insufficiency of labour, although that may prevent the shipowner from doing his part of the discharge, yet that is not due to any failure on his part in regard to something that it was in his power to do, and it is, therefore, not due to the default of the shipowner.

4.28 In the particular case, the court had to consider an inefficiency of labour rather than an insufficiency, resulting in a much slower rate of discharge than that required by the charterparty. This was eventually cured by the master offering increased payment. The court held that not only was there no fault on the part of the ship but that the charterers could not take advantage of a provision excusing the shipper for loss or damage arising without his neglect or default.

4.29 In London Arbitration 4/93,[33] the shipowners were able to secure a finding that where delay was caused by the failure of a windlass motor due to a latent defect which meant the vessel was unable to shift from the anchorage to the multi-buoy mooring where she was scheduled to load, there was no breach or fault on the part of the owners and, even if there was, it was excluded by a general exceptions clause. On the latter point, it is usually accepted that general exceptions clauses do not apply to laytime or demurrage[34] and on the former, whilst a latent defect is obviously not foreseeable, in the context of laytime and demurrage, it nevertheless meant that the vessel was unable to perform the service required of it and, to that extent, the owners were in default of their obligation to perform what was required, namely to shift from the anchorage to the loading mooring. Whilst the possibility

---

29. See also London Arbitration 21/95, 22/95 and 23/95—LMLN 421, 23 December 1995. Where an Owner fails to make all the hatches available or where a Charterer is unable to work one or more hatches because of problems with the hatch covers or cargo gear, it is normal for Arbitrators to either reduce the loading/discharging rate thus increasing the laytime allowed or pro rata the time used. In *The Sea Wind* LMLN 531 16 March 2000, New York Arbitrators held that there should be no reduction in the discharging rate where the Charterer chose to use only three out of five hatches made available to him.

30. *Budgett & Co* v. *Binnington & Co* [1891] 1 QB 35.

31. *William Alexander & Sons* v. *Aktieselskabet Dampskabet Hansa and others* (1919) 25 CC 13 (HL).

32. *Leeds Shipping Co Ltd* v. *Duncan Fox & Co Ltd* (1932) 37 CC 213, at p. 217. *See* also New York Arbitration—*The Tai Ning* LMLN 532, 30 March 2000.

33. London Arbitration 4/93—LMLN 351, 17 April 1993.

34. See *post* at paras 4.57 *et seq.*

of establishing that such a delay was due solely to a latent defect must be comparatively rare, it would seem that if it can be established, time will continue to run.

4.30 In London Arbitration 4/95,[35] the tribunal held that time spent by surveyors acting for the owners carrying out line displacements at a discharging berth to ascertain whether there was oil in the lines was not time lost by default of the owners.

4.31 In London Arbitration 14/96,[36] the tribunal considered whether a difference in description between the vessel as built and as described in *Lloyd's Register* could be held to be the fault of the owners and whether the design of the ship meant that the owners were in breach of their obligation to provide three "unobstructed" holds, where the absence of these meant that cargo operations took longer. On the facts, the tribunal held that the owners were not responsible for how the vessel was described in *Lloyd's Register* but they were responsible if the design of the vessel meant there were obstructions in the holds.

Bunkering

4.32 In *Ropner Shipping Co Ltd* v. *Cleeves Western Valleys Anthracite Collieries Ltd,*[37] the Court of Appeal had to consider a situation where a shipowner removed his vessel from a loading berth in order to bunker her. The particular charter had a clause excluding bunkering time from laytime and the appellate hearing proceeded on the basis that it was for the shipowner's own convenience that he chose to bunker prior to the end of loading but after the vessel had come on demurrage. At first instance, it was argued that since the charter did not mention bunkering during demurrage, it was not a wrongful act within the principle of *Budgett & Co* v. *Binnington & Co.*[38] Roche J said in reply he was inclined to think that it did not lie in the mouth of the shipowners to say that their act was not a wrongful act. In the Court of Appeal, however, Bankes LJ refused to endorse that view, preferring to leave the point open.[39] The court therefore put their decision on the slightly narrower grounds that a shipowner cannot claim his vessel is being detained by a charterer and therefore he is entitled to demurrage when for his own convenience he has removed the vessel for bunkering.

4.33 It is submitted, however, that notwithstanding the caution of the Court of Appeal, the inclination of Roche J was correct and that it would be a wrongful act to remove a vessel for bunkering during loading whether laytime was then still running or whether the vessel was on demurrage.

4.34 In *Ropner Shipping Co Ltd* v. *Cleeves Western Valleys Anthracite Collieries Ltd,*[40] the shipowners also sought to argue in the Court of Appeal that no cargo had been available, but the court refused to consider this point since it had not been raised in the original arbitration proceedings and declined to say what their answer would have been had the submission been made. However, in those circumstances, whether before or after demurrage commenced, it is submitted that there would have been no fault on the part of the shipowners and laytime or demurrage, as the case may be, would have continued to run. It is also suggested that the same answer would apply where a vessel was removed from a waiting berth to bunker where congestion had prevented her berthing on arrival,

---

35. London Arbitration 4/95—LMLN 403, 15 April 1995.
36. London Arbitration 14/96—LMLN 446, 7 December 1996.
37. *Ropner Shipping Co Ltd* v. *Cleeves Western Valleys Anthracite Collieries Ltd* (1927) 27 Ll L Rep 317.
38. *Budgett & Co* v. *Binnington & Co* [1891] 1 QB 35.
39. *Ropner Shipping Co Ltd* v. *Cleeves Western Valleys Anthracite Collieries Ltd* (1927) 27 Ll L Rep 317, at p. 319.
40. *Ibid.,* at p. 318.

providing, of course, she was an Arrived ship, and providing her removal did not result in a loss of turn.

4.35 A further finding by the Court of Appeal in the *Ropner* case[41] was that what was to be excluded was the whole period the vessel was away from the loading berth and not just the periods when bunkering was actually taking place. Again, it is suggested that this would apply not merely to demurrage, but to any period of laytime lost by the fault of the shipowner.

Ballasting and deballasting

4.36 On completion of their approach voyage, ships customarily discharge their ballast and similarly take on new ballast on completion of the carrying voyage as their cargo is discharged. Both these operations may or may not delay or interrupt cargo operations, and the principles that apply are not necessarily the same. In modern ships sea water is invariably used as ballast, but some of the principles that relate were laid down in the days when solid ballast was the rule. Thus in *Vaughan* v. *Campbell, Heatley & Co*[42] it was held that a ship could still be ready to load, notwithstanding the presence of ballast in the holds, where this was needed to keep the ship upright and stable. In *Houlder* v. *Weir*,[43] a case involving ballasting, it was claimed that whilst ballast was being taken in, the rate of discharge of the cargo was reduced. Dismissing the charterers' claim that the days concerned should not count as lay days, Channell J said:

In one sense the act of the shipowner may be said to have prevented the charterers from having the full benefit of the day, but the act which prevented the charterers from having a full day was not a breach of any obligation on the part of the shipowners . . . Here there has not been a breach of obligation, but merely the performance of a necessary operation, no less for the protection of the cargo than for the protection of the ship. It was an act similar to one beyond the control of the party, and not one like acts which are breaches of contract.

4.37 In London Arbitration 1/91,[44] it was held that the fact that one hold which charterers wished to load was in ballast, and the charter required all the holds that were to be used to be passed by the NCB/USDA, did not invalidate a Notice of Readiness where the vessel was waiting to enter the commercial limits of the port (the charter provided for notice to be given outside the commercial limits). In the particular case after the hold was deballasted and successfully inspected, the hold had to be reballasted to pass under a bridge to reach the loadport.

4.38 In tanker charterparties it is usual to exclude deballasting time from laytime, where this results in time being lost, and sometimes ballasting time as well. Thus, clause 14(*b*)(vi) of Part II of the Exxonvoy 84 form of charter provides for laytime and demurrage time not to count, if it is spent or lost "In ballasting or deballasting, cleaning of tanks, pumps, pipelines, bunkering or for any other purposes of vessel only, unless same is carried out concurrent with loading and/or discharging such that no loss of time is involved".

4.39 In the Asbatankvoy charter, the corresponding provision is clause 7 of Part II but this only applies to deballasting and not ballasting. The STB Voy charter has a very similar

---

41. *Ibid.*, at p. 320.
42. *Vaughan and others* v. *Campbell, Heatley & Co* (1885) 2 TLR 33.
43. *Houlder* v. *Weir* (1905) 10 CC 228.
44. London Arbitration 1/91—LMLN 299, 20 April 1991.

provision at clause 7(c) but also by clause 11 provides that laytime or demurrage, if the vessel is on demurrage, shall continue until the discharging hoses are disconnected, or ballasting begins at the discharge port(s), whichever occurs first. In a London arbitration,[45] it was held that this should be given a literal interpretation, notwithstanding that the vessel might start taking on ballast before all her cargo had been discharged. In argument, the owners concerned pointed out that where a ship has two ballasting systems, one constituting permanent ballast and the other being ballast for the unladen voyage, the ship could be freshening up her permanent ballast and not ballasting for the purpose of increasing her draught prior to sailing. The arbitrators commented that clause 11 was puzzling and suggested that it might have originally been intended to cover a situation where the shore connection was used for ballasting after completion of discharge. Nevertheless, they held that time on demurrage ended when ballasting began, even though this was some 36 hours before discharge of the cargo was completed. Although not put forward in this particular case, there would seem to be no reason why the owners should not have put forward a claim for detention during this period since the vessel was being detained for the charterers' purposes, namely discharge of the cargo.

4.40 In the absence of any specific clauses dealing with deballasting/ballasting then it is suggested the following principles apply:

A. If deballasting or ballasting can be carried out concurrently with cargo operations, then the vessel will not be prevented thereby from becoming an Arrived ship and laytime/demurrage will continue to run until cargo operations are complete.

B. If deballasting or ballasting are carried out/continue after cargo operations are complete, then laytime/demurrage will not be prolonged thereby.

C. If deballasting or ballasting delay/interrupt cargo operations, then if it is necessary for these operations to be carried out at the time they are carried out for the safety of the ship/cargo then the time lost will not be due to the fault of the shipowner and must count.

D. If deballasting or ballasting delay/interrupt cargo operations, then if it is *not* necessary for these operations to be carried out at the time they are carried out but they are done then for the convenience of the shipowner then the time lost will be due to his fault and will not count.[46]

Non-production of bills of lading

4.41 The general principle is that delivery of cargo should be against presentation of an original bill of lading. Bills of lading are usually prepared in sets of three. Delivery of the cargo against one of the three normally means that the remainder are null and void. Delivery of cargo without presentation of an original bill may prejudice the owners' P & I cover.

4.42 It therefore follows that the usual rule is that the master may refuse to commence discharge until an original bill is presented or the receivers/charterers produce a letter of indemnity acceptable to his owners, who are not bound to accept a letter of indemnity unless so provided for in the charter.

---

45. London Arbitration—LMLN 72, 5 August 1982. See also *post* at para. 5.65.
46. See also London Arbitration 9/91—LMLN 304, 29 June 1991. It is not clear from this brief report quite where or when deballasting was carried out, save that it was after arrival at the port. This decision should therefore be approached with some caution.

4.43 The exceptions to this principle may be in relation to:
A. a liner service;
B. by custom of the port.
For ships engaged in a regular liner service, it is customary for bills of lading to be presented to the line agents and for the vessel to discharge in accordance with the agents' instructions, even where the ship has been chartered in on a voyage basis for a single voyage.

4.44 So far as the second exception is concerned, there are many ports around the world where the port authorities will simply not allow a vessel to refuse discharge once it has berthed.

4.45 Subject to these exceptions, where a master refuses to give delivery without production of a bill of lading and discharge is consequently delayed, laytime nevertheless will continue to run and time on demurrage thereafter. A refusal to give delivery in these circumstances is not a default on the part of the vessel, neither are the owners entitled to pursue a claim for detention for the delay; the charterers are entitled to use their laytime for the period of delay.[47]

Communications with vessel

4.46 One London Arbitration[48] arose because of a delay caused by the port agents being unable to establish communications with the vessel concerned, which was lying in the roads, when a berth became unexpectedly available. The arbitrators held that a vessel waiting offshore must keep open communication channels to a reasonable degree and operate them on a reasonable schedule. The burden of proof was on the charterers to show that the vessel had failed to do this and in the absence of special arrangements it was up to the charterers to find a method of communication.

The Altus[49]

4.47 On completion of loading a cargo of crude oil from a barge via a sealine, the master of the *Altus* was asked by the terminal to flush the sealine and ballast the loading barge, which the terminal wished to move inshore for cleaning. The terminal indicated they would pay the cost of the operation. The master complied, and in subsequent proceedings between the owners of the *Altus* and the charterers, who were not the terminal operators, Webster J held that laytime continued to run during these operations. The judge then turned to consider whether laytime was suspended during these operations, drawing a distinction between them. He first, however, pointed out that neither was necessary for the operation or safety of the vessel, nor for the safety of the cargo on board.

4.48 The judge then held that when the terminal required the sealine to be flushed, they did so as the agent of, and in the interests of, the charterers. With regard to the ballasting of the barge, the judge said that the master complied because he feared that if he did not his vessel would have been detained; if it escaped, it or other vessels in the same ownership might have been blacked. However, when it made the request, the terminal was not acting on behalf of the charterers. Having considered the contractual obligations of the

47. London Arbitration 21/92—LMLN 329, 13 June 1992.
48. London Arbitration—LMLN 1, 15 November 1979.
49. *Total Transport Corporation of Panama* v. *Amoco Trading Co (The Altus)* [1985] 1 Lloyd's Rep 423.

shipowners, and having reviewed the authorities dealing with their obligations, Webster J continued[50]:

I would assume, therefore, that laytime can be suspended or interrupted by an act of a shipowner, which has the effect of preventing the completion of loading or the commencement of the voyage, even without a breach of contract on his part, if that act constitutes a fault falling short of a breach of contract, or if it lacks lawful excuse.

Applying that test to the facts of the present case which I have found, in my judgment the master, in complying with SEREPT's[51] request, was not at fault, nor is he to be regarded as having failed to proceed on the voyage without unreasonable delay, or having failed to do everything reasonably possible to co-operate with the defendants in securing the release of the vessel for that purpose. In my judgment, therefore, laytime was not interrupted or suspended.

Exclusion of fault

4.49 The question of what happens where there has been fault on the part of the shipowner, or those for whom he is responsible, but he claims that it is excused by a clause in the charter, was the question that was considered by Parker J in *The Union Amsterdam*.[52] The facts were relatively simple. The *Union Amsterdam*, the vessel concerned, had arrived at her discharge port and laytime had expired before a berth became available. She was therefore on demurrage when, a berth having become available, she grounded en route to the berth. The owners claimed that demurrage continued to run whilst she was aground because any fault that might be attributable to them because of the negligent navigation of the vessel was excused under the US Carriage of Goods by Sea Act (COGSA), which was incorporated into the charter.

4.50 Rejecting this argument, Parker J put forward three propositions. First, he said that the material clause said only that the vessel should not be held liable for any delay to the cargo for causes excepted by the US COGSA and under the general principle of construing exceptions clauses narrowly this should only assist an owner to defeat a claim by cargo for delay, not allow him to put forward a claim against the charterers for demurrage. He then went on to put forward two further more general propositions, which must, it is suggested, be considered as *obiter*.

4.51 The judgment continues:

In the second place a breach of duty remains a breach of duty, and therefore fault notwithstanding, that liability for the breach is excluded. In the third place, far from doing nothing to prevent the vessel being available, owners have, by negligent navigation or management, so prevented her and, as Lord Justice Bankes said, it does not lie in their mouths to say that the vessel was being detained by the charterers during the period when by their negligence she was grounded.

4.52 The reference to Bankes LJ is a reference to his judgment in *Ropner Shipping Co Ltd* v. *Cleeves Western Valleys Anthracite Collieries Ltd*, which was quoted earlier in Parker J's judgment and to which reference has already been made in this chapter.[53] One major difference between the *Ropner* case and *The Union Amsterdam* was, of course, that in the latter it was the shipowners' argument that their negligence was discounted by an exceptions clause. In the *Ropner* case, the Court of Appeal were not prepared to go so far

---

50. *Ibid.*, at p. 430.
51. Société de Recherche et d'Exploitation des Pétroles en Tunisie (SEREPT)—the terminal operators.
52. *Blue Anchor Line Ltd* v. *Alfred C Toepfer International GmbH (The Union Amsterdam)* [1982] 2 Lloyd's Rep 432.
53. See *ante* at para. 4.34.

as to find "fault" on the part of the shipowner[54] but proceeded on what would probably now be considered as estoppel. If such an estoppel does exist in the case of a deliberate withdrawal for the shipowner's convenience, whether this extends to negligence on the part of his servants must be open to question, particularly if such negligence is excused under the terms of the charter. In *The Union Amsterdam* it was not so excused, but that, of course, does not affect the underlying principles.

4.53 There is also a line of authority in a different but closely related context dealing with the point raised in Parker J's second and third propositions where the fault of the shipowner has been removed by an exceptions clause. Needless to say such an exceptions clause must cover the fault specifically to be effective.[55] This line of authority is drawn from cases on general average and the cases concerned were not cited to Parker J.

4.54 It is an accepted principle of general average that the right to claim contribution is lost if the danger which necessitated the sacrifice was caused by the "fault" of the claimant. Thus, an owner will be precluded from recovering a contribution where the loss has been caused by, for example, the negligence of those on board his vessel, unless he is protected from liability for their acts by the terms of the charter or bill of lading. In *The Carron Park*, Sir James Hannen P said[56]:

The claim for contribution as general average cannot be maintained where it arises out of any negligence for which the shipowner is responsible; but negligence for which he is not responsible is as foreign to him as to the person who has suffered by it.

4.55 That decision was affirmed by the House of Lords in *Dreyfus* v. *Tempus Shipping Co*.[57] A later analysis of the rule by Pearson J in *Goulandris Brothers Ltd* v. *B Goldman & Son*[58] also shows that an actionable wrong must have occurred before a claim for a contribution in general average can be defeated.

4.56 It is therefore respectfully suggested that whilst the decision in *The Union Amsterdam*[59] was correct on the first ground, namely that the particular clause did not cover the situation that was then being considered, nevertheless the wider principles put forward cannot be sustained. If, therefore, the "fault" is covered by an exclusion clause, time will, it is submitted, continue to run, whether it be laytime or demurrage time.

General exceptions clauses

4.57 Most charterparties have an all-embracing general exceptions clause as well as specific exceptions clauses. A typical example is that contained at clause 19 of Part II of the Asbatankvoy form of charter, which reads as follows:

GENERAL EXCEPTIONS CLAUSE. The Vessel, her Master and Owner shall not, unless otherwise in this charter expressly provided, be responsible for any loss or damage, or delay or failure in performing hereunder, arising or resulting from:— any act, neglect, default or barratry of the Master,

54. *Ropner Shipping Co Ltd* v. *Cleeves Western Valleys Anthracite Collieries Ltd* (1927) 27 Ll L Rep 317. See also *ante* at para. 4.34.

55. Although exceptions clauses are to be construed narrowly, the House of Lords has also said that they should not be construed artificially in order to restrict their natural meaning. See *George Mitchell (Chesterhall) Ltd* v. *Finney Lock Seeds Ltd* [1983] 3 WLR 163.

56. *The Carron Park* (1890) 15 PD 203, at p. 207.

57. *Dreyfus & Co* v. *Tempus Shipping Co* [1931] AC 726.

58. *Goulandris Brothers Ltd* v. *B Goldman & Son* [1958] 1 QB 74.

59. *Blue Anchor Line Ltd* v. *Alfred C Toepfer International GmbH (The Union Amsterdam)* [1982] 2 Lloyd's Rep. 432.

pilots, mariner or other servants of the Owner in the navigation or management of the Vessel; fire, unless caused by the personal design or neglect of the Owner; collision, stranding or peril, danger or accident of the sea or other navigable waters; saving or attempting to save life or property; wastage in weight or bulk, or any other loss or damage arising from inherent defect, quality or vice of the cargo; any act or omission of the Charterer, Owner, shipper or consignee of the cargo, their agents or representatives; insufficiency of packing; insufficiency or inadequacy of marks; explosion, unseaworthiness of the Vessel unless caused by want of due diligence on the part of Owner to make the vessel seaworthy, or properly manned, equipped and supplied; or from any other cause of whatsoever kind arising without the actual fault or privity of the Owner. And neither the Vessel nor Master or Owner, nor the Charterer, shall, unless otherwise in this charter expressly provided, be responsible for any loss or damage or delay or failure in performing hereunder, arising or resulting from:— Act of God; act of war; perils of the seas; act of public enemies, pirates or assailing thieves; arrest or restraint of princes, rulers or people; or seizure under legal process provided bond is promptly furnished to release the Vessel or cargo; strike or lockout or stoppage or restraint of labour from whatever cause, either partial or general; or riot or civil commotion.

4.58 The question of the mutuality or otherwise of exceptions clauses has already been considered.[60] Clearly, in this example only the exceptions in the second sentence are mutual in the sense that they are intended for the protection of both the owner and charterer. The larger list of exceptions contained in the first sentence are intended only for the benefit of the shipowner.

4.59 However, even where the exceptions are mutual, it is doubtful whether they apply to laytime and demurrage and, unless by express words or necessary implication to the contrary, they do not protect either party in respect of events which occur before the ship starts on her approach voyage to the port of loading.[61] In *Sametiet M/T Johs Stove* v. *Istanbul Petrol Rafinerisi A/S (The Johs Stove)*, where the charter concerned contained the exceptions clause quoted above, Lloyd J said[62]:

I agree with the arbitrator that a general exceptions clause such as cl. 19 will not normally be read as applying to provisions for laytime and demurrage, unless the language is very precise and clear.[63]

4.60 Interestingly enough, the Exxonvoy 84 form of charter, which is the successor to the Exxonvoy 69 or Asbatankvoy form, expressly provides by a subclause[64] that the exceptions clause set out above is not intended to apply to laytime or demurrage.

4.61 The applicability of clause 28 of the Sugar Charterparty 1969 form to laytime was considered in *The Solon*.[65] This clause reads, under the heading "Strikes and Force Majeure":

Strikes or lockouts of men, or any accidents or stoppages on Railway and/or Canal and/or River by ice or frost, or any other force majeure clauses including Government interference, occurring beyond the control of the Shippers or Consignees which may prevent or delay the loading and discharging of the vessel always excepted.

60. See *ante* at para. 4.6.

61. *Transworld Oil Ltd* v. *North Bay Shipping Corporation (The Rio Claro)* [1987] 2 Lloyd's Rep 173.

62. *Sametiet M/T Johs Stove* v. *Istanbul Petrol Rafinerisi A/S (The Johs Stove)* [1984] 1 Lloyd's Rep 38, at p. 41. See also *Freedom Maritime Corporation* v. *International Bulk Carriers SA and another (The Khian Captain)* [1985] 2 Lloyd's Rep 212.

63. For the meaning of "any other hindrances" in relation to congestion, see *Navrom* v. *Callitsis Ship Management SA (The Radauti)* [1987] 2 Lloyd's Rep 276 and [1988] 2 Lloyd's Rep 416. See also *post* at para. 000.

64. Clause 29(*b*)—the main exceptions clause is now 29(*a*).

65. *The Solon*, Case No 1999 Folio 736, judgment dated 11 Jan 2000; LMLN 529, 17 February 2000.

The cause of the delay sought to be relied on by the charterers was a strike at the load port.

4.62 In his judgment, Thomas J reviewed the cases of the *Kalliopi A*,[66] *The Forum Craftsman*[67] and *The Lefthero*.[68] He also mentioned the *dictum* from *The Johs Stove* quoted above. In relation to (i) a suggestion that a greater degree of certainty as to meaning might be required where it was suggested that an exceptions clause afforded protection after the vessel was on demurrage than whilst laytime was running, and (ii) the general application of the principle that an ambiguous clause is no protection, the judge first summarized the arguments put before him, saying:

> The owners submitted that there was nothing in principle or authority that supported what the arbitrator had said at GG [this was that a greater degree of certainty might be required in relation to demurrage exception clauses]; the charterers were under a primary obligation to load within the laydays and a secondary obligation to pay demurrage for exceeding that period. In *Photo Productions* v. *Securicor* [1980] AC 827 Lord Diplock had stated at page 850 that an exclusion clause was:
>> "one which excludes or modifies an obligation whether primary, general secondary or anticipatory secondary, that would otherwise arise under the contract by implication of law."
> Thus as a matter of principle it could not be said that less clarity was required to relieve the charterers from their primary obligation to load within the laydays than the clarity required to relieve them from their secondary obligation to pay demurrage for failing to do so.
>
> The charterers submitted there was a distinction. When an excepted peril operated when the vessel was on demurrage, then the charterer was already in breach of contract and so the exception had to be very clear. However, when an excepted peril operated during laytime, the charterer was not then in breach; the exception took effect by extending the time for performance so that the charterer continued not to be in breach of his obligation to load. It took effect in a manner similar to phrases such as "time not to count" which Hobhouse J had observed in *The Forum Craftsman* defined the obligation (see page 87 of the judgment). A provision which affected the obligation during the laydays was not in these circumstances an exception clause, but a clause which modified the performance; the words therefore did not have to be so clear, because the charterer was never in breach and did not need to be excused from the consequences of his breach.
>
> In my view the owners' submission is in substance correct. The rule "once on demurrage always on demurrage" can, as the cases point out, make for a lack of clarity; it is a phrase best confined, as Lloyd LJ suggested in *The Lefthero*, to the general proposition that the express exceptions to laytime do not apply when the vessel is on demurrage. When the question is whether a general exception clause applies to excuse performance of the relevant obligation during laytime or demurrage, the rule "once on demurrage always on demurrage" is not relevant; it is the general principle that an ambiguous clause is no protection which applies. That is because the issue is whether the clause excuses the charterer from his obligations under the charterparty; during laytime there is the primary obligation to load the vessel within the laydays and after the expiry of the laydays, although the primary obligation to load continues, there is the secondary obligation to pay demurrage for breach of the obligation to load within the laydays. In both cases the question is whether the clause is sufficiently clear to excuse the charterer from performance of the relevant obligation.

He therefore concluded that clause 28 did not provide an exception to the running of laytime.[69]

---

66. *The Kalliopi A* [1988] 2 Lloyd's Rep 101.
67. *The Forum Craftsman* [1991] 1 Lloyd's Rep 81.
68. *The Lefthero* [1992] 2 Lloyd's Rep 109.
69. See also London Arbitration 5/98—LMLN 481, 14 April 1998.

"Any other cause beyond the control of charterers"

4.63 This or a similar expression is commonly inserted in exceptions clauses where several causes of delay are excluded. The phrase often appears as the final words. If the vessel is delayed by a cause not specifically mentioned, the question arises as to whether the cause can be excluded by virtue of the catch-all phrase.

4.64 Before considering the cases where this point has arisen, it may be helpful to summarize the principles that have emerged.

A. If the preceding exceptions are of the same type, or as is sometimes said, of the same genus, then there is a presumption that only exceptions of that type or genus are excluded. This is the *ejusdem generis* rule of construction.[70]

B. If, however, there is no common thread running through the preceding exceptions then the words will be interpreted more widely and may be given a literal meaning.

C. If the final words of exclusion include the word "whatsoever", or something similar, then this will tend to exclude the *ejusdem generis* rule and even if the preceding exceptions are of the same type or genus, the final words will still normally be given a wide meaning.

CASES RELATING TO PRINCIPLE A

4.65 In the early case of *Lyndon* v. *Standbridge*, Pollock CB said[71]:

It is a general rule of construction that where a particular class is spoken of, and general words follow, the class first mentioned is to be taken as the most comprehensive, and the general words treated as referring to matters *ejusdem generis* with such class.

4.66 In *Crawford and Rowat* v. *Wilson, Sons & Co*,[72] the charter contained a clause which provided as follows:

The Act of God, the Queen's enemies, restraint of Princes and Rulers, fire, riots, stoppage of trains, strikes of pitmen and others, lock-outs, disputes with workmen, and all unavoidable accidents or hindrances, in procuring, loading and/or discharging the cargo . . . always excepted.

4.67 The *Port Crawford*, the vessel concerned, was ordered to Rio de Janeiro with a cargo of coal, but was delayed in discharge because of a revolution. The situation in Rio de Janeiro was described by Mathew J thus[73]:

the town of Rio was from time to time bombarded by the rebels, and there was constant firing of shot, shell and small arms between the ships of the insurgents and the forts and batteries of the Government on shore.

Mathew J concluded that the rebellion constituted an "unavoidable accident or hindrance in discharging the cargo" and the delay was therefore excluded.

4.68 The Court of Appeal considered the *ejusdem generis* rule in *Richardson* v. *M Samuel & Co*,[74] where the charter contained the following, amongst other exceptions:

---

70. The phrase is defined in Osborn, *A Concise Law Dictionary*, thus: "*ejusdem generis*. (Of the same kind or nature) The rule that where particular words are followed by general words, the general words are limited to the same kind as the particular words."
71. *Lyndon* v. *Standbridge* (1857) 2 M & N 45, at p. 51.
72. *Crawford and Rowat* v. *Wilson, Sons & Co* (1895) 1 CC 154.
73. *Ibid*., at p. 157.
74. *In the matter of an Arbitration between Richardson and M Samuel & Co.* (1897) 3 CC 79 (CA).

"strikes, lock-outs, accidents to railway . . . or other causes beyond charterers' control." An accident on the railway meant there was insufficient cargo for the vessel concerned to load at the load port. Loading was further delayed because the charterers' agent had discharged the men employed by him in loading the vessels because of the stoppage and when work was resumed there was an insufficiency of labour.

4.69 On the interpretation to be given to the final words of the clause, Smith LJ said[75]:

In my opinion, these words are to be read as applying to matters *ejusdem generis* with those which have been mentioned before—that is to say, matters which relate to the impossibility of getting the cargo down to the ship and into the ship, and cannot be read so as to cover acts of the charterers' agent, which he for his own purposes thinks fit to perform, Therefore, I am of opinion that the want of men does not come within this exception.

Rigby LJ agreed, adding[76]:

I am far from saying that in another case it might not very well be held that a dismissal of men by their employer is analogous to a lock-out, though not to a strike.

However, he concluded this was not so in the present case.

4.70 In *Shamrock Steamship Co Ltd* v. *Storey & Co*,[77] Bigham J held that delay caused by an abnormal number of colliers at Grimsby because of a strike in the South Wales coalfield did not come within an exceptions clause which excluded delay due to, "Commotions by keelmen, pitmen, or any hands striking work . . . or other acts or causes beyond the freighters' control".

4.71 The judge said[78]:

. . . the fact that the Welsh coal strike may have caused an unusual number of ships to seek cargoes at Grimsby has, in my view, no more to do with the case than if the same result had followed from a strike in German or Australian or Japanese collieries. The glut in shipping cannot, I think, be brought within the fair meaning of either of the particular or the general words of the exception, the general words having to be read as confined to matters *ejusdem generis* with the particular matters mentioned in front of them.

4.72 The case subsequently went to the Court of Appeal, who upheld the lower court on the alternative ground found by Bigham J relating to the incorporation of the colliery guarantee into the charter, but Lord Russell of Killowen CJ added a note of caution that he would require the matter to be further discussed before he would be prepared to accept Bigham J's views on the exceptions clause.[79]

4.73 A review of many of the earlier cases relating to the *ejusdem generis* rule was carried out by Vaughan Williams LJ in *Tillmans & Co* v. *The Steamship Knutsford Ltd*.[80] In particular the learned Lord Justice discussed at some length, and rejected, a suggestion from counsel, based on a non-maritime case,[81] that *prima facie*, general words should be given a wide meaning, unless limited by the preceding words, rather than that general words should normally be limited by the preceding words unless extended by the context.

---

75. *Ibid.*, at p. 84.
76. *Ibid.*, at p. 85.
77. *Shamrock Steamship Co Ltd* v. *Storey & Co* (1898) 4 CC 80.
78. *Ibid.*, at p. 82.
79. *Shamrock Steamship Co Ltd* v. *Storey & Co* (1899) 5 CC 21, at p. 24.
80. *Tillmans & Co* v. *The Steamship Knutsford Ltd* (1908) 13 CC 244, at pp. 248 *et seq.*
81. *Anderson* v. *Anderson* [1895] 1 QB 749.

In other words, which way around does the presumption lie? The House of Lords agreed[82] with the lower courts that a restricted meaning primarily attaches to such general words. In the particular case, it was held that the words "or any other cause" must be construed as *ejusdem generis* with the words "war" or "disturbance", as meaning some violent act attributable to human agency, and therefore that the words did not cover the case of a master deeming entry at a port unsafe in consequence of ice or perils of the sea.

4.74 In *Mudie* v. *Strick & Co Ltd*,[83] Pickford J held, at first instance, that a shortage of labour occasioned by plague, whereby discharging was delayed, did not excuse the charterers, inasmuch as it was not an "accident" or *ejusdem generis* with "strikes, lock-outs or civil commotions". On appeal, the Court of Appeal[84] ordered a new trial without commenting on the views expressed by Pickford J.

4.75 In *Thorman* v. *The Dowgate Steamship Co Ltd*,[85] Hamilton J again considered the *ejusdem generis* rule, saying of it[86]:

One must, of course, bear in mind that it is a canon of construction only. The object is to find out the intention of the parties. The instrument, the nature of the transaction, and the language, must all have due regard given to them, and the intention of the parties is to be ascertained by the consideration of their language in accordance with its ordinary and natural meaning.

4.76 In the instant case what was specifically excluded was delay due to:

. . . strikes of pitmen or workmen, frosts or storms, and delays at spouts caused by stormy weather, and any accidents stopping the working, loading or shipping of the said cargo, also restrictions or suspensions of labour, lock-outs, delay on the part of the railway company . . .

The vessel was, however, delayed by congestion, which Hamilton J found was a normal part of the trade at that port. Referring to the link between the various exceptions, the judge said[87]:

But it appears to me that the common category which covers all this is to be found in the circumstances that they clearly all refer to something extraordinary—something in the nature of a casualty, something accidental or abnormal . . .

He therefore concluded that the delay that occurred did not come within the closing words of the exceptions clause, "any other cause beyond my control . . . ".

4.77 McCardie J again considered the many authorities on the rule in *SS Magnhild (Owners of)* v. *McIntyre Brothers & Co*,[88] apparently disagreeing with Vaughan Williams LJ in *Tillmans* v. *Knutsford*[89] as to whether there is any presumption with regard to whether a wide or narrow meaning should be given to general words of exclusion which follow specific exceptions.

4.78 As to what constitutes a genus, McCardie J said[90]:

I confess that I find great difficulty in answering the question. How the language of natural history came to be applied to the construction of commercial documents or statutes, wills and deeds, I know not . . . So far as I can see, the only test seems to be whether the specified things which precede the

82. *Tillmans & Co* v. *The Steamship Knutsford Ltd* (1908) 13 CC 244.
83. *Mudie* v. *Strick & Co Ltd* (1909) 14 CC 135.
84. *Mudie* v. *Strick & Co Ltd* (1909) 14 CC 227 (CA).
85. *Thorman* v. *The Dowgate Steamship Co Ltd* (1909) 15 CC 67.
86. *Ibid.*, at p. 78.
87. *Ibid.*, at p. 86.
88. *SS Magnhild (Owners of)* v. *McIntyre Brothers & Co* (1920) 25 CC 347, at p. 351.
89. *Tillmans & Co* v. *The Steamship Knutsford Ltd* (1908) 13 CC 244, at p. 248.
90. *SS Magnhild (Owners of)* v. *McIntyre Brothers & Co* (1920) 25 CC 347, at p. 354.

general words can be placed under some common category. By this I understand that the specified things must possess some common and dominant feature.

A little later in his judgment, he continued[91]:

Speaking broadly, the judges in the past seem to have been somewhat acute to find, if reasonably possible, a common category in charterparties, bills of lading and policies of insurance . . . Must the particular facts in question be similar to one or other of the specified things ere they can be allowed to fall within the general words, or will it suffice if they fall within the genus? Even on this point there seems much doubt.

The judge also cited with approval a passage from *Scrutton on Charterparties*, where Scrutton LJ said[92]:

It must be remembered that the question is whether a particular thing is within the genus that comprises the specified thing. It is not a question (though the point is often so put in argument) whether the particular thing is like one or other of the specified things. The more diverse the specified things, the wider must be the genus that is to include them; and by reason of the diversity of the specified things, the genus that includes them may include something that is not like any one of the specified things.

4.79 In *Hain Steamship Co Ltd* v. *Canadian Transport Co Ltd*,[93] Atkinson J applied what had been said in *Thorman* v. *The Dowgate Steamship Co Ltd* by Hamilton J about the genus he was considering, which he said related to abnormal events. However, Atkinson J added[94]:

But it must be remembered that if frost, fog and bad weather are within the genus, then "abnormal" must not be given any extreme interpretation.

4.80 More recently, the New South Wales Supreme Court has held in *Caltex Oil (Australia) Pty Ltd* v. *Howard Smith Industries Pty Ltd (The Howard Smith)*[95] that a provision excluding "acts of God, restraint of Government and other circumstances beyond control of parties" did not exclude delays due to a strike of shore operators.

4.81 In London Arbitration 2/94,[96] the tribunal took a slightly different approach to some of the earlier cases and decided that the exceptions in the clause under consideration did not fall into one particular category, type or genus, but rather several. They decided therefore that the words "any other cause beyond the control of charterers" could under the *ejusdem generis* rule of construction only be applied to each of the categories mentioned. They therefore concluded that breakdowns of machinery elsewhere than "at the Mines, at Shippers or Receivers works or Wharf" were outside the general words of exception at the end of the clause.

CASES RELATING TO PRINCIPLE B

4.82 The case of *SS Magnhild (Owners of)* v. *McIntyre Brothers & Co*,[97] which has just been referred to, was in fact a time charter case which concerned an incident where a

---

91. *Ibid.*, at p. 355.
92. Quoted *ibid.*, at p. 356.
93. *Hain Steamship Co Ltd* v. *Canadian Transport Co Ltd* (1942) 73 Ll L Rep 80.
94. *Ibid.*, at p. 86.
95. *Caltex Oil (Australia) Pty Ltd* v. *Howard Smith Industries Pty Ltd (The Howard Smith)* [1973] 1 Lloyd's Rep 544.
96. London Arbitration 2/94—LMLN 385, 6 August 1994.
97. *SS Magnhild (Owners of)* v. *McIntyre Brothers & Co* (1920) 25 CC 347.

vessel grounded entering a French port. She remained aground for eight days and repairs took some two weeks thereafter. During the whole of this period the charterers put the vessel off-hire, but the owners disputed this. The relevant clause provided for the vessel to be off-hire "in the event of loss of time from deficiency of men, or owners' stores, breakdown of machinery or damage to hull or other accident preventing the working of the steamer . . . ".[98] The owners claimed that the words "accident preventing the working of the steamer" had to be read *ejusdem generis* with the preceding causes. However, McCardie J said that[99]:

I cannot create a genus (whether scientific or otherwise) out of the specific words. I see no common or dominating feature of such words. Default of the owners cannot, of course, be such a feature, for the matter mentioned in the specific words could arise either with or without such default. Unseaworthiness . . . cannot be a common or dominating feature inasmuch as damage to hull might supervene, although the ship was perfectly seaworthy. Human agency cannot be a common or dominating feature, for damage to hull might arise through tempest . . . If, then, there be no such common or dominating feature, the *ejusdem generis* rule cannot apply.

The judge also commented that if a genus could be found, then it would probably be so wide as to cover the present facts.[100]

4.83 The House of Lords reached a similar conclusion in *Nicholas E Ambatielos* v. *Anton Jurgens' Margarine Works*,[101] which arose out of a strike of dock labourers at Rotterdam, which delayed the vessels *Ambatielos* and *Panagis* from discharging. Both vessels were on charters which contained no specific strike clause, but contained the following provision:

Should the vessel be detained by causes over which the charterers have no control, viz., quarantine, ice, hurricanes, blockade, clearing of the steamer after the last cargo is taken over, etc., no demurrage is to be charged and lay days not to count.

4.84 The first issue considered by their Lordships was whether the specific instances given were intended to be exhaustive of the definition of detention and on this the majority held they were not. Turning then to consider what common thread ran through these examples, they concluded there was none.

4.85 The Lord Chancellor put it this way[102]:

We have to see whether . . . the well known rule *ejusdem generis* applies. My Lords, I know no authority for applying that rule to a case of this kind—a case where to begin with the whole clause is governed by the initial general words, secondly, where the expression to be construed is the expression *et cetera*, and thirdly, where as in this case there is no genus to which anyone can point which comprises all the five cases.

The House therefore concluded that the clause was effective to prevent time running during the strike.

---

98. There was also an exception to the off-hire clause which covered grounding on a bar at the entrance to a harbour, but that was not the situation here.
99. *SS Magnhild (Owners of)* v. *McIntyre Brothers & Co* (1920) 25 CC 347, at p. 357.
100. *Ibid.*
101. *Nicholas E Ambatielos* v. *Anton Jurgens' Margarine Works* (1922) 13 Ll L Rep 357.
102. *Ibid.*, at p. 359.

CASES RELATING TO PRINCIPLE C

4.86 The leading case on this point is *Larsen* v. *Sylvester & Co*,[103] a decision of the House of Lords. There the clause in question read:

The parties hereto mutually exempt each other from all liability arising from frosts, floods, strikes, lock-outs of workmen, disputes between masters and men, and any other unavoidable accidents or hindrances of what kind soever beyond their control, preventing or delaying the working, loading, or shipping of the said cargo occurring on or after the date of this charter until the actual completion of loading.

The *Mauranger*, the vessel concerned, arrived in dock in Grimsby to load a cargo of coal, but was delayed thereafter by congestion. The higher courts agreed that the *ejusdem generis* principle did not apply and the delay was excluded. Speaking of the *ejusdem generis* rule, Lord Robertson said[104]:

. . . the parties, I think, have realized, or, at least, may well be held to have realized, the applicability of that rule to such contracts, and they inserted these words "of what kind soever", simply for the purpose of excluding that rule of construction. The effect of the insertion of these words is this, it excludes the limitation that would naturally arise from the context and gives to the word "hindrances" its full and absolute meaning.

4.87 This decision of the House of Lords was followed in *France, Fenwick & Co Ltd* v. *Philip Spackman & Sons*[105] by Bailhache J. In this case, the clause provided:

Strikes of workmen, lock-outs, pay days, idle days or cavilling days, or riots or frost, rain or floods, or any accident or any cause whatsoever beyond the control of the charterer which may prevent or delay her loading or unloading excepted.

The vessel was delayed by a shortage of railway wagons at the discharging port, due to an abnormal demand for these at the time. The reason for that abnormal demand was said by Bailhache J to be as follows[106]:

As we all remember the summer of 1911 was quite exceptional; the fruit crop was heavy and the hops were moved some 14 days before the usual time; there were about this time some manoeuvres, partly of the territorial forces and partly of the regular army; and in addition there was the dislocation of the railway traffic owing to the few days' serious strike in August.

The judge continued, saying[107]:

It is sufficient for me to refer to *Larsen* v. *Sylvester*[108] and *Thorman* v. *Dowgate Steamship Co*.[109] In the former of these cases the general words were "of what kind soever", and the House of Lords held that by the use of those words there was a sufficient expression of intention to exclude the *ejusdem generis* rule. In *Thorman* v. *Dowgate Steamship Co*, the general words were "any other cause", and Hamilton J decided there was no sufficient indication to override the well-known *ejusdem generis* rule.

In this case, the judge concluded, the words were sufficient to exclude the rule.

4.88 A slightly different problem came before Mustill J in *The Mozart*.[110] In this case, the vessel concerned was chartered to carry a cargo of petcoke from the TOPCO terminal

103. *Larsen* v. *Sylvester & Co* (1908) 13 CC 328.
104. *Ibid.*, at p. 333.
105. *France, Fenwick & Co Ltd* v. *Philip Spackman & Sons* (1912) 18 CC 52.
106. *Ibid.*, at p. 56.
107. *Ibid.*, at p. 57.
108. *Larsen* v. *Sylvester & Co* (1908) 13 CC 328.
109. *Thorman* v. *The Dowgate Steamship Co Ltd* (1909) 15 CC 67.
110. *The Mozart* [1985] 1 Lloyd's Rep 239.

near Port Arthur to Rotterdam. At the load port the vessel was delayed for some days by a breakdown of a large mobile conveyor belt, called a stacker-reclaimer, used to transport petcoke to store from the railcars in which it arrived and from thence to the ship. The breakdown was due to poor maintenance by the terminal, who were not the shippers but independent contractors engaged by charterers' agents to store and load the petcoke. The charter was on an Americanized Welsh Coal Charter form and the charterers claimed to be excused for the delay by clause 3, which provided:

... Any time lost through riots, strikes, lock-outs, or any dispute between masters and men, occasioning a stoppage of pitmen trimmers or other hands connected with the working or delivery of the petcoke for which the Vessel is stemmed, or by reason of accidents to mines or machinery, obstructions, embargo or delay on the Railway or in the Dock; or by reason of fire, floods, frosts, fogs, storms or any cause whatsoever beyond the control of the Charterer affecting mining, transportation, delivery and/or loading of the petcoke not to be computed as part of the loading time (unless any cargo be actually loaded during such time) ...

In the original arbitration proceedings it was argued that the breakdown of the stacker-reclaimer was a breakdown of machinery, but that contention was rejected by the arbitrators, and before Mustill J it was argued that the breakdown came within the words "... any cause whatsoever beyond the control of the Charterer affecting ... loading of the petcoke".

4.89 Mustill J considered this question in two parts, the first being whether the words should be given a literal meaning and, secondly, if so, whether what happened was beyond the control of the charterers. On the first point, he said[111]:

If the clause is expressed widely, it must be applied widely.

He therefore held, without citing either of the previous cases, or indeed any authority, in favour of a literal meaning, thus excluding the *ejusdem generis* rule. On the second issue he held that the charterers were not vicariously liable for TOPCO's failure to maintain the stacker-reclaimer, since the charterers, via their agents, were in an arm's length relationship with the terminal.

4.90 Another issue that arose in this case was whether the charterers were disentitled to rely on the exceptions clause, because they failed to give notice of the stoppage as required by the final part of the clause. On this, the arbitrators and Mustill J agreed that the charterers could rely on the clause, since the owners were not prejudiced by the failure to give notice as, via the master, they were fully aware of what had happened.[112]

4.91 In *The Notos*,[113] owners sought unsuccessfully to argue that a clause which included the phrase

... any other cause of whatsoever nature or kind over which the charterer has no control

should be limited to causes relating to the vessel or her owners since some such were also expressly mentioned.

4.92 In *The Mastrogiorgis B*,[114] the US Court of Appeals (2nd Circuit) held that time lost as a result of congestion, itself resulting from a strike, came within the protection of

111. *Ibid.*, at p. 242.
112. The decision in *The Mozart* was followed by Bingham J in *Valla Giovanni & C SpA v. Gebr Van Weelde Scheepvaartkantoor BV (The Chanda)* [1985] 1 Lloyd's Rep 563.
113. *The Notos* [1987] 1 Lloyd's Rep 503, at p. 507.
114. *Orient Shipping Rotterdam BV v. Hugo Neu & Sons Inc (The Mastrogiorgis B)*, LMLN 451, 18 February 1997. *See* also *The Apostolis* [1999] 2 Lloyd's Rep. 292.

the phrase "beyond the charterer's/receiver's control" in a clause said to be drafted in the broadest possible language.

Overtime ordered by port authorities to count as laytime

4.93 A number of points of interest arose in a case called *President of India* v. *Edina Compania Naviera SA (The Stamatios G Embiricos)*,[115] a decision of Mocatta J.

4.94 The case concerned a charter for the carriage of grain from the US Gulf to Kandla and Bombay. The charter envisaged that, before the *Stamatios G Embiricos* could berth at Kandla, lightening would be necessary, and the charter therefore included as clause 11 the Centrocon lighterage clause, the significant part of which, as far as this was concerned, was the provision for time to commence 48 hours after the vessel's arrival at the lightening anchorage. The charter also contained the following terms:

12. ... If overtime work ordered by the Port Controller or Authorities at loading or discharging ports, the cost of such overtime shall be shared equally between Owners and Charterers, and half such time so used to count as laytime.
13. Vessel to work day and night including Saturdays after noon, Sundays and Holidays if requested to do so by Charterer or his Agents.
14(a) Cargo to be discharged by consignees' stevedores, free of risk and expense to vessel, at the average rate of 1000 tons of 2240 lbs. per weather working day of 24 consecutive hours Saturdays after noon, Sundays and Holidays excepted even if used, always provided the vessel can deliver at this rate.

4.95 The vessel arrived at the Kandla lightening anchorage at 06 00 on 29 September 1958, so that time began on 1 October at the same time. However, before time began to run, the port authority ordered that overtime be worked for certain periods and, from 1 October, the vessel worked around the clock on the instructions of the port authority, first at the anchorage and then alongside, until discharge of the Kandla cargo was complete.

4.96 The dispute concerned the interaction of the clauses mentioned and how the periods of overtime, (a) before laytime commenced, (b) during laytime and (c) during excepted periods, should be treated. The charterers argued that the final words of clause 12 only operated after laytime had commenced and thereafter meant that any overtime periods only counted as half time. The owners, on the other hand, said that the only periods that were to count as half time were those when, in the absence of this provision, laytime would not have run, either because it had not commenced or because it was an excepted period, e.g. Sundays or holidays. Mocatta J held that the owners were right. In the course of his judgment, the judge said[116]:

When in a charter words are used to the effect that a certain period of time is to count as laytime the natural and ordinary meaning of those words is that such period is to be treated as permitted laytime when otherwise it would not be. The addition of the word "half" does not alter that natural and ordinary meaning in its character, but only so far as quantum is concerned. Support for this view is afforded by the argument of Mr Diamond, which is in my judgment well founded, that the positive phrases in charters that a period is "to count" or is "to count as laytime" are commonly used for the benefit of the shipowner, so as to result in a decrease in dispatch money or an increase in demurrage, in contrast to the negative phrases that a period is "not to count" or is "not to count as

115. *President of India* v. *Edina Compania Naviera SA (The Stamatios G Embiricos)* [1965] 1 Lloyd's Rep 574.
116. *Ibid.*, at p. 582.

laytime", which are used for the benefit of the charterer so as to result in an increase in dispatch money or a decrease in demurrage.[117]

Congestion

4.97 Congestion is probably the most common cause of delay, although it is not usually expressly mentioned as an exception. It is usually excepted by reason of a more general phrase such as obstructions[118] or hindrances beyond the control of either party.

4.98 In *The Amstelmolen*,[119] the Court of Appeal held that such an exceptions clause applied, even where commencement of laytime was accelerated by virtue of a WIBON[120] provision. The general effect, therefore, in such a case is for laytime to commence, either because the vessel concerned has arrived at a point within the port where it is "at the immediate and effective disposition of the charterer" in the case of a port charter[121] or because there is a provision bringing forward the commencement of laytime,[122] and then be immediately suspended.

4.99 There are many cases on the meaning of "obstructions",[123] particularly in relation to congestion, but in *Navrom v. Callitsis Ship Management SA (The Radauti)*,[124] the High Court and Court of Appeal were agreed that in that case[125] "hindrances" protected charterers against similar delays.

4.100 One issue that arose in *The Radauti* was whether the likelihood of congestion made any difference. On this the courts were agreed. It did not, Lloyd LJ saying[126]:

> But if, as we are bound to hold, the word "obstructions" covers the inability of a vessel to get to her berth because of congestion, I can see no difference in principle whether there was one vessel in front of *Radauti* or a 100. The degree of congestion is clearly irrelevant. So also, in my view, is the likelihood of congestion. That was the view of Mr Justice Staughton in *The Adolf Leonhardt* [1986] 2 Lloyd's Rep 395. It was his view in the present case.[127] I share his view. The phrase "hindrances . . . delaying . . . the discharge of the cargo" should be given its ordinary meaning, even though on the facts some degree of hindrance was inevitable. The foreseeability of the congestion does not justify attaching an unusual or restricted meaning to the word "hindrances".

ADVERSE WEATHER

4.101 Periods of adverse weather are often excluded from laytime. This may be either because such periods do not come with the definition of the type of laytime allowed by the

---

117. The judge drew support for his decision from the cases relating to the phrase, "time lost in waiting for berth to count as laytime". For a discussion on these, see *ante* at para. 3.377.

118. See *post* at para. 4.319.

119. *The Amstelmolen* [1961] 2 Lloyd's Rep 1.

120. Whether in Berth or Not—see *ante* at para. 3.346.

121. See *ante* at para. 3.64.

122. See *ante* at paras 3.318 *et seq*. This would not apply where there is a "reachable on arrival" provision. See *ante* at para. 3.402 and *post* at para. 4.394.

123. See *post* at para. 4.319.

124. *Navrom v. Callitsis Ship Management SA (The Radauti)* [1987] 2 Lloyd's Rep 276; [1988] 2 Lloyd's Rep 416.

125. In *Marc Rich & Co Ltd v. Tourloti Compania Naviera SA (The Kalliopi A)* [1988] 2 Lloyd's Rep 101, charterers failed to show that an exceptions clause relating to "hindrances" applied to demurrage. In that case, the Court of Appeal emphasized that it had been agreed by the parties that laytime would run despite the clause, although in the light of the Court of Appeal decision in *The Radauti*, decided some months later, it would seem that this would not have been the case.

126. *The Radauti* [1988] 2 Lloyd's Rep 416, at p. 420.

127. Staughton J was the judge in the High Court.

charter, e.g. weather working days, or because they are excluded by a specific clause. In the former case, the reference is usually simply to "weather" in general; in the latter it may be the same or there may be a reference to a specific type of weather.

4.102 The word "weather" is a word in everyday use and therefore, unless it is used in an unusual sense, its meaning is to be determined as a question of fact. It is for the tribunal which determines any particular case to consider, not as law but as fact, whether in the whole circumstances the word does or does not as a matter of ordinary usage of the English language cover or apply to the facts which have been proved.[128]

4.103 The *Shorter Oxford English Dictionary, inter alia*, defines weather as:

The condition of the atmosphere (at given place and time) with respect to heat or cold, presence or absence of rain, etc.

The definition of weather is thus wide and although most natural phenomena which could interfere with cargo operations could be said to arise directly or indirectly as a result of the weather, there are limits to what the courts or arbitrators will accept.

4.104 A somewhat unusual set of circumstances gave rise to the decision in London Arbitration 5/94.[129] Here from time to time work was interrupted because, particularly in the heat of the day, bees attracted by sugar products discharged from earlier ships swarmed and the stevedores, not altogether surprisingly, stopped work.

4.105 One of the arguments put forward by the charterers as to why time should not count during these interruptions was that bees only swarmed in certain weather conditions and consequently they were entitled to rely on a weather exception. This the tribunal rejected saying that it was clear that "bees" were not themselves weather. Therefore, for the charterers to have any chance of relying upon the weather exception, they would have at least to show a direct causal link between the weather conditions and the effects said to result, namely the swarming of bees. To show that would require showing consistency and inevitability to a fairly high degree. The tribunal concluded that the charterers had not satisfied those requirements in the present case.

4.106 It must also be remembered that what might constitute bad weather for one vessel will not necessarily be the same for another, even though both are in the same port at the same time. Thus, periods of rain may well prevent the discharge of a cargo of bulk sugar, but would have no effect on the discharge of a cargo of crude oil from a tanker. The effect on laytime may even be different in the case of two similar ships with the same type of cargo, but different weather clauses in the charterparty. For example, if ship A has a port charter with laytime expressed in weather working days and ship B has a similar charter but with laytime expressed in working days, but with an additional clause excluding time lost due to adverse weather, and both are waiting at anchorage for a berth, then in the case of ship A rainy periods on working days will be excluded from laytime, but not in the case of ship B, assuming both have a type of cargo that would be affected by rain during cargo operations. This is because the causal element necessary is different for an interruption to laytime (i.e. where the periods concerned do not come within the definition of laytime) compared with that relating to an exception from laytime.[130]

---

128. *Brutus v. Cozens* [1972] 3 WLR 521, at p. 525 *per* Lord Reid.
129. London Arbitration 5/94—LMLN 386, 20 August 1994.
130. See *ante* at para. 4.1.

The limits of weather

4.107 Clearly, the weather must be adverse to be excluded and, as already mentioned, must be adverse to the particular type of cargo sought to be loaded or discharged.

4.108 The most common phenomena encountered can probably be put under the heading of atmospheric precipitation—rain, hail, snow and sleet. The next most common is probably high winds. With all of these, providing they are actually occurring at the place where cargo operations are or are intended to be carried out, there will usually be no difficulty in determining whether the weather was or would have been adverse to cargo operations.

4.109 In practice what is usually excluded is the actual period of adverse weather, notwithstanding that the charterer or other cargo interest may have had to decide in advance whether to book gangs of stevedores for a particular shift. A fear that loading or discharging will be interrupted is not enough to stop laytime from running.

4.110 In *The Maria G*,[131] Devlin J commented:

But no case has been cited to me in which a mere threat of bad weather which has suspended loading has been held to make a day not a weather working day, and certainly no case where the threat of bad weather has affected not the operation of the actual work of loading, but the safety of the ship in the particular place in which she was.

In that case, the *Maria G* was ordered to shift from her loading berth to buoys by the Calcutta harbour master because he feared damage both to the vessel and the berth from bore tides, which were expected and did in fact occur whilst the vessel was at the buoys. The charterers unsuccessfully claimed that time should not run whilst the vessel was at the buoys. Having been prepared to accept, without deciding, that bore tides were weather, Devlin J held that the threat of bad weather was insufficient to prevent time from counting.

4.111 The question of whether time should be excluded in anticipation of circumstances arising which, had they occurred, would have been excluded has been considered in relation to other types of exclusion clauses, notably ones dealing with clauses covering "restraint of princes". One such case was *Watts, Watts & Co Ltd* v. *Mitsui & Co Ltd*,[132] a decision of the House of Lords, where Lord Dunedin said:

Restraint of princes, to fall within the words of the exception, must be an existing fact and not a mere apprehension. This was held long ago by Lord Ellenborough in *Atkinson* v. *Ritchie*.[133] The more recent cases cited by the appellants, such as *Geipel* v. *Smith* and *Nobel's Explosives Co* v. *Jenkins*,[134] do not in any way touch that proposition. They only show that it may be possible to invoke the exception when a reasonable man in face of an existing restraint may consider that the restraint, though it does not affect him at the moment, will do so if he continues the adventure. It would be useless to try and fix by definition the precise imminence of peril which would make the restraint a present fact as contrasted with a future fear. The circumstances in each particular case must be considered.

4.112 In theory there would seem no reason why these principles should not also apply to a weather clause. The question would then be how imminent must adverse weather be to make the present weather itself be considered adverse. Common sense would suggest

---

131. *Compania Crystal de Vapores* v. *Herman & Mohatta (India) Ltd (The Maria G)* [1958] 1 Lloyd's Rep 616, at p. 621.
132. *Watts, Watts & Co Ltd* v. *Mitsui & Co Ltd* (1917) 22 CC 242, at p. 248.
133. *Atkinson* v. *Ritchie* (1809) 10 East 530.
134. *Geipel* v. *Smith* (1872) LR 7 QB 404; *Nobel's Explosives Co Ltd* v. *Jenkins* [1896] 2 QB 326.

that the answer will vary with different types of adverse weather. Thus with rain or snow, for instance, it is unlikely that the weather would be considered adverse until it actually started raining or snowing, as the case may be. When this happened the hatches could be quickly closed and cargo operations suspended.

4.113 In contrast, however, if the adverse weather feared was a typhoon, then it is suggested that there might be scope for invoking the principles set out above. Clearly, a typhoon would affect both cargo operations and the safety of the vessel/berth. It is therefore suggested that at the point where good seamanship dictates that cargo operations should cease and the vessel sail, that is the time at which the threat of adverse weather could itself be considered adverse weather, notwithstanding that at the moment, wind strengths had not yet risen so far as to of themselves justify suspending cargo operations.

4.114 In *The Maria G*,[135] it does not seem to have been argued that, had the vessel remained in berth, the effect of the bore tide would have prevented loading. In the course of his judgment, having pointed out that the charterers' argument was that the period when the berth was temporarily unsafe could be considered weather working days, Devlin J continued[136]:

> ... I should decide against it [charterers' argument] on the broad ground that, if the effect of weather is not to interfere with the operations of the loading and discharging, but is to render the presence of the vessel in a particular place unsafe, the time so lost is not what the parties contemplate when they are referring to weather working days.

Another illustration of the same point was provided in a London Arbitration.[137] The vessel concerned arrived at the loading port and commenced loading a cargo of bulk sulphur via a conveyor belt with the vessel being anchored offshore. Owing to bad weather the vessel had to leave the loading point but returned when the weather improved. An additional clause in the charter provided that time lost by reason of bad weather should not be computed in the loading time. However, the arbitrators held that whilst it was true that, indirectly, the loading operation was suspended because of the bad weather, nevertheless the effective cause of the cessation of loading was the vessel having to leave the loading point because of its unsafety. No evidence had been produced to show that the bad weather actually prevented the loading of sulphur through the conveyor belt, and the weather exclusion clause was therefore held inapplicable.

Particular types of weather

Frost

4.115 The temperature at which water vapour in the atmosphere condenses into water droplets is called the dew point. If the dew point is above freezing, condensation will be to water; if it is below freezing then moisture will be deposited on cold surfaces directly in the form of ice crystals, commonly known as frost. There is no doubt that frost is weather.

135. *Compania Crystal de Vapores* v. *Herman & Mohatta (India) Ltd (The Maria G)* [1958] 1 Lloyd's Rep 616.
136. *Ibid.*, at p. 621.
137. London Arbitration—LMLN 115, 29 March 1984.

4.116 The effect of frost was considered in the Scottish case of *Henry & MacGregor Ltd* v. *Galbraith & Roy.* The vessel concerned, the *Rattray Head,* arrived at Wisbech with a cargo of potatoes. At the time there was continual severe frost and other adverse weather and the commencement of discharge was delayed for some 11 days. The relevant charter had an additional clause stating that time lost during usual working hours owing to bad weather was not to count and a general exceptions clause specifically excluded time lost due to frost. The charterers argued that damage to the cargo would have been caused during and after discharge because of the frost. They conceded that the prevailing frost did not prevent the actual operation of discharge. They therefore claimed they were entitled to delay discharge until the risk of cargo damage had passed.

4.117 Rejecting this argument, Lord Russell said[138]:

Now, in my opinion, the exceptions in the charterparty which absolve the charterers from liability for demurrage on the happening of certain events (bad weather and frost) connote circumstances which affect the discharging or loading so as to render these operations physically impossible . . . In the present case I consider that neither expressly nor by clear implication do the words of the exceptions invoked by the charterers apply to the circumstances disclosed on record.

However, whatever may be the position under Scottish law, there is clear authority in English law that the effect of weather may be either physically to prevent cargo operations, e.g. high winds, or to risk damage to the cargo. An illustration of the latter is provided by *Compania Naviera Azuero SA* v. *British Oil and Cake Mills Ltd and others,*[139] where the laytime allowed was measured in weather working days, the cargo was grain and the dispute concerned certain periods of rain. Clearly, the principal effect of the rain would have been to cause damage to the cargo had cargo operations been carried out.

4.118 In so far as the decision in *Henry & MacGregor Ltd* v. *Galbraith & Roy* is to the effect that the exclusions clauses only applied to loading and discharging and not to anything that happened before or after that, it is submitted it is correct. In *British Steel Corporation* v. *National Dock Labour Board,*[140] the Court of Appeal held that in that case, which concerned discharge of iron ore by grab unloaders into a hopper and then on to a conveyor belt to the stock-yard, that discharge from the vessel was complete when the iron ore reached the conveyor. In *Henry & MacGregor Ltd* v. *Galbraith & Roy,*[141] Lord Russell apparently took the view that discharge ended when the cargo reached the quay. If, therefore, there was a risk of cargo damage by frost whilst the cargo was in the open hold or as it was being discharged, then it is submitted that the exceptions clause should have been effective, and the decision was wrong.

4.119 There is, of course, no reason why an exceptions clause should not be more widely drawn so as to cover delay by frost before loading or after discharge, and an illustration of the former is provided by *Pinch & Simpson* v. *Harrison Whitfield & Co,*[142] an early decision of Denning J, as he then was.

4.120 The case concerned a vessel fixed to carry loam from the River Thames to Middlesbrough. The loam came from a nearby quarry and was taken straight from being quarried to the vessel. The effect of frost was to prevent quarrying and also any loam

---

138. *Henry & MacGregor Ltd* v. *Galbraith & Roy* (1940) 66 Ll L Rep 71, at p. 73.
139. *Compania Naviera Azuero SA* v. *British Oil and Cake Mills Ltd and others* [1957] 1 Lloyd's Rep 312.
140. *British Steel Corporation* v. *National Dock Labour Board* [1971] 2 Lloyd's Rep 439.
141. *Henry & MacGregor Ltd* v. *Galbraith & Roy* (1940) 66 Ll L Rep 71.
142. *Pinch & Simpson* v. *Harrison, Whitfield & Co* (1948) 81 Ll L Rep 268.

stored overnight in trucks would tighten, so that it could not be tipped out. The charter had a provision excepting time lost, *inter alia*, through "frosts . . . preventing the loading or unloading or provision of cargo". By the time the vessel concerned was ready to load a severe frost had set in and provision of cargo was delayed.

4.121 Upholding the validity of the exceptions clause and having quoted it, Denning J continued[143]:

Those words show that a distinction is drawn between the act of loading and the provision of cargo. The loading is the actual operation of loading from the wharf or quay on to the ship. The provision of cargo applies to an earlier time—that is to say, in this case the actual provision of the loam from the quarry and its carriage down to the jetty. It applies, in my judgment, to the getting of the cargo, in that it has to be got out of the quarry. It applies not only to the carrying of it down to the jetty but to the actual picking of it out of the quarry.

Denning J also commented that the words "provision of cargo" were probably put in because "loading" was sometimes construed as applying only to the bare operation of loading from the wharf or quay on to the ship.

Ice

4.122 The usual effect of ice during laytime is to prevent the provision of cargo. With vessels trading to areas where ice is likely to delay cargo operations, it is common to include a specific clause to deal with the problem. Frequently this will cover not just the effect of ice on laytime but deal with the situation where ice prevents the vessel concerned from reaching her loading or discharging port or requires her to leave port early. One such clause is that contained in the Exxonvoy 84 form of charter, which reads as follows:

Clause 21 Ice

   (a) DURING VOYAGE. In case a nominated port or place of loading or discharging should be inaccessible due to ice, Master shall immediately notify Charterer by telegraph, telex or radio, requesting revised orders and shall remain safely outside the ice-bound area. Charterer shall give orders for another port or place which is free from ice and where there are facilities for the loading or discharging of the cargo in bulk. In this event, freight shall be paid at the rate stipulated in Part I(g) to such alternative port or place and any time by which the steaming time to such port or place exceeds that which would have been taken if Vessel had been ordered to proceed to such port or place in the first instance shall be compensated at the Deviation rate per running day and pro-rata thereof. In addition, Charterer shall pay for extra bunkers consumed during such excess time at Owner's documented actual replacement cost for such bunkers at the port where bunkers are next taken.
   (b) AT PORT. If, on or after Vessel's arrival at the loading or discharging port or place, it is dangerous to remain at such port or place for fear of Vessel being frozen-in or damaged, Master shall notify Charterer who shall give orders for Vessel either to proceed to another port or place where there is no danger of ice and where there are facilities for the loading or discharging of the cargo in bulk or to remain at such original port or place at Charterer's risk. If Vessel is ordered to proceed to another port or place, the sum in respect of freight and delay to be paid by Charterer shall be as stipulated in paragraph (a) of this clause. If Vessel remains at such original port or place, any time so lost on account of ice shall count as laytime or, if Vessel is on demurrage, as time on demurrage.

4.123 In this section it is intended to confine discussion on the effect of ice to problems relating to laytime.

143. *Ibid.* at p. 273.

4.124 The effect of an ice clause was considered by the House of Lords in *Michalinos & Co* v. *Louis Dreyfus & Co*.[144] The case concerned a charter for the carriage of wheat from a port on the River Danube to a port in the United Kingdom or on the Continent. Seventeen running days were allowed for loading and discharging. The ship concerned, the *Matheos*, arrived in the selected port, Braila, on 7 December 1921 and tendered Notice of Readiness. At Braila there were three usual and customary methods of loading grain—(a) at a quay in the docks from silos, (b) from lighters in midstream outside the docks, and (c) from the river bank by the use of gangways and manual labour. The charterers' intention was to load a small part of the cargo in the dock and the remainder in mid-river. On arrival at Braila, the *Matheos* berthed in the docks at the grain quay but outboard of another vessel which was still loading. On 12 December a severe frost set in and the dock became completely frozen over; from that date until 9 March the *Matheos* and all other vessels in the dock remained icebound. Clause 11 of the charter provided that "detention by . . . ice from Braila down to Sulina shall not count as lay days" and the charterers claimed to be protected by this clause. The owners, on the other hand, claimed that it only applied to the actual passage between the two ports named and although they were successful in the original arbitration proceedings in this argument, it was decisively rejected by the House of Lords and the courts below. The Lord Chancellor, Lord Cave, said the argument was quite untenable since the clause referred to lay days and there could be no question of lay days during the passage of the vessel down the Danube.

4.125 The second argument put forward by the shipowners was that loading was not absolutely prevented by the ice since the ship could have been loaded in the dock by manual labour, either from the quay or from lighters lying in the dock and the time afterwards spent in loading could have been saved. Whilst agreeing that it was physically possible, the House nevertheless rejected this contention and endorsed the arbitrator's finding that it was commercially impossible, since not only would it have been unrealistically expensive, but storing the wheat on board the *Matheos* for what was clearly going to be a prolonged period would have increased the risk of cargo damage.

4.126 The House also rejected an argument that had found favour with Rowlatt J that, to take advantage of the exceptions clause, the charterers had to show that ice prevented all three forms of loading in use at Braila. Lord Sumner put it this way[145]:

I agree with the view of the Court of Appeal. The *Matheos*, being an arrived ship, was entitled to have a usual loading intimated to her, but it was for the charterers to select for her, among the usual and proper places, one which thereupon becomes the place where her loading was to begin; and exceptions excusing delay in this loading attach and have relation to that place and mode of loading.

The House therefore held that having selected a method of loading, the charterers brought themselves within the exceptions clause if they showed that it covered that method.

4.127 The same cold winter of 1921 when the Danube froze earlier than usual also gave rise to the case of *T Lewis* v. *Louis Dreyfus & Co*,[146] a decision of the Court of Appeal. The facts were similar to the previous case and the ice clause the same. Again, Braila was the loading port. In this case, however, the vessel concerned, the *Newlands*, became stuck in the ice on its way up to Braila, arriving there eventually on 5 March. The dispute concerned a period of three days after the vessel's arrival at Braila, during which

144. *Michalinos & Co* v. *Louis Dreyfus & Co* (1925) 21 Ll L Rep 233.
145. *Ibid*., at p. 237.
146. *T Lewis* v. *Louis Dreyfus & Co* (1926) 24 Ll L Rep 333.

cargo could not be loaded because part of the cargo was in lighters in the docks which were still frozen and part was further upstream in lighters which could not be brought downstream because of the ice. The *Newlands* was moored in mid-stream during this period awaiting her cargo, the charterers having selected loading from lighters out of the three options available.

4.128 Having decided that the obstructions to loading by the method selected were only temporary, as would have been obvious at the time, the court went on to consider the general responsibilities of the charterers in this type of situation. On the question of whether a charterer should consider alternative methods of loading, Lord Hanworth MR said[147]:

In the present case the charterer had half his cargo in lighters ready to go alongside the ship. He might have had the whole cargo in lighters ready to go alongside the ship. The fact that for a day or two ice prevents loading being carried on alongside the ship ought not to compel him suddenly to alter the whole of his plans, to get the whole of the cargo out of the lighters, or to purchase other cargo out of warehouse, leaving the cargo in lighters on his hands as derelict. He is entitled to continue in the option he has exercised for a reasonable time; and I am not going to specify what a reasonable time is, because I cannot foresee all cases or events which will require him to change over to another form of loading at another place.

The court therefore concluded that the charterer was protected by the ice clause.

4.129 The question of whether ice could make a day not a weather working day was the issue in *Dampskibsselskabet Botnia A/S* v. *Bell & Co.*[148] The vessel concerned had been chartered to bring a cargo of pit props from Finland to Cardiff. The charter specified a rate of loading per weather working day and the practice at the place where loading was to take place was for the cargo to be towed out to the ship as rafts of timber. This operation was hampered by ice and eventually the ship had to sail with a part cargo since it was clear that no more cargo could be provided before the port was closed for the winter. The shipowners claimed deadfreight and the issue was whether the shippers had met the charterparty requirements for loading prior to the vessel having to sail. This in turn depended on whether ice could prevent time counting as weather working days. The shipowners unsuccessfully argued that ice was not weather but the result of weather. Bateson J, however, put it this way[149]:

I think the formation of ice by cold which prevents the loading is weather . . .

and later on:

I think it [i.e. weather] means loading weather and if you have ice which prevents you loading you are stopped from loading by the weather being unfit for loading. In other words, you have not got a weather working day.

The judge also pointed out that ice could very often be beautiful weather but at the same time bad weather when it prevented loading.[150]

Surf

4.130 In some ports it is customary to load and discharge vessels from and to lighters which are in turn loaded and discharged from a nearby beach. The practice was, of course,

147. *Ibid.*, at p. 339.
148. *Dampskibsselskabet Botnia A/S* v. *Bell & Co* (1931) 41 Ll L Rep 160.
149. *Ibid.*, at p. 162.
150. *Ibid.*, at p. 163.

more prevalent in former times, before proper port facilities developed and before the advent of containerization. However, there are still some parts of the world, particularly in South America and India, where the practice is still continued.

4.131 If the beach is affected by surf then clearly lighters cannot be loaded or discharged and this in turn may lead to congestion or shortage of lighters around the mother vessel, thus directly interfering with loading and discharging, although normally the lighters will be able to be cleared away to prevent this. A shortage of lighters would not normally arise from the default of the shipowner, whose responsibility usually starts or ends with the taking from or delivery to the lighters. Therefore normally, in the absence of an express clause, surf will not affect the laytime calculations even if the laytime allowed is expressed in weather working days. In comparison with ice which can so affect laytime, the distinction appears to be that surf affects the loading or discharging of the lighters and is therefore one step further back compared with ice which prevents their reaching the mother vessel.

4.132 One such express clause dealing with surf was considered in *Bennetts & Co v. J & A Brown*,[151] where delay by surf was excluded from laytime. Evidence was given by the charterers that, by a custom of the port of Valparaiso, surf days were not weather working days and that the port captain could declare what days were deemed to be surf days. Rejecting this argument, Walton J held that as the custom gave a meaning to the words "weather working days" different from their plain and natural signification, it could not be accepted. However, as there was some delay directly caused by the surf, the exception relating to surf applied in respect of those days.

4.133 In *British and Mexican Shipping Co Ltd v. Lockett Brothers & Co Ltd*,[152] the receivers sought to argue that by a custom of the port of Iquique surf days, as declared by the captain of the port, were not working days. At first instance, Hamilton J refused to accept this, but on appeal the Court of Appeal ruled on a preliminary point of law that the custom could constitute a defence to the shipowners' claim for demurrage. However, all the judges concerned stressed that their ruling was only on a preliminary point of law and Kennedy LJ in particular emphasized that his judgment proceeded on the basis that both parties knew of the custom. It is perhaps interesting to note that in the earlier Scottish case of *Holman v. Peruvian Nitrate Co*,[153] the Court of Session said that, despite this custom, the days concerned were still working days, which is, it is submitted, the better decision.

Swell

4.134 In some exposed ports and anchorages, swell is often the cause of interruptions to loading and discharging.[154] In one London Arbitration, the umpire said this about whether high swell constituted weather[155]:

151. *Bennetts & Co v. J & A Brown* (1907) 13 CC 110.
152. *British and Mexican Shipping Co Ltd v. Lockett Brothers & Co Ltd* (1910) 16 CC 75.
153. *Holman & Sons v. Peruvian Nitrate Co* (1878) 15 SLR 349.
154. For instance Bejaia and other Algerian ports are subject to a phenomenon known as the Ressac. When the Mistral and Tamentane winds blow from the coasts of France, a heavy swell occurs in Bejaia which at its onset may require vessels in harbour to be held on their berths by tugs and at its height the harbour master may close the port. See *Cosmar Compania Naviera SA v. Total Transport Corporation (The Isabelle)* [1982] 2 Lloyd's Rep 81; [1984] 1 Lloyd's Rep 366.
155. London Arbitration—LMLN 64, 15 April 1982.

There appeared to be no direct authority, nor was any cited to me, as to whether "high swell" is "weather". "Weather" certainly includes "storms". "Swell" is a phenomenon of the high seas and has been defined as "a slow, steady, continuous undulation of the sea unbroken by waves after a storm". It is the product of bad weather.

I found that "high swell" was analogous to storms, although to a lesser degree. The charterers would not have discharged during a storm, as not only would there have been a risk of damage to the cargo, there would have been a substantial risk of damage to the vessel. In the case of storm, the charterers would have been perfectly entitled to stop discharge and not to count the laytime. I therefore felt that this also disposed of the owners' argument that the charterers should not be entitled to the benefit of time lost. I found no merit in the "surf" argument as these cases covered loading or discharging lighters on a beach and not alongside the carrying vessel at an anchorage.

I therefore found that "high swell" was covered by "weather" and that the charterers were entitled to except such periods from laytime.

4.135 In *Dampskibsselskabet Botnia A/S* v. *Bell & Co*,[156] where the actual dispute concerned delays in loading due to ice, counsel for the receivers, who was trying to show that ice was weather, argued that if ice was not weather, then the waves (i.e. swell) which were produced by the wind and prevented lighters or rafts from coming alongside vessels, as did the ice in that case, would also not be weather. In response, Bateson J agreed that that was somewhat analogous and, since he found that ice was a form of weather, he presumably would have agreed that waves caused by wind (i.e. swell) were also weather.

4.136 To interfere with laytime, the swell must interrupt cargo operations. In the case of dry cargo vessels it may impose an undue strain on the vessel's cargo gear, causing the cargo then being loaded or discharged to be lost. In the case of liquid cargoes, there may be a risk of ruptured hoses with a consequent loss of cargo.[157]

4.137 It is perhaps interesting to note that under German law it would appear that swell is not considered bad weather on its own.[158]

4.138 Where swell encounters shallow water it breaks into waves and is often classed as rough seas. In this situation presumably similar principles apply.

Bore tides

4.139 A bore tide is a tidal wave of unusual height caused either by the meeting of two tides or by the rushing of the tide up a narrowing estuary. Bore tides are often at their most severe at the time of the equinoxes.

4.140 In *Compania Crystal de Vapores* v. *Herman & Mohatta (India) Ltd (The Maria G)*,[159] Devlin J assumed without deciding that a bore tide could be weather as in weather working days. He then went on to find that time was not interrupted on other grounds.[160] In side-stepping the issue, it is clear that Devlin J did not find it an easy question to decide whether a bore tide could be weather.

4.141 However, it is submitted that an examination of the meteorological and oceanographical principles involved suggests that a bore tide or indeed any ordinary tidal

---

156. *Dampskibsselskabet Botnia A/S* v. *C P Bell & Co* (1931) 41 Ll L Rep 160, at p. 162.
157. See for example London Arbitration 7/92—LMLN 323, 21 March 1992.
158. Hamburg Arbitration—LMLN 32, 22 January 1981.
159. *Compania Crystal de Vapores* v. *Herman & Mohatta (India) Ltd (The Maria G)* [1958] 1 Lloyd's Rep 616.
160. See *ante* at para. 4.110.

phenomenon is not weather. The dictionary defines weather as related to the condition of the atmosphere.

4.142 Wind is the movement of air in the atmosphere by differences in atmospheric pressure between two localities. These differences in pressure are caused by variations in temperatures of columns of air over different places. The atmosphere is always trying to achieve a uniform pressure distribution by transfer of air from one region, where an accumulated excess of air has resulted in high pressure, to another region, where a deficiency of air has resulted in low pressure. However, because of the rotation of the earth, the winds so caused do not blow direct from areas of high to areas of low pressure but blow in a circular manner around regions of low or high pressure. The moving air exerts a drag upon the water surface with which it is in contact, causing ripples and eventually waves which, whilst they are in the area where the wind is blowing, will grow to a size determined by the wind speed, the time for which the wind has been blowing, the distance over which the wind has blown and the depth of the water. When the wind dies down or the wave train moves outside the area of its birth, it may continue to travel thousands of miles before dying away. As it does so the wave lengths increase slowly and the heights decrease. Beyond the region in which they were generated, those wave trains are known as swell. When the swell encounters shallow water it may become surf. Thus, sea waves, swell and surf are all caused directly or indirectly by the condition of the atmosphere.

4.143 On the other hand, tides, including bore tides, owe their origin to the gravitational influence of the sun and moon and therefore their effect, it is suggested, will not normally be weather unless it can be shown that this has been influenced by something which is itself weather. Thus, strong winds against a spring tide may result in short steep seas which might impede cargo operations and so come within the definition of weather because of the effect of the wind.

Causation and weather

4.144 As previously mentioned,[161] interruptions to laytime are those periods when laytime does not run because they are outside the definition of laytime, whereas exceptions to laytime are within the definition but excluded by an additional clause. Different rules on causation apply in each case.[162]

Interruptions

4.145 The most common laytime clauses which provide for weather to interrupt time are those which measure allowed laytime in terms of:

weather working days
working or running days or hours, weather permitting.

161. See *ante* at para. 4.1.
162. As illustrations of evidential problems involved in causation and the onus of proof, see London Arbitration 12/97—LMLN 464, 16 August 1997 and London Arbitration 16/97—LMLN 466, 13 September 1997.

4.146 In *Dow Chemical (Nederland) BV* v. *BP Tanker Co Ltd (The Vorras)*, Sir John Donaldson MR said at the end of his judgment[163]:

There have been attempts to classify laytime provisions as either "descriptive" or exceptive, the latter importing a causative connection with the delay. I am not sure how much this adds to clarity. *Prima facie*, any clause defining laytime is descriptive and any clause providing that time shall not count against laytime so defined . . . is exceptive. If it matters, I would classify the expression "72 running hours weather permitting" as descriptive.

In a descriptive laytime clause, such as those above, although there need not be a causative connection with the delay to the ship concerned, nevertheless there must be a causative link between the weather and the possibility of loading or discharging, as the case may be.

4.147 The question to be asked seems to be: could cargo of the type intended to be loaded or discharged be safely loaded or discharged without undue risk due to the weather conditions then prevailing at the place where the parties intended cargo operations to be carried out? In answering this question it is irrelevant whether the vessel concerned is herself at the loading or discharging point. Clearly, if the vessel is in position then evidentially it is easier to establish but if she is not in position and no similar cargo is being worked at the loading/discharging position then the question will have to be determined on a theoretical basis. In *The Vorras*, dealing with a tanker, Sir John Donaldson said[164]:

In my judgment the weather prohibited any vessel of this general type from loading and it is nothing to the point that owing to the presence of another vessel in the berth, the prohibition was not the operative cause which prevented the vessel from loading.

4.148 In the tanker trade it probably makes little difference as to what particular cargo is being carried (on this point) and hence the reference to a "vessel of this general type", because the danger is likely to come from ruptured hoses which might also lead to loss and/or contamination of cargo, whatever was being carried. In the dry trade, however, although there appears to be no direct authority, it is suggested that it is necessary to ask the question in relation to the particular cargo since weather which would affect one type of cargo will not necessarily affect another. For instance, high winds might pose a risk to container loading and rain might affect loading grain or sugar.

4.149 It should be emphasized that it is only the effect of the weather on cargo operations that is important, not the safety of the vessel at the berth. The point was put succinctly by Devlin J in *The Maria G*[165]:

. . . if the effect of weather is not to interfere with the operations of the loading and discharging, but is to render the presence of the vessel in a particular place unsafe, the time so lost is not what the parties contemplate when they are referring to weather working days.

4.150 It is also irrelevant whether any actual work was intended. It is simply a day on which the weather would have permitted work to be done, whether or not anyone availed

---

163. *Dow Chemical (Nederland) BV* v. *BP Tanker Co Ltd (The Vorras)* [1983] 1 Lloyd's Rep 579, at p. 584.

164. *Ibid.*

165. *Compania Crystal de Vapores* v. *Herman & Mohatta (India) Ltd (The Maria G)* [1958] 1 Lloyd's Rep 616, at p. 621.

themselves of the opportunity. As Pearson J said about weather in relation to weather working days[166]:

The status of a day as being a weather working day, wholly or in part or not at all, is determined solely by its own weather, and not by extraneous factors, such as the actions, intentions and plans of any person.

Exceptions

4.151 Where the reference to adverse weather being excluded is not part of the clause defining laytime but is contained in an exceptions clause, then different considerations apply. In this case what must be shown is not only that the weather was adverse but that the adverse weather was the proximate cause of the loss of loading time or discharging time, as the case may be.

4.152 In *Burnett Steamship Co Ltd* v. *Joint Danube & Black Sea Shipping Agencies*[167] the relevant clause of what was in effect a charterparty provided that "Should any time be lost whilst steamer is in a loading berth owing to work being impossible through rain . . . the amount of actual time so lost . . . to be added to the loading time . . . ". In all, the rainy periods during loading came to a total of two days. However, the shipowners argued that nevertheless no time was lost because no cargo was available for loading, an argument that was upheld by a majority in the Court of Appeal. Greer LJ put it this way[168]:

There are two things that he [the charterer] has got to prove in order to entitle him to that extension of time, and if he fails to prove either of those two things he fails to establish his right to an extension of time. He has to prove that work became impossible through rain and that in consequence of that he lost time in loading; unless he proves both those circumstances he does not bring himself within the clause.

4.153 In *Stephens* v. *Harris*,[169] "400 tons per weather working day, weather permitting" was allowed for each loading. The vessel was to load ore which was to come from five miles away but which was delayed by bad weather. The weather therefore did not affect loading but only the transit to the ship prior to loading. In these circumstances, the court held that the running of laytime was not interrupted because the weather did not affect the loading of the vessel. Commenting on this in the *Reardon Smith* case, Lord Devlin said[170]:

. . . if the weather was to be treated as if it were an excepted peril excusing work only when it was actually operating, words could, of course, be found to do it. In *Stephens* v. *Harris & Co*, the Court of Appeal held that the phrase "weather permitting" in the laytime clause had that effect.[171]

4.154 *The Camelia and the Magnolia*[172] was another "weather permitting" case, and although the Court of Appeal have now held that when this phrase is part of the laytime

---

166. *Compania Naviera Azuero SA* v. *British Oil & Cake Mills Ltd and others* [1957] 1 Lloyd's Rep 312, at p. 329.
167. *Burnett Steamship Co Ltd* v. *Joint Danube & Black Sea Shipping Agencies* (1933) 46 Ll L Rep 231.
168. *Ibid.*, at p. 234.
169. *Stephens* v. *Harris & Co* (1887) 57 LJQB 203 (CA).
170. *Reardon Smith Line Ltd* v. *Ministry of Agriculture, Fisheries and Food* [1963] 1 Lloyd's Rep 12, at p. 41.
171. In *The Vorras* [1983] 1 Lloyd's Rep 579 the Court of Appeal disagreed about the meaning of *Stephens* v. *Harris* although no doubt agreeing with the first part of this quotation.
172. *Magnolia Shipping Co Ltd of Limassol* v. *Joint Venture of the International Trading & Shipping Enterprises and Kinship Management Co Ltd of Brussels (The Camelia and the Magnolia)* [1978] 2 Lloyd's Rep 182.

clause the clause is descriptive and not exceptive, nevertheless the principles there decided may still apply to a truly exceptive clause.

4.155 The dispute in that case related to whether periods of rain, which occurred whilst the vessels were waiting for a berth, should be excluded from laytime. The relevant charter provided for a rate of discharge "per weather permitting working day" and also contained a "berth occupied" clause providing for time to count from arrival in the roads when no cargo berth was available. The judgment of Brandon J was given on the basis that this was an exclusion from laytime.[173]

4.156 The judge posed two questions to himself, asking first what was the effect of weather after the ship was in berth, and secondly what was the effect on notional laytime before the ship was in berth. Having decided in answer to the first question that time would count unless work was actually prevented by the weather, he then went on to consider the effect of the "berth occupied" clause on the second question and held on the authority of *The Darrah*[174] that where adverse weather was excluded by an additional exclusion clause and there was also a "berth occupied" or "time lost in waiting for berth" clause providing for such waiting time to count as laytime, then any time which would have been lost if the vessel had been in berth should not count as laytime. In doing so, Brandon J summed up the respective arguments that had been put forward as follows[175]:

> ... it was contended for the shipowners that since the words were words of exception they could only result in time being excluded from laytime if discharge was actually prevented by the weather. So far as notional laytime is concerned, it was impossible for discharge to be actually prevented by the weather because, the ship not being in berth, she was *ex hypothesi* not engaged in discharging. For the charterers, on the other hand, it was contended that the object of clause 6 (the berth occupied clause) was to put both the parties in the same position when a berth was not available on arrival as they would have been if a berth had been available. Accordingly, if weather would have prevented discharge if the ship had been in berth although it did not do so because she was not, allowance should be made for the time which would notionally have been lost.

He then concluded that the shipowners' argument ran counter to the whole basis on which the House of Lords had decided *The Darrah*, and held that that case applied whether or not the exception only took effect if it was causative.[176]

4.157 Although Brandon J did not say what would have been the result had there been no "berth occupied" clause, the answer probably would have been that contended for by the shipowners, namely that laytime would have continued to run because there would have been no causal connection between the weather and the failure to discharge cargo.

4.158 In *The Darrah*[177] the point at issue had been whether a waiting provision was independent of a laytime provision, which was expressed in weather working days, so that all waiting time counted without exception. In holding that this was not so, although the speeches are couched in general terms and refer to broad principles, their Lordships do not actually refer to the point considered by Brandon J in *The Camelia and the Magnolia*.[178] Indeed, it could be argued that in holding, as they did, that a "berth occupied" clause had

---

173. For the difference between exclusions and interruptions, see *ante* at para. 4.1.
174. *Aldebaran Compania Maritima SA* v. *Aussenhandel AG* [1976] 2 Lloyd's Rep 359 (HL).
175. *The Camelia and the Magnolia* [1978] 2 Lloyd's Rep 182, at p. 184.
176. *Ibid.*, at p. 185.
177. *The Darrah* [1976] 2 Lloyd's Rep 359 (HL).
178. *The Camelia and the Magnolia* [1978] 2 Lloyd's Rep 182.

no effect in a port charter where the vessel concerned was an Arrived ship, the House of Lords could not have been intending that their decision should extend to situations where adverse weather was excluded by an exceptions clause. In this latter case there is a difference because in the absence of a "berth occupied" clause adverse weather will only be excluded when the vessel concerned is in berth. Only then can loading or discharging be interrupted by weather.

4.159 Of *The Darrah*,[179] Sir John Donaldson MR said in *The Vorras*[180]:

It is authority for the proposition that a time lost clause is immaterial in a port charterparty, at least after the vessel has arrived, since in such circumstances time lost waiting for berth is laytime.

Again, it is unclear whether this was intended to be a general proposition or one confined to descriptive laytime provisions.

4.160 Until the matter is once more considered by the courts, the only authority appears to be that of Brandon J in *The Camelia and the Magnolia*.[181] In principle, there would seem to be no reason why the effect of a "berth occupied" or "time lost in waiting" provision should not be to make the effectiveness of an exceptions clause excluding bad weather depend simply on the same circumstances that would have applied had the vessel reached her berth and thus remove the windfall benefit that would otherwise accrue to the shipowner when no berth is available. Even then, as Brandon J was careful to point out,[182] periods of rain or other adverse weather will only be excluded if they have a causative effect. Thus, if no cargo was available or there was no loading or discharging for some other reason other than the weather, then laytime would still continue to run.

4.161 In *Gebr Broere BV* v. *Saras Chimica SpA*,[183] Parker J considered a number of situations which a vessel might encounter in relation to weather.

4.162 The first of these was where the vessel, having got into berth had commenced to load, ceases loading due to weather. Assuming the relevant charter to have a weather exclusion clause, then whether this was exceptive or descriptive time would cease to count. If the weather then worsened so that the vessel had for her own safety to leave the berth, then whether time should count is a question of causation. In the *Gebr Broere* case Parker J took the view that the weather, having first prevented loading and then having the added effect of forcing the vessel to leave the berth, did not cease to have the former effect after the vessel had left the berth.

4.163 However, to bring himself within such a clause, the charterer must show that the loading operation was prevented by bad weather and it was not simply that the berth had become temporarily unsafe.[184]

4.164 In the *Gebr Broere* case,[185] Parker J then considered a situation where a vessel, for her own safety, refrained from going into berth and concluded that laytime would be interrupted if the weather was such that it would both have prevented loading and required

179. *The Darrah* [1976] 2 Lloyd's Rep 359 (HL).

180. *Dow Chemical (Nederland) BV* v. *BP Tanker Co Ltd (The Vorras)* [1983] 1 Lloyd's Rep 579, at p. 584.

181. *The Camelia and the Magnolia* [1978] 2 Lloyd's Rep 182.

182. *Ibid.*, at p. 185.

183. *Gebr Broere BV* v. *Saras Chimica SpA* [1982] 2 Lloyd's Rep 436, at p. 439. Although Parker J was dealing with a "weather permitting" laytime clause which was therefore a descriptive clause, the principles are still relevant.

184. See as an illustration London Arbitration—LMLN 115, 29 March 1984, and London Arbitration 7/92—LMLN 323, 21 March 1992.

185. *Gebr Broere BV* v. *Saras Chimica SpA* [1982] 2 Lloyd's Rep 436, at p. 440.

the vessel to leave had she been in berth. It would not be interrupted if she could not for safety reasons reach her berth (assuming she was an Arrived ship) if loading would not have been interrupted by weather had she been in berth.

4.165 Laytime also would not be interrupted if the intended berth was occupied, regardless of the effect of the weather on the vessel then in berth (in the absence of "time lost waiting for berth" clause) or if an insufficiency of water prevented her getting to the berth.[186]

4.166 In one New York Arbitration,[187] the tribunal were prepared to hold that an exceptions clause that referred to "prevention or stoppage of work", was sufficiently wide as to apply not only to delays due to weather which affected discharge from the vessel had she been alongside, but also which prevented the barge into which the cargo had been discharged at anchorage from discharging at the designated berth.

Conoco weather clause

4.167 This well-known clause, often used in conjunction with Asbatankvoy charters, provides as follows:

Delays in berthing for loading or discharging and any delays after berthing which are due to weather conditions shall count as one half laytime or, if on demurrage, at one half demurrage rate.

As will be apparent, it supplements and enlarges upon the half rate demurrage storm provision in clause 8 of the printed form of the Asbatankvoy form of charter so that owners and charterer in certain circumstances share the effect of delays even where the adverse weather does not amount to a storm and where the delay occurs before the vessel goes on demurrage.

4.168 The scope of the clause has been considered in a New York arbitral decision, *Medtank Ltd* v. *Adam Maritime Corporation (The Alaska)*,[188] which provides an interesting illustration of the working of the clause.

4.169 In this case, the owners contended that the clause should be narrowly construed to apply only to delays in getting into a berth which had already been designated by the charterer in accordance with the charterer's obligation under clause 9 of the Asbatankvoy form to procure a berth reachable on arrival. The owners also argued that the clause did not apply where the charterer had not as yet met its overriding obligation to procure a cargo for the vessel.

4.170 The panel considered two different periods of delay and found as follows:

The first delay occurred before the vessel's turn to berth had arrived and before a berth had been designated and procured by the charterer. The intended berth was occupied when NOR was tendered and the *Alaska* was third in the lineup for that berth. This was an Asbatankvoy form of charter, the same form as in *The Laura Prima* [1982] 1 Lloyd's Rep 1. There the charterers could not be excused for delays "getting into" berth but that distinction was not enough to excuse the charterer from its duty to designate and procure a berth "reachable on her arrival" under clause 9.

The Conoco Weather Clause did not go far enough to change that rule. It spoke of "berthing" rather than "getting into" berth but that distinction was not enough to excuse the charterer from its duty to designate and procure a berth "reachable on her arrival" under clause 9.

186. Assuming the vessel concerned was an Arrived ship. See however *Fina Supply Ltd* v. *Shell UK Ltd (The Poitou)* [1991] 1 Lloyd's Rep 452 where there was an express exclusion clause relating to delays in berthing.

187. *Sunward Overseas SA* v. *Cargill Inc (The Chios Faith)* (NY Arb), LMLN 349, 20 March 1993.

188. *Medtank Ltd* v. *Adam Maritime Corporation (The Alaska)* (NY Arb), LMLN 452, 1 March 1997.

The second delay was in a different category. A berth had become available, but its use had been lost for reasons other than bad weather. To take advantage of the Conoco Weather Clause the charterer had to prove that the "delays in berthing" were "due to weather conditions". The burden of proof was on the charterer . . .

An adverse weather clause did not protect a charterer from demurrage if there was no cargo to load . . .

In other circumstances i.e. where a berth and a cargo were available and berthing was clearly delayed because of the weather conditions, the Conoco Weather Clause would reduce the demurrage to one-half without the need to prove the weather bad enough to be a "storm" under Clause 8.

4.171 The crux of the decision is therefore that so far as concerns delays before berthing, the berth referred to in the opening words of the clause must be one which the charterer has procured which is reachable on arrival. If a berth is not available, then the clause is of no effect to that delay.

4.172 This interpretation mirrors exactly what the House of Lords held in the *Laura Prima*[189] in relation to the meaning of "berth" in clause 9 of Part II of the Asbatankvoy form.

HOLIDAYS

4.173 As with weather, holidays may either be outside the definition of laytime and thus an interruption to laytime, or may be an exception to laytime.[190] The principal examples of the former are where laytime is expressed in "working days", "weather working days" or variants thereof.[191] As an exception, the laytime clause may, for example, after defining laytime, add the phrase "Sundays and holidays excepted". However, unlike weather, even as an exception, it is not normally necessary to show causation. To incorporate an element of causation, it would be necessary for a "holiday" exception to be expressed in some such words as "Time lost due to holidays not to count as laytime". In this case if work was done, whether at normal or overtime rates, then clearly such time would not be lost. It would perhaps raise an interesting point in causation if work could have been done in these circumstances had the charterer been prepared to pay overtime rates. It is suggested that the answer might well depend on whether at the particular port it was normal to pay overtime to continue work on such days and therefore whether the charterer's refusal was reasonable. Exceptions in relation to holidays are inserted into charterparties in favour of charterers so that time does not count on such days when they cannot, or choose not to work, except possibly in the latter case where a casual element has been included.

What is a holiday?

4.174 At first instance in *British and Mexican Shipping Co Ltd* v. *Lockett Brothers & Co Ltd*,[192] Hamilton J drew a distinction between working days and non-working days, which he described as days for play or rest. He continued:

189. *The Laura Prima* [1982] 1 Lloyd's Rep 1.
190. For the distinction between "interruptions" and "exceptions" see *ante* at para. 4.1.
191. For the meaning of these phrases, see Chapter 2 *ante*. For holidays in relation to working days, see *post* at para. 4.199.
192. *British and Mexican Shipping Co Ltd* v. *Lockett Brothers & Co Ltd* [1911] 1 KB 264, at p. 273.

I think it is immaterial whether the days for play or rest are so for secular or religious reasons, and whether they are so by the ancient authority of the Church or by the present authority of the state.

Whilst the term "non-working days" may be somewhat different from holidays, since it also includes Sundays or the equivalent, nevertheless this description would also seem appropriate to holidays.

4.175 The *Charterparty Laytime Definitions 1980*, *Voylayrules 1993* and *Baltic Code 2000* have similar definitions of the word "holiday".[193] The last of these defines it in these terms:

HOLIDAY—a day other than the normal weekly day(s) of rest or part thereof, when by local law or practice the relevant work during what would otherwise be ordinary working hours is not normally carried out.

Whether a day is a holiday is a question of fact to be decided "according to the regulations or the practice or the custom or the law applicable in the port".[194] It is also clear

that the character of the day falls to be determined by reference to conditions on land at the port and not by reference to conditions on board the ship herself, the latter being determined by the terms of the articles and the law of the flag.[195]

Regulations and law

4.176 By this is meant any ordinance made by a competent authority. Whether this includes regional and local authorities was the question in issue in *Hain Steamship Co Ltd v. Sociedad Anonima Comercial de Exportación e Importación (Louis Dreyfus & Cia Lda)*.[196] The dispute arose in Argentina. Of the two days concerned, one was an official holiday throughout the province of Buenos Aires and the other was a holiday in the town and port of San Nicolas, having been so declared by the municipal authority. By a decree of the Federal Government, the Customs and other Federal offices in the port remained open on such holidays. Rejecting the suggestion that a holiday must be shown to be universally recognized or decreed throughout the whole of the country, MacKinnon J said[197]:

With limited exceptions, such as national holidays like July 4 in the United States and, I suppose, to some extent, bank holidays in England, holidays are necessarily things which vary as to particular days in particular parts of the country . . . holidays really are a local institution and only very exceptionally a national institution.

4.177 *The Mosfield*,[198] it was successfully argued that a provision of the Louisiana State Legislature made every Saturday a holiday at the port of Lake Charles. Dismissing a submission that the legislation was only intended to govern the closing hours of banks and government and legal institutions, Donaldson J added[199]:

193. See Appendix.
194. *A/S Westfal-Larsen & Co* v. *Russo-Norwegian Transport Co Ltd* (1931) 40 Ll L Rep 259, at p. 261.
195. *The Chief Controller of Chartering of the Government of India* v. *Central Gulf Steamship Corporation (The Mosfield)* [1968] 2 Lloyd's Rep 173, at p. 178 *per* Donaldson J.
196. *Hain Steamship Co Ltd* v. *Sociedad Anonima Comercial de Exportación e Importación (Louis Dreyfus & Cia Ltda) (The Tregantle)* (1932) 43 Ll L Rep 136.
197. *Ibid.*, at p. 139.
198. *The Mosfield* [1968] 2 Lloyd's Rep 173.
199. *Ibid.*, at p. 179.

Furthermore I do not consider that it matters what is the purpose of the legislation, if the chosen method is to declare certain days to be holidays. Act 210 of 1958 of the Louisiana Legislature declares all Saturdays to be holidays in an area which includes the Port of Lake Charles and this concludes the matter.

4.178 In both these cases, the relevant days were declared to be holidays by an authority having control of both the port area and the surrounding district and the holidays concerned applied to the local community in general. In *The Mosfield*, notwithstanding the status of Saturdays as holidays, work continued in the port, although at overtime rates.

4.179 In some parts of the world, however, it is common for the local Port Trust or Dock Labour Board to declare its own list of holidays, which may or may not coincide with similar lists published by the local civic authorities. Unless such port authorities have express authority under their local laws to declare holidays, then such declarations can only be effective, if at all, by virtue of custom and practice.

4.180 In some countries with a state system, the individual states are given authority to declare their own holidays under powers from the central government. In India, for example, the Negotiable Instruments Act 1881 enables each state to issue General Orders detailing Public and Government holidays. Although this Act is primarily concerned with banking, the relevant section, section 25, is of general application and not confined to banks. Care must, however, be taken to distinguish between public and government holidays. The former are general in nature and therefore apply to charterparties as holidays by law, whereas the latter are simply days on which government offices may be closed. An illustration of the working of the Act is provided by London Arbitration 23/87[200] relating to the port of Veraval in the state of Gujarat. On the days in dispute, which were held to be holidays, the port office was closed, but cargo work went on.

4.181 In *A/S Westfal-Larsen & Co* v. *Russo-Norwegian Transport Co Ltd*,[201] the point at issue was a possible conflict between law and practice. In an effort to improve productivity, the Soviet Government introduced what it called "the uninterrupted week". This involved the abolition of the pre-existing pattern of work, including holidays, and the introduction of a continuous shift system. The decrees changing the system were published in the middle of 1929 and the dispute concerned Christmas Day and Boxing Day at the end of that year and New Year's Day 1930. On all three days, work was apparently done. Nevertheless, on the evidence before him, Wright J found that the decrees had not on the material dates been put into practice at Leningrad, the port in question, and that the workers who had worked had been paid substantial overtime so to do. He also found that at that time the traditional religious festivals and feasts had continued to be recognized. It therefore seems that if there is a conflict between law and practice then practice will prevail.

4.182 A slightly different question fell to be answered in *Hain Steamship Co Ltd* v. *Sociedad Anonima Comercial de Exportación e Importación (Louis Dreyfus & Co Ltd)*.[202] Here the question was: can a local law making it illegal to work after a certain time on specific days have the effect of turning those days into holidays? The answer given was "no". In saying this, the judge (MacKinnon J) pointed out that there was no undertaking

---

200. London Arbitration 23/87—LMLN 212, 19 December 1987.
201. *A/S Westfal-Larsen & Co* v. *Russo-Norwegian Transport Co Ltd* (1931) 40 Ll L Rep 259.
202. *Hain Steamship Co Ltd* v. *Sociedad Anonima Comercial de Exportactión e Importación (Louis Dreyfus & Co Ltd) (The Trevarrack)* (1934) 49 Ll L Rep 86.

by either the ship or charterers that they would work contrary to the local law. The law was therefore irrelevant in construing the holiday in the laytime clause.

Custom and practice

4.183 In this sense, custom means a settled and established practice of the port. The custom may itself lay down holidays, either by specifying dates or establishing a formula, or may provide for a specified organization so to do.[203] In each of these cases, the words of Kennedy J in *Sea Steamship Co Ltd* v. *Price, Walker & Co Ltd*[204] remain apposite. In that case, Kennedy J said:

In my opinion, in order to establish a mercantile custom it is necessary, not only to show that a large number of influential people at the place have agreed that it would be a good thing . . . but also that the agreement was acted upon, because, unless it is acted on, no one will challenge it . . . A custom cannot be established merely by three or four important classes of persons in a community of a port agreeing that it is desirable. It must be enforced . . .

4.184 For a holiday to arise through custom or practice, it must be one that is observed by a sufficiently large proportion of the community to have become generally accepted as such. Thus in *Z Steamship Co Ltd* v. *Amtorg, New York*, Goddard J said[205]:

If it could be shown that certain trades—I do not think one would be enough—a certain number of trades had closed their doors in Boston on Saturdays so that a large number of working people regarded Saturday as a holiday, although you might persuade somebody to work on that day, more might be said, but I do not think you could make a holiday . . . merely because of some arrangement between employers and employees in a particular trade . . .

4.185 In *Denniston & Co* v. *Zimmerman*[206] there was a clause in the charterparty that holidays, fête days and colliers' monthly holidays were not to count as lay days. Under this, the Court of Appeal held that the four days of the Welsh National Eisteddfod were both holidays and fête days for the particular district.

4.186 In London Arbitration 18/87 and 22/87,[207] 8 November (Thomas W Gleason's birthday), 31 December (New Year's Eve) and 7 January (Clarence Henry's birthday) were all held not to be holidays in the southern United States, but merely "Longshoremen's holidays", namely days agreed between the union and the employers for which overtime would be payable.

4.187 Most religious holidays will be such by custom.

Particular types of holidays

4.188 It sometimes happens that a particular charterparty does not exclude holidays in general but only a specified type of holiday. In those circumstances it is only that type of holiday which is excluded.

---

203. For example, see *post* at para. 4.195 under charterparty holidays.
204. *Sea Steamship Co Ltd* v. *Price, Walker & Co Ltd* (1903) 8 CC 292, at p. 295.
205. *Z Steamship Co Ltd* v. *Amtorg, New York* (1938) 61 Ll L Rep 97, at p. 104.
206. *Denniston & Co* v. *Zimmerman* (1894) 11 TLR 113.
207. London Arbitration 18/87 and 22/87—LMLN 209, 7 November 1987.

"General or local holidays"

4.189 This was the phrase used in *Love and Stewart Ltd* v. *Rowtor Steamship Co Ltd*,[208] a Scottish appeal to the House of Lords. The principal issue was whether the laytime allowed, which provided for a rate of discharge daily "but according to the custom of the respective ports", was a fixed or customary laytime provision and therefore whether a custom of the particular port not to work during wet weather and half of each Saturday could be proved. The House were in no doubt that it was a fixed laytime clause and Lord Sumner, who gave the principal speech, then went on to hold that a Saturday half-holiday did not come within the phrase "general or local holidays".[209] He did not, however, elucidate on what the phrase did mean or whether there was any difference from holidays *simpliciter*.

4.190 If there is any difference it probably only relates to holidays arising by custom. There might be circumstances where in a particular country a specified day was a holiday by custom generally, although in the particular locality it was usual to treat it as a working day. If the relevant clause just excluded holidays then the day in question would probably not be excluded. If, however, "general or local holidays" were excluded the opposite result might be attained.

"Legal holidays"

4.191 This phrase is most likely to appear in charters involving voyages to countries with a large number of customary holidays, some of which might affect various sections of the community differently. Its effect, therefore, is to exclude only those holidays which arise or are recognized by law and not those by custom. Legal holidays include those declared by regional and local authorities, as well as those ordained at national level.[210]

"Official and local holidays"

4.192 *Z Steamship Co Ltd* v. *Amtorg, New York*,[211] Goddard J appears to have taken the view that an official holiday is one proclaimed so to be by "Government officials or under Government powers". If by Government is meant central Government, then this would exclude holidays declared by regional and local authorities. It might be argued that where official and local are joined together that this indeed is the intention. However, in principle, it would seem more logical to give "official" a wider definition so as to include at least regional decisions.

4.193 What is clear from Goddard J's decision is that to count as an official holiday there must be a direct edict to that effect and that it will not suffice if the so-called holiday only results indirectly from an official decision. The facts of the case provide an interesting illustration. The case arose out of the discharge of coal at Boston, US.

4.194 Under a Code of Fair Competition which had the force of law by virtue of the National Recovery Act 1933 men in the coal dock industry could not be required to work more than 40 hours per week, although if work was available and they so chose, they

---

208. *Love and Stewart Ltd* v. *Rowtor Steamship Co Ltd* [1916] 2 AC 527.
209. *Ibid.*, at p. 536.
210. *Hain Steamship Co Ltd* v. *Sociedad Anonima Comercial de Exportación e Importación (Louis Dreyfus & Cia Ltda) (The Tregantle)* (1932) 43 Ll L Rep 136.
211. *Z Steamship Co Ltd* v. *Amtorg, New York* (1938) 61 Ll L Rep 97, at p. 103.

could do additional hours at overtime rates. As a result all concerned in the trade agreed that the 40 hours should be worked between Monday and Friday and any work done on Saturday would be paid for at overtime rates whether or not the basic 40-hour week had been achieved. Because this agreement was made in implementing an official requirement it was said that this made Saturday an official holiday. Although Goddard J described the point as "a very, very difficult one" and one on which he had great difficulty in making up his mind,[212] he nevertheless held that the agreement was only for the convenience of the local trade and that Saturday was not an official holiday. He also went on to hold that as only one trade was affected, it was not a local holiday.

"Charterparty holidays"

4.195 In some countries a two-tier system of holidays exists. These include India, Bangladesh, Sri Lanka and the Province of Quebec in Canada. If all such holidays were to be excepted from laytime then the laytime allowed would be artificially increased, since for the most part work continues on such holidays, although at overtime rates. For this reason a system has evolved whereby some local organization, usually the local Chamber of Commerce, declares which holidays shall count for the purpose of charterparties. These declarations are often said to have a status of being a custom of the port, and are well established. In Bombay, for instance, such declarations have been made by the Bombay Chamber of Commerce for more than 90 years.

4.196 If a charterparty specifically refers to "charterparty holidays" then only such holidays are counted against laytime. If the charter refers to "holidays" and nothing else then it is unlikely that any such limitation could be implied.

"Non-working holidays"

4.197 These words have been held to refer to those holidays where only substantial extra payment will enable loading or discharging to continue, in contrast to "working holidays" where work continues at more or less normal rates of pay, although by law or custom the days concerned are undoubtedly holidays. This was the effect of the decision of Roche J in *Panagos Lyras (Owners)* v. *Joint Danube & Black Sea Shipping Agencies of Braila*.[213] There the charter referred to a rate of loading per running day "Sundays and non-working holidays excepted". The dispute actually concerned dispatch money and centred on Good Friday, Saturday in Holy Week and the Easter Tuesday, all of which were public holidays in Galatz, the port of loading. However, on each day work proceeded as normal. Having decided that the criterion was whether any substantial extra payment was made, the matter was referred back to the arbitrator. In sending it back, the judge indicated that it might be necessary to look at payments, not only to the labourers in the hold, but to the men working at the silos or elevators, and also whether extra payment was made to the dock authorities. The judge also commented[214]:

The mere fact of some extra payment need not make all the difference, but on the other hand, if the payments were of any large amount it might make all the difference.

---

212. *Ibid.*, at p. 102.
213. *Panagos Lyras (Owners)* v. *Joint Danube & Black Sea Shipping Agencies of Braila* (1931) 40 Ll L Rep 83.
214. *Ibid.*, at p. 86.

The BIMCO calendar

4.198 Each year the Baltic and International Maritime Council publishes a calendar of the different types of holidays to be observed at various ports in the forthcoming year. This is based on reports from each of the countries concerned and is intended as a guide for BIMCO members. As such, it normally has only persuasive standing, although there is, of course, no reason why a charterparty clause should not provide for the exclusion of holidays "as specified in the BIMCO Calendar".

Holidays and working days

4.199 The question is "Are holidays and working days mutually exclusive?" or can a day be a holiday at the place of loading or discharging and yet still be classed as a working day in the port? The question is clearly one of some importance in relation to interruptions to laytime where this is expressed in working or weather working days and holidays have not been specifically excluded. However, there appears to be no clear answer, but what authority there is appears to suggest that in certain circumstances the courts may now be prepared to recognize that although a day is a holiday in the community it might nevertheless be a working day for laytime purposes.

4.200 In the early case of *Cochran* v. *Retborg*,[215] Lord Eldon said of working days:

that is a construction which excludes Sundays and holidays . . .

4.201 In *Nielsen* v. *Wait*,[216] Lord Esher took a similar line, saying:

If by the custom of the port certain days in the year are holidays, so that no work is done in that port on those days, then working days do not include those holidays . . . Therefore "working days" means days on which, at the port, according to the custom of the port, work is done in loading and unloading ships . . .

4.202 In *Nelson & Sons Ltd* v. *Nelson Line (Liverpool) Ltd (No 3)*,[217] Channell J went so far as to say that where the charterparty said "working days", the mention of Sundays and holidays would be unnecessary as those days would not be working days.

4.203 In *Reardon Smith Line Ltd* v. *Ministry of Agriculture*, Lord Devlin cited these cases with approval[218] and later in his speech went on to say[219]:

. . . the character of a day as a working day cannot be determined by inquiring whether on that day or on a part of it work was done at standard rates.

4.204 There can be no doubt that the important thing in deciding whether a particular day was a working day is to look at what was happening in the port generally. It is almost certainly taking it too far to say that if work was being done either at normal or overtime rates then it must have been a working day. As MacKinnon J said in *Hain Steamship Co Ltd* v. *Sociedad Anonima Comercial de Exportación e Importación (Louis Dreyfus & Cia Ltda) (The Tregantle)*[220]:

215. *Cochran* v. *Retberg* (1800) 3 Esp 121, at p. 123.
216. *Nielsen & Co* v. *Wait, James & Co* (1885) 16 QBD 67, at p. 71.
217. *Nelson & Sons Ltd* v. *Nelson Line (Liverpool) Ltd (No 3)* (1907) 12 CC 185, at p. 193.
218. *Reardon Smith Line Ltd* v. *Ministry of Agriculture, Fisheries and Food* [1963] 1 Lloyd's Rep 12, at pp. 38, 39.
219. *Ibid.*, at p. 42.
220. *Hain Steamship Co Ltd* v. *Sociedad Anonima Comercial de Exportación e Importación (Louis Dreyfus & Cia Ltda) (The Tregantle)* (1932) 43 Ll L Rep 136, at p. 139.

... no doubt, it is possible to get people to work on the most universally recognized holidays in London, such as bank holidays, if you pay them sufficiently to make it worth their while.

4.205 If no work is being done in the port because of a holiday, then clearly that holiday prevents it being a working day. The difficulty comes when there is a holiday in the locality of the port but the work of loading and unloading ships continues, either at normal or overtime rates. This was substantially the position in *The Mosfield*, where Donaldson J said[221]:

There was a time when a finding that a day was a working day seems to have excluded the possibility that it was a holiday ... but in modern conditions this is no longer the case ... I doubt whether holidays would feature so regularly as an exception to laytime counted in working days if holidays and working days were in fact mutually exclusive.

However, in that particular case, holidays were expressly excluded and therefore the judge's finding that the Saturdays in question were working days as well as holidays under local legislation was not strictly necessary to decide the matter.

4.206 In the *Panagos Lyras (Owners)*[222] case, work in the port continued much as normal and at normal rates. If the laytime clause, instead of providing for a rate of loading per running day with holidays excepted, had said cargo to be loaded at so much per working or weather working days, then there might well have been a finding that, notwithstanding that the disputed days were holidays by ancient custom, they were also working days.

4.207 If this argument were to be taken to its logical conclusion then no holidays, or indeed Sundays, would interrupt laytime measured in working or weather working days if the port was working, unless there was a specific exception. Since whether a day is a working day is essentially a question of fact, one way in which the courts might avoid reaching this conclusion would be to say that whilst not all holidays prevent a day being a working day, if most of the port is on holiday then it is a holiday, notwithstanding the fact that some work is being done.

4.208 Since most charters specifically exclude holidays even if laytime is measured in working or weather working days, the question may well continue to remain an academic one.

Part holidays

4.209 It sometimes happens that by local law or custom, part or half-day holidays are declared. Whether such limited periods can count as holidays appears to depend on the wording of the laytime clause. Where this is simply in terms of working or weather working days, the day must be characterized as a whole and, therefore, if work is done on part of the day, it will normally be held to be a working day.[223] Commenting on this, one London Arbitration award held[224]:

---

221. *The Chief Controller of Chartering of the Government of India* v. *Central Gulf Steamship Corporation (The Mosfield)* [1968] 2 Lloyd's Rep 173, at p. 178.
222. *The Panagos Lyras (Owners)* v. *Joint Danube & Black Sea Shipping Agencies of Braila* (1931) 40 Ll L Rep 83. For a summary of the facts of the case see *ante* at para. 4.197.
223. *Reardon Smith Line Ltd* v. *Ministry of Agriculture, Fisheries and Food* [1963] 1 Lloyd's Rep 12 (HL). See *ante* at para. 4.203.
224. London Arbitration—LMLN 10, 20 March 1980.

... The day had to be considered as a whole. Subject to any express agreement to the contrary the English law was settled. The House of Lords in *Reardon Smith* v. *Ministry of Agriculture* ... had found that on some days the hours of work may vary but this could not transform a working day into a non-working day unless it was also effective to transform it into a holiday. The fact that no work was performed after 14 00 hours because of a local half-day could not derogate from the description of a day, as a whole, as a working day. It could not be described as a holiday because work was performed up to 14 00 hours and so the whole day must score up as laytime.

4.210 On the other hand, where "holidays" are specifically excluded, there would seem no reason in principle why this should not extend to holidays of less than a full day in suitable circumstances. The definition of holiday in the *Charterparty Laytime Definitions 1980* and in the *Voylayrules 1993* and Baltic Code 2000 all[225] both specifically refer to part(s) of a day. However, in the *Reardon Smith* case, Lord Devlin said[226]:

... Sundays and holidays are days of 24 hours, which, when excepted, are taken out of the lay days. They are taken out as a whole because, as Lord Sumner said in *Love and Stewart Ltd* v. *Rowtor Steamship Co Ltd*,[227] the exception of holidays is based on days and not on parts of days.

Whilst this might arguably be put forward as supporting the proposition that, even with an express exclusion, only whole day holidays should be excepted, there are two good reasons why it should not.

4.211 The first concerns the basis on which *Love and Stewart* v. *Rowtor* was decided. In that case laytime was measured on the basis of a daily rate of loading and there was also a specific holiday exception. The particular argument concerned Saturday afternoons, which were said to be half-day holidays by local custom, a proposition rejected by the House of Lords. The leading speech was by Lord Sumner who, as Lord Devlin said, excluded all part-day holidays.[228] However, it must be remembered that at that time, parts of days were counted as whole days.[229] Thus, in the particular case, both the laytime allowed and the time used were rounded up to the next whole day. Demurrage was treated differently because the charter expressly provided for a pro rata calculation of parts of a day. The decision would not therefore necessarily be the same now.

4.212 The second reason for not putting too much weight on what Lord Devlin said is because it was said in the context of a discussion on the meaning of "working days" and therefore, if anything, it should be confined to part holidays on working days.

4.213 In a New York Arbitration case,[230] the charterers sought unsuccessfully to argue that Ramadan was a series of part holidays and that six hours each day should be deducted from laytime. The owners relied on the BIMCO Holiday Calendar for the current year, which stated:

Ramadan. Ramadan is the ninth month of the Islamic year and is rigidly observed as a thirty days' feast, during the hours of daylight by all Muslims. As a consequence labour conditions may be difficult and in any event the labourers' capacity will drop. Thus the month of Ramadan is not in itself a holiday but the first day of the following month (Shawwal) is usually a holiday often called "Id-ul-Fitr", Ramadan end of feasting ...

225. See Appendix.
226. *Reardon Smith Line Ltd* v. *Ministry of Agriculture, Fisheries and Food* [1963] 1 Lloyd's Rep 12, at p. 39.
227. *Love and Stewart Ltd* v. *Rowtor Steamship Co Ltd* [1916] 2 AC 527.
228. *Ibid.*, at p. 536.
229. See *ante* at para. 2.7.
230. New York Arbitration (*The Ultramar*), LMLN 291, 29 December 1990.

The tribunal therefore concluded that laytime continued to count as a full day during the observance of Ramadan.

Saturdays

4.214 In the absence of anything in the charterparty or local law providing specifically to the contrary, Saturday is usually a normal working day and counted as such, regardless of what local arrangements there may be over hours of work or payment of overtime.[231]

4.215 The leading case on the treatment of Saturdays with regard to laytime is *Reardon Smith Line Ltd* v. *Ministry of Agriculture*.[232] Although normally known as such, the case was in fact a consolidated appeal by a number of shipowners against the Ministry of Agriculture, Fisheries and Food, which had chartered their vessels to carry wheat from Vancouver. A strike of elevator men at five out of the seven elevators at Vancouver for nearly three months caused considerable delay. The cases are sometimes collectively known as the *Vancouver strike* cases.

4.216 One of the points considered by the House of Lords was whether Saturday in Vancouver was wholly or in part a working day. The leading speech on this point was delivered by Lord Devlin, who embarked on a wide-ranging historical analysis of the meanings of both working day and weather working day, concluding that in both cases the word "working" described the character of the day rather than the number of hours worked and that it was irrelevant to this whether work was done at standard rates. Their Lordships therefore unanimously agreed that Saturday was a working day, although it was not part of the elevator men's normal working week and only Saturday morning was part of the longshoremen's week (the longshoremen were the other trade essential to the loading of wheat). They further held that even if no one in the port worked at standard rates on Saturday afternoons, Saturday afternoon could not be treated as a non-working part of the day.

4.217 In London Arbitration 15/97,[233] charterers sought unsuccssfully to argue that every Saturday morning was a holiday at Romanian ports. Dismissing the claim, the tribunal said:

... there were two considerations which militated against the proposition that Saturday mornings should not count against laytime. The first was that in almost the whole of the Western world nowadays, Saturdays were non-working days (at least for the bulk of the population); yet they were not commonly regarded as being "holidays" in any country. The second was that the relevant charter exceptions frequently (as in the present case) pointed up a distinction between Saturdays on the one hand and holidays on the other.

To amount to a holiday, a day had to be determined as such by law or as a matter of custom . . .

4.218 In *The Mosfield*,[234] it was successfully argued that a provision of the Louisiana state legislature made every Saturday a holiday at the port of Lake Charles.

---

231. See also London Arbitration 8/95—LMLN 408, 24 June 1995.
232. *Reardon Smith Line Ltd* v. *Ministry of Agriculture, Fisheries and Food* [1963] 1 Lloyd's Rep 12 (HL).
233. London Arbitration 15/97—LMLN 465, 30 August 1997.
234. *The Mosfield* [1968] 2 Lloyd's Rep 173. See also *ante* at para. 4.177.

Overtime

4.219 Another case to consider the effect of the payment of overtime on the status of Saturdays was *Corrado Società Anonima di Navigazione* v. *Exporthleb*.[235] In this case, which concerned loading at Russian ports, Sundays and holidays were excepted. The ports in question worked a continuous working day of three eight-hour shifts. On Saturdays, however, overtime was paid for the last two hours of each shift and it was argued that these periods of overtime were in fact covered by the exception. Rejecting this argument, the judge said that the question was whether at the time concerned it was customary that work should be done. Overtime was therefore irrelevant.

Custom

4.220 In *Love and Stewart Ltd* v. *Rowtor Steamship Co Ltd*,[236] the laytime clause provided for a daily rate of cargo working "during the ordinary working hours of the respective ports, but according to the custom of the respective ports". There was also a Sundays and holidays exception.

4.221 Rejecting a suggestion that the words quoted allowed a local custom for Saturday to be counted as a half day, Lord Sumner said[237]:

The intention to have fixed lay days is clear and must prevail. Furthermore, the days which are to be excepted in computing the lay days are the subject of an express provision which is complete in itself.

He then went on to hold that a Saturday half-day holiday did not come within the holiday exception, although, as discussed in the previous section, his reason for so holding, namely that the exception only applied to whole days, may not be good law today.

4.222 It should be noted, however, that in that case the days were running days which therefore leaves open the question as to whether, where laytime is expressed in working or weather working days, it can be proved that Saturday is a holiday or non-working day by custom. Clearly, on the strength of the *Reardon Smith* case,[238] any such designation would have to apply to the whole day.

4.223 In Vancouver, at the time the *Reardon Smith* case arose, some work was regularly done on Saturdays—the longshoremen worked on Saturday mornings, without overtime, as part of their normal working week—and both they and the elevator men were prepared to work all day to get a ship out.[239] On that basis it was not and could not have been argued that Saturdays were holidays. That some days might not be holidays, and yet not working days either, appears to have been recognized by Lord Devlin when he said[240]:

But there may, of course, be days in some ports, such as the Mohammedan Friday, which are not working days and yet cannot well be described as Sundays or holidays.

---

235. *Corrado Società Anonima di Navigazione* v. *Exporthleb* (1932) 43 Ll L Rep 509.
236. *Love and Stewart Ltd* v. *Rowtor Steamship Co Ltd* [1916] 2 AC 527.
237. *Ibid.*, at p. 536, an appeal to the House of Lords from the Court of Session in Scotland. The decision was followed in England in *The Robert Dollar Co* v. *Blood, Holman & Co Ltd* (1920) 4 Ll L Rep 343, at p. 350.
238. *Reardon Smith Line Ltd* v. *Ministry of Agriculture, Fisheries and Food* [1963] 1 Lloyd's Rep 12 (HL).
239. *Ibid.*, at p. 38.
240. *Ibid.*, at p. 39. For a discussion on holidays and non-working days, see *ante* at para. 4.199.

4.224 If there was a finding of fact that work was not normally done at a particular port on Saturdays, then there would seem to be no reason not to find that such days were not working days or weather working days, as the case may be.

4.225 In *Z Steamship Co Ltd* v. *Amtorg, New York*,[241] Goddard J did not rule out the possibility of a finding that Saturdays might be a holiday by custom, provided it was observed by a sufficiently large proportion of the community, although on the facts then before him, he did not so find. To exclude Saturdays on this basis, there would, of course, have to be a provision in the charter discounting holidays.

Local law

4.226 A local law may perfectly validly turn a Saturday into a holiday, whilst keeping it a working day in the port.

4.227 In *The Mosfield*,[242] Donaldson J found on the evidence before him that a Saturday was a working, although not a regular working, day in Lake Charles, Louisiana. He continued[243]:

The adjective "regular" might signify that it was not a day upon which work was regularly done or that it was not a day on which work was done at normal rates of pay. This ambiguity is resolved by the further statement that Saturday morning is a normal overtime working day.

Although thus finding that it was a working day, he also found that an Act of the Louisiana legislature declared all Saturdays to be holidays in an area which included the port of Lake Charles. It was therefore also a holiday.

4.228 As laytime was measured in "weather working days of 24 consecutive hours" with Saturday afternoons, Sundays and holidays excepted, this meant that the whole of Saturday did not count against laytime.

4.229 The effect of a law making it illegal to work after 1 p.m. on a Saturday was the question considered by MacKinnon J in *Hain Steamship Co Ltd* v. *Sociedad Anonima Comercial de Exportación e Importación (Louis Dreyfus & Co Ltd) (The Trevarrack)*.[244] In his judgment, MacKinnon J summed up the charterers' argument as follows[245]:

. . . in the Argentine not only is Saturday afternoon after 1 p.m. a non-working time, or a holiday, but it is a compulsory holiday in the sense that by the Argentine law it is illegal to work after 1 p.m. on the Saturday. Therefore, the charterers argue that as it was illegal to work after that time, that period when it was so illegal to work must be cut out of the period of 24 hours which is to constitute a "running day".

Rejecting this argument, the judge gave two reasons. First, he said, there was no undertaking by either the ship or the charterers that they would work on Saturday afternoon contrary to the Argentine law. The second reason, the judge said, was because in *Love and Stewart Ltd* v. *Rowtor Steamship Co Ltd*[246] it had been held that Saturday

241. *Z Steamship Co Ltd* v. *Amtorg, New York* (1938) 61 Ll L Rep 97, at p. 104.
242. *The Chief Controller of Chartering of the Government of India* v. *Central Gulf Steamship Corporation (The Mosfield)* [1968] 2 Lloyd's Rep 173.
243. *Ibid.*, at p. 178.
244. *Hain Steamship Co Ltd* v. *Sociedad Anonima Comercial de Exportación e Importación (Louis Dreyfus & Co Ltd) (The Trevarrack)* (1934) 49 Ll L Rep 86.
245. *Ibid.*, at p. 88.
246. *Love and Stewart Ltd* v. *Rowtor Steamship Co Ltd* [1916] 2 AC 527.

afternoon was not included in the term "holiday" and the fact that the holiday was compelled by a local law did not affect the situation.

4.230 With respect, however, although the decision of the House of Lords in *Love and Stewart Ltd* v. *Rowtor Steamship Co Ltd* is often cited for the proposition that Saturday afternoon is not a holiday, what Lord Sumner excluded in that case was any parts of a day, i.e. anything less than a whole day.[247] In his speech, having dealt with wet days, which were also sought to be excluded, he continued[248]:

Saturday afternoons are the more plausible case of the two, but the exception in the charter[249] is clearly based on days, not on parts of days. I do not think the term extends to the latter part of a weekday, on which it is usual not to work, although we all call it and enjoy it under the name of a Saturday half-holiday. Really it is a half-day, which while it lasts, is wholly holiday, and I do not think that "general or local holidays" cover it.

However, at that time and in that case, the general practice was only to consider whole days.[250] Nowadays, of course, it is normal to consider parts of days, often down to the nearest minute, and a laytime calculation based only on whole days would look very unusual. There would therefore seem no reason today why the word "holiday", as an exclusion, should be confined to a whole day. The considerations that led to the word "working" as in "working day" describing the character of the day as a whole need not apply to the word "holiday" and there would therefore seem no good reason why holidays should be so limited. This was clearly the view of those responsible for the *Charterparty Laytime Definitions 1980*[251] where holiday is defined to include a part of a day.

4.231 If this is right, then the decision in *The Trevarrack*[252] is wrong and a half-day holiday enforced by local legislation making it illegal to work should count as such.

4.232 In *The Trevarrack*, the laytime allowed was measured in running days. If it had been in working or weather working days without a holiday exception, then although Saturday afternoon was non-working, even allowing for the above, Saturday would still count as a full day because of the need to characterize the day as a whole as working or non-working.

Saturdays today

4.233 Notwithstanding what is said above about part-day holidays in general, the courts would still in most cases be unlikely to find that Saturday was in fact a half-day holiday in a port, simply because no work was done on Saturday afternoons. That no work in the port was done would certainly make it a non-working part of the day but, to show that it was a holiday, it would probably be necessary to prove that it was a holiday for the rest of the locality, not just the port, either by law as in *The Mosfield*[253] or by custom, as suggested as a possibility in *Z Steamship Co Ltd* v. *Amtorg, New York*.[254]

---

247. See also *ante* at para. 4.211.
248. *Love and Stewart Ltd* v. *Rowtor Steamship Co Ltd* [1916] 2 AC 527, especially at p. 536.
249. "Sundays, general or local holidays".
250. See *ante* at para. 2.7.
251. See Appendix.
252. *Hain Steamship Co Ltd* v. *Sociedad Anonima Comercial de Exportación e Importación (Louis Dreyfus & Co Ltd) (The Trevarrack)* (1934) 49 Ll L Rep 86.
253. *The Chief Controller of Chartering of the Government of India* v. *Central Gulf Steamship Corporation (The Mosfield)* [1968] 2 Lloyd's Rep 173.
254. *Z Steamship Co Ltd* v. *Amtorg, New York* (1938) 61 Ll L Rep 97, at p. 104.

Baltimore form C Saturday clause

4.234 This provides as follows:

1. Notwithstanding any custom of the port to the contrary Saturday shall not count as laytime at loading and discharging port or ports where stevedoring labour and/or grain handling facilities are unavailable on Saturday or available only at overtime and/or premium rates.
2. In ports where only part of Saturday is affected by such conditions, as described under "1" above, laytime shall count until the expiration of the last straight time period.
3. Where six or more hours of work are performed at normal rates, Saturday shall count as a full layday.

4.235 The meaning of the clause was considered in *Primula Compania Naviera SA* v. *Finagrain Cie Commerciale Agricole et Financière SA (The Point Clear)*.[255] The facts of the case were as follows. The *Point Clear*, the vessel concerned, had anchored at the Hook of Holland awaiting her turn to move to the suction elevators to discharge her cargo of grain. The dispute concerned the Saturday after her arrival and whether laytime, which had previously commenced, continued to run.

4.236 At Rotterdam day and night shifts were worked on Mondays to Saturdays inclusive. On Saturdays there was between one-third and one-half of the weekday labour force available, and therefore not all of the bulk grain discharging berths could be worked. The elevator operators made a flat rate charge to their customers for weekday day and night shifts and Saturday day shifts and a higher charge was made for Saturday night shifts, although the workers concerned received increased rates of remuneration for any work outside Monday to Friday day work. However, their contracts of employment required them to work a day shift every third Saturday.

4.237 The first question that arose was whether, if the vessel was not in berth, as here, it could be said that the requisite facilities were unavailable. In holding that they were available, Donaldson J said that the clause must be applied objectively to Rotterdam, and not subjectively to the vessel—the fact that the vessel was not in berth was therefore irrelevant.

4.238 The next question to be considered was whether the fact that only certain of the berths were being worked because of the reduced workforce meant that labour and facilities were unavailable in Rotterdam generally. In answering this question "no", Donaldson J pointed out that the clause used a negative formula of facilities and labour being unavailable on Saturdays. He continued[256]:

De minimis apart, this must mean wholly unavailable. Otherwise, the clause would have spoken of "partially unavailable" or "not wholly available" or "subject to a reduction in availability". On this particular Saturday, like other Saturdays, there was a substantial reduction in the availability of labour and grain discharging facilities, but neither was "unavailable".

4.239 The last question to be dealt with was whether the labour and facilities were only available at premium rates. It was common ground that what was in question was the Saturday day and not the Saturday night shift. In finding that the clause was clear, the judge said that the reference to overtime or premium rates must be to the charges paid by the customers to those who supplied the facilities and labour and therefore in Rotterdam they were not only available at such rates.

255. *Primula Compania Naviera SA* v. *Finagrain Cie Commerciale Agricole et Financière SA (The Point Clear)* [1975] 2 Lloyd's Rep 243.
256. *Ibid.*, at p. 248.

Weekend clause

4.240 Charters which exclude Sundays and holidays commonly also provide for periods to be excepted before and after. A typical clause would be[257]:

Time shall not count between noon on Saturday and 8 am on Monday, nor between 5 pm (noon if Saturday) on the last working day preceding a holiday and 8 am on the first working day thereafter.

4.241 Problems sometimes arise as to the application of such a clause to Friday in Moslem countries.[258] Although there would appear to be no specific authority on the point, it is suggested that the clause must be read as it stands and it would not be permissible to substitute Friday for Saturday. This means that where laytime is measured in (weather) working days, time would not count on Friday, because it is not a working day, and would also be suspended from noon Saturday until Monday morning. This may not be particularly fair but it is for the parties to provide for it if they envisage the situation.

4.242 In London Arbitration 6/91,[259] an unsuccessful attempt was made to assert that not only were weekends excluded but also from 5 p.m. each day to 8 a.m. the following morning on each working day.

4.243 In London Arbitration 7/97,[260] the clause in question read:

Vessel to be discharged at the rate of . . . Saturdays Afternoon, Sundays and Holidays excepted, even if used.

Time from 1700 hrs Saturday or day preceding a Holiday to 0800 hrs Monday or day following a Holiday not to count as laytime, even if used.

The issue was whether time between 12 00 and 17 00 on a Saturday should count. In the words of the *Lloyd's Maritime Law Newsletter*:

The tribunal considered that the phrase "Saturdays Afternoon" itself was a little strange. The tribunal was more accustomed to seeing "Saturdays after noon", and had those words appeared in the present charter it would perhaps have been arguable that there was a conflict between the two parts of the clause. Reading the clause as a whole, the parties' intention must be taken to have been that time should count until 1700 on Saturdays as well as on days preceding holidays, but not thereafter even if used. If there was ambiguity it had to be resolved against the charterers.

Working in excepted periods

4.244 This may arise in two sets of circumstances:
  A. Where provided for.
  B. Where not provided for.

Where provided for

4.245 The most common way of providing for laytime to count when work takes place in excepted periods is by the addition of the words "unless used" or "unless used, in which event only actual time used to count". The latter phrase clearly presents no difficulties since it spells out exactly what time is to count and it matters not how laytime

257. London Arbitration 21/87—LMLN 209, 7 November 1987.
258. For the treatment of Ramadan in Moslem countries see *ante* at para. 4.213. See also *Liquid Bulk Tanker Services Inc* v. *The Embassy of Bangladesh (The Westport Clipper)* (NY Arb), LMLN 360, 21 August 1993.
259. London Arbitration 6/91—LMLN 300, 4 May 1991.
260. London Arbitration 7/97—LMLN 459, 7 June 1997.

is expressed, whether in running hours, working days or weather working days. In each case the actual time used counts against laytime.

4.246 If, however, only the words "unless used" are included, it is sometimes argued that if any time on a particular day is used, then the whole day should count against laytime. Presumably this argument goes back to the days when, if any work was done on a particular day, then the whole day was counted against laytime.[261] Alternatively, it may be suggested that the words themselves mean that if any time is used then the day counts as a day of the type which the charter provides as lay days.

4.247 However, these days it is usual to work in fractions of days or even minutes and therefore it is suggested that the better view is that even if only the words "unless used" are included that only actual time used should count. Some support for this view can be gained from the *Charterparty Laytime Definitions 1980*,[262] which provide that:

"UNLESS USED" means that if work is carried out during the excepted days the actual hours of work only count as laytime.

4.248 In a similar vein, the *Voylayrules 1993* provide:

"UNLESS USED" (UU) shall mean that if laytime has commenced but loading or discharging is carried out during periods excepted from it, such time shall count.

4.249 More powerful support for the proposition that the actual time used should count is, however, contained in *Sofial SA* v. *Ove Skou Rederi (The Helle Skou)*,[263] another decision of Donaldson J. In that case, the relevant charter excluded time between 17 00 on Fridays until 08 00 on the following Monday, "unless used". In fact, some work was done on the Saturday in question, but about half of the time planned to be used was lost by rain. The owners argued that the whole of the weekend should count, whilst the charterers contended that only the period in which work was possible should be allowed against laytime. Neither side therefore actually argued that the whole of Saturday should count.

4.250 On the basis of the arguments then before him, Donaldson J decided that the charterers were right and only the time actually used should count. He concluded[264]:

The fallacy of the owners' argument lies in regarding time between 17 00 hours on a Friday and 08 00 hours on the following Monday as an indivisible period of time which is either used or not used. The basic rule, which is set out in the first sentence [of the laytime clause] is that laytime is calculated by aggregating individual moments of weather working time. The laytime clock ticks only so long as each succeeding moment can properly be described as weather working time. Between 17 00 hours on Fridays and 08 00 hours on Mondays, more than weather working time is required to make the clock tick. In addition, the weather working time has to be used, and it is only so long as it is used that the laytime clock will continue to tick.

Presumably in referring to weather working time, the judge meant all time spent working whether or not the day was a working day so that had work continued on Sunday time would have counted in the same way.

---

261. See *ante* at para. 2.8.
262. A similar definition to the *Voylayrules 1993* definition appears in *Baltic Code 2000*. See Appendix.
263. *Sofial SA* v. *Ove Skou Rederi (The Helle Skou)* [1976] 2 Lloyd's Rep 205.
264. *Ibid.*, at p. 214.

Where not provided for

4.251 After some initial uncertainty, it is now clear that the mere fact of work being carried out in excepted periods is insufficient to vary the express terms of a charterparty so as to allow time to count when no clause similar to those described above is included.

4.252 The first English[265] case in which this point was considered appears to be the *Brankelow Steamship Co Ltd* v. *Lamport & Holt*,[266] a decision of Lord Russell of Killowen CJ. In this case, Sundays were excepted, but nevertheless at the instance of the charterers, cargo was loaded throughout the day. In these circumstances, the judge concluded:

when a full day is occupied in loading by the charterers on the one hand, who were not bound to load, and in the receipt of cargo by the ship which was not bound to receive, the fair inference is that both parties agreed to treat that as a working day.

4.253 The next case to consider the question was *Houlder* v. *Weir*[267] where Channell J found that whether time should count depended upon the terms (if any) upon which permission to work was given. In that case the arbitrator had found that the terms were that Sundays upon which work was done would not count as laytime but the charterers would meet any extra expense. Upholding the arbitrator's findings, the judge commented that he was inclined to think that time would also not have counted if there had been no express agreement but the ship had simply assented to the work proceeding.

4.254 In *Houlder* v. *Weir*, one of the points in issue was whether the master had any authority to make the agreement he did concerning the terms on which work should proceed on the Sundays in question. However, in *Nelson & Sons Ltd* v. *Nelson Line (Liverpool) Ltd (No 3)*,[268] having referred to his earlier decision, Channell J said that whilst he felt that was correct on the facts of the case, nevertheless he was now prepared to accept that a master could agree on what basis as to laytime that work should be done in excepted periods. In the particular case he was then considering, he found there was no express agreement but concluded that the proper inference was that the parties meant to treat the excepted period as a working day. This decision at first instance was followed in *Whittall & Co* v. *Rahtkens Shipping Co Ltd*[269] by Bray J.

4.255 The Court of Appeal[270] then affirmed Channell J's judgment in *Nelson & Sons Ltd* v. *Nelson Line (Liverpool) Ltd (No 3)*, but on further appeal to the House of Lords, this was reversed. Lord Loreburn LC, giving his reasons, said[271]:

In my view it is a question, not of law, but of fact, whether or not there was an agreement varying the terms of the charterparty and providing that the holidays in question should count as lay days. I am unable to see any evidence of such an agreement.

---

265. The earlier Scottish case of *Holman & Sons* v. *Peruvian Nitrate Co* (1878) 5 Ct of Sess Cas (4th series) 657 had concluded that where the parties work on a Sunday or holiday such day is a working day.

266. The case is unreported but a note of part of the judgment dealing with this point is printed as a footnote to the first instance decision of Channell J in *Nelson & Sons Ltd* v. *Nelson Line (Liverpool) Ltd (No 3)* (1907) 12 CC 185, at p. 189. The case of *Brankelow Steamship Co Ltd* v. *Lamport & Holt* was heard some ten years earlier on 17 February 1897.

267. *Houlder* v. *Weir* (1905) 10 CC 228, at p. 235.

268. *Nelson & Sons Ltd* v. *Nelson Line (Liverpool) Ltd (No 3)* (1907) 12 CC 185, at p. 191.

269. *Whittall & Co* v. *Rahtkens Shipping Co Ltd* (1907) 12 CC 226.

270. *Nelson & Sons Ltd* v. *Nelson Line (Liverpool) Ltd (No 3)* [1907] 2 KB 705 (CA).

271. *Nelson & Sons Ltd* v. *Nelson Line (Liverpool) Ltd (No 3)* (1908) 13 CC 235, at p. 240 (HL).

4.256 In *Pteroti Compania Naviera SA* v. *National Coal Board*,[272] Diplock J considered the not dissimilar situation of work commencing before the time provided for in the laytime commencement clause. Having reviewed the evidence, the judge continued[273]:

> ... I draw attention to the decision in the House of Lords in *James Nelson & Sons Ltd* v. *Nelson Line (Liverpool) Ltd* ... and to a dissenting judgment of Lord Justice Fletcher Moulton (as he then was) in the Court of Appeal in the same case ..., which points out the principles on which the court should be prepared to infer agreements of that kind between the parties, and contains a warning against an easy inference of such agreements. I can see no ground whatsoever on which I could infer an agreement here that, because the charterers started to unload, and the shipowners' servants assisted in doing so, at 2.30 in the morning, there was an agreement between the parties that laytime should start then instead of at the time provided for (in my view) on the plain construction of clause 8.

4.257 It is clear, therefore, that in the absence of an express agreement varying the terms of the charter, the courts will be slow to infer such an agreement. Certainly more would be required than the work being done. Although the making of such an agreement may well be within the authority of the master, particularly if it is ratified by the shipowner, the point at issue is more likely to be whether the charterers' servants or agents had such a power and this, in turn, will probably depend on general principles of agency.

4.258 It should perhaps be noted that the *Voylayrules 1993* provide as follows:

"EXCEPTED" or "EXCLUDED" shall mean that the days specified do not count as laytime even if loading or discharging is carried out on them.

The *Charterparty Laytime Definitions 1980* and *Baltic Code 2000* have similar definitions.[274]

⌐STRIKES⌐

4.259 The exclusion of "strikes" from laytime is probably one of the most common exceptions to be found in fixed laytime charterparties and this may well explain why there is such a proliferation of cases on the subject. The most common strike clauses are the Centrocon strike clause, derived from the River Plate Charterparty 1914 and the Gencon strike clause from the Uniform General Charter (Gencon). The wording of the latter is the same in both 1922 and 1976 revisions. Both of these strike clauses will be considered.[275]

4.260 There are, however, certain broad principles applicable to strike clauses generally, and these will be first considered. Whether they apply to a specific clause will, of course, depend on the wording of that clause.

---

272. *Pteroti Compania Naviera SA* v. *National Coal Board* [1958] 1 Lloyd's Rep 245. See also *Liquid Bulk Tanker Services Inc* v. *The Embassy of Bangladesh (The Westport Clipper)* (NY Arb), LMLN 360, 21 August 1993.
273. [1958] 1 Lloyd's Rep 245, at p. 249.
274. See Appendix.
275. See *post* at para. 4.312 and para. 4.346.

Meaning of "strike"

4.261 This is now usually given a wide meaning to include most forms of disruption of work by employees, regardless of the cause or motive behind the interruption to work.[276] However, it still seems to be an essential requirement that the action taken in withdrawing their labour is a concerted one by a body of people. A refusal to work by one person is probably not a strike but how many people must act together appears not to have been decided. The number is probably very low and may even be as low as two.

4.262 In the nineteenth century, a narrower interpretation was given to the word "strike", confining its meaning to action related to wages. Thus, in *King* v. *Parker*,[277] Kelly CB held that a strike meant a refusal by the whole body of workers to work because the employers had refused an increase in wages or because the workers had refused to accept a diminution of wages, a not uncommon thing at that time. In a similar vein, Lord Coleridge CJ commented in *Stephens* v. *Harris & Co*[278]:

When one hears of persons striking, it does not mean a refusal to work because the weather happens to be hot, but a standing out for higher wages.

In that case, the courts held that "strikes" and "striking work" did not cover a stoppage of work by miners through fear of catching cholera. In *Re Richardson and M Samuel & Co*,[279] Smith LJ suggested that the words "strikes and lockouts" were confined to trade disputes.

4.263 However, in *Williams Brothers (Hull) Ltd* v. *Naamlooze Vennootschap W H Berghuys Kolenhandel*, Sankey J refused to follow earlier definitions of strike. The facts of the case were that the crew of a Dutch ship had in 1915 refused to sail from Hull because of a German threat to sink neutral shipping, Holland being at the time neutral. The shipowners sought to take advantage of a strike exception clause. In upholding their right to do so, the judge said[280]:

A strike does not depend merely upon the question of wages. At the same time, I do not think it would be possible to say the abstention of a workman from mere fear to do a particular thing or perform a particular contract would necessarily constitute a strike. I think the true definition of the word "strike", which I do not say is exhaustive, is a general concerted refusal by workmen to work in consequence of an alleged grievance.

4.264 In *Tabb & Burletson* v. *Briton Ferry Works Ltd*,[281] Greer J held that the term "strike" extended to a partial strike where workmen refused to work night shifts in an

276. A more specific definition of "strike" is sometimes recognized by English law. Thus, in the field of industrial relations, paragraph 11 of Schedule 1 of the Contracts of Employment Act 1963 defined strike, for the purposes of that Act, as follows: "the cessation of work by a body of persons employed acting in combination, or a concerted refusal or a refusal under a common understanding of any number of persons employed to continue to work for an employer in consequence of a dispute, done as a means of compelling their employer or any person or body of persons employed, or to aid other employees in compelling their employer or any person or body of persons employed, to accept or not to accept terms or conditions of or affecting employment." This is now in section 235(5) of the Employment Rights Act 1996. See also section 246 of the Trades Union and Labour Relations (Consolidation) Act 1992.
277. *King* v. *Parker* (1876) 34 LT 887, at p. 889.
278. *Stephens* v. *Harris & Co* (1887) 56 LJQB 516, at p. 517. Affirmed by the Court of Appeal at (1887) 57 LJQB 203.
279. *Re Richardson and M Samuel & Co* (1897) 3 CC 79, at p. 85.
280. *Williams Brothers (Hull) Ltd* v. *Naamlooze Vennootschap W H Berghuys Kolenhandel* (1915) 21 CC 253, at p. 257.
281. *Tabb & Burletson* v. *Briton Ferry Works Ltd* (1921) 6 Ll L Rep 181.

effort to force an improved minimum wage, although the day shift functioned as normal. In the not dissimilar case of *Naamlooze Vennootschap A C Lensen's Stoomvaart Maatschappij* v. *Muller & Co (London) Ltd*,[282] Roche J was prepared to hold that a refusal to work overtime by crane drivers and stevedores was at least analogous to a strike and therefore within a clause excluding time lost by any other similar cause to those listed.

4.265 The question of whether a failure to work for part of the day could amount to a strike was also considered in *Tramp Shipping Corporation* v. *Greenwich Marine Inc (The New Horizon)*, a decision of the Court of Appeal.[283] The case concerned a refusal by dock workers at St Nazaire to work night shifts in action designed to improve their conditions. Day shifts continued as usual. In so acting, the dock workers were not in breach of their contracts of employment, although it was customary for a 24-hour shift pattern to be worked. At first instance,[284] despite this and despite the refusal to work being limited only to a portion of the day, Ackner J held that this was a strike. On appeal, the Court of Appeal upheld his decision with Lord Denning MR giving his own definition of a strike in these terms[285]:

I think a strike is a concerted stoppage of work by men with a view to improving their wages or conditions, or giving vent to a grievance or making a protest about something or other, or supporting or sympathizing with other workmen in such endeavour. It is distinct from a stoppage which is brought about by an external event such as a bomb scare or by apprehension of danger.

On the case in question, he continued:

They were not in breach of contract. But it is none the less a strike. Many a strike takes place after a lawful notice; but it is still a strike. It was discontinuous. At work during the day-time, off work at night. But a strike need not be continuous. It can be discontinuous and the periods may be added up.

4.266 The *Voylayrules 1993* provide the following definition of strike[286]:

"STRIKE" shall mean a concerted industrial action by workmen causing a complete stoppage of their work which directly interferes with the working of the vessel. Refusal to work overtime, go-slow or working to rule and comparable actions not causing a complete stoppage shall not be considered a strike. A strike shall be understood to exclude its consequences when it has ended, such as congestion in the port or effects upon the means of transportation bringing or taking the cargo to or from the port.

The question as to whether an overtime ban amounts to a strike is not an easy one. The definition above is probably correct in so far as it purports to say that a refusal to work overtime which does not cause a complete stoppage is not a strike. However, if the effect of the overtime ban is to cause a complete stoppage, albeit for only certain hours each day, then on the authority of the *New Horizon*,[287] it probably is a strike. The key question is whether the industrial action results at any time in a complete cessation of work.

---

282. *Naamlooze Vennootschap A C Lensen's Stoomvaart Maatschappij* v. *Muller & Co (London) Ltd* (1921) 7 Ll L Rep 248.

283. *Tramp Shipping Corporation* v. *Greenwich Marine Inc (The New Horizon)* [1975] 2 Lloyd's Rep 314 (CA).

284. *Tramp Shipping Corporation* v. *Greenwich Marine Inc (The New Horizon)* [1974] 2 Lloyd's Rep 210.

285. *Tramp Shipping Corporation* v. *Greenwich Marine Inc (The New Horizon)* [1975] 2 Lloyd's Rep 314, at p. 317.

286. A similar definition appears in *Baltic Code 2000*. See Appendix.

287. *Tramp Shipping Corporation* v. *Greenwich Marine Inc (The New Horizon)* [1974] 2 Lloyd's Rep 210; [1975] 2 Lloyd's Rep 314 (CA).

4.267 In the earlier case of *Yewglen (Owners)* v. *Helical Bar & Engineering Co*,[288] where the exceptions clause covered "strikes, lock-outs, and employment disputes", the presiding judge in the Mayor's and City of London Court held that a "go-slow" came within the clause. Whilst there can be no doubt that such action does amount to time lost by an employment dispute, it is perhaps doubtful whether the time so lost could also be referred to as time lost due to a strike. It is suggested that to come within the term "strike", there must be a cessation of work, although this need not be continuous, nor need it be for the whole of each day. It might, however, be excepted where the exclusion clause covers not only strikes "but any other cause outside the control of charterers" as well.

4.268 As indicated by Lord Denning in *The New Horizon*[289] above, the dispute over which the strike has arisen need not be confined to ones between an employer and his employees, but may be in support of other wider causes. The term "sympathetic strike" is sometimes used to describe such matters.

4.269 An early case in which this point arose was *Seeberg* v. *Russian Wood Agency*, a decision of MacKinnon J, as he then was. The case concerned a strike of stevedores at Leningrad. The strike was directed only against Latvian ships, the remainder of the port was working normally. On this, the judge commented[290]:

... that is the curious incident of this strike, work was going on in this port and ships of many nationalities were being loaded with all due diligence, but the stevedores did not in fact load any cargo on Latvian ships, and it was said that it was a strike in sympathy with some labour grievance of some alleged unions or other workers on or connected with Latvian ships in Latvian and other ports. That was the nature of the strike.

The shipowners argued that, since effectively the stevedores and the shippers were both controlled by the Russian Government, the shippers could have taken steps to end the strike. However, on the evidence, this was rejected by the judge, who found it was a properly declared strike within the meaning of the strike clause.

4.270 A more recent case involving sympathetic strike action was *J Vermaas' Scheepvaartbedrijf NV* v. *Association Technique de L'Importation Charbonnière (The Laga)*.[291] In this case, the relevant laytime clause excluded "existing strikes". Shortly after the *Laga*'s arrival at Nantes with a cargo of coal, port labour refused to handle coal ships, thereby hoping to assist French miners who were on strike. Other ships were handled normally. Having reviewed the nineteenth century authorities, McNair J continued[292]:

Strikes in every sense of the word occur today which are not concerned directly with wages. They are concerned, for instance, with working conditions; and so I think one has got to bear in mind that the meaning of the term "strike" must change with the progress (if that is the right word) of industrial history and it may have a different meaning today from the meaning given to it a century ago.

Later in his judgment, having found there was no grievance between the strikers and their employers, the judge said[293]:

288. *Yewglen (Owners)* v. *Helical Bar and Engineering Co* (1926) 25 Ll L Rep 170.
289. *Tramp Shipping Corporation* v. *Greenwich Marine Inc (The New Horizon)* [1975] 2 Lloyd's Rep 314, at p. 317.
290. *Seeberg* v. *Russian Wood Agency Ltd* (1934) 50 Ll L Rep 146, at p. 149.
291. *J Vermaas' Scheepvaartbedrijf NV* v. *Association Technique de L'Importation Charbonnière (The Laga)* [1966] 1 Lloyd's Rep 582.
292. *Ibid.*, at p. 590.
293. *Ibid.*, at p. 591.

... the word "strike" is a perfectly good, appropriate word to use to cover a sympathetic strike and a general strike and there is no need for it today to have any ingredient of grievance between those who are refusing to work and their employers.

Dealing with the meaning of "existing" in the exceptions clause, he held that it had been inserted to limit time lost to the actual period of a strike, excluding any consequential delays.

Causation

4.271 To take advantage of a strike clause, it will normally be necessary to show causation between the strike and any loss of time. This requirement usually arises from the wording of the strike clause itself. Thus, the Centrocon strike clause has as its opening words, "If the cargo cannot be loaded by reason of ... a strike"[294] and the Asbatankvoy form of charterparty at clause 19 states that " ... neither the Vessel nor Master ... shall ... be responsible for any ... delay ... arising or resulting from ... strike".

4.272 The clauses quoted above also illustrate the two types of strike exclusion clauses that exist, namely clauses specifically referring to loading and discharging of cargo, and secondly, more widely drawn clauses, usually referred to as general exception clauses. Commenting on the latter type, and indeed the general exceptions clause in an Asbatankvoy or Exxonvoy 69 charter, Lloyd J said in *Sametiet M/T Johs Stove* v. *Istanbul Petrol Rafinerisi A/S (The Johs Stove)*[295]:

... a general exceptions clause, such as clause 19, will not normally be read as applying to provisions for laytime and demurrage, unless the language is very precise and clear.

The need to prove causation was emphasized in *Reardon Smith Line Ltd* v. *Ministry of Agriculture* (the *Vancouver strike* cases) in the Court of Appeal by Sellers LJ when he said[296]:

I would agree with Mr Justice McNair[297] that the decision[298] established and applies the principle that the mere existence of strike is not sufficient; it must have some causative effect upon the operations of the particular ship concerned.

4.273 Whilst the extent of any particular clause must always depend on its particular wording, as does the causation necessary in any particular case, nevertheless there are certain general aspects which can be considered under the following subheadings:
    A. Provision of cargo
    B. Congestion and consequential delays
    C. Duty to lessen effect
    D. Length of delay.

---

294. See *post* at para. 4.312.
295. *Sametiet M/T Johs Stove* v. *Istanbul Petrol Rafinerisi A/S (The Johs Stove)* [1984] 1 Lloyd's Rep 38, at p. 41.
296. *Reardon Smith Line Ltd* v. *Ministry of Agriculture, Fisheries and Food* [1961] 1 Lloyd's Rep 385, at p. 402.
297. At first instance: [1959] 2 Lloyd's Rep 229. The decisions of the lower courts were later upheld by the House of Lords: [1963] 1 Lloyd's Rep 12.
298. The decision referred to was that of the House of Lords in *Central Argentine Railway Ltd* v. *Marwood* [1915] AC 981.

A. Provision of cargo

4.274 The charterer's duty to have the cargo at the loading place ready for shipment at the right time is normally an absolute one and a strike exceptions clause will only apply to protect a charterer who has his cargo ready at the port of loading. If the cause of the delay lay in getting the cargo to the port of loading, then unless the exceptions clause is clearly worded to include this, it will be ineffective.[299]

4.275 The language of Lord Dunedin in *Arden Steamship Co* v. *Mathwin & Son* puts it very clearly[300]:

> ... the excuse must be very clearly expressed in the charter, because, unless this is very clearly expressed, the duty is, as I have phrased it, an absolute duty ... It is amply settled by authority that loading is one thing and providing a cargo is another; and an accident which may prevent a cargo coming forward is not to be construed as an accident which delays the loading, although of course, unless the cargo is forward the loading cannot go on.

4.276 Thus, in *H A Brightman & Co* v. *Bunge y Born*[301] there was a "work to rule" on one of five railways serving the port of Rosario, the port of loading, and this caused a delay in getting cargo to Rosario. The relevant charterparty excluded not only strikes but obstructions on the railways, which this was held to be in arbitration proceedings. Whilst doubting this conclusion, the Court of Appeal and the House of Lords held that nevertheless the only obstructions that could be relevant would be any which might occur on the port railway system.

B. Congestion and consequential delays

4.277 A common source of conflict between owners and charterers is where delay occurs to a vessel as a result of berth congestion following the end of a strike. Whether such consequential delays are excluded by the terms of a strike clause will, as usual, depend on the wording of the particular clause concerned. Also, it will often be a question of fact whether particular circumstances come within a specified clause. The cases that follow can only therefore be considered as guidance.

WHERE CONSEQUENTIAL DELAY ALLOWED

4.278 In *Leonis Steamship Co Ltd* v. *Joseph Rank Ltd (No 2)*,[302] the relevant clause provided: "If the cargo cannot be loaded by reason of ... any dispute between masters and men, occasioning a strike of railway employees or other labour connected with the working, loading or delivery of the cargo proved to be intended for the steamer ... , the time lost not to be counted as part of the lay days ... " A strike amongst railway men, which had ended before the vessel's arrival, had caused congestion on the railway resulting in a delay in delivery of the vessel's cargo. On these facts Bigham J held that the delay in transit of the cargo was covered by the exclusion clause.

299. *Grant* v. *Coverdale* (1884) 9 App Cas 470 and *Arden Steamship Co* v. *Andrew Weir & Co* [1905] AC 501.
300. *Arden Steamship Co* v. *Mathwin & Son*, 1912 SC 215.
301. *H A Brightman & Co* v. *Bunge y Born* (1924) 19 Ll L Rep 384 (CA), (1925) 22 Ll L Rep 395 (HL).
302. *Leonis Steamship Co Ltd* v. *Joseph Rank Ltd (No 2)* (1908) 13 CC 161. The strike clause also excluded time lost due to "obstructions ... in the docks or other loading places" and Bigham J also held that port congestion amounted to such an obstruction. On appeal, his judgment was affirmed on both points by the Court of Appeal (1908) 13 CC 295.

4.279 In the Scottish case of *Moor Line Ltd* v. *Distillers Co Ltd*, Lord Salvesen commented[303]:

> ... It is according to the good sense, and, I think, also according to the strict language of the contract, that in the case of delay arising as a consequence of a strike which has terminated, but the effects of which on the rate of discharge still continue, that to the extent that that delay is attributable, not to want of reasonable diligence on the part of the receiver, but to the after-effects of a strike or lock-out, he shall not be answerable for any delay . . .

4.280 In the more recent case of *The Johs Stove*, the arbitrators had found that the vessel had been delayed by congestion, but that this was due to the after-effects of a strike. The general exclusion clause excluded delay or failure in performing the charter "arising or resulting from . . . strikes". Although Lloyd J found that this did not excuse a failure by the charterers to nominate a berth "reachable on arrival", it does appear that he was prepared to accept the charterers' submission that a consequence does not have to be the immediate consequence of a particular cause in order to be said to arise or result from that cause.[304]

WHEN CONSEQUENTIAL DELAY NOT ALLOWED

4.281 The dispute that arose in *Shamrock Steamship Co Ltd* v. *Storey & Co* concerned a vessel due to load coal at Grimsby. However, at that time there was a coal strike affecting the South Wales collieries, which resulted in an accumulation of shipping at Grimsby, thereby delaying the vessel getting into berth. One of the arguments put forward concerned an exceptions clause in the charter excluding "commotions by keelmen, pitmen, or any hands striking work . . . or other acts or causes beyond the freighter's control which may prevent or delay the loading of the ship". Rejecting the submission that this could excuse the delay, Bigham J said[305]:

> It was admitted that there was no strike or interference with work at the collieries from which the defendants' coal was being procured, and the fact that the Welsh coal strike may have caused an unusual number of ships to seek cargoes at Grimsby has, in my view, no more to do with the case than if the same result had followed from a strike in German or Australian or Japanese collieries. The glut in shipping cannot, I think, be brought within the fair meaning of the particular or the general words of the exception.

However, in the Court of Appeal, Lord Russell of Killowen CJ, having decided the case on an alternative basis found by Bigham J,[306] commented that on the strike argument he would require further discussion before accepting the view of the court below.[307]

4.282 The Scottish case of *Westoll* v. *Lindsay*[308] concerned the after-effects of a strike of dock workers at Leith, the charter there providing that if cargo could not be loaded or discharged because of certain causes which included a strike of any essential workmen, "the days shall not count" during the continuance of the cause. The vessel concerned, the *Gladys Royle*, arrived seven days after the strike ended but did not get into berth until

---

303. *Moor Line Ltd* v. *Distillers Co Ltd*, 1912 SC 514, at p. 521.
304. *Sametiet M/T Johs Stove* v. *Istanbul Petrol Rafinerisi A/S (The Johs Stove)* [1984] 1 Lloyd's Rep 38, at p. 40.
305. *Shamrock Steamship Co Ltd* v. *Storey & Co* (1898) 4 CC 80, at p. 82.
306. Namely, that under terms of "the usual colliery guarantee" in use at Grimsby, time for loading did not begin to run until the ship was under the tip.
307. *Shamrock Steamship Co Ltd* v. *Storey & Co* (1899) 5 CC 21, at p. 24 (CA).
308. *Westoll* v. *Lindsay* (1916) Sess Cas 782.

some 11 days after she was ready to discharge. Lord Strathclyde, the Lord President, in holding the exclusion clause inapplicable, said[309]:

> The strike of the dock labourers did not, therefore, prevent the discharge of the *Gladys Royle*, but it did prevent the discharge and, it may be, the loading, of other vessels which arrived before her at the port, and were berthed before her but later than they otherwise would have been on account of the strike which delayed them. In short, there was a sufficiency of men essential to the discharge at the port, but an insufficiency of berths.[310]

4.283 Similarly, it seems that in both the Centrocon and Gencon strike exception clauses, where the strike ends prior to when time would otherwise commence, then any delay caused by the after effects of the strike is outside their strike provisions, although in the case of the Centrocon clause it may amount to an "obstruction".[311]

4.284 In *Union of India* v. *Compania Naviera Aeolus SA (The Spalmatori)*, Lord Reid said[312] that it was clear that the first part of the Centrocon strike clause did not apply to time lost except when the strike, etc., was continuing. He also suggested (without deciding) that the third part of the clause might cover delays after the end of the strike providing the strike was operative during the running of laytime. Lords Hodson and Guest, the remainder of the majority, also agreed that Part III was subject to Part I.

4.285 In *Salamis Shipping (Panama) SA* v. *Edm Van Meerbeck SA (The Onisilos)*, Donaldson J considered the same point in relation to the Gencon strike clause, holding *obiter* that that also did not extend to the after-effects of a strike, notwithstanding the reference in the opening words to the consequences of any strike. Explaining this, the judge said[313]:

> The use of the word "consequences" does not necessarily connote "after-effects" and in my judgment means no more in this context than "loss or damage" resulting from a strike or lock-out which prevents or delays the doing of something required to be done under the contract. So read, the clause makes complete sense, and if it is construed as being confined to prevention or delay caused directly by the strike rather than by its after effects, is coterminous in time with pars. 2 and 3 which deal with the special cases of loading and discharging . . .

Donaldson J also pointed out that in so construing the clause, he was taking the same approach as was adopted in *The Spalmatori*.[314]

C. Duty to lessen effect

ALTERNATIVE ACTION

4.286 Before a party for whose benefit a strike clause has been inserted in a charterparty can take advantage of it, the delay must be shown to be such as could not reasonably have been avoided. Thus, in *Bulman & Dickson* v. *Fenwick & Co*, Lord Esher MR said[315]:

---

309. *Ibid.*, at p. 787.
310. The judgments in this case were said by Lord Morris not to be convincing in his dissenting judgment in *The Spalmatori* [1962] 2 Lloyd's Rep 175, at p. 187.
311. See *Leonis Steamship Co Ltd* v. *Joseph Rank Ltd (No 2)* (1908) 13 CC 161 and later cases discussed at para. 4.305.
312. *Union of India* v. *Compania Naviera Aeolus SA (The Spalmatori)* [1962] 2 Lloyd's Rep 175, at p. 182. For details of the clause see *post* at para. 4.313.
313. *Salamis Shipping (Panama) SA* v. *Edm Van Meerbeck SA (The Onisilos)* [1970] 2 Lloyd's Rep 405, at p. 408. For fuller details of the clause see *post* at para. 4.346.
314. *Ibid.*
315. *Bulman & Dickson* v. *Fenwick & Co* [1893] 1 QB 179, at p. 185.

It is true that when the vessel arrived at the Regent's Canal there was a difficulty in taking delivery because of a strike of workmen; but a strike would in itself not be sufficient to exonerate the charterers from doing the best they could to accept delivery, and would not entitle them to fold their arms and do nothing.

4.287 It should be emphasized, however, that other clauses in the charterparty may limit what they can do or impose alternative courses of action. Whilst in one sense this requirement to consider alternative action could be viewed as a duty somewhat similar to that imposed upon a plaintiff to mitigate his loss, the better view is probably that it flows from the need to show a causal connection between a strike and any delay.

4.288 In dealing with strikes, the courts have long recognized their transient and unpredictable nature, and in *Reardon Smith Line Ltd* v. *Ministry of Agriculture*, McNair J commented[316]:

It is an obvious truism that no one can predict in advance how long a strike will last, and even when the contestants appear to be far apart, a strike may end suddenly without any advance warning.

Furthermore, *per* Scrutton LJ in *Metropolitan Water Board* v. *Dick, Kerr & Co*[317]:

. . . strikes have always been treated by the courts as subject to such unexpected termination that they cannot without more be treated as abrogating contracts . . .

ALTERNATIVE PORT

4.289 A charterparty may specify a range of ports for both loading or discharging. In *Reardon Smith Line Ltd* v. *Ministry of Agriculture*, McNair J and the Court of Appeal reviewed the authorities dealing with nomination of a strike-bound port and concluded that it would only be reasonable to nominate a port where a strike was in progress if it could be shown at the time of nomination that the vessel concerned was bound to suffer inordinate delay.[318] However, the very nature of strikes would make this almost an impossibility. Furthermore, once the port has been nominated, the charterer has no right or power to change it. In the *Reardon Smith* case in the Court of Appeal, Donovan LJ summed the point up in this way[319]:

Next the charterers are not, in my view, in breach of contract in not nominating a different port from Vancouver when it became clear that the strike would or might be a long one, or when it had lasted several weeks with no end actually in sight. If, as the authorities appear by implication to decide, the nomination of one of the optional ports of loading has the result that the port must be regarded as written into the charterparty from the beginning as the sole port of loading, the effect is as if the remaining ports were struck out . . . on that view, no port exists after such election as an alternative port except by fresh agreement. Apart from this, I do not think the charterparty ought to be read as containing an implied term that some alternative port shall be named if unreasonable delay occurs at the port first nominated.

---

316. *Reardon Smith Line Ltd* v. *Ministry of Agriculture, Fisheries and Food* [1959] 2 Lloyd's Rep 229, at p. 244.

317. *Metropolitan Water Board* v. *Dick, Kerr & Co* [1917] 2 KB 1, at p. 35.

318. *Reardon Smith Line Ltd* v. *Ministry of Agriculture, Fisheries and Food* [1959] 2 Lloyd's Rep 229, at pp. 248–250 *per* McNair J; *Reardon Smith Line Ltd* v. *Ministry of Agriculture, Fisheries and Food* [1961] 1 Lloyd's Rep 385, at p. 405 *per* Sellers LJ, at p. 419 *per* Willmer LJ, at p. 429 *per* Donovan LJ.

319. *Reardon Smith Line Ltd* v. *Ministry of Agriculture, Fisheries and Food* [1961] 1 Lloyd's Rep 385, at p. 429.

Both the court below and the Court of Appeal stressed the disadvantage that could result to the shipowner in allowing a further nomination, who might thereby incur the cost of clearance from the strike-bound port, passage to a second port and entry thereto.[320]

ALTERNATIVE CARGO

4.290 The question to be considered under this heading is whether the charterer is bound to load a different cargo if the cargo originally intended cannot be loaded because of a strike. The answer is that it depends on the terms of the charter as to what cargo the parties agreed should be loaded. The leading case is *Brightman & Co* v. *Bunge y Born Ltda Sociedad*,[321] a decision of the Court of Appeal.[322] The principles there established were said by Viscount Radcliffe in the *Reardon Smith* case to be as follows[323]:

(1) If a shipper has undertaken to ship a full and complete cargo made up of alternative commodities, as in the terms "wheat and/or maize and/or rye", his obligation is to have ready at the port of shipment a complete cargo within the range of those alternatives. Consequently, the fact that he is prevented from loading one of the possible types of cargo by a cause within the exceptions clause, even though that is the type that he has himself selected and provided for, is not an answer to a claim for demurrage. To protect him each of the alternatives or all the alternatives would have to be covered by an excepted clause.

(2) Consistently with this view the shipper's selection of one of the named commodities does not convert the primary obligation to ship a full cargo in one form or the other into a simple obligation to ship a full cargo of the commodity selected. In other words, his selection is not like the exercise of an option to name a port. He may change his mind and later his choice: he "retains control of his powers until the final ton is put on the ship", said Lord Justice Atkin.[324] This may not be a full statement of the nature and consequences of the right of selection, but I have no doubt that it describes the general situation.

(3) If a shipper finds himself stopped by an excepted cause (e.g. in that case, the government prohibition) from loading or continuing to load the type of cargo that he has provided for and genuinely intended to ship, he may still rely on delay as covered by the exceptions clause to the extent of a reasonable time "to consider the position and change his cargo" or "to deal with the altered conditions" or, simply "to change over".

4.291 Viscount Radcliffe then went on to question the last of these principles in the light of the commercial difficulties that might arise. He first, however, considered the basis on which an allowance of time for adjustment might arise and concluded that it could only derive from the general position of a shipper under such a charterparty and not from any construction of the exceptions clause itself. Having pointed out that in his opinion, there was much to be said in favour of the view taken by the judge at first instance in the *Bunge y Born* case,[325] though not adopted by the Court of Appeal, that given the two assumptions that a shipper is under a primary obligation to load a full cargo of one of the permitted commodities or some combination of them and that there is no excepted cause covering the loading of all those commodities, he is in default as soon as the lay days run out with

---

320. *Reardon Smith Line Ltd* v. *Ministry of Agriculture, Fisheries and Food* [1959] 2 Lloyd's Rep 229, at p. 246 *per* McNair J; [1961] 1 Lloyd's Rep 385 (CA), at p. 408 *per* Sellers LJ, at p. 422 *per* Willmer LJ, and at p. 429 *per* Donovan LJ.

321. *Brightman & Co* v. *Bunge y Born Ltda Sociedad* [1924] 2 KB 619.

322. The case went on to the House of Lords on a different point which is reported at (1925) 22 Ll L Rep 395.

323. *Reardon Smith Line Ltd* v. *Ministry of Agriculture, Fisheries and Food* [1963] 1 Lloyd's Rep 12, at p. 29.

324. *Brightman & Co* v. *Bunge y Born Ltda Sociedad* [1924] 2 KB 619, at p. 637.

325. *Brightman & Co* v. *Bunge y Born Ltda Sociedad* (1923) 16 Ll L Rep 200.

no further allowance of "reasonable time" to change commodities, Viscount Radcliffe continued[326]:

The risk is hardly more onerous than many others that commercial men have to assume. I must add, too, that the whole idea of "reasonable time" seems to me to remain in a good deal of uncertainty and that there is a wide and unexplored range of argument as to how long the thwarted shipper is to be allowed for the purpose of considering his position, what deployment of effort he is supposed to achieve in the pursuit of his alternative cargo, when he has decided on it, and how far he is allowed to set the time and expense of getting such a cargo to the port and, it may be, its unsuitability to his own current needs against the expected delay to the cargo originally intended.

Similar views were expressed by Lord Devlin[327] and apparently shared by the remainder of the House, although not expressly stated.

4.292 In the *Reardon Smith* case, however, the House of Lords held that the parties had not simply undertaken to ship and carry a full cargo of one of several commodities, but had agreed that one commodity be shipped with an option to ship alternatives. The House held there was no primary obligation on the charterers to ship a mixed cargo. The primary obligation was to provide a cargo of wheat, which was covered by the exceptions clause, and there was no obligation on the charterers to lose their protection by exercising their option to provide another kind of cargo unaffected by the delay.[328] Lord Devlin pointed out that: "In exercising the option, which he has acquired solely for his own advantage, the holder is not bound to consider the convenience or the interest of the other party."[329] He is, however, bound to exercise his option within a reasonable time and to communicate his election to the other party, failing which the option lapses. In the context of shipping cargo, the election must be made in time for the vessel to make appropriate preparations and for the cargo to be provided.[330]

4.293 A distinction must therefore be drawn between the right to select one of several cargoes when an inability to load that particular cargo will require a further type of cargo to be selected, and a requirement to load a particular cargo with an option exercisable by the charterer to his own advantage to load an alternative.

ALTERNATIVE METHODS OF LOADING/DISCHARGING AND/OR CHANGE OF BERTH WITHIN THE PORT

4.294 Whilst a strike, or indeed any other excepted cause, may affect cargo operations at the particular berth by the method chosen by the charterer, it may nevertheless be possible for them to continue either by another method and/or changing berth.

4.295 As with alternative cargoes, whether a charterer may or is bound to order the vessel to shift will depend on the terms of the particular charter in use. In *King Line Ltd v. Moxey, Savon & Co Ltd*, Goddard LJ said[331]:

... the ship is not bound, once she has arrived and made fast to a berth to which she has been ordered, to shift again from that berth for the purpose of taking on board part of the cargo which is the subject-matter of the charter.

326. *Reardon Smith Line Ltd* v. *Ministry of Agriculture, Fisheries and Food* [1963] 1 Lloyd's Rep 12, at p. 29.
327. *Ibid.*, at p. 37.
328. *Ibid.*, at p. 29 *per* Viscount Radcliffe.
329. *Ibid.*, at p. 35.
330. *Ibid.*, at pp. 36 and 37 *per* Lord Devlin.
331. *King Line Ltd* v. *Moxey, Savon & Co Ltd* (1939) 62 Ll L Rep 252, at p. 253.

4.296 It frequently happens, however, that a charter may include some such phrase as "vessel to proceed to 1/2 safe berth, 1/2 safe ports Red Sea and there load a full cargo . . . ". Alternatively, the charter may contain a clause similar to clause 16C of the Exxonvoy 84 charter, which reads:

SHIFTING. Charterer shall have the right to shift Vessel within any port of loading and/or discharging from one loading or discharging place back to the same or to another such place once or more often. . . .

4.297 Both these clauses allow the charterer to order the vessel to shift berth. In *Lewis* v. *Louis Dreyfus & Co*, one of the Danube ice cases, the ship concerned, the *Newlands*, was sent to Braila to load a cargo of grain. At Braila there were three places at which such a cargo could be loaded, one of which was in mid-stream where the cargo would be loaded using floating elevators. However, ice prevented the lighters containing the cargo from leaving the dock or coming downstream. Delays due to ice were excepted under the charter. As the delay was only a matter of days, the charterers made no attempt to shift the vessel to load at one of the other places. In holding that the charterers were right and did not have to move the vessel, Scrutton LJ said[332]:

. . . when you have in a port a way of loading in the river from lighters, a way of loading from carts by men alongside the river bank, and a way of loading from dock silos in the dock, the charterer is not bound to have a cargo ready at each place of loading for each alternative on the chance of some difficulty turning up. He may exercise his option and be ready for one method of loading and if something occurs to prevent him loading in the way which he had intended it must take something more than a mere day or two's prevention to require him to completely turn over his plans and start loading at another place in another way . . . They are entitled to continue in the option they have exercised for a reasonable time, and I am not going to specify, because I cannot foresee, all the cases which might happen to require them to change over to another form of loading at another place.

4.298 Because of the unpredictability of the duration of a strike, it is unlikely that the courts would be prepared to hold that a charterer should abandon his previous plan of loading and order the vessel to shift. As Scrutton LJ pointed out in *Lewis* v. *Louis Dreyfus & Co*,[333] it would have been unreasonable in that case to have held that the charterers should have taken all the cargo out of the lighters or purchased another cargo, leaving the first cargo as a sort of derelict. The whole question is one of commercial possibility. This being so, different considerations may apply in the case of discharge, providing, of course, that again there is a shifting provision. If discharge at another berth is feasible then, even in a strike situation, the courts might be prepared to hold that the vessel should have been ordered to shift.

4.299 Similar considerations apply to the use of different methods of loading or discharge at the same berth. In *Michalinos & Co* v. *Louis Dreyfus & Co*,[334] another of the Danube ice cases, it was argued that after the *Matheos*, the vessel concerned, had been frozen into the dock, loading could still have taken place by manual labour either from the quay or from the lighters lying in the dock. Rejecting this suggestion, the House of Lords held that whilst it was physically possible for this to happen, it was commercially impracticable. On commercial practicability, in *Lewis* v. *Louis Dreyfus & Co*, Scrutton LJ said[335]:

332. *Lewis* v. *Louis Dreyfus & Co* (1926) 31 CC 239.
333. *Ibid.*, at p. 250.
334. *Michalinos & Co* v. *Louis Dreyfus & Co* (1925) 21 Ll L Rep 233.
335. *Lewis* v. *Louis Dreyfus & Co* (1926) 31 CC 239, at p. 250.

There is a finding by the umpire that it was physically possible to load in the way suggested and that the only obstacle was cost; but cost generally is the obstacle and a thing is commercially impossible if it costs more than commercial men would contemplate as a reasonable way of carrying out the matter.

4.300 In *Reardon Smith Line Ltd* v. *Ministry of Agriculture* in the Court of Appeal, Sellers LJ commented[336]:

The argument based on an obligation to seek an alternative method of loading if one became unavailable, equally fails, for the unavailability would have to be of a permanent and not a temporary nature of an option which would exclude the obligation to load in one of the ways available at the port.

That statement, in fact, accurately reflects the headnote in *Lewis* v. *Louis Dreyfus & Co*,[337] although in that case what was being discussed was a combination of changing berth and method of loading. In that case Lord Hanworth MR also held that in the event of a change of berth or method of loading becoming necessary, then a reasonable time should be allowed the charterers to change their plans in the same way that in *Brightman & Co* v. *Bunge y Born*[338] it was suggested that a reasonable time should be allowed to change to an alternative cargo.

4.301 However, in *Reardon Smith Line Ltd* v. *Ministry of Agriculture*,[339] at least two members of the House of Lords had doubts about the practicality of allowing a reasonable time to change to an alternative cargo and presumably the same points would arise with regard to changing berth and/or method of loading.

ALTERNATIVE LABOUR

4.302 If the work of loading or discharging of the cargo is held up by a strike or if the prosecution of the voyage is delayed by a strike, then the party seeking to rely on a strike exceptions clause to excuse such delay must refute any suggestion that alternative labour could have been found.

4.303 Thus, in *Williams Brothers (Hull) Ltd* v. *Naamlooze Vennootschap W H Berghuys Kolenhandel*,[340] where the crew of a Dutch ship refused to carry coal from Hull to Rouen because of a German threat to sink neutral shipping, Sankey J held that every effort had been made to induce the crew to remain or procure substitutes and therefore the shipowners were entitled to rely on a strike exceptions clause.

4.304 In *D A Stathatos Steamship Co Ltd* v. *Cordoba Central Railway Co Ltd*,[341] charterers, who were also consignees, claimed that a delay in discharge at Rosario was due to a strike of stevedores. Under the relevant charter, the consignees were responsible for discharging the vessel but because they feared future boycotts, they refused to use non-union labour which was available. As a result, the master made his own arrangements and using non-union labour got the cargo discharged. The charterers, however, claimed that

336. *Reardon Smith Line Ltd* v. *Ministry of Agriculture, Fisheries and Food* [1961] 1 Lloyd's Rep 385, at p. 411.
337. *Lewis* v. *Louis Dreyfus & Co* (1926) 31 CC 239.
338. *H A Brightman & Co* v. *Bunge y Born Ltda Sociedad* [1924] 2 KB 619.
339. *Reardon Smith Line Ltd* v. *Ministry of Agriculture, Fisheries and Food* [1963] 1 Lloyd's Rep 12, at p. 29 *per* Viscount Radcliffe, and at p. 37 *per* Lord Devlin. See *ante* at para. 4.291.
340. *Williams Brothers (Hull) Ltd* v. *Naamlooze Vennootschap W H Berghuys Kolenhandel* (1915) 21 CC 253.
341. *D A Stathatos Steamship Co Ltd* v. *Cordoba Central Railway Co Ltd* (1931) 40 Ll L Rep 274.

they were excused from paying demurrage because of the strike. Rejecting the charterers' contentions, Wright J said[342]:

The question which has been debated is a question of fact, and it is whether the strike here did, as the whole or any part of the period of discharge, prevent or delay the discharging, and whether, in fact, if the charterers had done what was reasonable in order to obviate and assist in obviating the effects of the strike, the delay would have continued for the period which in fact it occupied.

Had the charterers used non-union labour, discharge would have been effected quicker and a fear of future boycotts by the union was not a valid reason for not using alternative sources of labour.

D. Length of delay

4.305 Even if a strike clause is applicable, the question remains as to how much time was lost. The point is well illustrated by two cases arising out of the same strike at Villa Constitución in Argentina in 1912. The strike, which was of railway engine drivers, stokers and crane drivers, began on 6 January and continued until 15 February. However, on 27 January there was a partial resumption of work which resulted in some cargo being discharged between then and the end of the strike. The usual method of discharge was directly into railway trucks which were then sent inland, there being no available storage space at the point of discharge.

4.306 In each case the laytime clause provided as follows:

Time to commence when steamer is ready to unload and written notice given, whether in berth or not. In case of strikes, lock-outs, civil commotions, or any other causes or accidents beyond the control of the consignees which prevents or delays the discharging, such time is not to count, unless the steamer is already on demurrage.

4.307 The first case to be considered by the courts was *London and Northern Steamship Co Ltd* v. *Central Argentine Railway Ltd*, a decision of Scrutton J.[343] This concerned the vessel *Holgate*, which arrived three days before the strike began, commenced discharging on 9 February and completed on 2 March. The railway argued that on any day that discharge was delayed, time did not count at all. This was rejected by Scrutton J, who said[344]:

In case of strikes which delay the discharging, time is consumed, and, in my view, what these businessmen meant when they said "such time" was the time they had spoken of inferentially in the words immediately preceding, the time which was lost by the complete prevention, or partial prevention or the delay of the discharging.

The judge then went on to hold that only part of the time was lost between the partial resumption of work and the end of the strike, time counting for the effective work done, but also holding that there was some delay due to the strike *after* work was resumed.

4.308 The second case was *Central Argentine Railway Ltd* v. *Marwood*, which eventually reached the House of Lords.[345] The ship in this case was the *Goathland*, which arrived during the strike on 12 January, berthed after the strike on 1 March and completed discharge on 23 March. The same argument was put forward by the railway and although

---

342. *Ibid.*, at p. 276.
343. *London and Northern Steamship Co Ltd* v. *Central Argentine Railway Ltd* (1913) 108 LT 527.
344. *Ibid.*
345. *Central Argentine Railway Ltd* v. *Marwood* [1915] AC 981.

it found favour at first instance, it was again rejected by the Court of Appeal and the House of Lords. In the House of Lords, the only argument concerned what allowance, if any, should be given for the partial resumption of work, the shipowners not arguing over the period of total strike.

4.309 On the point before them, their Lordships found that the work done during the period of partial work was the equivalent of $6\frac{1}{4}$ days' normal work and therefore held that this length of time should be debited against laytime. However, several of them also emphasized that they had not been asked to consider the earlier period. Lord Sumner commented[346]:

I think the words "which prevents or delays the discharging" means strikes which in themselves prevent or delay the discharging of the chartered ship herself, and do not extend to the case of strikes which only prevent the chartered ship from getting into a berth because they prevent some other ship from getting out of that berth.

4.310 It would seem from this that Lord Sumner, and possibly other members of the House, might have been prepared to hold, if it had been argued, that time continued to run in the earlier period. If this was so, then logically it should also have run in full during the period of partial working. An argument that time continued to run throughout the strike was put forward with regard to the *Holgate*,[347] but Scrutton J appears to have dealt with it on the basis that what was being suggested was that there was no strike, rather than there was no causation in relation to the time the vessel was waiting to berth.

4.311 However, these two cases would appear to establish that provided it can be shown that the strike exception applies, then the time actually lost is the time to be excluded and time may continue to be lost even after the end of the strike, provided this after-effect directly applies to the vessel concerned, as in the case of the *Holgate*, but not where the delay is consequential.

Centrocon strike clause

4.312 This clause was originally part of the River Plate Charterparty 1914 (Homewards), designed to cover trade from the River Plate to the United Kingdom. However, it is frequently used with many other types of charter.

4.313 Although referred to as a strike clause, it does in fact cover a number of additional exclusions. The full text of the clause, which was clause 30 in the Centrocon charter, is as follows:

If the Cargo cannot be loaded by reason of Riots, Civil Commotions or of a Strike or Lock-out of any class of workmen essential to the loading of the Cargo, or by reason of obstructions or stoppages beyond the control of the Charterers on the Railways, or in the Docks, or other loading places, or if the Cargo cannot be discharged by reason of Riots, Civil Commotions, or of a Strike or Lock-out of any class of workmen essential to the discharge, the time for loading or discharging, as the case may be, shall not count during the continuance of such causes, provided that a Strike or Lock-out of the Shippers' and/or Receivers' men shall not prevent demurrage accruing if by the use of reasonable diligence they could have obtained other suitable labour at rates current before the Strike or Lock-out. In case of any delay, by reason of the before-mentioned causes, no claim for damages or demurrage shall be made by the Charterers, Receivers of the Cargo or Owners of the Steamer. For

---

346. *Ibid.*, at p. 989.
347. *London and Northern Steamship Co Ltd* v. *Central Argentine Railway Ltd* (1913) 108 LT 527, at p. 528.

the purpose, however, of settling despatch rebate accounts, any time lost by the Steamer through any of the above causes shall be counted as time used in loading or discharging.

4.314 In *Navico AG* v. *Vrontados Naftiki Etairia PE*,[348] Donaldson J, as he then was, commented that the Centrocon form of charterparty and this clause in particular had kept lawyers in congenial employment for years. Whilst the ingenuity of lawyers will no doubt continue to find points to discuss, the main parameters of the clause are now reasonably settled.

4.315 As was pointed out by McNair J in *Union of India* v. *Compania Naviera Aeolus SA (The Spalmatori)*,[349] the clause falls naturally into four parts, all of which are however inter-related and must be considered together. This division will be followed here.

First part

4.316 This covers most of the first sentence but excludes the proviso, ending with the words "such causes". The nub of this part of the clause is that

If the Cargo cannot be loaded by reason of [specified causes] . . . or discharged by reason of [other specified causes] . . . the time for loading or discharging, as the case may be, shall not count during the continuance of such causes, . . .

4.317 In *The Spalmatori*,[350] at first instance, McNair J held that "time for loading or discharging" meant time *allowed* and not, as had been suggested, time used, a conclusion agreed with both by the Court of Appeal and the House of Lords.[351] Any time excluded by this part of the clause does not therefore count against the laytime allowed in other clauses of the charter. This means that this part of the clause can only apply where the strike or other excepted clause occurs during laytime and not if it happens after the vessel has gone on demurrage.

4.318 In *The Spalmatori*, in the House of Lords, Lord Reid put the parameters of this part of the clause this way[352]:

I think that the meaning of the first part is clear. It deals with periods during which no work can be done in loading or discharging by reason of one or more of the causes mentioned. It does not deal with any period during which the operation of any of these causes merely slows down the work and it does not deal with consequential delay after these causes have ceased to exist. Clearly, it applies if one of these causes exists at the beginning of the laytime or comes into operation during the laytime. Then, in the first event, the laytime does not begin to run until these causes have ceased or, in the latter event, the laytime is suspended.

THE SPECIFIED CAUSES

4.319 It will be noted that the list of causes relating to loading is longer than that relating to discharging and also includes "obstructions or stoppages beyond the control of the Charterers on the Railways, or in the Docks, or other loading places".

---

348. *Navico AG* v. *Vrontados Naftiki Etairia PE* [1968] 1 Lloyd's Rep 379, at p. 382.
349. *Union of India* v. *Compania Naviera Aeolus SA (The Spalmatori)* [1960] 1 Lloyd's Rep 112, at p. 114.
350. *Ibid.*, at p. 115.
351. *Union of India* v. *Compania Naviera Aeolus (The Spalmatori)* [1961] 1 Lloyd's Rep 132 (CA); [1962] 2 Lloyd's Rep 175 (HL).
352. *The Spalmatori* [1962] 2 Lloyd's Rep 175, at p. 180.

OBSTRUCTIONS BEYOND THE CONTROL OF THE CHARTERERS IN THE
DOCKS OR OTHER LOADING PLACES

4.320 The meaning to be given to this phrase has been the subject of many challenges since it was first held in *Leonis Steamship Co Ltd* v. *Joseph Rank Ltd (No 2)*[353] that "obstruction" includes port congestion by reason of which a berth is not available.[354] In *Ionian Navigation Co Inc* v. *Atlantic Shipping Co SA (The Loucas N)*, Lord Denning[355] commented "that it is an unsatisfactory decision which merchants and lawyers try to get out of".[356] However, the obstruction must be beyond the control of the charterers and the working of this part of the phrase may be illustrated by two cases.

4.321 The first is *Sir R Ropner & Co Ltd* v. *Bunge North American Grain Corporation*[357] where the *Ashby*, the ship concerned, was due to load grain at Mobile. The only elevator berth was occupied but the charterers offered to load by ship's tackle if the owners would pay the extra cost, which they refused. Nevertheless, the owners argued that as loading could have been carried out at another berth, there was no obstruction beyond the control of the charterers. However, in arbitration, the umpire held in an award affirmed by the court that charterers were not under any obligation to load by ship's tackle, that to do so would have been unreasonable in the circumstances. There was therefore an obstruction beyond the control of the charterers and the detention of the ship did not occur by default of the charterers or their agents.

4.322 On the other hand, in the second case, *Venizelos A N E of Athens* v. *Société Commerciale (The Prometheus)*[358] Mocatta J held that where the charterers did not nominate a berth for some 18 hours after the vessel's arrival the charterers could not rely on the berth of their choice being obstructed during this period unless they could also show that it was commercially impracticable to load at alternative berths. The crucial element was the charterers' failure to nominate a berth before the vessel's arrival.

OBSTRUCTIONS BEYOND THE CONTROL OF THE CHARTERERS ON THE
RAILWAYS

4.323 In *H A Brightman & Co* v. *Bunge y Born*, one of the issues concerned a "go slow" or "work to rule" on one of the railways used to bring cargo to the port. In the Court of Appeal both Bankes and Scrutton LJJ expressed some doubt whether, notwithstanding the

---

353. *Leonis Steamship Co Ltd* v. *Joseph Rank Ltd (No 2)* (1908) 13 CC 161; (1908) 13 CC 295 (CA).

354. In *Navrom* v. *Callitsis Ship Management SA (The Radauti)* [1988] 2 Lloyd's Rep 416, the Court of Appeal said that "hindrances" similarly protected charterers against delays due to congestion. See *ante*. at para. 4.99.

355. *Ionian Navigation Co Inc* v. *Atlantic Shipping Co SA (The Loucas N)* [1971] 1 Lloyd's Rep 215, at p. 218. The decision Lord Denning was referring to was that in *The Amstelmolen* [1961] 2 Lloyd's Rep 1, although that in turn was based on *Leonis Steamship Co Ltd (No 2)*, *supra*.

356. *Reardon Smith Line Ltd* v. *East Asiatic Co* (1938) 62 Ll L Rep 23; *Sir R Ropner & Co Ltd* v. *Bunge North American Grain Corporation* (1938) 62 Ll L Rep 111; *NV Reederij Amsterdam* v. *President of India (The Amstelmolen)* [1961] 2 Lloyd's Rep 1 (CA); *Ionian Navigation Co Inc* v. *Atlantic Shipping Co SA (The Loucas N)* [1971] 1 Lloyd's Rep 215 (CA); *Venizelos A N E of Athens* v. *Société Commerciale de Céréales et Financière SA of Zurich (The Prometheus)* [1974] 1 Lloyd's Rep 350; *R Pagnan & Fratelli* v. *Finagrain Compagnie Commerciale Agricole et Financière SA (The Adolf Leonhardt)* [1986] 2 Lloyd's Rep 395, at p. 401.

357. *Sir R Ropner & Co Ltd* v. *Bunge North American Grain Corporation* (1938) 62 Ll L Rep 111.

358. *Venizelos A N E of Athens* v. *Société Commerciale de Céréales et Financière SA of Zurich (The Prometheus)* [1974] 1 Lloyd's Rep 350.

findings of fact in the case, this type of industrial action could amount to an obstruction. Atkin LJ, on the other hand, held that[359]:

The word "obstruction" ... may include both the physical condition which interferes with the normal flow of traffic, and abnormal industrial conditions which cause the normal flow of traffic to be impeded.

However, all the members of the court and, later, the House of Lords, held that the only railways to which the clause applies are those within the port. Lord Dunedin put it this way[360]:

The word "railways" is in concatenation with the word "docks" and points, I think, to the use of a railway as one of the instruments of loading ...

4.324 In the *Owners of the SS Bassa* v. *Royal Commission on Wheat Supplies*,[361] Roche J considered delays on the railway caused by an accumulation of rolling stock following a strike. In addition to holding that the railway must be within the port, the judge also held that the clause was limited in time to the period of the obstruction and did not extend to consequential delays.

STOPPAGES

4.325 It would seem that, like "obstructions", stoppages applies to such events "on the Railways, or in the Docks, or other loading places". Although not so specifically stated in this clause, it appears that by "stoppage" is meant a stoppage of work by workmen rather than just a cessation of the loading operation for whatever cause. In the Chamber of Shipping Welsh Coal Charter, where the word also appears, the phrase used is "Any time lost through riots, strikes, lock-out, or any dispute between masters and men occasioning a stoppage of pitmen, trimmers or other hands ... ". On this Pickford J said[362] in *Akties Adalands* v. *Whittaker*:

I think "stoppage" looking at the wording of the clause, means an entire stoppage of work, not a delay and only just getting a small amount ...

4.326 The difficulties that might arise from accepting that a stoppage could include anything less than a total stoppage were discussed in *Miguel de Larrinaga Steamship Co Ltd* v. *D L Flack & Son*, again a case concerning the Welsh Coal Charter. In the Court of Appeal in that case, Sir Ernest Pollock MR said[363]:

What is a partial stoppage? How much is a partial stoppage? Are you to treat it as a stoppage when you are still able to get 50% of the coal loaded? Are you to say when you are getting a slower delivery than is normal that that is a stoppage? At what point can you stop? Having regard to these difficulties I think that the right course is to treat the word stoppage as bearing its meaning on its face and intended to mean complete stoppage.

By analogy with strikes,[364] whilst a stoppage must be complete it presumably need not be continuous and therefore broken periods may be excluded.

359. *H A Brightman & Co* v. *Bunge y Born* (1924) 19 Ll L Rep 384 (CA), at p. 387.
360. *H A Brightman & Co* v. *Bunge y Born* (1925) 22 Ll L Rep 395 (HL), at p. 396.
361. *Owners of the SS Bassa* v. *Royal Commission on Wheat Supplies* (1924) 20 Ll L Rep 243.
362. *Akties Adalands* v. *Whittaker* (1913) 18 CC 229, at p. 236. See also *Valla Giovanni & C SpA* v. *Gebr Van Weelde Scheepvaartkantoor BV (The Chanda)* [1985] 1 Lloyd's Rep 563.
363. *Miguel de Larrinaga Steamship Co Ltd* v. *D L Flack & Son* (1925) 21 Ll L Rep 284, at p. 287.
364. *Tramp Shipping Corporation* v. *Greenwich Marine Inc (The New Horizon)* [1975] 2 Lloyd's Rep 314. See also *ante* at para. 4.266.

4.327 However, it is not really clear whether the word "stoppage" does in fact add anything to the other excepted causes in the Centrocon clause. In *The Spalmatori*,[365] Lord Reid said that all the excepted causes only apply to periods when no work is done and not just to those periods when work slows down. Furthermore, in *H A Brightman & Co* v. *Bunge y Born*, in the Court of Appeal,[366] Atkin LJ was prepared to hold that obstruction included impediments caused by abnormal industrial conditions, thus making "stoppage" otiose. It may be that the word was included in the days when strikes were limited to disputes over wages[367] so as to include any form of wider dispute.

RIOTS AND CIVIL COMMOTION

4.328 Unlike the causes considered above, these and the remaining causes apply to both loading and discharging.

4.329 Under English law there are five elements which together make a riot. To constitute a riot there must be at least three people engaged in the execution or inception of a common purpose with an intent to help one another, by force if necessary, against any person who may oppose them and in so doing the force or violence must be such as to alarm at least one person of reasonable firmness and courage.[368]

4.330 A civil commotion, on the other hand, is probably a wider term. It is suggested that the principal differences may be that the number of people involved may be as few as two, as in an affray, and there need be no common purpose. Secondary picketing and demonstrations would certainly come within the definition. Whether acts of terrorism would is perhaps a debatable point.

STRIKE OR LOCK-OUT OF ANY CLASS OF WORKMEN ESSENTIAL TO THE LOADING/DISCHARGING

4.331 The term "strike" has already been considered in some detail and nothing further need be said about its use in this clause.

4.332 "Lock-out" has been defined as the closing of a place of employment or the suspension of work or the refusal by an employer to continue to employ any number of persons employed by him in consequence of a dispute, done with a view to compelling those persons, or to aid another employer in compelling persons employed by him, to accept terms and conditions of or affecting employment.[369] This definition is, however, not comprehensive, for a lock-out may be instituted for purposes other than compelling workers to accept terms and conditions of or relating to employment.

4.333 An illustration of the meaning of "workmen essential to the loading or discharging" is provided by *Dampskibsselskabet Svendborg* v. *Love & Stewart Ltd*.[370] In that case, time was not to count during any delay caused by strikes of workmen essential

---

365. *Union of India* v. *Compania Naviera Aeolus SA (The Spalmatori)* [1962] 2 Lloyd's Rep 175, at p. 180.
366. *H A Brightman & Co* v. *Bunge y Born* (1924) 19 Ll L Rep 384, at p. 387. See *ante* at para. 4.270. The case later went to the House of Lords.
367. See *ante* at paras 4.262 and 4.270.
368. *Field* v. *Receiver of Metropolitan Police* [1907] 2 KB 859, *per* Phillimore J.
369. Employment Protection (Consolidation) Act 1978, s. 151(1) and Sched. 13, para. 24; Employment Act 1982, s. 20(1) and Sched. 2, para. 7(1), now re-enacted in section 235(4) of the Trades Union and Labour Relations (Consolidation) Act 1992.
370. *Dampskibsselskabet Svendborg* v. *Love & Stewart Ltd*, 1915 SC 543.

to the discharge. Because of a strike of workmen in the charterers' yard, the railway company limited the number of wagons they were prepared to supply to avoid an accumulation of wagons in the yard. The indirect effect of this was to delay discharge, but it was held that the charterers could not rely on the exceptions clause since the strike was not of workmen engaged in the actual loading or discharging operations but only those involved in the further distribution of the cargo.

Second part

4.334 The second part of the Centrocon strike clause is the proviso at the end of the first sentence, which reads,

provided that a Strike or Lock-out of the Shippers' and/or Receivers' men shall not prevent demurrage accruing if by the use of reasonable diligence they could have obtained other suitable labour at rates current before the Strike or Lock-out.

The proviso limits the application of the first part in certain events. Although the requirements of the first part are satisfied—there is a strike during the laytime and it prevents any work being done—nevertheless laytime is not to be suspended, but is to continue to count if other labour can be obtained to carry on the work.

4.335 In *Union of India* v. *Compania Naviera Aeolus SA (The Spalmatori)*, Lord Reid said of this part of the clause[371]:

The reference to preventing demurrage accruing is not happy, but I think that the meaning is clear enough. The existence of the strike is not to prevent demurrage from beginning to accrue at the end of the stipulated laytime if other labour was available. Without the proviso demurrage would not have begun to accrue then: the first part of the clause would have prevented that and demurrage would only have begun to accrue at the end of the stipulated laytime, plus the time during which the strike prevented work.

4.336 There appears to be no clear authority as to what is meant by "Shippers' and/or Receivers' men" or why a different phrase is used to that which is being qualified, namely "workmen essential to the loading/discharge". In *The Spalmatori*, Lord Reid refers to "other labour being available" which tends to suggest that he considered there to be no distinction between the workmen referred to in the first part of the clause and those in the second, i.e. both parts encompass any workmen engaged to load or discharge the vessel whether those workmen be direct employees or simply independent contractors. In the vast majority of ports the stevedores, etc., will be independent contractors rather than direct employees of the shippers/receivers. However, in *Seeberg* v. *Russian Wood Agency Ltd*,[372] MacKinnon J took a narrow view of the phrase and held that in Leningrad state organized stevedores were not shippers' men where the shippers were also a state agency. Whilst the judge took the view that the phrase was confined to a strike of those in the direct employ of the shippers he nevertheless also held that the charterers, who were also the shippers, had to show there was no alternative labour that could be used. In his judgment, MacKinnon J said[373]:

---

371. *Union of India* v. *Compania Naviera Aeolus SA (The Spalmatori)* [1962] 2 Lloyd's Rep 175. at p. 181.
372. *Seeberg* v. *Russian Wood Agency Ltd* (1934) 50 Ll L Rep 146.
373. *Ibid.*, at p. 148.

I do not think it is sufficient for the charterers merely to say: "There is a strike and therefore we need not load." They must further prove that the cargo could not be loaded by reason of the strike, and if it is established that by taking some steps or adopting some reasonable course the cargo could, by or on behalf of Exportles, have been loaded notwithstanding the existence of the strike, then in those circumstances they would not have established under this clause that the cargo could not be loaded by reason of the strike . . .

4.337 The question of whether there is a duty on the charterers to mitigate the effects of a strike or whether this is simply part of the proof of causal connection has already been considered.[374] The inference from MacKinnon J's judgment is that he viewed this as a problem of causation, but Lord Reid, in *The Spalmatori*, took it that the causation required was simply that there was a strike which prevented work being done.[375]

4.338 In his speech, Lord Reid quoted from *Scrutton on Charterparties*[376] to the effect that for an exceptions clause to apply when a vessel is on demurrage, it must be clearly so worded. Later in his speech, he continued[377]:

There is no wholly satisfactory interpretation or explanation of the third part of the clause and one must choose between two almost equally unsatisfactory conclusions. In a case like this where a clause in common use has simply been copied one cannot try to find what the parties intended. They almost certainly never thought about things happening as they did. So I must fall back on the rule which I have already quoted from the work of Lord Justice Scrutton. I do not think it is an arbitrary rule for this reason. If a strike occurs before the end of the laytime neither party can be blamed in any way. But if it occurs after demurrage has begun to accrue the owner might well say: "True, your breach of contract in detaining my ship after the end of the laytime did not cause the strike, but if you had fulfilled your contract the strike would have caused no loss because my ship would have been on the high seas before it began: so it is more reasonable that you should bear the loss than that I should." So it seems to me right that if the respondents are to escape from paying demurrage during this strike they must be able to point to an exceptions clause which clearly covers this case. And in my judgment they cannot do that.

4.339 On the particular wording of the Centrocon clause, if alternative labour were available, then where there was a failure to load, the strike would be the direct reason but the failure to use the alternative labour would be the indirect reason.[378] If the indirect reason is sufficient to break the causal chain then the "proviso" would seem to have little meaning and therefore it would seem more logical to accept Lord Reid's view rather than that of MacKinnon J. In both decided cases the point was *obiter* but interestingly enough giving a narrow meaning to the phrase "Shippers' and/or Receivers' men" but accepting MacKinnon J's views on causation produces the same result as giving the phrase a wider meaning to include independent contractors but with Lord Reid's views on causation. With either approach, the shipper/receiver must show there was no alternative labour available before he can take advantage of the strike clause. This, it is suggested, is good commercial sense and whilst it is possible that in a future decision the courts might give a narrow meaning to the phrase "Shippers' and/or Receivers' men" and only require proof that the strike prevented work being done, without inquiring into what other labour was available, this would be commercially unrealistic. The better view is, therefore, it is submitted, that the effect of the proviso is that notwithstanding the existence of a strike

374. See *ante* at para. 4.271.
375. *The Spalmatori* [1962] 2 Lloyd's Rep 175, at p. 180.
376. *Ibid.*
377. *Ibid.*, at p. 182.
378. For a strike clause couched in terms of "time lost" the situation might be different and the failure to use alternative labour might be the principal cause of loss of time.

preventing cargo operations, laytime should nevertheless continue if other labour can be found to carry on the work.

Third part

4.340 This covers the second sentence and provides:

In case of any delay, by reason of the before-mentioned causes, no claim for damages or demurrage shall be made by the Charterers, Receivers of the Cargo or Owners of the Steamer.

The meaning of this part of the clause was the actual issue considered by the House of Lords in *Union of India* v. *Compania Naviera Aeolus SA (The Spalmatori)*.[379] In that case the strike arose after laytime had expired and the vessel was on demurrage. By the time the case reached the House of Lords it had been accepted that the first two parts of the clause were limited to the events occurring during laytime and the principal question was therefore whether the third part should be read independently of the first two. At first instance, McNair J held[380] that Part III, if any sense was to be given to it, was merely an inaccurate paraphrase of the detailed provisions preceding it or was leading up to Part IV dealing with despatch money. The Court of Appeal held[381] that this was not so and that Part III was independent of the remainder so that the receivers were not liable for demurrage during the strike, even though it commenced after the vessel came on demurrage. The House of Lords then reversed this by a majority of three to two, restoring the decision of McNair J holding that the third part was also limited to events occurring during laytime.

4.341 Whilst not necessary for the actual decision, the speeches of the majority do suggest that Part III also covers delays in loading/discharging which occur after the strike has ended but which result directly from the strike, provided that, as in the earlier parts, the strike was in operation when laytime would otherwise have commenced or occurred during the running of laytime. It does not, therefore, cover delay due to the after-effects of a strike where the strike finished before laytime commenced or would otherwise have commenced. However, the usual after-effect of such a situation is port congestion, which would normally be covered by the "obstruction" provision of the Centrocon strike clause.

4.342 Commenting on the illogicalities that this can produce, Lord Hodson said[382]:

It is represented on behalf of the respondents that this is an odd result since if the right to rely upon exception depends upon the date of the strike this has capricious results for a strike occurring before the beginning of the laytime would be of no avail to the respondents, whereas a strike occurring shortly after the laytime had begun to run would avail them. This may be true, but I cannot see that this affords any justification of construing the words under consideration in such a way as to cover the respondents from the effects of delay arising from a strike whenever occurring.

Lord Reid also suggested that whereas Part I only covered a complete cessation of work, Part III might cover a situation where, during the continuance of a strike, its effect was not to stop work completely but merely to slow down loading and unloading.

---

379. *Union of India* v. *Compania Naviera Aeolus SA (The Spalmatori)* [1962] 2 Lloyd's Rep 175 (HL).
380. *The Spalmatori* [1960] 1 Lloyd's Rep 112.
381. *The Spalmatori* [1961] 1 Lloyd's Rep 132 (CA).
382. *The Spalmatori* [1962] 2 Lloyd's Rep 175, at p. 189.

4.343 It is therefore clear that the effect of Part III is to widen that of Part I and not merely, as suggested by McNair J, to paraphrase it. The difficulties their Lordships faced in finding a sensible interpretation of this part of the clause in particular were illustrated by Lord Reid when he said[383]:

It is fairly obvious that the third part is not an original part of the clause, but is a later addition: I cannot imagine even the least legally minded draftsman drafting the clause as a whole in its present form.

Fourth part

4.344 This covers the last sentence of the clause, which reads as follows:

For the purpose, however, of settling despatch rebate accounts, any time lost by the Steamer through any of the above causes shall be counted as time used in loading or discharging.

4.345 Were it not for the presence of this clause, the effect of the earlier sections in stopping the laytime clock might result in the shipowner not only having to bear the cost of the time lost by one of the excepted causes, but if loading or discharging proceeded quicker than expected once the excepted cause ceased to have effect, ending up having to pay despatch as well. A more detailed analysis of this part of the clause will be made in the chapter on "Despatch".[384]

Gencon strike clause

4.346 This clause, which has appeared in the well-known Gencon Charterparty since 1922, is in the following terms:

Neither Charterers nor Owners shall be responsible for the consequences of any strikes or lock-outs preventing or delaying the fulfilment of any obligations under this contract.

If there is a strike or lock-out affecting the loading of the cargo, or any part of it, when vessel is ready to proceed from her last port or at any time during the voyage to the port or ports of loading or after her arrival there, Captain or Owners may ask Charterers to declare that they agree to reckon the lay days as if there were no strike or lock-out. Unless Charterers have given such declaration in writing (by telegram, if necessary) within 24 hours, Owners have the option of cancelling this contract. If part cargo has already been loaded, owners must proceed with same (freight payable on loaded quantity only) having liberty to complete with other cargo on the way for their own account.

If there is a strike or lock-out affecting the discharge of the cargo on or after vessel's arrival at or off port of discharge and same has not been settled within 48 hours, Receivers shall have the option of keeping vessel waiting until such strike or lock-out is at an end against paying half demurrage after expiration of the time provided for discharging, or of ordering the vessel to a safe port where she can safely discharge without risk of being detained by strike or lock-out. Such orders to be given within 48 hours after Captain or Owners have given notice to Charterers of the strike or lock-out affecting the discharge. On delivery of the cargo at such port, all conditions of this Charterparty and of the Bill of Lading shall apply and vessel shall receive the same freight as if she had discharged at the original port of destination, except that if the distance of the substituted port exceeds 100 nautical miles, the freight on the cargo delivered at the substituted port to be increased in proportion.

---

383. *Ibid.*, at p. 181.
384. See *post* at para. 7.30.

4.347 Although this clause has been in existence for over 60 years, there is remarkably little judicial authority as to its meaning. In *Salamis Shipping (Panama) SA* v. *Edm Van Meerbeck & Co SA (The Onisilos)*, Donaldson J commented[385]:

Carriers of goods by sea have traditionally shown an interest in developing and refining the law, which earns (amongst other things) the unbounded admiration of those lawyers who practise in this field. It was therefore with a sense of shock that I learned that there still remained an area which is totally unexplored—the general strike clause, which probably has appeared in the Gencon charterparty since 1922.

In the same case in the Court of Appeal, Lord Denning MR[386] stressed that the clause must be considered as one whole, in the same way that the corresponding clause in the Centrocon charter was construed.[387]

4.348 The two leading cases on the interpretation to be given to the Gencon strike clause are *Salamis Shipping (Panama) SA* v. *Edm Van Meerbeck & Co SA (The Onisilos)*[388] and *Superfos Chartering A/S* v. *NBR (London) Ltd (The Saturnia)*.[389] Strictly speaking, the comments on the construction of the clause in the latter were *obiter*, since both at first instance and in the Court of Appeal it was held that the clause did not apply as the vessel was on demurrage when the strike arose.

4.349 In the first of these cases, the ship concerned, the *Onisilos*, was fixed to carry a mixed cargo from Antwerp to Charleston, Mobile and Houston. On arrival at Charleston the vessel was unable to discharge because of a strike. On her arrival there laytime had not expired, but did so some six days later, the charterers having failed to order her to an alternative discharge port.

4.350 In *The Saturnia*, on the other hand, the facts were somewhat different. Here the vessel was chartered to carry sugar and some general cargo from Antwerp to Lagos, but no difficulties were encountered due to strikes until after the vessel's arrival at Lagos and until after laytime had expired.

4.351 Notwithstanding the need to consider the clause as a whole, it is probably now convenient to consider the parameters of each of the constituent paragraphs.

First paragraph

4.352 Taken on its own this is in very wide terms. As Sir Gordon Willmer commented in *The Onisilos*[390]:

. . . the charterers under the opening words of the general strike clause would be completely relieved of any liability to pay demurrage for the whole of the time during which the strike lasted, and even beyond that time if it were shown that the consequences of the strike still prevented discharge.

385. *Salamis Shipping (Panama) SA* v. *Edm Van Meerbeck & Co SA (The Onisilos)* [1970] 2 Lloyd's Rep 405, at p. 406.

386. *Salamis Shipping (Panama) SA* v. *Edm Van Meerbeck & Co SA (The Onisilos)* [1971] 2 Lloyd's Rep 29 (CA).

387. *Compania Naviera Aeolus SA* v. *Union of India (The Spalmatori)* [1962] 2 Lloyd's Rep 175 (HL). See also *ante* at para. 4.315.

388. *Salamis Shipping (Panama) SA* v. *Edm Van Meerbeck & Co SA (The Onisilos)* [1971] 2 Lloyd's Rep 29 (CA).

389. *Superfos Chartering A/S* v. *NBR (London) Ltd (The Saturnia)* [1984] 2 Lloyd's Rep 366; [1987] 2 Lloyd's Rep 43.

390. *The Onisilos* [1971] 2 Lloyd's Rep 29, at p. 35.

4.353 At first instance, Donaldson J suggested that this part of the clause might cover situations such as where a strike of tugs, pilots or seamen prevent the vessel concerned from reaching her loading or discharging port.[391] Although the Court of Appeal reversed the first instance finding that "consequences" did not extend to the after-effects of a strike, none of the judges apparently disagreed with Donaldson J's comments on tugs, etc. In *The Saturnia*, Bingham J said[392]:

It is evident that Part I . . . is drawn in very wide terms. It is for the potential benefit of both owners and charterers. It is not limited to strikes or lock-outs which prevent or delay the loading or discharging of the vessel. It would cover strikes of the crew, or of pilots or tugmen, as well as of stevedores or cranedrivers. Any strike which prevents or delays the fulfilment of any obligation under the contract falls within the apparent scope of the clause. So construed, the clause modifies the ordinary contractual position according to which neither party is relieved of his obligation to perform by supervening impossibility of performance, whether as a result of strikes or lock-outs or any other cause unless or until the contract is frustrated.

4.354 This part probably therefore also covers delays in the cargo reaching the port. This paragraph will also exclude delays not specifically covered by the second and third paragraphs. Thus, if there is a strike at the load port, which ends prior to the vessel sailing from her previous port of call, but the after-effects of which continue, then any delay will be excluded by this paragraph. Similarly, if there is a strike at the discharge port during the carrying voyage, which ends prior to the vessel's arrival, but where the after-effects cause delay, then the time so lost will also be excluded. However, in *The Saturnia*,[393] Bingham J held that where the strike arose after laytime had expired, the owners were right in saying that Part I did not excuse the charterers from their obligation to continue to pay demurrage, a conclusion upheld on appeal by the Court of Appeal[394] where the only reasoned judgment was given by Sir John Donaldson MR, who held that the clause as a whole did not apply if the strike arises after laytime has expired.

4.355 In *Armada Lines Continent Mediterranean Service Ltd* v. *Naviera Murueta SA*,[395] a vessel on a Gencon charter arrived at the discharging port during a strike, which delayed discharging. The strike was over in less than 48 hours and therefore only the first part of the Gencon strike clause might have applied. In arbitration, the owners argued unsuccessfully that the charterers were not entitled to rely on this provision because the strike was over in less than 48 hours and laytime had not expired. The arbitrator, however, held that the period of delay should be excluded from laytime. The case subsequently came before the High Court on an application to vary the award for excess of jurisdiction, but the judge did not express any view on the arbitrator's construction on this part of the strike clause, save for commenting that the correct application of the first paragraph of the clause had not been covered by direct authority, although it had been indirectly referred to in cases dealing with other paragraphs. However, it would seem on general principles that the arbitrator's decision was right.

4.356 The meaning of "strike" and "lock-out" have already been considered in general terms,[396] and although the wording of the first paragraph is wide, there must be industrial

---

391. *The Onisilos* [1970] 2 Lloyd's Rep 405, at p. 408.
392. *The Saturnia* [1984] 2 Lloyd's Rep 366, at p. 369.
393. *Ibid.*, at. p. 371.
394. *Superfos Chartering A/S* v. *NBR (London) Ltd (The Saturnia)* [1987] 2 Lloyd's Rep 43 (CA).
395. *Armada Lines Continent Mediterranean Service Ltd* v. *Naviera Murueta SA (The Elexalde)* [1985] 2 Lloyd's Rep 485.
396. See *ante* at para. 4.261 and para. 4.332.

action of the type specified. Thus, a refusal to work for part of each day would probably be included, but not a "go-slow" or "work to rule".

Second paragraph

4.357 This deals specifically with strikes or lock-outs affecting loading of the cargo. Whilst the word "affecting" could be given either a wide or narrow meaning, it seems likely that here it is intended that a reasonably wide meaning should be given. Had it been intended to confine the application of the paragraph (and the corresponding one on discharge) to strikes of those directly responsible for cargo operations, then some such word as "preventing" would have been more appropriate. Furthermore, since delays outside the scope of the paragraph may be totally excused under the first paragraph, it makes commercial sense to give a fairly broad interpretation to the words, "affecting loading of the cargo".

4.358 To come within the second paragraph, the strike must come into or be in existence when or after the vessel is ready to proceed from her last port, which could either be her previous discharge port or an earlier load port on the present voyage, provided that at the start of the strike, laytime has not expired. Thus, in *The Saturnia*, Bingham J said[397]:

> . . . Parts 1 and 2 seem to me to represent a coherent commercial bargain. If a strike or lock-out affects the loading of the vessel at the loading port after expiry of the agreed laytime, the charterer has no relief from his obligation to pay demurrage at the full rate. It is his fault that the vessel has not been loaded. There is no reason why the owner should suffer loss of his contractual demurrage when, but for the charterers' breach, the loading of the vessel would not have been affected by the strike or lock-out.

4.359 It would seem from the wording of the clause and some remarks of the judge in *The Saturnia*[398] that there is a positive onus on the vessel to ask for a declaration. If no such declaration is sought then the terms of the first paragraph come into play and laytime either does not start, or if the strike is after the vessel's arrival, it is suspended.

4.360 If, on the other hand, a declaration is sought and the charterers agree to laytime running then this would take effect from the vessel's arrival or the commencement of the strike as appropriate with full demurrage after laytime expires. However, if the charterers do not reply to the request for a declaration or refuse it then one of three things can happen. If no cargo has been loaded either at the strikebound or previous load ports, the owners can either wait for the strike to end, laytime not running by virtue of the first paragraph, or they can opt to cancel the contract.

4.361 If they take this second choice of cancellation, then the situation would seem somewhat analogous to the option given in a time charter to an owner to withdraw his vessel from hire upon non-payment of hire, i.e. the contract simply comes to an end without the withdrawal, or in this case, cancellation of itself giving rise to a claim for damages in addition. Presumably, to be effective, the option must be exercised by the owners timeously, possibly within 24 hours of the charterers' refusal or failure to respond.[399] If the owners do not respond within this period, the courts might well hold that

397. *The Saturnia* [1984] 2 Lloyd's Rep 366, at p. 370.
398. *Ibid.*
399. In *The Saturnia*, the judge did not appear to consider this specific point, which therefore remains moot.

they have elected to waive their option and remain until the end of the strike, with time not running by virtue of Part I.

4.362 Although the owners might normally be expected to seek a declaration from the charterers as soon as it takes effect or even before the vessel's arrival, there would seem no reason why they should not choose to wait for a while, laytime not running, to see whether the strike will end before seeking a declaration from the charterers. Short of the charterparty becoming frustrated, there would seem no limit on how long this waiting period could be, the only time constraints arising after the appropriate declaration has been sought.

4.363 The third thing that can happen after a declaration is sought and either refused or not responded to is when some cargo has already been loaded. In this situation the owners must order the vessel to sail with whatever cargo is on board, however little.

4.364 It may occasionally happen that the load port strike only affects one type of cargo. If so, there would seem no reason why the owners should not exercise the liberty contained in the last sentence of the paragraph by completing with other cargo at the original load port. However, in this situation, it would be likely that the charterers would opt to keep laytime running and themselves load alternative cargo, provided this was within the range of cargoes permitted by the charterparty. If no such cargo is available at the original load port, then the vessel must presumably sail as quickly as if she had completed loading a full cargo.

4.365 Sometimes to protect themselves against the consequences of having to sail with only a small amount of cargo and thus earning a minimal amount of freight, owners negotiate a lump sum freight. The effect of such a provision in relation to the term in the Gencon strike clause, providing for freight to be payable on the loaded quantity only, has been considered by London arbitrators,[400] who held that the "freight payable on loaded quantity only" was the lump sum freight. This was so because that was the freight payable no matter what quantity was loaded.

4.366 In this case, a further issue arose in that, notice of the intention to strike having been given, the charterers ordered the vessel to sail prior to the commencement of the strike and the owners argued that the second paragraph of the clause only applies where there is a strike or lock-out. On this point, the arbitrators agreed with the owners, and held that the clause did not apply to a prospective strike, but that on the evidence an *ad hoc* agreement had been made between the parties that it would apply prospectively.

4.367 The final point that arises on this part of the clause concerns the liberty to complete with other cargo at other ports. It will be noted that these ports must be on the way and therefore presumably reasonably proximate to the direct route. If, for instance, the shipowners chose initially to sail a short distance in the reverse direction then this would not be "on the way" and might, subject to the other clauses in the charter, amount to a deviation as against the cargo already loaded with the consequences that would involve.[401]

Third paragraph

4.368 This covers a strike or lock-out at the discharge port. The meaning of "affecting" has already been considered in relation to the second paragraph and presumably similar

---

400. London Arbitration—LMLN 91, 28 April 1983.
401. See *post* at para. 6.165.

considerations would apply to its use in the third paragraph. It should also be noted that the strike, and not merely its after-effects, must be in existence at the vessel's arrival at the discharge port, or come into existence thereafter, for the third paragraph to come into play. If the strike ends before the ship's arrival, then the situation is governed by the first paragraph. In *The Onisilos*, Lord Denning commented on this aspect in the context of a strike occurring on the vessel's arrival, but what he said would also be applicable to a strike which had finished before the vessel got there. He said[402]:

After the strike comes to an end, the ship is still unable to discharge her cargo because of congestion in the port. The ships are waiting in a queue to get in. This waiting is one of the "consequences" of the strike. According to Part I of the strike clause, the charterers would not be liable for demurrage during that period (of waiting for a berth) . . .

4.369 If, however, there is a strike or lock-out on or after the vessel's arrival, then the charterers may keep the vessel at that port—and, if they do, laytime continues to run and half demurrage is payable thereafter—or they may send the vessel to another discharge port unaffected by the strike. The mechanics of how these alternatives are to be exercised are set out in the paragraph. First, the vessel must give notice of the strike to the charterers, who must then choose which option they elect to exercise within 48 hours of receiving the notice.

4.370 In *The Onisilos*[403] no notice was given by the vessel to the charterers, although from the report it is clear that the receivers were of course aware of the strike, and no formal election was made by the charterers. Nevertheless, the arbitrators found as a mixed finding of fact and law, which was not challenged in the courts, that by failing to give orders to discharge at another port the charterers elected to keep the vessel at the original discharge port until the strike ended. No point was taken on the difference, if any, between the charterers and the receivers of the cargo.

4.371 If, however, the charterers could have shown that they were unaware of the strike, the vessel having given no notice, then presumably the situation would have been governed by the first paragraph and laytime would have been simply suspended. If, on the other hand, the vessel does give notice, but the charterers fail to respond, then clearly they must have been taken to elect to keep the vessel there.

4.372 The question also arises whether, if the charterers do elect to wait for the strike to end, does laytime (or half demurrage thereafter) run as if there had been no strike or only from the time of the charterers' election? In *The Onisilos*, since no actual notices were given, presumably time ran from the vessel's arrival.

4.373 It would seem logical that if the charterers do retain the vessel at the discharge port that time should run as if there had been no strike. If, however, the charterers elect to sail the vessel, then time would not run after the order to sail had been given, nor would it run prior to this whilst the vessel was affected by the strike because of paragraph I.

4.374 In *The Onisilos* one of the main issues was how long the vessel was to remain on half demurrage—was it until the end of the strike, until the completion of discharge at that discharge port, or until the completion of discharge at the last discharge port? In the High Court,[404] Donaldson J held that the answer was the end of the strike, but the Court

---

402. *Salamis Shipping (Panama) SA* v. *Edm Van Meerbeck & Co SA (The Onisilos)* [1971] 2 Lloyd's Rep 29, at p. 33.
403. *Salamis Shipping (Panama) SA* v. *Edm Van Meerbeck & Co SA (The Onisilos)* [1970] 2 Lloyd's Rep 405, at p. 406.
404. *The Onisilos* [1970] 2 Lloyd's Rep 405.

of Appeal[405] unanimously held that after laytime had expired, half demurrage ran for all periods in port until the completion of discharge at the last discharge port. In so doing, the Court of Appeal held that this included periods after the strike had ended when the vessel was held up by the after-effects of the strike, such as port congestion.

4.375 If, on the other hand, the charterers have elected to go to another discharge port then it would seem that on arrival at that port laytime will run in the normal way. If the vessel was on demurrage earlier or comes on demurrage at the alternative port, then full rate demurrage will be payable. In *The Saturnia* Bingham J put it this way[406]:

At such port, it would seem, any demurrage would have to be paid at the full rate. Again, it seems clear, as was accepted in *The Onisilos*, that the clause represents a commercial bargain attempting fairly to apportion the loss between the parties. The owner would suffer through losing the use of his ship for only half the contractual compensation, but he would at least recover that. The charterer would suffer either by paying demurrage at a half rate when his inability to discharge was due to no fault of his or by taking the risk of paying full demurrage at an alternative port, but at least his potential liability at the original port would be mitigated.

4.376 In *The Saturnia* the vessel was held up by a series of strikes during discharge, after laytime had expired, and the owners submitted that Part III, like Part I, had no application. Upholding this argument, the judge said[407]:

But there are four considerations which compulsively lead me to accept the owners' construction and thus differ from the umpire. First, the reference to paying half demurrage after expiration of the time provided for discharging does suggest that the draftsman had in mind a strike or lock-out taking effect before laytime had expired. Secondly, the charterers' construction entitling them to pay at the half rate from the expiry of the agreed laytime or the onset of the strike, whichever was later, does seem to me to involve writing into the text words which are not there but which very well could have been, had the draftsman's intention been to that effect. Thirdly, if, as I have concluded, the Part 2 options only obtain where the strike takes effect before the expiry of laytime at the loading port, it is more natural, and certainly more symmetrical, if the option at the discharge port similarly obtains only if the strike takes effect before the expiry of laytime. Fourthly, account may be taken of the fact, already referred to and put into the scales in the owners' favour in *The Spalmatori*, that once laytime has expired and the obligation to pay demurrage has accrued, the charterer is in breach and but for that breach the vessel would not be affected by the strike.

4.377 In the Court of Appeal, Sir John Donaldson MR dealt with this point more generally, saying[408]:

So I am left with the position that this is a clause which in all its essentials is in the nature of an exceptions clause. The general rule applies and unless there is something in the wording of the clause which shows that the parties intended to apply it to a situation in which the laydays had already expired, it will be ineffective. I have looked in vain through the clause for any such words.

4.378 The last sentence of the third paragraph deals with the question of additional freight payable if the charterers elect to send the vessel to another discharge port. If this other port is 100 miles or less from the original discharge port, then no additional freight is payable, but if it is more, then the freight is increased by the proportion that the additional distance bears to the original voyage. On the wording of the sentence it would seem that the additional freight is only payable on the cargo discharged at the substituted

405. *The Onisilos* [1971] 2 Lloyd's Rep 29 (CA).
406. *The Saturnia* [1984] 2 Lloyd's Rep 366, at p. 370.
407. *Ibid.*, at p. 371.
408. *The Saturnia* [1987] 2 Lloyd's Rep 43, at p. 45.

port. The vessel may well then have to either back-track or steam extra miles to get to any further discharge ports, but for this it would seem that no compensation is given to the shipowners and, furthermore, they will only receive half demurrage, if demurrage is payable. Where a lump sum freight was payable, however, this would presumably be increased, similarly notwithstanding that it might cover cargo for discharge not only at the substituted port, but at other ports as well.

4.379 It is possible, depending on the wording of the bills of lading, that a claim for deviation might arise if the charterers, at the request of the receivers of some of the cargo, sent the vessel to a substituted port, but consideration of this is largely outside the scope of the present work.[409]

SHIFTING AND LIGHTENING

Shifting

4.380 Shifting may be required:
- A. from anchorage to berth.
- B. from one berth to another.

Since different considerations apply, each will be considered separately.

From anchorage to berth

4.381 The cost of proceeding from anchorage to berth is traditionally considered to be part of the cost of the carrying voyage (both for load and discharge ports) irrespective of the type of charter. Whether time will count will depend on the terms of the charter.

4.382 In the case of a berth charter which has not been modified to provide to the contrary, time will not commence until arrival in berth. In the case of a port charter, then time will only run if the anchorage is within the port limits so that time commences on arrival at the anchorage (or a specified time thereafter) and time is not excluded by an exceptions clause or custom providing for passage time not to count, or, if the anchorage is outside the port limits, there is a "reachable on arrival" provision or an additional clause providing for time to count from arrival at the anchorage.

4.383 In one London Arbitration on a port charter, the sole arbitrator said[410]:

The traditional view was that, in the absence of provisions to the contrary, the charterers bore the risk of port congestion after the vessel reached her agreed destination and laytime had commenced and the shipowners bore the risk of navigational matters/bad weather preventing a vessel reaching a position where laytime could commence.

4.384 In another London Arbitration, the arbitrator commented[411]:

It was perhaps curious that, if the charterers had not been in breach of their "reachable on arrival" obligation and the ship had gone straight to her berth, the time spent travelling from the anchorage to the berth would not have counted, whereas in the circumstances of the present case, it did count. However that was a result which was not entirely without commercial justification, for there could be no doubt that the net transit time from anchorage to berth was considerably greater when a ship first had to anchor off the port than if she went straight into her berth. That was simply because of

409. For the effect of deviation on laytime and demurrage, see *post* at para. 6.165.
410. London Arbitration—LMLN 123, 19 July 1984.
411. London Arbitration 8/91—LMLN 304, 29 June 1991.

the time lost in slowing down, dropping anchor, weighing anchor and picking up speed on the resumed voyage. It might be thought not inappropriate that Charterers should have to pay for that additional time.

So far as shifting from an anchorage within the port is concerned, this would have been the same result had this been a port charter or a berth charter without the "reachable on arrival" provision, provided that in the latter case there was a clause accelerating the commencement of laytime to arrival within the port.[412]

CLAUSES PROVIDING FOR TIME NOT TO COUNT

4.385 Most tanker and some dry cargo charters seek to make the shipowner responsible for some or all of the time between the vessel's arrival at an anchorage within the port limits and the vessel's arrival in berth.[413] Precisely what time will be excluded will depend on the precise wording of the charter in question. In broad terms, however, what may be excluded will usually be:

A. time spent moving on an inward passage, e.g. Exxonvoy 84, Texacovoy 71, Intertankvoy 76, BPvoy 2, and Shellvoy 3 if the charterers order the vessel to wait at an anchorage

and/or

B. any delay in vessel getting into berth beyond the control of the charterer, e.g. STB Voy and Exxonvoy 69.

4.386 What is meant by "inward passage" will again depend on the wording used in the particular charter. It would appear that the phrase has a different meaning from charter to charter, depending on the words in conjunction with which it is used. Thus, in the Texacovoy 71 charter, the time excluded is that spent or lost

on an inward passage moving from anchorage or other waiting place . . . [414]

whereas in the BPvoy 2 charter, the corresponding clause excludes time

on an inward passage, including awaiting tide, pilot or tugs and moving from anchorage . . . [415]

4.387 Clearly, the second example quoted is much wider. The wording of the first example suggests that time does not start to be excluded until the vessel starts moving, i.e. the anchor is raised, whereas in the second example time will stop somewhat earlier. How much earlier is a question yet to be decided. It could be as early as receipt of orders to proceed and if delays awaiting tide are excluded, would weather be excluded? Does tide mean the next tide or does it include the transition from neaps to springs? These and other similar questions will unfortunately have to wait future litigation before an answer can be given.

4.388 However, as already mentioned, some charters such as the STB Voy not only exclude passage time but other delays beyond the control of the charterer as well. Thus, clause 6 of the STB charterparty provides as follows:

---

412. See para. 3.41 *ante.*
413. See as an example London Arbitration 27/91—LMLN 316, 14 December 1991.
414. Clause 8(*b*)(i).
415. Clause 17(i).

... However where delay is caused to vessel getting into berth after giving notice of readiness for any reason whatsoever over which charterer has no control such delay shall not count as laytime on demurrage.

4.389 In *SAMIR* v. *Notos Maritime Corporation of Monrovia (The Notos)*,[416] one of the issues raised concerned a period of delay during which, because of swell, no vessel of the relevant size was able to discharge at a sea-line, at which it was intended that the *Notos* should discharge. Rejecting an argument by the owners that clause 1(*b*) of the charter was a "reachable on arrival" provision, the arbitrators who originally heard the matter, the Commercial Court, the Court of Appeal and the House of Lords held that the delay was beyond the charterer's control and therefore excepted. Another of the issues raised in the same case was a second period of delay when the swell had abated and the sea-line was usable but another vessel which had arrived earlier than the *Notos* was using it. For this period, the arbitrators and the court held that time should run because the charterers controlled the sea-line.

CUSTOM

4.390 In *Nielsen* v. *Wait*,[417] to which more detailed reference will be made with respect to lightening, the Court of Appeal held that part of a custom allowing lightening of grain ships destined for Gloucester at Sharpness was that, notwithstanding that Sharpness was deemed to be within the port of Gloucester, the time taken to shift from Sharpness to Gloucester was excluded from laytime.

4.391 However, it is unlikely that the courts today would be prepared to hold that time taken in shifting from anchorage to berth would be excluded in the absence of a specific exclusion, although proof of a custom so providing is in theory possible.

SHIFTING FROM ANCHORAGES OUTSIDE THE PORT

4.392 Normally, if a vessel is forced to anchor outside the port, then time will not commence and time lost waiting at the anchorage and shifting to an anchorage within the port or to a berth will be a part of the voyage and therefore for the shipowner's account. However, there is no reason why, if this situation is foreseen, the parties should not provide for it. Such was the case in *Compania Naviera Termar SA* v. *Tradax Export SA (The Ante Topic)*, a decision which eventually reached the House of Lords.

4.393 The vessel concerned, the *Ante Topic*, was chartered for the carriage of a cargo of corn from the United States to London or Hull. In fact, the vessel was ordered to discharge at Hull and clause 17 of the charter provides as follows:

In the event of the vessel being ordered to Hull and being unable to berth immediately upon arrival on account of congestion, time to count from next working period after vessel's arrival at Spurn Head anchorage but time used in shifting from such anchorage to discharging berth in Hull not to count as laytime.

No berth was available on her arrival off the River Humber and the vessel accordingly anchored at the Spurn Head anchorage, some 22 miles from Hull. When a berth did become available she was unable to move upriver because of insufficient water and a

416. *SAMIR* v. *Notos Maritime Corporation (The Notos)* [1985] 1 Lloyd's Rep 149; [1985] 2 Lloyd's Rep 334; [1987] 1 Lloyd's Rep 503.
417. *Nielsen & Co* v. *Wait, James & Co* (1885) 16 QBD 67.

further four days elapsed before she was able to do so. The charterers claimed that this time should be excluded as being part of the time used in shifting; the owners argued that only the actual time of moving should not count. Before the umpire, the arbitrators having differed, and before Mocatta J, the charterers' view prevailed. In his judgment, the judge held that once the congestion had ended and permission to proceed was given, it was the duty of the owners to proceed to the discharging berth with due despatch and that the time taken in so doing included any periods of immobility. He continued[418]:

> I further do not consider that the wording of the clause is sufficient to alter the common law position so that the risks of delay, due to navigational and other hazards occurring after the cessation of inability to obtain a berth due to congestion, are made to fall upon the charterers save only for time taken in moving through the water or in preparation therefor.

However, a majority of the Court of Appeal and all the House of Lords disagreed, holding that the shipowners were right. In the Court of Appeal, Diplock LJ, part of the majority, said that the plain meaning of the words in the clause was that time used in shifting started when the vessel weighed anchor. He went on[419]:

> Why should not the words be given their ordinary meaning? I do not think that one solves this problem by arguing whether the *Ante Topic* was an "arrived" ship or not when she reached Spurn Head, or whether she had completed her contract voyage, or whether the risks of delay on voyage are normally accepted by owners, and of delay in discharge by charterers, or on any principle that once laytime begins to run it does not cease to do so unless some express term in the contract applies or further delay is caused by default of the owner. To give the words their ordinary meaning seems to me in this case to make business sense.

The House of Lords agreed,[420] the only short speech being given by Viscount Simonds, who said that "to shift" denoted activity. He also commented that there could not well be a less appropriate word to describe a vessel lying at anchor waiting for sufficient water to move.

REACHABLE ON ARRIVAL

4.394 The effect of such a clause on the commencement of time has already been considered, as have the cases in which it has been judicially considered.[421] In a port charter with such a clause time will commence on arrival at the anchorage (or the specified time thereafter)[422] if no berth is available and, if there is a clause excluding time shifting from anchorage to berth, such time will be excluded in the normal way.

4.395 If, however, the anchorage is outside the port limits or it is a berth charter then by virtue of a "reachable on arrival" provision, the shipowner will have a claim for detention from arrival at or off the port until the arrival of his vessel in berth if the vessel

418. *Compania Naviera Termar SA* v. *Tradax Export SA (The Ante Topic)* [1965] 1 Lloyd's Rep 198, at p. 206.
419. *Compania Naviera Termar SA* v. *Tradax Export SA (The Ante Topic)* [1965] 2 Lloyd's Rep 79, at p. 85.
420. *Compania Naviera Termar SA* v. *Tradax Export SA (The Ante Topic)* [1966] 1 Lloyd's Rep 566 (HL).
421. See *ante* at para. 3.402.
422. *Shipping Developments Corporation SA* v. *V/O Sojuzneftexport (The Delian Spirit)* [1971] 1 Lloyd's Rep 506 (CA). See also London Arbitration—LMLN 117, 26 April 1984. In that case the relevant charter also required a gas free certificate to be obtained before Notice of Readiness was tendered. On arrival, the port was congested and because of bad weather the appropriate inspector could not get out to the anchorage, but the weather was not such as would have prevented the vessel from berthing had it not been for the congestion.

proceeds there direct from the anchorage,[423] or until the vessel's arrival at the usual anchorage within the port limits if the vessel goes from one anchorage to another.[424] In the latter case, the usual rules will apply for the commencement of laytime and the application of any clause excluding time spent in shifting from anchorage to berth.

4.396 The interaction of a "reachable on arrival" clause and one excluding delay beyond the control of a charterer in the vessel concerned getting into berth was the point at issue in *Nereide SpA di Navigazione* v. *Bulk Oil International Ltd (The Laura Prima).*[425] The relevant clauses were clauses 6 and 9 of the Exxonvoy 1969 form of charter. These read as follows:

6. Notice of Readiness: Upon arrival at customary anchorage at each port of loading or discharge, the Master . . . shall give the Charterer . . . notice . . . that the vessel is ready to load or discharge cargo, berth or no berth, and laytime . . . shall commence upon the expiration of six (6) hours after receipt of such notice . . . However where delay is caused to Vessel getting into berth after giving notice of readiness over which Charterer has no control, such delay shall not count as used laytime.
9. Safe Berthing—Shifting: The vessel shall load and discharge at any safe place or wharf, or alongside vessels or lighters reachable on her arrival, which shall be designated and procured by the Charterer . . .

4.397 The facts in *The Laura Prima* were substantially not in dispute. The vessel arrived at the customary anchorage at Marsa El Hariga, within port limits, and gave Notice of Readiness to load. However, she was unable to proceed to berth for some days because of port congestion. The owners argued a breach of the "reachable on arrival" provision and the charterers claimed to be excused by virtue of the last sentence of clause 6. In arbitration the arbitrators appointed by each side differed and an award was published by the umpire, upholding the charterers' contentions. In so doing he found that the congestion was something over which the charterers had no control.

4.398 In the High Court[426] Mocatta J reversed this finding, holding that clauses 6 and 9 had to be read together and that this was a port charter with no express provision placing the risk of congestion on the owners. He went on to hold that the last sentence of clause 6 only applied and prevented laytime from running if the charterers had designated and procured a safe place, etc., reachable upon the vessel's arrival.

4.399 The Court of Appeal reversed this,[427] restoring the finding of the umpire. On further appeal, the House of Lords upheld the appeal, finding in favour of the owners and upholding the decision of Mocatta J.[428]

4.400 In the House of Lords the only speech was that given by Lord Roskill, who at the start of his speech emphasized, as had the lower courts, that the problem they were considering was the incidence of liability as between shipowners and charterers under a

423. *Sociedad Cargo Oceanica SA* v. *Idolinoele Vertriebsgesellschaft mbH (The Angelos Lusis)* [1964] 2 Lloyd's Rep 28.
424. *Inca Compania Naviera SA and Commercial and Maritime Enterprises Evanghelos P Nomikos SA* v. *Mofinol Inc (The President Brand)* [1967] 2 Lloyd's Rep 338.
425. *Nereide SpA di Navigazione* v. *Bulk Oil International Ltd (The Laura Prima)* [1980] 1 Lloyd's Rep 466.
426. *Ibid.*
427. *Nereide SpA di Navigazione* v. *Bulk Oil International Ltd (The Laura Prima)* [1981] 2 Lloyd's Rep 24 (CA).
428. *Nereide SpA di Navigazione* v. *Bulk Oil International Ltd (The Laura Prima)* [1982] 1 Lloyd's Rep 1 (HL).

voyage charterparty for delay in loading and discharging ports caused by congestion.[429] Later on he said[430]:

"Reachable on arrival" is a well-known phrase and means precisely what it says. If a berth cannot be reached on arrival, the warranty is broken unless there is some relevant protecting exception . . . The berth is required to have two characteristics; it has to be safe and it also has to be reachable on arrival.

Thus the end result of the case was that the owners succeeded in their claim for demurrage, which commenced when the notice period, plus the allowed laytime, expired and continued thereafter until the completion of loading.

THE LIMITS OF THE LAURA PRIMA DECISION

4.401 Since the House of Lords announced their decision in November 1981, its precise limits have been a matter of some speculation. Part of the problem arises from the fact that the earlier decisions on what was meant by "reachable on arrival" did not have to consider the effect of an exceptions clause such as that in the last sentence of clause 6, and part from whether the principles of *The Laura Prima* apply to causes of delay other than congestion.

4.402 To take the former first: in *The Laura Prima* it was not disputed that the vessel was an Arrived ship. Suppose, however, the facts had been as in *The President Brand*,[431] where the vessel concerned first anchored outside the port limits of Lourenço Marques then shifted to an anchorage within the port limits where she gave Notice of Readiness but was further delayed by congestion before she could move into berth. In that case there was no equivalent to the last sentence of clause 6 or a provision advancing commencement of laytime and Roskill J held that the owners could claim for detention from the vessel's arrival at the first anchorage until giving notice at the second anchorage. In addition, after the requisite period expired, thereafter laytime commenced and on that occasion discharge was completed within the laytime allowed. If, however, the charter had contained a clause excluding delay in getting into berth beyond the charterers' control similar to clause 6, how would that have affected the position? Clearly, it would not affect the claim for detention but would it affect the second period of delay? On the strength of the *The Laura Prima*, the answer must surely be "no". The failure to procure a berth "reachable on arrival" is not rectified by the commencement of laytime and the last sentence of clause 6 still does not apply. There can only be one arrival for the purpose of a "reachable on arrival" clause.

4.403 If in the case of an Asbatankvoy form of charter, clause 6 does not apply where there has been a breach of clause 9, what is the position where there has also been a breach of an additional clause? That was the question considered in London Arbitration 7/91,[432] although the charter in this case was a Tanker Motor Vessel Voyage form of charter. An additional clause provided:

Any time used in waiting for daylight, normal tide conditions, bad weather or port services such as pilotage and towage shall not count as laytime at ports of loading and discharging.

429. *Ibid.*, at p. 3.
430. *Ibid.*, at p. 6.
431. *The President Brand* [1967] 2 Lloyd's Rep 338.
432. London Arbitration 7/91—LMLN 303, 15 June 1991.

There was also a general exceptions clause which specifically referred to laytime.

4.404 The vessel was delayed and charterers sought to rely on these clauses as overriding a printed "reachable on arrival" provision, which the tribunal held they could. It is not clear from the short report of the case whether the delay that was the subject of the dispute occurred before or after the vessel berthed. If it was after then the effect of the breach of the "reachable on arrival" provision was clearly spent and the tribunal were obviously right.

4.405 If the delay was before, but after the vessel had reached a position from where Notice of Readiness could be tendered, the issue is more difficult. One way it could be justified would be to invoke the well-known rule of construction whereby an additional clause takes precedent over a printed clause.

4.406 The same point arises in relation to clause 8 of Part II of the Asbatankvoy form, which provides for half rate demurrage in certain circumstances and no demurrage in others. Does this mean that laytime continues until it expires and then, if the specified conditions are met, either half rate or no demurrage is payable?

4.407 One case where this arose was London Arbitration 2/90,[433] where the vessel concerned arrived at the discharge port still on laytime, but in the middle of a tug strike which continued after laytime expired. Tug strikes are one of the instances in which by clause 8 no demurrage is payable. In these circumstances, the arbitrator held the charterers were excused from liability.[434]

4.408 If this decision is correct, it means that whether charterers are protected will depend on whether the charter is a berth or port charter. In the case of the former, the claim would be one for detention but in the latter the demurrage exception would apply.

4.409 Whilst any definitive answer must await future judicial comment, it is suggested that it would be more logical to say that in the same way that the laytime exception in clause 6 relating to delay in getting into berth does not apply unless the charterers procure a berth "reachable on arrival" so should the demurrage exceptions in clause 8. To hold otherwise would be to seriously limit the effect of a "reachable on arrival" provision in the circumstances specified in that clause.

4.410 The more contentious issue, however, is whether the principles enunciated in *The Laura Prima* in relation to congestion apply equally to other forms of delay, particularly those which have been traditionally held to be shipowners' risks, such as weather and lack of water. On this point there have been opposing views between the legal and mercantile communities.[435]

4.411 To understand these it is necessary to consider the essential characteristics of a voyage charter. In *The Johanna Oldendorff*,[436] Lord Diplock divided such a voyage into four stages—the loading (approach) voyage, the loading operation, the carrying voyage and the discharging operation. Of these, the first and third call for acts of performance by the shipowner alone and the other two are joint acts, but for which the primary obligation rests with the charterer. It is for this reason that the provision of berths and hence

---

433. London Arbitration 2/90—LMLN 267, 27 January 1990.

434. See also the United States case of *Black Swan Inc* v. *Castle Supply and Marketing Inc* (*The Altus*) (NY Arb), LMLN 275, 19 May 1990, where New York arbitrators held clause 8 applied during a tug strike, but not to congestion resulting from it.

435. Sometimes euphemistically referred to as the inhabitants of the Temple and of the parish of St Mary Axe. See also *Commencement of Laytime* by Donald Davies.

436. *Oldendorff (EL) & Co GmbH* v. *Tradax Export SA* (*The Johanna Oldendorff*) [1973] 2 Lloyd's Rep 285 (HL).

congestion are normally held to be the charterer's responsibility. As Lord Diplock put it in *The Johanna Oldendorff*[437]:

> The standard forms of charterparty do not usually include an exception clause for delay caused by the inability of the vessel to load or to discharge her cargo because of congestion at the place, whether berth or dock or port, specified in the charterparty as the place of loading or discharge. So any loss due to delay from this cause falls upon the party who is thereby prevented from doing timeously what, by the terms of the charterparty, he had undertaken the primary obligation to secure was done.
>
> Herein lies the importance of the four stages into which the adventure is divided. Each must be completed before the next can begin. So until the vessel has reached the specified place of loading on the loading voyage or the specified place of discharge on the carrying voyage, the contractual obligation to bring the vessel there lies on the shipowner alone; and any loss occasioned by delay in doing so falls upon him.

4.412 The views of the mercantile community are well illustrated by two London Arbitration awards, the second of which involved a "reachable on arrival" provision. In the first, however,[438] the point strictly at issue was whether the vessel concerned was an Arrived ship. The vessel anchored in Brest Roads, within the limits of the port, but was unable to move into berth for some seven days because of insufficiency of water caused by neap tides. Because of this the arbitrators held that she was not at the effective disposition of the charterers and not an Arrived ship. The arbitrators commented that it was usual for owners to bear the risk of delays which occur because of low tides at a named port in the absence of any express provision to the contrary.

4.413 The second arbitration was on the Exxonvoy form and therefore a "reachable on arrival" provision was included. It is not clear from the limited report[439] of the case whether the vessel concerned had to lie off inside or outside the port limits but since the sole arbitrator based his award on the basis that clause 6 applied and laytime would otherwise run, presumably the vessel had to wait at the normal waiting area. It would appear that, having arrived at the normal waiting area, the vessel was unable to proceed further because of bad weather and, in particular, high winds. Having mentioned *The Angelos Lusis*,[440] *The President Brand*[441] and *The Laura Prima*[442] (in particular the decision of Mocatta J), the arbitrator continued:

> Although those decisions were logical within the context of port congestion, the judgments had left open the position when the facts were such that it was a useless exercise to designate and procure a berth in circumstances where it was impossible for the vessel to proceed into a berth because of bad weather. If the designation/procurement of a berth was irrelevant at the time of a vessel's arrival off a port, then clause 9 should be disregarded so that one was left with clause 6 only vis-à-vis the running of laytime and delay in berthing. The result would then be that delay in berthing because of bad weather would not count as laytime.
>
> It was impracticable to talk about designating/procuring a berth when a port was closed and a vessel could not enter because of bad weather. In practice, a tanker was told to lay off a port until the weather improved, after which time she was given berthing instructions. It was pointless to

437. *Ibid.*, at p. 305.
438. London Arbitration—LMLN 18, 10 July 1980.
439. London Arbitration—LMLN 123, 19 July 1984.
440. *Sociedad Cargo Oceanica SA* v. *Idolinoele Vertriebsgesellschaft mbH (The Angelos Lusis)* [1964] 2 Lloyd's Rep 28.
441. *Inca Compania Naviera SA and Commercial and Maritime Enterprises Evanghelos P Nomikos SA* v. *Mofinol Inc (The President Brand)* [1967] 2 Lloyd's Rep 338.
442. *Nereide SpA di Navigazione* v. *Bulk Oil International Ltd (The Laura Prima)* [1980] 1 Lloyd's Rep 466; [1981] 2 Lloyd's Rep 24 (CA); [1982] 1 Lloyd's Rep 1 (HL).

designate a berth in bad weather conditions. The sensible approach was that the charterers should have a berth available so that there was no delay between improvement in weather and the berthing of the vessel.

4.414 Earlier in the award, the arbitrator recognized that he was bound by the decision of Roskill J in *The President Brand*, where the first delay was caused by an insufficiency of water over the bar outside Lourenço Marques, but argued that this should not be extended to weather. Since the arbitrator also referred to the shipowner's traditional responsibility for navigational matters/bad weather preventing a vessel reaching a point where laytime can commence, presumably had it been open to him to so do, he would have disagreed with Roskill J and applied the principles set out later in his award, quoted above, to insufficiency of water.

4.415 The commercial or mercantile view, therefore, is that *The Laura Prima*[443] should be confined to delay caused by port congestion and the duty of the charterer should therefore be to procure a berth which is free and available in the sense of not being occupied at the time of the vessel's arrival off the port. In the event that notwithstanding this the vessel is unable to proceed to the berth because of lack of water, weather or other risk traditionally the responsibility of the shipowner, then the time lost must be borne by the shipowner either because the vessel has not become an Arrived ship or, if it has, because of the effect of clause 6. In other words "reachable on arrival" means simply "reachable without delay due to port congestion".

4.416 The contrary or legal view is equally simple and is that "reachable on arrival" means precisely what it says[444] and that all risks of delay from whatever cause are thereby put on the charterer unless he protects himself by a suitably worded exceptions clause. It therefore does not matter what the cause of the delay is or whether it is something that is traditionally laid at the door of the shipowner or at the door of the charterer. In *The President Brand*[445] the risk was one categorized as a shipowner's risk (lack of water); in *The Laura Prima*[446] the risk was a charterer's risk (congestion) but there was a specific finding of fact that there was nothing the charterer could have done about it.

4.417 In the arbitration referred to above,[447] the arbitrator distinguished weather and lack of water. In another arbitration[448] the tribunal held the contrary. In *Aden Refinery Co Ltd* v. *Ugland Management Co Ltd*,[449] Sir John Donaldson MR somewhat reluctantly upheld a refusal by the High Court to grant leave to appeal in a case involving delay due to weather.

4.418 However, in a series of cases in 1987, the issue did eventually reach the High Court. The first of these was *The Kyzikos*,[450] a non-tanker case, where an "always accessible" provision was held to be the same as one providing for a berth "reachable on arrival". In that case, a berth was available, but not accessible, because the vessel concerned could not proceed to it because of fog. Accepting that he was bound by *The*

---

443. *Ibid.*
444. *Per* Lord Roskill in *The Laura Prima* [1982] 1 Lloyd's Rep 1, at p. 3.
445. *The President Brand* [1967] 2 Lloyd's Rep 338.
446. *The Laura Prima* [1982] 1 Lloyd's Rep 1.
447. London Arbitration—LMLN 123, 19 July 1984.
448. See also London Arbitration—LMLN 151, 15 August 1985, where a majority of the arbitrators followed the *Laura Prima* decision although expressing disquiet about it when applied to adverse weather.
449. *Aden Refinery Co Ltd* v. *Ugland Management Co Ltd* [1986] 2 Lloyd's Rep 336.
450. *Seacrystal Shipping Ltd* v. *Bulk Transport Group Shipping Co Ltd (The Kyzikos)* [1987] 2 Lloyd's Rep 122.

President Brand,[451] Webster J drew a distinction between physical and non-physical reasons for the delay, applying such a provision only to the former. Fog and other forms of weather came under the latter and owners were not protected.

4.419 This was followed by *The Fjordaas*[452] and *The Sea Queen*.[453] In the former, the delay was due to a prohibition on night navigation[454] coupled with a requirement for compulsory pilotage plus bad weather, and in the latter, by a non-availability of tugs followed by bad weather. In both cases, charterers succeeded in arbitration, but were reversed on appeal. In both cases, charterers sought unsuccessfully to argue that delays could be divided into physical obstructions preventing the vessel from reaching the berth and other reasons. Included in the former were both congestion and lack of water, notwithstanding that that would normally be classed an owners' risk.

4.420 Although *The Kyzikos* subsequently reached the House of Lords,[455] this point was not considered above the High Court. There are, therefore, at present two High Court decisions applying *The Laura Prima* whatever the reason for the delay and one confining it to delay caused by physical obstructions.

4.421 Presumably sooner or later, the issue will have to come again before the higher courts. At the moment, however, the majority view is encapsulated by the *dictum* of Saville J, when he said in *The Sea Queen*[456]:

> . . . it seems to me that the charterers have warranted in clear and simple words that there will be a berth that the vessel will be able to reach on her arrival—so that, if there is not, for whatever reason, then the charterers have failed to perform this part of their bargain.

4.422 What is also clear is that if the "reachable on arrival" provision is complied with,[457]

> Then if some intervening event occurs causing delay over which the charterers have no control, such as the imposition of an embargo or an insufficiency of water, the last sentence of clause 6 will apply.

That is, of course, if the vessel is an Arrived ship. If not, the charterer will still be protected because the voyage will not have come to an end and the risk of delay will lie with the shipowner. The most likely cause for such delay will be what has been termed shipowner's risks, such as weather, insufficiency of water, collision, etc., although political and other risks normally borne by the charterer are also covered. However, where the risk is one normally allocated to the charterer, it should be emphasized that the delay must be beyond his control, which could give rise to some interesting questions in ports

---

451. *The President Brand* [1967] 2 Lloyd's Rep 338.
452. *K/S Arnt J Moerland* v. *Kuwait Petroleum Corporation (The Fjordaas)* [1988] 1 Lloyd's Rep 336.
453. *Palm Shipping Inc* v. *Kuwait Petroleum Corporation (The Sea Queen)* [1988] 1 Lloyd's Rep 500. For a report on the arbitration stage of the case, see London Arbitration 7/87—LMLN 197, 21 May 1987.
454. See also New York Arbitration (*The Luctor*), LMLN 349, 20 March 1993.
455. *Seacrystal Shipping Ltd* v. *Bulk Transport Group Shipping Co Ltd (The Kyzikos)* [1989] 1 Lloyd's Rep 1. Interestingly enough, the House of Lords restored the decision of Webster J on the main issue in the case, the meaning of Whether in Berth or Not, and it would be of interest to know what they would have thought on this point.
456. *The Sea Queen* [1988] 1 Lloyd's Rep 500, at p. 502. In *Novorossisk Shipping Co* v. *Neopetro Co Ltd (The Ulyanovsk)* [1990] 1 Lloyd's Rep 425, owners unsuccessfully sought to argue that orders not to berth on arrival were unlawful, because it would prevent the vessel from reaching the berth "reachable on arrival", which charterers were obliged to designate.
457. *The Laura Prima* [1980] 1 Lloyd's Rep 466, at p. 468 *per* Mocatta J.

dominated by a major charterer, particularly where that charterer was also a state organization.

From one berth to another

4.423 In the absence of an express stipulation permitting a charterer to load at more than one berth, a ship is not bound, once she has arrived and made fast to a berth to which she has been ordered, to shift again from that berth for the purpose of taking on board part of the cargo which is the subject-matter of the charter.[458]

4.424 However, it is common for a charter to include a provision allowing loading or discharging at more than one berth. This may either be done by a provision in the voyage instructions part of the charter and/or an additional clause. Thus, as an example of the former, a charter on the Baltimore berth grain form C, might read

... the ... Vessel ... shall proceed to 1/2 safe berths [nominated port] and there load [the specified cargo] ... and being so loaded shall therewith proceed to 1/2 safe berths [nominated port] and deliver the same ...

4.425 An example of the latter is clause 9 of the Exxonvoy 1969 (Asbatankvoy) form, the second sentence of which reads as follows:

The Charterer shall have the right of shifting the Vessel at ports of loading and/or discharge from one safe berth to another on payment of all towage and pilotage shifting to next berth, charge for running lines on arrival at and leaving that berth, additional agency charges and expense, customs overtime and fees and any other extra port charges or part expenses incurred by reason of using more than one berth.

4.426 Whichever form is used, however, laytime will continue to run during shifting in the absence of a provision to the contrary,[459] or a shift for the shipowner's own purposes which has the effect of withdrawing the ship from the immediate and effective disposition of the charterers. In *Surrey Shipping Co Ltd* v. *Compagnie Continentale (France) SA (The Shackleford)*, having distinguished a two-berth discharge from a two-port discharge, which of necessity must involve a second carrying voyage, Buckley LJ continued[460]:

A charter to discharge at one or more berths in a single port is a very different thing. The movement from one berth to another within the port is for the convenience of the charterers. It would be eminently reasonable to construe the charterparty in such a case so as to reckon shifting time from one berth to another, or, if laytime has started to run, from anchorage to berth of discharge, as counting against laytime or demurrage and not as part of the carrying voyage.

4.427 One of the shifts that occurred in this case was for bunkering, but since the period of bunkering took place whilst the vessel was waiting for a berth, the court held that this did not mean that time was lost purely for the shipowner's own purposes and therefore time continued to run during the shift to and from the bunkering berth and whilst bunkering.[461]

458. *King Line Ltd* v. *Moxey, Savon & Co Ltd* (1939) 62 Ll L Rep 252.

459. Since in a fixed laytime charter, laytime runs continuously once commenced unless there is an exception or interruption or default of the shipowner. See *ante* at para. 4.3.

460. *Surrey Shipping Co Ltd* v. *Compagnie Continentale (France) SA (The Shackleford)* [1978] 2 Lloyd's Rep 154, at p. 164.

461. *Ibid.*, at p. 163 *per* Sir David Cairns, and at first instance [1978] 1 Lloyd's Rep 191 *per* Donaldson J.

4.428 An illustration of time not counting during shifting is provided by *W I Radcliffe Steamship Co Ltd* v. *Exporthleb*,[462] where the relevant clause read "Charterers have the option of loading and discharging at two safe berths in one port without extra charge and time for shifting not to count".

4.429 Although the likelihood of a delay arising before a vessel is able to shift is probably less in a shift from one berth to another than in a shift from anchorage to berth, nevertheless a clause worded as above would probably only exclude the actual period of the move and not any waiting period beforehand.[463] However, if for any reason, something happened during the move which caused it to be prolonged, then that further delay would probably be considered as part of shifting time.

Enforced shifting

4.430 It not infrequently happens that a vessel is forced to shift at the behest of neither the shipowner nor the charterer. This may happen either because of the weather and/or on the orders of the port or other local authorities.

4.431 If, in this situation, laytime is measured in either weather working days or days/ working days weather permitting, then whether time will be interrupted will depend on whether the weather permitted loading/discharging at the berth at the time of the shift and during the vessel's absence from the berth. However, as Parker J pointed out in *Gebr Broere* v. *Saras Chimica SpA*,[464] if the weather first prevents loading (or discharging) and then has the added effect of forcing the vessel to leave her berth, it does not cease to have the former effect after the vessel has left the berth. Nevertheless, it is only when cargo operations are curtailed that time stops, not when the effect of the weather is to render the presence of the vessel unsafe.[465]

4.432 The leading case on enforced shifting is *Cantiere Navale Triestina* v. *Handelsvertretung der Russe Soviet Republik Naphtha Export*.[466] In this case, the *Dora*, an Italian ship, arrived at the Soviet port of Batum to load a cargo of oil. However, because of a dispute between the Soviet and Italian Governments, she was ordered to leave Russian waters shortly after her arrival. This she did, proceeding to Constantinople whilst representations were made on her behalf to the Soviet Government in Moscow. As a result of these, she returned to Batum some 17 days after she left. The shipowners claimed that time continued to run during this period and the Court of Appeal held that this was correct.

4.433 In his judgment, Atkin LJ said[467]:

Indeed, if one comes to think it out, there can be no reason why the absence of the ship from the harbour, once she has left and the lay days have begun to run, without any fault on the part of the owner, should prevent demurrage from running . . . it appears to me to make no difference whether

462. *W I Radcliffe Steamship Co Ltd, and another* v. *Exporthleb* (1939) 64 Ll L Rep 250. In this case the owners argued unsuccessfully that the provision quoted only allowed shifting from one berth to another in the same dock and not from one dock to another.
463. *Compania Naviera Termar SA* v. *Tradax Export SA (The Ante Topic)* [1966] 1 Lloyd's Rep 566 (HL).
464. *Gebr Broere BV* v. *Saras Chimica SpA* [1982] 2 Lloyd's Rep 436, at p. 439.
465. *Compania Crystal de Vapores* v. *Herman & Mohatta (India) Ltd (The Maria G)* [1958] 1 Lloyd's Rep 616, at p. 621.
466. *Cantiere Navale Triestina* v. *Handelsvertretung der Russe Soviet Republik Naphtha Export* (1925) 21 Ll L Rep 204.
467. *Ibid.*, at p. 211.

the vessel is in harbour 50 yards away from a berth and cannot get to the berth, or whether she is out of the harbour, say 50 miles away, and is unable to get to the berth.

4.434 During the case it was also argued that performance of the charter was illegal and that this, therefore, prevented time from running. However, on the facts, the court held that the orders given to the *Dora* were of an executive nature such as would be excluded by a "restraint of princes" clause had there been one in the charter. The court therefore left open the question of illegality.

4.435 In *The Maria G*,[468] illegality was also considered. In that case the harbour master at Calcutta, fearing the effect of a bore tide that was expected, ordered the ship to shift from an alongside berth to buoys. Laytime was measured in weather working days and Devlin J held that, assuming that a bore tide was weather, nevertheless time was not interrupted.[469] Turning to the question of illegality, the judge held that it was implicit in the finding of the umpire that the law in the Port of Calcutta was such as to authorize the harbour master to give orders of this character and that failure to comply with the order would have been a breach of the law.[470] He then went on to accept the owners' argument that, assuming the law made it an offence for the charterers to attempt to load during the period the vessel was away from the berth, laytime continued to run. This was because it was not enough to point to a law which made it an offence to load the vessel during a particular part of lay days, however large a part that might be.

4.436 How practical it was to load in the reduced period appears to have been considered irrelevant.[471] It therefore seems that to stop laytime on the basis of illegality, any prohibition must be of a permanent or, at least, indefinite nature.

4.437 If a vessel is required to shift, it is clear that laytime will only continue to run if the shift and absence from her berth is temporary. Thus, in *Petrinovic & Co Ltd* v. *Mission Française des Transports Maritimes*,[472] it was held that demurrage ceased when the vessel concerned was taken away from Bordeaux because of the military situation in France. Commenting on that decision in *Gem Shipping Co of Monrovia* v. *Babanaft (Lebanon) SARL (The Fontevivo)*, Donaldson J said[473]:

... the departure of the vessel was intended to be permanent. Such a departure must bring the contract of carriage to an end, whether it be a justified or an unjustified repudiation or whether it merely recognizes that in the events which were unfolding the contract had been frustrated. Once the contract of carriage is at an end, laytime must also cease to run.

Shifting expenses

4.438 Although strictly outside the terms of reference of this book, the question of shifting expenses will be mentioned briefly, since a frequent source of dispute concerns

---

468. *Compania Crystal de Vapores* v. *Herman & Mohatta (India) Ltd (The Maria G)* [1958] 1 Lloyd's Rep 616.

469. For a more detailed consideration of this aspect, see *ante* at para. 4.140.

470. *The Maria G* [1958] 1 Lloyd's Rep 616, at p. 623.

471. This part of the finding was based on *Steamship Induna Co Ltd* v. *British Phosphate Commissioners* (1949) 82 Ll L Rep 430, where it was held that a prohibition on discharge during specified night hours did not make it illegal to discharge at the rate specified in the charterparty, although it would have been difficult to achieve in the remaining period of the day.

472. *Petrinovic & Co Ltd* v. *Mission Française des Transports Maritimes* (1941) 71 Ll L Rep 208.

473. *Gem Shipping Co of Monrovia* v. *Babanaft (Lebanon) SARL (The Fontevivo)* [1975] 1 Lloyd's Rep 339, at p. 343.

who pays. This usually arises in connection with involuntary shifts; but before dealing with this, for the sake of completeness, other shifts will be considered.

4.439 The cost of shifting from anchorage to berth is invariably at the expense of the shipowner, whether it be a berth or a port charterparty. Illustration of this point is contained in London Arbitration 11/99,[474] where the owners unsuccessfully sought to get the charterers to pay part of the cost of tugs on the basis that the number used was excessive. Rejecting the claim, the tribunal held:

> ... in a voyage charter it was customary that owners met the cost of pilotage and tugs. The tribunal had not been informed of the size of the tugs or why five had been needed, although it did note that the vessel was the largest vessel to use the port. Whether the tugs were used for arrival or departure or both was unclear. The owners' claim had been put on the basis that if port charges were more than average in the permitted range for a particular port, then any excess had to fall to the charterers. Apart from the fact that no evidence had been produced as to what the norm might be, the tribunal would in any event reject that argument. The charterers were entitled to select any port in the permitted range and the consequential costs fell to the owners ...

Payment for shifts thereafter permitted under the terms of the charter and made on the orders of the charterer will depend on the terms of the charter. If this provides for cargo operations at more than one berth and nothing further is said, then payment is included in freight. However, particularly in tanker charters, subsequent shifts may be specifically said to be at the expense of the charterer, by some such clause as clause 9 of the Exxonvoy 1969 charter, to which reference has already been made.[475]

4.440 With regard to involuntary shifts, in *The Maria G* Devlin J was careful to say at the end of his judgment[476]:

> But, of course, it does not necessarily follow, as a matter of law, that, because the time lost in loading has to be included in the assessment of the laytime, the charterers have to pay the expenses incurred in the shifting of the vessel to the King George Dock Buoys.

4.441 One argument frequently advanced is that if the vessel is forced to leave the berth for the safety of the ship and cargo, whether because of weather, or because of other constraints such as in the *Petrinovic* case,[477] this must mean that the berth was unsafe.

4.442 The classic definition of a safe port/berth, however, is that set out by Sellers LJ in *The Eastern City*,[478] where he said that the question is whether the port and/or berth was such that the vessel could "reach it, use it and return from it without ... being exposed to danger which could be avoided by good navigation and seamanship". A further useful point was that made by Parker J in *The Polyglory*, where he said[479]:

> If the only dangers to which a properly manned and equipped vessel of the size and type in question will be exposed are dangers which can be avoided by the exercise of ordinary reasonable care and skill that port is not as a matter of law unsafe ... [480]

4.443 In leaving the berth, it follows that the danger is avoided and therefore, on the basis of the above, there has been no breach of the safe berth warranty, assuming it to be

---

474. London Arbitration 11/99—LMLN 510, 27 May 1999.
475. See *ante* at para. 4.425.
476. *Compania Crystal de Vapores* v. *Herman & Mohatta (India) Ltd (The Maria G)* [1958] 1 Lloyd's Rep 616, at p. 625.
477. *Petrinovic & Co Ltd* v. *Mission Française des Transports Maritimes* (1941) 71 Ll L Rep 208.
478. *Leeds Shipping Co Ltd* v. *Société Française Bunge (The Eastern City)* [1958] 2 Lloyd's Rep 127.
479. *Kristiandsands Tankrederi A/S* v. *Standard Tankers (Bahamas) Ltd (The Polyglory)* [1977] 2 Lloyd's Rep 353.
480. See also *The Notos* [1987] 1 Lloyd's Rep 503, at p. 507.

a continuing one, for which the cost of shifting would give rise to a claim for damages.

4.444 A somewhat unusual "safe berth" situation arose in *The Universal Monarch*.[481] In this case the ship in question was ordered to Leixoes in Portugal under a charter containing a safe port provision. Because of a previous accident, the port authorities would only allow a ship of that size to berth with the aid of six tugs, which was more than the number normally available at the port. For such a ship it was necessary for additional tugs to come from approximately 200 miles away at considerable extra expense. This additional expense was claimed by owners as a breach of the safe port warranty. In arbitration they were unsuccessful, but this was reversed on appeal by Gatehouse J. It should, however, be noted that the judgment was extempore none of the leading cases relating to what is a safe port were cited and the merits of the appeal were dealt with on an application for leave to appeal. The judge concluded his judgment saying[482]:

In my judgement, once the arbitrators had found that on the vessel's arrival the port was not safe in the absence of the Lisbon tugs, a proper approach must have led them to conclude that the charterers were in breach of the safe port warranty and that the cost of obtaining the tugs from a distance represented by 16 hours steaming time in order to remedy their breach and render the port safe was for the charterers to bear.

4.445 However, the leading case on shifting expenses is probably *Cosmar Compania Naviera SA* v. *Total Transport Corporation (The Isabelle)*,[483] a decision of Robert Goff J. The case subsequently went to the Court of Appeal, where the decision at first instance was upheld completely with the court adopting the reasoning of the lower court in a very short judgment.[484]

4.446 The charterers, Total, ordered the *Isabelle* to proceed to Bejaia to load a cargo of oil supplied by the Algerian National Oil Co (Sonatrach). However, Bejaia is subject to a phenomenon known as the "Ressac". When the Mistral and Tamentane winds blow from the coasts of France, a heavy swell occurs in Bejaia and vessels which remain in port are liable to damage and there is risk of ruptured hoses. In such an event it is usual for the harbour master to close the port if he considers this necessary. If a vessel is completing loading when the Ressac starts, the harbour master sometimes instructs the vessel to use tugs to hold her steady and minimize the risk. At other times he may order the vessel to leave the berth and wait at the anchorage until the Ressac has passed.

4.447 The *Isabelle* was delayed getting into berth because of the Ressac and congestion arising therefrom. However, after eventually getting into berth and commencing loading, the *Isabelle* started to surge heavily and two tugs were ordered to keep the vessel in place. In spite of this, the ship continued to surge and she was ordered to leave the berth and proceed to the anchorage. Some eight days later she returned to the berth and completed loading.

4.448 The first area of dispute concerned the period prior to the vessel first berthing and, with regard to this, Robert Goff J held that time did not run because it was a berth charter and the only clause advancing time related to a situation where the charterers ordered the vessel not to proceed to berth, which did not apply in the present case. Any

---

481. *Palm Shipping Inc* v. *Vitol SA (The Universal Monarch)* [1988] 2 Lloyd's Rep 483.
482. *Ibid.*, at p. 485.
483. *Cosmar Compania Naviera SA* v. *Total Transport Corporation (The Isabelle)* [1982] 2 Lloyd's Rep 81.
484. [1984] 1 Lloyd's Rep 366 (CA).

instructions from the port authority to wait whilst other vessels loaded were given in the exercise of their own administrative function, and not as agents for the charterers.

4.449 The second point raised concerned payment for the tugs ordered to hold the vessel at the berth. The owners claimed that they were required as part of loading. However, the judge held that it was for the owners to bring the vessel to the berth for loading and it was for them to keep the vessel at the berth for that purpose and the owners could not therefore claim the cost of the tugs in maintaining the vessel at the loading berth simply as part of the expenses of loading the vessel.

4.450 The last issue concerned shifting expenses. As to these, it was held that the order to shift was given by the port authority in pursuance of its function as administrator of the port, not as the charterers' agent. Although the charter contained the usual tanker shifting clause allowing the charterers to order the vessel to load/discharge at more than one berth, that contemplated a positive order by the charterers and no such was given. The owners' claim for reminbursement of shifting expenses therefore failed.

4.451 It is therefore clear that, in most cases, the cost of involuntary shifting will fall to the shipowners, notwithstanding that laytime will continue to run.

Warping

4.452 Warping is where a vessel shifts using the vessel's winches to haul herself along the jetty, sometimes assisted by the engines. It is necessary to differentiate between warping in the same berth and warping to a new berth.

4.453 The former sometimes happens where cranes cannot plumb and it is necessary for the vessel to shift a few yards either forwards or backwards. Obviously there is no change of berth in these circumstances and it is irrelevant as to how many berths are allowed to charterers in the charterparty. So far as any costs are concerned, it is not uncommon for the crew to do it if they can. Sometimes the charter contains an additional clause providing for the crew to assist with this operation if allowed by port regulations and that warping within the same berth should not count as a shift of berth. If port regulations do not allow the crew to warp the vessel or there is no clause of this type and the crew refuse to do it, at least without payment, then any costs are logically part of the loading or discharging expenses. Normally time would continue to run during the operation.

4.454 So far as warping to a new berth is concerned (even though this is on the same frontage), the situation may be different. The first question to ask is who requires this to be done. If it is the port authority, it is an involuntary shift and any cost probably falls where it lies. This may be with the owners. However if the charterers or shippers/receivers were billed, the cost would lie with them.

4.455 If it is a voluntary shift for the convenience of the shippers/receivers then the situation is exactly the same as any shift of berth. Does the charter allow for cargo operations at more than one berth? Does the charter provide for who is to pay for shifting between berths? If the answer to the first question is "no" then it is a matter of negotiation with the owners to effectively change the charter provisions to allow for it and no doubt they would agree provided time continued to run and the cost was for charterers' account. If the answer is "yes" but there is nothing in the charter about time or expense, then time would probably run but the cost would fall to the owners.

Lightening

4.456 If the charterparty allows the charterer to choose the discharging port out of a range of ports, then there will be a breach of charter if a port, or for that matter a berth, is nominated which the vessel cannot get into without lightening first. Thus in *The Alhambra*,[485] the vessel concerned was ordered to Lowestoft but, because of her draught, she could not lie afloat there at low water. The charter provided for her to proceed to a safe port "or as near thereto as she can safely get, and always lie and discharge afloat". The receiver of the cargo offered at his own expense to lighten the vessel in the roads but the master refused and proceeded to Harwich to discharge the cargo, the nearest safe port. On these facts it was held that he was justified in doing so.

4.457 If the charter, as in *The Alhambra*, contains an "as near as she may safely get" provision then laytime will start in the usual way when the vessel arrives at the nearest place where she can safely discharge. If there is no such provision then, it is suggested, the situation is analogous to one where the charterer fails to nominate a discharge port[486] and there is *prima facie* a claim for detention for the period of discharge, although the charterer would, however, be entitled to set off the amount of laytime against the delay arising from his breach of contract.[487]

4.458 In *Nielsen* v. *Wait*,[488] the Court of Appeal had held that, by custom, the time taken in shifting from Sharpness to Gloucester was excluded from laytime. That case was distinguished by Day J in *Reynolds & Co* v. *Tomlinson*,[489] where the master refused a request to discharge so much of the cargo at Sharpness as would enable her to proceed up the canal to Gloucester, the nominated port, and he discharged the whole cargo at Sharpness. It was held that he was entitled to act as he did since Gloucester was not a safe port in the circumstances. The judge also pointed out that the question of whether Gloucester was a safe port was not considered in *Nielsen* v. *Wait*.[490]

4.459 However, if he wishes, the master may agree to discharge part of his cargo as a lightening operation and, if he does, the charterer or consignee will be liable for the costs incurred.[491] If the ship concerned has already become an Arrived ship prior to lightening, then in the absence of anything to the contrary in the charterparty, laytime will continue to run during lightening, whether it takes place at the option of the master or because it is permitted by the charterparty, and during shifting to the principal discharge berth.

4.460 If lightening takes place before the vessel has become an Arrived ship, then *prima facie* laytime does not run. In *Nielsen* v. *Wait*, Lord Esher dealt with the matter on the basis that Sharpness was part of the Port of Gloucester, but he continued[492]:

If it is not within the Port of Gloucester, it is obvious to my mind that the shipowner would not be entitled to count the time spent in unloading as lay days; and if it is without the Port of Gloucester, it seems to be impossible to say that the defendants are liable.

485. *The Alhambra* (1881) 6 PD 68.
486. *Zim Israel Navigation Co Ltd* v. *Tradax Export SA (The Timna)* [1971] 2 Lloyd's Rep 91 (CA). See also *ante* at para. 3.22.
487. London Arbitration—LMLN 117, 26 April 1984.
488. *Nielsen & Co* v. *Wait, James & Co* (1885) 16 QBD 67.
489. *Reynolds & Co* v. *Tomlinson* [1896] 1 QB 586.
490. *Nielsen & Co* v. *Wait, James & Co* (1885) 16 QBD 67.
491. *Hall Steamship Co* v. *Paul* (1914) 19 CC 384.
492. *Nielsen & Co* v. *Wait, James & Co* (1885) 16 QBD 67, at p. 74.

4.461 However, in the Scottish case of *Dickinson* v. *Martini & Co*[493] it was held that the shipowners were entitled to count time spent in lightening outside the port. In that case, a ship had been chartered to discharge at a "safe port in the United Kingdom, or so near thereunto as she may safely get always afloat at any time of the tide". Glasgow was nominated as the discharge port but, because of her draught, part of the cargo had to be discharged at Greenock. In respect of that cargo, the Court of Session held that the voyage had been completed at Greenock and time spent in lightening was to be included in used laytime.

4.462 If, on the other hand, there is no "as near as she may safely get" clause in the charter but the master agrees to lighten, then time will still count as a form of detention,[494] either because the operation has been carried out at the request of the charterer, or because the charterer is in breach in nominating a port or berth where lightening is required. Such lightening will normally cease when the last lighter leaves the vessel.[495] It should, of course, be emphasized that in talking of a need to lighten what is meant is not that there will be a delay getting into berth because of the state of the tides, but that the vessel would never be able to berth safely because of insufficiency of water.

4.463 One exception to what has been said above is where the discharging port is named in the charter. In that case, the charterer had the right to select a berth, but he is not entitled to choose one which has insufficient water to take the vessel's draught fully laden if there are other suitable berths which could be used without lightening being necessary. If, however, there is no berth in the named port which the vessel can get into without lightening first, then, it is suggested, lightening expenses will be for the shipowner's account and time will not run during lightening whether before or after the vessel has become an Arrived ship. The reason for this is that by accepting the named port as the place of discharge, the shipowner impliedly warrants that the vessel will be able to get into the port with the contractual quantity of cargo on board without unreasonable delay in the conditions that are to be expected to prevail at the time of year in question. Thus, in these circumstances, it is the shipowner that is in default.

4.464 Charterparties, however, frequently make explicit provision for lightening, especially tanker charterparties. An example of a particularly comprehensive lightening clause is that contained at clause 15 of the Exxonvoy 1984 form of charter, which reads:

15. LIGHTENING/DISHARGE AT SEA

(a) Except when required by reason of fault attributable to Vessel, any lightening or discharge at sea or at a place outside a port shall be at the expense of Charterer and, . . . time used for such lightening or discharge shall count as laytime or as time on demurrage, as provided below:

(i) If Vessel is lightened at sea or at a place outside a port, laytime or, if Vessel is on demurrage, time on demurrage shall commence when Vessel arrives at the lightening site designated by Charterer and shall end when disconnecting of the cargo hoses from the last cargo receiving vessel has been completed.

(ii) If Vessel is fully discharged at sea or at a place outside a port, laytime or, if Vessel is on demurrage, time on demurrage shall commence upon the expiration of six (6) hours after Vessel arrives at the lightening site designated by Charterer or when Vessel is all fast alongside the first

---

493. *Dickinson* v. *Martini & Co* (1874) 1 R (Sess Cas) 1185.

494. But as with the situation where the cargo is discharged at the nearest safe port, the charterer will be entitled to set off any remaining laytime against the delay if the vessel has reached its specified destination. However, the delay will only encompass the period of lightening and will not include the time taken in shifting from the lightening place to the discharging berth.

495. See as an illustration of this London Arbitration 10/99—LMLN 510, 27 May 1999.

cargo carrying vessel, whichever occurs first, and end when disconnection of the cargo hoses from the last cargo receiving vessel has been completed.

(b) ... If Vessel is lightened at sea, the lightening site shall not constitute a port or place additional to those specified in Part I(D) ... Charterer, however, shall reimburse Owner for any time by which the steaming time to the final discharging port or place exceeds that which would have been taken if Vessel had not lightened at the Deviation rate per day or *pro rata* for a part thereof. In addition, Charterer shall pay for extra bunkers consumed ...

4.465 Under clause 16, the charterer undertakes to discharge sufficient cargo into vessels and/or lighters within port limits to enable the vessel to safely reach and lie at the designated berth, always afloat.

4.466 In London Arbitration 9/98,[496] the tribunal held that the anchorage position where intermediate lightening took place did not constitute a berth within the meaning of clause 9 of the Asbatankvoy form of charter. It should be noted that in this case there was a provision expressly stating that any lighterage area should not be considered as an additional port or berth.

Time used in lightening

4.467 In *Clerco Compania Naviera SA* v. *The Food Corporation of India (The Savvas)*,[497] two questions arose for determination. The first concerned what was the time used in lightening and the second was whether laytime should be calculated on the amount of cargo carried before or after lightening.

4.468 The *Savvas*, the vessel concerned, arrived at Bombay and gave Notice of Readiness on arrival, which under the terms of the charter took effect on 21 October, said the owners. However, the charterers alleged that time did not start until after lightening because of an additional clause providing for lightening to be at the owners' risk and expense and time used not to count as laytime. Unfortunately, lightening did not start until 6 November, continuing until 13 November. During this period 5,520 tons of cargo were discharged out of a total of 31,604 tons.

4.469 On these facts, the High Court held that time used in lightening covered only the actual period of the lightening operation and the owners' argument was correct. In giving judgment, Parker J commented[498]:

As a matter of language, time sitting at Bombay from Oct. 20 to Nov. 6 doing nothing is not time used in lightening, any more than Sundays, holidays and Saturday afternoons are times used in discharging unless discharging operations are taking place.

4.470 On the second point, the judge held that the charterers were entitled to calculate laytime on the basis of a full cargo, since it was a matter of commercial sense that this should happen if they were to have laytime running against them as from the moment when the fully laden vessel arrived at the port.

4.471 In the Court of Appeal the decision below was upheld on both points. The principal judgment was given by Ackner LJ, who on the first point said[499]:

---

496. London Arbitration 9/98—LMLN 488, 21 July 1998.
497. [1981] 1 Lloyd's Rep 155.
498. *Ibid.*, at p. 158.
499. *Clerco Compania Naviera SA* v. *The Food Corporation of India (The Savvas)* [1982] 1 Lloyd's Rep 22, at p. 24.

To my mind "lightening" and "time spent waiting for lighters to arrive" are two quite different matters. Clause 22 is an unusual clause, in as much as it imposes upon the owners what is normally the charterers' liability. If it had been intended to extend the meaning of the word "lightening" to cover that which is not normally included in its ordinary meaning, then clear words were required and could, without any great difficulty, have been supplied: specific provision could have been made for time lost in waiting for lightening not to count against laytime.

On the second point, he said[500]:

I agree with the learned judge's observations with regard to the commercial sense of the matter. It is obviously of importance to charterers to know the total period of laytime that they have purchased in the freight which they have agreed to pay.

500. *Ibid.*, at p. 26.

CHAPTER 5

Other Laytime Matters

COMPLETION OF LAYTIME

5.1 Laytime ends in one of two ways. It may either end upon the expiry of the laytime allowed and the commencement of demurrage, or upon the completion of cargo operations if these are concluded within the laytime allowed. It is with the second alternative that this chapter is concerned. It is important to remember, however, that what constitutes loading and discharging for the purpose of apportioning responsibility for cargo, e.g. under the Hague Rules and similar enactments, will not necessarily be decisive of when cargo operations are complete for the purpose of deciding when laytime ends.

5.2 What constitutes the end of cargo operations will be considered first in relation to dry cargo and secondly in relation to liquid cargoes, since different problems arise between the dry cargo and tanker trades.

5.3 Before discussing these, there are, however, a number of general points to be considered to bring the subject into context.

5.4 The laytime allowed is allowed for the benefit of the charterers. As Lord Denning MR said in *Shipping Developments Corporation SA* v. *V/O Sojuzneftexport*[1]:

. . . they have bought their laytime and paid for it in the freight, and are entitled to use it in the way which suits them best . . .

5.5 The shipowner cannot therefore complain if work does not commence immediately the ship is in a position to load or discharge cargo or if there are delays during the running of laytime caused by the charterers' inactivity. Thus, in *Petersen* v. *Dunn & Co*,[2] a vessel was chartered to load a cargo of coal in 12 colliery working days, the charter providing specifically that loading was to be "at once, and lay days to count when vessel ready and notice given". However, loading did not commence for several days after the vessel was ready and was then prevented by a strike, time lost due to strikes being excluded from laytime. After the strike was over, the cargo was loaded in two colliery working days. If the strike period was excluded, then the whole cargo was loaded during the permitted period, but the question that arose was whether the charterers were entitled to defer the commencement of loading. Mathew J held that they were. Of the additional provision relating to loading at once, he said[3]:

---

1. *Shipping Developments Corporation SA* v. *V/O Sojuzneftexport (The Delian Spirit)* [1971] 1 Lloyd's Rep 506, at p. 509.
2. *Petersen* v. *Dunn & Co* (1895) 1 CC 8.
3. *Ibid.*

The written clause was not intended to qualify the proviso as to "twelve colliery working days". The main object of the written clause is to show when the lay days begin . . . The charterparty allowed 12 days for the loading and the plaintiff in effect says that it only allowed seven. The case is perfectly clear, and the defendants are entitled to judgment.

It was after seven days that the strike broke out.

5.6 In *Novorossisk Shipping Co* v. *Neopetro Ltd (The Ulyanovsk)*,[4] charterers anticipating a fall in the market price of the cargo they intended to buy ordered the vessel only to tender Notice of Readiness at the load port to themselves and not to berth and commence loading until so instructed by charterers. Contrary to his voyage instructions, the master tendered notice to the refinery and shippers, berthed and commenced loading shortly after arrival. The purchase price of the cargo was linked to the date of the bill of lading—after which the market continued to fall, resulting in a substantial loss to charterers.

5.7 In resisting charterers' claim to recover this loss, owners argued, amongst other things, that charterers were not entitled to delay loading since that would have meant the allowed laytime would have been exceeded. This argument was rejected without hesitation by the arbitrators and by Steyn J in the High Court. In the course of his judgment, the judge said[5]:

In terms of the charterparty the charterers were given a total laytime of 72 running hours. They bought that laytime and paid for it in the freight. They are entitled to use that laytime as they wish. Even if they can load in less than the stipulated laytime, they may keep the ship for the whole of the laytime. Their right to the whole of the laytime is not to be abridged by requiring them to commence loading at any particular time.

5.8 The case of *The Eurus*[6] does, however, appear to show that there may be some doubt as to the extent to which a charterer is entitled to order a vessel not to load.

5.9 The charter in question at clause 36 had a provision entitled "Adherence to Voyage Instructions" which made the owners responsible for losses suffered by the charterers by any failure to comply fully with voyage instructions. The vessel was ordered on several occasions not to tender notice to the loading terminal before 11 00 on 31 January. The charterers hoped that by so doing, loading would not be completed before 1 February and therefore February bills of lading would be issued. The charterers knew that the price of the cargo would be significantly lower for a February bill of lading but what was not known was that it was the local practice for January bills to be issued if loading was completed before 08 00 on 1 February.

5.10 In the event, the vessel berthed at 03 00 on 31 January and started loading at 06 36. At 11 00, after loading had been under way for some hours, the master gave notice to the terminal. Loading was completed at 01 30 on 1 February but, because of the 8 o'clock rule, January bills were issued.

5.11 The arbitral tribunal which first heard the matter held that the master was in breach in berthing early and that an instruction not to tender Notice of Readiness before a certain time amounted to an instruction not to present or berth before that time, but that the application of the 8 o'clock rule, or the loss that would result because of it, was not

---

4. *Novorossisk Shipping Co* v. *Neopetro Co Ltd (The Ulyanovsk)* [1990] 1 Lloyd's Rep 425.
5. *Ibid.*, at p. 431.
6. *The Eurus* [1998] 1 Lloyd's Rep 351.

foreseeable. They went on to hold that clause 36 was an indemnity and therefore the owners were liable whether the loss was foreseeable or not.

5.12 The principal issue in the High Court and the Court of Appeal was whether clause 36 was an indemnity clause; on that, both courts agreed it was not and therefore the charterers had to show foreseeability before they could recover.

5.13 The question of whether the charterers could give the order not to berth they did was not in issue in this case, because the owners and master accepted the order, albeit the master did not obey it. Commenting on this *obiter*, Staughton LJ said[7]:

I would agree it as open to question whether the charterers were entitled to give those orders, either in the literal sense or with the addition of the arbitrators' interpretation.[8] The charter-party certainly contemplates that the charter-party [this should probably read "charterers"] may give some orders, such as the nomination of loading and discharging ports, the quantity of cargo, and whether it shall comprise one or two grades of oil. There is also an express term (Scanport cl. 6) allowing the charterers to divert the vessel during the voyage—at their expense. No doubt on many occasions a shipowner will be prepared to acquiesce in an order which the charterer could not otherwise insist upon, provided that the shipowner is recompensed. But this was a voyage charter-party not a time charter. The owners contracted for a voyage that was more or less defined in return for the freight specified. I can think of quite a number of reasons why in other circumstances they might not have wished to accept the charterers' orders—delay to their next engagement, for example, or imminent bad weather on the voyage, war or political interference.

The problem does not arise in the present case, and has not been argued before us. The owner acquiesced in the orders that were given; and it was not argued before the arbitrators that the orders were unlawful, save in the narrow point that they were not in accordance with the custom of the trade (cl. 36), as to which Mr Kazantzis dissented. No doubt the parties had regard to the decision of Mr Justice Steyn in *Novorossisk Shipping Co* v. *Neopetro Co Ltd* [1990] 1 Lloyd's Rep 425. Leave to appeal was refused in that case on the ground that the point was "not realistically arguable" and a certificate under s. 1 of the Arbitration Act, 1979 was also refused. I wish only to say that, not having heard argument on this point, I would not lend the authority to this Court in that decision.

It is clear from the above that Staughton LJ had some doubts about the correctness of the *Ulyanovsk*[9] decision.

5.14 The charter in the present case was on an Asbatankvoy form and therefore a port charter. The delay which the charterers sought was after the vessel's arrival off the port and therefore after arrival at the point at which the vessel was entitled to give Notice of Readiness. The voyage had therefore ended and as between the owners and the charterers the laytime clock was ticking. Whilst an order to delay during the voyage stage would probably be something the charterers were not entitled to give, it is difficult to see why they should not use their laytime as they chose. The comments of Staughton LJ were clearly *obiter* and insofar as there is a difference with what was said in *The Ulyanovsk*,[10] the latter probably currently represents the law.

5.15 However, as the cases that follow show, even keeping the ship for the whole of laytime does not mean that they can keep it once loading or discharge has been completed;

---

7. *Ibid.*, at p. 355.
8. This appears to be a reference to the fact that the arbitrators equated an order not to tender notice with one not to berth.
9. *The Ulyanovsk* [1990] 1 Lloyd's Rep 425.
10. *Ibid.*

but they can adjust the speed and timing of cargo operations for their own convenience.

5.16 In *Margaronis Navigation Agency Ltd* v. *Henry W Peabody & Co of London Ltd*,[11]
a ship was chartered to load maize at Cape Town. By the end of work on 29 December,
which was a Friday, virtually all the cargo had been loaded. However, the charterers
insisted on keeping the vessel over the holiday weekend and loading the last few tons on
the following Tuesday. Their reason for so doing was so that January bills of lading could
be issued. The small amount of cargo remaining could have been loaded on either Friday
or Saturday upon payment of overtime.

5.17 In the High Court the owners argued *inter alia* that Mathew J, in *Petersen* v. *Dunn
& Co*,[12] could not have intended to decide that the charterers in that case were entitled to
keep the ship for the whole of the allowed lay days even though they could have loaded
in less. Rejecting this, Roskill J said[13] that it was a necessary inference from that decision.
The other argument that was pursued by the owners was that the ship had a full and
complete cargo on the Friday evening and that the principle "*de minimis non curat lex*"
applied to the balance.

5.18 On the question as to how and for what the permitted laytime should be used, the
judge said[14]:

A charterer is entitled to have that time to load, but once he has loaded, he must not use that time
for some other purpose. But, so long as he has not completed loading, that time is his, and he is
under no obligation to accelerate that rate of loading so as to shorten the time to which he is
otherwise entitled.

This particular point was not pursued before the Court of Appeal, but the court did
consider the application of the *de minimis* rule to commercial contracts. On that aspect,
Diplock LJ said[15] that the question was whether it was commercially practicable to get
closer to the required quantity, and on that he concluded that it was.

5.19 In London Arbitration 24/95,[16] the tribunal held that where the charterparty
concerned provided for two-port loading but no cargo was available at the first load port,
time ceased to run when the charterers instructed the vessel to proceed to the second load
port.

Dry cargo

Loading

5.20 In *Svenssons Travaruaktiebolag* v. *Cliffe Steamship Co Ltd*[17] the point primarily at
issue was the seaworthiness of the vessel, but before it could be decided whether there was
a breach of the shipowner's duty to have the vessel seaworthy at the commencement of
each stage of the voyage, it was necessary to decide whether the previous stage, in this

11. *Margaronis Navigation Agency Ltd* v. *Henry W Peabody & Co of London Ltd* [1964] 1 Lloyd's Rep 173;
[1964] 2 Lloyd's Rep 153.
12. *Petersen* v. *Dunn & Co* (1895) 1 CC 8.
13. *Margaronis Navigation Agency Ltd* v. *Henry W Peabody & Co of London Ltd* [1964] 1 Lloyd's Rep 173,
at p. 187.
14. *Ibid.*, at p. 186.
15. *Margaronis Navigation Agency Ltd* v. *Henry W Peabody & Co of London Ltd* [1964] 2 Lloyd's Rep 153,
at p. 159.
16. London Arbitration 24/95—LMLN 421, 23 December 1995.
17. *Svenssons Travaruaktiebolag* v. *Cliffe Steamship Co Ltd* (1931) 41 Ll L Rep 262.

case loading of the cargo, had been completed. The case arose out of an incident that occurred whilst a deck cargo of timber was being loaded on board the steamship *Headcliffe* at Burea in Sweden. When the last lifts of timber were being loaded, the vessel, which had developed a slight list to port earlier, suddenly began listing first to starboard and then to port. The sudden oscillations caused the deck cargo to shift and a considerable quantity was lost overboard.

5.21 Having held that the accident occurred as the last sling was loaded, Wright J continued[18]:

If it were necessary to decide the matter, but it is not, I should also hold that on the facts of this case the lashing was a necessary part of the operation of loading . . . the crew were actually engaged in lashing the after-deck cargo when the accident occurred—and I think it is an integral part of the operation of loading in the case of a vessel situated like this and lying with her deck cargo in an exposed roadstead.

The judge also said a little earlier in his judgment, as a general proposition[19]:

I think that in a case like this, and, indeed, in most cases, the mere reception or dumping down of the cargo on the ship does not involve the completion of the loading, because I think the operation of loading involves all that is required to put the cargo in a condition in which it can be carried.

5.22 A similar question arose in *Argonaut Navigation Co Ltd* v. *Ministry of Food.*[20] This case concerned a 'tweendecker loading grain in Sorel on the St Lawrence. Under local regulations, such a ship was not permitted to sail until a certificate had been produced from the Port Warden confirming that all the appropriate regulations had been complied with. These included a provision that in the case of a 'tweendecker, only the lower holds were to be loaded with bulk grain and any cargo carried in the 'tween decks was to be bagged. The relevant charter provided for the carriage of a full and complete cargo and to load this amount some of the cargo had to be carried in the 'tween decks. All loading was in bulk by elevators and, to comply with the regulations, a reduced flow was arranged when the lower holds had been filled and the loose grain was bagged by stevedores employed by the owners. The full amount of bulk grain permitted had been loaded by 08 45 on 17 October and a further amount required for bagging was loaded by 13 00, bagging being completed at 15 00 on the same day. The dispute was as to whether loading was completed at 08 45, 13 00 or 15 00. The ship was already on demurrage at 08 45 and a second question asked was whether this made any difference.

5.23 The High Court and the Court of Appeal were in no doubt that loading did not complete until 15 00, and that it made no difference whether the vessel was already on demurrage or not. Sellers J summed up the matter in this way[21]:

In the case of the loading of a general cargo, time is of necessity taken in placing and stowing the cargo as it arrives in the hold. Often the delivery of cargo on board a vessel is slowed down because of the difficulty of stowing certain kinds of cargo or of stowing it in a place particularly difficult of access or by reason of its structure or some obstruction. I have never heard it suggested in such a case that in assessing the time taken in loading for purposes of demurrage an apportionment should take place (on some estimated basis for accuracy would be impossible) between time taken in stowing and time taken in bringing the goods to the hold. I can see no reason why it should be

---

18. *Ibid.*, at p. 267.
19. *Ibid.*
20. *Argonaut Navigation Co Ltd* v. *Ministry of Food* (1948) 81 Ll L Rep 371; (1949) 82 Ll L Rep 223 (CA).
21. *Argonaut Navigation Co Ltd* v. *Ministry of Food* (1948) 81 Ll L Rep 371, at p. 377.

different with bulk cargo, which has to be trimmed, or, to some extent, put into bags, for the purpose of safety or for complying with enforceable regulations, the object of which is safety. It cannot, I think, make any difference that the time so occupied arises from time to time in the course of loading, or at the end when all the cargo is on board, or at any particular stage of the operation.

5.24 The judge also said that it was immaterial who had to pay the costs of loading or whose task in the joint effort might finish first. The shipper would normally finish his work of delivery before the ship receives it, but, decided the judge, loading could not be said to be completed when the shipper (or charterer) had done all that was required of him. The ship could not therefore be said to be loaded until the cargo had been loaded and bagged, if required for safety or by regulation, and therefore, to avoid demurrage, the cargo must be delivered in sufficient time within the lay days for this to be done before laytime expired.

5.25 In the Court of Appeal, Bucknill LJ said[22]:

... loading is not complete until the cargo is so placed in the ship that the ship can proceed on her voyage in safety.[23]

5.26 A different question arose in the *Owners of the Steamship Nolisement* v. *Bunge and Born*.[24] The facts of the case are important, since what was decided can easily be exaggerated. The case concerned a period of delay after loading was completed before bills of lading were presented by the charterers for signature by the master. The reason why the charterers delayed was because they had not made up their minds about where the ship should be discharged. The charter specifically provided for bills of lading to be signed by the master. Several ports were named, to one of which, at the master's option, the vessel was to proceed for orders. Upon arrival there notice was to be given to the consignees, who were then required to nominate the actual discharge port within 24 hours of receiving notice. Alternatively, the charterers had the option of nominating the discharge port on signing bills of lading and it was this option which the charterers purported to exercise. Loading was completed well within the allowed laytime but thereafter the vessel was delayed for three days. The parties *agreed* and in arbitration proceedings the umpire found that the charterers had the right to keep the ship for 24 hours for the purpose of settling accounts and therefore the dispute only concerned the remaining two days.

5.27 In the High Court, Atkin J found in favour of the charterers, holding that[25]:

the true view is that the charterer has a stipulated period of lay days during which he may delay the ship at the port of loading without incurring liability for demurrage or for damages; in other words, he commits no breach by detaining the ship for that particular period.

5.28 Disagreeing with the width of this *dictum*, Swinfen Eady LJ said, in the same case in the Court of Appeal[26]:

Of course, it may well be that if all the lay days are consumed in loading, there is no breach for which the charterer is liable; but in a charterparty in this form, where the ship is loaded at an accelerated rate, the charterer has no right to detain the ship after she is loaded ...

---

22. *Argonaut Navigation Co Ltd* v. *Ministry of Food* (1948) 82 Ll L Rep 223, at p. 229.
23. Different considerations apply where it is necessary for similar measures to be taken on completion of a part discharge before proceeding to a second discharge port. On this, see *post* at para. 5.37.
24. *Owners of the Steamship Nolisement* v. *Bunge and Born* (1916) 22 CC 135.
25. Quoted by Swinfen Eady LJ in the Court of Appeal, *infra*, at p. 142.
26. *Owners of the Steamship Nolisement* v. *Bunge and Born* (1916) 22 CC 135, at p. 142.

5.29 On the specific question as to how long should be allowed for signature of the bills of lading, the Court of Appeal endorsed what was said by Lord Esher MR in *Oriental Steamship Co* v. *Tylor* when, having commented that bills of lading could only be signed after completion of loading and before sailing unless the vessel's agent was authorized to sign on the master's behalf, his Lordship said[27]:

... the time for the signing of these bills of lading is to be calculated from the time of the loading on board ... the charterers ought to have presented that bill of lading almost immediately.

This, said the Court of Appeal, meant within a reasonable period and on the facts of this particular case that meant 24 hours, as agreed by the parties. One factor that might have induced the parties to agree this figure was the fact that the charter provided for a delay of at least this period had the charterers exercised their alternative option and sent the vessel to one of the named ports for orders.

5.30 There is no doubt that such a lengthy period would not be allowed today, when probably little more than an hour would be allowed.[28] However, in London Arbitration 9/99,[29] where there was a problem over cargo documentation which resulted in the vessel being delayed from 08 00 to 17 00, the tribunal in that case apparently allowed the full period and no "free period". Unlike tankers, there is no general practice in the case of dry cargo vessels.

5.31 Perhaps more important, however, where there has been a substantial delay is the question of whether this would be laytime or would give rise to a claim for detention.

5.32 In London Arbitration 16/89,[30] the question to be considered was a delay caused by owners wishing to clause a bill of lading to reflect that some cargo was loaded during rain on charterers' orders, during which owners said laytime continued to run. The arbitrators disagreed, saying the delay could not possibly be said to be so closely connected with loading as to allow it to be termed part of the loading operation. The problem was caused by a problem over the form of the bills of lading and, more particularly, a difficulty in getting the shippers' agreement. That was not something closely bound up with the operation of loading. It did, however, give rise to a claim for damages for detention.

5.33 It therefore seems on the basis of the cases quoted above that laytime will run until loading is completed and the vessel can proceed on her voyage in safety, but that any delay relating to signing of bills of lading or other problems relating to cargo documentation or draft surveys[31] would be beyond the completion of laytime but might give rise to a claim for damages for detention.

---

27. *Oriental Steamship Co* v. *Tylor* [1893] 2 QB 518, at p. 523.
28. Although a similar time scale probably applies in the case of tankers, different considerations apply because tanker charters frequently expressly provide for laytime to end on disconnection of hoses and although it is common to allow a reasonable period thereafter, it is not laytime. Where, however, as sometimes happens, time is allowed to count until cargo documents are put on board, then such time is laytime. See *post* at para. 5.44.
29. London Arbitration 9/99—LMLN 510, 27 May 1999.
30. London Arbitration 16/89—LMLN 253, 15 July 1989.
31. In London Arbitration 11/98—LMLN 488, 21 July 1998, where there was a delay in providing cargo documents due to the fact that a draft survey was carried out on completion of loading, the time taken for this to be carried out was held not to be laytime. However, the brief report of the case does not say whether the tribunal considered whether the time lost gave rise to a claim for detention, which it almost certainly would.

Discharge

5.34 The question of whether discharge can be considered complete for all practical purposes when a small amount of cargo remains was the issue in *Robert Dollar Co* v. *Blood, Holman & Co Ltd.*[32] This concerned a sailing ship which brought a cargo of bagged barley to Sharpness from Panama. Although the transatlantic crossing was uneventful, virtually everything that could go wrong did after her arrival at Barry Roads. However, she eventually reached Sharpness and discharged virtually all of her cargo of approximately 4,000 tons by the end of work on 2 January 1920. However, quite a number of the bags of barley had split accidentally, or, in quite a lot of cases, been split deliberately by the crew to improve the stowage on loading. After most of the cargo had been discharged, the crew collected the remaining barley from various nooks and crannies and some of this was damaged. Five tons were extracted on Saturday 3 January and eight tons on Monday 5 January. The shipowners claimed that discharge would not be considered complete until 5 January. Rejecting this, McCardie J said[33]:

I hold otherwise. The question concerned is when the discharge was in substance completed, i.e. in a practical business sense.

In my opinion, this completion took place on Jan. 2. It was regarded by both parties as the ship's duty to collect the grains beneath boards. I think that the ship collected it rather for its own convenience than for the benefit of the defendants, and the matter is so regarded according to the practice at Sharpness.

The judge went on to emphasize that he was reinforced in his view because he was satisfied that the quantity of under-board loose grain was largely due to the over-bleeding of the bags on loading by the crew.

5.35 In the discharge of bagged or bulk cargo, there is inevitably a certain amount of sweeping up and rebagging loose cargo for delivery to the receivers and it is the normal practice for the time taken in doing this to count as laytime or demurrage, if the vessel is on demurrage. The case just considered does not, it is submitted, detract from this, but should be considered on its own facts as an illustration of the practice then prevailing at the particular port or possibly as an instance of default by the shipowner, since the comparatively large amount of sweepings was due to the activities of the crew on loading.[34]

5.36 It is also suggested that, just as with loading,[35] the question of which of the parties is responsible for discharge should not affect when the operation is deemed to be completed.

5.37 However, it is clear that, unlike on loading, there is no obligation on completion of discharge for the vessel to be left in a seaworthy trim so that she is fit to proceed immediately on her next voyage, unless the parties have specifically agreed to the contrary. If, therefore, on completion of discharge, it is necessary for the vessel to ballast,

---

32. *Robert Dollar Co* v. *Blood, Holman & Co Ltd* (1920) 4 Ll L Rep 343.

33. *Ibid.*, at p. 349.

34. See also the reference to discharge being completed when "the last grain . . . was put off", *per* Denning LJ (as he then was) in *Chandris* v. *Government of India* [1956] 1 Lloyd's Rep 11, at p. 17 (*post* at para. 5.40) and a discussion of the *de minimis* rule in relation to loading, which would presumably equally apply to discharge, in *Margaronis Navigation Agency* v. *Henry W Peabody & Co of London Ltd* [1964] 2 Lloyd's Rep 153, at p. 159 *per* Diplock LJ (*ante* at para. 5.16).

35. See *ante* at para. 5.24.

then the time taken in so doing after all the cargo has been discharged does not count as laytime or for demurrage if the vessel is on demurrage.

5.38 This also applies to any time taken in putting the vessel back into a seaworthy trim for passage to a second discharge port. Laytime at the first discharge port ends when all the cargo destined for that port has been discharged. This was the effect of the decision of the Court of Appeal in *Chandris* v. *Government of India*.[36] In that case, the *Evgenia Chandris*, the vessel concerned, had been fixed on a Centrocon charter to carry wheat from Argentina to India. The charter also contained a seaworthy trim clause from the Austral charterparty. This provided in part:

> ... any expense incurred by the shipowners at the first port of discharge in shifting, discharging and/or reloading any cargo either for the purpose of putting the vessel into seaworthy trim for the passage to the second port or to enable the cargo for discharge at the first port to be conveniently so discharged shall be paid by the charterers ...

On loading, the master insisted that approximately 10% of the cargo should be supplied in bags, the remainder being in bulk. To ensure safe stowage, the bags were placed on top of the bulk grain, there being no shifting boards.

5.39 The charterers ordered that 2,900 tons of cargo be discharged at Cochin and the rest at Bombay. The physical discharge of the Cochin parcel, which was all in bulk, was completed at 4.30 p.m. on Saturday 27 November 1948, but the vessel was unable to sail for a further 21 hours whilst the remainder of the wheat was trimmed in the lower holds, covered with tarpaulins and the bagged wheat stacked on top. Only then would the port authorities allow the vessel to sail.

5.40 The owners claimed that the reference to expenses in the seaworthy trim clause should also include compensation for the delay and before Devlin J they were successful.[37] The Court of Appeal, by a majority, disagreed,[38] holding that the term "expense" was limited to specific disbursements. In the course of his judgment, Denning LJ said[39]:

> Mr Roskill next contended that the time should count as lay days because it was time occupied in discharging the cargo, in that the discharge could not be said to be completed until the ship was made trim again ready to proceed on her voyage.[40] The answer is, however, that the discharge was completed as soon as the last grain of the 2,900 tons was put off. The time occupied thereafter in trimming the ship is another matter altogether, and must be recovered under the Seaworthy Trim Clause or not at all.

On this last point, the remainder of the court agreed, Morris LJ saying[41]:

> If the parties had wished to provide that, in the stipulated circumstances, any time occupied at the first port of discharge in shifting cargo for the purpose of putting the vessel into seaworthy trim for passage to the second port should count as part of the lay days, it would have been easy for them so to provide and to use language comparable to that used where in various events they were agreeing that time should for certain purposes count.

---

36. *Chandris* v. *Government of India* [1956] 1 Lloyd's Rep 11 (CA).
37. *Chandris* v. *Government of India* [1955] 2 Lloyd's Rep 212.
38. Denning and Hodson LJJ. The third member of the court, Morris LJ, was prepared to hold that the shipowner should be allowed to recover his net loss, i.e. the cost of running his ship, within the term "expense".
39. *Chandris* v. *Government of India* [1956] 1 Lloyd's Rep 11, at p. 17.
40. As with loading.
41. *Chandris* v. *Government of India* [1956] 1 Lloyd's Rep 11, at p. 22.

5.41 This decision was followed in *J C Carras & Sons (Shipbrokers) Ltd* v. *President of India (The Argobeam)*,[42] a decision of Mocatta J. The facts were essentially similar, except that the first discharge port, Madras, was intended only as a lightening port, with final discharge at Calcutta. At Madras, after discharge of the cargo, the receivers' stevedores filled 9,900 bags with grain and stowed them on the surface of the remaining bulk cargo to prevent there being a free surface. By an additional clause, the vessel was to be left in seaworthy trim to shift between ports.

5.42 The charterers argued that this was not intended to apply where the vessel was only lightening, applied only to make them liable for ensuring an even distribution of cargo in the holds, or was declaratory only and had no legal effect. Mocatta J rejected these arguments and also said[43]:

> ... when all the cargo to be unloaded at a first or lightening port has been landed on the quay, or into lighters when these are used, discharge at such port has, in my judgment, ended and laytime does not continue to run during the time taken to put the vessel in seaworthy trim.

The owners were therefore entitled to the expenses they incurred in the vessel shifting to buoys to be put in a seaworthy trim, but not to be compensated for the time taken.

Liquid cargo

5.43 In London Arbitration 2/92,[44] the parties originally agreed for the carriage of a single parcel of cargo for a lump sum freight with no option to complete in favour of owners. However, having been approached by another potential shipper, it was agreed that the original charterers should themselves become charterers for the additional parcel. In the event, there was a shortfall in the quantity shipped in the original parcel but because this was carried for a lump sum freight, it made no difference to the freight that was payable. However, the owners argued that they were entitled to additional freight above the quantity actually shipped under the first parcel rather than the quantity intended to be shipped. They also said there should be separate laytime calculations. Whether there should depended on whether what had been agreed was a separate charter or simply a variation of the original charter allowing charterers to load further cargo. In this particular case, the tribunal held that there was only one agreement, which had been varied.

5.44 Most tanker and liquid cargo charters contain specific provisions dealing with the end of laytime. Whilst, as will be seen shortly, individual charters differ slightly, nevertheless in most cases they either provide that laytime shall run until loading/discharging hoses are disconnected or, in the case of loading, until the relevant cargo documentation has been placed on board. One that did not was considered in London Arbitration 11/91.[45] The vessel in question was chartered on a Tanker Voyage Charterparty Form (Vegoilvoy 1/27/50) and the problem concerned a delay of one hour between the completion of loading and the disconnection of hoses. The charterers submitted that their obligation to load the cargo within the laytime was limited to the actual operation of loading and did not include the connection or disconnection of hoses.

---

42. *J C Carras & Sons (Shipbrokers) Ltd* v. *President of India (The Argobeam)* [1970] 1 Lloyd's Rep 282.
43. *Ibid.*, at p. 291.
44. London Arbitration 2/92—LMLN 319, 25 January 1992.
45. London Arbitration 11/91—LMLN 304, 29 June 1991.

5.45 The tribunal held that generally loading was complete when all was done that was necessary to be done to put the cargo in a condition to be carried, but did not in the absence of any additional provision include anything further, such as closing of hatches or preparation of documents. It was therefore necessary to consider whether, after the loading operation had ceased, the loading lines were drained to the ship, thus adding a small extra amount of cargo, or to the shore. In the absence of any specific evidence, they concluded that the lines were probably drained to the ship, as is the normal practice, and time should continue to run since draining down to the ship was part of the loading cycle.

5.46 Amongst those charters that do provide for loading/discharging to continue until hoses are disconnected are the following:

Exxonvoy 69/Asbatankvoy	— Clause 11
Shellvoy 3	— Clause 14
BPvoy 2	— Clause 16
Mobilvoy	— Clause 12

Typical of these is clause 11 of the Exxonvoy 69 form of charter, which in part provides:

11. HOSES: MOORING AT SEA TERMINALS. Hoses for loading and discharging shall be furnished by the Charterer and shall be connected and disconnected by the Charterer, or, at the option of the Owner, by the Owner at the Charterer's risk and expense. Laytime shall continue until the hoses have been disconnected.[46]

5.47 In London Arbitration 14/93,[47] in a case on the Asbatankvoy Form, the owners failed in their claim that laytime continued until cargo documents were put on board, the delay in that case being in excess of eight hours.

5.48 Where, as here, the charter does not expressly provide for any delay beyond the disconnection of hoses, it is nevertheless usual to allow a short period for the necessary documentation relating to loading to be produced. In such circumstances, the time allowed is such as is reasonable if the documentation must be on board before sailing, it cannot be produced before completion of loading and the charter is silent on the time to be allowed. As was said by Blackburn J in *Ford and others* v. *Cotesworth and another*[48]:

... whenever a party to a contract undertakes to do some particular act, the performance of which depends entirely on himself, so that he may choose his own mode of fulfilling his undertaking, and the contract is silent as to time, the law implies a contract to do it within a reasonable time under the circumstances. And if some unforeseen cause, over which he has no control, prevents him from performing what he has undertaken within that time, he is responsible for the damage.[49]

5.49 Whilst each case must be considered on its own facts dependent on the actual documentation involved, a period of either one or two hours is frequently allowed. Such time, however, is not laytime and if the time allowed is exceeded, then the shipowner's claim is one for detention for the excess.

5.50 Amongst the charters providing for laytime to run beyond disconnection of hoses on completion of loading are the following:

---

46. The remaining sentence of the clause deals with Mooring at Sea Terminals.
47. London Arbitration 14/93—LMLN 358, 24 July 1993.
48. *Ford and others* v. *Cotesworth and another* (1868) 4 QB 127, at p. 133.
49. Blackburn J then went on to contrast what he had said with situations which require activity on the part of both parties where what is implied is that each party should act with reasonable diligence. See also *Sunbeam Shipping Co Ltd* v. *President of India (The Atlantic Sunbeam)* [1973] 1 Lloyd's Rep 482, and *ante* at para. 3.166.

Bimchemvoy	— Clause 10
Intertankvoy 76	— Clause 9
Finavoy	— Clause 15
Exxonvoy 84	— Clause 13

5.51 The first two of those listed provide for laytime to continue until the hoses are disconnected, or, if later, until "all necessary cargo documents for which Charterers are responsible have been received on board" (Bimchemvoy)/"Charterers or their agents have fulfilled their obligation to produce any necessary documents" (Intertankvoy 76). With both of these charters laytime continues to run until the documentation is received or until it expires. It follows also that, as used laytime, it is subject to the application of any laytime exceptions clauses there may be in the charter.

5.52 The other two charters in this second group provide for specific periods of delay and, since the terms of each are somewhat different, each will be considered in turn.

5.53 The last part of clause 15 of the Finavoy charter provides:

Time shall continue to count as laytime, or if the vessel is on demurrage, for demurrage, until cargo hoses have been disconnected, and such disconnection shall be effected promptly. Time spent awaiting cargo documents in excess of three hours after disconnection of hoses shall count as laytime, or if the vessel is on demurrage, for demurrage.

5.54 As will be apparent, the clause provides expressly for what is to happen where the delay exceeds three hours and in such cases the effect thereafter is the same as with the last two charters considered, i.e. the excess time counts as used laytime. What the clause does not say is what happens if the delay does not exceed three hours or, if it does, what happens to the first three hours. The implication presumably is, however, that it should be considered a free period of detention for which no recompense is payable. It is perhaps also worth noting that three hours for the production of documents is somewhat longer than usually allowed.

5.55 The equivalent clause in the Exxonvoy 84 charter is clause 13(*b*), which states:

The laytime specified in Part I(I) shall be allowed free of expense to Charterer for the purpose of loading and discharging cargo and all other Charterer's purposes. Laytime or, if Vessel is on demurrage, time on demurrage, shall continue until all cargo hoses have been completely disconnected upon the final termination of the loading or discharging operation. Disconnection of all cargo hoses shall be promptly effected. If vessel is delayed in excess of two (2) hours after such disconnection of cargo hoses solely for Charterer's purposes, laytime or, if Vessel is on demurrage, time on demurrage shall be deemed to have continued without interruption from the disconnection of the cargo hoses until the termination of such delay.

5.56 This avoids some of the difficulties found with the previous charter, since it provides for what happens to the first two hours where the delay exceeds this. It does not, however, expressly say what happens where the delay is two hours or less. Presumably, again, it is to count as a period of free detention.

5.57 It is also interesting that, unlike any of the other charters in this group, the cause of the permitted delay is wider than awaiting documents and extends to anything connected with the charterer's role. The precise limits of this have yet to become apparent, although presumably in practice cargo documentation will probably be the main cause of delay.

5.58 It may be appropriate at this point to expand a little on what is meant by cargo documentation in this context. Before doing so, however, to put the subject into context, it is necessary to consider a little about tanker procedures.

5.59 When loading is complete, it is usual for the chief officer of the vessel concerned, together with the charterer's inspector, to ullage the vessel's tanks. This involves measuring the space between the top of the liquid in the tank and the tank top. It is then possible, knowing the temperature of the cargo and the trim of the vessel, to calculate the amount of cargo loaded, using standard tables for the vessel. The figure so produced will be the ship's loading figure. At the same time, the terminal will calculate a corresponding shore loading figure, based on before and after readings of the shore tank on which the bill of lading figure will be based. Inevitably, there will be some difference between ship and shore figures and, if possible, the terminal will wish to see the calculated ship's figure before presenting the bill of lading to the master for signature. The significance of this difference lies in the realm of cargo claims and as such is beyond the scope of this book. However, for the present purposes, it is sufficient to say that the calculation of the ship and shore figures will take some little while and therefore if the charter requires the bill of lading to be signed by the master then some delay will be inevitable.

5.60 Any dispute between the ship and shore over the correctness of the figures which causes delay may give rise to a claim for detention,[50] but unless expressly provided for in the charter, such delay will not be laytime.

5.61 In addition to bills of lading, some or all of the following documents may have to be placed on board before the vessel's departure:

Certificates of Quantity and Quality
Certificate of Origin of the Cargo
Cargo Manifest
Documentation relating to Customs Clearance
Certificate of Discharge.

5.62 Whilst most of these will be self-evident, it is perhaps worth explaining that a certificate of discharge is something that is particular to cargo which is loaded in Arab countries. It is a certificate showing the cargo loaded which, on discharge, must be notarized at the port of discharge to show where the cargo has been landed.

5.63 Some loading terminals, however, operate what is called an "early departure" procedure. Under this, the master is required, either in conformity with the charter (e.g. STB Voy, Exxonvoy 84) or by subsequent agreement, to authorize the charterer's agents to sign the bills of lading on his behalf so that the vessel may depart as soon as loading is completed. If this procedure is followed then the documents listed, with the exception of any relating to Customs clearance, are not put on board prior to sailing and therefore, unless the charter provides for a fixed period for documentation, any time allowed must be very short.

5.64 One slightly unusual tanker charter with regard to the ending of laytime is the STB Voy form of charter. The second sentence of clause 11 of this provides:

Laytime or, if the Vessel is on demurrage, time on demurrage shall continue until the hoses have been connected, or until ballasting begins at the discharge port(s), whichever occurs first.

5.65 The meaning of the last part of this sentence has been considered by London arbitrators.[51] What happened was that the vessel started to ballast a considerable time

---

50. As an illustration, see *Boukadora Maritime Corporation* v. *Société Anonyme Marocaine de L'Industrie et du Raffinage (The Boukadora)* [1989] 1 Lloyd's Rep 393.
51. London Arbitration—LMLN 72, 5 August 1982.

before completion of discharge and, indeed, finished ballasting over 12 hours before the completion of discharge. Finding in favour of the charterers that time stopped on commencement of ballasting, the arbitrators commented:

Clause 11 was puzzling. It may be that in days of old the clause had some meaning if the shore connection were used for ballasting after completion of discharge, but this did not take place at Mohammedia. There was no doubt that in Roads exposed to adverse weather such as likely to occur in early March, the master felt it safer to increase his draught to avoid having a light ship at the mercy of sudden gusts. Clause 11 was not a sensible clause, but the parties had accepted it. Accordingly, demurrage time stopped when ballasting began, even though the cargo had only partially been discharged.[52]

There would seem no reason why this should not also apply to laytime.

5.66 Another case involving the end of tanker laytime was *Total Transport Corporation of Panama* v. *Amoco Trading Co (The Altus)*.[53] Here, the *Altus* was loaded a cargo of crude oil from a barge four miles offshore. A sealine ran from the barge to the bottom of a buoy $1\frac{1}{2}$ miles away and the *Altus* was secured to the buoy by chain. Loading hoses ran from a swivelling manifold at the top of the buoy to the *Altus*.

5.67 Prior to completion of loading, the terminal operator requested the *Altus* to flush the sealine and ballast the loading barge so that it could be moved inshore for cleaning. The dispute concerned whether laytime ran until flushing of the sealine began or until hoses were disconnected. The charter, which was on the Exxonvoy form, provided for laytime to continue until hoses had been disconnected.

5.68 Webster J was in no doubt that the end of laytime was when hoses were disconnected, whether or not the flushing of the pipeline was required by the charterer. The flushing operation could not possibly be said to be part of the carrying voyage and there was no hiatus or interval between the commencement of that and the end of the loading operation. A further reason for the finding was that there was no default by the master.

AVERAGING AND REVERSING

5.69 A fixed laytime charterparty may provide either for a single allowed period of laytime to cover both loading and discharging or may alternatively provide separate periods for each. The former is the almost invariable practice in tanker charters. The latter is commonly used for bulk cargoes where the laytime allowed is based on rates of loading and discharging, where, dependent on the methods used, one operation will usually be quicker than the other.

5.70 If a charter does provide for separate rates, even if the actual rate is the same, then separate laytime calculations must be produced for loading and discharging. If the charter provides for despatch as well as demurrage, then, dependent on the time used, despatch or demurrage will be payable at the end of loading and the same on completion of discharge.

---

52. There would however seem to be no reason why the time spent ballasting after the end of laytime/demurrage should not give rise to a claim for detention. See *ante* at paras 4.38 *et seq* and *post* at para. 000.

53. *Total Transport Corporation of Panama* v. *Amoco Trading Co (The Altus)*, LMLN 140, 14 March 1985; [1985] 1 Lloyd's Rep 423.

5.71 It would seem that from about 1885 it became common to include a clause in charters, which provided for separate loading and discharging laytime, which enabled the time saved in one operation to be taken into account in offsetting demurrage due from the other, and vice versa. Thus, in *Molière Steamship Co Ltd* v. *Naylor, Benzon & Co*,[54] such a clause was said to have been in common use for 10 years.

5.72 In those early days, the clause commonly in use read:

Charterers to be at liberty to average the days for loading and discharging in order to avoid demurrage . . .

5.73 Although in form this purported to be a clause allowing averaging, as will be seen shortly, the meaning given to it was what today would be called reversing. The first cases where averaging and reversing were given their modern meanings were apparently in 1910[55] and 1916.[56] The current usage of these terms is shown by the meanings given in the *Voylayrules 1993*[57]:

"TO AVERAGE" means that separate calculations are to be made for loading and discharging and any time saved in one operation is to be set against any excess time used in the other.

"REVERSIBLE" means an option given to the charterer to add together the time allowed for loading and discharging. Where the option is exercised the effect is the same as a total time being specified to cover both operations.

5.74 The example that follows may make this a little clearer, as well as showing that a different result can follow, depending on which term is used.

5.75 In this case two weather working days have been allowed for loading, four weather working days for discharging, and the demurrage/despatch money rates are US $4000 and US $2000 respectively.

Laytime "averaged"

Loading

	Time allowed			Time saved		
	D	H	M	D	H	M
Sat, 1 June, laytime commences at 1200	—	12	—			
Sun, 2 June	—	—	—			
Mon, 3 June, loading completed at 1200	1	—	—		12	—
Tues, 4 June, laytime expires at 1200	—	12	—		12	—
	2	—	—	1	—	—

---

54. *Molière Steamship Co Ltd* v. *Naylor, Benzon & Co* (1897) 2 CC 92, at p. 99.
55. *Watson Brothers Shipping Co Ltd* v. *Mysore Manganese Co Ltd* (1910) 15 CC 159.
56. *Love and Stewart Ltd* v. *Rowtor Steamship Co Ltd* [1916] 2 AC 527 and Baltic Code 2000.
57. See Appendix. The *Charterparty Laytime Definitions 1980* provided similar definitions.

Discharging

	Time allowed			Excess time		
	D	H	M	D	H	M
Tues, 11 June, laytime commencing at 1200	—	12	—			
Wed, 12 June	1	—	—			
Thurs, 13 June	1	—	—			
Fri, 14 June	1	—	—			
Sat, 15 June, laytime expires at 1200		12	—		12	—
Sun, 16 June				1	—	—
Mon, 17 June				1	—	—
Tues, 18 June				1	—	—
Wed, 19 June, discharging completed at 1200					12	—
	4	—	—	4	—	—

Time saved in loading	1 day
Time exceeded in discharging	4 days

Demurrage incurred	3 days @ US $4000 per day—US $12000

"Reversible" laytime

	Time allowed			Excess time		
	D	H	M	D	H	M
Sat, 1 June, loading commences at 1200		12	—			
Sun, 2 June	—	—	—			
Mon, 3 June, loading completed at 1200		12	—			
Tues, 11 June, discharging commences at 1200	—	12	—			
Wed, 12 June	1	—	—			
Thurs, 13 June	1	—	—			
Fri, 14 June	1	—	—			
Sat, 15 June	1	—	—			
Sun, 16 June	—	—	—			
Mon, 17 June, laytime expires at 1200		12	—		12	—
Tues, 18 June				1	—	—
Wed, 19 June, discharging completed at 1200					12	—
	6	—	—	2	—	—

Demurrage incurred	2 days @ US $4000 per day—US $8000

5.76 Using the same figures, if there had been no averaging or reversing provision, then a still different answer would have resulted. In that case, one day's despatch money would be payable in respect of loading and four days' demurrage for discharge, i.e. a total of US $14,000.

Cases on averaging

5.77 The case of *Molière Steamship Co Ltd* v. *Naylor, Benzon & Co*[58] has already been mentioned. In that case Kennedy J held that where a liberty to average the laytime for loading and discharge was given, this meant that the charterers might add together both amounts of laytime and apply the time used against the total. He did so on the basis that

---

58. *Molière Steamship Co Ltd* v. *Naylor, Benzon & Co* (1897) 2 CC 92.

as the provision was on its face open to more than one meaning, he was entitled to receive evidence of how it was applied in practice, and this was the meaning he ascribed to it. As will be obvious, this is the meaning that would now be given to a clause providing for laytime to be reversible. The argument that the shipowners unsuccessfully put forward that the time saved at the discharging port could be used to partially offset the demurrage incurred at the load port was rejected, although that is precisely how such a clause would be interpreted today. In the later case of *Alma Shipping Co SA* v. *VM Salgaoncar e Irmaos Ltda*,[59] Devlin J accepted an argument from counsel that the *Molière Steamship* case was not a decision on the construction of the clause concerned and appeared to consider that it was anomalous.

5.78 Two years after the *Molière Steamship* case was decided, the case of *Oakville Steamship Co Ltd* v. *Holmes*[60] came before Bigham J. In this case, loading was quick and discharge slow, with the result that apart from the provision on averaging, despatch money would have been payable on loading and demurrage on discharge. The principal issue before the court was whether the charterers, having agreed the load port despatch money with the master and having had it endorsed on the bill of lading as an advance of freight, were nevertheless entitled to rescind this agreement and average loading and discharging times. On this issue Bigham J said[61]:

I think that when the defendant (the charterer) asked for and obtained his dispatch-money at Cartagena . . . he exercised once for all his option as to averaging the loading and discharging days—that is to say, he elected not to average; and it was too late for him to change his mind after the discharge at Maryport.

5.79 Interestingly enough, the earlier case was cited in argument by the charterer, but it appears to have been accepted on all sides that the averaging calculation, if it was permissible, should be done by deducting the time saved at loading from the excess discharge time. Another point of interest is that two of the counsel involved in this case were also involved in the next case,[62] where the basis of the modern doctrine was laid down.

5.80 This was the case of *Watson Brothers Shipping Co Ltd* v. *Mysore Manganese Co Ltd*,[63] a decision of Hamilton J. This concerned a charterparty for the carriage of iron ore from Marmagoa to England. The charter envisaged loading and discharging "at the rate of 500 tons per clear working day of 24 hours (weather permitting), Sundays and holidays always excepted". There were a certain number of exceptions and an averaging clause which anticipated there being more than one voyage, since it provided "Days to be averaged over all voyages performed under and during the entire currency of this charter to avoid demurrage". As events transpired, there was, however, only one voyage.

5.81 On arrival at Marmagoa, the *Benvrackie*, the ship concerned, had to wait for almost a month before a berth became available. This was caused by congestion at the port, which in turn was partially caused by a shortage of workmen available to work ships; there had been an outbreak of plague earlier in the year and the workforce was depleted.

59. *Alma Shipping Co SA* v. *V M Salgaoncar E Irmaos Ltda* [1954] 1 Lloyd's Rep 220, at p. 227.
60. *Oakville Steamship Co Ltd* v. *Holmes* (1899) 5 CC 48.
61. *Ibid.*, at p. 52.
62. Mr J A Hamilton was for the shipowners and Mr T E Scrutton was junior counsel for the defendant, the charterer's agent. In the next case Mr T E Scrutton KC was leading counsel for the shipowners and the case was tried by Hamilton J.
63. *Watson Brothers Shipping Co Ltd* v. *Mysore Manganese Co Ltd* (1910) 15 CC 159.

It would seem that discharge was completed within the allowed laytime, which was some 10 days, with the same for loading.

5.82 Before Hamilton J, the charterers argued unsuccessfully that they were entitled to add the 10 days for discharging to the 10 days allowed for loading. Part of the dispute also concerned what constituted "a working day of 24 hours" and that aspect of the case has already been considered.[64] On the present issue, the judge said that the question turned on what was meant by the word "average". A little further on in his judgment, he continued[65]:

In my opinion, the meaning of the average clause is that a number of days for shipment having been stipulated, and then a number of like days for discharge having been stipulated, the vessel's right to demurrage must be determined upon the events which happen at the port of loading and according to the number of days allowed for loading there, though subsequent events at the port of discharge may entitle the charterers to abate the amount of demurrage incurred at the port of loading by taking credit for the number of days saved, if any, at the port of discharge.

The earlier cases were apparently not cited.

5.83 In *Alma Shipping Co SA* v. *V M Salgaoncar e Irmaos Ltda*,[66] Devlin J reviewed the earlier decisions, having first set out the three alternative methods of computation proposed by the parties. These were:

A. (by shipowners): That demurrage incurred at the port of loading should be deducted from the lay days allowed for discharging, and that the charterers were liable in demurrage for the time spent in discharging in excess of the net lay days remaining.

B. (by charterers): That the total time spent in loading and discharging should be deducted from the aggregate of the lay days allowed for loading and discharging.

C. (in the alternative): That time spent in loading and discharging should be considered separately, and that a balance should be struck between them (i.e. in this case, the time saved in discharging should be set off against the excess time spent in discharging).

5.84 The case concerned a charter for the carriage of iron ore from Mormugao[67] to Rotterdam. Loading took over three weeks and discharge was completed in just over a day. The loading rate provided was 500 tons per day and the discharge rate 1,500 tons. Clause 9 of the charter, which was on the C(ore) 7 form, provided:

Charterers to have the right to average the days allowed for loading and discharging.

By methods "B" and "C", despatch money was payable and method "A" resulted in a small amount of demurrage being payable.

5.85 Having reviewed the authorities and considered the three methods, Devlin J held that "C" was the correct method. In so holding, the judge followed the decision of Hamilton J in the *Watson Brothers* case,[68] saying[69]:

---

64. See *ante* at para. 2.122.
65. *Watson Brothers Shipping Co Ltd* v. *Mysore Manganese Co Ltd* (1910) 15 CC 159, at p. 167.
66. *Alma Shipping Co SA* v. *V M Salgaoncar E Irmaos Ltda* [1954] 1 Lloyd's Rep 220.
67. Although the spelling is different, this was apparently the same port as the *Benvrackie* loaded at in the *Watson Brothers* case ((1910) 15 CC 159). See *ante* at para. 5.80.
68. *Watson Brothers Shipping Co Ltd* v. *Mysore Manganese Co Ltd* (1910) 15 CC 159.
69. *Alma Shipping Co SA* v. *V M Salgaoncar E Irmaos Ltda* [1954] 1 Lloyd's Rep 220, at p. 228.

... I reach the conclusion that a distinction must be drawn when the word "average" is used in a clause of this type from a clause which, though no doubt with similar intent, is phrased so as to use other terms which are quite so commonly used.

Earlier in his judgment he had explained what he had in mind, when he said[70]:

These clauses, the authorities show, adopt various forms. The use of the word "average" is very common; the use of the word "reversible" is also common; and sometimes there is a clause which simply provides, quite clearly and simply, for the addition of the two lots of lay days together.

The judge also said that for his part[71]:

I am bound to say that if the matter were *res integra* I think a lot might be said for treating all these types of clauses as if they were intended to achieve the same thing, whether the words used were "averaging", "adding" or "reversible", but in the face of that decision, which clearly distinguishes between the clauses which use the word "average" and clauses which use the word "adding" or have a similar effect to using the word "adding", I do not conceive that I can do so.

Cases on reversing

5.86 The earliest case where the term "reversible" is specifically used was a decision of the House of Lords, on appeal from the Scottish courts, *Love and Stewart Ltd* v. *Rowtor Steamship Co Ltd*.[72] There a charter for the carriage of a cargo of pit props provided for them "to be loaded at the rate of 125 fathoms daily and discharged at the rate of 125 fathoms daily reversible . . . ". This meant that 13 days each were allowed for loading and discharging. Explaining the meaning of "reversible", Lord Sumner said[73]:

My Lords, at Kristinestad the whole cargo was loaded in nine days, and the effect of the word "reversible" in the charter is that the receivers were entitled to 17 lay days under the charter for discharging the ship at Newport.

5.87 The next case where there was reversible laytime was *Verren* v. *Anglo-Dutch Brick Co (1927) Ltd*,[74] where the charter which was one of a series provided for "Cargo to be loaded and discharged together within five reversible working days . . . ". There was also a provision that any days saved on this charter were to be deducted from the owners' claim for demurrage under an earlier charter.

5.88 The case concerned a three-masted schooner, which also had an engine, which had been employed in carrying bricks from Belgium to the River Thames. The master was also the owner. Part of the argument was as to whether lay days were interchangeable between the various voyages and on this Roche J and the Court of Appeal agreed that it was only against a claim arising under the earlier charter that any deduction could be made. Clearly the charterers, who were the appellants in the Court of Appeal, failed to secure the sympathy of Scrutton LJ, who said[75]:

This case involves a sum of about £150, and a decision has to be arrived at by considering a series of minute facts about the voyages of a minute coaster. Mr Justice Roche, with incredible patience, listened for three days to the discussion of these various minute points and in the end came to a

---

70. *Ibid.*, at p. 225.
71. *Ibid.*, at p. 227.
72. *Love and Stewart Ltd* v. *Rowtor Steamship Co Ltd* [1916] 2 AC 527.
73. *Ibid.*, at p. 536.
74. *Verren* v. *Anglo-Dutch Brick Co (1927) Ltd* (1929) 34 Ll L Rep 56; (1929) 34 Ll L Rep 210 (CA).
75. (1929) 34 Ll L Rep 210, at p. 211.

conclusion . . . The defendants thought it right to appeal. Mr Stranger has addressed us for a day with equal minuteness. I am afraid we have not listened with equal patience.

On the reversing provision, the learned Lord Justice said[76]:

Now the whole of the first part of the charter relates to one voyage, and on that one voyage the cargo is to be loaded and discharged together within five reversible working days. I do not know who was the ingenious person who first thought the word "reversible" might possibly express what he meant to say. "Reversible" seems to mean that you may use days for either loading or discharging. The case of *Love and Stewart Ltd* v. *Rowtor Steamship Co Ltd* [1916] 2 AC 527 appears to show that that is the meaning.

5.89 In *Z Steamship Co Ltd* v. *Amtorg, New York*,[77] Goddard J agreed that a reversible provision meant that there had to be separate calculations for loading and discharging. However, he also added[78]:

So the charterers have a right to say directly the loading is finished: "We have saved you four days; pay us four days' dispatch money." If that is paid there is an end of the claim for dispatch money. It is quite true that in calculating the number of days that the ship had got to discharge you can add those four days on to the discharging time, because the charter says they are reversible; but it does not mean that you can get paid over again . . .

Unfortunately, the judge also suggested that if despatch money was paid at the load port, the time so saved could still be used to offset discharging port demurrage, although it could not be taken into account in calculating discharge port despatch if discharging was completed in less than the time allowed. In *The Atlantic Sun*,[79] doubt was rightly cast on this and it is now generally accepted that payment of despatch money at the load port wipes out all obligations with respect to the time so saved.

5.90 In the *Vancouver strike* cases,[80] one of the many issues considered by McNair J at first instance was a reversible laytime provision and the method of applying it. The relevant clauses were clause 27, which provided:

Loading and discharging time shall be reversible

and clause 17, which stated:

. . . if charterers elect to treat lay days in loading and discharging as per Clause No. 27 despatch or alternatively demurrage to be settled on completion of discharge . . .

5.91 As to the method of calculating the sum due, the judge said[81]:

On the authorities cited as to reversible lay days and in principle, it seems to me that where, as here, dispatch is payable on "time saved including Sundays and holidays", the result is as follows: First, you ascertain the number of days of the particular quality specified in the charter which are allowed for loading and discharging, which days so ascertained form a pool. For example, eight weather working days for loading; 12 weather working days for discharging; total 20 weather working days. If at the loading port less than the quantity of days allowed for loading had been used, the balance

---

76. *Ibid.*, at p. 212.
77. *Z Steamship Co Ltd* v. *Amtorg, New York* (1938) 61 Ll L Rep 97.
78. *Ibid.*, at p. 102.
79. *Fury Shipping Co Ltd* v. *State Trading Corporation of India Ltd (The Atlantic Sun)* [1972] 1 Lloyd's Rep 509, at p. 512.
80. *Reardon Smith Line Ltd* v. *Ministry of Agriculture, Fisheries and Food* [1959] 2 Lloyd's Rep 229. The case subsequently went on to the Court of Appeal ([1961] 1 Lloyd's Rep 385) and the House of Lords ([1963] 1 Lloyd's Rep 12) on other points.
81. *Reardon Smith Line Ltd* v. *Ministry of Agriculture, Fisheries and Food* [1959] 2 Lloyd's Rep 229, at p. 266.

of the days of that quality, say three weather working days, is carried forward to the discharging port or if more than the number of such days have been used for loading, you draw on the days of that quality available for discharge to meet the excess, with the result that there are fewer days of that quality (say 12 days less five) left for discharging. Finally, you ascertain how many days of the specified quality have been used at the discharging port; if the days so used exceed the number of days available for discharge whether that number has been increased (i.e. 12 plus three) or diminished (i.e. 12 minus five) demurrage is payable on such excess; but if the days so used are less than the number of days available for discharge, whether that number has been increased or diminished, dispatch money is payable on the number of days of that quality by which the days used is less than the number of days of that quality available.

5.92 With respect, however, if the last part of this statement was intended to say that demurrage or despatch is to be measured in days of the specified quality then this is not so, as will be evident from the examples given at the start of this chapter. The point of the calculation must surely be to establish either when laytime expired or, if it had not expired when discharging was complete, when it would have expired. Having established that, then normally the demurrage or despatch due is based on the number of running days between when laytime expired (or would have expired) and the completion of discharge. The only exception will be where the despatch clause clearly intends that time saved be working rather than all time saved.

5.93 As McNair J explained, it does not matter if normal working hours are different at the load and discharge ports when the laytime specified is measured in weather working days, because for example[82]:

... the factor that the working day is a period of eight hours at the loading port and a period of 24 hours at the discharging port is only brought into play in determining how many working days or parts have been used at the loading and discharging port respectively. What is carried forward or drawn on is a number of weather working days or parts of such days.

5.94 Fractions of a day should therefore be dealt with in a similar fashion to interruptions by weather.[83] Thus, in the example quoted by McNair J, if loading completed on a particular day four hours after the normal time for commencing work, then that would count as a half weather working day. If this meant that a half weather working day was carried forward to the discharge port where 24-hour working was the rule, then this means allowing 12 hours.

5.95 A different issue arose for determination in *The Atlantic Sun*.[84] Here the question the parties wanted answered was whether a reversing provision meant that laytime had to be reversed or did the charterers have an option, depending on whether the answer came out in their favour? Before answering this, Mocatta J first reviewed the earlier cases. He then concluded that the charterers did indeed have an option on the wording of the clauses in the charter then before him. The particular provisions with which the judge was concerned were clauses 9 and 28, which read as follows:

9. If the Vessel is detained longer than the time allowed for loading and/or discharging, demurrage shall be paid at £350 per running day or *pro rata* and despatch money for all time saved each end to be paid to Charterers at half demurrage rate per running day and *pro rata*.
28 ... Laytime allowed for loading and discharging to be reversible.

82. *Ibid.*
83. See *ante* at para. 2.59.
84. *Fury Shipping Co Ltd* v. *State Trading Corporation of India Ltd (The Atlantic Sun)* [1972] 1 Lloyd's Rep 509.

5.96 In his judgment, the judge said[85] that the principal textbook writers and editors had taken the view that "reversible" conferred a choice upon the charterer. Turning to clause 9, he said[86]:

... in my judgment, clause 9 supports the view that the words "to be reversible" confer an option on the charterers. This is the view, as I said earlier, which to my mind is preferable as a matter of construction of the words used apart altogether from authority. I find nothing in the decided cases pointing to a contrary conclusion and some support for the optional view in earlier editions of *Scrutton on Charterparties* of authority.

Mocatta J also rejected a finding by the umpire that the interpretation customarily given to the word "reversible" was that it was not intended to grant an option and said that such a finding did not amount to a finding of a custom.

Other similar clauses

5.97 In *Rederi Aktiebolaget Transatlantic* v. *La Compagnie Française des Phosphates de L'Océanie*,[87] the Court of Appeal had to consider a clause to the effect that:

... any days or part of days not consumed in loading may be added to the time for discharging, and any extra time consumed in loading may be deducted from the time for discharging ...

5.98 The case concerned a charter under which a vessel called the *Anten* was fixed to carry a cargo of phosphate from Makatea, in the South Pacific, to ports in Sweden. Loading took over 22 days more than the stipulated lay days, but only 12 days were occupied in discharging, some 10 days less than that allowed. Laytime was expressed in weather working days of 24 consecutive hours. The dispute centred on whether the extra time consumed in loading was measurable in demurrage days or weather working days.

5.99 The court were in no doubt that like must be taken with like and therefore what was important was the number of extra weather working days consumed in loading. Having established that, the same number and type of days had to be deducted from the time allowed for discharging. As Scrutton LJ said[88]:

It would seem reasonable that if you have saved days from your loading time, you should only add to your discharging time so many of those days as you would be bound to work on, and therefore, not add such days as were Sundays or non-weather working days. For the days you add to discharging time must be of the same quality as the discharging days ... [89]

MULTIPLE CHARTERS

5.100 It is possible, and now relatively common in the case of parcel tankers, for a vessel to be under more than one voyage charter at the same time, carrying separate cargo under each charter. Where multiple chartering is envisaged, it is usual for each charter to state that it is in respect of a specified quantity of cargo, that this is a part cargo and that the

---

85. *Ibid.*, at p. 512.
86. *Ibid.*, at p. 513.
87. *Rederi Aktiebolaget Transatlantic* v. *La Compagnie Française des Phosphates de L'Océanie* (1926) 26 Ll L Rep 253.
88. *Ibid.*, at p. 255.
89. This quotation was part of a passage cited with approval by Viscount Dilhorne in *Aldebaran Compania Maritima SA* v. *Aussenhandel AG (The Darrah)* [1976] 2 Lloyd's Rep 359, at p. 369.

shipowner is entitled to enter into other charters concurrently. The provision agreeing that the shipowner may so do is sometimes referred to as a "liberty to complete" clause. An early example of such a provision is the Centrocon completion clause, the salient parts of which provide:

Owners have the liberty to complete with other . . . merchandise from port or ports to port or ports en route for owners' risk and benefit, but . . . same not to hinder the loading or discharging of this cargo.

5.101 A more sophisticated clause is that in the Bimchemvoy charterparty, clause 24 of which states under the heading "Segregation/Commingling/Rotation":

If the Vessel is carrying different parcels, same always to be safely segregated but commingling of some commodities is permissible by written consent of all the Charterers concerned. If part cargo fixed, Owners shall have the option of loading and of discharging other cargo(es) for account of other Charterers or Shippers from port or ports en route or not en route to port or ports en route or not en route.
Rotation
Rotation of loading/discharging ports to be at Owners' option.

5.102 Similar principles apply where a voyage charter is supplemented by part cargoes carried pursuant to one or more booking notes or bills of lading with their own provisions covering demurrage and possibly laytime as well.

Are the charters to be read separately or together?

5.103 It occasionally happens that a vessel is under two charters between the same parties at the same time. The question then arises as to whether this is really a multiple charter situation or whether the two charters should be read together.

5.104 The two cases which follow provide interesting illustrations of this problem: in the first the Court of Appeal held that they should be read together and, in the second, Parker J held that they should be read separately.

5.105 In *Sarma Navigation SA v. Sidermar SpA (The Sea Pioneer)*,[90] the owners let their vessel for the carriage of a part cargo of steel bars, somewhat less than half what the vessel could have carried. The owners' right to load a completion cargo was expressly excluded. Three days later the parties concluded a second charter by which the vessel was to proceed to load a further parcel of steel coils at a second load port for discharge at a second discharge port. However, pursuant to a provision in the first charter, both parcels were discharged at the same port, discharge being consecutive with a small period of overlap.

5.106 The owners argued that each charter had to be looked at separately, so that time at the discharge port ran concurrently with demurrage being payable under each charter for the periods during which discharge of each parcel exceeded the allowed laytime. The charterers, on the other hand, contended that the charters had to be read together so that laytime ran consecutively and demurrage was only payable at the rate specified in each charter (not the total thereof) for the excess period after both laytimes had expired. At first instance, Lloyd J held,[91] reversing the decision of the umpire in the earlier arbitration

---

90. *Sarma Navigation SA v. Sidermar SpA (The Sea Pioneer)* [1982] 1 Lloyd's Rep 13 (CA).
91. *Sarma Navigation SA v. Sidermar SpA (The Sea Pioneer)* [1979] 2 Lloyd's Rep 409.

proceedings, that the charterers were right, a view upheld by the Court of Appeal.[92] The basis for so finding was that since there were specific references in the second charter to the first and an agreed addendum to the first charter to lift the restriction on the owners loading further cargo, the parties must be taken to have intended that the two charters should be read together as if all their provisions had been contained in the same contract. Having so concluded, the courts held that the laytime provided for must be calculated on a consecutive or cumulative basis, with demurrage at the rate common to each charter becoming payable thereafter.

5.107 In the second case, *Transamerican Steamship Corporation* v. *Tradax Export SA (The Oriental Envoy)*,[93] apart from the cargo carried under the two charters with which the court was concerned, the vessel carried other parcels of cargo, most of which were discharged at destinations en route. In his judgment, Parker J noted other differences between the two cases, saying of the earlier case[94]:

That case was very different from the present case. There, there was the same named vessel in each charter. Here, in each case the vessel was to be nominated, and it is expressly found in the case that at the time when each of the two charters was concluded it was not in the contemplation of the charterers that the same vessel would be nominated under both fixtures, or that any particular vessel would be nominated under either fixture. Furthermore, in as much as owners made no nomination under the June charter until four days after the July charter, and no nomination under the July charter until 14 days later, it appears that the owners also had nothing specific in mind at the date of either charter. Again, in *The Sea Pioneer*, the demurrage and laytime provisions were the same, whereas here the demurrage rates are different, and there is a difference in the laytime provisions. There is thus no basis upon which the two charters could be read together.

5.108 A slightly different question arose in *The Mexico I*,[95] amongst other issues. There the same charterers arranged for the carriage of a second parcel of cargo and in the second set of negotiations which took place some months after the first, changed the original discharge port providing for both parcels to be discharged at the same place. In arbitration the question argued was whether there was one contract or two. However, the High Court and the Court of Appeal said that was not the correct formulation of the issue, which was whether the effect of the second contract was to annul the provisions in the first for the computation of laytime and substitute for them a new set of laytime arrangements covering a composite cargo. Giving the judgment of the Court of Appeal, Mustill LJ said[96]:

I believe not. It is true that the two contracts contained substantially identical provisions as to rate of discharge, rate of demurrage and so on. It may also be true that if the parties had addressed their minds to the implications for laytime of having two charters in existence for the same ship at the same time, they might have worked out a solution which would have eliminated all dispute. But they did not do so. . . The case seems to me quite different from *The Sea Pioneer*,[97] where the two charters were knitted together by express cross-references in the second and an express amendment to the first.

92. *Sarma Navigation SA* v. *Sidermar SpA (The Sea Pioneer)* [1982] 1 Lloyd's Rep 13 (CA).
93. *Transamerican Steamship Corporation* v. *Tradax Export SA (The Oriental Envoy)* [1982] 2 Lloyd's Rep 266.
94. *Ibid.*, at p. 270.
95. *Transgrain Shipping BV* v. *Global Transporte Oceanico SA (The Mexico I)* [1988] 2 Lloyd's Rep 149; [1990] 1 Lloyd's Rep 507.
96. *The Mexico I* [1990] 1 Lloyd's Rep 507, at pp. 515–516.
97. *Sarma Navigation SA* v. *Sidermar SpA (The Sea Pioneer)* [1979] 2 Lloyd's Rep. 409; [1982] 1 Lloyd's Rep 13.

5.109 Some charters do in fact specifically envisage their being read in conjunction with another charter in certain circumstances, e.g. clause 5 of the Vegetable Oil Charterparty (Vegoil).[98]

5.110 It is essentially a question of law whether two charters can be read together, but these cases show the sort of points the court will look for, apart from the fact that the parties are the same and so is the vessel.

Commencement and running of laytime

5.111 The discussion that follows will for simplicity's sake be based on two charters. However, the same principles will apply where there are more than two charters.

5.112 In general, the normal rules apply to the commencement and running of laytime of each charter in a multiple charter situation.[99] Thus, where both charters are port charters and loading or discharging, as the case may be, is to take place at the same port then the vessel may in the usual way give Notice of Readiness under both charters on arrival within the port, provided that, in the case of the discharge port, both cargoes are freely accessible. If one of the cargoes is overstowed in part or in whole, then laytime cannot run in respect of the charter until all the cargo is accessible.

5.113 In *Government of Ceylon* v. *Société Franco-Tunisienne d'Armement-Tunis (The Massalia (No. 2))*,[100] Diplock J had to consider when laytime began in relation to overstowed cargo. In that case the *Massalia* arrived at Colombo with a part cargo of flour, some of which was overstowed by general cargo carried under a separate contract of carriage. On berthing, discharge began of that part of the flour cargo that was accessible, together with the general cargo. Pointing out that, in the case of loading, a vessel could not be said to be ready until all the holds were ready, the judge held that the same applied to discharge, saying[101]:

I take the view, therefore, that the charterers are right in their contention that laytime did not begin to run until all the flour cargo was accessible . . .

5.114 In so far as this passage is taken to mean that the earliest that laytime can run is when the particular cargo is accessible, a similar decision was reached in *The Mexico I*,[102] although the main issue in that case related to Notice of Readiness.

5.115 If both cargoes are accessible, then laytime under both charters will run concurrently after arrival. If loading or discharging of each cargo is to take place at the same berth, then time, laytime or demurrage, will continue to run during this operation, ending in respect of each charter when the cargo carried under it is loaded or discharged. However, if there are periods when cargo operations in respect of one cargo have to be suspended whilst cargo operations take place in respect of a different cargo, then the periods lost to the first charterer will not count against laytime or demurrage.[103] If the cargoes are to be loaded/discharged at different berths, then if the second berth is

---

98. See *post* at para. 5.145.

99. Time will therefore run separately under each charter and must be calculated separately.

100. *Government of Ceylon* v. *Société Franco-Tunisienne d'Armement-Tunis (The Massalia (No 2))* [1960] 2 Lloyd's Rep 352.

101. *Ibid.*, at p. 357.

102. *Transgrain Shipping BV* v. *Global Transporte Oceanico SA (The Mexico I)* [1988] 2 Lloyd's Rep 149; [1990] 1 Lloyd's Rep 507. On the NOR point, see *ante* at para. 3.257.

103. See as an illustration of this London Arbitration 9/99—LMLN 510, 27 May 1999.

unavailable whilst the vessel is at the first, time will run under both charters, but if the second berth is available, then time will only run under the charter under which cargo operations are being carried out since the vessel will thereby be unavailable to the other charterers.[104]

5.116 If one or both of the charters are berth charters, then time in respect of that charter will not run until the vessel is in berth and, in the case of discharge, the cargo is freely accessible. In London Arbitration 3/97,[105] where the charter concerned was a berth charter on an Amwelsh form, the tribunal held that a provision that ordinary delays be shared pro rata meant that where there were delays which affected the discharge of all the cargoes on board, the time lost should be shared between charterers in proportion to their respective cargo quantities.

Time lost in waiting for berth

5.117 Clause 4 of the Gencon form of charter provides that time lost in waiting for a berth is to count as laytime. The cases show clearly[106] that the clause applies to delays due to congestion and that it is not necessary for the ship concerned to have reached its specified destination if it cannot do so because all berths are occupied. In that sense it applies before Notice of Readiness can be given.

5.118 The question has, however, arisen in relation to multiple charters whether, when a vessel is waiting for a berth under a charter with such a clause but where the cargo carried is overstowed by other cargo, the waiting time still counts as laytime. As has been discussed in the previous section, Notice of Readiness cannot be given in such circumstances because the cargo is not accessible and the vessel cannot say that she is in all respects ready to discharge the overstowed cargo. Does the clause make any difference so as to enable time to count?

5.119 The answer given by the cases appears to show a difference of opinion. Before commenting further it may be as well to consider the cases.

5.120 The first case where the point arose was *The Massalia*,[107] to which reference has already been made. Strictly speaking, in that case there was only one charter, the additional cargo being carried under bills of lading, but that does not affect the issue.[108]

5.121 In *The Massalia* both the flour and the general cargo, which was the additional cargo, could be discharged at the same berth. On the *Massalia*'s arrival at Colombo, because of congestion, she was forced to wait at an anchorage until a berth became free. On arrival alongside she began discharging flour from those holds where the flour was accessible and general cargo from the remaining holds. Some three days later all the flour was accessible. Notice of Readiness had, however, been given on arrival at the anchorage, but under the *Aello*[109] doctrine which then held sway, this would have been ineffective in

104. This seems to follow from *Ropner Shipping Co Ltd* v. *Cleeves Western Valleys Anthracite Collieries Ltd* (1927) 27 Ll L Rep 317. See also the London Arbitration award referred to in LMLN 71, 22 July 1982.

105. London Arbitration 3/97—LMLN 450, 1 February 1997.

106. See *ante* at para. 3.377.

107. *Government of Ceylon* v. *Société Franco-Tunisienne d'Armement-Tunis (The Massalia (No 2))* [1960] 2 Lloyd's Rep 352.

108. So said Donaldson J in *Agios Stylianos Compania Naviera SA* v. *Maritime Associates International Ltd Lagos (The Agios Stylianos)* [1975] 1 Lloyd's Rep 426, at p. 431.

109. *Agrimpex Hungarian Trading Co for Agricultural Products* v. *Sociedad Financiera de Bienes Raices SA (The Aello)* [1960] 1 Lloyd's Rep 623 (HL). See *ante* at para. 3.90.

any event since the anchorage, although within port limits, was not a part of the port at which cargo operations were carried out.

5.122 Although Diplock J held that the vessel could not claim to be ready until all the flour was accessible, he also held that under the time lost clause the shipowners could claim the time the vessel waited for a berth. As far as the flour charter was concerned, time started after arrival,[110] stopped on shifting to the berth, and started again when all the flour was accessible.

5.123 In argument, the charterers had sought to argue that readiness was a condition precedent to time counting under a time lost clause. In support, they quoted a passage from Parker LJ's judgment in *The Radnor*,[111] where he said:

... If in any case a charterer could show that, even if a berth had been available, the vessel could not have been ready for cargo, he would be able to say that all the time occupied in waiting for a berth had not been "lost", but the finding here is that at 9.30 a.m. on June 3, 1951, the vessel was "dunnaged, matted and all hatches ready for cargo".

Rejecting this argument, Diplock J said[112]:

I think—indeed I am quite sure—that Lord Parker, in making that *dictum*, did not have in mind the sort of case with which I am concerned here. I see no reason, in reason or authority, to make me depart from what seems to me to be the natural meaning of the words, that time lost as a result of this waiting for a berth should count as, and be, extra time which it took her to finish discharging this cargo as a result of waiting for a berth.

5.124 In the next case to consider the matter, Donaldson J took a different view. This concerned a vessel called the *Agios Stylianos*,[113] whose owners had entered into two separate charters for the carriage of cargo from Constantza to Lagos. One was in respect of vehicles and the other cement, which was wholly overstowed by the vehicles. On arrival at Lagos, the vessel waited 14 days for a berth and, after berthing, discharged the vehicles and then the cement, both cargoes being discharged at the same berth. Having recovered demurrage from the vehicle charterers for the waiting time, the owners then sought unsuccessfully to maintain a similar claim against the cement charterers.

5.125 Distinguishing *The Massalia*,[114] Donaldson J said[115]:

However, Mr Rix has advanced a new argument which was not before the court in *The Massalia*. It is that "time lost waiting for berth" in the cement charterparty must mean "time lost waiting for the cement berth". This seems to me to be right and to be supported by the decision in *The Massalia* that "cargo" in that charterparty meant "flour". He goes on to submit that none of the time spent, lost or wasted before the vehicles had been discharged was spent, lost or wasted waiting for the cement berth. This is right. The vessel was waiting for a vehicle discharging berth. Once the vehicles had been discharged the cement charterers had the right and duty to nominate a berth, but this did not arise at any earlier point of time. In fact they nominated the same berth, but so far as the charter was concerned, they could have nominated one or two other berths in Lagos. Time waiting for that berth or berths would indeed have counted as discharging time, but that situation never arose.

110. By concession, the shipowners agreed time should start from when their purported Notice of Readiness would have taken effect had it been effective.
111. *North River Freighters Ltd* v. *President of India (The Radnor)* [1955] 2 Lloyd's Rep 668, at p. 680.
112. *The Massalia (No 2)* [1960] 2 Lloyd's Rep 352, at p. 358.
113. *Agios Stylianos Compania Naviera SA* v. *Maritime Associates International Ltd Lagos (The Agios Stylianos)* [1975] 1 Lloyd's Rep 426.
114. *The Massalia (No 2)* [1960] 2 Lloyd's Rep 352.
115. *The Agios Stylianos* [1975] 1 Lloyd's Rep 426, at p. 431.

5.126 The problem was also touched upon in *The Tropwave*,[116] where the court was primarily concerned with other matters. However, in his judgment, having referred to *The Massalia*, Parker J said[117]:

Since, however, in that case, as in the present, it was provided that time lost waiting for berth should count as discharging time and since in that case owners were permitted pursuant to that clause to add time waiting for berth notwithstanding that the cargo was then overstowed, it would seem to follow that, if the charterparties were all in the same form, the owners would at least *prima facie* be entitled to recover demurrage in respect of all three cargoes.

5.127 *The Agios Stylianos*[118] was not cited, but it would appear that Parker J took the same view as Diplock J in *The Massalia*.[119]

5.128 The difficulty of overstowed cargo in relation to a time lost clause has also been considered by London arbitrators. In this case, it would seem that, unlike the other cases, more than one berth was involved. The dispute before the arbitrators concerned a part cargo of fertilizer. On arrival off the discharge port, the ship tendered Notices of Readiness to the various receivers. At that time the average waiting time for a fertilizer berth was 40 days but less for the other cargoes, which were stowed on top of the fertilizer. The ship started discharging the other cargoes first and by the time a fertilizer berth became available, all the fertilizer was accessible.

5.129 The ship therefore shifted to the fertilizer berth as soon as it became free and discharged the fertilizer and the remaining part cargo concurrently. The charterers contended that, in a port charter, a time lost clause effectively added nothing and did not allow the counting of time which could not be counted as laytime ordinarily because a ship was unfit for discharge. They contended that initially the vessel was waiting for a berth at which she could discharge the cargoes stowed on top of the fertilizer and then, until the fertilizer berth became available, she was discharging cargo other than fertilizer at berths where she was put for that purpose. Therefore, she was not in either period waiting for a fertilizer berth. Also, so it was said, the ship was profitably employed in performing other contracts and so could not be said to be losing time.

5.130 Rejecting these arguments, the arbitrators said[120]:

If the ship had had the same cargoes on board on arrival at the discharge port, but none of them had obstructed access to the fertiliser, the first notice of readiness would have been valid and laytime would have started . . . Assuming events had thereafter followed as they did, laytime would have continued to count, notwithstanding the ship's other activities, for it would seem that *Ropner* v. *Cleeves*[121] would have been decided in favour of the owners if it had been shown that the charterers there were unable to work the ship during her period of unavailability, as was the case here. If that were right, and if it were also correct (a) that "time lost" provisions might operate even when a ship could not give a valid notice of readiness, and (b) that "time lost" was to be counted as if it were laytime counting under ordinary laytime provisions, it followed that all the time should count in this case.

116. *Maritime Transport Operators GmbH* v. *Louis Dreyfus et Cie (The Tropwave)* [1981] 2 Lloyd's Rep 159.
117. *Ibid.*, at p. 166.
118. *The Agios Stylianos* [1975] 1 Lloyd's Rep 426.
119. *The Massalia (No 2)* [1960] 2 Lloyd's Rep 352.
120. London Arbitration—LMLN 71, 22 July 1982.
121. *Ropner Shipping Co Ltd* v. *Cleeves Western Valleys Anthracite Collieries Ltd* (1927) 27 Ll L Rep 317. In that case, the shipowner removed his vessel from the cargo berth to bunker her after the vessel was on demurrage.

This also seemed a commercially just result since the ship would have waited for a fertiliser berth as long as she did in any event, and the charterers lost nothing by her other activities. What the owners might have earned under their other fixtures appeared irrelevant, for the charterers knew they were only getting part of the ship, and they gave express permission for completion cargoes to be loaded.

5.131 This decision has been quoted extensively because it sums up the underlying difficulties and arguments. Although not always expressly stated, there always seems to be the background contention that the shipowners are being unjustly enriched and are receiving double demurrage. As Parker J pointed out in *The Oriental Envoy*,[122] this may not always be so since it is quite possible that the demurrage rate which the owner has been able to secure may well reflect the quantity and nature of cargo carried rather than the size of the carrying vessel.

5.132 Support for this approach is also to be found in another London Arbitration, London Arbitration 3/93.[123] In this case, both cargoes were to be discharged at the same berth, although discharge of the overstowed cargo did not commence until later the same day that the first cargo began to be discharged. The arbitrators put forward two principles: first, the time which it was sought to count must have been lost in waiting for the berth for the cargo in question; and secondly, another charter covering the same voyage was not to be taken into account unless it was apparent on a reading of the charters in question that they did overlap or were intended to impinge on one another, particularly in relation to arguments about double demurrage.

5.133 Arguably, the cases quoted provide three different answers to the question posed at the start of this section as to whether waiting time may be claimed where the cargo in respect of which it is sought is overstowed by other cargo.

5.134 The answer given by *The Massalia*[124] is that it may always be claimed, even where discharge is subsequently delayed by the need to remove the other cargo. One interpretation of *The Agios Stylianos*[125] is that the period whilst the vessel is also waiting to discharge the other cargo is never waiting time. Clearly, any further delay once the other cargo is removed will be the responsibility of the charterer whose cargo had been overstowed. The third and most logical alternative is that provided by the London Arbitration award referred to above,[126] namely that it depends on whether the other cargo can be removed before a berth becomes available. Thus, if there is a delay caused by the need to discharge other cargo, the shipowner cannot claim that any earlier delay was time lost in waiting to discharge that cargo. If this approach is applied to the facts of *The Agios Stylianos*[127] then the result would be the same, as it would whenever discharge was a single berth.

5.135 In *The Agios Stylianos*[128] Donaldson J, as has already been mentioned, referred to the point in time when the charterers' duty to nominate a berth arose, i.e. when all the cargo was accessible, and apparently accepted counsel's suggestion that time could not be lost before then. However, with respect, that is not necessarily so. The reason why the

122. *Transamerican Steamship Corporation* v. *Tradax Export SA (The Oriental Envoy)* [1982] 2 Lloyd's Rep 266, at p. 271. See *ante* at para. 5.107.
123. London Arbitration 3/93—LMLN 351, 17 April 1993.
124. *The Massalia (No 2)* [1960] 2 Lloyd's Rep 352.
125. *The Agios Stylianos* [1975] 1 Lloyd's Rep 426.
126. London Arbitration—LMLN 71, 22 July 1982.
127. *The Agios Stylianos* [1975] 1 Lloyd's Rep 426.
128. *Ibid.*, at p. 431.

charterers' duty to nominate a berth arose then was because that was when the vessel became an Arrived ship and it has long been accepted that it is not a prerequisite for a time lost clause to take effect that the vessel must be an Arrived ship.[129] If counsel was, however, referring to the readiness aspect, then that was the argument specifically rejected by Diplock J in *The Massalia*.[130]

5.136 There is some support in *The Darrah* for the arbitrators' approach of asking what was the operative cause of the delay—congestion or congestion plus the overstowage of the cargo—and if the answer is the former, holding it to be within the time lost clause. In *The Darrah*, Lord Diplock, as he had by then become, said[131]:

"Time lost in waiting for berth" in the context of the adventure contemplated by a voyage charter, as it seems to me, must mean the period during which the vessel would have been in berth and at the disposition of the charterer for carrying out the loading or discharging operation, if she had not been prevented by congestion from reaching a berth at which the operation could be carried out.

It is true that, in the same case, Lord Diplock also suggested[132] that a time lost clause was superfluous in a port charter so far as time spent in waiting within port limits was concerned, but it would seem that the point now under discussion may be an exception. It is also difficult to reconcile Lord Diplock's view in *The Darrah* that congestion must be the operative cause of the delay with his decision in *The Massalia*.

5.137 The *Charterparty Laytime Definitions 1980* definition[133] of time lost also adopts the causal approach, since it provides that congestion must be the main reason for the delay. Whilst this definition only applies where it is specifically incorporated, that it is so framed is again some support for this approach.

5.138 From the point of view of the parties involved, this approach does have some drawbacks. The biggest difficulty is that it is not possible to say with any certainty at the time the charter is made who will be responsible for any delay due to congestion at the discharge port, since that will depend on whether the cargo is in fact overstowed by other cargo, whether all the cargo carried is discharged at the same or more than one berth, and in which order the berths become available.

5.139 Any definitive answer to the question will therefore have to await further litigation. It is probable, however, that the problem is confined to dry cargoes since it is only with these that overstowage arises. In the tanker trade, whilst a parcel tanker can and does carry a large number of different parcels, in theory, at least, they are equally accessible.

Demurrage

5.140 In the case of multiple charters each will specify its own demurrage rate and if, under the terms of the various charters, demurrage is due, then the shipowner is entitled to claim the cumulative amount.[134] In a number of cases, efforts have been made,

---

129. See *ante* at para. 3.384.
130. *The Massalia (No 2)* [1960] 2 Lloyd's Rep 352, at p. 358. See *ante* at para. 5.127.
131. *The Darrah* [1976] 2 Lloyd's Rep 359, at p. 364.
132. *Ibid.*
133. As do the *Voylayrules 1993* and *Baltic Code 2000* definitions. See Appendix.
134. For a consideration of the similar problem in relation to demurrage due under a number of different bills of lading issued under the same charter, see *post* at para. 6.263.

unsuccessfully, to suggest that this means that the shipowner can get double damages. Rejecting one such argument, Parker J said in *The Tropwave*[135]:

Provisions for demurrage are in a sense provisions for liquidated damages for detention and, as such, there is no absolute yardstick of what is the total damage suffered which could enable it to be said that there was double or treble indemnity. It would, for example, be perfectly possible for an owner with three charterparties covering three cargoes in different holds to fix his demurrage rate under each charterparty at one third of that which he would charge were there only one charterparty and one cargo . . . In my judgment, the arbitrator's conclusion that the possibility of overlapping claims does not in any way affect the owners' claim is entirely correct.

The judge then went on to suggest that before any such contention could succeed, the charterers would first have to displace the demurrage provision altogether so that the owners were driven to claim unliquidated damages for detention.

5.141 In *The Oriental Envoy*,[136] Parker J developed this theme further, particularly when the identity of the carrying vessel was not decided at the time of entering the fixture, saying[137]:

If a charter provides for the carriage of 10000 tons in a vessel to be named, but reserves a liberty to the owners to load his own cargo, he may provide a vessel capable of carrying the 10000 tons and no more, or he may provide a vessel which is capable of carrying, and which does carry, say, an additional 5000 tons. In such a case, the demurrage rate cannot be fixed in relation to the size of the vessel for it is not known. It can only be fixed in relation to the cargo. If a vessel capable of carrying only the stipulated cargo is provided, a rate fixed in relation to the cargo may coincide with the rate which would be appropriate for the vessel . . .

On the other hand, if a bigger vessel is provided and the excess space is filled then, said the judge, the total demurrage may well coincide with the level of damages that might be awarded for delay in the absence of demurrage provisions.

5.142 Parker J then went on to comment on the nature of demurrage itself, about which he said[138]:

In my view, however, while demurrage can no doubt be regarded as being in the nature of damages for detention, it is not to be equated with such damages. It is very different. It is a simple contractual obligation by the charterer to pay a certain sum if he fails to complete discharge within the stipulated laytime, the commencement and calculation of which is itself a matter of agreement.

5.143 In London Arbitration 26/89,[139] having decided that owners could claim full demurrage in respect of each parcel, the arbitrators said:

It was appreciated that it might be said that the conclusion in the present case might give a windfall to the owners. However, it was clearly established that laytime and demurrage could be calculated separately without regard to other part cargoes unless the parties had agreed that there was to be a single calculation of all the laytime and demurrage.

5.144 In *The Mexico I*,[140] Mustill LJ commented:

---

135. *Maritime Transport Operators GmbH* v. *Louis Dreyfus et Cie (The Tropwave)* [1981] 2 Lloyd's Rep 159, at p. 167.
136. *Transamerican Steamship Corporation* v. *Tradax Export SA (The Oriental Envoy)* [1982] 2 Lloyd's Rep 266.
137. *Ibid.*, at p. 271.
138. *Ibid.*
139. London Arbitration 26/89—LMLN 262, 18 November 1989.
140. *Transgrain Shipping BV* v. *Global Transporte Oceanico SA (The Mexico I)* [1990] 1 Lloyd's Rep 507, at p. 516.

Mention was made in argument of the possibility that the charterers might on this view be liable for two sets of demurrage at the same time ... I will suggest only that the possibility of multiple demurrage where there are parallel contracts has been recognised by the law for more than a century (see *Porteous* v. *Watney* (1878) 2 QBD 534), and also that where the recipient of the demurrage would in each case be the same person, arbitrators or the court might not find it too hard to devise a way of ensuring that he did not recover liquidated damages more than once for the same loss.

Carriage of edible vegetable oils

5.145 There is an extensive trade in the carriage of edible vegetable oils. Such cargoes are carried in sophisticated parcel tankers, each of which may have several dozen different parcels carried under multiple charterparties. Loading and discharging may be from or to a combination of shore tanks, barges or smaller feeder vessels, tanker lorries and railtankcars.

5.146 Whilst the Tanker Voyage Charter Party (Vegoilvoy) is commonly used, other forms of charter may also be used.

5.147 There are a number of aspects of this trade where practice differs from conventional charters.

Nomination of loading and discharging berths

5.148 In most charters, it is for the charterers to choose at which berths the vessel should load and discharge. In this trade it is often the owners who choose the berth and the shippers/receivers are invited to provide and take their cargoes from that berth.

Commencement of laytime and waiting time

5.149 Clause 4 of the Vegoilvoy charter provides as follows:

4. NOTICE OF READINESS AND COMMENCEMENT OF LAYTIME
  (a) When the vessel has arrived at the port of loading or discharge and is ready to load or discharge, a notice of readiness shall be tendered to the charterer or its agent by the master or agent, by letter, telegraph, wireless or telephone. The vessel shall be deemed ready within the meaning of this clause whether she arrives during or outside business hours, whether she is in or out of berth, or whether or not she has ballast water or slops in her tanks. Laytime shall commence either at the expiration of (6) running hours after tender of notice of readiness, vessel in or out of berth, except that any delay to the vessel in reaching her berth caused by the fault of the vessel or owner shall not count as used laytime; or immediately upon the vessel's arrival in berth (i.e. finished mooring when at a sealoading or discharging terminal and all fast when loading or discharging alongside a wharf) with or without notice of readiness, whichever first occurs.
  (b) Notwithstanding anything in paragraph (1) of this clause, laytime shall commence when the vessel arrives at the loading or discharging port, whether or not berth is available; provided that notice of readiness shall always be tendered as therein stipulated.

5.150 Despite the fact that the charterers have no control over where the ship berths, nevertheless they are required collectively to contribute to any time lost whilst the vessel is waiting to berth. The time taken from commencement of laytime until connection of the first cargo hose is pro-rated between all the cargo to be loaded/discharged at that terminal.

Laytime and demurrage

5.151 Clauses 5 and 11 of the Vegoilvoy charter read as follows:

5. LAYTIME

(a) The number of running hours specified as laytime in Part I shall be permitted the charterer for loading. discharging and used laytime; but any delay due to breakdown or inability of the vessel's facilities to load or discharge the cargo within the time allowed shall not count as used laytime. If regulations of the owner prohibit loading or discharging of the cargo at night, time so lost shall not count as used laytime; if the charterer, shipper or consignee, or the port authorities prohibit loading or discharging at night, time so lost shall count as used laytime. The vessel shall have the right to sail from all ports immediately upon the completion of loading or discharging whether or not laytime has expired.

(b) Where commingled shipment or separate shipments are loaded or discharged concurrently at the same installation, the laytime allowed to each shipper shall be the gross number of hours allowed any of the commingled or separate shipments, it being conclusively presumed that loading and discharging of all such shipments shall commence simultaneously.

11. DEMURRAGE

(a) Charterer shall pay demurrage per running hour and pro rata for a part thereof at the rate stipulated in Part I for all time that loading and discharging and used laytime as elsewhere herein provided exceeds the allowed laytime herein specified. If however demurrage shall be incurred at ports of loading and/or discharge because of fire or explosion in or about the plant, or because of breakdown of machinery or loading or discharging facilities of the charterer, shipper or consignee of the cargo, the rate of demurrage shall be reduced to one-half the rate stipulated in Part I hereof per running hour and pro rata of such reduced rate for part of an hour for demurrage so incurred.

(b) Where commingled or separate shipments are loaded or discharged at the same installation, demurrage shall be apportioned among such shipments in proportion to the ratio which each bears to the aggregate thereof; provided however, that where the cause of the delay results from the act of any specific charterer or shipper, the total demurrage on the vessel shall be charged against such charterer or shipper and such shipment.

Their meaning has been considered in a number of cases on both sides of the Atlantic.

5.152 In a case reported as London Arbitration 26/89,[141] the tribunal considered the relationship of clauses 5 and 11 in the context of loading, rejecting the conclusion of an earlier New York Arbitration decision of *Parcel Tankers Inc* v. *Lever Brothers Company*, where the arbitrators had held that the drafters of the Vegoil form could not have intended clause 5(*b*) to be restricted to truly concurrent cargo operations but that it must have been intended to cover consecutive operations. In the London case in question, it was stated that no other cargo had been loaded concurrently, but by inference it would seem that at least one other cargo was loaded, presumably consecutively. The tribunal held that clauses 5(*a*) and 11(*a*) had to be read together, as did clauses 5(*b*) and 11(*b*).

5.153 The tribunal also held that clause 11(*b*) clearly contemplated there being only one total demurrage obligation and that in turn could only be achieved by applying one laytime allowance, which, in the case of separate shipments, could only be achieved by the application of clause 5(*b*).

5.154 Having concluded that there was no concurrent loading, the tribunal held that in that case, clauses 5(*a*) and 11(*a*) were the ones that governed the situation. It was not therefore necessary for the tribunal to determine what laytime would have been allowed had clauses 5(*b*) and 11(*b*) applied.

5.155 Unfortunately, in the abridged report of the case it is not entirely clear what the tribunal concluded should be the meaning of "concurrent" in clause 5(*b*), save that it should be given "its natural, clear and correct meaning". One possibility is that this means that commencement and completion of loading or discharge must begin and end at exactly

141. London Arbitration 26/89—LMLN 262, 18 November 1989.

the same time. However, it is highly unlikely that even if there were only two parcels of cargo, such cargo operations would begin and end at exactly the same time. At a busy port like Rotterdam there could be 15 or more parcels of cargo, discharged partly to shore tanks, partly into railtankcars and partly into barges.

5.156 To restrict the operation of clauses 5(*b*) and 11(*b*) in this way would seem to be unreasonably restrictive. It would also mean that the presumption at the end of clause 5(*b*) that loading and discharging of all such shipments should be deemed to have commenced simultaneously would be unnecessary.

5.157 The second case where these clauses were considered, which in part supports this approach, was a decision of New York arbitrators reported in *BIMCO Bulletin* 2/90. Much of the discussion in this case centred on the assertion that these clauses were intended to prevent a "windfall profit" accruing to the owners.

5.158 As already stated, English law does not, however, recognize the concept of a windfall profit. There is nothing in English law to prevent an owner from negotiating two or more separate charters for part cargoes, possibly with different laytime allowances, and claiming the full amount of demurrage allowed under each charter. It is even possible for laytime to be still running under one charter with the owner claiming demurrage under the second, even though the ship is not in any way detained under the second charter, because English law recognizes the freedom of the parties to make whatever agreement they wish. Equally, of course, the parties may by the clauses inserted in the charters provide for a relationship between the different charters; and that is the situation, it is suggested, which is provided for by clauses 5(*b*) and 11(*b*).

5.159 Commenting on clause 5(*b*), the New York tribunal said:

There is no question that clause 5(*b*) has been imperfectly drafted, nor that—so long as it exists in its current form—it will always be subjected to scrutiny and differing opinions under the many fact patterns which can and do arise in this specialised trade. It is quite possible that there is no clause which will clearly, fairly and succinctly satisfy the many different situations which arise in parcel tanker operations.

Looking at 5(*b*), it is immediately apparent that "gross number of hours allowed any of the commingled or separate shipments" makes little or no sense at first reading. The word "gross" clearly means an aggregate of more than one, whereas "any" is an indefinite word meaning "any one", without specifying which one. The clause is further complicated by stating that there is a clear presumption that "loading and discharging of all shipments shall commence simultaneously".

Later on, they continued:

Given the nature of parcel tanker operations, it is seldom in practice that multiple cargo operations commence simultaneously, except by coincidence . . . The panel finds that the presumption of simultaneous commencement of loading and/or discharging does not mean that the operations must literally commence simultaneously in order for 5(*b*) to apply. Rather it is a presumption that if the operations can begin simultaneously i.e. they are not limited by ship or shore delivery or receiving capability, or other restrictions, the laytime must first be calculated as if they did commence simultaneously. Thereafter if demurrage results, it is allocated under the provisions of clause 11(*b*). In this connection, we find that there should normally be no reason to handle multiple cargoes consecutively at the same installation, unless by design or restriction. In such case, the liability for the additional time taken must be borne by the one creating the restriction.

5.160 The tribunal then went on to conclude that the correct approach was to first determine which was the biggest shipment and then to divide the total of that by the loading or discharging rate, as the case may be, for that particular cargo.

5.161 These cases and the wording of the clauses in question seem to lead to the following conclusions:

A. Clauses 5(*a*) and 11(*a*) should always be applied together, as should clauses 5(*b*) and 11(*b*). Clauses 5(*a*) and 11(*a*) alone deal with full cargoes. Clauses 5(*b*) and 11(*b*) alone deal with commingled cargoes. Where there are part cargoes, then either pair of clauses may apply. Where clauses 5(*a*)/11(*a*) do apply, there should be one laytime calculation per charter for loading and one for discharging based on the provisions of Part I of the charter, irrespective of the number of installations at which these operations occur. Where clauses 5(*b*)/11(*b*) apply, separate laytime calculations should be made in respect of each installation.

B. If clauses 5(*a*)/11(*a*) apply, the quantity of cargo carried for that particular charterer determines the laytime allowed.

C. As already suggested, where clauses 5(*a*)/11(*a*) apply, *waiting time* between Notice of Readiness taking effect and connection of the first loading/discharging hoses (not the hoses relating to the cargo of the particular charterer) should be apportioned between the various charterers in relation to the proportion their cargoes bear to the total cargo loaded or discharged at that installation by custom of the trade.

D. Under clauses 5(*a*)/11(*a*), if there is a delay (after the vessel berths) in connecting hoses to load/discharge a particular charterer's cargo whilst cargoes under other charters are being loaded/discharged because of a limitation on the facilities available at the loading/discharging installation (ie the terminal cannot cope with the number of part cargoes being handled), such time does not count.

E. Where clauses 5(*a*)/11(*a*) apply, if there is a delay after hoses are connected to load/discharge cargo carried for particular charterers during which cargo operations are suspended because the vessel chooses to load/discharge cargo for other charterers, whether or not this involves disconnection of hoses, such time will not count against the charterers whose operations have been halted. If the delay, however, arises not from what is happening to other charterers' cargoes but, for instance, from a limitation applied by the port authority to the number of barges allowed alongside, and the barges are involved in discharging the particular charterer's cargo, then time runs during that delay, the crucial question being whose cargo is causing the delay. But it is only if there is a complete cessation of cargo operations on particular charterers' cargo that time as against those charterers ceases to run.

F. Laytime or time on demurrage, whichever the case may be, ends in any event with disconnection of hoses. In the case of operations under clauses 5(*a*)/11(*a*), it is hoses relating to the particular charterer's cargo, whereas under 5(*b*)/11(*b*), it is in relation to the last parcel of cargo to be loaded/discharged irrespective of whose cargo it is.

G. The key as to which pair of clauses should apply when separate cargoes are loaded (or discharged) at the same installation is whether the loading (or discharging) of *all* of the parcels takes place concurrently, or could have taken place concurrently. The separate parcels may be of different sizes and/or might be allocated different loading (discharging) rates. There are concurrent operations when they take place as a co-ordinated overlapping arrangement. It is not necessary for cargo operations to begin and end nearly simultaneously. However, from the commencement of the whole cargo operation until its end, there must not be periods in which a substantial parcel of cargo is commenced, worked and completed entirely on its own. This is to adopt the remarks and approach of the New York tribunal referred to above, particularly the last full paragraph there quoted, and the reference to restrictions.

H. If it is determined that this is a concurrent cargo operations situation, it is both permissible and necessary to consider the terms of the other charters.

I. If clauses 5(b)/11(b) apply, it is necessary to determine which shipment consists of the largest quantity of cargo, since that will provide the benchmark for the laytime allowed. In theory, if each particular shipment was loaded/discharged at the same rate commencing at the same time, the one with the greatest quantity would be the last to finish. The ship would not therefore be detained in a practical sense (by any of the charterers) until cargo operations involving that shipment have been completed. That theoretical calculation has to be adapted to allow for different loading/discharge rates between shipments and that is done by identifying the one with the greatest laytime allowance, which will be referred to as the "benchmark shipment".

J. Under clauses 5(b)/11(b), and assuming that there is no attributable delay, the demurrage payable by particular charterers is calculated by first ascertaining the period of time used from commencement of laytime until all hoses are finally disconnected at that installation, then subtracting the laytime allowed by reference to the benchmark shipment and then apportioning the balance of time so calculated in proportion to the amount of cargo loaded/discharged for particular charterers against the total loaded/discharged at that installation. In this way the owners receive compensation by way of demurrage jointly from the various charterers. The question of "unjust enrichment", which was the approach of the New York tribunal, simply does not arise because the parties have agreed by clauses 5(b)/11(b) that there should be a sharing of liability for whatever demurrage is incurred.

K. The onus of proof in demonstrating that a particular cargo operation is one to which the concurrent loading/discharging rules should apply is on the party asserting it.

Squeegeeing and sweeping

5.162 Clause 7(e) provides:

Squeegeeing—squeegeeing to be paid by the owner and time used is not to count as used laytime.

Crude palm oil is solid at ambient temperatures and the residues are scraped off the sides of the vessel's tanks and swept up. Refined palm oils are liquid at ambient temperatures and have to be mopped up or "squeegeed" to get the tanks clean. It is of course not only a question of getting the tanks clean but of ensuring that the maximum quantity of this very expensive type of cargo is discharged.

5.163 Although Clause 7(e) refers only to squeegeeing and not sweeping, common sense suggests that both practices should be treated alike and covered by the clause.

Transhipment

5.164 In the vegetable oil trade, it is common practice for a mother vessel to load parcels of cargo for various charterers, notably in Malaysia and Indonesia, for carriage to Europe. At certain recognized transhipment ports, such as Rotterdam and Hamburg, individual parcels of cargo are transhipped into smaller vessels which deliver the cargo to its ultimate destination.

5.165 The time taken to tranship the cargo does not count against discharge laytime but it is common practice for the discharge laytime/demurrage calculation to be based on events at the ultimate discharge port.

5.166 An illustration of this practice is provided by the case of *The Christos*.[142] The owners of the vessel *Christos* agreed to carry a cargo of palm oil from Belawan in Indonesia to Tuapse in the Black Sea. In the event, the cargo was discharged at Novorossisk from a daughter vessel, having been transhipped at Piraeus. The owners claimed demurrage based on the time taken to discharge at Novorossisk.

5.167 Clause H of Part 1 of the charterparty provided, *inter alia*:

Owners have the option to tranship this cargo on a single vessel to the discharge port.

The charterers, however, claimed that the demurrage provisions in the charterparty were specific to the vessel *Christos* and that, once transhipment had been effected, the owners' right to demurrage fell away as the charterers were only obliged to pay demurrage in respect of the vessel named in the charterparty. They did, however, subsequently concede in the High Court that there would probably have to be an implied duty to discharge with due diligence and a common law liability for unliquidated damages in default.

5.168 In argument, the charterers sought to contrast transhipment with substitution, but, whilst noting the factual difference, Mance J does not appear to have considered it of significance. His conclusion, therefore, was that the decision of the majority of the tribunal from which the appeal lay—that the discharge laytime and demurrage provisions in the mother vessel charter applied as between the parties to that charter in relation to discharge from the daughter vessel—was correct.

---

142. *The Christos* [1995] 1 Lloyd's Rep 106.

CHAPTER 6

Demurrage

Meaning and nature

6.1 The *Voylayrules 1993* define demurrage as follows[1]:

"DEMURRAGE" shall mean an agreed amount payable to the Owner in respect of delay to the vessel beyond the laytime for which the Owner is not responsible. Demurrage shall not be subject to laytime exceptions.

6.2 However, this definition avoids what at one time was unclear, namely whether a failure to complete loading and discharging in the allowed laytime of itself constituted a breach of charter. The current view is that demurrage is liquidated damages for such a breach. In origin, however, demurrage did not mean a sum payable for breach of contract but a sum payable under and by reason of a contract for detaining a ship at the port of loading or discharge beyond the allowed time.[2] In *Lockhart* v. *Falk*, Cleasby B said[3]:

The word demurrage no doubt properly signifies the agreed additional payment for an allowed detention beyond a period either specified in or to be collected from the instrument: but it has also the popular or more general meaning of compensation for undue detention; and from the whole of each charterparty containing the clause in question we must collect what is the proper meaning to be assigned to it.

6.3 On the other hand, in *Harris* v. *Jacobs*, having said in the course of argument that demurrage is an elastic term, Brett MR said in his judgment[4]:

Demurrage is the agreed amount of damage which is to be paid for the delay of the ship caused by a default of the charterers at either the commencement or the end of the voyage.

Ten years later, in *Lilly* v. *Stevenson*, Lord Trayner took the view[5]:

Days stipulated for by the merchant on demurrage are just lay days, but lay days that have to be paid for. If a charterparty provides that the charterer shall have 10 days to load cargo, and 10 days further on demurrage at a certain rate per day, the shipper has 20 days to load, although he pays something extra for the last 10, loading within 20 days is fulfilment of the obligation to load . . .

6.4 The Court of Appeal in *Steel, Young & Co* v. *Grand Canary Coaling Co* took a similar view, Collins MR saying[6]:

---

1. See Appendix. A similar definition appears in *Baltic Code 2000*.
2. *Trading Society Kwik-Hoo-Tong of Java* v. *The Royal Commission on Sugar Supply* (1924) 19 Ll L Rep 90, at p. 92 *per* Roche J, and *Trading Society Kwik-Hoo-Tong* v. *Royal Commission on Sugar Supply* (1923) 15 Ll L Rep 24, *per* Rowlatt J.
3. *Lockhart* v. *Falk* (1875) LR 10 Ex 132, at p. 135.
4. *Harris* v. *Jacobs* (1885) 15 QBD 247, at p. 251.
5. *Lilly* v. *Stevenson* (1895) 22 Rett 278, at p. 286.
6. *Steel, Young & Co* v. *Grand Canary Coaling Co* (1902) 7 CC 213, at p. 217.

... it was also contended that the charterparty was broken by the vessel being allowed to go on demurrage; but this is not so, for the payment of demurrage is merely a payment for the use of the ship, and not damages for a breach of charterparty

and in the same case Mathew LJ said[7]:

There is no ground for suggesting that the obligation to pay demurrage is by way of damages for breach of charterparty. It is merely a payment for use of the ship.

In *Inverkip Steamship Co* v. *Bunge & Co*, Scrutton LJ suggested that both views were tenable, saying[8]:

The sum agreed for freight in a charter covers the use of the ship for an agreed time for loading or discharging, known as "the lay days", and for the voyage. But there is almost invariably a term in the agreement providing for an additional payment known as demurrage for detention beyond the agreed lay days. This is sometimes treated as agreed damages for detaining the ship, sometimes as an agreed payment for extra lay days.

6.5 The Gencon charter (Uniform General Charter 1976) provides for the possibility of a limited period on demurrage, as did many early charters, and if the vessel is further delayed beyond that, then the shipowner's claim is one for detention. Most modern charters do not put any fixed time limit on demurrage. In *Aktieselskabet Reidar* v. *Arcos Ltd*,[9] Bankes LJ suggested that charters where only a limited demurrage time was allowed might be considered as an example of where demurrage could arise without there being a breach of charter. Having quoted what Cleasby B said in *Lockhart* v. *Falk*,[10] Bankes LJ continued[11]:

It will be noted that the learned judge draws the distinction between the "allowed detention", and the "undue detention". It may well be that where a charterparty ... provides for a given number of days ... on demurrage, as much of the much-discussed judgment of Lord Trayner in *Lilly* v. *Stevenson*,[12] ... as holds that days stipulated for by the merchant on demurrage are just lay days, but lay days that have to be paid for, is well founded.

However, he did add a caveat that it was not necessary to decide the point in the case then under consideration.

6.6 More recently, in *Union of India* v. *Compania Naviera Aeolus SA (The Spalmatori)*, Lord Guest said[13]:

Lay days are the days which parties have stipulated for the loading or discharge of the cargo, and if they are exceeded the charterers are in breach; demurrage is the agreed damages to be paid for delay if the ship is delayed in loading or discharging beyond the agreed period.[14]

In *Dias Compania Naviera SA* v. *Louis Dreyfus Corporation*,[15] Lord Diplock said:

If laytime ends before the charterer has completed the discharging operation he breaks his contract. The breach is a continuing one; it goes on until discharge is completed and the ship is once more available to the shipowner to use for other voyages.

---

7. *Ibid.*
8. *Inverkip Steamship Co* v. *Bunge & Co* (1917) 22 CC 200, at p. 204.
9. *Aktieselskabet Reidar* v. *Arcos Ltd* (1926) 25 Ll L Rep 513.
10. *Lockhart* v. *Falk* (1875) LR 10 Ex 132, at p. 135. See *ante* at para. 6.2.
11. *Aktieselskabet Reidar* v. *Arcos Ltd* (1926) 25 Ll L Rep 513, at p. 515.
12. *Lilly* v. *Stevenson* (1895) 22 Rett 278, at p. 286. See *ante* at para. 6.3.
13. *Union of India* v. *Compania Naviera Aeolus SA (The Spalmatori)* [1964] AC 868, at p. 899.
14. Lord Reid also took the view that failure to complete loading/discharging within the allowed laytime was a breach of contract. See [1962] 2 Lloyd's Rep 175, at p. 182.
15. *Dias Compania Naviera SA* v. *Louis Dreyfus Corporation* [1978] 1 WLR 261, at p. 263.

In *The Lips*,[16] Lord Brandon put it this way:

> ... I deal first with what demurrage is not. It is not money payable by a charterer as the consideration for the exercise by him of a right to detain a chartered ship beyond the stipulated lay days. If demurrage were that, it would be a liability sounding in debt. I deal next with what demurrage is. It is a liability in damages to which a charterer becomes subject because, by detaining the chartered ship beyond the stipulated lay days, he is in breach of his contract. Most, if not all, voyage charters contain a demurrage clause, which prescribes a daily rate at which the damages for such detention are to be quantified. The effect of such a claim is to liquidate the damages payable: it does not alter the nature of the charterer's liability, which is and remains a liability for damages, albeit liquidated damages. In the absence of any provision to the contrary in the charter the charterer's liability for demurrage accrues *de die in diem* from the moment when, after the lay days have expired, the detention of the ship by him begins.

Whilst strictly speaking demurrage is the money payable for time in excess of the allowed laytime, it is often used to describe the period during which such money is payable. The *Charterparty Laytime Definitions 1980* also provide that[17]:

> "ON DEMURRAGE" means that the laytime has expired. Unless the charterparty expressly provides to the contrary the time on demurrage will not be subject to the laytime exceptions.[18]

6.7 It is, of course, true that demurrage normally only commences when the allowed laytime has expired. However, if they wish, there is no reason why the parties should not agree that demurrage should be payable for any delay at an earlier stage. Indeed, the Australian Grain Charters 1928 and 1972 contain an express provision allowing demurrage for waiting time in specified circumstances before the vessel concerned becomes an Arrived ship.[19]

6.8 Under such a provision demurrage may run, cease on the vessel becoming an Arrived ship, and then start again on expiry of the allowed laytime.

Length of demurrage

6.9 As already mentioned, a charter may either provide a specific duration for demurrage or, more commonly, just provide for a demurrage rate, leaving the period unspecified.

6.10 Where the period was unstated, it used to be said that demurrage would run for a reasonable period with any further delay thereafter forming a claim for detention. That view, however, has been superseded and it is now the case that demurrage will run until the contract becomes frustrated or repudiated. Similarly, it was the law that the shipowner could depart from the port of loading once the specified demurrage period had expired, or if the charter only stated a demurrage rate, after a reasonable period had elapsed. How judicial thinking changed will now be considered in more detail.

6.11 In *Dimech* v. *Corlett*,[20] it was held that if the charter provides for a fixed number of demurrage days, the ship must wait for those days to expire before sailing if the charterer requires it and there is ground for believing that further cargo will be loaded. In

---

16. *President of India* v. *Lips Maritime Corporation (The Lips)* [1987] 2 Lloyd's Rep 311, at p. 315.
17. See Appendix.
18. For a discussion on exceptions clauses in relation to demurrage, see *post* at para. 6.97.
19. For a discussion on such provisions, see *ante* at para. 3.484.
20. *Dimech* v. *Corlett* (1858) 12 Moo PC 199.

Lilly v. *Stevenson*,[21] to which reference has already been made, Lord Trayner also said[22]:

Where the days on demurrage are not limited by contract, they will be limited by law to what is reasonable in the circumstances.

6.12 In *Wilson and Coventry Ltd* v. *Otto Thoresen's Linie*,[23] Bray J had to consider a charter which provided for customary laytime with indefinite demurrage thereafter. The shipowner had undertaken to load a full and complete cargo of straw but had sailed early because of later commitments. Bray J found that a reasonable time for loading would have been $2\frac{1}{2}$ days but that the vessel had sailed before that had elapsed. He then went on to hold that not only should the ship have remained until the laytime had expired, but a reasonable time thereafter. However, in *Western Steamship Co Ltd* v. *Amaral Sutherland & Co Ltd*,[24] the same judge said that if a shipowner chose to remain after a reasonable time on demurrage had elapsed, where the charter did not provide for a fixed time on demurrage, then demurrage remained payable and the shipowner was not entitled to claim damages for detention thereafter.

6.13 Although the case went to the Court of Appeal,[25] they sent the case back, saying that the point of law involved should not have been decided as a preliminary issue without going into all the facts. They declined, however, to express any opinion at that stage on Bray J's decision in the court below. As the case was subsequently settled they were thus denied any further opportunity.

6.14 Such an opportunity did, however, arise some three years later in *Inverkip Steamship Co* v. *Bunge & Co*.[26] At first instance, Sankey J held that Bray J had been right in the *Western Steamship Co* case[27] and Lord Trayner in *Lilly* v. *Stevenson*[28] had been wrong. He said that the clause in the charter with regard to demurrage, which simply provided for a rate, was exhaustive on the subject and that this rate applied to the whole period during which the ship was detained. The shipowners were not therefore entitled to claim damages exceeding the demurrage rate for the period the steamer was detained beyond a reasonable time after the termination of the lay days. The Court of Appeal agreed. Scrutton LJ pointed out some of the difficulties that might arise if it were to be held that demurrage ran for a reasonable period, particularly with customary laytime charters where the laytime itself was measured in terms of a reasonable time. How could there be a second reasonable time thereafter? Said Scrutton LJ[29]:

Her days on demurrage are part of an unreasonable time for loading. Is the court to determine what is a reasonable degree of unreasonableness? In my view, the test of reasonable time is not one that is applicable. To enable the ship to abandon the charter without the consent of the charterer, I think the shipowner must show either such a failure to load as amounts to a repudiation of, or final refusal to perform, the charter, which the shipowner may accept as a final breach and depart claiming damages—*Mersey Steel Co* v. *Naylor, Benson & Co*[30]—or such a commercial frustration of the

---

21. *Lilly* v. *Stevenson* (1895) 22 Rett 278.
22. *Ibid.*, at p. 286.
23. *Wilson and Coventry Ltd* v. *Otto Thoresen's Linie* (1910) 15 CC 262.
24. *Western Steamship Co Ltd* v. *Amaral Sutherland & Co Ltd* (1913) 19 CC 1.
25. *Western Steamship Co Ltd* v. *Amaral Sutherland & Co Ltd* (1914) 19 CC 272 (CA).
26. *Inverkip Steamship Co* v. *Bunge & Co* (1916) 22 CC 147; (1917) 22 CC 200 (CA).
27. *Western Steamship Co Ltd* v. *Amaral Sutherland & Co Ltd* (1913) 19 CC 1.
28. *Lilly* v. *Stevenson* (1895) 22 Rett 278.
29. *Inverkip Steamship Co* v. *Bunge & Co* (1917) 22 CC 200, at p. 204.
30. *Mersey Steel Co* v. *Naylor, Benson & Co* (1884) 9 App Cas 434, at p. 439.

adventure by delay under the doctrine of *Jackson* v. *Union Marine Insurance Co*[31] as puts an end to the contract.

6.15 Scrutton LJ, however, went on to disagree[32] with what Bray J had said in *Wilson and Coventry Ltd* v. *Otto Thoresen's Linie*[33] about a ship being able to sail a reasonable time after the expiration of lay days, which must thus be considered overruled. It therefore follows that a ship must normally remain for the full period of allowed laytime and thereafter on demurrage until loading or discharging is complete, or the contract has come to an end in one of the ways suggested by Scrutton LJ.

6.16 The reason why a shipowner must keep his vessel at the port of loading, discharge or call, as the case may be, after the time allowed to the charterer to fulfil his obligations there was considered by the Court of Appeal in *Aktieselskabet Reidar* v. *Arcos Ltd*.[34]

6.17 Having pointed out that previous decisions[35] had left open the question whether this was because of an implied term in the charter or upon the necessity that the master should remain for a reasonable time before he would be in a position to say that the conduct of the charterers amounted to a repudiation of the contract, Bankes LJ went on to set out what is the present position, saying[36]:

I see no sufficient reason for construing the provision for demurrage as contained in the charterparty in the present case as a contractual extension of the lay days either for a reasonable time or for any other time, or as an implied term of the contract that the vessel shall remain for any time. I prefer to rest the necessity for remaining upon the ground that, time not being of the essence of the contract, the shipowner will not, except under some exceptional circumstances, be in a position to assert that the contract has been repudiated unless the vessel does remain for a sufficient time to enable that question to be tested.

6.18 In a similar vein, Lord Diplock said in *Dias Compania Naviera SA* v. *Louis Dreyfus Corporation*[37]:

But unless the delay in what is often, though incorrectly, called re-delivery of the ship to the shipowner, is so prolonged as to amount to a frustration of the adventure, the breach by the charterer sounds in damages only. The charterer remains entitled to continue to complete the discharge of the cargo, while remaining liable in damages for the loss sustained by the shipowner during the period for which he is being wrongfully deprived of the opportunity of making profitable use of his ship.

6.19 It therefore seems that in contractual terms, laytime provisions relating to the amount of laytime allowed are warranties rather than conditions, and therefore a breach only results in damages being payable unless the delay is such as to bring the charter to an end by frustration or by a repudiation of the charter.

Rate and payment of demurrage

6.20 As Lord Diplock also said in *Dias Compania Naviera SA* v. *Louis Dreyfus Corporation*[38]:

31. *Jackson* v. *Union Marine Insurance Co* (1874) LR 10 CP 125.
32. *Inverkip Steamship Co* v. *Bunge & Co* (1917) 22 CC 200, at p. 206.
33. *Wilson & Coventry Ltd* v. *Otto Thoresen's Linie* (1910) 15 CC 262.
34. *Aktieselskabet Reidar* v. *Arcos Ltd* (1926) 25 Ll L Rep 513.
35. *Ethel Radcliffe Steamship Co* v. *Barnett Ltd* (1926) 24 Ll L Rep 277; *Proctor, Garratt, Marston Ltd* v. *Oakwin Steamship Co* (1925) 22 Ll L Rep 518.
36. *Aktieselskabet Reidar* v. *Arcos Ltd* (1926) 25 Ll L Rep 513, at p. 515.
37. *Dias Compania Naviera SA* v. *Louis Dreyfus Corporation* [1978] 1 WLR 261, at p. 263.
38. *Ibid.*

It is the almost invariable practice nowadays for these damages to be fixed by the charterparty at a liquidated sum per day and *pro rata* for part of a day (demurrage) which accrues throughout the period of time for which the breach continues.

6.21 Whilst most charters do provide for demurrage on a daily basis or a method of so calculating, there is no reason why demurrage should not be specified on an hourly or some other basis. An example of an hourly basis was the charter considered in *Rayner* v. *Rederiaktiebolaget Condor*[39] which provided for laytime of 72 hours and "if longer detained to pay 16s 8d per like hour demurrage".

6.22 Unless the charter provides for portions of a day, then *prima facie* the shipowner is entitled to a whole day's demurrage if any time is used. Thus, in *Commercial Steamship Co* v. *Boulton*,[40] the charterer provided for seven days' laytime and "ten days on demurrage over and above the said lying days . . . ". Laytime expired at midnight on a Tuesday and discharging ended at 8 a.m. the following Thursday. Finding that the shipowners were entitled to two days' demurrage, Lush J said[41]:

There is no ground for saying that in the case of demurrage there can be any division of a day, without express stipulation to that effect.

6.23 Lush J's decision was followed and applied in *South Australian Voluntary Wheat Pool* v. *Owners of the Riol*,[42] where a $31\frac{1}{2}$-hour delay resulted in two days' demurrage. In *Stewart Line (Belfast)* v. *Wallace Brothers Ltd (Dublin)*,[43] however, the charter provided for the cargo to be discharged in 24 running hours, with demurrage 2s per gross ton per day. Gordon J agreed[44] that where fixed days were appointed for discharge and these were exceeded if only by one hour, that a full day's demurrage must be awarded in respect of that hour, but, he continued, in this charter it was fixed hours that were named for laytime and demurrage was to be paid at the rate of so much per day. With some doubt, he arrived at the conclusion that the intention and meaning of the charter was that demurrage should be calculated on a per hour basis.

New Worldscale—Full Title: New Worldwide Tanker Nominal Freight Scale[45]

6.24 In tanker charters, it is usual to specify freight rates in terms of a percentage of a scale published as a standard of reference by means of which rates for voyages can be compared. Worldscale provides for standard demurrage rates according to ships' sizes based on deadweight capacity. Thus in the absence of any provision to the contrary, the size of the ship is critical and not the amount of cargo carried. The freight scale is based on a standard tanker of 75,000 tonnes[46] (summer deadweight). For any particular voyage Worldscale will publish freight rates based on New Worldscale 100. If the parties agree another figure, e.g. New WS50, then the freight rates will be that percentage of the published figures.

---

39. *Rayner* v. *Rederiaktiebolaget Condor* (1895) 1 CC 80.
40. *Commercial Steamship Co* v. *Boulton* (1875) LR 10 QB 346.
41. *Ibid.*, at p. 349.
42. *South Australian Voluntary Wheat Pool* v. *Owners of the Riol* (1926) 24 Ll L Rep 363.
43. *Stewart Line (Belfast)* v. *Wallace Bros Ltd (Dublin)* (1921) 7 Ll L Rep 98.
44. *Ibid.*, at p. 99.
45. New Worldscale applies for all voyages on which loading was commenced on or after 1 January 1989.
46. Worldscale, which applied up to 31 December 1988, was based on what was said to be the standard tanker when it was first introduced, a vessel of 19,500 long tons (summer deadweight).

Payment

6.25 Whilst the entitlement to demurrage accrues usually on a day-by-day basis, payment is normally made on completion of the voyage after the vessel has departed for her next fixture. However, it would seem that if the delay is substantial, then it is possible to apply to London arbitrators (assuming the charter provides for London arbitration) for an interim award of demurrage before discharge has been fully completed.[47] Such an award will probably only cover an undisputed amount and is unlikely to include interest, which will be dealt with when the final calculation can be made.

Damages in addition to demurrage[48]

6.26 As has already been pointed out,[49] once the allowed laytime has expired and demurrage becomes payable, it will continue to be payable until the loading and discharging operations are completed, unless the charter provides for a limited period on demurrage. There is thus normally no point at which demurrage becomes replaced by damages at large. The question now under consideration, however, is whether damages can ever be payable in addition to demurrage, where the shipowner's proved losses exceed the moneys payable as demurrage.

6.27 This, unfortunately, is a question of some complexity and whilst the general principles are now reasonably clear, the precise scope of their application is not.

6.28 The leading cases on this point are the Court of Appeal decision in *Aktieselskabet Reidar* v. *Arcos Ltd*,[50] some aspects of which have already been mentioned, and the House of Lords' decision, usually referred to as the *Suisse Atlantique* case,[51] where their Lordships agreed on this aspect with what had been said in the lower courts. The effect of these cases is that where there has been a breach of the charter laytime provisions by the charterer failing to load and discharge in the period allowed, resulting in a detention of the ship and a consequent loss of earnings to the shipowner, then the only damages payable are the liquidated damages, i.e. demurrage provided for in the charter. If, however, the shipowner can prove a separate breach of charter, although arising from the same circumstances, then he may recover damages at large if he can show that the consequences extended beyond the detention of his vessel.

6.29 In *Inverkip Steamship Co* v. *Bunge & Co*,[52] owing to a late change in loading port occasioned by a natural phenomenon affecting the original load port, there was a delay in loading and in fact no cargo was loaded before the vessel went on demurrage. The shipowner's principal argument was that the demurrage rate provided for in the charter should only apply for a reasonable period and that thereafter damages should be at large. That point was rejected by the court, as has already been considered.[53] However, an

47. London Arbitration—LMLN 74, 2 September 1982. See also London Arbitration 11/90—LMLN 285, 6 October 1990, on a requirement to provide supporting documentation within a specified period.
48. For damages in lieu of demurrage, see *post* at paras 8.29 *et seq.* See also *The Sea Wind* LMLN 531 16 March 2000 where New York Arbitrators allowed demurrage for part of the delay and damages for detention for the remainder.
49. See *ante* at para. 6.9.
50. *Aktieselskabet Reidar* v. *Arcos Ltd* (1926) 25 Ll L Rep 513.
51. *Suisse Atlantique Société d'Armement Maritime SA* v. *NV Rotterdamsche Kolen Centrale (The General Guisan)* [1966] 1 Lloyd's Rep 529 (HL). A somewhat notorious case, not on this aspect but on the wider question of what constitutes a fundamental breach, which was also discussed by the House of Lords (a doctrine which is no longer in favour).
52. *Inverkip Steamship Co Ltd* v. *Bunge & Co* (1917) 22 CC 200.
53. See *ante* at para. 6.14.

additional argument put forward was that there was a further breach by the failure to provide a cargo. Whilst the court accepted that the obligation to load and the obligation to provide a cargo were separate and distinct obligations, they nevertheless held that the result of a breach of either was the same. Scrutton LJ put it this way[54]:

> If there was a breach in not having cargo ready on August 25 the only consequence is detention of the ship, and the damages for that, which is the same detention, however it arises, are agreed in the charter and have been paid.

6.30 The next case that considered the question was *Aktieselskabet Reidar* v. *Arcos Ltd*,[55] where a vessel was fixed to carry a full cargo of timber from the White Sea to an English port. She arrived at Archangel on 3 October, lay days began the following day, loading actually started on 8 October and completed on 23 October. The significance of the dates was that had she completed loading within the allowed laytime, she would have arrived in England by 31 October and therefore could have loaded to her summer loading line, thus carrying more cargo and earning more freight. The case concerned the cargo that had thereby been shut out, for which deadfreight was claimed, and allowed, in addition to demurrage.

6.31 Whilst Greer J in the High Court[56] and Bankes, Atkin and Sargant LJJ in the Court of Appeal[57] were all agreed that this should be the result, their reasoning differed somewhat.[58] Greer J, Atkin and Sargant LJJ all held that there was a breach of the obligation to load a full and complete cargo, Greer J and Atkin LJ holding that the amount to be loaded to meet this requirement was to be determined at the end of the lay days. Sargant LJ, on the other hand, said that[59] " . . . the time at which that [amount of] cargo must be ascertained is . . . the time when the charterers received the ship for loading . . . and not the time at which they ceased to load in fact". However, even if it is quantified on commencement of laytime, that quantification must presumably take into account the length of laytime and what effect, if any, this would have on the application of regulations at the intended discharge port. Interestingly enough, Atkin LJ appears to have considered[60] the demurrage payable in the particular case as a part mitigation of the loss suffered by the shipowner from the failure to load a full and complete cargo, a loss that could never be fully extinguished by the payment of demurrage because of the change in the regulations after 31 October.

6.32 Bankes LJ differed[61] from his colleagues by holding that the date on which a full and complete cargo was to be ascertained was the actual date of completion of loading. However, he then went on to say that the shipowner could recover his additional loss as a separate head of damage.[62] Detailed analyses of the judgments in this case are contained

---

54. *Inverkip Steamship Co Ltd* v. *Bunge & Co* (1971) 22 CC 200, at p. 206. See also *per* Warrington LJ, at p. 202.
55. *Aktieselskabet Reidar* v. *Arcos Ltd* (1926) 25 Ll L Rep 513 (CA).
56. *Aktieselskabet Reidar* v. *Arcos Ltd* (1926) 25 Ll L Rep 30.
57. *Aktieselskabet Reidar* v. *Arcos Ltd* (1926) 25 Ll L Rep 513 (CA).
58. Judicial comment on the various judgments is to be found by Devlin J in *Chandris* v. *Isbrandtsen-Moller Co Inc* (1950) 83 Ll L Rep 385, at pp. 397–398, by all the courts who considered the *Suisse Atlantique* case (see *post* at para. 6.35), and by Webster J in *The Altus* [1985] 1 Lloyd's Rep 423.
59. *Aktieselskabet Reidar* v. *Arcos Ltd* (1926) 25 Ll L Rep 513, at p. 517.
60. *Ibid.*, at p. 516.
61. *Ibid.*, at p. 515.
62. *Ibid.*, at p. 516.

in most of the subsequent cases, particularly by Webster J in *The Altus*[63] and by Potter J in *The Bonde*.[64]

6.33 Another case where similar issues arose was *Chandris* v. *Isbrandtsen-Moller Co Inc*,[65] a decision of Devlin J, as he then was. This concerned a cargo of general merchandise shipped from the United States to Liverpool during the Second World War. Amongst the cargo was some 1,546 tons of turpentine in steel drums, a dangerous cargo and as such excluded under the terms of the relevant charter.

6.34 Whilst Devlin J was prepared to hold that this breach would have entitled the shipowner to repudiate the charter, nevertheless, as the cargo had been accepted by the vessel, the owner was held to be limited to claiming damages. The damages claimed before Devlin J arose from what happened during discharge at Liverpool. Two days after commencing discharge the vessel was moved out of dock and ordered to complete discharge into barges in the River Mersey because of the dangerous nature of turpentine, with the result that discharge took 16 days longer than it would otherwise have done. For those days the shipowner claimed the full amount of the loss as well as demurrage for the first two days when the vessel was already on demurrage, plus the extra costs of discharge. The shipowner's argument was rejected by Devlin J, who held that damages were limited to demurrage plus the extra costs of discharge. Much of the case concerned whether loading a dangerous cargo was a fundamental breach of the charter or, put another way, a breach of a primary obligation so that the demurrage clause did not apply, an argument which Devlin J declined to accept. However, it would seem that, like Bankes LJ in *Aktieselskabet Reidar* v. *Arcos Ltd*,[66] Devlin J accepted that if damages were recoverable in addition to liquidated damages for detention then it was because they could be shown to be a separate head of damage, rather than because there had been a breach of a separate obligation. Of what the Court of Appeal had decided, the judge said[67]:

That case decided a point up to then left undetermined. *Inverkip Steamship Co Ltd* v. *Bunge & Co*[68] . . . had decided that damages for detention for breach of the obligation to provide a cargo were covered by the demurrage clause. But supposing that the breach of such an obligation gave rise to damages of a different character, not for detention at all. The demurrage clause could not then provide the measure. Ought the clause to be construed as exhaustive, so that no damages which could not be measured by it could be recovered at all, or ought it to be construed merely as applying to damages for detention, leaving damages of any other character to be assessed at large? The Court of Appeal decided the latter.

6.35 The other important case to consider the exclusivity of demurrage for detention was the *Suisse Atlantique* case.[69] The facts were relatively simple. A charter was entered into by the owners of a vessel called the *General Guisan* for the carriage of coal from the US to Europe for a two-year period, during which some eight voyages were performed. Except for first loading, on each occasion of loading or discharging demurrage was incurred. Had loading and discharge been completed within the allowed laytime, a

63. *Total Transport Corporation of Panama* v. *Amoco Trading Co (The Altus)* [1985] 1 Lloyd's Rep 423, at p. 423.
64. *Richco International Ltd* v. *Alfred C Toepfer International GmbH (The Bonde)* [1991] 1 Lloyd's Rep 136, at pp. 141, 142.
65. *Chandris* v. *Isbrandtsen-Moller Co Inc* (1950) 83 Ll L Rep 385.
66. *Aktieselskabet Reidar* v. *Arcos Ltd* (1926) 25 Ll L Rep 513, at p. 516.
67. *Chandris* v. *Isbrandtsen-Moller Co Inc* (1950) 83 Ll L Rep 385, at p. 397.
68. *Inverkip Steamship Co Ltd* v. *Bunge & Co* (1917) 22 CC 200.
69. *Suisse Atlantique Société d'Armement Maritime SA* v. *NV Rotterdamsche Kolen Centrale (The General Guisan)* [1966] 1 Lloyd's Rep 529 (HL).

substantial number of additional voyages could have been performed on which the profit earned would have exceeded the demurrage paid on the reduced number of voyages. The charter did not provide for any minimum number of voyages during the two-year period. All three courts[70] rejected the shipowners' claim to recover the losses they said they had incurred.

6.36 One of the reasons why so few voyages were performed was because the freight rate agreed for the whole fixture was relatively high and the demurrage rate did not reflect the high freight rates that could be earned at the start of the charter. However, soon after the fixture was entered into, freight rates dropped and the owners claimed that the charterers had deliberately kept the number of voyages low because of this. If this was so, then it was irrelevant, said Mocatta J, and this aspect was not pursued in the higher courts. On the question of whether damages could be claimed apart from demurrage, Mocatta J said[71]:

Were it not for *Reidar* v. *Arcos*,[72] I would readily have accepted Mr Donaldson's argument that the loss suffered by the owners was indistinguishable in principle from that suffered by a shipowner under a single voyage charter when his ship is detained beyond her lay days. In consequence, I would have decided without much doubt that, just as the consequential loss of future freight in such a case would be a loss by detention covered by the demurrage provisions, so should losses of freight under the additional voyages that could have been performed under the charter be treated as covered by demurrage.

The judge pointed out[73] that the case of *Aktieselskabet Reidar* v. *Arcos Ltd*[74] had the special feature that the delay in loading affected the quantity of cargo that could be carried on the very voyage in which the delay arose, unlike the case he was then considering. He therefore concluded[75]:

. . . the general principle agreed by all members of the Court of Appeal must apply, namely that for a claim for detention by a shipowner due to the laytime provisions in a charter being exceeded, the demurrage provisions quantify the damages recoverable.

6.37 When the case came before the Court of Appeal, Sellers LJ said of the earlier case[76]:

The dead freight claim which the court allowed was an additional and independent loss unrelated to the loss of use. The length of detention was not relevant to the loss from failure to load a full and complete cargo, which was a loss of a different kind. If the vessel had sailed within her laytime with 300 tons short the claim for dead freight would still have succeeded. I do not find that the *Reidar* v. *Arcos* case, *supra*, supports the argument which is advanced here—that there is some damage to be assessed on a separate ground or as a separate head by reason of the detention of this vessel. The figure of demurrage was the parties' agreed assessment of what was to be paid . . .

Harman LJ and Diplock LJ also agreed that the owners' claim must fail, Diplock LJ saying[77]:

---

70. *Suisse Atlantique* [1965] 1 Lloyd's Rep 166 (Mocatta J); [1965] 1 Lloyd's Rep 533 (CA); [1966] 1 Lloyd's Rep 529 (HL).
71. *Suisse Atlantique* [1965] 1 Lloyd's Rep 166, at p. 177.
72. *Aktieselskabet Reidar* v. *Arcos Ltd* (1926) 25 Ll L Rep 513 (CA).
73. *Suisse Atlantique* [1965] 1 Lloyd's Rep 166, at p. 177.
74. (1926) 25 Ll L Rep 513.
75. *Suisse Atlantique* [1965] 1 Lloyd's Rep 166, at p. 178.
76. *Suisse Atlantique* [1965] 1 Lloyd's Rep 533, at p. 539.
77. *Ibid.*, at p. 540.

The nature of the damage of which the parties have estimated the quantum in their agreed sum for demurrage is that during the period of detention the vessel is unable to earn freight; and in so far as the complaint of the claimants here is that the vessel has been unable to earn freight, it is covered, in my view, by their own assessment of the damage to be payable, namely, the daily demurrage rate.

6.38 By the time the case reached the House of Lords, it had become complicated by an additional claim from the shipowners that there had been a fundamental breach by the charterers, which they said precluded reliance on the demurrage clause since that was a form of exceptions clause. The House, however, decided that such a clause was for the benefit of both parties and was not an exceptions clause. Nevertheless, their Lordships went on to consider the doctrine of fundamental breach in what was subsequently described in a later case by one of their Lordships as "lengthy" and "sometimes indigestible" speeches.[78] However, on the question of whether damages might be payable in certain circumstances in addition to demurrage, and the meaning of the Court of Appeal's decision in *Aktieselskabet Reidar* v. *Arcos Ltd*,[79] Viscount Dilhorne said[80]:

I do not consider that this decision affords any basis for the contention that, where demurrage provisions apply, it is possible to obtain more than the demurrage payments for the detention of a vessel.

On these issues I agree with, and do not think that it is necessary to add to, the judgments of the Court of Appeal and Mr Justice Mocatta.

If, in this case, the appellants had been able to establish a breach of the charterparty other than by the detention of the vessel then *Reidar* v. *Arcos, supra*, is authority for saying that the damages obtainable would not be limited to the demurrage payments. In my opinion they have not done so.

Lord Hodson said of the earlier case[81]:

There was a breach separate from although arising from the same circumstances as the delay, and it was in these circumstances that damages were awarded.

Lord Upjohn took a similar view[82]:

In the view of Mr Justice Greer at first instance and the majority of the Court of Appeal there were in that case breaches of two quite independent obligations; one was demurrage for detention (as here), the other was a failure to load a full and complete cargo, which had become impossible owing to the onset of winter conditions and, therefore, entirely different considerations applied to that case.

The remaining members of the House did not specifically comment on this point.

6.39 In *Bedford Steamship Co Ltd* v. *Navico AG (The Ionian Skipper)*,[83] the question arose as to how deadfreight should be calculated. Under the terms of the relevant charter, the charterers were to load a full and complete cargo of wheat for carriage from Antwerp to Alexandria. In fact, the quantity supplied was some 1,570 tonnes short, for which a claim for deadfreight was made in addition to demurrage. Initially, the charterers claimed to be entitled to laytime based on a full and complete cargo, the charter providing for

---

78. By Lord Wilberforce in *Photo Production Ltd* v. *Securicor Transport Ltd* [1980] 2 WLR 283, at p. 287. Lord Wilberforce was the only Law Lord common to both cases.
79. *Aktieselskabet Reidar* v. *Arcos Ltd* (1926) 25 Ll L Rep 513 (CA).
80. *Suisse Atlantique* [1966] 1 Lloyd's Rep 529, at p. 539.
81. *Ibid.*, at p. 549.
82. *Ibid.*, at p. 555.
83. *Bedford Steamship Co Ltd* v. *Navico AG (The Ionian Skipper)* [1977] 2 Lloyd's Rep 273.

loading and discharging at specified rates, but by the time the case came before the High Court, both sides had agreed that laytime should be based on the quantity loaded. Amongst the issues that were contested, however, was whether the deadfreight calculation should take into account the changes in despatch and demurrage because a reduced quantity had been shipped and also whether the charterers were entitled to re-open the calculation of deadfreight, which had already been paid, without changes in demurrage/despatch being taken into account.

6.40 On what is meant by deadfreight, Parker J said[84]:

Prima facie such damages would be the freight which would have been payable on the quantity short-loaded but there would have to be deducted from that any benefits to the owner, e.g. by having his vessel available earlier as a result of having had to load and discharge a smaller quantity or any increased demurrage or saving in dispatch money which might result from the smaller quantity of cargo actually loaded and discharged. Any savings in dispatch and increase in demurrage so resulting would be dependent upon two things. Firstly, the time at which laytime would have expired had the full cargo been loaded and discharged, and secondly, how long it would have taken to load and discharge the full cargo.

As this information was not available, the case was remitted to the arbitrators. On the second question, Parker J held that the charterers were entitled to re-open the calculation of deadfreight.

6.41 The particular complication considered by Parker J on calculation of deadfreight will only arise where the laytime allowed is dependent upon the amount of cargo carried. However, another complication may arise in such circumstances where the demurrage rate is linked to the actual quantity of cargo loaded, as in some tanker charters where a part cargo is carried, and this was one of the issues considered in *Total Transport Corporation v. Amoco Trading Co (The Altus)*.[85] Here was a claim for deadfreight and a claim for demurrage, which under the normal rules would have been payable at a higher rate had the full quantity been loaded.

6.42 Having reviewed the judgments in *Aktieselskabet Reidar* v. *Arcos Ltd*[86] in some detail, Webster J said[87]:

In these circumstances it seems to me that I must treat the *ratio decidendi* of the case as being that where a charterer commits any breach, even if it is only one breach, of his obligation either to provide the minimum contractual load or to detain the vessel for no longer than the stipulated period, the owner is entitled not only to the liquidated damages directly recoverable for the breach of the obligation to load (deadfreight) or for the breach of the obligation with regard to detention (demurrage), but also for, in the first case, to the damages flowing indirectly or consequentially from any detention of the vessel (if it occurs) and, in the second case, to damages flowing indirectly or consequentially from any failure to load a complete cargo if there is such a failure.

The judge then continued[88]:

---

84. *Ibid.*, at p. 277.

85. *Total Transport Corporation of Panama* v. *Amoco Trading Co (The Altus)* [1985] 1 Lloyd's Rep 423. As the Worldscale system provides demurrage rates based on the deadweight tonnage of the vessel, this would give the shipowner an exaggerated demurrage rate for a part cargo. It is therefore not uncommon, as in this case, for the demurrage rate for a part cargo to be based not on the actual size of the vessel but on a notional vessel for which the part cargo would be a full load.

86. *Aktieselskabet Reidar* v. *Arcos Ltd* (1926) 25 Ll L Rep 513 (CA).

87. *Total Transport Corporation of Panama* v. *Amoco Trading Co (The Altus)* [1985] 1 Lloyd's Rep 423, at p. 435.

88. *Ibid.*, at pp. 435–436.

If that *ratio decidendi* is applied to the circumstances of this case, it follows that the plaintiffs are entitled in addition to the deadfreight which they have already received, to the difference between the demurrage rates as damages for the loss of demurrage consequent upon the defendants' failure to load the minimum agreed cargo.

The judge also said that either the deadfreight clause was not a liquidated damages clause, or, if it was, then on the authority of the *Aktieselskabet Reidar* case[89] the additional damages claimed were also recoverable. He then added[90]:

The defence ought in any event, in my view, to fail for a third reason, namely that the defendants should not be able to benefit, by paying a lower demurrage rate, from their own wrong in failing to load a full and complete cargo.[91]

The shipowners therefore effectively received the demurrage rate, which would have been applicable to the intended cargo.

6.43 Commenting on the reasoning in this case in *The Bonde*, Potter J said of Webster J[92]:

In that case he appeared to be of the view that Lord Justice Atkin was [in the *Reidar* v. *Arcos* case], like Lord Justice Bankes a "one breach" man. However, surprisingly, he appears not to have had the decision in *Suisse Atlantique* brought to his attention and helpful as I have found the analysis which Mr Justice Webster gave to the *Reidar* case, I do not find it reliable for that reason.

6.44 In *The Adelfa*,[93] Evans J suggested that the *dicta* in *Suisse Atlantique* did not necessarily preclude the possibility that an independent head of damages (as opposed to damages for a separate breach of contract) might be recoverable in certain circumstances. However, what those circumstances were is not specified and this view was described as *obiter* by Potter J in *The Bonde* where he went on to conclude[94]:

... the opinion which I have formed upon analysis of the cases ... is that where a charter-party contains a demurrage clause, then in order to recover damages in addition to demurrage for breach of the charterers' obligation to complete loading within the lay days, it is a requirement that the plaintiff demonstrate that such additional loss is not only different in character from loss of use but stems from breach of an additional and/or independent obligation.

An illustration of the working of this principle is contained in the case of *R & H Hall plc* v. *Vertom Scheepvaart en Handelsmaatschappij BV*[95] before Steyn J.

6.45 The vessel concerned, the *Lee Frances*, was to discharge at Cork and the charter contained a provision that if the vessel was ready for discharge by a certain date and time, the charterers would guarantee the date of completion of discharge. However, by the time the guarantee period expired she had still not been able to berth, presumably because of congestion. There was a dispute about what ready for discharge meant in the context of Arrived ship, berth or port charters, etc., which the judge sidestepped, but the other issue was whether damages were claimable in addition to demurrage. On this the judge said:

89. *Aktieselskabet Reidar* v. *Arcos Ltd* (1926) 25 Ll L Rep 513 (CA).
90. *The Altus* [1985] 1 Lloyd's Rep 423, at p. 436.
91. The same issue could have been raised in *Kawasaki Steel Corporation* v. *Sardoil SpA* [1977] 2 Lloyd's Rep 552.
92. *Richco International Ltd* v. *Alfred C Toepfer International GmbH (The Bonde)* [1991] 1 Lloyd's Rep 136, at p. 142.
93. *The Adelfa* [1988] 2 Lloyd's Rep 466.
94. *The Bonde* [1991] 1 Lloyd's Rep 136, at p. 142.
95. *R & H Hall plc* v. *Vertom Scheepvaart en Handelsmaatschappij BV (The Lee Frances)*, LMLN 253, 15 July 1989 (Com Ct).

The broad purpose of the guarantee was plainly to confer on the owners rights in respect of delay over and above the rights contained in the conventional laytime and demurrage code. There is no hint in the language of the guarantee, or elsewhere in the charterparty, that the remedy for breach of the guarantee would be the recovery of demurrage. That would have been a surprising construction, but I am satisfied that there is no textual or contractual support for it.

But it was suggested that the co-existence of a right to recover demurrage and unliquidated damages in some way creates inconsistent rights. That is not so. If the owners recover demurrage and then seek to recover unliquidated damages under the guarantee, they must obviously give credit for the liquidated damages (i.e. the demurrage) already received. So the two contractual remedies create no inconsistency. I have therefore come to the conclusion that damages for breach of the charterparty are at large.

6.46 A different sort of difficulty that may arise on the question of whether damages are payable in addition to demurrage is illustrated by the following London Arbitration decision.[96]

6.47 During discharge, a dispute arose between the charterers and the consignees and on the charterers' instructions discharge was stopped. At the time the vessel was on demurrage. The shipowners were not a party to the dispute and were simply obeying the instructions given to them. Eventually the dispute was sorted out and discharge completed. However, because of the stoppages in discharge, the owners had become liable to the port authority for much higher berthage, which was assessed on a progressive scale. This the charterers refused to pay, saying that the owners were only entitled to demurrage.

6.48 This contention was rejected by the arbitrators, who held that by stopping discharge the charterers had committed an additional and independent breach of contract to that which arose when the vessel went on demurrage. Applying *The Atlantic Sunbeam*[97] they held that it was the charterers' duty to act with reasonable diligence in discharging the vessel, a duty they breached in stopping discharge. The altercation had nothing to do with the discharging operations and the delay resulting from it could not fall within the ambit of discharging time even by way of the broadest interpretation. Because of this independent cause of action the owners were entitled to recover the loss they had suffered by having to pay increased berthage, as well as being entitled to demurrage.

6.49 However, it is the author's view that the decision was wrong. There can be no doubt that had there been no dispute and discharge had simply taken longer than allowed, with the result that higher berthage had become payable, then this would not have been recoverable. Does the dispute therefore make any difference? The arbitrators felt it did, relying on a breach of a duty to act with reasonable diligence in discharging the vessel. There is, however, clear authority[98] that, at least during laytime, if there is any such duty, it does not mean that discharge must be continuous and the charterers are entitled to suspend discharge for their own purposes. Does the duty change, therefore, once demurrage becomes payable? The answer is probably "No". Failure to complete discharge in the allowed time is a breach of charter and that breach remains until discharge is completed. A temporary suspension of discharge does not create a further breach any more than the charterers' policy of minimizing the number of voyages in the *Suisse Atlantique* case.[99]

---

96. London Arbitration—LMLN 19, 24 July 1980.

97. *Sunbeam Shipping Co Ltd* v. *President of India (The Atlantic Sunbeam)* [1973] 1 Lloyd's Rep 482. See *ante* at paras 3.166 and 3.327.

98. See *ante* at para. 5.5 and the cases discussed there.

99. *Suisse Atlantique Société d'Armement Maritime SA* v. *NV Rotterdamsche Kolen Centrale (The General Guisan)* [1966] 1 Lloyd's Rep 529 (HL)—see *ante* at para. 6.35.

Mitigation and proof of loss

6.50 It is normally accepted that where the parties to a contract have agreed liquidated damages for breach,[100] then implicit in this is an agreement that it is not necessary for the plaintiff to prove an actual loss[101] or to take steps to mitigate his loss. The latter point has, however, come up in New York Arbitration. Thus in a case called *The Antalya*[102] the charterers, having declared the discharge port as Bhavnagar, subsequently sought to change this to the nearby port of Bedi Bunder after the vessel's arrival at the nominated port. At the alternative port discharge could have been effected considerably quicker. The terms on which the owners were prepared to accept the change were unacceptable to the charterers and the vessel therefore discharged at Bhavnagar. Had she discharged at Bedi Bunder, discharge would have been shortened by 25 days. The charterers claimed the owners were under a duty to mitigate their loss by minimizing the amount of demurrage payable.

6.51 This argument was rejected by the tribunal, who held that whilst there might be some circumstances in which, from a commercial point of view, it would be unreasonable for the owners to sit stubbornly and earn demurrage when they could take some trifling step which would expedite the discharge, the present case did not come within that category. It is likely that London arbitrators would adopt the same approach.

6.52 So far as actual loss is concerned, all that is necessary is for the owners to show a breach of contract. Indeed, as has been shown in the previous section, if the loss is greater than the liquidated damages, then it will be irrecoverable unless the same set of circumstances can be demonstrated to have given rise to two different breaches, only one of which is covered by the liquidated damages provision. Like all general principles, however, this can be negated by specific terms in the relevant contract. The cases that follow are best considered as illustrations of this point.

6.53 In *Leeds Shipping Co Ltd v. Duncan, Fox & Co Ltd*,[103] the shipowners successfully claimed the reimbursement of additional expenses which they had incurred in order to lessen the amount of demurrage which would otherwise have been payable. The case concerned the discharge of a cargo of wheat at Callao which had been shipped from Australia. The charter provided for discharge at 450 tons per weather working day (with the usual exceptions) with demurrage payable thereafter.

6.54 At that time, in Callao, it was usual for shipowners to engage local stevedores for their part in discharge. However, the inefficiency of the best of the local stevedores was such as to cause the judge to remark,[104] "the methods of the port appeared to be a paradise for the workman who wants to do as little work as possible and get as much money as possible". As discharge was taking an inordinately long time, the master came to an arrangement with the stevedores by which they were to be paid double, the effect of which was to enable discharge to be completed much quicker. The time saved quantified at the demurrage rate was more than the additional payments.

---

100. For other examples of damages and demurrage, see *Adelfamar SA v. Mangimi & Martini SpA (The Adelfa)*, LMLN 218, 12 March 1988; *R & H Hall v. Vertom Scheepvaart en Handelsmaatschappij BV (The Lee Frances)*, LMLN 253, 15 July 1989.

101. *Clydebank Engineering & Shipbuilding Co Ltd v. Don Jose Ramos Yzquierdo y Castoneda* [1905] AC 6, at p. 11.

102. *Oceansky Co Ltd v. Hugo New & Sons Inc (The Antalya)* (NY Arb), LMLN 291, 29 December 1990.

103. *Leeds Shipping Co Ltd v. Duncan, Fox & Co Ltd* (1932) 42 Ll L Rep 123.

104. *Ibid.*, at p. 125.

6.55 The charterers argued that any delay was due to the slow working of the stevedores engaged by the shipowners and therefore the shipowners were not entitled to demurrage. They also argued that not only was it customary at Callao for shipowners to pay double rates but for them to reimburse the charterers for the additional sum they were forced to pay their workers in consequence, a sum the charterers deducted from freight in this case. Rejecting any suggestion that that could be right, MacKinnon J said[105]:

Well, if that is applied to the position when the charterers have undertaken to have the discharge done in a fixed time it seems to be a delightful port in which the charterer can fulfil such an obligation.

6.56 Of the argument that the delay of the stevedores was a default of the shipowners, MacKinnon J held that the situation was governed by the rule in *Budgett* v. *Binnington*,[106] saying[107]:

The effect of a charterparty in this form for discharge in a fixed time really amounts to a guarantee by the charterer that the discharge shall be completed in that fixed time, and if the discharge is not completed in that fixed time the charterer is liable to pay the agreed demurrage unless the failure to have the ship discharged in the agreed time is due to the fault of the shipowner in that the shipowner has not done his part in regard to something which it was within his power to do. The result is that supposing there is a strike or an insufficiency of labour, although that may prevent the shipowner from doing his part of the discharge, yet that is not due to any failure on his part in regard to something that it was in his power to do, and it is, therefore, not due to the default of the shipowner.

6.57 On the shipowners' claim for reimbursement of the additional sums paid to the stevedores, the judge, having described it as a bribe and having found that two days had been saved, said[108]:

The demurrage on those two days is £130. He therefore spent £123 and to that extent saved the defendants £130 demurrage, and he claims to recover that as an amount expended by him in the interests of the defendants in mitigation of his damages and to save them demurrage.

This sum was therefore awarded to the shipowners. However, it should be noted that counsel for the charterer did not seriously dispute the shipowners' claim once the judge had found that demurrage was payable[109] and also that the judge considered demurrage as more in the nature of an agreed payment for delay rather than as liquidated damages for breach of contract.[110] In *Cazalet* v. *Morris*[111] a shortage of railway wagons delayed discharge. After the vessel concerned had gone on demurrage, the shipowners completed discharge by discharging some of the cargo into lighters. As this resulted in a saving of time, the shipowners were held entitled to claim their expenses up to the amount of demurrage saved. Whether there is a general principle that shipowners are entitled to claim any expense in reducing demurrage up to the amount saved is perhaps more doubtful, although it does seem that there is a greater willingness to allow this than there is to impose a duty on the owners to take steps which would have the effect of reducing the demurrage payable.

---

105. *Ibid.*, at p. 126.
106. *Budgett & Co* v. *Binnington & Co* [1891] 1 QB 35.
107. *Leeds Shipping Co Ltd* v. *Duncan, Fox & Co Ltd* (1932) 42 Ll L Rep 123, at p. 126.
108. *Ibid.*, at p. 127.
109. *Ibid.*, at p. 128.
110. *Ibid.*
111. *Cazalet* v. *Morris* [1916] Sc 952.

6.58 It would seem that in some American courts it is possible to avoid demurrage by showing that no loss occurred. Thus in *D'Amico Mediterranean Pacific Line Inc* v. *Procter and Gamble Manufacturing Co (The Giovanni D'Amico)*,[112] the shipowner contracted to carry a part cargo of tallow from Wilmington, California, to Spain with other cargo for different shippers. The contract of carriage provided for demurrage to be payable if a berth or cargo was not available at the load port provided a notice provision was complied with. On arrival, there was a delay of over two weeks before the tallow was provided for loading, but even after it had been loaded the vessel was not free to depart since the remaining cargo had not been loaded.

6.59 In these circumstances, the US District Court held that demurrage was not payable because there had been no actual loss suffered by the shipowner, who would have been bound to wait anyway for the remaining cargo.

6.60 In England, it would seem that the question would be approached as one of construction as to whether the contracts should be read together or separately. If the latter, then it would seem that demurrage is payable even though the shipowner has suffered no loss. Thus, in *Transamerican Steamship Corporation* v. *Tradax Export SA (The Oriental Envoy)*, Parker J considered[113] an argument that payment of more than one amount of demurrage for the same vessel would be "double demurrage" since demurrage, it was said, was detention of the whole ship. Rejecting this, and drawing a distinction between damages for detention and demurrage, the judge said[114]:

If the matter is properly to be regarded as damages for detention, each will be paying a limited sum for the detention of the ship, the two sums together adding up to a figure which will properly compensate the owner for the loss of the use of the vessel. In my view, however, while demurrage can no doubt be regarded as being in the nature of damages for detention, it is not to be equated with such damages. It is very different. It is a simple contractual obligation by the charterer to pay a certain sum if he fails to complete discharge within the stipulated laytime, the commencement and calculation of which is itself a matter of agreement.

If the agreement provides for demurrage to be payable in any given circumstances, then it would seem that, as far as English law is concerned, that is an end to the matter and the money is payable.

Default of charterer

6.61 This is not normally a question that arises with regard to demurrage, since if by the terms of the charter the charterer has agreed to load or discharge within a fixed period of time, that is an absolute and unconditional engagement for the non-performance of which he is answerable, whatever may be the nature of the impediments which prevent him from performing to time,[115] unless these are covered by exceptions in the charter[116] or arise from the loading or unloading being illegal by the law of the place where they are to be carried out,[117] or arise from the fault of the shipowner or those for whom he is

112. *D'Amico Mediterranean Pacific Line Inc* v. *Procter and Gamble Manufacturing Co (The Giovanni D'Amico)* [1975] 1 Lloyd's Rep 202.
113. *Transamerican Steamship Corporation* v. *Tradax Export SA (The Oriental Envoy)* [1982] 2 Lloyd's Rep 266, at p. 271.
114. *Ibid.*
115. *Postlethwaite* v. *Freeland* (1880) 5 App Cas 599, at p. 608 *per* Lord Selborne LC.
116. See *post* at para. 6.97.
117. See *ante* at para. 4.16.

responsible.[118] It is, of course, not uncommon for delays to occur without the fault of either the shipowner or the charterer. From time to time efforts have been made by charterers to exclude their liability for demurrage in such circumstances by the addition of limiting words to the relevant demurrage clause. A typical example might be a clause providing for demurrage to be payable

provided such detention shall occur by default of charterer or his agents.[119]

6.62 This type of clause does not appear to have found much favour with the courts since, in effect, it goes contrary to the whole concept of fixed laytime. No doubt, however, human ingenuity could devise a clause sufficiently clear to achieve this aim.

6.63 An early example of this type of clause is to be found in *Kokusai Kisen Kabushiki Kaisha* v. *Wm H Muller & Co (Inc)*,[120] a decision of the Court of Appeal. In that case the charter provided for a demurrage rate of £50 per day "provided such detention shall occur by default of charterers". The vessel concerned had been chartered to load wheat and/or Indian corn and/or rye but because of congestion on the railways following a miners' strike the intended cargo of wheat could not be brought to the port for loading. Before the Court of Appeal it was contended that the case should be sent back to the court of first instance to consider a suggestion that the charterers should have been allowed a period to make alternative arrangements, but the court refused, saying they were satisfied that the charterers had no intention of doing anything except waiting for the original cargo to become available. The court also held that the proviso did not excuse the absolute liability of the charterers for demurrage.

6.64 In *Leeds Shipping Co Ltd* v. *Duncan, Fox & Co Ltd*,[121] one of the arguments raised was that the charterers need only pay demurrage where this arose through their default because the charter incorporated the Australian equivalent of the Hague Rules, which by Article IV(3) provide:

The shipper shall not be responsible for loss or damage sustained by the carrier or the ship arising or resulting from any cause without the act, fault or neglect of the shipper, his agent or his servants.

In that case the delay arose through the incompetence of the shipowners' stevedores. No point appears to have been taken that the Hague Rules refer to the shipper rather than the charterer, but it was argued that demurrage was a "loss or damage" and thus excluded without fault.

6.65 The argument, however, did not find favour with MacKinnon J, who, although expressing some doubt as to whether demurrage was in fact an agreed sum as liquidated damages,[122] said that even if it was and even if the clause had been expressly written into the charter, it would still have required clearer words to avoid liability for demurrage by showing that the failure to discharge was due to the fault of the shipowner.[123]

---

118. See *post* at para. 6.70.
119. This example was that used in *Argonaut Navigation Co Ltd* v. *Ministry of Food* (1948) 81 Ll L Rep 371; (1948) 82 Ll L Rep 223 (CA).
120. *Kokusai Kisen Kabushiki Kaisha* v. *Wm H Muller & Co (Inc)* (1925) 21 Ll L Rep 290 (CA).
121. *Leeds Shipping Co Ltd* v. *Duncan, Fox & Co Ltd* (1932) 42 Ll L Rep 123.
122. *Ibid.*, at p. 128. It is now generally accepted that demurrage is a form of liquidated damages, at least where the charter does not provide for a limited period on demurrage. See *ante* at paras 6.1 *et seq.*
123. *Ibid.*

6.66 In *Argonaut Navigation Co* v. *Ministry of Food*,[124] the main issue concerned when loading was complete. The charter provided for demurrage to be payable but only when this arose by default of the charterer or his agents. On the question of what constituted such a default, Sellers J said[125]:

To detain the vessel beyond the lay days was a breach of the contract by the charterers (*Aktieselskabet Reidar* v. *Arcos Ltd* [1927] 1 KB 352). They remained in default and without any protection under the charterparty until the loading was completed. The shipowners have therefore established all that is necessary for them to recover demurrage under the relevant clause of the charterparty.

The Court of Appeal agreed. Singleton LJ said[126]:

The default of the charterers lay in not providing the cargo at the proper time and place. It was through that default that the detention occurred. The detention was due to the default of the charterers.

6.67 Another example of this type of clause arose in *NV Reederij Amsterdam* v. *President of India (The Amstelmolen)*.[127] Here, the vessel was delayed in berthing at the load port because of congestion. Much of the argument concerned whether the charter provided for fixed or customary laytime and, if the former, whether the delay was excepted by virtue of an amended Centrocon strike clause. On these points, Pearson J held that this was a fixed laytime charter, but that delay through congestion was excluded by the strike clause, it not being in dispute that neither party could be blamed for the congestion. However, Pearson J also considered in some detail what was meant by the proviso attached to the demurrage clause. The questions he asked himself were[128]:

What is the meaning of the word "default"? Does it necessarily involve moral fault or negligence or does it simply mean a breach of contract? If it means a breach of contract, does it have to be some breach which is antecedent to, or otherwise different from, the mere detention of the ship beyond the specified period? Or does the mere detention of the ship beyond the specified period constitute default of the charterers unless the detention was caused by an excepted risk or owners' breach of contract?

Having reviewed the earlier authorities, he put his answers as a series of propositions, with the first being the answer to an earlier question as to whether this was a fixed or customary laytime charter. He continued[129]:

Secondly, the word "default" does not necessarily involve moral fault or negligence: it means a breach of contract.

Thirdly, it is not necessary to look for any antecedent breach of contract, because the mere detention of the ship beyond the specified laytime constitutes a breach of contract, and therefore a default of the charterers, unless the detention has been caused by an excepted risk or a breach of contract by the owners.

Fourthly, can one in reliance on the American cases[130] . . . find in, or derive from the proviso a general exception of *vis major*? . . .

124. *Argonaut Navigation Co Ltd* v. *Ministry of Food* (1948) 81 Ll L Rep 371.
125. *Ibid.*, at p. 377.
126. *Argonaut Navigation Co Ltd* v. *Ministry of Food* (1948) 82 Ll L Rep 223, at p. 231.
127. *NV Reederij Amsterdam* v. *President of India (The Amstelmolen)* [1960] 2 Lloyd's Rep 82.
128. *Ibid.*, at p. 90.
129. *Ibid.*, at p. 94.
130. Earlier in his judgment, at p. 93, he considered three American authorities: *The Hans Maersk*, 266 Fed 806 (1920), which in turn cited *Crossman* v. *Burrill*, 179 US 100 (1900) on the meaning of *vis major*; *The Marpesia*, 292 Fed 957 (1923); *Continental Grain Co* v. *Armour Fertiliser Works*, Fed Supp 49 (1938), concerning a ship called the *Buffalo Bridge*.

6.68 In answer to this last question, the judge concluded that it would be difficult to include the concept of *vis major* since that concept does not belong to English law, but in any event, said the judge, the Centrocon strike clause provided its own limits in that direction. He therefore decided that ultimately the question was whether the charterers were protected by that clause, which he held they were.

6.69 Whilst the judge's comments on the meaning of this type of proviso were without doubt *obiter*, nevertheless they tie in closely with the earlier decisions and now probably provide a definitive statement on the principles involved.

Default of shipowner[131]

6.70 As has already been mentioned, demurrage will not be payable where it arises from "the fault of the shipowner or those for whom he is responsible". This raises two questions: what is meant by fault? And for whom is he responsible? The converse of this, that if the shipowner is "prevented from carrying out his part of the discharge by the acts of persons over whom he has no control" he is not responsible for the delay, is sometimes referred to as the rule in *Budgett* v. *Binnington*.[132]

6.71 Unfortunately, the answers given by the courts to the two questions posed have not always been as separate and clear as might have been hoped for. Before considering what principles have emerged, the cases must first be discussed.

6.72 The earliest case to consider the problem was *Budgett* v. *Binnington* itself.[133] There, a ship on a fixed laytime charter was delayed during discharge by a strike of dock labourers, there being no strike exception in either the bill of lading or charter. The strike started during the period of laytime and came to an end some days after laytime had expired. Some of the dock labourers had been employed by the shipowners to do their part in the discharge and some by the consignees, who argued that since they could not do their part of the joint operation until after the shipowners had performed their part, they should be excused.

6.73 Holding that the consignees must be responsible for the delay, Lord Esher said[134]:

Now, has the shipowner failed in this duty through any default of his own, or of persons for whom he is responsible? The persons for whom he is responsible are the persons who represent him in his absence. If, for instance, the master refused to discharge the cargo, the owner would be responsible. How much further this rule of liability extends I am not prepared to say—whether, for instance, it extends to the case of the crew refusing to work . . .

A little later he added[135] that the non-delivery (i.e. delay) was occasioned by something which the shipowners could not have foreseen and by the acts of people over whom they had no control, that is, the workmen employed by the stevedore who were in breach of their contract of employment.

6.74 The next case to consider for whom the shipowner should be held responsible came some two years later and was *Harris* v. *Best, Ryley & Co.*[136] This case is somewhat

---

131. See also paras 4.17 *et seq.*
132. *Budgett & Co* v. *Binnington & Co* [1891] 1 QB 35, at p. 39 *per* Lord Esher.
133. *Budgett & Co* v. *Binnington & Co* [1891] 1 QB 35.
134. *Ibid.*, at p. 38.
135. *Ibid.*, at p. 39.
136. *Harris* v. *Best, Ryley & Co* (1892) 68 LT 76 (CA).

difficult to reconcile with the earlier decision, which is all the more surprising since the division of the Court of Appeal which considered it included both Lord Esher and Lopes LJ, who had both been party to the earlier decision.

6.75 The facts were somewhat different, however, to the earlier case. What happened here was that a ship was chartered to load cargo at both Leith and London. During the voyage between these ports the vessel encountered heavy weather, some of the cargo becoming damaged and some shifting. On arrival at London it was necessary to land the damaged cargo for reconditioning and to restow the cargo which had shifted. It also became necessary to shift some of the other cargo to enable the London cargo to be properly stowed. Owing to these matters and to some delay on the part of the stevedore, who under the terms of the charter was appointed by the charterers but employed by the owners, the vessel was delayed by three days.

6.76 On these facts, the court held that the stevedore was the servant of the owners and that the charterers were not liable for demurrage arising either from his delay or from the necessity of moving the cargo and the charterers were also not liable for the additional expense involved. The earlier case, although cited in argument, was not mentioned in the judgment of Lord Esher, the only full judgment to be given.

6.77 In his judgment, Lord Esher stressed that loading was a joint act between the shipper or charterer and the shipowner,[137] and that whilst each was to do his own part, he was also to do whatever was reasonable to enable the other to do his. Thus, it was the shipper's duty to bring the cargo alongside and then the shipowner's duty to load and stow it. However, the shipper must bring the cargo alongside in sufficient time to enable it to be loaded within the lay days.

6.78 The joint nature of loading and discharging was mentioned in the Scottish case of *William Alexander & Sons* v. *Aktieselskabet Dampskabet Hansa and others*,[138] a decision of the House of Lords, in which was also cited the decision of Lord Esher in *Budgett* v. *Binnington*,[139] apparently with approval. In this case, discharge of a cargo of timber was held up by a shortage of labour. At Ayr, the port in question, it was by custom of the port the duty of the shipowners to put the cargo on the quay and of the charterers to remove it. The same stevedore was employed for both operations and, as he could not get enough men, both were delayed.[140] For this the House said the charterers must be responsible.

6.79 It would seem, therefore, that because loading and discharging are joint acts, where some extraneous event, e.g. a strike in *Budgett* v. *Binnington*[141] or a shortage of labour in the Scottish case,[142] effectively delays both parties from performing their respective parts, then that is the fault of neither but, because of the nature of fixed laytime, demurrage will be payable if the time allowed is exceeded.

6.80 If, however, the extraneous event only affects one of the parties and that party is the shipowner, then demurrage will not be payable if the delay is caused by somebody for whom he is alone responsible. Thus, in *Harris* v. *Best, Ryley & Co*,[143] the delay was caused by the acts and omissions of the master and the stevedore, who under the terms of the particular charter was also deemed to be employed by the shipowner.

---

137. *Ibid.*, at p. 77.
138. *William Alexander & Sons* v. *Aktieselskabet Dampskabet Hansa and others* (1919) 25 CC 13 (HL).
139. *Budgett & Co* v. *Binnington & Co* [1891] 1 QB 35.
140. See the speech of Viscount Finlay, (1919) 25 CC 13, at p. 14.
141. *Budgett & Co* v. *Binnington & Co* [1891] 1 QB 35.
142. *William Alexander & Sons* v. *Aktieselskabet Dampskabet Hansa and others* (1919) 25 CC 13 (HL).
143. *Harris* v. *Best, Ryley & Co* (1892) 68 LT 76.

6.81 More recently, the question of a shipowner's responsibility for the acts and omissions of stevedores was considered by Donaldson J, as he then was, and by the Court of Appeal in *Overseas Transportation Co* v. *Mineralimportexport (The Sinoe).*[144] The main issue in the case was the effect of a cesser clause but an important subsidiary point was who was responsible for a considerable delay caused by the incompetence of the discharging stevedores. The charter provided for them to be employed and paid for by the charterers and for the cargo to be carried on f.i.o. terms. However, by an additional clause, it was provided that they should be considered "as Owners' servants and subject to the orders and direction of the Master".

6.82 In his judgment, Donaldson J said[145]:

If I had to decide this point, I should hold that the charterparty does not sufficiently clearly make the owners responsible for the fault of the stevedores to rebut the *prima facie* liability of the charterers to pay for the detention of the vessel. Fortunately, I do not have to decide it because even if I were to be in the charterers' favour on that point, they have, in my judgment, no answer to the owners' rejoinder, that in employing or causing or allowing these particular stevedores to be employed, the charterers were in breach of their duty to the owners. If this is right, the charterers are unable to rely upon the neglect of the stevedores as barring the owners' claim to demurrage or alternatively are liable to the owners in a like amount as damages for breach of their obligation to employ competent stevedores.

6.83 All the Court of Appeal agreed that the charterparty was not sufficiently clearly worded to make the owners responsible for the default of the stevedores and a majority of the Court (Lord Denning MR and Megaw LJ) also agreed with the judge that, even if they were the owners' servants, the true cause of the delay was the charterers' appointment of incompetent stevedores. Therefore the charterers were ultimately responsible for the delay. Lord Denning put it this way[146]:

Let me suppose, however, that clause 23 is sufficient to make the stevedores in some respects the servants of the owners. Even then the charterers are not, in my opinion, able to rely on it, and for this reason: it was the charterers who appointed the stevedores. It was their duty to appoint stevedores who were competent to do the discharging. The stevedores here turned out to be utterly incompetent. I do not think the bad conduct of the stevedores can be the fault of the owners, when the real cause of it was the fault of the charterers in appointing stevedores who were incompetent.

Megaw LJ agreed[147]:

Whether or not the appointment of incompetent stevedores would have been a breach of contract on the part of charterers, at any rate, the fact that that appointment was their responsibility under the contract does to my mind produce the result that vis-à-vis the shipowners the charterers cannot say that the exceeding of the laytime was caused by the fault of the shipowners. For the true cause was the appointment of incompetent stevedores . . .

At first instance, Donaldson J had also commented[148]:

Mr Lloyd also relied upon a passage in the judgment of Lord Esher MR in *Budgett & Co* v. *Binnington & Co* [1891] 1 QB 35, which suggested that the class of persons for whom the owners were responsible in this context might be very limited indeed—perhaps extending no further than

---

144. *Overseas Transportation Co* v. *Mineralimportexport (The Sinoe)* [1971] 1 Lloyd's Rep 514; [1972] 1 Lloyd's Rep 201 (CA).
145. *The Sinoe* [1971] 1 Lloyd's Rep 514, at p. 520.
146. *The Sinoe* [1972] 1 Lloyd's Rep 201, at p. 205.
147. *Ibid.*, at p. 207.
148. *The Sinoe* [1971] 1 Lloyd's Rep 514, at p. 519.

the master. Whatever the basis for this suggestion, Lord Esher MR had revised his views two years later in *Harris* v. *Best, Ryley & Co* [1892] 68 LT 76, when he held that charterers were not liable to pay demurrage in respect of stevedores employed by the shipowners.

6.84 Whether delays caused by stevedores will prevent demurrage from accruing will therefore depend on the terms of the charter concerned. If the stevedores are appointed by the charterers or someone for whom they are responsible, then it seems that they must be competent if liability for their actions or defaults is to be transferred to the shipowners under the charter, and, what is more, clear and unambiguous language must be used.

6.85 We now turn to the other question posed at the start of this section as to what acts of the shipowner or his servants suffice to prevent demurrage becoming payable.[149]

6.86 What is clear is that it is not every act of the shipowner or those for whom he is responsible which results in delay that will suffice. Thus, in *Houlder* v. *Weir*,[150] Channell J held that where discharge of the cargo was held up because of a need by the ship to take on ballast, this was not in any sense culpable conduct on the part of the shipowner. In his judgment, Channell J said[151]:

In order that the charterers may succeed on that point, they must, in my opinion, show that the delay was caused by an act of the shipowners or some one for whom they are responsible, which amounts to a breach of obligation on the part of the shipowners. Here there has not been a breach of obligation, but merely the performance of a necessary operation, no less for the protection of the cargo than for the protection of the ship.

6.87 In *Ropner Shipping Co Ltd* v. *Cleeves Western Valleys Anthracite Collieries Ltd*,[152] the Court of Appeal considered a situation where a shipowner chose to stem bunkers after demurrage had commenced for his own convenience. Had this operation been carried out during laytime, then the time taken would have been excluded by an express provision. As a result, loading was interrupted. Whilst the Court of Appeal were not prepared to endorse the finding of the High Court that this was a wrongful act by the shipowner, preferring to leave the point open, they nevertheless held that demurrage was not payable for the whole period during which the vessel had been withdrawn from the charterers' service and not as argued by the shipowner only for the working hours lost. Sargant LJ put it this way[153]:

It appears to me, in order that demurrage may be claimed by the shipowners, that they must at least do nothing to prevent the vessel from being available and at the disposal of the charterers for the purpose of completing the loading of the cargo.

The court[154] were at pains to make it clear that their decision was solely on the basis that the shipowner had withdrawn the vessel for his own convenience—there was no question of choosing a time when no cargo was available so that no time was lost. If bunkering could be carried out at a time when it could be done without causing delay, then

---

149. See *Associated Bulk Carriers Ltd* v. *Shell International Petroleum Co Ltd (The Nordic Navigator)* [1984] 2 Lloyd's Rep 182 on an owner's duty to clean holds and tanks, and the effect of not so doing on demurrage.
150. *Houlder* v. *Weir* (1905) 10 CC 228.
151. *Ibid.*, at p. 236. A contrary conclusion in relation to deballasting was reached in London Arbitration 15/85—LMLN 160, 19 December 1985, but some doubt must be cast on this decision.
152. *Ropner Shipping Co Ltd* v. *Cleeves Western Valleys Anthracite Collieries Ltd* (1927) 27 Ll L Rep (CA).
153. *Ibid.*, at p. 320.
154. *Ibid.*, at p. 318 *per* Bankes LJ.

presumably there would be no breach of the shipowner's duty to make his vessel available and at the disposal of the charterers.

6.88 It would seem that it makes no difference whether the non-availability of the vessel is a deliberate decision of the shipowner or is inadvertent (provided it is blameworthy). Thus, in *The Union Amsterdam*,[155] a vessel of that name grounded while proceeding from an anchorage to the discharging berth in dense fog. As laytime had expired and the vessel was on demurrage, the owners claimed that this continued to run during the five days that she remained aground. The arbitrator, in a decision upheld by Parker J, concluded that whilst the vessel had taken a considerable number of precautions to avoid this, nevertheless the very fact that she grounded meant either that she should not have proceeded or that if it was in fact safe for her to do so, then there had been negligence. The owners, however, whilst unsuccessfully challenging this finding, also submitted that they were excused from the consequences of this because clause 35 of the charter excepted liability for any loss of or damage to the cargo for causes excepted by the US Carriage of Goods by Sea Act, clause 4(2) of which excluded liability for acts, etc., done in the navigation or management of the ship.

6.89 Dismissing this contention, the judge gave three reasons.[156] First, he held that the exclusion clause relied on did not cover the circumstances of the case, since what was excluded was only liability to cargo for delay. However, he then went on to give two further reasons saying[157]:

In the second place a breach of duty remains a breach of duty, and therefore fault, notwithstanding that liability for the breach is excluded. In the third place, far from doing nothing to prevent the vessel being available, owners have, by negligent navigation or management, so prevented her and . . . it does not lie in their mouths to say that the vessel was being detained by the charterers during the period when by their negligence she was grounded.

However, there is an analogous line of authorities, which were not cited in this case, but which suggest that where the fault or breach of duty is covered by an exceptions clause then there is no longer any breach. This is certainly the position in general average and there would seem no reason why, despite the *dicta* above, the same should not be true in claims for demurrage. Thus, in *The Carron Park*, Sir James Hannen P said[158]:

The claim for contribution as general average cannot be maintained where it arises out of any negligence for which the shipowner is responsible; but negligence for which he is not responsible is as foreign to him as to the person who has suffered by it.

6.90 That decision was affirmed by the House of Lords in *Dreyfus* v. *Tempus Shipping Co*[159] and a later analysis of the rule by Pearson J in *Goulandris Brothers Ltd* v. *B Goldman & Son*[160] also shows that an actionable wrong must have occurred before a claim for a contribution in general average can be defeated.

6.91 Needless to say, any exceptions clause which the shipowner puts forward to excuse the non-availability of his vessel would have to be very clearly worded to achieve this object. As can be seen from the first reason given by Parker J in *The Union*

155. *Blue Anchor Line Ltd* v. *Alfred C Toepfer International GmbH (The Union Amsterdam)* [1982] 2 Lloyd's Rep 432.
156. *Ibid.*, at p. 436.
157. *Ibid.*
158. *The Carron Park* (1890) 15 PD 203, at p. 207.
159. *Dreyfus & Co* v. *Tempus Shipping Co* [1931] AC 726.
160. *Goulandris Brothers Ltd* v. *B. Goldman & Son* [1958] 1 QB 74.

Amsterdam,[161] this object is unlikely to be achieved by incorporating the Hague Rules or similar enactments into the charter. Furthermore, it would seem that the courts are unlikely to be willing to hold that a general exceptions clause, such as that at clause 19 of the Exxonvoy 69/Asbatankvoy forms of charter, which makes the owner not liable for delay arising from acts, etc., of the master and other servants of his in the navigation or management of the vessel, has this effect. Thus, in *Sametiet M/T Johs Stove* v. *Istanbul Petrol Rafinerisi A/S (The Johs Stove)*, Lloyd J commented[162]:

I agree with the arbitrator that a general exceptions clause such as clause 19 will not normally be read as applying to provisions for laytime and demurrage, unless the language is very precise and clear.

6.92 A slightly unusual set of circumstances arose for consideration in London Arbitration 29/84,[163] which concerned a charter on the Gencon form. After the voyage, the owners presented a demurrage claim showing laytime starting at 14 00 on 29 December. On that basis laytime expired at 14 00 on 31 December and the ship was then on demurrage until 19 30 on 5 January. The New Year holiday and weekend therefore counted against demurrage. Subsequently, the charterers were informed that the vessel had been delayed on sailing from the load port by reason of the temporary absence, for personal reasons, of the chief engineer. Had there been no delay, the vessel would have arrived at the discharge port on 23 December and completed discharging on 30 December. The Christmas holidays and adjacent weekend would have fallen whilst the ship was on laytime and would not therefore have counted. The charterers therefore sought a refund of alleged overpaid demurrage.

6.93 The arbitrators held that the owners were in breach of contract and that, at the time the ship should have sailed from the load port, she was unseaworthy, being without her chief engineer. Clause 2 of the Gencon form did not protect the owners since the phrase "loss or damage or delay" had been held to be limited to goods.[164] However, said the arbitrators, it was a fundamental principle that only those damages were recoverable which were "on the cards" or "not unlikely to occur" as a result of the breach viewed at the date when the parties entered into their contract. The answer given by the arbitrators was "There is a possibility that a weekend will fall within laytime rather than within a demurrage period, but since the ship will be carrying only a small quantity of cargo which will not take more than about 36 hours to discharge, and only 48 hours' laytime is being allowed, it is not likely that such a happening will occur". Thus, as at the date of entering into the contract, it could not be said that what subsequently happened was reasonably foreseeable and the charterers' claim therefore failed.

6.94 The arbitrators, however, stressed that if the discharging time could reasonably have been expected to be greater than 48 hours, then the answer would have been different, and it would have been very much on the cards that at least the weekend would fall within laytime, if not the Christmas holidays.

---

161. [1982] 2 Lloyd's Rep 432.
162. *Sametiet M/T Johs Stove* v. *Istanbul Petrol Rafinerisi A/S (The Johs Stove)* [1984] 1 Lloyd's Rep 38, at p. 41.
163. London Arbitration 29/84—LMLN 134, 20 December 1984.
164. *Louis Dreyfus & Cie* v. *Parnaso Cia Naviera SA* [1959] 1 QB 498.

6.95 In *The Mobil Courage*,[165] the master's refusal to sign a triplicate bill of lading against presentation of which the cargo could be discharged, as required by the charter, was held to disentitle owners to demurrage for the delay that ensued. In *The Anna Ch*[166] the vessel concerned was destined for Bandar Khomeini, but the majority of officers and crew refused to proceed beyond Bandar Abbas, where the ship was waiting for a convoy, because of the risk of becoming involved in the Iran/Iraq war. Eventually charterers ordered the ship to discharge at Bandar Abbas and a dispute arose over the payment of demurrage for the period between the refusal to join the convoy and the vessel proceeding into Bandar Abbas to discharge. In arbitration it was held that the owners were entitled under the charter to refuse to proceed to Bandar Khomeini and an award of demurrage for the period in question was upheld on the basis of absence of fault by owners and any relevant exceptions clause.

6.96 A somewhat unusual set of circumstances arose in *The Forum Craftsman*.[167] What happened was that the ship was removed from her discharging berth because it was found that some of the cargo had been damaged by ingress of sea water through the hatches. At the time this happened, the vessel was already on demurrage and it was a further 79 days before she was allowed to re-berth, mainly caused by bureaucratic delay. In arbitration a delay of 7 days was allowed against the vessel with demurrage running for the remainder of the period, a conclusion upheld on appeal.

Exceptions clauses and demurrage[168]

6.97 One of the most commonly quoted phrases in relation to demurrage is the maxim "once on demurrage, always on demurrage" and, like most sayings, it is true in part. What it is usually taken to mean is that unless an exceptions clause specifically refers to demurrage, it will only apply during the running of laytime. This is because by exceeding laytime, the charterer is in breach of contract, notwithstanding that the parties have agreed the payment of demurrage as liquidated damages for such a breach and, once there has been such a breach, even clearer words are necessary to prevent time running. As Lord Reid said in the course of argument in *Union of India* v. *Compania Naviera Aeolus SA (The Spalmatori)*[169]:

The loss must fall on someone, and one would think business people who made the contract would regard it as reasonable that the man whose fault it is should pay for it. That seems to me to be the basis of the rule, "Once on demurrage, always on demurrage".

The *Charterparty Laytime Definitions 1980* provide[170]:

28. "ON DEMURRAGE" means that the laytime has expired. Unless the charterparty expressly provides to the contrary the time on demurrage will not be subject to the laytime exceptions.

---

165. *Mobil Shipping and Transportation* v. *Shell Eastern Petroleum (Pte) Ltd (The Mobil Courage)*, LMLN 202, 1 August 1987.
166. *Islamic Republic of Iran Shipping Lines* v. *The Royal Bank of Scotland plc (The Anna Ch)* [1987] 1 Lloyd's Rep 266.
167. *Islamic Republic of Iran Shipping Lines* v. *Ierax Shipping Co (The Forum Craftsman)*, LMLN 276, 2 June 1990; [1991] 1 Lloyd's Rep 81.
168. See also *ante* at para. 4.1.
169. *Union of India* v. *Compania Naviera Aeolus SA (The Spalmatori)* [1962] 2 Lloyd's Rep 175, at p. 179.
170. See Appendix.

This definition was left out of the *Voylayrules 1993* and *Baltic Code 2000*.

6.98 In *Saxon Ship Co Ltd* v. *Union Steamship Co Ltd*,[171] a coal charter provided for demurrage at the load port "as per colliery guarantee".[172] The colliery guarantee excluded Sundays and holidays, and time lost by strikes from the loading period. It also excluded time on Saturdays from 5 p.m. and on Mondays until 7 a.m. However, said the House of Lords (reversing the Court of Appeal), the exception as to time lost through strikes only applied to the lay days and not to the time when the ship was on demurrage. They also held that, in calculating the period of demurrage, no account was to be taken of Sundays and holidays and that the demurrage period included the time from 5 p.m. to midnight on Saturdays and from midnight to 7 a.m. on Mondays. In so holding, they overruled an earlier decision of the Court of Appeal, *Clink* v. *Hickie, Borman & Co (No 2)*.[173]

6.99 In *Rederi Aktiebolaget Transatlantic* v. *La Compagnie Française des Phosphates de L'Océanie*[174] the Court of Appeal considered an exceptions clause which provided for lay days not to count and "demurrage not to accrue" during certain specified situations. This, said the court, meant that the exceptions clause was intended not just to apply during the running of laytime but also after the vessel had gone on demurrage. Of the words, "demurrage not to accrue", Bankes LJ said[175]:

Having regard to the whole tenor of the charterparty I think that they are inserted for a set purpose and in order to prevent the operation of the ordinary rule that when once a vessel comes on demurrage the time she is detained is to be calculated by running days or calendar days, as opposed to charterparty days.

The court also pointed out that although, for example, bad weather was excluded by the exceptions clause, time continued to run on Sundays and holidays whilst the vessel was on demurrage because the exceptions clause did not apply to those days, although such days would have been excluded from laytime.

6.100 In *Union of India* v. *Compania Naviera Aeolus SA (The Spalmatori)*, Lord Reid said of the general rule relating to exceptions clauses and demurrage[176]:

Counsel were agreed that the general rule was accurately stated by Lord Justice Scrutton in his work on charterparties in words which now appear in the 16th edn., at p. 353[177]:
    "When once a vessel is on demurrage no exceptions will operate to prevent demurrage continuing to be payable unless the exceptions clause is clearly worded so as to have that effect."

6.101 Whether a particular exceptions clause applied after laytime had expired was the point at issue in *Dias Compania Naviera SA* v. *Louis Dreyfus Corporation (The Dias)*, a case which eventually reached the House of Lords.[178] In August 1973 the *Dias* had loaded a cargo of wheat at Philadelphia for carriage to Hsinkang in China. In November of the same year, whilst the vessel was waiting in the roads to discharge, the receivers (for whom

171. *Saxon Ship Co Ltd* v. *Union Steamship Co Ltd* (1900) 5 CC 381 (HL).
172. For an explanation of the working of "colliery guarantees", see *ante* at para. 2.38.
173. *Clink* v. *Hickie, Borman & Co (No 2)* (1899) 4 CC 292.
174. *Rederi Aktiebolaget Transatlantic* v. *La Compagnie Française des Phosphates de L'Océanie* (1926) 26 Ll L Rep 253 (CA).
175. *Ibid.*, at p. 254.
176. *Union of India* v. *Compania Naviera Aeolus SA (The Spalmatori)* [1962] 2 Lloyd's Rep 175, at p. 180.
177. *Scrutton on Charterparties*, 16th edn., 1955. The current edition is the 20th.
178. *Dias Compania Naviera SA* v. *Louis Dreyfus Corporation (The Dias)* [1978] 1 Lloyd's Rep 325 (HL).

the charterers were responsible) had the cargo fumigated. At the time, the vessel was on demurrage. Clause 15 of the charter provided:

At discharging, Charterers . . . have the option at any time to treat at their expense ship's . . . cargo and time so used to not count . . .

The arbitrators disagreed, but the umpire held that demurrage continued to accrue whilst fumigation was taking place. This view was upheld by Mocatta J,[179] reversed by the Court of Appeal,[180] but finally upheld by the House of Lords. In his speech, Lord Diplock said[181]:

Since demurrage is liquidated damages, fixed by agreement between the parties, it is possible by apt words in the charterparty to provide that, notwithstanding the continuance of the breach, demurrage shall not be payable in respect of the period when some event specified in the charterparty is happening . . .

Lord Diplock then went on[182] to endorse what Lord Guest had said in *The Spalmatori*[183] that an ambiguous clause was no protection. He therefore concluded[184]:

For my part, I think that when construed in the light of established principles, clause 15 is unequivocal. It means that time used in fumigation is not to be taken into account only in the calculation of laytime. The provision that "time is not to count" has no further application once laytime has expired.[185] But even if I were persuaded that the clause was in some way ambiguous, this would not be enough to save the charterers from their liability to pay demurrage during the period while fumigation was being carried out after laytime had expired.

6.102 In *The Tsukuba Maru*,[186] charterers unsuccessfully sought to argue that because in an Exxonvoy 69 (Asbatankvoy) charter, the demurrage clause provides for demurrage to be payable for all time "used laytime" as specified elsewhere in the charter is exceeded, this meant that various laytime exceptions applied. A similar approach also failed in London Arbitration 13/85.[187]

6.103 In *Action SA* v. *Britannic Shipping Corporation (The Aegis Britannic)*,[188] Staughton J commented:

. . . where there are exceptions to a provision that a ship shall be loaded or discharged within the laydays . . . those do not apply when the laydays have expired because of the rule "once on demurrage, always on demurrage". That result can only be displaced by clear words and not by words which would merely be sufficient in the ordinary use of the English language.

---

179. *The Dias* [1976] 2 Lloyd's Rep 395.
180. *The Dias* [1977] 1 Lloyd's Rep 485 (CA).
181. *The Dias* [1978] 1 Lloyd's Rep 325, at p. 328.
182. *Ibid.*, at p. 328.
183. *The Spalmatori* [1962] 2 Lloyd's Rep 175, at p. 191.
184. *The Dias* [1978] 1 Lloyd's Rep 325, at p. 329.
185. See also the *Food Corporation of India* v. *Carras Shipping Co Ltd (The Delian Leto)* [1983] 2 Lloyd's Rep 496.
186. *Nippon Yusen Kaisha* v. *Société Anonyme Marocaine de L'Industrie du Raffinage (The Tsukuba Maru)* [1979] 1 Lloyd's Rep 459. See also *Huyton SA* v. *Inter Operators SA (The Stainless Emperor)* [1994] 1 Lloyd's Rep 298.
187. London Arbitration 13/85—LMLN 160, 19 December 1985. See also a decision of New York arbitrators—*The Pasadena*, LMLN 266, 13 January 1990, where *The Tsukuba Maru* was on this occasion followed by the majority of the panel.
188. *Action SA* v. *Britannic Shipping Corporation Ltd (The Aegis Britannic)*, LMLN 148, 4 July 1985. The case actually concerned the effect of a cesser clause on a claim for stevedore damage, and these remarks were very much *obiter*.

Clearly, Staughton J disapproved of this, but felt constrained to follow established doctrine.

6.104 A case on this subject which has been the subject of some discussion and debate is *The John Michalos*.[189] The facts were simple enough. The ship in question was delayed by a strike at the discharge port after laytime had expired. The charter contained a modified Centrocon strike clause relating to discharge, an additional clause expressly referring to interruptions in loading caused by a wide variety of causes, including strikes, and a further additional clause, which in essence read:

> 62. Charterers shall not be liable for any delay in loading or discharging including delay due to the unavailability of cargo which delay or unavailability is caused in whole or in part by . . .

There followed a whole range of exclusions, including strikes, ending with "and any other causes beyond the control of charterers".

6.105 As to this clause, Leggatt J held that it was more naturally to be read as a corollary to the other two exclusion clauses, which excluded laytime, thereby extending the specified exclusions to demurrage. In *The Kalliopi A*,[190] it was said that *The John Michalos* was the only case which counsel could find where a clause which did not expressly mention demurrage had been held to provide an exemption from it.

6.106 In *The Kalliopi* itself, the delay was due to congestion and again the clause on which charterers relied did not expressly mention demurrage. The crux of the clause was:

> The act of God, restraint of Princes and Rulers . . . and all and every other unavoidable hindrances which may prevent the loading and discharging and delivery during the said voyage always mutually [excepted].

Charterers sought only to argue that this clause protected them from payment of demurrage and not the running of laytime. Although the charterers succeeded in the High Court, they were unsuccessful in arbitration and in the Court of Appeal. Suggestions by counsel that *The John Michalos*[191] was wrongly decided were sidestepped, with the Court of Appeal content to say that was a different clause.

6.107 In *The Forum Craftsman*,[192] the dispute centred on one of the issues on clause 28 of the Sugar charterparty and its applicability to demurrage. In that case the delay was due partly to cargo damage, but mainly to government interference. The clause read:

> Strikes or lockouts of men, or any accidents or stoppages on railway and/or canal and/or river by ice or frost or any other *force majeure* causes including government interferences, occuring beyond the control of the shippers or consignees, which may prevent or delay the loading and discharging of the vessel, always excepted.

Both the previous cases were cited in argument, but the court concluded the clause was not sufficiently clear to invoke an intention to exclude demurrage.

6.108 There was a similar result in *The Lefthero*,[193] a decision of the Court of Appeal, although in the High Court it had been held that the clause in question in relation to

---

189. *President of India* v. *N G Livanos Maritime Co (The John Michalos)* [1987] 2 Lloyd's Rep 188.
190. *Marc Rich & Co Ltd* v. *Tourloti Compania Naviera SA (The Kalliopi A)* [1988] 2 Lloyd's Rep 101, at p. 106.
191. *President of India* v. *N G Livanos Maritime Co (The John Michalos)* [1987] 2 Lloyd's Rep 188.
192. *Islamic Republic of Iran Shipping Lines* v. *Ierax Shipping Co (The Forum Craftsman)*, LMLN 276, 2 June 1990; [1991] 1 Lloyd's Rep 81. See also London Arbitration 5/94—LMLN 386, 20 August 1994.
193. *Ellis Shipping Corp* v. *Voest Alpine Intertrading (The Lefthero)* [1991] 2 Lloyd's Rep 599; [1992] 2 Lloyd's Rep 109.

restraint of princes not only protected owners from a claim by the charterers for the cost of forwarding cargo to Bandar Khomeini because the vessel was too slow to keep up with the convoy system then in operation, but also protected the charterers from payment of demurrage. This latter conclusion was reversed by the higher court.

6.109 It would therefore seem that the decision in *The John Michalos*[194] should be considered as confined to its own facts and not indicative of the law as it now stands.

6.110 London Arbitrations 10/89[195] and 2/90[196] considered the effect of clause 8, the demurrage exceptions clause of the Asbatankvoy form, and in both cases the arbitrators held that the clause protected charterers even where the cause of action arose before demurrage began and the vessel was still on laytime. In the latter case, the tribunal went further and held that it applied despite the "reachable on arrival" provision in the charter.[197] In the American case of *The Altus*,[198] New York arbitrators held that congestion following a tug strike did not come within the tug strike exception in clause 8, a conclusion which, it is suggested, would be followed in this country.

Shifting

6.111 Whether time shifting from anchorage to berth is excluded once demurrage has begun to run will normally depend on whether there is an appropriate exceptions clause in the charter. In London Arbitration 13/85,[199] the arbitrators held there was no such clause in an Asbatankvoy charter. However, in an f.o.b. contract of sale dispute, one panel of arbitrators[200] was prepared to hold that there were various activities which were naturally for the account of the buyers (owners) irrespective of whether they occurred during laytime or demurrage. One such was shifting, which was not an exception to laytime, but an allocation of time for an act of navigation which occurred as part of the sea passage to the port concerned and which would not have counted had the vessel proceeded directly to her berth irrespective of whether on arrival she was on laytime or demurrage. Whilst this, broadly speaking, is true, it is doubtful whether it means that where a vessel does come to a stop prior to berthing and demurrage commences, demurrage is then interrupted during shifting to berth unless there is a clear provision to this effect in the contract of sale or charter under which demurrage is claimed.

Half rate demurrage

6.112 Most tanker charters contain a provision that in certain specified circumstances the demurrage payable shall be at half rate.[201] Typical of such provisions is that contained in clause 8 of the Exxonvoy 69/Asbatankvoy forms of charter. This provides:

8. DEMURRAGE. Charterer shall pay demurrage per running hour and *pro rata* for a part thereof at the rate specified in Part 1 for all time that loading and discharging and used laytime as elsewhere herein

---

194. *The John Michalos* [1987] 2 Lloyd's Rep 188.
195. London Arbitration 10/89—LMLN 247, 22 April 1989.
196. London Arbitration 2/90—LMLN 267, 27 January 1990.
197. See *ante* at para. 4.394.
198. *Black Swan Inc v. Castle Supply & Marketing Inc (The Altus)*, LMLN 275, 19 May 1990.
199. London Arbitration 13/85—LMLN 160, 19 December 1985.
200. London Arbitration 15/85—LMLN 160, 19 December 1985.
201. In London Arbitration 13/89—LMLN 251, 17 June 1989, the charter provided for the proportion of demurrage payable to be inserted, but it was left blank and the tribunal refused to insert a half or indeed any other proportion.

provided exceeds the allowed laytime elsewhere herein specified. If, however, demurrage shall be incurred at ports of loading and/or discharge by reason of fire, explosion, storm or by a strike, lock-out, stoppage or restraint of labor or by breakdown of machinery or equipment in or about the plant of the Charterer, supplier, shipper or consignee of the cargo, the rate of demurrage shall be reduced one-half of the amount stated in Part 1 per running hour or *pro rata* for part of an hour for demurrage so incurred . . .

6.113 Of the similar provision in the STB Voy form of charter, where there is also a term excluding the charterer's liability for demurrage for events over which he has no control, Leggatt J said in *The Notos*[202]:

Here, all that the draftsman need be supposed to have done is to have prescribed those misfortunes in respect of which half demurrage is payable and left the rest to result in the payment of full demurrage or not according to whether they were or were not the fault of the charterer.

6.114 Commenting on this in the House of Lords, Lord Goff said[203]:

It is right that I should record that there was a difference of opinion between the judge and the Court of Appeal as to the effect of the second sentence of cl. 8, on which the arbitrators had relied. The judge took the simple view that, if the relevant event was specified in the second sentence, the half demurrage rate applied; and that the last sentence of cl. 8 would have no application in such a case, even though such cause of delay was in fact beyond charterers' control. The Court of Appeal[204] took a different view, considering that, for example, delay by storm, although storm is a cause of delay specified in the second sentence, would always fall within the third sentence. For my part, I prefer the view of the judge, considering that, since delay by storm is expressly included in the somewhat arbitrary list of events specified in the second sentence, the half demurrage rate must apply in respect of such a delay, even though delay by storm must be a delay by a cause over which the charterers have no control.

6.115 The meaning of that part of the clause relating to breakdown of equipment was considered by Robert Goff J in *Olbena SA* v. *Psara Maritime Inc (The Thanassis A)*.[205] What happened in this case was that two days before the relevant charter was made, the jetty and the pipes running along it were damaged when another ship collided with it. As a result, part of the facility was completely destroyed and the *Thanassis A* was delayed whilst it was repaired. The charterers claimed that only half demurrage should be payable because there had been a breakdown of equipment in or about the plant of the charterer, supplier or shipper of the cargo at the loading port. The arbitrator rejected that contention and, on appeal, the judge held that so far as the damage to the jetty was concerned this could not properly be described as a breakdown of machinery or equipment. Plainly the jetty was not machinery and neither was it equipment. Furthermore, complete destruction of part of the facility appeared to involve something more than a breakdown.

6.116 In *Nippon Yusen Kaisha* v. *Société Anonyme Marocaine de L'Industrie du Raffinage (The Tsukuba Maru)*,[206] one of the many issues raised in the original arbitration proceedings concerned a number of periods when discharge was interrupted because of leakage from the sealine into which the cargo was being discharged. By the time the case

202. *Société Anonyme Marocaine de L'Industrie du Raffinage* v. *Notos Maritime Corporation (The Notos)* [1985] 1 Lloyd's Rep 149, at p. 154.
203. *The Notos* [1987] 1 Lloyd's Rep 503, at p. 508.
204. *The Notos* [1985] 2 Lloyd's Rep 334 (CA).
205. *Olbena SA* v. *Psara Maritime Inc (The Thanassis A)*, LMLN 68, 10 June 1982.
206. *Nippon Yusen Kaisha* v. *Société Anonyme Marocaine de L'Industrie du Raffinage (The Tsukuba Maru)* [1979] 1 Lloyd's Rep 459.

came before the High Court, the parties had agreed that half demurrage was payable for these periods.

Storm

6.117 One of the circumstances under which half rate demurrage becomes payable under clause 8 of the Exxonvoy 69/Asbatankvoy forms of charter is when time is lost due to a "storm". The actual wording is that half rate demurrage is payable where it is "incurred . . . by reason of . . . storm". Although not the clearest wording, the inclusion of "by reason of" is presumably intended to introduce a causal requirement.

6.118 The word "storm", however, is differently interpreted in London and New York. In one New York Arbitration,[207] the arbitrators held that a storm must be weather that is violent enough or turbulent enough to have caused something of an unusual commotion or disturbance in the port. They also held that the standards applied to "weather working days" were inappropriate and that storm meant more than simply bad weather which interfered with cargo operations. The mere closing of the port for rough seas or heavy swell was not enough.

6.119 In London, however, the word "storm" is usually given a more rigid meaning and taken to be those weather conditions which are described as storm on the Beaufort Scale, i.e. wind force 10 (48–55 knots) with sea conditions as follows:

Very high waves with long overhanging crests. The resulting foam, in great patches, is blown in dense white streaks along the direction of the wind. On the whole, the surface of the sea takes on a white appearance. The tumbling of the sea becomes heavy and shock-like. Visibility affected.[208]

6.120 One reason sometimes put forward against this definition is that the Beaufort Scale is intended to describe the weather in the open sea and that it is therefore inappropriate to use it to define "storm" for the purpose of demurrage which is only likely to be incurred when the vessel concerned is in comparatively sheltered waters. Such an argument is, however, it is suggested, misdirected. It is not the definition of storm that is inappropriate, it is its inclusion in the list of circumstances that give rise to half rate demurrage. It may well be that "severe weather" or some such might be a better phrase but that is not the wording used in these charters and therefore, since "storm" has a recognized nautical meaning, that, it is submitted, is the correct definition. Interestingly enough, the Exxonvoy 84 form of charter drops the word "storm" in favour of "weather and/or sea conditions".

6.121 There is no direct judicial authority under English law for the meaning of "storm", but there are two cases which are of some relevance. The first is *The Tsukuba Maru*[209] where the learned umpire, who was also a master mariner, applied the Beaufort Scale definition, although he used force 11 rather than force 10 to describe storm-force winds. "Storm" was the description formerly applied to force 11 winds, although this was changed in 1958 (force 10 was previously described as "severe gale"). The correct description of "storm" is now winds of force 10. In the subsequent High Court

207. New York Arbitration—SMA 1437, LMLN 24, 2 October 1980.
208. The original description put forward by Admiral Beaufort in relation to a man-of-war was: "That which she could scarcely bear with close-reefed main topsail and reefed foresail."
209. *Nippon Yusen Kaisha* v. *Société Anonyme Marocaine de L'Industrie du Raffinage (The Tsukuba Maru)* [1979] 1 Lloyd's Rep 459. The umpire was Mr H S Keswani.

proceedings, counsel for the charterers did not argue that the use of the Beaufort Scale was wrong.[210]

6.122 The other case that involved the meaning of "storm" was *S & M Hotels Ltd* v. *Legal and General Assurance Society Ltd*.[211] That, however, was not a case on demurrage or even a marine case, it was one involving house insurance, and concerned an insurance policy covering "storm, tempest or flood". For the purposes of such a policy, Thesiger J held simply that a storm was something more prolonged and widespread than a gust of wind.

Notices of readiness, periods of notice and commencement of demurrage

6.123 Notice of Readiness is a prerequisite to the commencement of laytime at common law at the first load port and usually expressly at second and subsequent load ports and discharge ports.[212]

6.124 As has been discussed earlier,[213] it is common in charters to provide that time should count only after a given period has elapsed after Notice of Readiness has been given. In most tanker charters the period chosen is six hours; in dry cargo charters it often varies.

6.125 Two questions that have come before the courts are whether notice provisions apply where a ship arrives at a second load port or discharge port already on demurrage, and whether any period specified thereafter before the commencement of time also applies to the commencement of demurrage. In the absence of any express provisions to the contrary, the answer given is generally "No" to both questions.

6.126 In *R Pagnan & Fratelli* v. *Tradax Export SA*,[214] Donaldson J had to consider this problem in relation to a Baltimore form "C" grain charterparty, which provided:

Notification of the Vessel's readiness must be delivered [–to–] . . . the Charterers . . . and the lay days will then commence at 7 a.m. on the next business day, whether in berth or not.

In finding that the notice provision had no effect where the vessel was already on demurrage on her arrival, the judge said that the provision had to be governed by its own terms; in that case there were no lay days left to commence at 7 a.m. on the next business day and the clause was clearly intended to deal only with a situation where the whole of the laytime was not exhausted at the loading port (the dispute concerned the discharge port). It was only in that case that the notice provision remained in effect. Donaldson J, having found the whole of the clause to be ineffective, then went on to deal with the law where there was no notice provision or where it was ineffective, saying[215]:

---

210. In London Arbitration 2/86—LMLN 166, 13 March 1986, the arbitrator held that the Beaufort Scale should be used for construing "storm" on the basis of an undisputed submission, whilst commenting that the arguments considered in an article at pages 343–359 of *Lloyd's Maritime and Commercial Law Quarterly* (August 1985) raised some interesting questions.

211. *S & M Hotels Ltd* v. *Legal and General Assurance Society Ltd* [1972] 1 Lloyd's Rep 157.

212. See *ante* at para. 3.212.

213. See *ante* at para. 3.242.

214. *R Pagnan & Fratelli* v. *Tradax Export SA* [1969] 2 Lloyd's Rep 150.

215. *Ibid.*, at p. 154.

The common law rule, that is to say, the rule which applies in the absence of any charterparty provision to the contrary, is that no notice of readiness is required of a vessel that is discharging.[216] Laytime or demurrage, as the case may be, begins to run from the moment of the arrival of the vessel in port, if it is a port charter, or in berth, if it is a berth charter. There is nothing in this charterparty which displaces a common law rule unless there is still an unexpired portion of laytime. Accordingly, the common law rule applies and the vessel was on demurrage from the moment of her arrival.

Presumably, had it been a second load port and not the discharge port, the situation would have been the same, since, as already mentioned, at common law notice need only be given at the first load port.

6.127 This case was followed by Mocatta J in *The Tsukuba Maru*[217] to which reference has already been made.[218] That case concerned a tanker charter[219] where the period that had to elapse was, as usual, six hours. Mocatta J, however, held that, as in the previous case where a vessel arrived on demurrage, then under the terms of the charter he was considering the period of delay was inapplicable.

6.128 In the course of his judgment, he also referred to two New York Arbitration awards. In the first, concerning a vessel called the *Atlantic Monarch*, the arbitrators held that even where a vessel arrived on demurrage, this did not commence until six hours after Notice of Readiness was given and, in the second, the arbitrators held that time on demurrage began immediately. This second decision was apparently given within days of the first.[220]

6.129 A subsequent version of this charter (Exxonvoy 84) provided expressly that Notices of Readiness were required whether the vessel was still on laytime or on demurrage and that in both cases the period of delay specified was to take effect.[221]

6.130 It also follows from the *dicta* of Donaldson J quoted above[222] and the general principle that laytime clauses do not apply to time on demurrage[223] that if there is a provision advancing the commencement of laytime in a berth charter, such as a WIBON provision or a "time lost" clause,[224] it will be inapplicable where a vessel arrives at load or discharge ports on demurrage and in the absence of any provision to the contrary, time will not start until the vessel berths. This is because in a berth charter the voyage stage does not end until the vessel is in berth.[225]

6.131 If there is a "reachable on arrival" or "always accessible" clause, the owner will have a claim for detention for any delay. However, it is suggested that in the absence of

---

216. In London Arbitration 18/89—LMLN 254, 29 July 1989, on somewhat different facts, the tribunal recognized that a clause imposing a deadline for claims for demurrage which specified certain documents, including Notices of Readiness, to be submitted with the claim might have to be read in certain circumstances as saying Notices of Readiness "if such exist". See also London Arbitration 11/90—LMLN 285, 6 October 1990.

217. *Nippon Yusen Kaisha* v. *Société Anonyme Marocaine de L'Industrie du Raffinage (The Tsukuba Maru)* [1979] 1 Lloyd's Rep 459. See also *Total Transport Corporation of Panama* v. *Amoco Trading Co (The Altus)* [1985] 1 Lloyd's Rep 423.

218. See *ante* at para. 6.121.

219. Exxonvoy 69 form.

220. See also the New York Arbitration award referred to in LMLN 25, 16 October 1980, which held there should be no delay after notice where the vessel arrives on demurrage.

221. Clauses 11 and 13(*a*). See also London Arbitration 9/90—LMLN 285, 6 October 1990, where the charterparty concerned had a similar provision.

222. *R Pagnan & Fratelli* v. *Tradax Export SA* [1969] 2 Lloyd's Rep 150. See *ante* at para. 6.126.

223. See *ante* at para. 6.97.

224. See *ante* at paras 3.346 and 3.398.

225. See *ante* at para. 3.30.

such a clause, there will be no such claim, since, as already discussed,[226] to recover damages for delay off subsequent load ports as well as demurrage at the discharge port(s) the owner must show a separate breach of charter. The owner may therefore be in a worse position in such circumstances, as bearing the risk of delay, than if laytime had not expired.

Tanker warranties

6.132 Most oil tanker charters provide for a total laytime of 72 running hours. However, they usually also contain an additional clause whereby, in its simplest form, the vessel warrants that it can discharge its entire cargo in 24 hours or maintain 100 p.s.i. back pressure at the ship's manifold.[227] There may also be a further additional clause requiring either that the cargo be maintained at loaded temperature or alternatively heated, usually to a maximum of 135 degrees F, on discharge.

6.133 Alleged breaches of these two clauses probably account for most demurrage disputes arising from tanker charters. As well as giving rise to disputes over demurrage, such breaches will also result in substantial cargo claims, since it may not be possible for the vessel to discharge all the cargo. That which is left is usually referred to by the initials R O B (Remaining On Board) and will be classed as pumpable or unpumpable. If the former, then the charterers may be entitled to deduct its value from freight under an Amoco retention clause or a similar clause.

6.134 Whilst the technical aspects of pumping warranties, cargo claims and freight retention clauses are outside the scope of the present work, it is probably necessary to say something about the carriage of bulk liquid cargoes, and its associated problems, since the demurrage problems that arise do so because of the nature of the cargo carried.

6.135 With any bulk liquid cargo some will inevitably be lost during the voyage, either because of evaporation of the higher fractions or because it remains as clingage covering the internal surfaces of the tanks in which it has been carried. Inevitably, some will also be lost because it is inaccessible to the ship's pumps, although the design of the tanks and the use of stripping lines to get out any that cannot be reached by the main pumps should keep this as low as possible. In the case of crude oil, the amount lost may be minimized by the modern technique of Crude Oil Washing (C O W) by which the cargo is recirculated and used to wash down the internal surfaces of the tanks.

6.136 Whilst the loading and discharging terminals will inevitably produce their own figures, the vessel's tanks will also be ullaged after loading and prior to discharge to determine any in-transit loss. In the case of crude oil, it has in the past traditionally been the practice to allow as acceptable an in-transit loss of 0.5%.[228] On completion of discharge the ship's tanks are again ullaged to determine whether any cargo remains and, if so, whether it is pumpable or unpumpable.

6.137 With some crude oils and refined products it may be necessary for them to be heated during transit, depending on the location of the load and discharge ports and the

---

226. See *ante* at paras 6.26 *et seq.*

227. The Exxonvoy 84 form of charter has a more sophisticated graded warranty. See London Arbitration 10/84—LMLN 121, 21 June 1984, as an illustration of the working of these alternative warranties. For a slightly unusual set of alternative warranties, see London Arbitration 4/98—LMLN 481, 14 April 1998.

228. Some charters now provide for a lesser figure as an acceptable in-transit loss and some recent cargo decisions have upheld a lower percentage as the customary allowance or required proof of any in-transit loss.

time of year of the voyage.[229] For any particular cargo, there will be optimum transit and discharge temperatures, the latter usually higher. The heating clause in the charter must take account of these temperatures if difficulties are to be avoided.

6.138 Two other temperatures which are important are the cloud point and pour point for the particular cargo. The cloud point is the temperature at which the waxes in the cargo first begin to settle out and be held in suspension. If the cargo falls below the cloud point then it is necessary for it to be heated considerably above, if the effect is to be reversed. In other words, the precipitation of the waxes is not irreversible but simply heating the cargo to the cloud point will not achieve this. The meaning and significance of the pour point is self-explanatory.[230]

6.139 As oils get colder they become thicker and more difficult to pump. As they start to solidify, pools of liquid will become trapped by deposits of waxy residues. Any such pools, although still liquid, will not be pumpable since the residues will prevent it reaching the pumps.

6.140 The cost of heating, which may well be considerable, is usually included in the freight. If the cargo heating requirement is only to maintain loaded temperature then little or no heating may be required if the vessel is in tropical waters, but as it moves to colder climes then heating will become necessary. If the vessel delays heating too long then there may be insufficient time to bring the cargo back to loaded temperature or it may have become so cold as to be no longer possible for it again to become pumpable. With some vegetable oils, for example, if the cargo is allowed to become semi-solid then applying heat will melt the oil around the heating coils but not that further away, with the result that the pools of liquid around the coils get hotter and hotter, eventually damaging that portion of the cargo.

6.141 In a less extreme case, if the vessel arrives with a cold cargo where the heating provision has not been met then discharge will be prolonged. In such a case the alternative in the pumping warranty of maintaining 100 p.s.i. may well have been met, but the ship will not be entitled to demurrage for the excess pumping time because of the breach of the heating provision.

6.142 In *Cia Argentina de Pesca* v. *Eagle Oil & Shipping Co Ltd*,[231] Branson J had to consider just such a situation. The case concerned a vessel, which was described as a whaling factory, which carried a cargo of 7,000 tons of fuel oil from Curaçao to Shell Haven. The charter provided for the cargo to be heated in accordance with cargo suppliers' instructions and they instructed the vessel to arrive at the port of discharge with a cargo temperature of between 130 and 140 degrees F. Except for one tank, the cargo temperatures were below the minimum and laytime was exceeded by 111 hours 20 minutes. As well as alleging a breach of the express warranty, the charterers alleged a breach of an implied term that the cargo would be heated during discharge at sufficient temperature to achieve a reasonable discharge rate and a breach of a further implied term that the pipework between the tanks and the pumps would be of sufficient size to enable this rate to be achieved. All these contentions were upheld in arbitration. In the High

229. See the comments of Bingham J on the need to heat crude oil in transit in *Gatoil International Inc* v. *Tradax Petroleum Ltd (The Rio Sun)*, LMLN 127, 13 September 1984.

230. There are sometimes said to be two pour points, a higher and a lower one with 5 degrees F between, the higher one being defined as 5 degrees F above that temperature at which the oil is observed to just fail to flow.

231. *Cia Argentina de Pesca* v. *Eagle Oil & Shipping Co Ltd* (1939) 65 Ll L Rep 168.

Court, the suggestion that there were errors of law upon the face of the award got short shrift, the judge saying:

The result is that it seems to me that those conclusions as to the proper construction of the contract, whether you use the expression "implied term", or whether you simply read the terms as meaning that the parties who have undertaken to do those various acts have to do them in a reasonable way, come to the same thing, and that the arbitrator was quite correct, upon the finding of fact which he has made, in coming to the conclusion which he did.

It should be noted that it is only in respect of the extra discharge time that the vessel will be disentitled to demurrage. The calculation of this may give rise to considerable problems.

6.143 One question that sometimes arises is whether the duty to heat the cargo or maintain its temperature is an absolute one. In most cases, the answer will depend on the terms of the charter. Thus, the Intertankvoy 76 form of charter contains a warranty in Part I by the owner that, at the date of making the charter, the heating coils were in good working order and capable of maintaining a cargo temperature not in excess of a given temperature, and then by clause 19 provides that, when heating of the cargo is required by the charterers, that the owners will exercise due diligence to maintain the temperature requested on passage to and whilst at the discharging port or place.

6.144 Most tanker charters contain a warranty either that the heating coils are in good condition at the time the fixture is made or will be when the vessel presents for loading. They also usually contain some form of exceptions clause relieving the owner from liability for latent defects in equipment which arise thereafter and are not discoverable by due diligence.

6.145 There are three main reasons why a vessel might not meet the cargo heating requirements in the charter:

A. The short duration of the voyage.

B. Failure by the crew to heat sufficiently early.

C. Breakdown of equipment.

6.146 Of these, the first is obviously only applicable to a requirement to increase the cargo temperature. Clearly, there must be a limit to what a vessel can reasonably be expected to do in this respect on a short voyage and there is probably an implied term that the cargo will be supplied at a sufficient temperature to come within what is practical. A failure by the crew to apply heat is unlikely to be excused by the terms of the charter, but a breakdown of equipment probably will be, provided it was working initially and the owner can show due diligence in maintenance.

6.147 Unless the charter provides to the contrary or the charterer has asked for a greater heating effort than he is entitled to under the charter, then the costs of cargo heating are not recoverable by the shipowner from the charterer.

6.148 Apart from problems with heating, there may be other reasons why the pumping warranty has not been met. In its common form, the warranty provides:

Owners warrant vessel is capable of discharging her entire cargo within 24 hours or maintaining 100 p.s.i. at ship's rail provided shore facilities permit.

Although in this form, described as a warranty of capability, it is invariably taken to mean not only that the vessel is capable of so doing, but will actually so perform, it is unlike speed and performance warranties in a time charter which, unless expressed to be ongoing, only normally relate to capability at the start of the charter.

6.149 A more complex warranty is that contained at clause 18(*f*) of the Exxonvoy form of charter, which reads:

Vessel shall load at rates required by Charterer having due regard for the safety of the vessel. Owner warrants that Vessel shall discharge entire cargo within twenty-four (24) hours pumping time or maintain pressure at Vessel's rail during the entire period of discharge as specified below, provided shore facilities permit.

Vessel kDWT per part T(A)	Rail Pressure, psi
Less than 60	100
60 to 160	125
Greater than 160	150

All time lost as a result of Vessel being unable to discharge its cargo in accordance with the pumping warranty above shall not count as laytime or, if Vessel is on demurrage, as time on demurrage. If the terminal or place of discharging does not allow or permit Vessel to meet the above warranty or requires discharging grades consecutively, Master shall forthwith issue a letter of protest (which should, if practical, be acknowledged) to such terminal or place and shall immediately advise Charterer by telegraph, telex or radio. If Master fails to issue the letter of protest, Owner shall be deemed to waive any rights to contest that time was lost as a result of Vessel's failure to comply with the above pumping warranty. Any pumping time lost solely due to restrictions imposed by the terminal or place of discharging shall count as laytime or, if Vessel is on demurrage, as time on demurrage.

6.150 Disputes often arise because the charterer simply deducts all time in excess of 24 hours. Owners usually assert in reply that the extended discharge was the fault of the terminal, often in providing hoses which are insufficient in number or size. Records as to the back pressure maintained at the ship's manifold and the shore side are sometimes missing or incomplete.

6.151 In fact there are remarkably few reported instances of such disputes reaching litigation. Some that have reached arbitration are as follows.[232]

6.152 In London Arbitration 10/84,[233] discharge had exceeded 24 hours, but the vessel had maintained 100 p.s.i. at the ship's rail. Only one shore line had been provided for discharge. The arbitrators held that if additional lines, or one of sufficient diameter, had been provided the ship could have discharged much more quickly and undoubtedly within 24 hours. The owners had therefore satisfied one of the alternative warranties and were prevented from fulfilling the other by charterers' failure to provide adequate facilities. The charterers had therefore failed to show any breach and were not entitled to reduce the amount of demurrage due.

6.153 In London Arbitration 19/87,[234] the vessel had been provided with a single 8-inch line and had been told to discharge at rather less than 100 p.s.i. at the ship's rail. The master protested and the receivers replied that under similar circumstances, other ships had discharged at a far greater rate than did this one. This argument was rejected by the arbitrators who further held that where a ship was not permitted to discharge at the back pressure required by the charter, and especially where she was provided with only

---

232. See also London Arbitration 26/98—LMLN 499, 22 December 1998.
233. London Arbitration 10/84—LMLN 121, 21 June 1984.
234. London Arbitration 19/87—LMLN 209, 7 November 1987.

one small diameter line, the burden was on the charterers to show clearly that there was a breach by the owners of the pumping warranty. This they had been unable to do.[235]

6.154 In London Arbitration 19/93,[236] the relevant pumping clause, as well as providing for the usual warranties, also contained a provision "requesting" the master to protest whenever pumping time exceeded the warranted period, failing which the charterers could deduct excessive pumping time.

6.155 At the discharge port in question, there had been no protest by the ship although only one shore line—a 16-inch line—was apparently provided. After puzzling over the meaning of the word "request", the tribunal concluded that discharging into two lines would have produced more satisfactory results, commenting that two pumps discharging into one line could create problems with back pressure (although see below). However, taking a broad approach to the problem and in view of the lack of protest, the tribunal made what they considered to be an appropriate reduction in owners' claim, reducing the discharging time by approximately 25 per cent.

6.156 In London Arbitration 11/99,[237] part of the dispute related to allegedly slow discharge. The charterers contended that only one pump and only one line had been flushed out and that the master had refused to flush the remaining cargo pumps and lines. The disponent owners said the master had been expecting to discharge through an 8-inch hose but only a 6-inch hose had been provided by the terminal operators. Nonetheless, 100 p.s.i. pressure had been maintained throughout discharge. On these facts, the tribunal held that the charterers intended to discharge through a single hose and that the vessel had maintained the warranted pressure through the hose provided.

6.157 In London Arbitration 14/99,[238] the charterers claimed that the owners were in breach of a provision that they could discharge the cargo at half the agreed laytime or maintain 100 p.s.i. at the ship's manifold. However, discharge was effected through portable pumps because the number of different cargoes loaded was greater than could be loaded within the vessel's natural segregation, which was the maximum the owners had undertaken to load. The tribunal therefore held that not only should the cost of hire of the portable pumps fall to the charterers' account, but that, since the use of the portable pumps was beyond the owners' control, even if there was a slower rate of discharge than the owners had guaranteed (as to which the evidence was inconclusive), the owners would not have been in breach of warranty.

6.158 A slightly unusual set of circumstances arose in a New York Arbitration relating to a chemical tanker called the *Bow Princess*[239] which the charterers had been forced to charter for the carriage of crude oil because the vessel originally fixed was unable to perform the charter. The problem here concerned loading and, of course, the 24-hour/100 p.s.i. warranty only applies to discharge. Nevertheless the charterers sought to argue a breach of clause 7 of Part II of the Asbatankvoy form of charter which provides that "any delay due to the vessel's condition or breakdown or inability of the vessel's facilities to load or discharge within the time allowed shall not count as used laytime". The vessel had 43 tanks which it was sought to load through one loading arm. The tribunal concluded in

---

235. See also London Arbitration 10/90—LMLN 285, 6 October 1990, where the arbitrators held that if charterers established a *prima facie* case, the burden shifted to owners to show that the fault lay with the shore facilities.
236. London Arbitration 19/93—LMLN 363, 2 October 1993.
237. London Arbitration 11/99—LMLN 511, 10 June 1999.
238. London Arbitration 14/99—LMLN 511, 10 June 1999.
239. *The Bow Princess* (NY Arb), LMLN 349, 20 March 1993.

the event that the burden of proving that specific delays were caused by deficiencies of the vessel remained with the charterers, which they had failed to do.

6.159 In strictly theoretical terms, the provision of one 8-inch hose would restrict the throughput to between 5,000 bbls/hr and 7,500 bbls/hr, dependent on whether the hose in question was light/medium duty or heavy duty. On this basis, the maximum cargo that could be discharged within 24 hours would be somewhere around 17,000/25,500 tonnes. If the cargo to be discharged exceeds that sort of figure then it could be argued that provision of hoses is not only usually the charterers' express responsibility under the charter, but that the hoses are part of the "shore facilities" referred to in the pumping warranty and therefore the warranty is wholly invalid. Whilst maintainable, such an argument would probably not be unduly attractive to commercial arbitrators, whose natural inclination would be to split the claim dependent on the relative degree of fault on each side.

6.160 Apart from the size and number of hoses, one factor that is sometimes introduced is the distance between the shore tanks and the jetty, particularly where the former are elevated. Whilst this may be something to be considered, its importance can be over-emphasized. Where it does have an effect, a relatively low or non-existent pressure drop across the shore manifold can be expected.

6.161 Sometimes, even with modern, well-maintained tankers, there can be an unexplained failure by the vessel to maintain 100 p.s.i. at the ship's rail, often blamed by the vessel on the fact that a single hose has been provided. In theory at least, this should not matter. Indeed, arguably it should be easier for a tanker to maintain 100 p.s.i. back pressure where it is pumping into a restricted opening, although what sort of line that in turn discharges into may be relevant. Such modern vessels may well have a relatively high number of pumps, each competing for a share of the cargo, but resulting in most of the cargo being re-circulated rather than discharged through the shore line. The answer in such circumstances is to reduce the number of pumps in use. Once there is a proper match between ship and shore, the back pressure will probably increase.

6.162 It sometimes happens that, as in the second case mentioned above, the terminal will ask the vessel to reduce its pumping rate. Needless to say, the vessel should ensure that any such request is made in writing. In that case, it would seem that the vessel pumped at a reduced rate throughout discharge, but that would be relatively unusual. It is far more common for the terminal to require a reduced rate for one or more periods of a couple of hours or so. Even this can result in discharge taking longer than 24 hours, but such periods are usually treated as being outside the warranty, provided the vessel maintains 100 p.s.i. (or such figure as is required by the charter) during the period when no restrictions apply.

6.163 In theory, if discharge exceeds 24 hours, the vessel should maintain the warranted pressure until the very moment discharge is complete. However, in practice that is impossible, since even if stripping[240] out of some cargo tanks is carried out concurrently with main discharge from others, there will eventually be the last two or three tanks to strip out, when discharge pressure is bound to fall. Most charterers are prepared to recognise this and, although few charters contain an express provision relating to stripping out, provided the time taken is not excessive such time will be allowed.

---

240. A stripping line is a small discharge line right at the bottom of a tank through which the last of the cargo in that tank can be discharged.

6.164 Whilst pumping warranties can by themselves generate quite complex problems for which a knowledge of fluid dynamics would be more useful than law, the issues can be even more involved when combined with an allegation of breach of heating warranty, which may explain why so many cases settle and so few get to be reported.

The effect of deviation on demurrage

6.165 Where there is an unjustified deviation during the currency of the charter, then demurrage may not be claimable under the terms of the charter and an alternative claim for detention can only be due in so far as it would be due at common law, or under the law relating to bailment, i.e. under the rules relating to customary laytime.[241]

6.166 The classic definition of deviation is a departure without justification or necessity from the proper and usual course of an agreed voyage, thereby altering the character and nature of what has been agreed between the parties. Unless extended by express agreement, a deviation is only permissible if it is, or is reasonably thought to be, necessary for the safety of the ship or cargo or in order to save life. As long ago as 1779 Lord Mansfield said in *Lavabre* v. *Wilson*,[242] in relation to the effect of deviation on a policy of marine insurance:

A deviation from necessity must be justified both as to substance and manner; nothing more must be done than what the necessity requires. The true objection to a deviation is not the increase of the risk. If that were so it would only be necessary to give an additional premium. It is that the party contracting has voluntarily substituted another voyage for that which has been insured.

The principle expressed in this statement applies equally to contracts of carriage.[243]

6.167 A not untypical liberty to deviate clause is that contained in clause 27(*b*)(vi) of the Exxonvoy 84 form of charter, which provides[244]:

DEVIATION. Vessel shall have liberty to sail with or without pilots, to tow or be towed, to go to the assistance of vessels in distress, to deviate for the purpose of saving life or property or of landing any ill or injured person on board, and to call for fuel at any port or ports in or out of the regular course of the voyage.

6.168 It should be emphasized that what is now under consideration is what happens with regard to demurrage if the deviation is held to be unjustified, either at common law or by the terms of the charter.

6.169 In *Davis* v. *Garrett*,[245] Tindal CJ held that a shipowner who deviated from an agreed voyage stepped out of the contract, so that clauses in the contract, such as exceptions or limitations, which were designed to apply to the contracted voyage were held to have no application to the deviating voyage. In *Joseph Thorley Ltd* v. *Orchis Steamship Co Ltd*[246] the facts were that in the course of discharging at London the shipowners' stevedores damaged part of the cargo, consisting of locust beans, by allowing the beans to become mixed with a poisonous earth called terra umber. During the carrying

---

241. As to when demurrage becomes payable under customary laytime, see *ante* at para. 2.278.
242. *Lavabre* v. *Wilson* (1779) 1 Doug KB 284.
243. Delay, if sufficiently long, may also give rise to a deviation—*Brandt and others* v. *Liverpool, Brazil, and River Plate Steam Navigation Co Ltd* (1923) 29 CC 57.
244. See also the London Arbitration award referred to in LMLN 102, 29 September 1983, concerning the equivalent provision in the Exxonvoy 69 (Asbatankvoy) form of charter.
245. *Davis* v. *Garrett* (1830) 6 Bing. 716.
246. *Joseph Thorley Ltd* v. *Orchis Steamship Co Ltd* (1907) 12 CC 251 (CA).

voyage the vessel had deviated, calling in at a number of additional ports. Refusing to allow the shipowner to rely on an exemption clause excluding liability for stevedore damage, the Court of Appeal held, relying on the earlier case of *Balian* v. *Joly, Victoria & Co*,[247] that[248]:

A deviation is a breach of a condition in a contract or a warranty in the sense of that word when it is used in connexion with seaworthiness, and the effect of that condition or warranty not being complied with is to displace the contract altogether. It goes to the root of the contract, and its performance is a condition precedent to the right of the shipowners to put in suit the liability of the other party to the contract. It is true that that condition may be broken, and yet circumstances may have arisen between the shipowner and the bill of lading holder—the consignee—which may give rise to some implied obligation on the part of the bill of lading holder to pay the freight, and, it may be, to perform other provisions such as would be implied from the mere fact of the cargo having been carried on the ship by the shipowner for the benefit of the owner of the goods.

6.170 The effect of this decision was considered by Pickford J in *Internationale Guano-En Superphosphaatwerken* v. *Robert MacAndrew & Co*[249] where the judge went on to find that, following a deviation, a shipowner loses the protection of any exceptions clauses not only in respect of damage to the cargo after the deviation, but also for any damage occurring prior to it. The judge also held that, in such a case, the shipowner was in the same position as a common carrier.

6.171 The consequences of deviation were also considered in *Kish & Co* v. *Taylor*, a case which eventually reached the House of Lords.[250] The main point at issue, however, was whether there was, in fact, a deviation. At first instance,[251] Walton J decided there was not. This was reversed by the Court of Appeal,[252] who were in turn reversed by the House of Lords.[253] In the Court of Appeal, Fletcher Moulton LJ said of the consequences of deviation in relation to the contract evidenced by the bills of lading, which he referred to as the special contracts of affreightment[254]:

... it does away with the special contract of affreightment altogether. The shipowner by his own default has substituted a different voyage from that to which the special contract (whether it be a contract of insurance or a special contract of affreightment) refers, and he cannot claim that contractual exceptions or obligations that relate to the one should be deemed to be transferred to the other.

In the House of Lords, the only reasoned speech was given by Lord Atkinson, who appeared to accept[255] that an unwarranted deviation might render the contract of affreightment void *ab initio*, as was decided by the Court of Appeal in *Thorley* v. *Orchis Steamship Co Ltd*[256] but on the facts decided the deviation was justified. It is of some significance that the claim by the shipowners was one for deadfreight and the right to that clearly arose before the deviation. Nevertheless, their claim would have failed if their deviation had been held to be unjustified and presumably the same would be true had the claim been one for demurrage arising before the deviation.

---

247. *Balian* v. *Joly, Victoria & Co* (1890) 6 TLR 345.
248. *Joseph Thorley Ltd* v. *Orchis Steamship Co Ltd* (1907) 12 CC 251, at p. 258 *per* Collins MR.
249. *Internationale Guano-En Superphosphaatwerken* v. *Robert MacAndrew & Co* (1909) 14 CC 194.
250. *Kish & Co* v. *Taylor* (1910) 16 CC 59 (CA); (1912) 17 CC 355 (HL).
251. *Kish & Co* v. *Taylor* (1910) 15 CC 268.
252. *Kish & Co* v. *Taylor* (1910) 16 CC 59 (CA).
253. *Kish & Co* v. *Taylor* (1912) 17 CC 355 (HL).
254. *Kish & Co* v. *Taylor* (1910) 16 CC 59 (CA), at p. 69.
255. *Kish & Co* v. *Taylor* (1912) 17 CC 355 (HL), at p. 366.
256. *Joseph Thorley Ltd* v. *Orchis Steamship Co Ltd* (1907) 12 CC 251 (CA).

6.172 The question of demurrage after a deviation arose in *United States Shipping Board* v. *Bunge y Born*, which again went to the House of Lords[257] where again the principal issue was whether the deviation was justified. On this occasion all the courts were agreed that the arbitrator was wrong in holding that the shipowners were entitled to deviate. They therefore held that the shipowners were not entitled to demurrage, which apparently arose at the second discharge port, *after* the deviation. The Court of Appeal[258] left open the question as to whether the charterers had waived their right to allege deviation by claiming arbitration, since that was not one of the points raised in the special case.[259]

6.173 Some 12 years later, the House of Lords once more had to consider the question of deviation, this time in *Hain Steamship Co Ltd* v. *Tate and Lyle Ltd*, where Lord Atkin, with whose views Lord Thankerton and Lord Macmillan agreed, said[260]:

... the effect of a deviation upon a contract of carriage by sea has been stated in a variety of cases but not in uniform language ... Occasionally language has been used which suggests that the occurrence of a deviation automatically displaces the contract, as by the now accepted doctrine does an event which "frustrates" a contract. In other cases where the effect of deviation upon the exceptions in the contract had to be considered language is used which ... shows that the sole effect is, as it were, to expunge the exceptions clause, as no longer applying to a voyage which from the beginning of the deviation has ceased to be the contract voyage. I venture to think that the true view is that the departure from the voyage contracted to be made is a breach by the shipowner of his contract, a breach of such a serious character, that however slight the deviation, the other party is entitled to treat it as going to the root of the contract, and to declare himself as no longer bound by any of the contract terms ...

6.174 A little later he continued[261]:

... If this view be correct, then the breach by deviation does not automatically cancel the express contract, otherwise the shipowner by his own wrong can get rid of his own contract. Nor does it affect merely the exceptions clauses. This would make those clauses alone subject to a condition of no deviation, a construction for which I can find no justification. It is quite inconsistent with the cases which have treated deviation as precluding enforcement of demurrage provisions. The event falls within the ordinary law of contract. The party who is affected by the breach has the right to say, "I am not now bound by the contract whether it is expressed in charterparty, bill of lading or otherwise" ... I am satisfied that once he elects to treat the contract as at an end he is not bound by the promise to pay the agreed freight any more than by his other promises. But, on the other hand, as he can elect to treat the contract as ended, so he can elect to treat the contract as subsisting; and if he does this with knowledge of his rights he must in accordance with the general law of contract be held bound ...

6.175 In the *Suisse Atlantique* case,[262] these principles were again affirmed, the passages quoted above being cited by Viscount Dilhorne.[263] In *Photo Production Ltd* v. *Securicor Transport Ltd*, Lord Wilberforce suggested[264] that the deviation cases might "be

257. *United States Shipping Board* v. *Bunge y Born* (1924) 18 Ll L Rep 422, Bailhache J; (1924) 20 Ll L Rep 97 (CA); (1925) 23 Ll L Rep 257 (HL).
258. *United States Shipping Board* v. *Bunge y Born* (1924) 20 Ll L Rep 97, at p. 99.
259. In *Verren* v. *Anglo-Dutch Brick Co (1927) Ltd* (1929) 34 Ll L Rep 210, Scrutton LJ suggested that the effect of deviation by delay was to make the vessel a common carrier so that exceptions and the demurrage provisions did not apply and only a reasonable freight was payable.
260. *Hain Steamship Co Ltd* v. *Tate and Lyle Ltd* (1936) 41 CC 350, at p. 354.
261. *Ibid.*, at p. 355.
262. *Suisse Atlantique Société d'Armement Maritime SA* v. *NV Rotterdamsche Kolen Centrale (The General Guisan)* [1966] 1 Lloyd's Rep 529 (HL).
263. *Ibid.*, at p. 539.
264. *Photo Production Ltd* v. *Securicor Transport Ltd* [1980] 2 WLR 283, at p. 291.

considered as a body of authority *sui generis* with special rules derived from historical and commercial reasons". In the same case Lord Diplock,[265] developing a theme he had earlier put forward in *Lep Air Services* v. *Rolloswin Ltd*,[266] drew a distinction between primary and secondary obligations under a contract, the duty not to deviate being an example of a primary obligation. Any breach of such an obligation, he said, entitled the other party to elect to put an end to all primary obligations of both parties remaining unperformed. The secondary obligation that arose in its place was for damages to be paid by the party in default.

6.176 Lord Diplock continued[267]:

The bringing to an end of all primary obligations under the contract may also leave the parties in a relationship, typically that of bailor and bailee, in which they owe to one another by operation of law fresh primary obligations of which the contract is the source.

Both in this case and in the earlier case,[268] Lord Diplock suggested that notwithstanding the ending of the contract, the mutual promises to submit disputes to arbitration might remain,[269] presumably without affecting the right of the innocent party to treat the contract as repudiated. As has already been mentioned, this point was left open by the Court of Appeal in *United States Shipping Board* v. *Bunge y Born*.[270] Despite this, an innocent party might consider it prudent to enter a caveat if responding to arbitration proceedings brought against him to recover demurrage or if seeking a declaration on non-liability to do so before the courts. Clearly, difficult questions could arise as to whether the party affected by the breach has elected to treat the contract as subsisting so as to make him liable for demurrage.

6.177 In the absence of such an election, however, the law is fairly clear that the shipowner is not entitled to claim demurrage for any delay after the deviation although he may be able to claim damages for detention if he would be so entitled under the rules relating to customary laytime. Whether he is entitled to claim demurrage arising before the deviation is perhaps more arguable. It may be that a distinction must be drawn between charters providing for separate laytime at load and discharge ports, and those which combine the laytime calculation. In the case of the former it might be possible to argue that liability remains, but in the case of the latter the same principles that apply to demurrage following a deviation almost certainly apply.

The end of demurrage—permanent and temporary absence from the port

6.178 In most cases demurrage will cease on completion of loading or discharging, as the case may be. When that is will be as already discussed in Chapter 5 under "Completion of Laytime". There are, however, a few cases in which demurrage has stopped at some different point, either temporarily or permanently, and it is these which will now be considered.

265. *Ibid.*, at p. 294.
266. *Lep Air Services Ltd* v. *Rolloswin Ltd* (otherwise reported as *Moschi* v. *Lep Air Services Ltd*) [1972] 2 WLR 1175, at p. 1185.
267. *Photo Production Ltd* v. *Securicor Transport Ltd* [1980] 2 WLR 283, at p. 295.
268. *Lep Air Services Ltd* v. *Rolloswin Ltd* [1972] 2 WLR 1175, at p. 1185.
269. Citing *Heyman* v. *Darwins Ltd* [1942] AC 356 as authority.
270. *United States Shipping Board* v. *Bunge y Born* (1924) 20 Ll L Rep 97, at p. 99.

6.179 In *Tyne & Blyth Shipowning Co Ltd* v. *Leach and others*[271] a ship was sent to Poti to load under a port charter. Owing to congestion she was forced to wait in the roads and whilst there was struck by another vessel without any fault on her part. Because of the damage she sustained, her master took her to Constantinople for repair. On return she again had to wait for a berth. On these facts, Kennedy J held that demurrage ceased when the accident occurred, but resumed again when she returned to Poti.

6.180 A slightly different set of circumstances fell to be considered in *Petrinovic & Co Ltd* v. *Mission Française des Transports Maritimes*.[272] What happened here was that a neutral ship arrived in Bordeaux in 1940 to discharge her cargo. At the time the port was under the control of the French authorities but before discharge could be completed the master, fearing, as was found, reasonably, for the safety of his vessel, sailed from the port with the intention of not returning but discharging the remainder of the cargo elsewhere. At the time, German forces were advancing on the town and, notwithstanding that his was a neutral ship, he feared her seizure. Finding that demurrage ceased on sailing, Atkinson J said[273]:

It is quite true that a charterer may continue to be liable to pay demurrage, although the discharging is interfered with by, for example, temporary or by voluntary departures of the ship, such as being driven out to sea, or some temporary inability of the ship to discharge, if, for instance, she is damaged by a collision; but I think it is perfectly clear that the obligation to pay demurrage cannot continue if the ship is taken away finally for her own purpose, for her own safety, under such circumstances as to make it quite clear that there is no intention whatever of her coming back to the port of discharge to enable the discharge to be completed.[274]

It is clear, however, that demurrage can continue to run if the vessel's absence from the port is only temporary. Support for that view can be found in the decision of the Court of Appeal in *Cantiere Navale Triestina* v. *Handelsvertretung der Russe Soviet Republik Naphtha Export*,[275] in particular in the judgment of Atkin LJ. In that case an Italian vessel was chartered to load at Batum. After she had arrived there, and laytime had begun to run, she had to leave Batum because of a dispute which had broken out between the Italian and Russian Governments. She was taken to Constantinople, eventually returning to Batum to complete loading. It was argued that time ceased to run during the period the vessel was away from Batum, an argument that was rejected by Atkin LJ, who said[276]:

... Indeed, if one comes to think of it, there can be no reason why the absence of the ship from the harbour, once the lay days have begun to run, without any fault on the part of the owner, should prevent the lay days from continuing to run and the ship going on demurrage. A ship may be prevented from loading by causes quite outside the will of either the shipowner or the charterer and yet the charterer is liable for demurrage. It appears to me to make no difference whether the vessel is in harbour 50 yards away from a berth and cannot get to it or whether she is 50 miles away.

---

271. *Tyne & Blyth Shipowning Co Ltd* v. *Leach and others* (1900) 5 CC 155.
272. *Petrinovic & Co Ltd* v. *Mission Française des Transports Maritimes* (1941) 71 Ll L Rep 208.
273. *Ibid.*, at p. 216.
274. See also as an illustration of this point *Silver Coast Shipping Co Ltd* v. *Union Nationale des Co-opératives Agricoles des Céréales (The Silver Sky)* [1981] 2 Lloyd's Rep 95. The *Silver Sky* was seized by one of the factions involved during a period of unrest in Angola and ordered to cease discharge and take a large number of Portuguese refugees to Walvis Bay. On sailing from Angola, it was clear she would not return and demurrage therefore ceased.
275. *Cantiere Navale Triestina* v. *Handelsvertretung der Russe Soviet Republik Naphtha Export* (1925) 21 Ll L Rep 204 (CA).
276. *Ibid.*, at p. 211.

6.181 A somewhat unusual set of circumstances arose for consideration in *Ricargo Trading SA* v. *Spliethoff's Bevrachtingskantoor BV (The Tassos N).*[277] What happened was that the *Tassos N* arrived in Aqaba with a cargo of timber from Finland. Her owners had chartered her for a time charter trip to Dan-Med, who had sub-chartered her on a voyage charter. Because of congestion, it was apparent after she had been in Aqaba for a while that there would be a considerable further delay before she got a berth and it was therefore agreed between the owners, the time charterers and the sub-charterers that she should proceed to Mersin and that the sub-charterers would pay demurrage direct to the owners, including a lump sum and any expenses of diverting the vessel to Mersin. The dispute concerned whether demurrage was payable during the passage from Aqaba to Mersin. Holding that it was, since the carrying voyage had been completed on arrival at Aqaba, Lloyd J commented[278]:

> The facts of the present case are unusual; it is perhaps unlikely that the courts will ever have to consider again whether time runs continuously between two ports of loading or discharging, as the case may be, where the charter provides for a single port only. But on principle the answer must be that it does. Although catch phrases seldom help and sometimes confuse legal analysis, this is, it seems to me, a true case where one can apply the phrase "Once on demurrage, always on demurrage".

6.182 A special provision in a charterparty which fell to be considered by London arbitrators[279] read as follows:

> 2 SP(s) Leixoes-Hamburg range . . . charterers option further on discharge port, charterers paying all port costs and laytime counting from taking inward pilot to dropping outward pilot third discharge port.

The charterers exercised their option for a third discharge port and the dispute concerned whether demurrage ended on completion of discharge or on dropping the outward pilot. The matter was further complicated by the fact that the vessel remained in port for almost two days on completion of discharge for the owners' own purposes but nevertheless they claimed two hours 45 minutes thereafter until the pilot disembarked.

6.183 In finding in favour of this contention by the owners, the arbitrators held that, although demurrage could only accrue after laytime had expired, the whole provision regarding the option of the third discharge port showed the intention of the parties to have been that time should count, whether as laytime or demurrage, until the dropping of the pilot.

LIABILITY FOR DEMURRAGE

General principles

6.184 Liability for demurrage can be one of the most complicated aspects of laytime and demurrage: it can also be one of the simplest. It all depends on the terms of the relevant contract and how the party on whom liability is sought to be imposed has become liable under that contract.

---

277. *Ricargo Trading SA* v. *Spliethoff's Bevrachtingskantoor BV (The Tassos N)* [1983] 1 Lloyd's Rep 648.
278. *Ibid.*, at p. 652.
279. London Arbitration—LMLN 80, 25 November 1982.

6.185 Under a voyage charter which contains a demurrage clause, the charterer is ordinarily the person with whom responsibility for the payment of demurrage lies. In the case of a vessel operating directly on a liner trade, then payment of demurrage will be governed by the relevant contract of carriage, usually evidenced by a bill of lading.

6.186 Apart from the charterer, holders of the bills of lading issued for the voyage may also become liable, either in addition to or in substitution for the charterer. They may become liable under an express term or, more commonly, by virtue of a lien clause either directly in the bill of lading or because the bills of lading incorporate the terms of the charter, which in turn includes an express lien upon the cargo for demurrage.[280] Such a lien is often combined with a cesser clause, intended to relieve the charterer from liability for demurrage.

6.187 A lien is "the right to hold the property of another as security for the performance of an obligation". In this case it is the right to retain the cargo or secure payment of the demurrage due either from the charterer or the bill of lading holder, as the case may be. It should be emphasised that a lien may only be exercised once the obligation to pay has arisen. Thus, if the obligation to pay demurrage only arises after completion of discharge or at some specified time in the future, it cannot be exercised before the time for payment falls due.[281]

6.188 In order to preserve his lien, a shipowner must retain continuous possession of the goods. He may, however, warehouse them and preserve his lien, if so allowed by local law. In London Arbitration 4/96,[282] the owners were held to be entitled to be reimbursed for storage expenses incurred in connection with their exercise of a lien to recover outstanding freight and demurrage. The introduction of local law of course complicates still further what is already a complicated subject.

6.189 If the shipowner's lien is sought to be exercised in the United Kingdom by landing the goods then they must remain under the shipowner's exclusive control or that of his agent.[283]

6.190 Of the lien clause in the Exxonvoy 1969 form of charter,[284] Lord Diplock said[285]:

... I deliberately refrain from expressing any view upon the effect of this curiously drafted lien clause, except to say that the time may be ripe for this House to re-examine this and other standard forms of lien clauses around which there seems to have accumulated a mystique which cries out for clarification and simplification.

However, he concluded that the case then under consideration did not afford the occasion for the House to embark upon this topic.

280. A lien for demurrage can only arise by agreement between the parties, unlike liens for freight, contributions in general average and salvage expenditure which derive from the common law.
281. See, for example, London Arbitration 21/92—LMLN 329, 13 June 1992.
282. London Arbitration 4/96—LMLN 426, 2 March 1996.
283. Originally enacted into law in the Merchant Shipping Act 1894 Part VII.
284. By this charterer agrees in favour of the owner that:
"21 LIEN. The owner shall have an absolute lien on the cargo for all freight, deadfreight, demurrage and costs, including attorney fees, of recovering the same, which lien shall continue after delivery of the cargo into the possession of the Charterer, or of holders of any Bills of Lading covering the same or of any storageman".
285. *Miramar Maritime Corporation* v. *Holborn Oil Trading Ltd (The Miramar)* [1984] 2 Lloyd's Rep 129, at p. 134.

6.191 A somewhat unusual argument arose as to liability for demurrage in a case called *The Christos*.[286] The charter in question allowed the owners to substitute another vessel to perform the charter and/or tranship the cargo into another vessel during the voyage, which the owners chose to do. However, the charterers said that by so doing they lost the right to claim demurrage, the demurrage provision being confined to the vessel into which the cargo was originally loaded. This argument was rejected by a majority of the tribunal in arbitration and an appeal to the High Court was dismissed. Had the case gone the other way, it would presumably have meant that discharge would have had to be governed by the rules of customary laytime.

Incorporation of charterparty terms into bills of lading

6.192 Most bills of lading do not contain an express provision making their holders liable for demurrage[287] and therefore the first step in seeing whether they are so liable is to see whether any of the provisions in the charterparty in association with which they have been issued, which relate to demurrage, have been incorporated.

6.193 In *Fidelitas Shipping Co Ltd* v. *V/O Exportchleb*,[288] Pearson LJ said[289]:

It appears from the decided cases that there are limitations on the incorporation of charterparty provisions into the bill of lading. Those which would be, as provisions of the bill of lading, "insensible or inapplicable", have to be rejected.

After considering a number of decisions[290] relating to the question under consideration, he concluded[291]:

From those authorities, it appears that a lien for demurrage, as it affects what the receiver has to pay in order to obtain delivery of the goods, is an apt thing, perhaps the most apt thing, to be introduced into the bill of lading by incorporation of the charterparty conditions.

In that case, the way the charter was incorporated into the bill of lading was described in the following terms[292]:

The words "All terms and conditions as per Charter Party" were typed in on the face of the bill of lading in a prominent position and would catch the eye of any shipper or receiver taking the bill of lading and would convey to him the impression that he was accepting, subject to any proper limitation, the terms and conditions of the charterparty.

6.194 The question of whether not only the lien clause was incorporated but the actual demurrage provision of the charter, and, if it was, whether for "charterer" could be read "receiver", was the question considered by the House of Lords in *Miramar Maritime Corporation* v. *Holborn Oil Trading Ltd (The Miramar)*.[293] At the discharge port, the shipowner exercised a lien over the remaining cargo part way through discharge against

286. *E G Cornelius & Co Ltd* v. *Christos Maritime Co Ltd (The Christos)* [1995] 1 Lloyd's Rep 106.
287. In optional clauses the Conlinebill and Conlinethrubill provide for payment of demurrage expressly.
288. *Fidelitas Shipping Co Ltd* v. *V/O Exportchleb* [1963] 2 Lloyd's Rep 113 (CA).
289. *Ibid.*, at p. 124.
290. Amongst the cases referred to were: *Porteus* v. *Watney* (1878) 3 QBD 534 (CA); *Serraino & Sons* v. *Campbell* [1891] 1 QB 283; *Gray* v. *Carr* (1871) LR 6 QB 522; *Gullischen* v. *Stewart Brothers* (1884) 13 QBD 317; *Gardner & Sons* v. *Trechmann* (1884) 15 QBD 154; *Manchester Trust* v. *Furness* [1895] 2 QB 539; *Andreas Vergottis* v. *Robinson David & Co* (1928) 31 Ll L Rep 23.
291. *Fidelitas Shipping Co Ltd* v. *V/O Exportchleb* [1963] 2 Lloyd's Rep 113, at p. 125.
292. *Ibid.*, at p. 124 *per* Pearson LJ.
293. *Miramar Maritime Corporation* v. *Holborn Oil Trading Ltd (The Miramar)* [1984] 2 Lloyd's Rep 129 (HL).

demurrage then due. This resulted in the receivers providing an undertaking to pay up to US$150,000 if found liable, the total amount due being considerably in excess. The principal issue before the courts that considered the matter was whether the receivers could be held liable, in addition to the charterer, for all the demurrage due, but before Mustill J it was also contended that if it were to be found that liability was limited to the charterer, then it would be wrong to allow the lien clause to operate so as to enable the shipowner to recover against the undertaking given in respect of that part of the cargo against which he purported to exercise a lien.

6.195 Rejecting this alternative submission, Mustill J also held that whilst the terms of the charter were incorporated into the bills of lading, this did not mean that the charterer's liability for demurrage under the charter could impose a corresponding liability on the receiver under the bill of lading only that liability contained in the lien clause, a conclusion upheld by the higher courts.[294] On the question, however, of incorporation of charterparty provisions into bills of lading, the judge said[295]:

> For present purposes, it seems to me sufficient to say that the court must ask itself: (1) Whether the words of the bill of lading evince a clear intention to bind the bill of lading holder to the rights and duties created by the relevant term of the charterparty . . . (2) Whether the language of the charterparty clause is such that, when the clause is inserted into the context of the bill of lading, it is effective to create in the consignee the rights or duties relied upon . . . A provision for discharging port demurrage is a term which (to use an expression found in more than one of the cases) relates to the shipment, carriage or discharge of the cargo.

The judge also added that some degree of manipulation of the language of the charter was permissible in order to put the intention of the parties into effect.

6.196 In the House of Lords, Lord Diplock added a note of caution[296]:

> . . . where in a bill of lading there is included a clause which purports to incorporate the terms of a specified charterparty, there is not any rule of construction that clauses in that charterparty which are directly germane to the shipment, carriage or delivery of goods and impose obligations upon the "charterer" under that designation, are presumed to be incorporated in the bill of lading with the substitution of (where there is cesser clause), or inclusion in (where there is no cesser clause), the designation "charterer", the designation "consignee of the cargo" or "bill of lading holder".

Liability of shippers, consignees, indorsees and receivers

6.197 The contract of carriage evidenced by the bill of lading is usually between the shipowner and the shipper in c.i.f.[297] contracts and sometimes also in f.o.b.[298] contracts. Under the classic f.o.b. contract, the buyer has to arrange for carriage and insurance, but sometimes such contracts provide for the seller to make such arrangements at the expense of the buyer. Devlin J described the difference between these two types of f.o.b. contracts in *Pyrene Co Ltd* v. *Scindia Navigation Co Ltd* as follows[299]:

> The f.o.b. contract has become a flexible instrument. In . . . the classic type . . . the buyer's duty is to nominate the ship, and the seller's to put the goods on board for account of the buyer and procure a bill of lading in terms usual in the trade. In such a case the seller is directly a party to the contract of carriage at least until he takes out the bill of lading in the buyer's name . . . Sometimes the seller

---

294. *The Miramar* [1984] 1 Lloyd's Rep 142 (CA); [1984] 2 Lloyd's Rep 129 (HL).
295. *The Miramar* [1983] 2 Lloyd's Rep 319, at p. 323.
296. *The Miramar* [1984] 2 Lloyd's Rep 129, at p. 134.
297. Cost Insurance Freight (The "C" is often erroneously said to mean "Carriage").
298. Free On Board.
299. *Pyrene Co Ltd* v. *Scindia Navigation Co Ltd* [1954] 2 QB 402, at p. 424.

is asked to make the necessary arrangements; and the contract may then provide for his taking the bill of lading in his own name and obtaining payment against the transfer, as in a c.i.f. contract. Sometimes the buyer engages his own forwarding agent at the port of loading to book space and to procure the bill of lading . . . In such a case the seller discharges his duty by putting the goods on board, getting the mate's receipt and handing it to the forwarding agent to enable him to obtain the bill of lading.

6.198 The party with whom the shipowner concludes the contract of carriage evidenced by the bill of lading, usually the shipper, will only be liable for demurrage where there is an express demurrage clause or where the charterparty is incorporated by reference in the bill of lading and, as has just been seen, where the terms of the demurrage clause are such as to make the owners of the cargo so liable.[300]

6.199 If the bill of lading does directly or indirectly so provide, then the question arises as to whether the shipper's liability thereunder ceases on transfer of the bill of lading and what responsibility is assumed by the various parties into whose hands the bill of lading may pass before delivery of the cargo. Before this question can be answered, it is necessary first to say something about the way in which ownership of cargo may be transferred during the course of the voyage.

6.200 In the case of goods sold under a specific export order, there will probably only be one transfer of title during this period and that will be from seller to buyer. In such a case the buyer, consignee and receiver may well be the same person. However, in the case of bulk cargoes, both dry and liquid, there may be several sales and in such a case the principal purpose of the bill of lading is to enable the person entitled to the goods represented by the bill of lading to dispose of the goods whilst in transit. By mercantile custom, possession of the bill is in many respects equivalent to possession of the goods and transfer of the bill has usually the same effect as transfer of the goods it represents. Bills of lading can, however, only be used in this way to the extent that they are negotiable. In the case of the specific export order, the bill will be made out in favour of a named consignee, usually the buyer. Alternatively, if the bill is to be negotiable, it will be made out "To Order" with a "Notify Party", usually the first buyer, who may also be the consignee. One description of a consignee was "a person residing at the port of delivery to whom the goods are to be delivered when they arrive there".[301] The consignee must, of course, first produce evidence of his entitlement to receive the goods, which is usually done by production of the bill of lading. He may or may not, however, be the owner of the goods. At any time before parting with the bill of lading or entering into a contract so to do, the shippers may withdraw the instruction to the master which they made by inserting the consignee's name in the bill of lading, as by so doing no contract was created with the consignee.

6.201 Whilst the right to enforce a contract may be assigned,[302] at common law obligations may only be similarly dealt with by the consent of the party entitled to enforce them. It therefore follows that the obligation to pay demurrage contained in the contract evidenced by the bill of lading cannot be transferred at common law without the agreement of the shipowner. However, in certain specified circumstances obligations and

---

300. In this section it is intended only to deal with express liability for demurrage. Where the right given is a right to the shipowner to exercise a lien will be dealt with separately: see *post* at para. 6.220. See also *Sucre Export SA* v. *Northern River Shipping Ltd (The Sormovskiy 3068)*, LMLN 380, 28 May 1994.
301. *Wolff* v. *Horncastle* (1798) 1 B & P 316, at p. 322 *per* Buller J.
302. Law of Property Act 1925, s. 136.

rights under a bill of lading may be transferred by virtue of the provisions of the Bills of Lading Act 1855,[303] section 1 of which provides as follows:

1. Every consignee of goods named in a bill of lading and every endorsee of a bill of lading to whom the property in the goods therein mentioned shall pass, upon or by reason of such consignment or endorsement, shall have transferred to and vested in him all rights of suit, and be subject to the same liabilities in respect of such goods as if the contract in the bill of lading had been made with himself.

Commenting on the preamble to the statute, Lord Bramwell said in *Sewell* v. *Burdick*[304]:

... I think there is some inaccuracy of expression in the statute. It recites that, "by the custom of merchants a bill of lading being transferable by indorsement the property in the goods may thereby pass to the indorsee ... ". Now the truth is that the property does not pass by the indorsement, but by the contract in pursuance of which the indorsement is made. If a cargo afloat is sold, the property would pass to the vendee, even though the bill of lading was not indorsed. I do not say that the vendor might not retain a lien, nor that the non-indorsement and non-handing over of the bill of lading would not have certain other consequences. My concern is to show that the property passes by the contract.

6.202 The current law relating to the sale of goods is the Sale of Goods Act 1979 as amended by the Sale and Supply of Goods Act 1994. Section 17 of the 1979 Act deals with the passing of property in ascertained goods and provides[305]:

17—(1) Where there is a contract for the sale of specific or ascertained goods the property in them is transferred to the buyer at such time as the parties to the contract intend it to be transferred.

Section 18 then goes on to lay down a series of rules for ascertaining the intention of the parties where this is not expressly covered in the contract of sale. The Sale of Goods (Amendment) Act 1995 deals with specified quantities of unascertained goods, forming part of an ascertained bulk.

6.203 It is important to note that if the property in the goods passes otherwise than "upon or by reason of" the consignment or endorsement then the rights of suit and obligations do not pass under the 1855 Act. Thus, in *Gardano & Giampieri* v. *Greek Petroleum George Mamidakis & Co*,[306] McNair J held that, in the contract of sale he had under consideration, property passed on delivery from the terminal at the discharge port and therefore section 1 of the Act did not apply. On the other hand, in *K/S A/S Seateam Co* v. *Iran National Oil Co and others (The Sevonia Team)*,[307] Lloyd J pointed out that there had long been a difference of academic opinion on whether the words "upon or by reason of" in section 1 of the Act should be given a narrow or wider view, the latter being that all that was necessary to comply with the provision was that property should pass under a contract in pursuance of which the goods were consigned or endorsed. Having pointed out that it was unnecessary to decide the point in the case then under consideration, the judge nevertheless indicated that he favoured the wider view.

303. One of the very few statutory interventions into this area of law.
304. *Sewell* v. *Burdick* (1884) 10 App Cas 74, at p. 105 (HL).
305. Re-enacting the similarly numbered provision in the Sale of Goods Act 1893.
306. *Gardano & Giampieri* v. *Greek Petroleum George Mamidakis & Co* [1961] 2 Lloyd's Rep 259.
307. *K/S A/S Seateam Co* v. *Iran National Oil Co and others (The Sevonia Team)* [1983] 2 Lloyd's Rep 640.

6.204 If the Bills of Lading Act does not apply, then liability for demurrage will remain with the party to whom the bill of lading was issued. If the Act does apply, either to the first or subsequent transfers of the bill of lading, then a further question arises as to whether endorsers of the bill retain any residual liability after transfer. In the case of intermediate parties, it would seem fairly clear that they do not. In *Smurthwaite* v. *Wilkins*[308] cargo was carried from Odessa to England under a bill of lading making it deliverable to a named firm or their assigns. The cargo was sold twice during the voyage and subsequently the shipowners sought to claim freight from the intermediate owners of the cargo. Rejecting this claim, Erle CJ explained that at common law the original concept had been that the assignee of the cargo, in receiving the cargo, was assumed to have agreed to pay freight and demurrage in return for the master agreeing to relinquish his lien over the cargo. He therefore concluded that in passing the Act, Parliament had similarly only intended assignees who received the cargo to bear liability, saying of the shipowners' claim[309]:

The consequences which this would lead to are so monstrous, so manifestly unjust, that I should pause before I consented to adopt this construction . . . it seems to me that the obvious meaning is that the assignee who receives the cargo shall have all the rights and bear all the liabilities of a contracting party; but that if he passes on the bill of lading by indorsement to another, he passes on all the rights and liabilities which the bill of lading carries with it.

6.205 The position, however, of the original contracting party, usually the shipper, is not so clear. It would seem that he may retain his liability for demurrage, notwithstanding transfer of the bill of lading. In *Gardano & Giampieri* v. *Greek Petroleum George Mamidakis & Co*,[310] McNair J said that a shipper could sue the shipowner under the bill of lading for damage to the cargo notwithstanding its subsequent transfer in accordance with the Act, and if the right of suit remains it would seem at least arguable that liability for demurrage should survive as well. Some support for this contention may be drawn from the terms of section 2, which states that the Act does not prejudice the shipowner's rights of stoppage in transit or his right to claim freight from the shipper. If this provision is merely declaratory and not an express reservation, then there would seem no reason why the shipowner should not also be able to sue the shipper under the original contract if he fails to get his demurrage from the party receiving the cargo.

6.206 In the case of the actual receiver of the cargo, it would seem that his liability to pay demurrage may arise in two ways. It may arise because he is a consignee or indorsee to whom property has passed upon or by reason of such consignment or indorsement, in which case his liability will arise by virtue of the Act, as has just been explained. However, if the Act does not apply he may still be liable because, as the holder of the bill of lading, he is the one who presents it to the shipowner in return for the cargo. In such a case he is deemed to accept the terms contained in the bill. A useful summary of the law relating to this point is contained in *Brandt and others* v. *Liverpool, Brazil and River Plate Steam Navigation Co Ltd*.[311] In that case it was the holder of the bill of lading who was

308. *Smurthwaite* v. *Wilkins* (1862) 11 CB (NS) 842.
309. *Ibid.*, at p. 848.
310. *Gardano & Giampieri* v. *Greek Petroleum George Mamidakis & Co* [1961] 2 Lloyd's Rep 259.
311. *Brandt and others* v. *Liverpool, Brazil and River Plate Steam Navigation Co Ltd* (1923) 29 CC 57 (CA).

trying to sue the shipowner, which the Court of Appeal held he could. In his judgment, Bankes LJ said[312]:

We have been referred to three authorities[313] . . . By those authorities it has been clearly established that where the holder of a bill of lading presents it and offers to accept delivery, if that offer is accepted by the shipowner the bill of lading holder does come under an obligation to pay the freight and to pay the demurrage, if any.

Atkin LJ explained how the law had developed, saying[314]:

Before the Bills of Lading Act it had been held in a series of decisions that the indorsee of the bill of lading, who came to the shipowner and claimed delivery under the bill of lading, was liable to the shipowner in respect of liabilities, which, I think, on the decisions gradually increased.

He then described how this came to include liability for demurrage and how effectively it became an offer to be bound by the terms of the bill of lading.

6.207 In a series of cases heard together, the Court of Appeal has now decided[315] that for this principle to apply it makes no difference whether the bill of lading is actually tendered in exchange for delivery of the goods or whether the receiver simply undertakes to surrender the bill at some future date as soon as it comes into his possession.

6.208 If the holders of the bill of lading, e.g. by virtue of a pledge, do not have property in the goods, then they do not get this by entering into possession and becoming liable under the terms of the bill. Similarly, the acceptance of a pledge without taking possession will not make the pledge liable under the terms of the bill. This, said Scrutton LJ in the *Brandt* case, was the effect of the House of Lords' decision in *Sewell* v. *Burdick*.[316]

6.209 It would seem, however, that the holder of a bill of lading, who would not otherwise have become liable for demurrage except for presenting the bill, may nevertheless still avoid liability by disclaiming liability for freight and demurrage. If, despite the disclaimer, the shipowner still releases the goods to the bill of lading holder, then effectively he accepts the disclaimer. It follows, of course, that the disclaimer must be made before presentation of the bill.

6.210 In *Sanders* v. *Vanzeller*[317] a cargo of wool was shipped from the River Danube to London. The bills of lading were assigned to buyers who, because of a dispute about the quality of the wool, refused to pay freight. Upholding their refusal, Tindal CJ said[318]:

. . . there would have been no promise implied by law, though there would have been evidence to warrant the jury in finding that there was such a contract; and it has been so much the practice for the indorsee of such a bill of lading to pay the specified freight, if he accepts the goods under it, that there is little or no doubt that the jury would, on such a question, have found in favour of the shipowner if the indorsee received the goods without a disclaimer of his liability to the freight.

---

312. *Ibid.*, at p. 62.
313. *Stindt* v. *Roberts* (1818) 5 D & L 460; *Young* v. *Moeller* (1855) 5 E & B 755; *Allen* v. *Coltart* (1883) 11 QBD 782.
314. *Brandt and others* v. *Liverpool, Brazil and River Plate Steam Navigation Co Ltd* (1923) 29 CC 57, at p. 72.
315. *Ilyssia Compania Naviera SA* v. *Ahmed Bamaodah (The Elli 2); Kition Compania Naviera SA* v. *Ahmed Bamaodah (The Toulla); Lemythou Compania Naviera SA* v. *Ahmed Bamaodah (The Eleni 2)* [1985] 1 Lloyd's Rep 107.
316. *Sewell* v. *Burdick* (1884) 10 App Cas 74 (HL).
317. *Sanders* v. *Vanzeller* (1843) 4 QB 260.
318. *Ibid.*, at p. 295.

It must be remembered that this case was before the Bills of Lading Act and, although the case related to freight, similar principles would apply to liability for demurrage.

6.211 The same principle was held to apply in a case after the Act, *SS County of Lancaster Ltd* v. *Sharp & Co.*[319] Here the consignees took delivery of part of the cargo, the shipowners exercising a lien over the remainder. Property had not passed under the Bills of Lading Act and the shipowners were aware that the consignees were acting as agents. Rejecting a claim for demurrage, Mathew J said[320]:

... it appears that they took delivery on the express understanding that they agreed to pay freight, but did not agree to pay demurrage.

Liability of charterers as bill of lading holders

6.212 In addition to their role as charterers, the charterers may also become the owners of the cargo being carried and/or bill of lading holders. They may have been the owners of the cargo prior to shipment or may have bought the cargo either from the shippers or from a previous indorsee of the bill of lading. In such circumstances, it may be necessary to decide whether the operative contract is that under the bill of lading or the contract contained in the charterparty.

6.213 In *President of India* v. *Metcalfe Shipping Ltd*,[321] the Indian Government bought a cargo of bagged urea from Italian sellers to be carried to Madras in a ship chartered in for the purpose by the Indian Government. The bill of lading received by the sellers was indorsed to the charterers. The dispute that arose concerned an alleged cargo shortage and whether such a claim was time barred. This, in turn, depended on whether the claim was made under the charter or the bill of lading. Upholding a decision of the High Court that the charter was the governing contract, Lord Denning said[322]:

The bill of lading here was not separate or severable from the charterparty. It was issued in pursuance of it. The Italian sellers . . . had already contracted to sell the fertiliser to the Government of India: and the Government had chartered the ship to carry it. The bill of lading was a mere instrument to carry out these contracts. It did not evidence any separate contract at all. As between charterers and shipowners, it was only a receipt for the goods.

6.214 Where the shippers are also the charterers, the rights of the shipowner to claim demurrage will usually be governed by the charterparty and any terms in the bill of lading that are inconsistent will not apply unless it can be shown that by the issue of the bill of lading it was mutually intended to vary the charterparty.

6.215 Most of the cases that have arisen on whether the contract of carriage is that evidenced by the bill of lading or by the charter have done so in the context of alleged cargo damage or the applicability of arbitration clauses. One of the few such cases where demurrage was actually one of the points at issue was *Love and Stewart Ltd* v. *Rowtor Steamship Co Ltd*.[323] This concerned a cargo of pit props bought by the charterers. Thirteen days were allowed under the charter for loading and the same for discharging, time being reversible. In fact, loading was completed in nine days but the bill of lading accepted by the shippers and indorsed to the charterers showed, incorrectly, 13 days as

319. *Steamship County of Lancaster Ltd* v. *Sharp & Co* (1889) 24 QBD 158.
320. *Ibid.*, at p. 161.
321. *President of India* v. *Metcalfe Shipping Ltd* [1969] 2 Lloyd's Rep 476.
322. *Ibid.*, at p. 483.
323. *Love and Stewart Ltd* v. *Rowtor Steamship Co Ltd* [1916] 2 AC 527 (HL).

being used for loading. As discharge took $17\frac{1}{2}$ days, the shipowners claimed $4\frac{1}{2}$ days' demurrage on the basis of the bill of lading. The House of Lords, however, held, reversing the Scottish court from which the case originated, that they were only entitled to a half day. The shipowners were bound by the reversible provision in the charter.

6.216 There are, however, some authorities which show, as already mentioned, that in some circumstances the courts may be prepared to hold that the parties intended to vary the terms of the charter and did so by expressing the terms of the variation in the bills of lading.[324] At the end of the day, therefore, each case must depend on its own facts; but the general principle is that stated above, that, in most cases, the charter will be the governing contract.

6.217 One exception to this principle is that where the charterers are the consignees and the bill of lading incorporates the terms of the charter, they cannot rely on the cesser clause for discharging port demurrage, although depending on the terms on which it is expressed, the cesser clause may be effective for load port demurrage.

6.218 In *Gullischen* v. *Stewart Brothers*,[325] the charter provided for charterers' liability to cease as soon as the cargo was on board, the shipowner being granted a lien for freight and demurrage. The bill of lading named the charterers as consignees, "they paying freight, and all other conditions as per charterparty". The shipowners claimed demurrage from them as consignees and the Court of Appeal held that the cesser clause was inapplicable. The charterers were therefore liable, Brett LJ commenting[326]:

Pushed to its logical conclusion, the argument for the defendants (charterers) would free them from liability for freight.

6.219 On the other hand, in *Sanguinetti* v. *Pacific Steam Navigation Co*[327] the Court of Appeal held that a cesser clause was effective in relation to load port demurrage. In that case the vessel was given a lien "for all freight and demurrage" but the ship did not exercise the lien at the discharge port for the demurrage incurred at the load port. On completion of discharge, they unsuccessfully claimed it from the receivers, who were also the charterers. The court, however, held that they were to have nothing as a remedy except their lien, which they failed to exercise.

Nature of lien for demurrage

6.220 As mentioned at the start of this section, a lien for demurrage is the right to retain possession of cargo granted expressly by contract. Its commercial effect is to enforce payment of moneys due, in this case demurrage, to secure the release of the cargo. A lien clause by itself only gives a right of possession, it does not give a right to sell the cargo to realize the demurrage due and it does not give a right of action against the owner of the cargo for the demurrage. Whether there is any such right will depend on the other clauses in the bill of lading and, if incorporated, the charterparty. As Kerr J said in *The Cunard Carrier*[328]:

---

324. *Gullischen* v. *Stewart Brothers* (1884) 13 QBD 317; *Bryden* v. *Niebuhr* (1884) C & E 241; *Steamship Calcutta Ltd* v. *Andrew Weir & Co* [1910] 1 KB 759.
325. *Gullischen* v. *Stewart Brothers* (1884) 13 QBD 317 (CA).
326. *Ibid.*, at p. 318.
327. *Sanguinetti* v. *Pacific Steam Navigation Co* (1887) 2 QBD 238 (CA).
328. *The Cunard Carrier, Eleranta and Martha* [1977] 2 Lloyd's Rep 261, at p. 263.

The fact that it may be impossible to exercise a lien would not, of course, relieve the receivers from liability for demurrage if, as here, the bill of lading makes them liable to pay any demurrage which may accrue.

Thus, for example, the Conlinebill used in liner trades provides that "The carrier shall be paid demurrage at the daily rate of . . . " or the charter, if incorporated, may simply provide for the payment of demurrage without specifying who by. In both those cases there will be a right of action[329] against the receiver for demurrage. If, on the other hand, the bill is silent about demurrage and the charter specifies that demurrage is to be paid by the charterer,[330] then there will be no right of action against the receiver.

6.221 If there is no such right of action, only a lien clause, then if the lien is not or cannot be exercised, the shipowners' only remedy will be against the charterer and, if there is a cesser clause, whether he can do that may depend on why the lien was not exercised.

6.222 If the ship is delayed because of the exercise of a lien and it was reasonable to keep the goods on board rather than land them to a warehouse, then demurrage will be payable for the delay. This was one of the points that arose in *Lyle Shipping Co Ltd* v. *Corporation of Cardiff*, where at first instance Bigham J said[331]:

Then if the plaintiffs were acting rightly in exercising their lien, can they claim damages for detention of the ship during its exercise?[332] This depends, in my opinion, upon whether they exercised their lien in a reasonable manner. If it was the cheaper course to keep the cargo on board the ship, rather than to warehouse it under the Merchant Shipping Act, then they acted reasonably in keeping it on board. If, on the other hand, it would have been cheaper to put the cargo into warehouse, then they acted unreasonably in keeping it on board.

6.223 In *The Boral Gas*,[333] Evans J found that the shipowners would be entitled to refuse to discharge the cargo if they were validly exercising a lien either for freight or demurrage. On the running of demurrage whilst a lien was being enforced, he concluded[334]:

. . . I hold that demurrage does not cease to accrue merely by reason of the shipowners' reasonable and lawful exercise of their lien.

6.224 Similarly in *Gill & Duffus SA* v. *Rionda Futures Ltd*,[335] Clarke J held that the shipowners' exercise of a lien, in that case for general average, provided it was both lawful and reasonable, did not prevent a valid Notice of Readiness being tendered.

6.225 Although it is common to refer to lien clauses as granting a lien, more accurately what they do is to give a future power—the right to lien the cargo does not actually arise until the cargo is shipped. As Pearson LJ said in *Fidelitas Shipping Co Ltd* v. *V/O Exportchleb*[336]:

---

329. For liability of receivers for demurrage generally, see *ante* at paras 6.197 *et seq.*
330. As, for example, in most tanker charters. See also *Miramar Maritime Corporation* v. *Holborn Oil Trading Ltd (The Miramar)* [1984] 2 Lloyd's Rep 129, and *ante* at para. 6.194.
331. *Lyle Shipping Co Ltd* v. *Corporation of Cardiff; Churchill and Sim* (1899) 5 CC 87, at p. 98. The case went on to the Court of Appeal, the report of which is at (1900) 5 CC 397.
332. The claim was one for detention because the charter provided for customary laytime at the discharge port. If it had been a fixed laytime charter then, it is submitted, demurrage would have been payable.
333. *Rashtriya Chemicals and Fertilizers Ltd* v. *Huddart Parker Industries Ltd (The Boral Gas)* [1988] 1 Lloyd's Rep 342.
334. *Ibid.*, at p. 349.
335. *Gill & Duffus SA* v. *Rionda Futures Ltd* [1994] 2 Lloyd's Rep 67.
336. *Fidelitas Shipping Co Ltd* v. *V/O Exportchleb* [1963] 2 Lloyd's Rep 113, at p. 122.

... The second part of the clause, even when it is expressed in participial form "the owner or his agent having a lien on the goods", creates a lien prospectively, in the sense of providing that a lien shall arise upon shipment of the goods: ...

On shipment of the goods the lien comes into existence ...

6.226 In *Redieriaktieselskabet Superior* v. *Dewar and Webb*,[337] holders of a bill of lading sought to argue that a lien clause did not apply in respect of demurrage incurred at the port of lading on the basis that the demurrage clause provided for demurrage to be paid "day by day as falling due". However, Bray J and the Court of Appeal disagreed. At first instance, Bray J said[338]:

I have searched to see whether there is any authority for the proposition that you cannot have a lien for a sum payable in advance or due before the time when the lien is to attach. I can find none. It is clear that under a general lien a carrier can have a lien not only in respect of freight not then earned, but for freight which has been earned and is overdue.

Cesser clauses

6.227 A cesser clause is a clause in a charter which purports to release the charterer from liability for specified payments to the shipowner after the goods have been shipped. It usually arises in conjunction with a lien clause giving the shipowner the right to retain possession of the cargo to secure payment of the sums due.

6.228 In *The Sinoe*,[339] Donaldson J said of such clauses:

Cesser clauses are curious animals because it is now well established that they do not mean what they appear to say, namely that the charterers' liability shall cease as soon as the cargo is on board. Instead, in the absence of special wording ... they mean that the charterers' liability shall cease if and to the extent that the owners have an alternative remedy by way of lien on the cargo.

6.229 In *Fidelitas Shipping Co Ltd* v. *V/O Exportchleb*, Pearson LJ commented on cesser and lien clauses, saying[340]:

... there has not been uniformity in their provisions and different wordings have naturally and rightly produced different decisions.

6.230 A not untypical lien clause is that contained in the Gencon charterparty, which states[341]:

Owners shall have a lien on the cargo for freight, dead freight, demurrage and damages for detention. Charterers shall remain responsible for dead freight and demurrage (including damages for detention) incurred at port of loading. Charterers shall also remain responsible for freight and demurrage (including damages for detention) incurred at port of discharge, but only to such extent as the Owners have been unable to obtain payment thereof by exercising the lien on the cargo.

6.231 Another type of cesser clause was that considered by Kerr J in *The Cunard Carrier*, based on the Australian grain form of charter[342]:

The charterers' liability under this charter shall cease, except as regards clause 5 (viz. payment of freight in London) when the cargo is shipped (provided it is worth the freight, deadfreight and

337. *Rederiaktieselskabet Superior* v. *Dewar and Webb* (1909) 14 CC 320 (CA).
338. *Rederiaktieselskabet Superior* v. *Dewar and Webb* (1909) 14 CC 99, at p. 108.
339. *Overseas Transportation Co* v. *Mineralimportexport (The Sinoe)* [1971] 1 Lloyd's Rep 514, at p. 516.
340. *Fidelitas Shipping Co Ltd* v. *V/O Exportchleb* [1963] 2 Lloyd's Rep 113, at p. 122.
341. Uniform General Charter 1976 (Gencon).
342. *The Cunard Carrier, Eleranta and Martha* [1977] 2 Lloyd's Rep 261.

demurrage upon arrival at port of discharge), the shipowners or their agent having an absolute lien on the cargo for freight . . . demurrage . . . at port of discharge.

6.232 There are many reported cases on cesser clauses and some of these will now be considered in more detail. However, the following general principles may be said to apply:

A. The lien and cesser clauses must be co-extensive.
   1. As a matter of construction of the charter.
   2. In practice.
B. A cesser clause may apply to liabilities accruing before as well as after shipment.

Construction of the charter

6.233 The charterparty itself must contain appropriate provisions for a lien to be created. If, as a matter of construction of the charter, it can be seen that the shipowner might have no lien, or only an inadequate lien, then the charterer's liability must continue or only cease in part.

6.234 Under a cesser and lien clause, the charterer's liability does not cease in respect of any subject-matter for which no lien is created, e.g. for damages for the detention of the ship, if the lien is only for demurrage in the ordinary sense of the word.[343] In *Clink* v. *Radford*[344] a cesser clause provided for charterer's liability to cease on the cargo being loaded, the owners having a lien on the cargo for freight and demurrage. The charter provided for laytime and demurrage at the discharge port, but at the load port the charter envisaged customary laytime with detention thereafter. However, although the ship was delayed unreasonably at the load port, the charterers denied liability for detention on the basis of the cesser clause, a claim rejected by the Court of Appeal. Lord Esher MR also said[345]:

. . . the main rule to be derived from the cases as to the interpretation of the cesser clause in a charterparty, is that the court will construe it as inapplicable to the particular breach complained of, if by construing it otherwise the shipowner would be left unprotected in respect of that particular breach, unless the cesser clause is expressed in terms that prohibit such a conclusion . . .

6.235 A similar outcome was the result in *Dunlop & Sons* v. *Balfour, Williamson & Co*, where Lord Esher said[346]:

If there were nothing else in the charterparty to which the word demurrage would be applicable, it may be—though I do not say it would be—that the court would then be obliged to say that the lien for demurrage must apply to such uncalculated damages.

However, in the case then under consideration, there was something to which the lien could apply, i.e. demurrage, and the court refused to hold that a right to lien the cargo for demurrage extended to a claim for detention.

---

343. Amongst the early cases where a demurrage lien was held not to apply to a claim for detention are: *Gray* v. *Carr* (1871) LR 6 QB 522; *Lockhart* v. *Falk* (1875) LR 10 Ex 132; *Gardiner* v. *Macfarlane, M'Crindell & Co* (1889) 26 Sc LR 492.
344. *Clink* v. *Radford & Co* [1891] 1 QB 625 (CA).
345. *Ibid.*, at p. 627.
346. *Dunlop & Sons* v. *Balfour, Williamson & Co* [1892] 1 QB 507, at p. 519.

6.236 In *Hansen* v. *Harrold Brothers*[347] there was a cesser and lien clause and a power for the charterers to sub-charter at any rate of freight with the master being required to sign bills of lading at the current or any rate of freight required without prejudice to the charter. Lord Esher MR, in the course of his judgment, with which Lopes LJ concurred, said[348]:

... where the provision for cesser of liability is accompanied by the stipulation as to lien, then the cesser of liability is not to apply in so far as the lien, which by the charterparty the charterers are enabled to create, is not equivalent to the liability of the charterers. Where in such a case, the provisions of the charterparty enable the charterers to make such terms with the shippers that the lien which is created is not commensurate with the liability of the charterers under the charterparty, then the cesser clause will only apply so far as the lien which can be exercised by the shipowner is commensurate with such liability.

6.237 In *Jenneson Taylor & Co* v. *Secretary of State for India in Council*,[349] the charter contained a cesser and lien clause, but it also provided that the master should sign bills of lading in a prescribed form and the prescribed form did not contain any provision as to lien. Consequently, when the bills of lading had been duly signed and issued there was no lien and, furthermore, the rate of discharge laid down in the charter was not incorporated into the bills, with the result that had the cesser clause been effective then the shipowner would not have been able to sue either the receiver or the charterer for the delay judged by the terms of the charter. This conclusion Rowlatt J refused to accept, holding that the charterer's liability did not cease as provided for in the cesser clause.

6.238 In *Anglo-Oriental Navigation Co Ltd* v. *T & J Brocklebank Ltd*, Roche J summed up the law thus[350]:

... it is possible for parties to provide by their contract in absolute terms that at a certain point the liability of the charterers shall cease, and that nothing shall keep it open, but in many contracts ... the true construction of the cesser clause, although it may be apparently absolute in its terms, having regard to the other provisions of the document and particularly to the nature and scope of the clause or clauses conferring liens for liabilities, may be that its operation is correlative and coextensive with the operation of the clause or clauses which confer a lien. That is to say, liability ceases if and so far as a lien is conferred, and does not cease if a lien is not conferred.

6.239 Similar sentiments were expressed by Goddard J in *Z Steamship Co Ltd* v. *Amtorg, New York*[351]:

The doctrine is now well settled that the lien, or rather the exemption granted to the charterer against liability for freight, must be co-extensive with the lien which is conferred on the shipowner, and if the lien which is conferred on the shipowner does not cover the whole of the matters which may materialize, then the charterer will be liable. The most common case has been where a lien is given for demurrage, and demurrage in the strict sense has not been incurred, but what has been incurred is damages for detention. Then the question has arisen whether the charterer is freed from liability because the lien is not co-extensive with the exemption granted.

6.240 In *The Athinoula*,[352] Mocatta J had to consider a charter which not only had a cesser/lien clause which provided for the charterers to remain liable for discharge port

347. *Hansen* v. *Harrold Brothers* [1894] 1 QB 612 (CA).
348. *Ibid.*, at p. 618.
349. *Jenneson, Taylor & Co* v. *Secretary of State for India in Council* [1916] 2 KB 702.
350. *Anglo-Oriental Navigation Co Ltd* v. *T & J Brocklebank Ltd* (1927) 27 Ll L Rep 359, at p. 360.
351. *Z Steamship Co Ltd* v. *Amtorg, New York* (1938) 61 Ll L Rep 97, at p. 100.
352. *Bravo Maritime (Chartering) Est* v. *Alsayed Abdullah Mohamed Baroom (The Athinoula)* [1980] 2 Lloyd's Rep 481.

demurrage in so far as the owners were unable to obtain payment by exercising their lien, but also had a further clause requiring the owners to submit time sheets and statements of fact, which, of course, they were unable to do until discharge was complete, by which time the possibility of their exercising a lien would have vanished. The judge therefore concluded that the two clauses could not be reconciled and, since the clause requiring presentation of the time sheets, etc., was an additional clause, that must prevail. Therefore, he said[353]:

... it does not become necessary to investigate whether at Jeddah there were possibilities for discharging these cargoes into warehouses and thereby retaining a lien for demurrage since to do so would be inconsistent with the provisions of the second paragraph of clause 18.

6.241 In *The Kavo Peiratis*,[354] Kerr J held that because the bill of lading did not include the terms of the relevant charter but incorporated different lien and demurrage provisions, the cesser clause did not apply as the owners were never able to assert the lien in the charter.

6.242 In *Action SA* v. *Britannic Shipping Corporation Ltd (The Aegis Britannic)*,[355] Staughton J held that a cesser clause was ineffective to prevent a shipowner claiming against the charterer for the negligence of his stevedores, where the lien given was for freight and demurrage. He clearly did so with some reluctance, since he said:

I have some regret at being compelled to reach that result. If a fair reading of the words in a contract on their ordinary meaning points to a particular result, it seems to me undesirable that a different result should be reached merely because the parties have not introduced some special phrase or shibboleth which the law requires in order to make their meaning plain beyond doubt. Those who frame their contracts with an intimate knowledge of *Scrutton on Charterparties* will achieve the results they desire; those who rely merely on an adequate knowledge of the English language will fail to do so. However, established doctrine prevents me from giving effect to that sentiment.

6.243 In *The Boral Gas*,[356] Evans J held that a charter on an Asbatankvoy form which under the cargo section of Part I was described as for eight consecutive voyages, but which thereafter made no further mention of multiple voyages, took effect as a single voyage to be performed eight times and this therefore meant that demurrage which accrued on the earlier voyages could not be secured by exercising a lien on the cargo carried on the last voyage.

Effectiveness of the lien

6.244 Even if the wording of the charter is appropriate to grant a theoretically effective lien, it may not be effective in practice. Perhaps the most common reason why this should be so is because the authorities at the port of discharge do not recognize the existence of the lien, either as a matter of law or as a matter of discretion. The latter is particularly common in a number of countries, particularly where the cargo is destined for a state or state-controlled agency.

---

353. *Ibid.*, at p. 487.
354. *Granvias Oceanicas Armadora SA* v. *Jibsen Trading Co (The Kavo Peiratis)* [1977] 2 Lloyd's Rep 344.
355. *Action SA* v. *Britannic Shipping Corporation Ltd (The Aegis Britannic)*, LMLN 148, 4 July 1985.
356. *Rashtriya Chemicals and Fertilizers Ltd* v. *Huddart Parker Industries Ltd (The Boral Gas)* [1988] 1 Lloyd's Rep 342.

6.245 Another possible reason why the lien may not be fully effective is because the value of the cargo is less than the total sum for which the lien is exercised. Whichever of these is the reason, it would seem that in the absence of agreement to the contrary, clearly expressed, the cesser clause will be inoperative to the extent that it is ineffective. However, the lack of effectiveness must not be due to any failure on the part of the vessel. As Goddard J said in relation to a claim for freight in *Z Steamship Co Ltd* v. *Amtorg, New York*[357]:

... the shipowner never exercised his lien and therefore there is no extent to which the charterers' liability can remain.

6.246 There are, however, a couple of *dicta* which suggest that a right of lien is enough even though it is not effective. In *Brankelow Steamship Co Ltd and others* v. *Canton Insurance Office Ltd*, Vaughan Williams LJ said[358]:

... nor do I think that it would have made any difference to the "cesser" of liability even if the shipowners had no lien or no effective lien ...

In that case it was freight that was under consideration, but when the matter was considered by the House of Lords, the point was expressly kept open.[359] The other case in which similar sentiments were expressed was *Fidelitas Shipping Co Ltd* v. *V/O Exportchleb*, in which Pearson LJ referred to the cesser clause as containing a participial phrase ("the owner *having* a lien" etc.) and said[360]:

If the shipowners' argument were correct, the participial phrase would have to do double duty: it would still have to create the lien and it would also have to mean "if and in so far as the owners have a lien which is effective at the time of discharge of the cargo".

Pearson LJ evidently thought that the clause should not be made to do double duty. In his view it was sufficient for the owner to have a right of lien—it was not necessary for it to be effective at the time of discharge of the cargo. The other judges, however, did not apparently take the same view and the case was decided on another point altogether.

6.247 Those *dicta* were disapproved by Lord Denning in *The Sinoe*,[361] where the point came up for decision directly. This is now the leading modern case on the need for a lien to be effective.

6.248 One aspect of the case has already been considered.[362] Briefly the facts were that discharge of a cargo of bags of cement was unduly prolonged due to the incompetence of the discharging stevedores. The charter contained a clause purporting to make the stevedores owners' servants and also a lien and cesser clause. On both grounds the charterers denied liability for demurrage. However, both at first instance[363] and in the Court of Appeal,[364] the courts were agreed that the cesser clause had to be effective in practice, as well as in theory. In the case under consideration it was not effective because no lien could be exercised, either on board or ashore, because the cargo was destined for

357. *Z Steamship Co Ltd* v. *Amtorg, New York* (1938) 61 Ll L Rep 97, at p. 101.
358. *Brankelow Steamship Co Ltd* v. *Canton Insurance Office Ltd* [1899] 2 QB 178, at p. 189.
359. In the House of Lords, the case is reported under the name of *Williams & Co and the Brankelow Steamship Co Ltd* v. *Canton Insurance Office Ltd* [1901] AC 462. See at pp. 467 and 476.
360. *Fidelitas Shipping Co Ltd* v. *V/O Exportchleb* [1963] 2 Lloyd's Rep 113, at p. 124.
361. *Overseas Transportation Co* v. *Mineralimportexport (The Sinoe)* [1972] 1 Lloyd's Rep 201 (CA).
362. See *ante* at para. 6.81.
363. *The Sinoe* [1971] 1 Lloyd's Rep 514.
364. *The Sinoe* [1972] 1 Lloyd's Rep 201 (CA).

the Government of the country concerned, and, at the time, a proclamation of emergency had allowed the Government to suspend all laws.

6.249 In the High Court, Donaldson J said of the decisions in *Clink* v. *Radford*[365] and *Hansen* v. *Harrold Brothers*[366]:

These two decisions show that whether or not there is a cesser of liability depends upon the true construction of the contract documents, but that the extent of the cesser can depend upon their application, properly construed, to events which occur subsequent to the contracts.[367]

The Court of Appeal agreed. Lord Denning said of the cesser and lien parts of the clause under consideration[368]:

... once it is accepted that the two parts of the clause are to be co-extensive, then it is sensible to require that the lien should be an effective lien. It is no use for the shipowner to be given a right of lien unless he can exercise it so as to get the money due to him. A right without a remedy is a vain thing. So I would hold that the lien for demurrage must be effective at the time of discharge of the cargo—unless it is so, the charterers are not relieved of their liability.

Megaw LJ agreed, saying[369]:

The onus of establishing that the lien is not effective at the port of discharge rests upon the shipowners: it is for them to show, if they can, by convincing evidence, that the lien is not effective, either because of illegality, or because of impossibility, the word "impossibility" means impossibility. It is not enough for the shipowners to show merely commercial inconvenience or difficulty. It must be impossibility.

6.250 The case was followed by Kerr J in *The Cunard Carrier*, where the judge said[370]:

The mere presence of a lien clause in the charter is not enough; the lien must be effective. Any remaining doubts about this were laid to rest by the decision of the Court of Appeal in *Overseas Transportation Co* v. *Mineralimportexport (The Sinoe)* [1972] 1 Lloyd's Rep 201.

In *Granvias Oceanicas Armadora SA* v. *Jibsen Trading Co (The Kavo Peiratis)*,[371] which was also decided by Kerr J, the judge suggested that depending on the wording of the cesser clause, the burden of proof might also be different.[372]

6.251 The question of what is meant by impossibility was one of the points that arose in *The Tropwave*,[373] which concerned the discharge of a cargo of rice at Bandar Shahpour. The owners did not attempt to exercise a lien and the charterers sought to argue that this meant that they could not subsequently claim impossibility. Summing up the charterers' arguments, Parker J said[374]:

Now in the present case the arbitrator's findings are such as to bring the owners squarely within the decision in *The Sinoe*, not as to legal but as to practical ineffectiveness. The charterers accept this as to the exercise of the lien on shore but attack it as to the exercise of the lien on board, saying that

365. *Clink* v. *Radford & Co* [1891] 1 QB 625.
366. *Hansen* v. *Harrold Brothers* [1894] 1 QB 612.
367. *The Sinoe* [1971] 1 Lloyd's Rep 514, at p. 518.
368. *The Sinoe* [1972] 1 Lloyd's Rep 201 at p. 204.
369. *Ibid.*, at p. 206.
370. *The Cunard Carrier, Eleranta and Martha* [1977] 2 Lloyd's Rep 261, at p. 263.
371. *Granvias Oceanicas Armadora SA* v. *Jibsen Trading Co (The Kavo Peiratis)* [1977] 2 Lloyd's Rep 344.
372. *Ibid.*, at p. 351.
373. *Maritime Transport Operators GmbH* v. *Louis Dreyfus et Cie (The Tropwave)* [1981] 2 Lloyd's Rep 159.
374. *Ibid.*, at p. 166.

all there is to be found in the case to support it is that any attempt to exercise the lien on board would have resulted in the vessel being sent to the back of the queue. This, they say, is no more than commercial inconvenience or difficulty and it does not in any event follow because the receivers might have paid.

However, the judge rejected these arguments, pointing out that much more had been shown in the way of practical ineffectiveness in the present case than in *The Sinoe*.[375] It would seem that the question as to what amounts to an impossibility will largely be left to arbitrators to decide as a question of fact and the courts will be reluctant to intervene.

Waiver of cesser clause

6.252 In *Rederi Aktiebolaget Transatlantic* v. *Board of Trade*,[376] Roche J held that a cesser clause could be waived with regard to freight and in *Fidelitas Shipping*, at first instance, Megaw J appeared to infer that this might also apply to demurrage.[377]

Liabilities before and after shipment

6.253 In most cases, if the cesser clause is operative, it applies both to liabilities which have accrued prior to its coming into operation and to those which have yet to accrue. Thus, it is usual for a cesser clause to provide for the charterers' liability to cease on completion of shipment and, in the absence of a provision to the contrary, it will mean that the receivers will become liable not only for discharge port demurrage but for load port demurrage as well. As Davey LJ said in *Hansen* v. *Harrold*[378]:

... the intention is that the liabilities of the charterer shall cease when the vessel is loaded, and that there shall be in the place of them a lien for all freight and demurrage under the charterparty.

6.254 In a similar vein, Pearson LJ commented in *Fidelitas Shipping Co Ltd* v. *V/O Exportchleb*[379]:

... it is not reasonable to suppose that the shipowner gives up his accrued right *in personam* against the charterer except in return for a corresponding lien on the goods.

6.255 In *Francesco* v. *Massey*, the lien and cesser clause provided for "Charterer's liability to cease when the ship is loaded, the Captain having a lien upon the cargo for freight and demurrage". The shipowners unsuccessfully tried to claim demurrage and damages for detention at the load port from the charterers. Bramwell B said of the cesser clause[380]:

It is impossible to say that this would not give a lien for demurrage incurred as well at the port of loading as at the port of discharge, and so for the demurrage sued for; and it seems impossible to hold that the matters as to which the liability was to cease were not the matters as to which the lien was given.

375. *The Sinoe* [1972] 1 Lloyd's Rep 201 (CA). *The Sinoe* was also considered in *Gerani Compania Naviera SA* v. *Alfred C. Toepfer (The Demosthenes V) (No 2)* [1982] 1 Lloyd's Rep 282.
376. *Rederi Aktiebolaget Transatlantic* v. *Board of Trade* (1924) 20 Ll L Rep 241.
377. *Fidelitas Shipping Co Ltd* v. *V/O Exportchleb* [1963] 1 Lloyd's Rep 246, at p. 255.
378. *Hansen* v. *Harrold Brothers* [1894] 1 QB 612, at p. 620.
379. *Fidelitas Shipping Co Ltd* v. *V/O Exportchleb* [1963] 2 Lloyd's Rep 113, at p. 122.
380. *Francesco* v. *Massey* (1873) LR 8 Ex 101.

6.256 A similar conclusion was reached in *Kish* v. *Cory*, where Cleasby B said[381]:

So far as the position of the shipowner, as well as the charterer, is concerned, it makes no difference whatever whether the demurrage accrues at the port of loading or at the port of discharge. In either case the shipowner has his lien, and it does not appear to be reasonable to hold that, if the demurrage accrued at the port of discharge, the charterer should be released, as the shipowner could look to his lien, but if it occurred at the port of loading he could not.

6.257 In the *Fidelitas* case, Pearson LJ cited the cases referred to above as authority for the proposition that[382]:

The cessation of liability on shipment involves not only incurring liability in respect of events occurring after shipment, but also a release from liability incurred before shipment.

6.258 The lien and cesser clause in the Gencon form of charter is an exception to the general principle set out above, since that provides for the charterer to remain liable for load port demurrage. The wording of the clause runs:

Owner shall have a lien on the cargo for freight, deadfreight, demurrage and damages for detention. Charterers shall remain responsible for deadfreight and demurrage (including damages for detention) incurred at port of loading. Charterers shall also remain responsible for freight and demurrage (including damages for detention) incurred at port of discharge but only to such extent as the Owners have been unable to obtain payment thereof by exercising the lien on the cargo.

Master's rights to claim demurrage

6.259 Normally claims for demurrage are put forward by the owners of the ship concerned. There are, however, a number of old cases dealing with what rights the master may have to bring an action for demurrage. Whilst these are probably now only of academic interest, nevertheless, for the sake of completeness, they will be mentioned briefly.

6.260 The general principle appears to be that where the contract is made with the master, then he may sue for any breach but he may not where the contract is with the shipowner. In *Jesson* v. *Solly*,[383] where the bill of lading signed by the master contained a provision as to demurrage, the master was allowed to sue for it. On the other hand, in *Brouncker* v. *Scott*,[384] decided in the same year, it was held that the master, not being an owner, could not bring an action on the implied promise in the bill of lading not to detain the ship improperly, and that was followed in *Evans* v. *Forster*.[385]

6.261 In *Cawthron* v. *Trickett*,[386] the master, who was a part-owner and managing owner, was held entitled to sue the consignor for failure to discharge the vessel in regular turn. It would seem that Erle CJ considered the master to have been personally a party to the bill of lading and therefore entitled to sue, whether or not he was a part-owner.

6.262 What is clear is that a master has no authority to waive or compromise a claim for demurrage and if he purports to do so then any such agreement will not be enforceable against the shipowner.[387]

---

381. *Kish* v. *Cory* (1875) LR 10 QB 553, at p. 561.
382. *Fidelitas Shipping Co Ltd* v. *V/O Exportchleb* [1963] 2 Lloyd's Rep 113, at p. 122.
383. *Jesson* v. *Solly* (1811) 4 Taunt 52.
384. *Brouncker* v. *Scott* (1811) 4 Taunt 1.
385. *Evans* v. *Forster* (1830) 1 B & Ad 118.
386. *Cawthron* v. *Trickett* (1864) 15 CB (NS) 754.
387. *Portofino (Owners)* v. *Berlin Derunaptha* (1934) 49 Ll L Rep 62.

Liability of bills of lading holders inter se

6.263 The question under consideration under this heading is how demurrage, both in terms of time and quantum, is to be calculated where liability for it rests with the holders of a number of bills of lading issued under the same charter. The answer to this question appears to be that there should usually be one calculation of the laytime allowed and used, even if more than one port of discharge is involved and that, in theory at least, the holder of each bill of lading may be held liable for all the demurrage due.[388]

One calculation or many calculations

6.264 The leading case on this point is *Compania Naviera Azuero SA* v. *British Oil & Cake Mills Ltd and others*,[389] a decision of Pearson J. In that case, the facts were that the *Azuero* loaded a cargo of grain in bulk at Philadelphia and discharged it at Belfast and Avonmouth. In all, some 14 bills of lading were issued, of which eight were held by a single receiver in Belfast and the remaining six, relating to the Avonmouth part of the cargo, were distributed amongst four receivers. The bills of lading incorporated the terms of the charter, which provided for a rate of discharge of 1,000 tons per weather working day and also contained a lien and cesser provision.

6.265 The shipowners argued that there should be separate calculations in respect of discharge at each port, whereas the receivers at Avonmouth (the Belfast receiver did not take part in the action) contended for one calculation. If the sums were done separately, then they resulted in despatch being payable at Belfast and a larger amount of demurrage being due at Avonmouth. If done together, then a lesser amount of demurrage was due. These results arose because discharge at Belfast had been quicker than the charterparty rate, but slower at Avonmouth. A third option of 14 separate calculations was mentioned but not pursued.

6.266 Having analysed the terms of the charter, Pearson J concluded that the intention of the charter was that there should be one calculation. In his judgment,[390] he quoted some words from an earlier case, which he said were apt to the present case. In that case Croom-Johnson J had said[391]:

This is, I think, after all is said and done, a perfectly simple situation. This is one adventure and one enterprise. If the parties wanted to make an agreement under which they were going to pay demurrage for delay at one point and only get one-third of the demurrage back, so to speak, or credit for the equivalent of one-third of the demurrage, for any time they saved at the other port, they could no doubt have framed an appropriate clause which would have produced that result.

He continued in that case:

It is quite plain that they have not done it, and it seems to me that, looking at this charterparty as a whole, when I see "cargo to be discharged at the average rate of" so-and-so, I think those words really mean what they say. It looks to me as if it would have been so simple to say, "cargo to be discharged at the average rate of so-and-so at each port". But they never did it.

It would seem that the fact that this was a bulk cargo and therefore the portions belonging to each bill of lading holder were unascertained before discharge did not play any part in

---

388. Different principles apply in the case of multiple charters—see *ante* at para. 5.140.
389. *Compania Naviera Azuero SA* v. *British Oil & Cake Mills Ltd and others* [1957] 1 Lloyd's Rep 312.
390. *Ibid.*, at p. 324.
391. *United British Steamship Co. Ltd* v. *Minister of Food* [1951] 1 Lloyd's Rep 111, at p. 115.

the judge's reasoning, and the decision would have been the same had the cargo been identifiable consignments.

6.267 Commenting on the final lines of the second passage from Croom-Johnson J's judgment, the tribunal in London Arbitration 7/97 said[392]:

The owners had placed reliance on those closing words [in the case then before them]. However it was difficult to understand precisely what the judge was trying to say. The judgment was extempore. As a matter of logic it was not clear why it should make any difference whether there should be a reference only to an "average rate" or whether there should be one to an "average rate at each port". It was possible that what the judge had in mind was two different rates being provided for, one for each port, although that was not what he had said.

To displace the underlying presumption by using a form of logic which involved second-guessing what a judge had said, particularly when it was *obiter*, was an unsure and inappropriate basis of decision, and it was not right to adopt it.

In *Compania Naviera Azuero SA* v. *British Oil and Cake Mills Ltd* [1957] 1 Lloyd's Rep 312 the judge had approved the words cited above from the *United British* decision, but that was in the context of his own decision that the charter with which he was concerned provided for only one calculation. He was dealing with a different charter, and since he was approving the positive decision made by an earlier judge, there was no reason to infer that he was approving the *obiter* passage and even if he was, such approval could hardly reinforce what was, to put it at its lowest, a highly ambiguous *dictum*.

The underlying presumption referred to in the passage quoted above was explained earlier in the report of the award in the following terms:

... the underlying presumption was that there would be one laytime calculation prepared for loading, and one for discharging, however many ports were used in each operation. That presumption was of course rebuttable, depending upon the actual words used by the parties in their contract.

It seems from the cases that very clear words will be necessary to rebut this underlying presumption.

6.268 A slightly different problem arose in London Arbitration 24/92.[393] Here the vessel in question was to load a cargo of corn and soyabean meal. The loading port laytime was simply four weather working days of 24 consecutive hours. However, the discharging port laytime clause provided for an average rate of discharge and went on to specify specific rates for the corn and for the soya-bean meal. The owners argued that there should be separate calculations for each commodity. This was rejected by the tribunal, who held that the correct approach was simply to arrive at a single figure representing the total laytime allowed based on the quantities actually loaded. They commented: "Had the final tonnage of each commodity been known at the time of fixing, it might well be that the parties would have agreed an overall rate or an overall period for discharging laytime."

How much must each pay?

6.269 The early cases of *Leer* v. *Yates*,[394] *Straker* v. *Kidd*,[395] and *Porteus* v. *Watney*[396] appear to suggest that, in theory at least, the shipowner may be able to recover the specified demurrage from each of the bill of lading holders, although there appear to be

---

392. London Arbitration 7/97—LMLN 459, 7 June 1997.
393. London Arbitration 24/92—LMLN 336, 19 September 1992.
394. *Leer* v. *Yates* (1811) 3 Taunt. 387.
395. *Straker* v. *Kidd* (1878) 3 QBD 223.
396. *Porteous* v. *Watney* (1878) 3 QBD 227; (1878) 3 QBD 534 (CA).

no reported cases where this has actually happened. In *Porteus* v. *Watney*, in the Court of Appeal, Thesiger LJ[397] suggested that if the shipowner received the full amount of demurrage due from one consignee, then any other sued could contend that the terms of the charter had been met so that no liability remained. However, in *The Lizzie*, in the Divisional Court, Horridge J appeared to accept that each consignee could be held liable for the full sum, although in that case the shipowner did not attempt to recover more than the charterparty rate from the consignees jointly. The charter was incorporated into the bills of lading and with respect to demurrage provided simply "Should the steamer be detained beyond the time stipulated as above for loading or discharging, demurrage shall be paid at twenty five pounds per day, and *pro rata* for any part thereof".

6.270 Explaining this part of the shipowner's claim, Horridge J said[398]:

The plaintiff says that the vessel ought to have been discharged within seven days. He says that . . . the ship was kept on demurrage . . . and that the various assignees of the cargo are jointly and severally liable for 11 days' demurrage. Mr Compston now says that he is content with a joint judgment against the three receivers of the cargo for the whole amount of the demurrage, and that he does not want them each to pay separately the whole amount of the demurrage.

Finding in favour of the shipowner, the judge said of the meaning to be given to the demurrage clause[399]:

Now, it seems to me that is an agreement by each of the holders of bills of lading that if the steamer is detained beyond the time stipulated for discharging, demurrage shall be paid at £25 per day, and *pro rata* for any part thereof.[400]

6.271 In *Roland-Linie Schiffahrt* v. *Spillers Ltd and others*,[401] three bill of lading holders were held liable for demurrage under a clause providing that if a discharging place should not be immediately available, demurrage should be payable for the period of waiting and the amount due was divided amongst the three defendants.

6.272 In the *Azuero* case,[402] which has already been considered on the question of whether there should be one calculation or more than one, having found that there should only be one, Pearson J then went on to hold that the total demurrage for the voyage calculated at the charterparty rate was due from the bill of lading holders who were parties to the action, who were the holders of six of the 14 bills of lading. However, in that case, the method of calculation having been decided by the court, the sum actually due was fixed by agreement. Interestingly enough, the demurrage clause that was operative provided for "the Receivers" to pay demurrage at a specified rate and presumably, therefore, it was felt that this meant that the total liability of all the receivers should not exceed this sum.

6.273 It would therefore seem that if the shipowner chooses so to do, he may recover his demurrage at the charter rate from any of the bill of lading holders, who could then, no doubt, bring in the other bill of lading holders as third parties. Whilst theoretically possible, the courts would no doubt be reluctant to allow the shipowner to recover the full amount of demurrage more than once under different bills of lading.

397. (1878) 3 QBD 534, at p. 540.
398. *The Lizzie* (1918) 23 CC 332, at p. 334.
399. *Ibid.*, at p. 335.
400. The case subsequently went on to the Court of Appeal and House of Lords, not on this point but on whether laytime had been exceeded: (1918) 24 CC 117 (CA); (1919) 25 CC 83 (HL).
401. *Roland-Linie Schiffahrt GmbH* v. *Spillers Ltd and others* [1956] 2 Lloyd's Rep 211.
402. *Compania Naviera Azuero SA* v. *British Oil & Cake Mills Ltd and others* [1957] 1 Lloyd's Rep 312.

Demurrage time bars

6.274 It is not uncommon to find an additional clause in voyage charters requiring owners to submit any claim for demurrage within a specified period, often 90 days, failing which the claim will be deemed to have been waived. Apart from a desire to dispose of any such claim promptly, the reason behind the inclusion of such a clause is often that there is a corresponding provision in the relevant contract of sale of the cargo, requiring the charterers to submit their claim against the shippers or receivers within a specified period.

6.275 The courts and arbitration tribunals are willing to uphold the validity of such clauses. However, they will only do so where the words which give rise to a time bar defence are clear and unambiguous and any such clause will be construed *contra proferentem* the party who seeks to rely on it. The cases that follow are illustrations of these principles.

6.276 In *The Oltenia*,[403] the relevant clause required the claim to be in writing with "all available supporting documents". Commenting on the purpose of the clause and the meaning of this phrase, Bingham J said[404]:

The commercial intention underlying this clause seems to me plainly to have been to ensure that claims were made by the owners within a short period of final discharge so that the claims could be investigated and if possible resolved while the facts were still fresh . . . This object could only be achieved if the charterers were put in possession of the factual material which they required in order to satisfy themselves whether the claims were well-founded or not. I cannot regard the expression "all available supporting documents" as in any way ambiguous: documents supporting the owners' claim on liability would of course be included, but so would a document relating to quantum only, just as a doctor's bill would be a document supporting a claim for personal injury. The owners would not, as a matter of common sense, be debarred from making factual corrections to claims presented in time . . . nor from putting a different legal label on a claim previously presented, but the owners are in my view shut out from enforcing a claim the substance of which and the supporting documents of which (subject always to *de minimis* exceptions[405]) have not been presented in time.

6.277 In London Arbitration 18/89,[406] the tribunal recognized that a clause imposing a deadline for claims for demurrage which specified certain documents, including Notices of Readiness, to be submitted with the claim, might have to be read in certain circumstances as saying Notices of Readiness "if such exist".

6.278 In London Arbitration 11/90,[407] the relevant clause required any claim to be submitted to the charterers within 90 days of final discharge, failing which it was deemed to be "waived and absolutely banned" (this should probably read "barred").

6.279 The clause did not define what was meant by supporting documents but no dispute arose on that aspect. The problem was that whilst the disponent owners had the required discharge port documentation they did not have the corresponding documentation from the load port, where the agents were owners' agents although nominated by charterers. However, they did not particularly press the agents until the last moment and eventually obtained the necessary documents from the head owners but outside the 90-day

403. *The Oltenia* [1982] 1 Lloyd's Rep 448.
404. *Ibid.*, at p. 453.
405. See also London Arbitration 21/98—LMLN 493, 29 September 1998 as an illustration of the *de minimis* principle.
406. London Arbitration 18/89—LMLN 254, 29 July 1989.
407. London Arbitration 11/90—LMLN 285, 6 October 1990.

period. On these facts, the tribunal concluded the disponent owners' claim was time barred.

6.280 In London Arbitration 18/91,[408] there was a similar provision but the problem was slightly different. What happened here was that the owners, having presented their demurrage claim with supporting documentation within the stipulated period, subsequently increased it outside the 90-day limit. In so doing, they relied on the same documentation as had previously been put forward. The tribunal held that they were entitled so to do, the clause did not limit the amount due.

6.281 In London Arbitration 25/92,[409] the clause required the claim to be "presented to charterers in writing with supporting documents", again within 90 days. The owners sent their claim through the broking chain but apparently it was only passed on by the charterers' brokers to their principals two months after it was sent to them. Hasteners apparently went unanswered. On these facts, the tribunal held the claim to be time barred. However, it is not clear from the brief report of the case whether the original claim documents went missing between the intermediate brokers and the charterers' brokers or were simply sat on by the charterers' brokers who then ignored the hasteners. If it was the latter alternative, it is suggested that the owners would have had a good argument that presentation to the charterers' brokers was, under the normal principles of agency, sufficient to meet the requirements of presentation to the charterers. If the charterers' brokers had the documents in sufficient time to pass them to the charterers within the 90 days, but simply failed to do so, and ignored further hasteners (even though these were outside the 90-day period), it is difficult to see what further the owners could have done, except start the hastening process earlier.

6.282 In London Arbitration 26/92,[410] the relevant time bar provision simply referred to "supporting documents", (including, but not limited to, vessel timesheets signed by the ship's agents and terminal log). The only document the owners failed to send timeously was a load port Notice of Readiness, which took some time to get from the agents, who were the charterers' agents. As a load port Notice of Readiness was not specifically required by the clause and the information it would have contained was evidenced by the appropriate statement of facts, the tribunal held that the owners had met their obligations.

6.283 Although not specified in the brief report of this case, it is perhaps significant that it was the charterers' agents who were slow in producing the missing document and there is no doubt that where the problem arises with someone on the charterers' side of the fence, arbitrators will be reluctant to allow the charterers to take advantage of a time bar provision.

6.284 In London Arbitration 4/98,[411] the tribunal followed the decision in London Arbitration 18/89[412] in holding that in relation to documents, the requirement that they be produced was subject to the proviso "if they exist". In that case the documents in question were terminal time logs.[413]

---

408. London Arbitration 18/91—LMLN 308, 24 August 1991.
409. London Arbitration 25/92—LMLN 337, 3 October 1992.
410. London Arbitration 26/92—LMLN 337, 3 October 1992.
411. London Arbitration 4/98—LMLN 481, 14 April 1998.
412. London Arbitration 18/89—LMLN 254, 29 July 1989.
413. See also *The Voltaz* [1997] 1 Lloyd's Rep 35 and *Mira Oil Resources of Tortola* v. *Bocimar NV* [1999] 2 Lloyd's Rep 101.

Time of payment

6.285 A more controversial decision, however, is that reported as London Arbitration 13/91.[414] In this case, an additional typed clause provided:

Demurrage, if any, to be settled 90 days after completion of discharge and charterers having received all relevant load/discharge documents duly signed.

This, said the tribunal, meant that liability for demurrage (and therefore interest) did not arise until 90 days after receipt of the documents. It should be noted that, in this case, failure to send the documents within 90 days would not have resulted in the claim being time barred.

6.286 There are two difficulties with this case. The first is whether, as the tribunal found, the 90-day period should run from the receipt of documents. Whilst it is largely a matter of impression, it is suggested that a more logical interpretation would be that the 90-day period runs from completion of discharge and there is an added requirement that the charterers should have received the relevant documents. Admittedly this leaves open the question as to what happens if the charterers do not receive the documents within the 90-day period. This gives rise to the second difficulty and a point that, so far as the report of the case is concerned, was not considered by the tribunal, namely the meaning of the word "settled".

6.287 The meaning of this word was considered by the House of Lords in a case called *The Lips*,[415] where the main issue was whether damages could be claimed for late payment of demurrage where the owners had suffered a loss because a clause in the charter required payment to be made in sterling (although the demurrage rate was in US dollars) at the rate of exchange prevailing at the date of the bills of lading. The relevant clause, however, referred to "demurrage/despatch settlements". Quoting the earlier case of *The Pearl Merchant*,[416] Lord Mackay appeared to accept that "settlement" means calculation and not payment. That construction was followed by Hirst J and the Court of Appeal in *The Antclizo (No 2)*,[417] where, in the High Court, Hirst J reviewed earlier authorities dealing with the meaning of the word "settlement" including the decision of Staughton J in *The La Pintada*,[418] where he held the word to mean payment. There is, however, now authority from the House of Lords (*The Lips*) and the Court of Appeal (*The Antclizo (No 2)*) that settlement does not mean payment but agreement. That would of course accord with the general principle that demurrage accrues and theoretically should be paid from day to day as it arises.[419] If "settled" means agreement or determination, what the clause in London Arbitration 13/91[420] is doing is setting a time limit for owners' claim to be agreed by the charterers and not setting a date from which interest should run.

---

414. London Arbitration 13/91—LMLN 304, 29 June 1994.
415. *The Lips* [1987] 2 Lloyd's Rep 311 (HL).
416. *The Pearl Merchant* [1978] 2 Lloyd's Rep 193.
417. *The Antclizo (No 2)* [1991] 2 Lloyd's Rep 485; [1992] 1 Lloyd's Rep 558.
418. *The La Pintada* [1983] 1 Lloyd's Rep 37.
419. *Per* Lord Brandon in *The Lips* [1987] 2 Lloyd's Rep 311, at p. 315, quoted *ante* at para. 66.
420. London Arbitration 13/91—LMLN 304, 29 June 1994.

CHAPTER 7

Despatch

7.1 Despatch[1] is the money which a shipowner is sometimes required under a charter to pay to the charterer for completing loading or discharging in less than the allowed laytime. It only arises where the charter expressly so provides and is virtually unknown in tanker charters.

7.2 Since the full amount of laytime has been paid for in the freight,[2] despatch is sometimes referred to as a rebate on freight. It is the opposite of demurrage. As Devlin J said in *Compania de Navigación Zita SA* v. *Louis Dreyfus & Cie*[3]:

The shipowner's desire is to achieve a quick turnround; time is money for him. The object of fixing lay days and providing for demurrage and dispatch money is to penalize dilatoriness in loading and to reward promptitude.

The *Voylayrules 1993*[4] provide as follows:

"DESPATCH MONEY" or "DESPATCH" shall mean an agreed amount payable by the owner if the vessel completes loading or discharging before the laytime has expired.

"DESPATCH ON (ALL) WORKING TIME SAVED" (WTS) or "ON (ALL) LAYTIME SAVED" shall mean that despatch money shall be payable for the time from the completion of loading or discharging to the expiry of the laytime excluding any period excepted from the laytime.

"DESPATCH ON ALL TIME SAVED" (ATS) shall mean that despatch money shall be payable for the time from the completion of loading or discharging to the expiry of the laytime including any periods excepted from the laytime.

Where despatch is payable, the rate is almost always half the demurrage rate.

7.3 The most common interpretation given to despatch clauses is to say that the clause provides for the shipowner to pay for all time saved to the ship, rather than working time saved, calculated in the way in which demurrage would be calculated, namely, without taking any account of the laytime exceptions. The alternative, but less common, meaning is to allow for such exceptions.

7.4 The difference between "all time saved" and "working time saved" can be illustrated as follows. If a charter allows 10 working days for loading and the operation actually takes five working days ending on a Wednesday, a projection of when laytime would have expired if the full amount of time allowed had been taken would show that

---

1. Often spelt "dispatch".
2. See *Inverkip Steamship Co Ltd* v. *Bunge & Co* [1917] 2 KB 193, at p. 200 *per* Scrutton LJ, and *Shipping Developments Corporation SA* v. *V/O Sojuzneftexport (The Delian Spirit)* [1971] 1 Lloyd's Rep 506, at p. 509 *per* Lord Denning: " . . . they have bought their laytime and paid for it in the freight . . . "
3. *Compania de Navigación Zita SA* v. *Louis Dreyfus & Cie* [1953] 2 Lloyd's Rep 472, at p. 475.
4. See Appendix.

laytime would end the following Tuesday, i.e. a further five days excluding Sunday, a non-working day. The time therefore saved is six days on an "all time saved" basis and five days on a "working time saved" basis. Another way of expressing the same thing would be to say that six actual days or five working days have been saved.

7.5 Despatch clauses often require separate calculations for loading and discharging. However, where there are more than one load or discharge ports, the time taken at all the load ports or all the discharge ports must first be added together. Separate calculations are not normally made for each port, although where each port has a different loading (or discharging) rate, this may not be so.[5]

7.6 A useful summary of the principles involved in construing despatch clauses was given by Bailhache J in *Mawson Steamship Co* v. *Beyer*, where he said[6]:

Accepting, however, as I must and do, the authorities as they stand, I think I may safely say that the conclusions to be drawn from them are: 1. *Prima facie* the presumption is that the object and intention of these despatch clauses is that the shipowner shall pay to the charterer for all time saved to the ship, calculated in the way in which, in the converse case, demurrage would be calculated: that is taking no account of the lay day exceptions . . .

2. This *prima facie* presumption may be displaced, and it is displaced where either (a) lay days and time saved by despatch are dealt with in one clause and demurrage in another clause; or (b) lay days, time saved by despatch and demurrage are dealt with in the same clause, but upon the construction of that clause the court is of opinion, from the collocation of the words, or other reason, that the days saved are referable to and used in the same sense as the lay days as described in the clause, and are not referable to or used in the same sense as days lost by demurrage.

7.7 The authorities cited by the judge in support of proposition 1 were: *Laing* v. *Holloway*[7] and *Re Royal Mail Steam Packet Co and River Plate Steamship Co*[8]; in support of 2(a): *The Glendevon*[9]; and for 2(b): *Nelson & Sons Ltd* v. *Nelson Line*.[10] These will now be considered further.

7.8 *Laing* v. *Holloway*[11] is usually taken as the start point for any consideration of despatch. In that case demurrage and despatch money were dealt with in one clause, and omitting unnecessary words, the clause ran "demurrage, if any at the rate of 20s per hour . . . Despatch money, 10s per hour on any time saved in loading and/or discharging". By an earlier clause the cargo was to be loaded "at the rate of 200 tons per running day (Sundays and holidays excepted), and to be discharged as fast as ship can deliver, not exceeding 200 tons per working day, weather permitting". Four days were saved in loading and five days in discharging. No one suggested that a Sunday did not count for despatch but the shipowners contended that a lay or working day was a day of 12 hours, and that what had been saved was nine working days of 12 hours each, equal to 108 hours. The charterers, on the other hand, contended that they had saved the ship nine days of 24 hours each, equal to 216 hours. The court held that there was no ground for the suggestion

5. *United British Steamship Co Ltd* v. *Minister of Food* [1951] 1 Lloyd's Rep 111, at p. 115 *per* Croom-Johnson J, and *Compania Naviera Azuero SA* v. *British Oil & Cake Mills Ltd and others* [1957] 1 Lloyd's Rep 312, at p. 324 *per* Pearson J.
6. *Mawson Steamship Co* v. *Beyer* (1913) 19 CC 59, at p. 67. See also London Arbitration 12/98–LMLN 488, 21 July 1998.
7. *Laing* v. *Holloway* (1878) 3 QBD 437.
8. *Re Royal Mail Steam Packet Co and River Plate Steamship Co* (1910) 15 CC 124.
9. *The Glendevon* [1893] P 269.
10. *Nelson & Sons Ltd* v. *Nelson Line (Liverpool) Ltd (No 3)* [1907] 2 KB 705 (CA).
11. *Laing* v. *Holloway* (1878) 3 QBD 437.

that the length of a day should be the working portion of the day, i.e. 12 hours,[12] and that "time saved" meant time saved to the ship. Judgment was therefore given to the charterers. Bramwell LJ said, in delivering the judgment of the court[13]:

It is admitted on both sides, and it is clear, that "time saved" means if the ship is ready earlier than she would be if the charterers worked up to their maximum obligation only all the time by which she is the sooner ready is "time saved" within the meaning of the charterparty. The question is by how much time is she sooner ready? The answer is, nine times twenty four hours. Really the reason of the thing is that way. The owner would sail away, by what has happened, 216 hours sooner than he would have done but for the defendant's despatch.

The judge also pointed out that it was admitted that demurrage would be payable on this basis, so why not despatch? he asked.

7.9 It was suggested by Bray J in *Re Royal Mail Steam Packet Co*[14] that the general principle laid down by Bramwell LJ was *obiter*, but in *Mawson Steamship Co* v. *Beyer*, Bailhache J said of this comment[15]:

It may be so, but the judgment is a reasoned judgment on the construction and objects of the clause and purports to lay down a principle.

7.10 The next case chronologically where despatch was considered was a decision of the Divisional Court in Admiralty, *The Glendevon*.[16] There, discharging and despatch were dealt with in the same clause, which provided: "Steamer to be discharged at the rate of 200 tons per day, weather permitting (Sundays and fête days excepted) . . . and if sooner despatched to pay at the rate of . . . for every hour saved." In the time saved were a fête day and a Sunday, and the charterers claimed despatch money in respect of them. The court held they were wrong, accepting the owners' argument that because weather was an exception, if there was persistent bad weather then laytime would be indefinitely extended and the charterers would be able to claim despatch money until the weather improved. This point was also dealt with by Fletcher Moulton LJ in *Nelson & Sons Ltd* v. *Nelson Line*,[17] where he suggested that the way around what clearly would be an absurdity would be to say that the projection forward of when laytime would have expired must be carried out at the moment when loading or discharging, as the case may be, is completed and any unforeseeable extensions of laytime beyond that point should be ignored. This view was also shared by Bailhache J in the *Mawson Steamship* case.[18]

7.11 Another point taken by the President, Sir Francis Jeune, in *The Glendevon* was that the demurrage clause was a separate clause containing no exceptions, and that as the lay day and despatch clauses were one clause, which did contain exceptions, those exceptions must be taken as equally applying to despatch days. As will be seen shortly, the decision in *The Glendevon* has been the subject of some criticism in the later cases.

12. In *Thomasson Shipping Co Ltd* v. *Henry W Peabody & Co of London Ltd* [1959] 2 Lloyd's Rep 296, some 80 years later, a similar argument was put forward. There, the shipowners unsuccessfully claimed that the working time saved should be calculated in hours during which work would have been carried out and then divided by 24.
13. *Laing* v. *Holloway* (1878) 3 QBD 437, at p. 441.
14. *Re Royal Mail Steam Packet Co and River Plate Steamship Co* (1910) 15 CC 124, at p. 132.
15. *Mawson Steamship Co* v. *Beyer* (1913) 19 CC 59, at p. 65.
16. *The Glendevon* [1893] P 269.
17. *Nelson & Sons Ltd* v. *Nelson Line (Liverpool) Ltd (No 3)* [1907] 2 KB 705, at p. 721.
18. *Mawson Steamship Co* v. *Beyer* (1913) 19 CC 59, at p. 65.

7.12 The next case was *Nelson & Sons Ltd* v. *Nelson Line*, where, although the case went to the House of Lords,[19] the question of despatch was dealt with by the Court of Appeal.[20] In that case the lay days, demurrage and despatch were all dealt with in the same clause, which stated: "Seven weather working days (Sundays and holidays excepted) to be allowed by owners to charterers for loading . . . For any time beyond the periods above provided the charterers shall pay to the owners demurrage . . . For each clear day saved in loading the charterers shall be paid or allowed by the owners . . . " The days saved included a Sunday but the charterers' claim in respect of it was disallowed by the Court of Appeal, Fletcher Moulton LJ dissenting. The judgment of the court was given by Buckley LJ, who held that *The Glendevon*[21] was rightly decided and that *Laing* v. *Holloway*[22] was also rightly decided, but had no bearing upon the point raised in that case. In his judgment, Buckley LJ said[23]:

They (the charterers) say, and quite truly, that the departure of the ship has been accelerated, not by three days but by four, because she got the benefit of Sunday . . . If this contract had been that the charterers should have so much a day for each day saved to the ship, this would have been right, but it does not so provide. The provision is that they shall have so much for each clear day saved in loading . . . the relevant words are "seven days to be allowed for loading" and "for each clear day saved in loading" the charterers shall be paid. In this language no trace is to be found of saving delay to the ship. The payment is to be made for any saving effected in the seven days allowed for loading.

In his dissenting judgment, Fletcher Moulton LJ suggested that *The Glendevon*[24] was wrongly decided and that, in the present case, the general presumption should apply so that what mattered was the time saved to the ship. As already mentioned, he did, however, say that even on that basis, the effect of weather should be discounted in calculating when laytime would have expired so that only Sundays and holidays would be taken into account. In two later cases which will shortly be considered,[25] the judges also expressed their doubts on the finding in *The Glendevon* and expressed support for Fletcher Moulton LJ's views. This support, however, appears to be limited to how the principles set out at the start of this section should be applied to particular clauses, rather than any criticism of the principles themselves.

7.13 In the *Re Royal Mail* case,[26] loading, demurrage and despatch were again dealt with in the same clause, which, having provided for the laytime and demurrage allowed, then continued with a similar provision for discharging. After that the clause went on: "The owners of the ship to pay £10 per day despatch money for each running day saved. Parts of days to count as parts of days, and demurrage or despatch money to be paid *pro rata*." The issue between the parties concerned weekends between 1 p.m. on Saturdays and 7 a.m. on Mondays, the charterers claiming payment and the owners resisting. Bray J held that the charterers were right.

---

19. *Nelson & Sons Ltd* v. *Nelson Line (Liverpool) Ltd (No 3)* (1908) 13 CC 235 (HL).
20. [1907] 2 KB 705 (CA).
21. *The Glendevon* [1893] P 269.
22. *Laing* v. *Holloway* (1878) 3 QBD 437.
23. *Nelson & Sons Ltd* v. *Nelson Line (Liverpool) Ltd (No 3)* [1907] 2 KB 705, at p. 724.
24. *The Glendevon* [1893] P 269.
25. *Re Royal Mail Steam Packet Co and River Plate Steamship Co* (1910) 15 CC 124, at p. 135 *per* Bray J; *Mawson Steamship Co* v. *Beyer* (1913) 19 CC 59, at p. 67 *per* Bailhache J.
26. *Re Royal Mail Steam Packet Co and River Plate Steamship Co* (1910) 15 CC 124.

7.14 It is worth noting that although the form of the clause and the collocation of words were the same as in the *Nelson* case,[27] in the last part of the clause, dealing with pro rata payment, demurrage and despatch are treated as being on the same footing. The judge therefore concluded that as demurrage ran on an uninterrupted basis so should despatch money.

7.15 In *Mawson Steamship Co* v. *Beyer*,[28] Bailhache J reviewed the cases just considered and then added[29]:

I should, I fear, have decided all the four reported cases in favour of the charterer. It would serve no useful purpose, and would perhaps be hardly respectful, to criticize the judgments of the court in *The Glendevon* and of Buckley LJ in the *Nelson* case; but if the test is as Buckley LJ says, whether there is to be found in the language used "a trace of saving delay to the ship", I should have thought that in all the cases more than a trace is to be found in that part of the language used which provides that the ship is to pay and, in *The Glendevon* in particular, the words "if sooner discharged" I should not have found in that case a trace of anything else.

The judge then summed up the conclusions and principles he drew from the cases as set out at the start of this section. As far as the case under consideration was concerned, where the laytime, demurrage and despatch money provisions were in separate clauses, he concluded that there was nothing to defeat the *prima facie* object and intention of the despatch clause that the shipowners should pay for all time saved to the ship calculated in the same way as demurrage.

7.16 It must be emphasized that these guidelines given by Bailhache J are only pointers and as always each case must be considered afresh. As will already be apparent, even small differences in the wording of particular clauses or the way in which they are incorporated with other clauses may lead to a different result. As Morris J said in *Themistocles (Owners)* v. *Compagnie Intercontinentale de L'Hyperphosphate of Tangier*[30]:

Parties who contract in reference to the charter of a vessel are free to provide for dispatch money or not as they wish. They are free to agree that dispatch money shall be calculated by any one of several possible methods. Unless terms of art are used, or unless the court is bound by some decision relating to a contract in virtually identical form, then, while deriving such assistance as the decisions afford, the task of the court, as it seems to me, is merely one of the construction of particular words as used in their context in a particular contract.

Some later cases

7.17 In the *Australian Wheat Board* v. *British India Steam Navigation Co Ltd and Associated Companies*,[31] the court was asked to construe a clause which read:

Steamer to pay charterers one-third demurrage rate per day every day saved in loading, and if steamer discharge elsewhere than in the United Kingdom, excluding Sundays and holidays saved.

27. *Nelson & Sons Ltd* v. *Nelson Line (Liverpool) Ltd (No 3)* [1907] 2 KB 705 (CA).
28. *Mawson Steamship Co* v. *Beyer* (1913) 19 CC 59.
29. *Ibid.*, at p. 67.
30. *Themistocles (Owners)* v. *Compagnie Intercontinentale de L'Hyperphosphate of Tangier* (1948) 82 Lloyd's Rep 232, at p. 239.
31. *Australian Wheat Board* v. *British India Steam Navigation Co Ltd and Associated Companies* (1923) 14 Ll L Rep 117.

The case concerned two vessels, both of which discharged outside the United Kingdom. The owners, however, argued that despatch was not due, saying that the reference to discharge outside the United Kingdom should read as provided discharge was outside, etc—in other words, that the clause only applied to loading and then only if discharge was not in the United Kingdom. This the court rejected, holding that despatch was due for time saved in loading and time saved in discharge if that occurred outside the United Kingdom.

7.18 In the *Themistocles* case[32] one of the issues raised concerned the meaning of the despatch provision. This was contained in the same clause as the provision relating to demurrage and the clause read:

11. Demurrage, if any, at loading port to be paid to owners at the rate of US$1000 per running day or pro rata.

On all time saved at port of loading, owners to pay to shippers dispatch money at half of demurrage rate per day (portions of a day pro rata).

The shipowners argued that there was a significance in the fact that the demurrage part of the clause referred to running days and the despatch provision referred to time saved. Rejecting this argument and finding in favour of the charterers' contention that the normal rule applied, Morris J said of these provisions[33]:

In my judgment, those words have reference to the whole time which is saved as a result of the vessel being able to leave the port of loading on some date or at some time earlier than she would have left had the shippers kept the vessel as long as they could have kept her.

7.19 In *Thomasson Shipping Co Ltd* v. *Henry W Peabody & Co of London Ltd*,[34] the principal dispute concerned not whether excepted periods should be excluded from the despatch calculation, but how the time saved should be worked out in terms of hours and days.[35] The despatch clause was a separate provision and provided for despatch money to be payable in respect of all working time saved.

7.20 In the course of his judgment however, McNair J said[36]:

It seems to me that the addition of the word "working" here merely has the effect of excluding from the time saved Sundays and holidays, and possibly—though I express no concluded opinion upon it—rainy days.[37]

Notice provisions

7.21 Charters frequently provide for laytime to commence a certain period after Notice of Readiness is tendered. Sometimes they provide that if work commences during this period then time is to count and sometimes for it not to count. Normally, such provisions do not

---

32. *Themistocles (Owners)* v. *Compagnie Intercontinentale de L'Hyperphosphate of Tangier* (1948) 82 Ll L Rep 232.

33. *Ibid.*, at p. 249.

34. *Thomasson Shipping Co Ltd* v. *Henry W Peabody & Co of London Ltd* [1959] 2 Lloyd's Rep 296.

35. At the time this case was heard, the Court of Appeal doctrine of calculating adverse weather interruptions in weather working days laid down in *Alvion Steamship Corporation Panama* v. *Galban Lobo Trading Co SA of Havana (The Rubystone)* [1955] 1 Lloyd's Rep 9 (CA) held sway and the arguments were based on that case, which has now been overruled.

36. *Thomasson Shipping Co Ltd* v. *Henry W Peabody & Co of London Ltd* [1959] 2 Lloyd's Rep 296, at p. 304.

37. In earlier cases, it was held that no account should be taken of such weather interruptions. See *ante* at para. 7.10.

cause any complication in calculating despatch since it is simply a question of applying the terms of the charter to work out the amount of laytime used and when laytime would have expired.

7.22 One case, however, where the despatch clause itself referred to notice time was *Sir R Ropner & Co Ltd* v. *W S Partridge & Co.*[38] In this case, the laytime allowed, commencement of laytime, demurrage and despatch were all dealt with in the same clause. Laytime was to commence 48 hours after notice, unless work commenced earlier and the last part of the clause provided, "No despatch to be paid on the 48 hours free time".

7.23 The owners claimed that for the purpose of despatch calculations, time should commence from the giving of notice. The charterers contended that time should commence in the normal way and that the last part of the clause meant that if loading was completed within 48 hours of the tendering of Notice of Readiness then, as far as despatch was concerned, it should be deemed to have taken 48 hours.

7.24 Deciding that the charterers were right, Branson J said[39]:

... you do not get the peculiar circumstance of having to apply to lay days for the purposes of demurrage a different calculation from that (applying to the same lay days) for the purposes of despatch.

Reversing and double despatch

7.25 In *Rowland and Marwood's Steamship Co Ltd* v. *Wilson, Sons & Co Ltd*,[40] the relevant charter provided for "Any hours saved in loading to be added to the hours allowed for discharging". Despatch was payable for time saved in discharging. Loading took $2\frac{3}{4}$ days less than the time allowed and discharging $7\frac{1}{2}$ days less; the charterers therefore claimed despatch of $10\frac{1}{4}$ days. The shipowners, however, only allowed $7\frac{1}{2}$ days, pointing out there was no provision which directly allowed despatch for time saved in loading. Bruce J held that the shipowners were right and that the clause allowing time saved in loading to be added to discharging time only applied to calculation of demurrage.

7.26 A not dissimilar point was one of several issues which arose for consideration in *Z Steamship Co Ltd* v. *Amtorg, New York*.[41] In that case, the despatch clause (clause 20) provided for "Owners to pay charterers £15 (fifteen pounds) per day or *pro rata* despatch money for all time saved in loading and discharging, to be settled at each end if required by charterers". There was a further clause that time allowed for loading and discharging should be reversible. Of the meaning of the despatch clause, Goddard J said[42]:

... the charterers have a right to say directly the loading is finished: "We have saved you four days; pay us four days' despatch money." If that is paid there is an end of the claim for despatch money.

7.27 Of the provision for reversing, the judge said this did not mean that you can get paid over again. He therefore held that whether payment was made immediately after loading or not, the particular despatch clause required separate calculations of despatch money for loading and discharging. The time saved in loading could not be claimed in

38. *Sir R Ropner & Co Ltd* v. *W S Partridge & Co* (1929) 33 Ll L Rep 86.
39. *Ibid.*, at p. 88.
40. *Rowland and Marwood's Steamship Co Ltd* v. *Wilson, Sons & Co Ltd* (1897) 2 CC 198.
41. *Z Steamship Co Ltd* v. *Amtorg, New York* (1938) 61 Ll L Rep 97.
42. *Ibid.*, at p. 102.

despatch money and at the same time carried forward to be added to the laytime allowed for discharge, thus enhancing the despatch due on discharge. Goddard J did however suggest that the same time saved in loading could be carried forward to prevent demurrage accruing at discharge as well as being used to claim despatch for loading. The judge put it this way[43]:

In my opinion, in view of clause 20 of the charterparty, the dispatch money has to be calculated independently; that is to say, loading time has got to be paid for separately from discharging time, although, in fact, demurrage will not be incurred if having saved time at the loading port she exceeds the time granted at the port of discharge but does not exceed it by more than the time that she has saved at the loading port.

7.28 In *The Atlantic Sun*, Mocatta J said of this passage and Goddard J's views on the relationship between the despatch and reversible laytime provisions[44]:

The reconciliation of these two provisions favoured by Goddard J, namely, that if despatch were paid at the end of loading, time then could still be used to avoid or lessen demurrage that would otherwise have been incurred in discharge, has been thought to give rise to difficulties and was not relied upon . . .

Logically, if the time saved in loading is paid for with despatch money then that ought to be an end to the matter for all purposes and one should not be able to use the same time again to offset discharge port demurrage, since that would effectively mean double payment for the same time.

7.29 A slightly different point was considered by Morris J in *The Themistocles*.[45] The despatch provision referred to "all time saved at port of loading" and was contained in the same clause as the demurrage provision. There were in fact two load ports and because the passage time between the two was very short and loading at both ports very quick, it meant that there was an overlap of days saved, so that the dates of the days saved from the first load port partly coincided with the dates saved at the second load port. Dismissing the shipowners' claim that this meant that they were paying twice for the same time, Morris J said[46]:

It is said, however, that the charterers are counting certain days twice over. In my judgment, this argument is fallacious.

A little later in his judgment, the judge said[47]:

As a broad, though not precise, test, it may be pointed out that the vessel could, for loading purposes have been retained at Sfax until Nov 12. If she had been, the voyage to Casablanca would then have occupied until approximately Nov 19. The lay days at Casablanca would have covered the period from then until approximately Nov 25 or 26. The vessel could therefore, for loading purposes, have been kept until such date without obligation to pay demurrage. In fact, loading was completed on Monday, Nov 10. There would, on this basis, be a saving of about 15 days.

---

43. *Ibid.*
44. *Fury Shipping Co Ltd* v. *State Trading Corporation of India Ltd (The Atlantic Sun)* [1972] 1 Lloyd's Rep 509, at p. 512.
45. *Themistocles (Owners)* v. *Compagnie Intercontinentale de L'Hyperphosphate of Tangier* (1948) 82 Ll L Rep 232.
46. *Ibid.*, at p. 240.
47. *Ibid.*

The Centrocon strike clause

7.30 The main parts of this clause have already been considered in some detail.[48] The last sentence of the clause, however, deals with how the excepted time should be treated for the purpose of working out despatch, and provides:

For the purpose, however, of settling despatch rebate accounts, any time lost by the Steamer through any of the above causes shall be counted as time used in loading or discharging.

The meaning of this part of the clause was considered by Donaldson J in *Navico AG* v. *Vrontados Naftiki Etairia PE*.[49] The *Costis*, the ship concerned, was ordered to load grain at Necochea and Bahia Blanca. On arrival at Necochea, she was unable to berth due to congestion and, although this was a port charter, under the rules then prevailing[50] laytime did not commence. It was not in dispute that congestion was one of the excepted causes under the Centrocon strike clause, but where the parties disagreed was to whether the despatch provision quoted above included time lost before laytime began. The owners argued simply that "any time lost" meant just that and drew support for their argument from the cases relating to the "time lost in waiting" provision in the Gencon form of charter.[51] On the other hand, the charterers said that the entitlement to despatch started with a calculation which takes as its start point the giving of Notice of Readiness, and this part of the clause was a defence to a claim so calculated. Deciding in favour of the charterers that the despatch provision did not apply to time lost before laytime commenced, Donaldson J said[52]:

The merits of the respective arguments are finely balanced, but, in my judgment, that of the charterers should prevail. I appreciate the force of the submission based upon the use of the words "any time lost" rather than "any laytime lost", but the decisive factor to my mind is the fact that the provision relating to dispatch is included in clause 30 [the Centrocon strike clause] and is not a separate clause.

The judge also pointed out[53] that the provision was in the nature of an exceptions clause operating on the *prima facie* entitlement to despatch and any doubt must therefore be resolved against the interests of the party seeking to rely upon the exception.

7.31 The general rule, therefore, seems to be that if the excepted cause arises after laytime has commenced then the shipowner has a defence to a claim for despatch; but if the excepted cause is operative on the vessel's arrival at the port and laytime does not commence, then this provision does not assist the shipowner. In the latter situation the crucial question therefore becomes whether the vessel can tender Notice of Readiness. Even if immediately thereafter laytime is suspended by virtue of the earlier parts of the strike clause, then the shipowner can resist a claim for despatch; but if he cannot give a Notice of Readiness then he has no protection.

7.32 One question that was raised in this case, but not decided, was: if this part of the clause does apply, is the time lost time measured in terms of running days or do the laytime exceptions apply so that the only time that counts is the time that would have

---

48. See *ante* at para. 4.312.
49. *Navico AG* v. *Vrontados Naftiki Etairia PE* [1968] 1 Lloyd's Rep 379.
50. As laid down in *Agrimpex Hungarian Trading Co for Agricultural Products* v. *Sociedad Financiera de Bienes Raices SA (The Aello)* [1960] 1 Lloyd's Rep 623 (HL). See *ante* at para. 3.90.
51. See *ante* at para. 3.377.
52. *Navico AG* v. *Vrontados Naftiki Etairia PE* [1968] 1 Lloyd's Rep 379, at p. 386.
53. *Ibid.*

counted against laytime? The answer, it is suggested, is the latter. It therefore becomes necessary to work out how time would have run had it not been for the excepted cause and then for the purposes of the despatch calculation apply it against the laytime allowed. Where the laytime allowed is measured in weather working days, the exceptions allowed will, it is submitted, include interruptions due to weather. In this respect, the calculation is therefore different to a despatch calculation, where the saving is measured in terms of laytime saved.[54]

7.33 An earlier version of the Centrocon strike clause omitted the last two words, so that time lost through any of the excepted causes was only to be counted as time used in loading. The effect of this was the point raised in *Chadwick Weir & Co Ltd* v. *Louis Dreyfus & Co.*[55] Here, there was a saving of time at the load port and the shipowner had paid despatch to the charterer on this. However, at the discharge port there was a strike, which caused discharge to be prolonged. The time lost was an excepted cause so no demurrage was payable, but the shipowner claimed that since the time so lost was to count as loading time, the despatch money should be repaid. He said that any advantage he might have got from getting his ship away earlier from the load port was lost by the delay at the discharge port. Rejecting that claim, Greer J said[56]:

> In the judgment of the umpire, and in my judgment, this clause with regard to the time lost by the steamer through any of the above causes being set up against the dispatch money only applies to the settlement of dispatch money accounts, which had to be settled by the charterers at the port of loading, where it is impossible to deduct anything except time which has been lost by any of those causes at the port of loading.

The judge also said that he was influenced in the interpretation he gave by the presence of a cesser clause, under which the charterers' liability was to cease after loading.

Delay after loading or discharging

7.34 In the *Owners of the Steamship Nolisement* v. *Bunge and Born*,[57] the owners claimed damages for detention for a delay which occurred after all the cargo had been loaded. Under the charter, despatch money was to be, and indeed was, paid for all time saved in loading. Whilst the owners were held entitled to the damages claimed, nevertheless the charterers were held entitled to retain the despatch money. In his judgment, Swinfen Eady LJ said[58]:

> . . . the charterers had earned and were entitled to retain the despatch money . . . The time was saved in loading. When once it is ascertained that $19\frac{1}{4}$ days were saved in loading the ship, then the despatch money became payable for that time; and the charterers were entitled to receive and retain it, although they might also be liable in damages for afterwards detaining the ship.

---

54. See *ante* at para. 7.2.
55. *Chadwick Weir & Co Ltd* v. *Louis Dreyfus & Co* (1923) 14 Ll L Rep 108.
56. *Ibid.*, at p. 110.
57. *The Owners of the Steamship Nolisement* v. *Bunge and Born* (1916) 22 CC 135 (CA).
58. *Ibid.*, at p. 142.

CHAPTER 8

Detention

8.1 A claim for detention will arise where a vessel is delayed by default of the charterer, or those for whom he is responsible, either on the approach voyage or carrying voyage, or at the port of loading or discharge. Unliquidated damages are recoverable for such delay, except where it occurs after the vessel has reached its specified destination and loading and/or discharging have not been completed, when any remaining laytime may be offset against the delay, or if the vessel is on demurrage, when demurrage will be payable.[1]

It is, however, quite common for the parties to agree that even where unliquidated damages are payable, these should be assessed at the demurrage rate, plus, if the delay occurs whilst the vessel is under way, the cost of additional bunkers consumed.[2] In *The Boral Gas* Evans J commented[3]:

> The agreed demurrage figure nevertheless may be regarded as the appropriate amount to award as unliquidated damages—this is a question of fact for the arbitrators to consider and decide.

Commenting on how the arbitrators had approached the problem in that case, he continued:

> ... they appear to reflect three possible but distinct approaches to the assessment of loss. The first ... is to consider whether the vessel would have earned more demurrage than she in fact did if she had ... proceeded ... without delay... Secondly the shipowners may say that if the first voyage had not been extended by the period of delay ... the vessel would have completed all ... voyages sooner, and the shipowners therefore lost eight days earnings after the charter was complete ... Thirdly the arbitrators could be invited to assess the actual loss caused by the delay which in fact occurred ...

8.2 It sometimes happens, particularly in the tanker trade, that a charterer asks a shipowner to interrupt the carrying voyage, either because there has been some obstacle in completing the contract or contracts of sale, or because he anticipates a more advantageous sale because the price of that commodity is rising, and agrees damages for the detention of the vessel thereby caused. Where this possibility is anticipated before the charter is executed, there may well be included an additional provision allowing, say, for the vessel to be detained for up to 30 days as floating storage. In such circumstances, payment for this period is usually made on the basis of a daily rate of hire, either inclusive or exclusive of additional bunkers consumed. In effect, the clause therefore turns the

---

1. For detention in relation to lightening, see *ante* at para. 4.457.
2. The demurrage rate usually includes an allowance for bunkers based on harbour consumption. The additional bunkers will be those required for propelling the vessel.
3. *Rashtriya Chemicals and Fertilizers Ltd* v. *Huddart Parker Industries Ltd*, (*The Boral Gas*) [1988] 1 Lloyd's Rep 342, at p. 346.

charter from a voyage charter into a time charter for the period of detention. This, however, is an exception to the normal unforeseen situation, where damages for detention are broadly comparable with demurrage.

8.3 In London Arbitration 12/90,[4] the question arose as to whether a clause providing for compensation for delay and/or deviation resulting from the charterers giving late orders or changing orders, to be paid for at the demurrage rate, was sufficient to cover a situation where, having loaded a cargo, the vessel was instructed to wait first 10 days before charterers nominated the discharge port and then a further 11 days before being instructed to proceed. In these circumstances the owners argued that they should be entitled to compensation reflecting the vessel's market rate which was twice the demurrage rate. However, the tribunal held that the clause was sufficient to cover the circumstances.

8.4 In *Harris and Dixon* v. *Marcus Jacobs & Co*,[5] Brett LJ described damages for detention as a payment "in the nature of demurrage". This description indicates the similarity in function of the two payments, which are both intended to compensate the shipowner for the delay suffered by his vessel.

8.5 Like demurrage, damages for detention are calculated on a running day basis, i.e. the laytime exceptions do not apply[6]; and neither normally will demurrage exceptions. For convenience, consideration of this topic will be divided up into delays occurring during the following periods:

    A. Before the vessel reaches its specified destination.

    B. During the running of laytime.

    C. During the running of demurrage (where provided for).

    D. After the end of laytime and/or demurrage.

    E. Delay by agreement.

Delay before the vessel reaches its specified destination

8.6 Such delays may occur on the approach or carrying voyage or, in the case of a berth or dock charter, prior to the vessel's arrival in berth or dock, as the case may be. However, most delays occur after the vessel has ceased to be under way, as the following cases show.

8.7 In a case called *Owners of the Breynton* v. *Theodoridi & Co*,[7] the delay occurred after the carrying voyage had commenced. What happened was that the *Breynton* had been chartered on a Chamber of Commerce Danube berth contract, which provided for her to load at "one or two safe places in the Danube not above Braila". The cargo so loaded was for carriage to London.

8.8 Having loaded at Braila and Tulcea, the *Breynton* proceeded over the bar of the River Danube to Constantza, where further cargo was loaded from lighters, taking some six days so to do, and it was for this period that the owners claimed the vessel had been detained. Under the charter, the master had the option, which he exercised, of asking for part of the cargo to be loaded outside the bar of the river from lighters because for her to have been loaded at the upriver ports would have meant that the vessel's draught would

4. London Arbitration 12/90—LMLN 286, 20 October 1990.
5. *Harris and Dixon* v. *Marcus Jacobs & Co* (1885) 15 QBD 247, at p. 251.
6. See, for example, London Arbitration 11/92—LMLN 324, 4 April 1992.
7. *Owners of the Breynton* v. *Theodoridi & Co* (1924) 20 Ll L Rep 314.

have been too much for her to get over the bar. The cost of lighterage was to be for the owners' account. However, the owners argued that because the cargo loaded by lighters came from Constantza, and not from the upriver ports, this was not what was intended in the charter. The Master of the Rolls, Sir Ernest Pollock, rejected this argument, however, saying of the meaning of lighterage[8]:

It means that although the cargo has not come down the river from the port above the Bar at which it might have been offered, although it is offered at a place more convenient to the vessel, yet when the cargo is so provided at Constantza it is to be treated as lighterage cargo, and for that purpose the cost and the delay caused by the transfer from lighters to the vessel shall fall on the owners.

8.9 In *Mikkelsen* v. *Arcos Ltd*,[9] a vessel was ordered from Leningrad to Yarmouth with a cargo of timber. After arriving at Yarmouth, the vessel was instructed to proceed to Boston, Lincs., which she did. The owners claimed, *inter alia*, for the time the vessel was detained at Yarmouth. Holding that the owners were justified, MacKinnon J said that in addition to payment for the voyage from Yarmouth to Boston for which reasonable remuneration should be made[10]:

I think that in that reasonable remuneration he is entitled to such payment as is reasonable for the service of keeping the goods in the ship while the arrangements for her going to Boston were being made.

Presumably, what was reasonable was the loss suffered by the shipowners, i.e. unliquidated damages.

8.10 In the days before instant communication with ships at sea became the norm, it was common for charters to include a provision that the vessel concerned should call at some intermediate port for further orders. It was usual for such a provision to provide that further orders should be given within 24 hours of receipt by the charterers of a cable from the master advising of arrival at the intermediate port. Failure to provide orders timeously meant the owners were entitled to claim damages for detention at a specified rate. In the *Ethel Radcliffe Steamship Co Ltd* v. *W R Barnett Ltd*[11] the charter concerned had such a provision. However, the charterers had not completed their arrangements for the sale of the cargo and they deliberately detained the vessel, accepting that they had to pay liquidated damages for the delay. The shipowners challenged this and sought damages at large.

8.11 In his judgment, Rowlatt J held that the charterers were not entitled to act as they did but nevertheless held that liquidated damages were payable. The significance of the fact that the charterers' breach was deliberate lay in that if it continued it would evince an intention by the charterers not to be bound by the charter, which repudiation the shipowners could accept. However, if the shipowners chose not to so act, then liquidated damages continued to be payable.

8.12 The case of the *Owners of Panaghis Vergottis* v. *William Cory & Son*[12] concerned a vessel under charter to load at Barry Dock under a dock charter. The vessel anchored at Barry Roads but was unable to gain admittance to the dock because the shipper failed to

---

8. *Ibid.*, at p. 315.
9. *Mikkelsen* v. *Arcos Ltd* (1925) 23 Ll L Rep 33.
10. *Ibid.*, at p. 35.
11. *Ethel Radcliffe Steamship Co Ltd* v. *W R Barnett Ltd* (1925) 23 Ll L Rep 2797.
12. *Owners of Panaghis Vergottis* v. *William Cory & Son* (1926) 25 Ll L Rep 64.

have one-third of the cargo available for loading, as required by the dock authority. Greer J held that the charterers were liable for the detention of the vessel because[13]:

I think there is an implied term in the charterparty that the defendants would do whatever was reasonable in order to enable the plaintiff's ship to get into the dock and so become an arrived ship.

8.13 A similar conclusion was reached in the Privy Council case of *Samuel Crawford Hogarth and others* v. *Cory Brothers & Co Ltd*.[14] There, the *Baron Ardrossan*, the ship concerned, was delayed getting into berth at Calcutta for a month and a half. The charter was a berth charter and the owners claimed the delay was because the charterers were not ready to load but the charterers claimed the delay was occasioned by causes for which they were not responsible. The Privy Council, however, held that the delay was due to a failure to furnish a cargo. Had cargo been available, the port authorities would have been able to furnish a berth.

8.14 Giving the judgment of the Judicial Committee, Lord Phillimore said[15]:

If a ship is prevented from getting to a loading berth owing to an obstacle created by the charterer, or owing to the default of the charterer in performing his duty, then it is well established that the shipowner has done all that is needful to bring the ship to the loading place, and that the charterer must pay for the subsequent delay.

Lord Phillimore also commented[16] that it did not appear to have been decided in previous cases whether the shipowner should receive damages for the delay or whether the lay days should be ante-dated, but the point did not arise for decision in this case because both sides accepted the decision of the appellate court in Bengal, from which the appeal came, which treated the question as one of damages. It is respectfully submitted that this approach is correct.

8.15 Another case concerning a delay arising out of a failure to give notice of the first load port was *Societa Ligure di Armamento* v. *Joint Danube & Black Sea Shipping Agencies of Braila*,[17] a decision of MacKinnon J. The delay was some four days 17 hours and the question was whether the charterers were entitled to use some of their allowed laytime against the time lost. In holding that the charterers were right and they were allowed to count the delay against laytime, the judge said that the deciding factor was the demurrage clause, which referred to demurrage being payable if the vessel was detained beyond the stipulated time. Since various times had been stipulated, including the time allowed for waiting for orders, it must mean the waiting time could be offset against laytime. The decision, however, is perhaps best seen as an interpretation of a particular charter, rather than establishing any general principle.

8.16 In *The Timna*,[18] the dispute concerned a delay arising from a failure by the charterers to nominate a discharge port in sufficient time to avoid the delay. The ship concerned was chartered on a Baltimore form C charterparty to carry grain from Norfolk, Virginia, to European ports. Part of the cargo was soya-bean meal for delivery at Bremen

---

13. *Ibid.*, at p. 67.
14. *Samuel Crawford Hogarth and others* v. *Cory Brothers & Co Ltd* (1926) 25 Ll L Rep 464 (PC).
15. *Ibid.*, at p. 468.
16. *Ibid.*, at p. 468.
17. *Societa Ligure di Armamento* v. *Joint Danube & Black Sea Shipping Agencies of Braila* (1931) 39 Ll L Rep 167.
18. *Zim Israel Navigation Co Ltd* v. *Tradax Export SA (The Timna)* [1971] 2 Lloyd's Rep 91 (CA).

and part maize for an unspecified destination. It was common ground that Bremen was intended as the second discharge port on approaching Land's End. At that time, the charterers instructed the vessel to proceed to the River Weser and said they would name which port later. On reaching the Weser light-vessel, at the mouth of the river, firm orders had still not been given. The following day, therefore, the master took the vessel upriver to Bremerhaven, but the charterers refused to accept the Notice of Readiness tendered there by the master, saying the vessel was intended for Brake, further upriver. However, the owners did not regard this as an order to proceed to Brake and the vessel remained at Bremerhaven waiting for orders, which were not received until some 16 days later. The owners claimed demurrage and/or detention. In the High Court Donaldson J held[19] that the demurrage claim failed. The vessel was never an Arrived ship at Bremerhaven and there was no room for an implied term that if the charterers failed to nominate the port of discharge within the time provided in the charter, or some further period thereafter, the master could himself make the nomination. However, he also held that the detention claim succeeded, a finding upheld by the Court of Appeal,[20] who held that to constitute a valid order to proceed to a port of discharge, the order must be a firm one. They also held that where a charterer fails to nominate a port of discharge, he is *prima facie* liable in damages and the shipowner does not have to prove that if the charterer had nominated that port the vessel could not get there.[21]

8.17 If a charterer delays in nominating the discharge port, the vessel concerned may have to reverse its track or otherwise alter course when the orders are received. In such a case, the shipowner is entitled to compensation for the extra distance steamed and time taken. The usual way of calculating this is to compare the actual route with the direct one, measure the additional mileage and, using the vessel's passage speed, ascertain the additional time taken. Although strictly speaking actual losses should be established, it is nevertheless common in practice to simply apply the additional time to the vessel's daily sea bunker consumption (giving allowance for harbour consumption which is included in the demurrage rate) to find the additional bunkers consumed, and apply the additional time to the demurrage rate to calculate the cost of the delay.

8.18 The vessel may be further delayed at the port of discharge because of the late nomination. For example, at Milford Haven, 48 hours' notice is required of the arrival of a VLCC. This is so that an appropriate number of tugs can be provided. A vessel coming north from Gibraltar heading towards Rotterdam might not be able to give this notice if nomination of Milford Haven was left to the last minute, with the result that the vessel might have to wait off Milford Haven. Whether such delay would give rise to a claim for damages for detention will, it is suggested, depend on whether the charter is a port or berth charter. If the latter, then a claim will lie, but if the former, then the charterer is entitled to offset any unused laytime or, if the vessel is on demurrage, then demurrage will be payable during the delay.

19. *Zim Israel Navigation Co Ltd* v. *Tradax Export SA (The Timna)* [1970] 2 Lloyd's Rep 409.
20. *Zim Israel Navigation Co Ltd* v. *Tradax Export SA (The Timna)* [1971] 2 Lloyd's Rep 91 (CA).
21. See also on the question of nomination of a discharge port *Gatoil Int Inc* v. *Tradax Petroleum Ltd (The Rio Sun)*, LMLN 127, 13 September 1984, and *Heinrich Hanno Co BV* v. *Fairlight Shipping Co Ltd; Hanse Schiffahrtskontor GmbH* v. *Andre SA (The Kostas K)*, LMLN 135, 3 January 1985.

8.19 In *The Delian Spirit*,[22] which concerned a "reachable on arrival" provision, where it was held that the vessel was an Arrived ship when she anchored in the roads to await a berth, Sir Gordon Willmer said[23]:

... I prefer to say no more upon the difficult question which might have arisen if the vessel had not been found to be an arrived ship at the time when she was lying in the Roads. But I certainly do not wish to be taken as accepting that, even in that situation, the owners would necessarily be entitled to prosecute an independent claim for damages, without giving credit for the laytime to which the charterers were entitled, and for which, as we have been reminded, they paid when they paid the freight.

8.20 However, in the other "reachable on arrival" cases which preceded *The Delian Spirit, The Angelos Lusis*[24] and *President Brand*,[25] Megaw J and Roskill J held that that was precisely what the owners were entitled to do, and despite the caveat entered by Sir Gordon Willmer, it is submitted that the puisne judges were indeed right. If laytime could be used to offset delays during the voyage stages of the charter, in the absence of any specific term so providing, then it would tend to erode the boundary between the voyage stages of the adventure and the loading/discharging operations,[26] which was something the House of Lords refused to allow in *The Maratha Envoy*,[27] when the Court of Appeal[28] sought to suggest that a vessel reached its specified destination under a port charter when it arrived at the usual waiting anchorage for that port, whether this was inside or outside the limits of the port.[29]

8.21 In *The Boral Gas*,[30] the owners let their vessel for eight consecutive voyages carrying anhydrous ammonia. Under the terms of the charter, the shippers were to supply ammonia for purging and pre-cooling. Three days after the vessel arrived, the charterers advised they had made arrangements with the shippers for purging and loading but it subsequently transpired they only made a contract to supply ammonia eight days after the vessel arrived. The vessel was kept waiting for a total of nine days. Under the terms of the charter Notice of Readiness could not be tendered until after purging and pre-cooling, so technically the delay occurred during the approach voyage stage of the charter.

8.22 In arbitration, a majority of the arbitrators held that the charterers were in breach by virtue of a failure by the shippers to provide ammonia for purging and pre-cooling and awarded eight days' damages for detention at the demurrage rate. On appeal, Evans J held that the charterers had undertaken to procure delivery by the shippers of the quantity of ammonia required within a reasonable time of receiving notice of the vessel's require-

---

22. *Shipping Developments Corporation SA* v. *V/O Sojuzneftexport (The Delian Spirit)* [1971] 1 Lloyd's Rep 506 (CA).

23. *Ibid.*, at p. 512.

24. *Sociedad Carga Oceanica SA* v. *Idolinoele Vertriebsgesellschaft mbH (The Angelos Lusis)* [1964] 2 Lloyd's Rep 28.

25. *Inca Compania Naviera SA and Commercial and Maritime Enterprises Evanghelos P Nomikos SA* v. *Mofinol Inc (The President Brand)* [1967] 2 Lloyd's Rep 338.

26. See the speech of Lord Diplock in *Oldendorff (EL) & Co GmbH* v. *Tradax Export SA (The Johanna Oldendorff)* [1973] 2 Lloyd's Rep 285, at p. 304, where his Lordship divided the adventure contemplated by a voyage charter into four successive stages.

27. *Federal Commerce and Navigation Co Ltd* v. *Tradax Export SA (The Maratha Envoy)* [1977] 2 Lloyd's Rep 301 (HL).

28. *The Maratha Envoy* [1977] 1 Lloyd's Rep 217 (CA).

29. See *ante* at para. 3.105. In *The Sea Wind* LMLN 531 16 March 2000, New York Arbitrators allowed two days demurrage and then damages for detention for breach of an always accessible clause in a berth charter. London Arbitrators would probably have allowed damages for detention for the whole period.

30. *Rashtriya Chemicals and Fertilizers Ltd* v. *Huddart Parker Industries Ltd (The Boral Gas)* [1988] 1 Lloyd's Rep 342.

ments. As he found this arose from the express terms of the charter, he declined to comment on a finding by a majority of the arbitrators for an alternative approach leading to the same conclusion by reference to an implied duty upon the charterers to co-operate in enabling the vessel to become an Arrived ship, based on the principles set out in *The Atlantic Sunbeam.*[31]

8.23 Having held the charterers liable, the judge remitted the matter back to the arbitrators to give further consideration to the amount to be awarded. In similar circumstances, it would seem prudent for the vessel to give notice of its requirements prior to arrival since the obligation on the charterers may well only be to procure pre-coolant within a reasonable period.

8.24 In London Arbitration 13/87,[32] the question arose as to whether the owners could claim their vessel was detained by the charterers where they had interrupted the voyage purporting to exercise a lien for unpaid freight. The charter in question related to the carriage of coal to Turkey and provided for 90 per cent freight to be paid within seven days of release of the bills of lading. Some 12 days after that period had expired, at which time the vessel was off Port Said, having passed through the Suez Canal, freight had still not been received and the owners ordered the vessel to anchor. They had previously been advised that exercise of their lien in Turkey was legally possible but not practical or commercially advisable. In fact had the vessel proceeded direct to Turkey and exercised a lien there of the same duration, the vessel would still have berthed at the same time. The arbitrators were, however, prepared to hold that the failure by the charterers to pay freight did amount to a detention of the vessel by them, although the orders to interrupt the voyage came from the owners, and that a lien for freight could be exercised short of the discharge port.

8.25 There have been a number of decisions as to whether the exercise by owners of a lien resulting in delay to the vessel during the carrying voyage can give rise to a claim for detention during the period of delay.

8.26 These appear to show that a lien can be exercised prior to arrival at the port where the cargo on which it is sought to exercise a lien is to be discharged if it can be shown that exercise of the lien at the discharge port would not be practical or commercially advisable, even though legally possible. However, the owners must show an actual loss as the result of the delay.

8.27 In *The Chrysovalandou Dyo,*[33] a case involving a time charter, Mocatta J rejected an assertion by charterers that for a lien to be exercised, there had to be a demand for possession of the cargo and therefore a lien could only be exercised when the vessel had reached the actual place of discharge. This, he said, would seriously limit the commercial value of any lien granted in a charter. The same principle would of course apply to a voyage charter.

8.28 In London Arbitration 12/91,[34] on similar facts, the owners failed because they could not show that had they not exercised their lien, the vessel would have completed the voyage any earlier. This was presumably a berth charter and the delay to the vessel during the voyage made no difference to when she actually completed the voyage stage of the

31. *Sunbeam Shipping Co Ltd* v. *President of India (The Atlantic Sunbeam)* [1973] 1 Lloyd's Rep 482, at p. 494. See also *ante* at paras 3.166 and 3.344.
32. London Arbitration 13/87—LMLN 205, 12 September 1987.
33. *The Chrysovalandou Dyo* [1981] 1 Lloyd's Rep 159.
34. London Arbitration 12/91—LMLN 304, 29 June 1991.

charter. The owners also failed to show that the delay made any difference to the vessel's next fixture.

Delay after arrival at the specified destination and during the running of laytime

8.29 If a breach of the charter or other default by the charterer results in the vessel being delayed after it has reached its specified destination, then the general rule is that damages for detention are not claimable and the charterer is entitled to apply his laytime against the delay.

8.30 In *The Delian Spirit*,[35] at first instance, Donaldson J had held that where the charterers were in breach of a "reachable on arrival" provision, the shipowners were entitled to claim damages and at the same time laytime continued to run, since the vessel had become an Arrived ship. The Court of Appeal,[36] however, said this would be wrong since the charterers would be made liable twice over—in damages and for demurrage once laytime had expired. In his judgment, Lord Denning said[37]:

The answer is given by a long line of cases which establish that where the charterers have been guilty of a breach causing delay, they are entitled to apply their laytime so as to diminish or extinguish any claim for the delay, leaving the shipowners to claim for demurrage at the agreed rate for any extra delay over and above the laytime. The reason is because they have bought their laytime and paid for it in the freight, and are entitled to use it in the way which suits them best, and in particular to use it so as to wipe out or lessen any delay for which they would otherwise be responsible.

Amongst the cases cited by Lord Denning were *Inverkip Steamship Co Ltd* v. *Bunge & Co*[38]; *Margaronis Navigation Agency Ltd* v. *Henry W Peabody & Co of London Ltd*[39]; and *Inca Compania Naviera SA, Commercial and Maritime Enterprises Evanghelos P Nomikos SA* v. *Mofinol Inc (The President Brand)*[40] and London Arbitration 20/92.[41]

8.31 In *Inverkip Steamship Co Ltd* v. *Bunge & Co*, Scrutton LJ said[42]:

One main argument of the shipowners' counsel as I understood it was that as the charterer was bound to have a cargo ready for loading, and had not such a cargo, the demurrage provision did not apply. This is in my experience an entirely novel argument. Ships with 20 lay days have frequently loaded no cargo for, say, 12 days because none was there and either finished in their lay days or in some demurrage days; but it has never been contended or understood to be the law that because there was no cargo there when the ship was ready to load the charterer had lost the benefit of the demurrage days or lay days and was bound to load in a reasonable time or pay damages for detention . . .

In *The President Brand*, Roskill J said[43]:

---

35. *Shipping Developments Corporation SA* v. *V/O Sojuzneftexport (The Delian Spirit)* [1971] 1 Lloyd's Rep 64.
36. *Shipping Developments Corporation SA* v. *V/O Sojuzneftexport (The Delian Spirit)* [1971] 1 Lloyd's Rep 506 (CA).
37. *Ibid.*, at p. 509.
38. *Inverkip Steamship Co Ltd* v. *Bunge & Co* [1917] 2 KB 193 (CA).
39. *Margaronis Navigation Agency Ltd* v. *Henry W Peabody & Co of London Ltd* [1964] 2 Lloyd's Rep 153.
40. *Inca Compania Naviera SA and Commercial and Maritime Enterprises Evanghelos P Nomikos SA* v. *Mofinol Inc (The President Brand)* [1967] 2 Lloyd's Rep 338.
41. London Arbitration 20/92—LMLN 328, 30 May 1992.
42. *Inverkip Steamship Co Ltd* v. *Bunge & Co* [1917] 2 KB 193, at p. 202.
43. *The President Brand* [1967] 2 Lloyd's Rep 338, at p. 352.

... it is trite commercial law that a charterer is entitled to the laytime for which his contract provides. If he is to be deprived by one clause of that which is expressly given by another clause, very, very clear words indeed would be required to produce that startling result. I think that the charterers are entitled to the benefit of all the time from the time notice of readiness was given ...

It should be noted that Roskill J refers to the time when notice is given and not when it takes effect. The charterers are therefore entitled to use not just their laytime to offset any delay, but laytime as extended by any period before the Notice of Readiness takes effect and by any excepted periods.

8.32 This point is illustrated by the facts of *The World Navigator*,[44] a commodity case. Put simply this involved a f.o.b. contract for the sale of maize to be loaded at Rosario on the Parana River. The vessel nominated by the buyers was the *World Navigator*. Under the terms of the contract, the buyers were to give the sellers at least 15 days' Notice of Readiness to load.

8.33 The vessel reached Zona Commun off Buenos Aires on 13 June 1985 and tendered Notice of Readiness to load. (Under the sale contract this she was apparently entitled to do, notwithstanding that Zona Commun is approximately 250 miles downriver from Rosario.) Had there not been a problem with the shippers' documentation she would have berthed at Rosario on 25 June and, even though that was before the 15 days expired, laytime would have commenced on arrival in berth. Because of problems over the documentation, some six vessels loaded ahead of her and she did not in fact berth until 18 July, completing loading of the relevant cargo on 22 July.

8.34 The buyers claimed that the sellers were in breach of their obligations in not having the goods ready to load at the time the vessel would have been ready to receive them, 25 June, and they claimed as damages for detention what they, the buyers had to pay by way of demurrage to the owners of the *World Navigator* for the period between that date and completion of loading on 18 July.

8.35 The sellers said they were not in breach of any obligation and that even if they were, the buyers had suffered no loss because even if the vessel had kept her turn on 25 June, laytime would not have expired by the time loading was complete on 18 July.

8.36 The Court of Appeal considered three issues. The one that is relevant to this section of the book is: on what basis should damages be assessed if the sellers were in breach?

8.37 The buyers contended that the proper course was to consider what would probably have happened had there been no breach. On that basis, given that loading took only four days, had she berthed on 25 June or shortly after loading would have been completed by 1 July. Therefore in relation to the period between 25 June and 18 July, their loss was the demurrage they paid between 1 and 18 July.

8.38 This argument was rejected by the Court of Appeal who held that the sellers were entitled to the whole of their laytime and, since that would not have expired even if the vessel had berthed promptly, the buyers' claim failed.

8.39 A somewhat unusual set of circumstances arose in London Arbitration 5/93.[45] Here the charterers had difficulty in providing all the cargo promptly at the loading port. After the ship had been loading for about a day, the owners threatened to sail because they feared delay in providing further cargo. Because of the threats, the charterers agreed to pay

44. *The World Navigator* [1991] 2 Lloyd's Rep 23 (CA).
45. London Arbitration 5/93—LMLN 351, 17 April 1993.

detention until the ship sailed. However, in arbitration they were able to avoid this agreement on the grounds of economic duress.

8.40 A different conclusion was reached in at least one decision of New York arbitrators in a case called *The Sugar Islander.*[46] What happened here was that the vessel presented Notice of Readiness to the charterers' agents at the opening of the laycan spread, which was accepted. However, the grain terminal from which the vessel was to load refused to call the vessel forward to load because the appropriate letters of credit were not in place. As a result, the vessel remained idle for two weeks. The tribunal concluded that the owners' losses resulted from a breach of the third party contract between the charterers and the shippers. They therefore concluded:

Parties to a contract owed a good faith obligation to co-operate in the venture to mutual benefit. The rapid loading and despatch of the vessel would have been beneficial to both owner and charterer. The owners would have had the vessel in position for her next cargo 16 days earlier had the charterers obtained the release of the cargo in a timely manner as it was their obligation to do.

Delays to vessels attributable to circumstances beyond the control of charterers, i.e. port congestion, strikes, etc., unless otherwise provided for in the applicable charterparty fell within the laytime provisions of the charter. Delays due to charterers' breach of their obligations to provide the cargo to a vessel tendering within laydays and ready to load were not normal or reasonable and resulted in claims for detention damages based not upon laytime but rather on the measure of loss or damage. The present case fell into the latter category.

Whilst that may have been a just result in this particular case, it is suggested that had the case been tried before London arbitrators, the result would have been that the owners would have lost because of the authorities quoted above.

Delay during the running of demurrage

8.41 It is now generally accepted that demurrage payments are payments of liquidated damages for delay beyond the laytime allowed during the loading and discharging operations. As such, demurrage is an exclusive remedy and the shipowner is properly compensated for any delay by the payment of demurrage.[47]

Delay after the end of laytime and/or demurrage

8.42 In customary laytime charters, it is comparatively unusual for the charter to provide for demurrage to be payable and, since by definition the laytime allowed[48] is such time as is reasonable in the circumstances, the only delay for which the shipowner is entitled to be compensated is any period by which loading or discharging, as the case may be, has been unreasonably extended. For such period the shipowner is entitled to claim damages for detention, if this is through the default of the charterer.

8.43 In a fixed laytime charter, demurrage may either be payable for a fixed period[49] or an indefinite period. If the charter provides for a fixed period, then a claim for detention

---

46. *California and Hawaiian Sugar Co* v. *The National Cereal and Produce Board of Kenya (The Sugar Islander)* (NY Arb), LMLN 318, 11 January 1992.
47. For a discussion on the exclusivity of demurrage as a remedy, see *ante* at para. 6.26.
48. See *ante* at para. 2.278.
49. See *ante* at para. 6.9.

arises for any time after this has expired until the completion of loading or discharging.

8.44 In both sorts of charter, there may be delays after the loading or discharging operations are complete, when again the shipowner may claim for detention if he can show that this arises from the default of the charterer.

8.45 The cases which follow are instances where such delays have occurred.

8.46 In *Lyle Shipping Co Ltd* v. *Corporation of Cardiff*,[50] the shipowner let his ship on a charter which provided for customary laytime at Cardiff, the discharge port. By a custom of the port, the cargo was discharged into railway wagons. Any wagons could be employed, but it was usual to contract with one railway company to supply all the wagons needed to discharge a particular vessel. The indorsees of the bill of lading, whose terms included those of the charter, entered into an arrangement with a railway company in order to take delivery of the cargo, under which the cargo would be carried in the company's wagons from the ship's side to a depot. Unfortunately owing to a press of work, the railway company did not supply sufficient wagons, and the discharge of the vessel was thereby delayed by some 22 working days. The shipowner claimed damages for detention for this period. However, the Court of Appeal held, affirming the decision of the court below, that the claim failed as the defendants, the indorsees of the bill of lading, "did their best to get the appliances which were available at the port at the time, and which were customarily used for the purpose of discharging vessels". In other words, there was no default of cargo interests and the delay was one of the ordinary incidences of risk in the particular port at that time, which therefore fell to the account of the shipowner under a customary laytime charter.

8.47 A different form of delay arose for consideration by the Court of Appeal in the *Owners of the Steamship Nolisement* v. *Bunge and Born*.[51] This concerned the right of the charterers to detain a vessel further once loading had been completed. In this case, loading was completed within eight days, being some 19 days before laytime expired. On completion of loading, the master applied to the charterers for his bills of lading and orders as to destination, but they were not forthcoming for three days, as the charterers had not made up their minds as to where the vessel should proceed. *By concession*, the parties agreed that 24 hours' delay was reasonable, but the shipowners claimed damages for the further two days.

8.48 The court held that the charterers had no right to detain the steamer, after her loading was completed, for the full period of the lay days, and that they were under an obligation to present bills of lading for the master's signature within a reasonable time after the ship was loaded, and that as the charterers had not done so, they had committed a breach of contract and were liable for the detention of the vessel.

8.49 In the tanker trade, it is customary to allow a short period of one or two hours for the necessary documentation relating to loading to be produced. Such a period is not laytime, but is in effect a free period of detention. If the documentation is not provided within this period, then a claim will usually lie for the excess period.[52] A claim for

---

50. *Lyle Shipping Co Ltd* v. *Corporation of Cardiff* (1900) 5 CC 397 (CA).
51. *Owners of the Steamship Nolisement* v. *Bunge and Born* (1916) 22 CC 135 (CA).
52. Some tanker charters contain specific provisions relating to the time allowed for production of documentation. For a discussion on this and other aspects relating to the end of loading generally, see *ante* at Chapter 5, at paras 5.26 (dry cargo) and 5.47 (tankers).

detention may also be appropriate where discharge continues after ballasting begins where the vessel concerned is chartered on an STB form of charter.[53]

8.50 In the *Owners of the Spanish Steamship Sebastian* v. *Sociedad Altos Hornos de Vizcaya*,[54] the vessel was delayed for a different reason. The case involved the shipment of coal from Norfolk, Virginia, to Spain. After the charter had been entered into, but before loading commenced, the United States Government prohibited the export of coal to Spain without a licence. This was not forthcoming until almost 15 days after loading was complete, despite the efforts of the charterers' agents, who were also the shippers' and owners' agents, to get it earlier. Loading was completed within the allowed laytime, but the owners claimed damages for detention, or alternatively, demurrage for the delay thereafter. In his judgment, Bailhache J said[55]:

In these circumstances it seems to me that the position of the charterers was this: They had become bound to obtain this licence, and it was their duty to obtain it without unreasonable delay, and the arbitrators have set down that they did procure the licence to export this coal from the United States to Spain without any delay; that they did all that was necessary to proceed with the matter, and in these circumstances it appears to me impossible to hold that the delay in this case should fall on the charterers rather than on the shipowners.

8.51 It would therefore seem that where, on completion of loading or discharging, some further step must be taken by the charterers to enable the vessel to sail, or permission obtained, the duty of the charterers is to take all reasonable steps to enable the ship to sail as soon as possible, but that the period of delay whilst these are taken if not unreasonable will not form the basis of a claim for detention. Presumably, the level of diligence required by the charterers would be the same as that required to enable a vessel to become an Arrived ship.[56] In this latter context, in *The Atlantic Sunbeam*, Kerr J said[57]:

A requirement of a high standard of initiative, let alone any excessive zeal, cannot be implied in a situation of this nature, however much one would like to see it used. Something of that kind would require an express term. If, for instance, there were two procedures in a certain port whereby a vessel's documentation can be dealt with, one on paying an expedition fee or taking some special steps, and the other one the ordinary procedure, then it seems to me that the charterers would be under no implied obligation to use the speedier and unusual procedure.

8.52 It should be noted that it is only where the fault of the charterers or those for whom they are responsible exists that a claim for damages may be presented. Whether charterers should be responsible for delay caused by cargo consignees was the issue in London Arbitration 12/87[58] where sailing of the vessel was delayed for 28 hours after discharge was complete. It seems the consignees asked owners' agents to delay clearance of the vessel, possibly in order to verify the condition and quantity of the cargo that had been discharged.

---

53. See *ante* at para. 4.38 and para. 5.65.
54. *Owners of the Spanish Steamship Sebastian* v. *Sociedad Altos Hornos de Vizcaya* (1919) 1 Ll L Rep 500.
55. *Ibid.*, at p. 501.
56. See *ante* at para. 3.166.
57. *Sunbeam Shipping Co Ltd* v. *President of India (The Atlantic Sunbeam)* [1973] 1 Lloyd's Rep 482, at p. 488. But see the comments of Staughton LJ in *The World Navigator* [1991] 2 Lloyd's Rep 23 at p. 30, quoted at para. 3.345 as to whether the obligation on the charterers in respect of arrival is an absolute one, as suggested in *The Aello* [1960] 1 Lloyd's Rep 623, or one of reasonable diligence/best endeavours, as suggested in this case. This of course leaves open the question whether any obligation relating to departure is the same as that relating to arrival.
58. London Arbitration 12/87—LMLN 204, 29 August 1987.

8.53 The question was whether the charterers were liable for the improper intervention of the consignees. On this, the arbitrators held the charterers were only liable for those acts of the consignees where they were ones which under the charter fell to be performed by the charterers, such as loading or unloading. In this case, the charterers' obligations ceased on completion of discharge and whatever happened thereafter was not their responsibility. The owners' claim therefore failed.

8.54 If, however, there was unreasonable delay, then it must follow that the shipowners would have a claim for detention for the excess period.

8.55 In *J C Carras & Sons (Shipbrokers) Ltd* v. *President of India (The Argobeam)*,[59] the owners claimed damages for the period of delay taken to put the vessel back in a seaworthy trim after lightening part of a cargo of grain. The relevant clause in the charter provided for the vessel to be left "in seaworthy trim to shift between ports". However, Mocatta J held that this meant that the charterers had to pay the expense of so doing, not that the owners were entitled to compensation for the time taken. In so finding, the judge followed the earlier Court of Appeal decision in *Chandris* v. *Government of India*,[60] where the owners unsuccessfully sought to argue in relation to a similar provision that discharge was not complete until the vessel was put into a seaworthy trim.[61]

8.56 In *The Boukadora*,[62] the dispute concerned a disagreement about the quantity of cargo to be shown in the bills of lading. Charterers presented inaccurate figures and refused to accept the master's qualification of them. In the High Court, Evans J held that the indemnity provision in the charter, which was on the STB Voy form, included liability for delay caused by the presentation of inaccurate figures. The charterers were therefore liable for the delay. It should be noted however that there was an express finding that the actions of the master had been reasonable throughout.

8.57 In London Arbitration 6/92,[63] a dispute arose as to whether the charterers should be liable to pay for the delay whilst a draft survey was carried out after loading. As the survey had been organized by the charterers, who also paid for it, it was reasonable that they should meet the cost of the delay to the vessel since the laytime clock stopped on completion of loading.

Delay by agreement

8.58 Detention is by definition an involuntary delay. However, as already mentioned,[64] it does sometimes happen that owners agree to a delay usually during the approach or carrying voyages.

8.59 Whilst remuneration for such delay is often at the demurrage rate, an illustration of where a different rate was held to be applicable is provided by *The Saronikos*.[65]

8.60 The facts of the case were simple. The vessel was chartered for the carriage of bagged sugar from Antwerp to Aqaba. At the request of the charterers the vessel waited

59. *J C Carras & Sons (Shipbrokers) Ltd* v. *President of India (The Argobeam)* [1970] 1 Lloyd's Rep 282.
60. *Chandris* v. *Government of India* [1956] 1 Lloyd's Rep 11 (CA).
61. For a further discussion on both these cases, see *ante* at paras 5.38 and 5.41.
62. *Boukadora Maritime Corporation* v. *Société Anonyme Marocaine de L'Industrie et du Raffinage (The Boukadora)* [1989] 1 Lloyd's Rep 393.
63. London Arbitration 6/92—LMLN 321, 22 February 1992.
64. See *ante* at para. 8.2. See also London Arbitration 12/90—LMLN 286, 20 October 1990.
65. *Greenmast Shipping Co SA* v. *Jean Lion et Cie SA (The Saronikos)* [1986] 2 Lloyd's Rep 277.

off Aqaba for about nine days to resolve problems that had arisen over the sale of the
cargo.

8.61 It was common ground that the owners were entitled to reasonable remuneration
but the issue was the basis on which it should be assessed. An important fact was that the
demurrage rate was less than the running costs of the vessel, although the arbitrators found
that the vessel could have been traded at that time on the market at a profit. They also
found that if the vessel had not been delayed but had proceeded straight to Aqaba and the
same delay had occurred there, the vessel would still have completed discharge before
laytime expired. The arbitrators therefore held that the owners were only entitled to the
cost of extra bunkers consumed whilst steaming off Aqaba during the period of delay.

8.62 The arbitrators' approach was criticized by Saville J in the High Court, who drew
a distinction based on an earlier Court of Appeal decision in *Steven v. Bromley & Son*,[66]
where charterers had loaded a mixed cargo of steel billets and general merchandise
although they had contracted to load only steel billets and the owners were held entitled
to freight at a higher rate for the general merchandise. The important distinction made in
that case and applied by Saville J in *The Saronikos* was that if the claim is based on breach
of contract the owners can only claim their actual loss however that be assessed, but if the
claim is based on an implied contract for a *quantum meruit* they are entitled to a fair
commercial rate for the use of the vessel outside the terms of the charterparty. On the facts
of the particular case the judge held that the owners were entitled to their running costs,
the extra bunker costs plus the profit margin they could have traded the vessel at, at the
time the vessel was delayed.

8.63 Depending on the circumstances of the case, therefore, it may be that an owner
might be entitled to more remuneration where the delay arises from agreement than when
it is involuntary.

Exception clauses

8.64 As already mentioned, laytime and demurrage exceptions do not normally apply to
claims for detention. However, it is possible to exclude such claims by an appropriate
wording. Thus, in the Scottish case of *Moor Line Ltd* v. *Distillers Co Ltd*,[67] which
concerned the carriage of grain from Russia to Scotland, the charter involved contained a
clause which provided that "in case of any delay by reason of" a strike "no claim for
damages" shall be made. The charter also specified a limited time on demurrage and it
was demurrage that the shipowners claimed, the question being principally whether a
claim for demurrage was a claim for damages, which the court held it was. However, in
the course of his judgment, Lord Salvesen said of both claims for demurrage and
detention[68]:

A claim under either head is a claim in respect of detention, and is in the nature of a claim of
damages.

The wording of this clause would therefore seem sufficient to exclude claims for
detention, provided the necessary causal connection can be established.

---

66. *Steven* v. *Bromley & Son* [1919] 2 KB 722 (CA).
67. *Moor Line Ltd* v. *Distillers Co Ltd*, 1912 SC 514.
68. *Ibid.*, at p. 520.

Lien for damages for detention

8.65 Although a period when demurrage is payable is a period of detention, it does not mean that the two are the same; and therefore it follows that if a charter contains a provision giving a lien for demurrage over the cargo carried, this does not usually entitle the shipowner to exercise a lien over the cargo in respect of a claim for detention. Since he cannot so do, then any cesser clause will be ineffective as regards a claim for detention if the only lien granted is one for demurrage. These conclusions have been affirmed by the courts in a series of cases, including *Gray* v. *Carr*,[69] *Lockhart* v. *Falk*,[70] *Gardiner* v. *Macfarlane, M'Crindell & Co*,[71] *Clink* v. *Radford & Co*[72] and *Dunlop & Sons* v. *Balfour, Williamson & Co*,[73] the last two being decisions of the Court of Appeal.

8.66 In *Clink* v. *Radford & Co*, Lord Esher MR said of the lien given for freight and demurrage[74]:

The word "demurrage" must mean demurrage as used in the charterparty; that is, as I have just stated, demurrage at the port of discharge, and the shipowner has no lien according to this charterparty in respect of detention of the ship at the port of loading.

8.67 However, a possible exception to the rule that a lien for demurrage does not include a lien for detention was suggested by Lord Esher MR in *Dunlop & Sons* v. *Balfour, Williamson & Co*, where he said[75]:

If there were nothing else in the charterparty to which the word demurrage would be applicable, it may be—though I do not say it would be—that the court would then be obliged to say that the lien for demurrage must apply to such uncalculated damages. But there is in the charterparty a matter to which the lien can apply, and it cannot be a proper mode of construction to say that, where there is that to which the lien can fitly apply, it is also to be applicable to something to which in ordinary circumstances it would not be applicable.

69. *Gray* v. *Carr* (1871) LR 6 QB 522.
70. *Lockhart* v. *Falk* (1875) LR 10 Ex 132.
71. *Gardiner* v. *Macfarlane, M'Crindell & Co* (1889) 26 Sc LR 492.
72. *Clink* v. *Radford & Co* [1891] 1 QB 625 (CA).
73. *Dunlop & Sons* v. *Balfour, Williamson & Co* [1892] 1 QB 507 (CA).
74. *Clink* v. *Radford & Co* [1891] 1 QB 625, at p. 629.
75. *Dunlop & Sons* v. *Balfour, Williamson & Co* [1892] 1 QB 507, at p. 519.

CHAPTER 9

Frustration

9.1 As Lord Atkinson said in *Larrinaga Steamship Co* v. *Société Franco-Américaine*[1]:

The phrase "frustration of a contract" is an incorrect phrase. It is the performance of the contract which is frustrated, with the result that the contract itself is thereby dissolved.

9.2 Whether or not a charter is frustrated is a question of law. The date, however, on which it became frustrated, if in dispute, is a question of fact and therefore to be determined by the arbitrators or other fact-finding tribunal.

9.3 In *Tsakiroglou & Co* v. *Noblee Thorl GmbH*,[2] the House of Lords had to consider a dispute which arose out of the closing of the Suez Canal, as a result of which the sellers of a cargo of Sudanese groundnuts refused to ship them, claiming the contract was frustrated. An appeal board upheld an award by an umpire in arbitration proceedings, who had found that shipping the cargo around the Cape of Good Hope,[3] instead of through the Suez Canal, was not commercially or fundamentally different. However, the House of Lords refused to accept this as a finding of fact, since it involved a question of law, although apparently accepting that the finding had evidential value.

9.4 More recently, however, there appears to have been a change of emphasis. Thus, in *Pioneer Shipping* v. *BTP Tioxide*, Lord Roskill said[4]:

My Lords, when it is shown on the face of a reasoned award that the appointed tribunal has applied the right legal test, the court should in my view only interfere if on the facts found as applied to that right legal test, no reasonable person could have reached that conclusion. It ought not to interfere merely because the court thinks that upon those facts and applying that test, it would not or might not itself have reached the same conclusion, for to do that would be for the court to usurp what is the sole function of the tribunal of fact.

9.5 Lord Roskill then went on[5] to suggest that in some of the reported cases the court had erred in imposing its own view and that, in future, the court should be more reluctant to interfere unless the wrong test had been used, or the conclusion was one which no reasonable person could have reached on the facts found.

9.6 In *The Evia*,[6] the House of Lords also refused to decide when a particular charter had become frustrated, although in several similar disputes arising out of the same

---

1. *Larrinaga Steamship Co* v. *Société Franco-Américaine* (1923) 29 CC 1, at p. 12.
2. *Tsakiroglou & Co* v. *Noblee Thorl GmbH* [1962] AC 93 (HL).
3. In *Denny, Mott & Dickson Ltd* v. *Jas B Fraser & Co* [1944] AC 265 (HL), Lord Wright said, at p. 276: "The event is something which happens in the world of fact, and has to be found as a fact by the judge. Its effect on the contract depends on the meaning of the contract, which is a matter of law."
4. *Pioneer Shipping Ltd* v. *BTP Tioxide Ltd (The Nema)* [1981] 3 WLR 292, at p. 312.
5. *Ibid.*, at p. 313.
6. *Kodros Shipping Corporation* v. *Empresa Cubana de Fletes (The Evia)* [1982] 3 WLR 637 (HL).

circumstances, different dates had been chosen by different arbitrators. On this occasion, Lord Roskill commented[7]:

The discharge of cargo may have been completed on a different date. The several masters, officers and crew may have left their ships on different dates. A host of differing factors may have arisen, and in common with all your Lordships I resolutely decline to investigate the facts found in other cases to see which choice of date is to be preferred. The choice of date in this case, as in the others, was for the umpire or arbitrator concerned and is not a matter for your Lordships' House.

9.7 In a voyage charter, laytime, and demurrage thereafter, will normally run until loading or discharging, as the case may be, has been completed or until the contract becomes frustrated. It is, of course, with this latter possibility that this section is concerned.

9.8 In broad terms, there are three types of event which may prevent further performance:

    A. Destruction of the Ship or Cargo.

    B. Inordinate Delay.

    C. Illegality.

9.9 Before discussing these in more detail, it may be useful to say something about the basis of the doctrine of frustration, since there appears to have been a change of judicial thinking. Up to about 1940, many of the cases proceed on the basis of an implied term. In *Tamplin Steamship Co* v. *Anglo Mexican Petroleum Co*, having said that a court has no power to change a contract, Earl Loreburn continued[8]:

. . . a court can and ought to examine the contract and the circumstances in which it was made, not of course to vary it, but only to explain it, in order to see whether or not from the nature of it the parties must have made their bargain on the footing that a particular thing or state of things would continue to exist. And if they must have done so, then a term to that effect will be implied, though it be not expressed in the contract.

In a similar vein, Lord Sumner said in *Bank Line Ltd* v. *Arthur Capel & Co*[9]:

The theory of dissolution of a contract by the frustration of its commercial object rests on an implication, which arises from the presumed common intention of the parties.

9.10 An early criticism of the implied term theory came from Lord Wright in *Fibrosa Spolka Akcyjna* v. *Fairbairn, Lawson*, where he said[10]:

No one who reads the reported cases can ignore how inveterate is this theory or explanation in English law. I do not see any objection to this mode of expression so long as it is understood that what is implied is what the court thinks the parties ought to have agreed on the basis of what is fair and reasonable, not what as individuals they would or might have agreed.

9.11 In *Denny, Mott & Dickson Ltd* v. *Jas B Fraser & Co*, Lord Wright again took up the same theme, saying[11]:

To my mind, the theory of the implied condition is not really consistent with the true theory of frustration. It has never been acted on by the court as a ground of decision, but is merely stated as a theoretical explanation . . .

---

7. *Ibid.*, at p. 660.
8. *Tamplin Steamship Co* v. *Anglo Mexican Petroleum Co* [1916] 2 AC 397, at p. 403.
9. *Bank Line Ltd* v. *Arthur Capel & Co* [1919] AC 435, at p. 455.
10. *Fibrosa Spolka Akcyjna* v. *Fairbairn, Lawson* [1943] AC 32, at p. 70.
11. *Denny, Mott & Dickson Ltd* v. *Jas B Fraser & Co* [1944] AC 265, at p. 276.

In *The Eugenia*, Lord Denning MR said, with characteristic directness[12]:

The theory of an implied term has now been discarded by everyone, or nearly everyone, for the simple reason that it does not represent the truth.

9.12 More recently, the basis of the doctrine of frustration has been considered by the House of Lords in a non-maritime case, *National Carriers Ltd* v. *Panalpina Ltd*.[13] In his speech,[14] Lord Hailsham LC suggested that at least five theories had been put forward at various times. Lord Simon of Glaisdale said, more simply[15]:

... a number of theories have been advanced to clothe the doctrine of frustration in juristic respectability, the two most in favour being the "implied term theory" (which was potent in the development of the doctrine and which still provides a satisfactory explanation of many cases) and the "theory of a radical change in obligation" or "construction theory" (which appears to be the one most generally accepted today).

9.13 It seems likely that no one theory can explain all the reported cases, although the "construction theory" explains most. This view was first put forward in *Davis Contractors Ltd* v. *Fareham Urban District Council*, where Lord Radcliffe said[16]:

... frustration occurs whenever the law recognizes that without default of either party a contractual obligation has become incapable of being performed because the circumstances in which performance is called for would render it a thing different from that which was undertaken by the contract. *Non haec in foedera veni*—It was not this that I promised to do.

9.14 This encapsulation was cited with approval by Lord Hailsham LC in the *National Carriers* case[17] and by Lord Roskill in *The Nema*,[18] where he said:

It should therefore be unnecessary in future cases, where issues of frustration of contracts arise, to search back among the many earlier decisions in this branch of the law when the doctrine was in its comparative infancy. The question in these cases is not whether one case resembles another, but whether, applying Lord Radcliffe's enunciation of the doctrine, the facts of the particular case under consideration do or do not justify the invocation of the doctrine, always remembering that the doctrine is not lightly to be invoked to relieve contracting parties of the normal consequences of imprudent commercial bargains.

A. Destruction of ship or cargo

9.15 In *D/S A/S Gulnes* v. *ICI Ltd*,[19] the *Gulnes* was chartered by ICI to carry ore from Spain to Manchester. A marginal clause provided:

If Steamer is detained at San Juan by any cause arising from the civil war in Spain, riots, strikes &c., charterers agree to pay demurrage and/or dead freight.

After arrival at the load berth, the vessel was hit by a bomb, before loading commenced and suffered such extensive damage that she was eventually towed to Gibraltar to be

---

12. *The Eugenia* [1964] 2 QB 226, at p. 238.
13. *National Carriers Ltd* v. *Panalpina (Northern) Ltd* [1981] 2 WLR 45 (HL). The case concerned the application of the doctrine of frustration to a lease on property.
14. *Ibid.*, at p. 51.
15. *Ibid.*, at p. 65.
16. *Davis Contractors Ltd* v. *Fareham Urban District Council* [1956] AC 696, at p. 729.
17. *National Carriers Ltd* v. *Panalpina (Northern) Ltd* [1981] 2 WLR 45, at p. 52.
18. *Pioneer Shipping Ltd* v. *BTP Tioxide (The Nema)* [1981] 3 WLR 292, at p. 312.
19. *D/S A/S Gulnes* v. *ICI Ltd* (1937) 59 Ll L Rep 144.

scrapped. Rejecting the owners' claim for deadfreight, demurrage and/or damages for detention, Goddard J said[20]:

I think we have here a case which brings it within the ambit of the line of cases of which *Taylor* v. *Caldwell*[21] is a leading example. Here you have a frustration by the destruction of the subject-matter which the parties must have contemplated would always remain in existence. I do not think this clause makes provision for the destruction or damaging of the ship to such an extent that it no longer remains a cargo-carrying ship.

9.16 In *Imperial Smelting Corporation Ltd* v. *Joseph Constantine Steamship Line Ltd*,[22] the charterers claimed damages for a failure by a vessel called the *Kingswood* to load their cargo. On arrival at the load port, prior to the vessel becoming an Arrived ship, there was a major explosion in the vicinity of the auxiliary boiler, which caused such damage that she could not perform the charterparty, which the owners claimed was frustrated. The cause of the explosion was uncertain and the main issue between the parties was whether the onus lay on the owners to show that it happened without their fault. The House of Lords were in no doubt that the onus lay on the party who asserted there was fault. Viscount Simon LC said[23]:

In this connection it is well to emphasize that when "frustration" in the legal sense occurs, it does not merely provide one party with a defence in an action brought by the other: it kills the contract itself and discharges both parties automatically. The plaintiff sues for breach at a past date and the defendant pleads that at that date no contract existed. In this situation the plaintiff could only succeed if it were shown that the determination of the contract was due to the defendant's "default", and it would be a strange result if the party alleging this were not the party required to prove it.

9.17 A case in which it was alleged that a charter had been frustrated by the destruction of the intended cargo was *E B Aaby's Rederi A/S* v. *LEP Transport Ltd*.[24] What happened in this case was that a ship had been chartered to load a part cargo of "about but not exceeding 65,000 cubic feet of wool in bales" for delivery at Rostock. On the day the ship gave Notice of Readiness to load, all but 167 bales of the intended cargo were destroyed in a fire at the warehouse in which the goods were stored prior to shipment. In these circumstances, it was held that the charter was not frustrated because it was not for the carriage of the specific goods that were destroyed—the charterers could have performed their contract by getting a different cargo and, in any event, the undamaged cargo could have been shipped. The court also held that 167 bales was not *de minimis*.

B. Inordinate delay

9.18 This is perhaps the most common cause for claiming frustration of a contract and the law reports contain many instances where this has been asserted. Many of the cases concern vessels under time charter, with regard to which similar principles apply as far as

20. *Ibid.*, at p. 147.
21. *Taylor* v. *Caldwell* (1863) 3 B & S 826. A contract for the hire of a music hall was held to be frustrated when it burned down.
22. *Imperial Smelting Corporation Ltd* v. *Joseph Constantine Steamship Line Ltd* (1941) 70 Ll L Rep 1 (HL). In this case, Viscount Maugham mentioned (at p. 11) that the doctrine of frustration had been considered in more than 50 reported cases.
23. *Ibid.*, at p. 9.
24. *E B Aaby's Rederi A/S* v. *LEP Transport Ltd* (1948) 81 Ll L Rep 465.

this point is concerned. The cases that follow are best considered as examples of how the courts approach the problem of deciding whether there has been an inordinate delay.

9.19 The general principles involved were summarized by Bailhache J in *Admiral Shipping Co Ltd* v. *Weidner Hopkins & Co*, thus[25]:

The commercial frustration of an adventure by delay means . . . the happening of some unforeseen delay without the fault of either party to a contract of such a character as that by it the fulfilment of the contract in the only way in which fulfilment is contemplated and practicable is so inordinately postponed that its fulfilment when the delay is over will not accomplish the only object or objects which the parties to the contract must have known that each of them had in view at the time they made the contract, and for the accomplishment of which object or objects the contract was made.

9.20 The question of whether a contract has been frustrated has to be considered as at the time when the parties came to know of the facts giving rise to the delay and had to assess its likely duration before deciding what action to take. Subsequent events are only of value to the extent of showing what the probabilities at the time really were.

9.21 Some frustrating events, such as the outbreak of a general war or the blocking of a major waterway as the result of a local war, will almost certainly result in the frustration of voyage charters. Other events such as strikes, or natural phenomena such as ice or neap tides, are unlikely to result in such charters becoming frustrated. However, each case must be considered on its own facts and, as some of the cases show, if the courts hold that the contract has been frustrated but the delay subsequently turns out not to be as long as was expected, then the parties have no further redress.

9.22 In *Embiricos* v. *Sydney Reid & Co*,[26] a Greek steamer was chartered to carry a cargo of grain from Temriuk in the Sea of Azov to the United Kingdom. After loading commenced, the Turkish Government detained all Greek vessels passing through the Dardanelles and war between Greece and Turkey was declared on 18 October 1912, the charterers having declined to continue loading after 7 October. On 21 October the charterers purported to cancel the charter, although lay days did not expire until 22 October. In fact, as events transpired, had the vessel been fully loaded, she would have been able to leave without being detained through the Dardanelles between 16 and 24 October or between 12 and 19 November. As it was, she was forced to remain in the Black Sea until the end of the war.

9.23 Scrutton J held that the contract was at an end, saying[27]:

. . . an excepted peril, restraint of princes, prevented the charter from being carried out by the vessel proceeding on her voyage, and was, in the language of Lush J in *Geipel* v. *Smith*,[28] "likely to continue so long, and so to disturb the commerce of merchants, as to defeat and destroy the object of a commercial adventure like this". If there is such a likelihood and probability, the fact that unexpectedly the restraint is removed for a short time does not involve that the parties should have foreseen this unexpected event, and proceeded in the performance of an adventure which at the time seemed hopelessly destroyed. As Lord Gorell said in *The Savona*[29]: "I do not think this case can be decided by what happened afterwards, except as a test of what was the true state of things at the time when the question of breach has to be considered", and the whole of his subsequent remarks are valuable on this point. Commercial men must not be asked to wait till the end of a long delay to find

---

25. *Admiral Shipping Co Ltd* v. *Weidner Hopkins & Co* [1916] 1 KB 429, at pp. 436–437.
26. *Embiricos* v. *Sydney Reid & Co* (1914) 19 CC 263.
27. *Ibid.*, at p. 271.
28. *Geipel* v. *Smith* (1872) LR 7 QB 404.
29. *The Savona* [1900] P 252, at p. 259.

out from what in fact happens whether they are bound by a contract or not; they must be entitled to act on reasonable commercial probabilities at the time when they are called upon to make up their minds.

9.24 On the question of whether a strike can be a frustrating event, Bailhache J said in *Ropner & Co v. Ronnebeck*[30]:

Strikes, of course, vary in length. No man can say when a strike begins whether it will be a long strike or a short one. I do not think that a charterer is entitled, merely because a strike is on foot, to say that he expects it will be of long duration and will frustrate the commercial object of his venture and that therefore he is entitled to refuse to load. In my opinion the doctrine has no application to cases of strikes . . .

9.25 One of the leading cases on frustration by delay is a time charter case, *Tamplin* v. *Anglo-Mexican Co*,[31] which arose out of the requisition of a vessel by the British Government on the outbreak of the First World War. The case eventually reached the House of Lords, and the principles established were used to determine the many cases that arose during and after the war as to whether requisition had frustrated the charter in force at the time of requisition. In the case of single voyage charters, the answer would almost certainly be "yes", but the principles laid down are of some general importance even in voyage charters.

9.26 The case concerned a tank steamship under a five-year charter for the carriage of oil. On the outbreak of war, the ship was requisitioned when the charter had nearly three years to run. The vessel came under Admiralty control, who altered her to become a troop transport. The charterers argued that requisition did not frustrate the charter and this was upheld by a majority of the House of Lords, who held that if, at the time of requisition, the business probability was that the requisition would last for practically the whole period of the charter, the common object of the adventure would be frustrated. However, if there was no probability of the requisition lasting for so long, then the charter continued in force. In this particular case, the House's holding that the probability was that the period of requisition would be less than that remaining under the charter proved to be incorrect. However, there was no way the owners could reopen the matter once the House had reached their conclusion.

9.27 One of the most likely possibilities for frustration to occur in a voyage charter setting is where the parties have agreed a series of consecutive voyages. This may either be for a fixed number of voyages or for an indefinite number, but a fixed period. *The Penelope*[32] is an example of the latter, where the period was to be 12 months, and *James Curley* v. *Barrellier & Francastel*[33] an example of the former, being for six voyages. In either case, if there is a substantial delay in prosecuting the voyages without the fault of either party, taking into account their number and duration, then the agreement may become frustrated. In *The Penelope*,[34] a delay of six months was held to frustrate the

---

30. *Ropner & Co v. Ronnebeck* (1914) 20 CC 95, at p. 99.
31. *Tamplin Steamship Co v. Anglo Mexican Petroleum Co* [1916] 2 AC 397.
32. *The Penelope* [1928] P 180.
33. *James Curley* v. *Barrellier & Francastel* (1923) 16 Ll L Rep 42.
34. *The Penelope* [1928] P 180. The delay was caused by the coal strike of 1926 which prevented any export of coal from South Wales ports for over six months. The case is also of interest as being one of the few reported cases where an agreement was frustrated by a strike.

agreement, whereas in *James Curley* v. *Barrellier & Francastel*,[35] a delay of two months seven days was held to be insufficient.

9.28 A more recent example of frustration affecting a series of voyage charters is *BTP Tioxide Ltd* v. *Pioneer Shipping Ltd (The Nema)*.[36] The *Nema* had been chartered for six consecutive voyages carrying titanium slag from Sorel to Europe, starting in April and ending in December 1979. The charterers exercised an option for a seventh voyage. Clause 5 excluded time lost due to strikes and clause 27 allowed the owners the option to cancel the charter in the event of a general strike.

9.29 One voyage was performed, but loading for the second voyage was prevented by a strike. An addendum to the charter postponed the second voyage, allowed an intermediate voyage, and required performance of voyages 2–7 thereafter. The shipowners also agreed to lift a further seven cargoes in the 1980 season. The strike continued and after a month, as the owners had been unable to fix their vessel for an intermediate voyage, the charterers agreed to pay US $2000 per day until such a voyage could be arranged. Another voyage was fixed, but when that was completed, the strike at Sorel was still on. A dispute then arose as to whether yet a further intermediate voyage should be carried out and, contrary to the charterers' wishes, the owners insisted on so doing. At that time the strike had been in existence for over two months and some four months had elapsed since the agreement was entered into. As both parties were well aware, all the voyages had to be completed within an eight-month period, because thereafter Sorel was only open for ice-reinforced vessels, which the *Nema* was not.

9.30 The dispute went to arbitration, the arbitrator giving his decision at the end of September. At that time the strike was still in operation and it finally ended on 5 October 1979.

9.31 In his award, the arbitrator held that the charter was frustrated as far as the seven voyages planned for 1979 were concerned, but said that he had not considered the addendum covering 1980. On appeal, Robert Goff J held[37] that the charter and addendum comprised one indivisible contract, which was not frustrated. The Court of Appeal then upheld[38] an appeal by the owners, holding that the arbitrator was right in his conclusion that by the date of his decision the contract was frustrated. On further appeal by the charterers, the House of Lords dismissed the appeal, holding that the contemplated voyages for 1979 and 1980 were distinct, separate and independent adventures and the arbitrator had rightly considered whether or not the charterparty for the 1979 season had been frustrated.

9.32 In this case, one of the principal issues was whether the series of voyages planned for 1980 was severable from those arranged for 1979. In other cases, the question has been whether each of the voyages was severable. In any particular case, it will depend on the terms of the individual agreement.

9.33 In *The Nema*, Lord Roskill set out the approach to be taken by the tribunal, saying[39]:

---

35. *James Curley* v. *Barrellier & Francastel* (1923) 16 Ll L Rep 42. In this case, the delay arose out of the need to repair a vessel following a collision on an earlier voyage.
36. *BTP Tioxide Ltd* v. *Pioneer Shipping Ltd (The Nema)* [1982] AC 724 (HL).
37. *The Nema* [1980] 1 Lloyd's Rep 519n.
38. *The Nema* [1980] QB 547 (CA).
39. *The Nema* [1981] 3 WLR 292, at p. 381.

... in some cases where it is claimed that frustration has occurred by reason of the happening of a particular event, it is possible to determine at once whether or not the doctrine can be legitimately invoked. But in others, where the effect of that event is to cause delay in the performance of contractual obligations, it is often necessary to wait upon events in order to see whether the delay already suffered, and the prospects of further delay from that cause, will make any ultimate performance of the relevant contractual obligations "radically different", to borrow Lord Radcliffe's phrase,[40] from that which was undertaken by the contract. But, as has often been said, businessmen must not be required to await events too long. They are entitled to know where they stand. Whether or not the delay is such as to bring about frustration must be a question to be determined by an informed judgment based upon all the evidence of what has occurred and what is likely thereafter to occur. Often it will be a question of degree whether the effect of delay suffered and likely to be suffered will be such as to bring about frustration of the particular adventure in question. Where questions of degree are involved, opinions may and often legitimately do differ.

9.34 In some cases, whilst the actual delay may not be sufficiently long to frustrate the charter, it may, taken in conjunction with other factors, show an impossibility of performance before the delay will become so long as to frustrate the venture.[41]

9.35 Another case where the duration of a delay was considered was *Unitramp* v. *Garnac Grain Co Inc (The Hermine)*.[42] The *Hermine* was delayed for a number of reasons from 27 January 1974 until 12 March 1974 after completion of loading a cargo of grain at Destrehan, on the River Mississippi. The causes of the delay were: congestion following severe fog which had restricted navigation through the South West Pass; a blocking of the Pass by the grounding of the *Texaco Florida*; a lack of water thereafter; and finally the grounding of another vessel, the *Mary Lou*, at the entrance to the Pass. The principal allegation was that Destrehan was an unsafe port, a contention rejected by the Court of Appeal, but in the course of his judgment Roskill LJ said of the delay[43]:

I confess that I find the phrase "commercially unacceptable" a rather difficult concept because I am uncertain by what standards that test falls to be applied. Do you apply it from the point of view only of the shipowner or of the charterer as well? If it means that if the shipowners appreciated the possibility of this delay they would not have entered into a charterparty in these terms, that may well be so. Contracts are often entered into without the parties appreciating possible results that may arise if certain events happen. But the fact that something may, with hindsight, be commercially unacceptable does not of itself involve that there has been a breach of contract.

There has been, without doubt, a tendency in recent years, when considering problems of delay such as arise in this case and have arisen where a charterer had failed to supply any cargo to load, to hold that the owner is not entitled to seek to rescind the contract unless and until the delay occasioned by the failure to supply a cargo is such as to frustrate the adventure. The classic case which enunciated that principle is *Universal Cargo Carriers' Corporation* v. *Citati*.[44]

9.36 In London Arbitration 2/84,[45] the question arose as to whether a voyage charter was frustrated by pipeline disruption at the loading port. The charter was for the carriage of a cargo of crude oil from a range of ports in West Africa. The vessel arrived off the load port on 25 January 1982, although laytime did not commence until 29 January. On 28 January the suppliers of the cargo made a declaration of *force majeure*, informing the charterers that, because of a burst pipeline, they would be unable to supply any oil.

---

40. *Davis Contractors Ltd* v. *Fareham Urban District Council* [1956] AC 696, at p. 729. See *ante* at para. 9.13.
41. *Universal Cargo Carriers Corporation* v. *Pedro Citati* [1957] 1 Lloyd's Rep 174.
42. *Unitramp* v. *Garnac Grain Co Inc (The Hermine)* [1979] 1 Lloyd's Rep 212 (CA).
43. *Ibid.*, at p. 217.
44. *Universal Cargo Carriers Corporation* v. *Pedro Citati* [1957] 1 Lloyd's Rep 174.
45. London Arbitration 2/84—LMLN 113, 1 March 1984.

Repairs were expected to be completed within four weeks. On the following day, the charterers claimed the charter was frustrated. On 1 February there was a newspaper report that the damage would take at least two weeks to put right, and the pipeline went back into normal operation on 15 February. The shipowners claimed that the charterers had wrongfully repudiated the charter: the charterers contended the charter was frustrated.

9.37 The arbitrators said that their approach in matters of delay might be rather different to that adopted by lawyers. However, they were of the view that a party could not snatch at some fortuitous event and claim frustration without, at the very least, waiting a little time in order to get a clearer idea of the changed circumstances and their effects. There was everything to be said for businessmen knowing, as soon as possible, where they stood. However, other than in very exceptional circumstances, there had to be a period of taking stock before a decision was made and communicated to the other party regarding the frustration of a contract.

9.38 In this case, said the arbitrators, the charterers had acted too quickly and had not even waited until the end of the lay days. Even if the charterers did prove that loading was impossible at the nominated load port, it was still for them to show that they could not load at any of the other ports in the permitted range.

9.39 In one New York Arbitration involving a vessel called the *Elevit*,[46] the owners successfully persuaded the tribunal that notwithstanding the provision of security by the charterers in respect of freight and demurrage in a sum sought by the owners nevertheless the owners were entitled to order the vessel to sail once laytime had expired and no cargo had been provided. Apart from various American cases, the English case of *Universal Cargo Carriers Corporation* v. *Pedro Citati*,[47] was also cited to the tribunal, who in their award said:

Furthermore the exchange of communications between the parties showed that the Charterers had expressed a desire to hide from the Owners the steps taken to obtain delivery [of the cargo] or even to name their contractors. Not to be overlooked also was the statement from the Charterers that they could not perform the contract to Djibouti and the request/suggestion that the Owners should allow other destinations to replace Djibouti.

Those events demonstrated a pattern of conduct amounting to a repudiation by the Charterers of the original charterparty. The Charterers had breached their obligation to supply the cargo and the Owners were justified in withdrawing from the charterparty.

It should be noted that whilst laytime was running, which was some 23 days, the owners had made extensive enquiries of the charterers and others to confirm the cargo availability, loading berth, agents and other relevant matters.

9.40 This should therefore be considered a case decided on its own facts and certainly not one which establishes a principle that if laytime expires without any cargo being provided, the charter comes to an end whether by repudiation or by frustration. It will normally be considerably after laytime has expired that non-provision of cargo would amount to a repudiation or frustration of the charter.

---

46. *Hanjin Shipping Co Ltd* v. *R J International Inc (The Elevit)* (NY Arb), LMLN 372, 5 February 1994.
47. *Universal Cargo Carriers Corporation* v. *Pedro Citati* [1957] 1 Lloyd's Rep 174.

C. Illegality

9.41 Illegality by the law of the country where performance is required may generally provide a defence to a failure to perform contractual obligations. The position of English law on this subject was summed up by Scrutton LJ in *Ralli Brothers* v. *Compania Naviera Sota y Aznar*, where he said[48]:

... where a contract requires an act to be done in a foreign country it is, in the absence of very special circumstances, an implied term of the continuing validity of such a provision that the act to be done in the foreign country shall not be illegal by the law of that country. This country should not, in my opinion, assist or sanction the breach of the laws of other independent states.

If a contract becomes frustrated by illegality, e.g. because of legislation passed subsequently in the country of performance, then it does so because of the impossibility of performance of the contract. It follows from this that the performance must be impossible and not merely difficult or only possible in some other way than that envisaged by the parties when they entered into the contract.

9.42 In *Brunner* v. *Webster and another*,[49] rice was shipped from Rangoon to Galatz. Whilst their vessel was at Beirut, the shipowners were told by a Government official at Galatz that, if the ship arrived there, discharge of the rice would not be permitted. The advice they were given was wrong and the law of Romania did not in fact prohibit the importation of rice. However, the shipowners ordered their vessel not to proceed to Galatz, but to proceed to London where the rice was sold at a loss. The shipowners were subsequently sued successfully by the holders of the bills of lading, Kennedy J holding that the shipowners were not justified in treating the contract of carriage as being impossible of performance. In his judgment, Kennedy J said[50]:

I am far from saying that a *de facto* restraint may not be a sufficient justification, if it lasts long enough to frustrate the adventure, in a commercial sense, but here no actual restraint was put upon the vessel for any time at all.

9.43 In some of the early cases,[51] it was sometimes held that the presence of an exclusion clause, limiting liability in the circumstances that actually arose, was sufficient to prevent those circumstances being a frustrating event. This was usually put on the basis that there was then no room for an implied term bringing the contract to an end. That view, however, no longer normally prevails. As Viscount Simon LC said in *Fibrosa Spolka* v. *Fairbairn*[52]:

The principle is that where supervening events, not due to the default of either party, render the performance of a contract indefinitely impossible, and there is no undertaking to be bound in any event, frustration ensues, even though the parties may have expressly provided for the case of a limited interruption.

However if, of course, the parties have provided for more than a limited interruption, then it must be doubtful how much scope remains for the doctrine of frustration. Thus, in *Isles*

48. *Ralli Brothers* v. *Compania Naviera Sota y Aznar* (1920) 25 CC 227, at p. 241.
49. *Brunner* v. *Webster and another* (1900) 5 CC 167.
50. *Ibid.*, at p. 174.
51. See the comments of Lord Parker in *Tamplin Steamship Co* v. *Anglo Mexican Petroleum Co* [1916] AC 397, at p. 426. However, in *Bank Line Ltd* v. *Capel* [1919] AC 435, at p. 443, Lord Finlay LC said that the proposition that a "restraint of princes" clause would exclude the doctrine of frustration should not be regarded as forming part of the judgment of the House in the earlier case.
52. *Fibrosa Spolka Akcyjna* v. *Fairbairn, Lawson* [1943] AC 32, at p. 40.

Steam Shipping Co Ltd v. Theodoridi & Co,[53] there was an additional clause providing for the charter to be null and void in the event of a prohibition of export of grain and seed at the load port. What happened was that there was a restriction on the export of grain, and in arbitration proceedings the umpire held that this was not a prohibition within the meaning of the clause, a conclusion upheld by the court. On the alternative argument of frustration, MacKinnon J said[54]:

I do not think it is possible to invoke that doctrine in this case. It would mean that the contract was impossible of performance by them by virtue of certain circumstances arising, and that as a matter of construction one ought to hold that it was an implied term of contract that upon these events arising to make performance impossible the contract should be void. I do not think that this contract contained any such implied provision having regard to the fact that there is an express provision dealing with these matters . . .

9.44 As already discussed,[55] the theory that frustration is based on an implied term no longer holds sway. Nevertheless, there would seem to be no reason why the parties should not make express provision for what might otherwise be considered a frustrating event.

9.45 Another case which concerned a partial restriction on loading was *Kawasaki Steel Corporation v. Sardoil SpA (The Zuiho Maru)*.[56] In this a tanker was to load a cargo of crude oil at Ras Tanura, in Saudi Arabia. After the charter had been made, the only oil supplier in Ras Tanura was ordered to cut production by 10 per cent by the Saudi Arabian Government and, because of a policy of rationing the available supplies, the vessel concerned only received 93 per cent of her intended cargo. The charterers argued that the whole charter had become frustrated and that the voyage performed was a *quantum meruit* voyage rather than the contractual one. However, this contention was rejected by Kerr J, who added[57]:

Without resort to any definition of the nature of a frustrating event, it is self evident that any short-fall of this kind could never be capable of giving rise to frustration, because there is nothing like a sufficiently fundamental change of circumstances.

9.46 A not dissimilar case came before Kerr J, almost at the same time. This was *Seabridge Shipping Ltd v. Antco Shipping Ltd (The Furness Bridge)*.[58]

9.47 This concerned a tanker charter for a lifting from a range of ports in the Mediterranean to the Caribbean. After the fixture had been made, the Arab/Israel war of October 1973 occurred. As a result of this, Libya, where it had been intended to load, imposed an embargo on shipments to certain countries, which prevented the lifting. In arbitration, the charterers claimed frustration and also sought to rely on a "restraint of princes" clause in the charter. The arbitrator found that whilst the charterers had established that they were unable to ship a cargo from Libya, they had failed to prove that they were prevented from loading at any other country within the nominated range. The question of frustration was not pursued and in the High Court Kerr J held that they could not take advantage of the "restraint of princes" clause, since they had failed to show that shipment from any contractual non-Libyan port was also commercially impossible. It is

---

53. *Isles Steam Shipping Co Ltd v. Theodoridi & Co* (1926) 24 Ll L Rep 362.
54. *Ibid.*, at p. 363.
55. See *ante* at para. 9.9.
56. *Kawasaki Steel Corporation v. Sardoil SpA (The Zuiho Maru)* [1977] 2 Lloyd's Rep 552.
57. *Ibid.*, at p. 555.
58. *Seabridge Shipping Ltd v. Antco Shipping Ltd (The Furness Bridge)* [1977] 2 Lloyd's Rep 367.

suggested that, had it been pursued, a claim for frustration would have failed for the same reason.

Self-induced frustration

9.48 There cannot be a finding of frustration where the reason why the contract cannot be performed is that the impossibility is due to the fault of either party. Thus, in *Bank Line v. Capel*, Lord Sumner said[59]:

It is now well settled that the principle of frustration of an adventure assumes that the frustration arises without blame or fault on either side. Reliance cannot be placed on a self-induced frustration; indeed, such conduct might give the other party the option to treat the contract as repudiated.

9.49 In *Ocean Trawlers Ltd* v. *Maritime National Fish Ltd*,[60] a trawler was chartered for fishing with an otter trawl, which required a licence. The charterers already operated a number of other vessels, and when they were limited to three such licences the vessels they nominated for these three licences did not include the one that was the subject of these proceedings, and they claimed that because of the limit that had been imposed upon them, the charter was frustrated. This suggestion was rejected by the Privy Council in a speech given by Lord Wright, who concluded[61]:

... It was the appellants' own default which frustrated the adventure. The appellants cannot rely on their own default to excuse them from liability under the contract.[62]

The Law Reform (Frustrated Contracts) Act 1943

9.50 Section 2(5) excludes voyage charters from the operation of the Act. The question of sums due, such as demurrage, is therefore governed by common law, which provides for them to be recoverable for any period up to the date of frustration. As Lord Sumner said in *Hirji Mulji* v. *Cheong Yue Steamship Co*[63]:

Though the contract comes to an end on the happening of the event, rights and wrongs, which have already come into existence, remain, and the contract remains too, for the purpose of giving effect to them.

59. *Bank Line Ltd* v. *Arthur Capel & Co* [1919] AC 435, at p. 452.
60. *Ocean Trawlers Ltd* v. *Maritime National Fish Ltd* (1935) 51 Ll L Rep 299 (PC).
61. *Ibid.*, at p. 304.
62. The burden, however, of proving that the supervening or frustrating event was self-induced is on the party alleging it. Thus, in *Constantine Line* v. *Imperial Smelting Corporation* [1942] AC 164, the House of Lords held that where an explosion had virtually wrecked a ship, the owners were not bound to prove that it was not due to their fault.
63. *Hirji Mulji* v. *Cheong Yue Steamship Co* [1926] AC 497, at p. 511.

APPENDIX

A. Laytime Definitions

In 1980, a set of 31 definitions of words and phrases commonly used in voyage charterparties in a laytime context was published jointly by BIMCO, CMI, FONASBA and GCBS (now Chamber of Shipping) under the title *Charterparty Laytime Definitions 1980*.

After some years' experience of how the definitions were working in practice and the extent to which they were being incorporated into charterparties, the four sponsoring organisations set up a Joint Working Group to revise and update the definitions. The Joint Working Group also included a representative from INTERCARGO (International Association of Dry Cargo Shipowners) who had expressed an interest in participating in the work of the Joint Working Group.

The result of their deliberations is the *Voylayrules 1993* which have been officially adopted by the governing bodies of the sponsoring organizations.

The following definitions which appear in the 1980 Definitions have been left out of the 1993 Rules.

"SAFE PORT"
"SAFE BERTH"
"CUSTOMARY DESPATCH"
"AS FAST AS THE VESSEL CAN RECEIVE/DELIVER"

The following definitions have been combined.

"DEMURRAGE/ON DEMURRAGE"
"WEATHER WORKING DAY/WEATHER WORKING DAY OF 24 HOURS/WEATHER WORKING DAY OF 24 CONSECUTIVE HOURS"

The definitions listed below have been added.

"UNLESS SOONER COMMENCED"
"VESSEL BEING IN FREE PRATIQUE AND/OR HAVING BEEN ENTERED AT THE CUSTOM HOUSE"
"DESPATCH ON ALL WORKING TIME SAVED"
"STRIKE"

The meaning attributable to the following terms has been significantly changed.

"REACHABLE ON ARRIVAL"
"WEATHER WORKING DAY"
"WHETHER IN BERTH OR NOT"

Comments on the terms added and changed are included, where appropriate, in the main body of the book under the appropriate headings.

Both the *Charterparty Laytime Definitions 1980* and the *Voylayrules 1993* are reproduced here with the permission and authority of BIMCO.

More recently, the Baltic Exchange in London have produced their own set of charterparty and laytime definitions for the guidance of their members as part of *Baltic Code 2000*. These are based on their understanding of English law as it currently stands.

There are differences between these definitions and those in the *Voylayrules 1993* in respect of the following definitions.

"REACHABLE ON HER ARRIVAL or ALWAYS ACCESSIBLE"
"WHETHER WORKING DAY" and variants thereof
"NOTICE OF READINESS"
"WHETHER IN BERTH OR NOT"

These differences are dealt with in the main body of the book under the appropriate headings. These definitions are reproduced here with the permission and authority of the Baltic Exchange.

All three sets of definitions will only apply to charterparties where they are expressly incorporated into the relevant charterparty.

B. Charterparty Laytime Definitions 1980

PREAMBLE

The definitions which follow (except such as are expressly excluded by deletion or otherwise) shall apply to words and phrases used in the charterparty, save only to the extent that any definition or part thereof is inconsistent with any other express provision of the charterparty. Words used in these definitions shall themselves be construed in accordance with any definition given to them therein. Words or phrases which are merely variations or alternative forms of words or phrases herein defined are to be construed in accordance with the definition (e.g. "Notification of Vessel's Readiness", "Notice of Readiness").

LIST OF DEFINITIONS

1. "PORT"
2. "SAFE PORT"
3. "BERTH"
4. "SAFE BERTH"
5. "REACHABLE ON ARRIVAL" or "ALWAYS ACCESSIBLE"
6. "LAYTIME"
7. "CUSTOMARY DESPATCH"
8. "PER HATCH PER DAY"
9. "PER WORKING HATCH PER DAY" or "PER WORKABLE HATCH PER DAY"
10. "AS FAST AS THE VESSEL CAN RECEIVE/DELIVER"
11. "DAY"
12. "CLEAR DAY" or "CLEAR DAYS"
13. "HOLIDAY"
14. "WORKING DAYS"
15. "RUNNING DAYS" or "CONSECUTIVE DAYS"
16. "WEATHER WORKING DAY"
17. "WEATHER WORKING DAY OF 24 CONSECUTIVE HOURS"
18. "WEATHER PERMITTING"
19. "EXCEPTED"
20. "UNLESS USED"
21. "TO AVERAGE"
22. "REVERSIBLE"
23. "NOTICE OF READINESS"
24. "IN WRITING"
25. "TIME LOST WAITING FOR BERTH TO COUNT AS LOADING/DISCHARGING TIME" or "AS LAYTIME"
26. "WHETHER IN BERTH OR NOT" or "BERTH NO BERTH"
27. "DEMURRAGE"
28. "ON DEMURRAGE"
29. "DESPATCH MONEY" or "DESPATCH"

30. "ALL TIME SAVED"
31. "ALL WORKING TIME SAVED" or "ALL LAYTIME SAVED"

DEFINITIONS

1. "PORT"—means an area within which ships are loaded with and/or discharged of cargo and includes the usual places where ships wait for their turn or are ordered or obliged to wait for their turn no matter the distance from that area.

If the word "PORT" is not used, but the port is (or is to be) identified by its name, this definition shall still apply.

2. "SAFE PORT"—means a port which, during the relevant period of time, the ship can reach, enter, remain at and depart from without, in the absence of some abnormal occurrence, being exposed to danger which cannot be avoided by good navigation and seamanship.

3. "BERTH"—means the specific place where the ship is to load and/or discharge.

If the word "BERTH" is not used, but the specific place is (or is to be) identified by its name, this definition shall still apply.

4. "SAFE BERTH"—means a berth which, during the relevant period of time, the ship can reach, remain at and depart from without, in the absence of some abnormal occurrence, being exposed to danger which cannot be avoided by good navigation and seamanship.

5. "REACHABLE ON ARRIVAL" or "ALWAYS ACCESSIBLE"—means that the charterer undertakes that when the ship arrives at the port there will be a loading/discharging berth for her to which she can proceed without delay.

6. "LAYTIME"—means the period of time agreed between the parties during which the owner will make and keep the ship available for loading/discharging without payment additional to the freight.

7. "CUSTOMARY DESPATCH"—means that the charterer must load and/or discharge as fast as is possible in the circumstances prevailing at the time of loading or discharging.

8. "PER HATCH PER DAY"—means that laytime is to be calculated by multiplying the agreed daily rate per hatch of loading/discharging the cargo by the number of the ship's hatches and dividing the quantity of cargo by the resulting sum. Thus:

$$\text{Laytime} = \frac{\text{Quantity of Cargo}}{\text{Daily Rate} \times \text{Number of Hatches}} = \text{Days.}$$

A hatch that is capable of being worked by two gangs simultaneously shall be counted as two hatches.

9. "PER WORKING HATCH PER DAY" or "PER WORKABLE HATCH PER DAY"—means that laytime is to be calculated by dividing the quantity of cargo in the hold with the largest quantity by the result of multiplying the agreed daily rate per working or workable hatch by the number of hatches serving that hold. Thus:

$$\text{Laytime} = \frac{\text{Largest Quantity in One Hold}}{\substack{\text{Daily Rate per Hatch} \times \text{Number of Hatches} \\ \text{Serving that Hold}}} = \text{Days.}$$

A hatch that is capable of being worked by two gangs simultaneously shall be counted as two hatches.

10. "AS FAST AS THE VESSEL CAN RECEIVE/DELIVER"—means that the laytime is a period of time to be calculated by reference to the maximum rate at which the ship in full working order is capable of loading/discharging the cargo.

11. "DAY"—means a continuous period of 24 hours which, unless the context otherwise requires, runs from midnight to midnight.

12. "CLEAR DAY" or "CLEAR DAYS"—means that the day on which the notice is given and the day on which the notice expires are not included in the notice period.

13. "HOLIDAY"—means a day of the week or part(s) thereof on which cargo work on the ship would normally take place but is suspended at the place of loading/discharging by reason of:

(i) the local law; or

(ii) the local practice.

14. "WORKING DAYS"—means days or part(s) thereof which are not expressly excluded from laytime by the charterparty and which are not holidays.

15. "RUNNING DAYS" or "CONSECUTIVE DAYS"—means days which follow one immediately after the other.

16. "WEATHER WORKING DAY"—means a working day or part of a working day during which it is or, if the vessel is still waiting for her turn, it would be possible to load/discharge the cargo without interference due to the weather. If such interference occurs (or would have occurred if work had been in progress), there shall be excluded from the laytime a period calculated by reference to the ratio which the duration of the interference bears to the time which would have or could have been worked but for the interference.

17. "WEATHER WORKING DAY OF 24 CONSECUTIVE HOURS"—means a working day or part of a working day of 24 hours during which it is or, if the ship is still waiting for her turn, it would be possible to load/discharge the cargo without interference due to the weather. If such interference occurs (or would have occurred if work had been in progress) there shall be excluded from the laytime the period during which the weather interfered or would have interfered with the work.

18. "WEATHER PERMITTING"—means that time during which weather prevents working shall not count as laytime.

19. "EXCEPTED"—means that the specified days do not count as laytime even if loading or discharging is done on them.

20. "UNLESS USED"—means that if work is carried out during the excepted days the actual hours of work only count as laytime.

21. "TO AVERAGE"—means that separate calculations are to be made for loading and discharging and any time saved in one operation is to be set against any excess time used in the other.

22. "REVERSIBLE"—means an option given to the charterer to add together the time allowed for loading and discharging. Where the option is exercised the effect is the same as a total time being specified to cover both operations.

23. "NOTICE OF READINESS"—means notice to the charterer, shipper, receiver or other person as required by the charter that the ship has arrived at the port or berth as the case may be and is ready to load/discharge.

24. "IN WRITING"—means, in relation to a notice of readiness, a notice visibly expressed in any mode of reproducing words and includes cable, telegram and telex.

25. "TIMES LOST WAITING FOR BERTH TO COUNT AS LOADING/DISCHARGING TIME" or "AS LAYTIME"—means that if the main reason why a notice of readiness cannot be given is that there is no loading/discharging berth available to the ship the laytime will commence to run when the ship starts to wait for a berth and will continue to run, unless previously exhausted, until the ship stops waiting. The laytime exceptions apply to the waiting time as if the ship was at the loading/discharging berth provided the ship is not already on demurrage. When the waiting time ends time ceases to count and restarts when the ship reaches the loading/discharging berth subject to the giving of a notice of readiness if one is required by the charterparty and to any notice time if provided for in the charterparty, unless the ship is by then on demurrage.

26. "WHETHER IN BERTH OR NOT" or "BERTH NO BERTH"—means that if the location named for loading/discharging is a berth and if the berth is not immediately accessible to the ship a notice of readiness can be given when the ship has arrived at the port in which the berth is situated.

27. "DEMURRAGE"—means the money payable to the owner for delay for which the owner is not responsible in loading and/or discharging after the laytime has expired.

28. "ON DEMURRAGE"—means that the laytime has expired. Unless the charterparty expressly provides to the contrary the time on demurrage will not be subject to the laytime exceptions.

29. "DESPATCH MONEY" or "DESPATCH"—means the money payable by the owner if the ship completes loading or discharging before the laytime has expired.

30. "ALL TIME SAVED"—means the time saved to the ship from the completion of loading/discharging to the expiry of the laytime including periods excepted from the laytime.

31. "ALL WORKING TIME SAVED" or "ALL LAYTIME SAVED"—means the time saved to the ship from the completion of loading/discharging to the expiry of the laytime excluding any notice time and periods excepted from the laytime.

C. Voyage Charterparty Laytime Interpretation Rules 1993

CODE NAME: VOYLAYRULES 93

Issued jointly by BIMCO, CMI, FONASBA and INTERCARGO.

PREAMBLE

The interpretations of words and phrases used in a charterparty, as set out below, and the corresponding initials if customarily used, shall apply when expressly incorporated in the charterparty, wholly or partly, save only to the extent that they are inconsistent with any express provision of it.

When the word "charterparty" is used, it shall be understood to extend to any form of contract of carriage or affreightment including contracts evidenced by bills of lading.

LIST OF RULES

1. "PORT"
2. "BERTH"
3. "REACHABLE ON HER ARRIVAL" or "ALWAYS ACCESSIBLE"
4. "LAYTIME"
5. "PER HATCH PER DAY"
6. "PER WORKING HATCH PER DAY" (WHD) or "PER WORKABLE HATCH PER DAY" (WHD)
7. "DAY"
8. "CLEAR DAYS"
9. "HOLIDAY"
10. "WORKING DAY" (WD)
11. "RUNNING DAYS" or "CONSECUTIVE DAYS"
12. "WEATHER WORKING DAY" (WWD) or "WEATHER WORKING DAY OF 24 HOURS" or "WEATHER WORKING DAY OF 24 CONSECUTIVE HOURS"
13. "WEATHER PERMITTING" (WP)
14. "EXCEPTED" or "EXCLUDED"
15. "UNLESS SOONER COMMENCED"
16. "UNLESS USED" (UU)
17. "TO AVERAGE LAYTIME"
18. "REVERSIBLE LAYTIME"
19. "NOTICE OF READINESS" (NOR)
20. "IN WRITING"
21. "TIME LOST WAITING FOR BERTH TO COUNT AS LOADING OR DISCHARGING TIME" or "AS LAYTIME"
22. "WHETHER IN BERTH OR NOT" (WIBON) or "BERTH OR NO BERTH"

431

23. "VESSEL BEING IN FREE PRATIQUE" and/or "HAVING BEEN ENTERED AT THE CUSTOM HOUSE"
24. "DEMURRAGE"
25. "DESPATCH MONEY" or "DESPATCH"
26. "DESPATCH ON (ALL) WORKING TIME SAVED" (WTS) or "ON (ALL) LAYTIME SAVED"
27. "DESPATCH ON ALL TIME SAVED" (ATS)
28. "STRIKE"

RULES

1. "PORT" shall mean an area, within which vessels load or discharge cargo whether at berths, anchorages, buoys, or the like, and shall also include the usual places where vessels wait for their turn or are ordered or obliged to wait for their turn no matter the distance from that area. If the word "PORT" is not used, but the port is (or is to be) identified by its name, this definition shall still apply.

2. "BERTH" shall mean the specific place within a port where the vessel is to load or discharge. If the word "BERTH" is not used, but the specific place is (or is to be) identified by its name, this definition shall still apply.

3. "REACHABLE ON HER ARRIVAL" or "ALWAYS ACCESSIBLE" shall mean that the charterer undertakes that an available loading or discharging berth be provided to the vessel on her arrival at the port which she can reach safely without delay in the absence of an abnormal occurrence.

4. "LAYTIME" shall mean the period of time agreed between the parties during which the owner will make and keep the vessel available for loading or discharging without payment additional to the freight.

5. "PER HATCH PER DAY" shall mean that the laytime is to be calculated by dividing (A), the quantity of cargo, by (B), the result of multiplying the agreed daily rate per hatch by the number of the vessel's hatches. Thus:

$$\text{Laytime} = \frac{\text{Quantity of Cargo}}{\text{Daily Rate} \times \text{Number of Hatches}} = \text{Days}$$

Each pair of parallel twin hatches shall count as one hatch. Nevertheless, a hatch that is capable of being worked by two gangs simultaneously shall be counted as two hatches.

6. "PER WORKING HATCH PER DAY" (WHD) or "PER WORKABLE HATCH PER DAY" (WHD) shall mean that the laytime is to be calculated by dividing (A), the quantity of cargo in the hold with the largest quantity, by (B), the result of multiplying the agreed daily rate per working or workable hatch by the number of hatches serving that hold. Thus:

$$\text{Laytime} = \frac{\text{Largest Quantity in One Hold}}{\text{Daily Rate per Hatch} \times \text{Number of Hatches Serving that Hold}} = \text{Days}$$

Each pair of parallel twin hatches shall count as one hatch. Nevertheless, a hatch that is capable of being worked by two gangs simultaneously shall be counted as two hatches.

7. "DAY" shall mean a period of twenty-four consecutive hours running from 0000 hours to 2400 hours. Any part of a day shall be counted pro rata.

8. "CLEAR DAYS" shall mean consecutive days commencing at 0000 hours on the day following that on which a notice is given and ending at 2400 hours on the last of the number of days stipulated.

9. "HOLIDAY" shall mean a day other than the normal weekly day(s) of rest, or part thereof, when by local law or practice the relevant work during what would otherwise be ordinary working hours is not normally carried out.

10. "WORKING DAYS" (WD) shall mean days not expressly excluded from laytime.

11. "RUNNING DAYS" or "CONSECUTIVE DAYS" shall mean days which follow one immediately after the other.

12. "WEATHER WORKING DAY" (WWD) or "WEATHER WORKING DAY OF 24 HOURS" or "WEATHER WORKING DAY OF 24 CONSECUTIVE HOURS" shall mean a working day of 24 consecutive hours except for any time when weather prevents the loading or discharging of the vessel or would have prevented it, had work been in progress.

13. "WEATHER PERMITTING" (WP) shall mean that any time when weather prevents the loading or discharging of the vessel shall not count as laytime.

14. "EXCEPTED" or "EXCLUDED" shall mean that the days specified do not count as laytime even if loading or discharging is carried out on them.

15. "UNLESS SOONER COMMENCED" shall mean that if laytime has not commenced but loading or discharging is carried out, time used shall count against laytime.

16. "UNLESS USED" (UU) shall mean that if laytime has commenced but loading or discharging is carried out during periods excepted from it, such time shall count.

17. "TO AVERAGE LAYTIME" shall mean that separate calculations are to be made for loading and discharging and that any time saved in one operation is to be set off against any excess time used in the other.

18. "REVERSIBLE LAYTIME" shall mean an option given to the charterer to add together the time allowed for loading and discharging. Where the option is exercised the effect is the same as a total time being specified to cover both operations.

19. "NOTICE OF READINESS" (NOR) shall mean the notice to charterer, shipper, receiver or other person as required by the charterparty that the vessel has arrived at the port or berth, as the case may be, and is ready to load or discharge.

20. "IN WRITING" shall mean any visibly expressed form of reproducing words; the medium of transmission shall include electronic communications such as radio communications and telecommunications.

21. "TIME LOST WAITING FOR BERTH TO COUNT AS LOADING OR DISCHARGING TIME" or "AS LAYTIME" shall mean that if no loading or discharging berth is available and the vessel is unable to tender notice of readiness at the waiting-place then any time lost to the vessel shall count as if laytime were running, or as time on demurrage if laytime has expired. Such time shall cease to count once the berth becomes available. When the vessel reaches a place where she is able to tender notice of readiness laytime or time on demurrage shall resume after such tender and, in respect of laytime, on expiry of any notice time provided in the charterparty.

22. "WHETHER IN BERTH OR NOT" (WIBON) or "BERTH OR NO BERTH" shall mean that if no loading or discharging berth is available on her arrival the vessel, on reaching any usual waiting-place at or off the port, shall be entitled to tender notice of readiness from it and laytime shall commence in accordance with the charterparty. Laytime or time on demurrage shall cease to count once the berth becomes available and shall resume when the vessel is ready to load or discharge at the berth.

23. "VESSEL BEING IN FREE PRATIQUE" and/or "HAVING BEEN ENTERED AT THE CUSTOM HOUSE" shall mean that the completion of these formalities shall not be a condition precedent to tendering notice of readiness, but any time lost by reason of delay in the vessel's completion of either of these formalities shall not count as laytime or time on demurrage.

24. "DEMURRAGE" shall mean an agreed amount payable to the owner in respect of delay to the vessel beyond the laytime, for which the owner is not responsible. Demurrage shall not be subject to laytime exceptions.

25. "DESPATCH MONEY" or "DESPATCH" shall mean an agreed amount payable by the owner if the vessel completes loading or discharging before the laytime has expired.

26. "DESPATCH ON (ALL) WORKING TIME SAVED" (WTS) or "ON (ALL) LAYTIME SAVED" shall mean that despatch money shall be payable for the time from the completion of loading or discharging to the expiry of the laytime excluding any periods excepted from the laytime.

27. "DESPATCH ON ALL TIME SAVED" (ATS) shall mean that despatch money shall be payable for the time from the completion of loading or discharging to the expiry of the laytime including periods excepted from the laytime.

28. "STRIKE" shall mean a concerted industrial action by workmen causing a complete stoppage of their work which directly interferes with the working of the vessel. Refusal to work overtime, go-slow or working to rule and comparable actions not causing a complete stoppage shall

not be considered a strike. A strike shall be understood to exclude its consequences when it has ended, such as congestion in the port or effects upon the means of transportation bringing or taking the cargo to or from the port.

D. Baltic Code 2000 Charterparty and Laytime Terminology and Abbreviations

1. PORT—an area, within which vessels load or discharge cargo whether at berths, anchorages, buoys, or the like, and shall in most cases also include the usual places where the vessels wait for their turn or are ordered or obliged to wait for their turn no matter the distance from that area. If the word PORT is not used, but the port is (or is to be) identified by its name, this definition shall still apply.

2. BERTH/ANCHORAGE—in most cases the place within a port where the vessel is to load or discharge. If the word BERTH is not used, but the specific place is (or is to be) identified by its name this definition shall still apply.

3. REACHABLE ON HER ARRIVAL OR ALWAYS ACCESSIBLE—means that the charterer undertakes that an available and accessible loading or discharging berth will be provided to the vessel on her arrival at or off the port which she can reach safely without delay proceeding normally. Where the charterer undertakes the berth will be ALWAYS ACCESSIBLE, he additionally undertakes that the vessel will be able to depart safely from the berth without delay at any time during or on completion of loading or discharging.

4. LAYTIME—the period of time agreed between the parties during which the owner will make and keep the vessel available for loading or discharging without payment additional to the freight.

5. PER HATCH PER DAY—means that the laytime is to be calculated by dividing the quantity of cargo (A) by the result of multiplying the agreed daily rate per hatch by the number of the vessel's hatches (B).

$$\text{Laytime} = \frac{\text{Quantity of Cargo (A)}}{\text{Daily Rate} \times \text{Number of Hatches (B)}} = \text{Days.}$$

Each pair of parallel twin hatches shall count as one hatch. Nevertheless, a hatch that is capable of being worked by two gangs simultaneously shall be counted as two hatches.

6. PER WORKING HATCH PER DAY OR PER WORKABLE HATCH PER DAY—means that the laytime is to be calculated by dividing the quantity of cargo in the hold with the largest quantity (A) by the result of multiplying the agreed daily rate per working or workable hatch by the number of hatches serving that hold (B).

$$\text{Laytime} = \frac{\text{Largest Quantity in One Hold}}{\text{Daily Rate per Hatch} \times \text{Number of Hatches Serving that Hold}} = \text{Days.}$$

Each pair of parallel twin hatches shall count as one hatch regardless of the number of gangs that are capable of operating in that hatch. (Nevertheless, a hatch that is capable of being worked by two gangs simultaneously can, if agreed, be counted as two hatches.)

7. DAY—a period of 24 consecutive hours running from 0001 hours to 2400 hours. Any part of a day shall be counted pro rata.

8. CLEAR DAYS—consecutive days commencing at 0001 hours on the day following that day on which a notice is given and ending at 2400 hours in the last day of the number of days stipulated.

9. HOLIDAY—a day other than the normal weekly day(s) of rest, or part thereof, when by local law or practice the relevant work during what would otherwise be ordinary working hours is not normally carried out.

10. WORKING DAYS (WD)—days not expressly excluded from laytime.

11. RUNNING DAYS or CONSECUTIVE DAYS—days which follow one immediately after the other.

12. WEATHER WORKING DAY (WWD)—a working day or part of a working day during which it is or, if the vessel is still waiting for her turn, it would be possible to load/discharge the cargo without interference due to the weather. If such interference occurs (or would have occurred if work had been in progress), there shall be excluded from the laytime a period calculated by reference to the ratio which the duration of the interference bears to the time which would have or could have been worked but for the interference.

13. WEATHER WORKING DAY OF 24 CONSECUTIVE HOURS—a working day of 24 consecutive hours except for any time when weather prevents the loading or discharging of the vessel or would have prevented it had work been in progress, whether the vessel is in berth or still waiting for her turn.

14. WEATHER WORKING DAY OF 24 HOURS—a period of 24 hours made up of one or more working days during which it is or, if the vessel is still waiting for her turn, it would be possible to load/discharge the cargo without interference due to the weather. If such interference occurs (or would have occurred if work had been in progress), there shall be excluded from laytime the actual period of such interference.

15. WEATHER PERMITTING (WP)—any time when weather prevents the loading or discharging of the vessel, or would have prevented work if the vessel is still waiting for her turn, shall not count as laytime.

16. EXCEPTED or EXCLUDED—the days specified do not count as laytime even if loading or discharging is carried out on them.

17. UNLESS SOONER COMMENCED—if laytime has not commenced but loading or discharging is carried out, time used shall count against laytime.

18. UNLESS USED (UU)—if laytime has commenced but loading or discharging is carried out during periods excepted from it, such time shall count.

19. TO AVERAGE LAYTIME—separate calculations are to be made for loading and discharging and any time saved in one operation is to be set off against any excess time used in the other.

20. REVERSIBLE LAYTIME—an option given to the charterer to add together the time allowed for loading and discharging. Where the option is exercised the effect is the same as a total time being specified to cover both operations.

21. NOTICE OF READINESS (NOR)—the notice to charterer, shipper, receiver or other person as required by the charterparty that the vessel has arrived at the port or berth, as the case may be, and is ready to load or discharge. (Alternatively: the notice may be specified to relate to the vessel arriving **at/off** the port or berth.)

22. IN WRITING—any visibly expressed form of reproducing words; the medium of transmission can include electronic communications such as radio communications and telecommunications.

23. TIME LOST WAITING FOR BERTH TO COUNT AS LOADING OR DISCHARGING TIME OR AS LAYTIME—if no loading or discharging berth is available and the vessel is unable to tender notice of readiness at the waiting-place then any time lost to the vessel is counted as if laytime were running, or as time on demurrage if laytime has expired. Such time ceases to count once the berth becomes available. When the vessel reaches a place where she is able to tender notice of readiness, laytime or time on demurrage resumes after such tender and, in respect of laytime, on expiry of any notice time provided in the charterparty.

24. WHETHER IN BERTH OR NOT (WIBON) or BERTH OR NO BERTH—if the designated loading or discharging berth is not available on her arrival, the vessel on reaching any usual waiting place within the port, shall be entitled to tender notice of readiness from it and laytime shall commence as provided under the charterparty.

25. VESSEL BEING IN FREE PRATIQUE and/or HAVING BEEN ENTERED AT THE CUSTOM HOUSE—the completion of these formalities shall not be a condition precedent to tendering notice of readiness, unless the charterparty expressly requires their completion before notice is tendered. If it does not, any time lost by reason of delay on the part of the vessel in the completion of either of these formalities shall not count as laytime or time on demurrage.

26. DEMURRAGE—an agreed amount payable to the owner in respect of delay to the vessel beyond the laytime, for which the owner is not responsible. Demurrage shall not be subject to exceptions which apply to laytime unless specifically stated in the charterparty.

27. DESPATCH MONEY or DESPATCH—an agreed amount payable by the owner if the vessel completes loading or discharging before the laytime has expired.

28. DESPATCH ON (ALL) WORKING TIME SAVED (WTS) or ON (ALL) LAYTIME SAVED (LTS)—despatch money shall be payable for the time from the completion of loading or discharging to the expiry of the laytime excluding any periods excepted from the laytime.

29. DESPATCH ON ALL TIME SAVED (ATS)—despatch money shall be payable for the time from the completion of loading or discharging to the expiry of the laytime including periods excepted from the laytime.

30. STRIKE—a concerted industrial action by workmen causing a complete stoppage of their work which directly interferes with the working of the vessel. Refusal to work overtime, go-slow or working to rule and comparable actions not causing a complete stoppage shall not be considered a strike. A strike shall be understood to exclude its consequences when it has ended, such as congestion in the port or effects upon the means of transportation bringing or taking the cargo to or from the port.

Index

References to the Appendices are given as eg App A

Acceptance
of notice of readiness, 3.274–3.301
of repudiation, demurrage and, 1.35
Accident, completion of demurrage and, 6.179
Action
alternative, 4.286–4.288
shipowner's, preventing demurrage, 6.86–6.96
Adventure
control of, 1.13–1.14
four stages of, 1.10–1.11, 3.2
Adverse weather, 4.101–4.106
see also Weather
as interruption to laytime, 1.23
bore tide, 4.139–4.143
causation and, 4.144
Conoco weather clause, 4.167–4.172
exceptions, 4.151–4.166
frost, 4.115–4.121
ice, 4.122–4.129
interruptions, 4.145–4.150
limits of, 4.107–4.114
storm, 6.117–6.122
surf, 4.130–4.133
swell, 4.134–4.138
Agent, 3.201–3.208, 3.240
Agreement, delay by, 8.58–8.63
"All time saved", 7.4
The Altus
claim for deadfreight and claim for demurrage
and, 6.41–6.43
completion of laytime and, 5.66–5.68
exceptions clauses and demurrage and, 6.110
interruptions and exceptions to laytime and,
4.47–4.48
Always accessible clause *see* Reachable on arrival
clause
Amwelsh charter, 5.116
Anchorage
see also Berth; Port; Shifting
arrived ship and, 3.90–3.92, 3.98–3.102, 3.108
notice of readiness and, 3.263–3.264
Apportionment of risk, 1.14
Approach voyage, 1.10
Area
commercial, of port, 3.84, 3.87–3.88, 3.93–3.95
dock and port compared, 3.62
geographical, 3.4–3.6
Arrived ship
anchorage and, 3.90–3.92, 3.98–3.102, 3.108

Arrived ship—*cont.*
at immediate and effective disposition of
charterer, 3.64–3.113
ballasting and, 4.40
berth and, 3.37, 3.86
berth charter and, 3.6, 3.72
charterer's duty to act to enable vessel to become,
3.339–3.345
charterer's duty to have cargo at loading place
ready for shipment and, 4.16
commencement of laytime and, 1.22, 3.88–3.94
conditions for, 3.1, 3.29
delay and, 3.326–3.327
demurrage and, 6.7–6.8
destination and, 3.48–3.50
detention and, 8.19, 8.30, 8.51
dock and, 3.45–3.49, 3.75–3.79
dock charter and, 3.70, 3.72, 3.85
estimated time of arrival (ETA) and, 3.238–3.241
Laura Prima decision, 4.396–4.400
lightening and, 4.460
notice in advance and, 3.238–3.241
notice of readiness and, 3.292
Parker test and, 3.92–3.101
port and, 3.102–3.103
port charter and, 3.48, 3.73–3.75, 3.104–3.107,
3.268
reachable on arrival and, 3.403–3.407,
3.410–3.411
Reid test, 3.48–3.49, 3.102
weather permitting and, 2.93
weather working day and, 2.55
"whether in port or not" and, 3.371–3.373
ASBA II, 3.13
Asbatankvoy charter (formerly *Exxonvoy 69* charter)
ballasting and, 4.39
demurrage and, 6.91, 6.102, 6.110, 6.112, 6.117
general exceptions clause, 4.57
Laura Prima decision and, 4.396
lien clause, 6.190
nomination of port and, 3.13
notice of readiness and, 3.209, 3.265–3.273
shifting and, 4.425
storm and, 6.117
tanker warranties and, 6.158
Australian Grain charters, 3.484–3.490, 6.7
Averaging of laytime, 1.26, 5.69–5.72
calculation of, 5.74–5.76
cases on, 5.77–5.85

Averaging of laytime—*cont.*
  defined, 5.73
  demurrage and, 5.70–5.77
  loading time added or deducted from discharging
    time, 5.97–5.99

Ballasting, 4.36–4.40, 6.86
Baltic Code 2000, 1.7, App D
  always accessible, 3.428
  berth or no berth, 3.363
  excepted, 4.258
  excluded, 4.258
  holiday, 4.175
  notice of readiness, 3.207
  reachable on her arrival, 3.428
  whether in berth or not, 3.363
Baltimore berth form C charter
  detention and, 8.16
  notice of readiness and demurrage and, 6.126
  Saturday clause, 4.234–4.239
  shifting and, 4.424
  work before laytime commences and, 3.315
Beaufort scale, 6.119–6.121
Berth
  see also Anchorage; Port; Loading and
    discharging; Reachable on arrival clause; So
    near thereto as she may safely get clause;
    Waiting time; Whether in berth or not
  arrived ship and, 3.37, 3.86
  Charterparty Laytime Definitions 1980 and, 3.363
  congestion and, 3.332–3.338
  defined, 3.20–3.32
  delay and, 3.37, 3.483
  destination and, 3.34
  failure to provide on arrival, 2.236–2.239
  nomination of, 3.6, 3.17–3.18, 5.135, 5.148
  shifting and, 4.423–4.429
  Voylayrules 1993 and, 3.30, 3.363
  warping and, 4.452–4.455
Berth charter
  see also Whether in berth or not
  arrived ship and, 3.6, 3.72
  commencement of laytime and, 1.22, 3.30–3.37
  delay and, 1.21
  demurrage and, 6.130
  destination and, 1.21
  detention and, 8.13–8.14
  in regular turn/in usual turn and, 3.464
  liability for delay and, 1.21
  multiple charters and, 5.116
  port charter distinguished, 3.35
  readiness and readiness and, 3.303–3.305
  specified destination reached and, 1.21
  work before laytime commences and, 3.315
Berth occupied cause, 2.98, 2.100
Bill of lading
  demurrage and, 6.95, 6.192–6.196, 6.212–6.219
  incorporation of charterparty terms into,
    6.192–6.196
  non-production of, 4.41–4.45
Bimchemvoy charter
  cancellation of charter and, 3.306

Bimchemvoy charter—*cont.*
  condition of tanks on loading and, 3.140
  liquid cargo, completion of laytime and, 5.51
  readiness and readiness and, 3.306
  segration/commingling/rotation clause, 5.101
  time lost when vessel not ready to load/discharge
    and, 3.301
BIMCO calendar, 4.198
Bore tide, 2.56–2.57, 4.139–4.143
Budgett v. *Binnington* rule, 6.70
Bunkering
  demurrage and, 6.87
  fault of shipowner, 4.32–4.35

Calculation
  averaging and reversing of laytime, 5.74–5.76
  demurrage, 6.262–6.264
  despatch, 7.5, 7.19–7.24, 7.27, 7.32
  lay days, 2.12
  weather interruptions in weather working days,
    2.59–2.79
Calendar day, 2.6–2.13
Cancellation of charter, 3.302–3.308
Cargo
  see also Working cargo
  accessible, 5.113–5.115, 5.121–5.122
  alternative, 4.290–4.293
  damaged, 6.96
  dangerous, 6.33–6.34
  destruction of, 9.15–9.17
  dry
    discharge, 5.34–5.42
    loading, 5.20–5.33
  failure to have in readiness, 2.240–2.244
  full and complete, 6.30–6.32
  fumigation of, 6.101
  liquid, 5.43–5.68
  loss of, 6.33
  non-provision of
    demurrage and, 6.29, 6.58–6.60
    detention and, 8.13–8.14, 8.30–8.40
    frustration and, 9.39–9.40
  overstowed, 3.147–3.149, 5.128–5.134
  proportion to be loaded/discharged at obstructed
    port, 3.462–3.463
  strike and, 4.272–4.276
Carrying voyage, 1.10
Causation
  strike and, 4.271–4.273
  weather and, 4.144
Centrocon charter
  completion clause, 5.100
  strike clause, 4.271, 4.312–4.315
    delay and, 4.340–4.343
    demurrage and, 1.30, 6.67, 6.68
    despatch and, 4.334–4.345, 7.30–7.33
    obstructions, 4.320–4.324
    "provided that a strike or lock-out of the
      shippers' and/or receivers" men shall not
      prevent demurrage accruing', 4.334–4.339
    riot and civil commotion, 4.328–4.330
    specified causes, 4.316–4.319

Centrocon charter—*cont.*
  strike clause—*cont.*
    stoppage, 4.325–4.327
    strike or lock-out of any class of workman
      essential to loading/discharging,
      4.331–4.333
Certificate, Gas Free, 3.189–3.191
Cesser clause
  construction of charter and, 6.233–6.243
  demurrage and, 1.31, 6.217–6.219, 6.227–6.232
  Gencon charter and, 6.258
  waiver of, 6.252
Changes to beginning of laytime, 3.317–3.319
  see also Reachable on arrival clause; So near
    thereto as she may safely get clause
  charterer's duty to act to enable vessel to become
    arrived ship, 3.339–3.345
  custom, 3.320–3.325
  custom and practice, 3.479–3.480
  delay after berthing, 3.483
  demurrage in respect of waiting time, 3.484–3.490
  how time lost should be counted, 3.394–3.397
  in regular turn/in usual turn, 3.464–3.477
  limits of delay, 3.478
  loss of turn, 3.481–3.482
  Norgrain charter—waiting for berth, 3.400–3.401
  obstacles created by charterers, 3.326–3.328
    congestion due to charterer's other
      commitments, 3.332–3.338
    failure to have cargo available or arrangements
      for discharge, 3.329–3.331
  time lost in waiting for berth to count as laytime,
    3.377–3.393
  time lost in waiting for berth to count in full,
    3.398–3.399
  time to commence on being reported at Custom
    House, 3.491–3.494
  to be loaded as per colliery guarantee,
    3.495–3.496
  "whether in berth or not" and, 3.346–3.369
  "whether in port or not" and, 3.370–3.376
Charter. *See* Charterparty
Charterer
  "any other cause beyond control of", 4.63–4.92
  arrived ship at immediate and effective
    disposition of, 3.64–3.113
  control of adventure by, 1.13–1.14
  delay and, 1.17–1.18, 2.235–2.273, 8.52–8.57
  demurrage and, 1.31, 6.61–6.69, 6.212–6.219
  duty to act to enable vessel to become arrived
    ship, 3.339–3.345
  duty to have cargo at loading place ready for
    shipment, 4.15–4.16
  obstacles created by, 3.326–3.345
  obstructions beyond control of, 4.320–4.324
Charterparty
  see also individually named types of charter;
    Multiple charters
  customary laytime and, 2.274–2.277
  effect of express terms in determining reasonable
    time, 2.274–2.277

Charterparty—*cont.*
  establishment of standard form and development
    of law, 1.3–1.4
  incorporation of terms into bill of lading,
    6.192–6.196
Charterparty Laytime Definitions 1980, 1.7, App B
  berth or no berth, 3.363
  excepted, 4.258
  excluded, 4.258
  holiday, 4.175
  laytime per working hatch per day and, 2.161
  on demurrage, 6.6, 6.97
  party holiday and, 4.210
  per hatch per day, 2.168
  time lost waiting for berth to count as loading/
    discharging time or as laytime, 3.380
  unless used, 4.247
  weather working day, 2.44
  weather working day of 24 consecutive hours,
    2.140
  whether in berth or not, 3.363
Christmas, demurrage and, 6.92–6.94
Civil commotion, 4.328–4.330
Clearances. *See* Customs clearance; *Free pratique*
Cloud point, 6.138
Colliery guarantee
  demurrage and, 6.98
  loading as per, 3.495–3.496
Colliery working day, 2.37–2.40
Commencement of laytime
  see also Changes to beginning of laytime;
    Readiness to load and discharge
  arrived ship and, 1.22, 3.88–3.94
  berth charter and, 1.22, 3.30–3.37
  carriage of edible vegetable oils and, 5.149–5.150
  colliery guarantee and, 3.495–3.496
  conditions to be satisfied, 3.1
  congestion and, 3.332–3.338
  conventional days and, 2.14–2.16
  customs clearance and, 3.188, 3.200–3.206
  despatch and, 7.22–7.24
  destination and, 3.2–3.29
  dock charter and, 3.38–3.47
  estimate time of arrival (ETA) and, 3.238–3.241
  multiple charters and, 5.111–5.116
  port charter and, 3.48–3.113
  'whether in berth or not' and, 1.22, 3.368–3.369
  work before, 3.309–3.316
Commercial area of port, 3.84, 3.87–3.88, 3.93–3.95
Communication with vessel, 4.46
Completion of demurrage, 6.178–6.183
  delay after, detention and, 8.42–8.57
Completion of laytime, 1.25, 5.1–5.19
  ballasting and, 5.65
  Bimchemvoy and, 5.51
  demurrage and, 1.35
  detention and, 8.42–8.57
  discharging operation and, 5.34–5.43
  documentation and, 5.61–5.63
  dry cargo and, 5.20–5.42
  Exxonvoy 84 and, 5.55
  Finavoy and, 5.53

Completion of laytime—*cont.*
hoses and, 5.44–5.60, 5.64–5.68
Intertankvoy 76 and, 5.51
liquid cargo and, 5.43–5.68
loading operation and, 5.20–5.33
ullaging and, 5.55
Congestion
berth and, 3.332–3.338
Centrocon strike clause and, 4.277–4.285
commencement of laytime and, 3.332–3.338
customary laytime and, 2.231
dock charter and, 3.42
exceptions to laytime and, 4.97–4.100
free pratique and, 3.186–3.187
strike and, 4.277–4.285
"whether in berth or not" and, 3.367
Conlinebill, 6.220
Conoco weather clause, 4.167–4.172
Consecutive running days, 2.13
Consecutive voyages
detention and, 8.21–8.23
frustration and, 9.27–9.31
Consignee, liability for demurrage, 6.197–6.211
Construction principles, despatch clause, 7.6–7.7,
7.16
Construction theory, frustration and, 9.12–9.14
Contra proferentem rule, 4.5–4.12
Conventional day, 2.14–2.16
Custom
changes to beginning of laytime and, 3.320–3.325
effect of, customary laytime and, 2.216–2.224
holidays and, 4.183–4.187
local, consecutive running days and, 2.13
of port, 3.479–3.480
Saturdays and, 4.220–4.225
shifting and, 4.390–4.391
Customary laytime, 2.205
bill of lading and, 2.277
commencement of obligation to load and
discharge, 2.225–2.234
delay and, 1.16, 2.235–2.273
effect of custom on, 2.216–2.224
exceeded, 2.278–2.279
exceptions to laytime and, 4.4
fallen into disuse, 1.19
laytime allowed under, 1.16
loading in daylight, 2.275
reasonable time and, 2.206–2.215, 2.274
strike clause and, 2.276
Customs clearance, 3.188, 3.200–3.206

Damages
for detention, 8.1–8.5, 8.29, 8.42, 8.52, 8.65–8.67
for loading and discharging not completed within
laytime allowed, 1.28
in addition to demurrage, 6.26–6.49
Days
see also Holiday
calendar, 2.6–2.13
colliery working, 2.37–2.40
consecutive running, 2.13
conventional, 2.14–2.16

Days—*cont.*
part, 2.10, 2.16, 6.22–6.23
running, 2.17–2.22
running working, 2.35
weather working
calculation of weather interruptions in,
2.59–2.79
custom of the port and, 2.48–2.51
Deadfreight, demurrage and, 6.30–6.32, 6.37,
6.39–6.44
Default
see also Fault
delay arising without shipowner's or charterer's,
2.253–2.273
Definitions
see also Words and phrases
introduction of standardised, 1.7
Delay
see also Congestion; Detention
after berthing, 3.483
after loading or discharging, despatch and, 7.34
arrived ship and, 3.326–3.327
ballasting and, 4.40
berth and, 3.37, 3.483
by agreement, 8.58–8.63
charterer and, 1.17–1.18, 2.235–2.273, 8.52–8.57
communication with vessel and, 4.46
customary laytime and, 1.16, 2.235–2.273
discharging operation and, 1.14
dock charter and, 1.21, 3.42
due to charterer/shipper/receiver, 2.235–2.252
inordinate, 9.18–9.40
length of, 3.457, 4.305–4.311
liability for, 1.21
limits of, 3.478
loading operation and, 1.14
loss of turn and, 3.481–3.482
risk of, 1.14–1.18
strike and, 4.277–4.285, 4.305–4.311
Demurrage
see also Completion of demurrage; Exceptions to
demurrage; Liability for demurrage
arrived ship and, 6.7–6.8
Asbatankvoy and, 6.91, 6.102, 6.110, 6.112, 6.117
Australian Grain charters and, 3.484–3.490, 6.7
averaging and, 5.68–5.77
ballasting and, 6.86
bill of lading and, 6.95, 6.192–6.196, 6.212–6.219
bunkering and, 6.87
calculation of, 6.264–6.268
cargo and, 6.30–6.34
carriage of edible vegetable oils and, 5.151–5.161
Centrocon strike clause and, 1.30, 6.67, 6.68
cesser clause and, 1.31, 6.217–6.219, 6.227–6.232
Charterparty Laytime Definitions 1980 and, 6.6,
6.97
colliery guarantee and, 6.98
completion of laytime and, 1.35
damages in addition to, 6.26–6.49
deadfreight and, 6.30–6.32, 6.37, 6.39–6.44
default of charterer and, 6.61–6.69
default of shipowner and, 6.70–6.96

Demurrage—*cont.*
 defined, 6.1–6.8
 despatch and, 7.8–7.9, 7.12–7.15, 7.18
 detention and, 1.34, 6.34–6.38, 6.60, 8.41
 development of law, 1.1–1.6
 deviation effect, 6.165–6.177
 discharging operation and, 6.46–6.49, 6.116
 equipment breakdown and, 6.115
 frustration and, 1.35–1.36
 Gencon charter and, 6.5, 6.92, 6.93
 grounded vessel and, 6.88–6.89
 half rate, 6.112–6.122
 holidays and, 6.92–6.94
 implied term and, 6.17, 6.142
 in respect of waiting time, 3.484–3.490
 length of, 6.9–6.19
 lien for, 1.31
 loading and discharging not completed within
  time allowed, 1.28
 Master's right to claim, 6.259–6.262
 mitigation and, 6.50–6.60
 multiple charters and, 5.140–5.144
 notice of readiness and, 6.123–6.132
 once on demurrage, always on demurrage, 1.30,
  6.97, 6.100, 6.103
 part days and, 6.22–6.23
 payment of, 6.20–6.23, 6.25, 6.285–6.287
 proof of loss and, 6.50–6.60
 rate of, 1.29, 6.20–6.24
 repudiation and, 1.35
 restraint of princes clause and, 6.106, 6.108
 right to claim, 1.31, 6.259–6.262
 shifting and, 6.111
 standardised definitions, 1.7
 STB Voy and, 6.113
 strike commencing after vessel on, 1.30
 Sugar Charterparty and, 6.107
 tanker warranties and, 6.132–6.164
 time bars, 6.274–6.284
 time of payment, 6.285–6.287
 transhipment and, 5.165–5.168
 Vegoilvoy charter and, 5.151
 Voylayrules 1993 and, 1.9, 6.1
 war and, 6.95
 Worldscale and, 6.24
Despatch
 "all time saved" and "working time saved"
  differentiated, 7.4
 calcuation, 7.5, 7.19–7.24, 7.27, 7.32
 Centrocon strike clause and, 7.30–7.33
 construction of clause, 7.6–7.7, 7.16
 defined, 7.1–7.3
 delay after loading or discharging, 7.34
 demurrage and, 7.8–7.9, 7.12–7.15, 7.18
 discharge outside United Kingdom and, 7.17
 discharging operation and, 7.10, 7.13, 7.17, 7.25,
  7.34
 double, 7.25–7.29
 exceptions and, 7.11, 7.30–7.33
 loading operation and, 7.34
 loading and discharging completed in laytime
  allowed, 1.32–1.33

Despatch—*cont.*
 meaning of provision, 7.18
 notice of readiness and, 7.21–7.24
 reversing, 7.25–7.29
 reversible laytime and, 7.28
 time saved and, 7.19–7.20
 Voylayrules 1993 and, 7.1–7.3
Destination, 1.21
 arrived ship and, 3.48–3.50
 berth charter and, 3.34
 change of, 3.14–3.21
 commencement of laytime and, 3.2–3.29
 detention and
  delay after arrival and during running of
   laytime, 8.29–8.40
  delay before vessel reaches, 8.6–8.28
 dock charter and, 3.39–3.47
 geographical area and, 3.4–3.6
Detention
 see also Damages, for detention
 arrived ship, 8.19, 8.30, 8.51
 claim arising, 1.34
 delay and
  after arrival at specified destination and during
   running of laytime, 8.29–8.40
  after end of laytime and/or demurrage,
   8.42–8.57
  before vessel reaches specified destination,
   8.6–8.28
  by agreement, 8.58–8.63
 demurrage and, 1.34, 6.34–6.38, 6.60, 8.41
 documentation and, 8.47–8.51
 exceptions clauses and, 1.30, 8.64
Deviation, 6.165–6.177
Discharge. *See* Discharging operation
Discharge at sea. *See* Lightening
Discharge guarantee, 6.45, 6.56
Discharging operation, 1.10
 see also Loading and discharging
 alternative methods of, 4.294–4.301
 ballasting and, 4.36, 4.40
 control of, 1.13, 1.17
 delay and, 1.14
 demurrage and, 6.46–6.49, 6.116
 despatch and, 7.10–7.13, 7.17, 7.25, 7.34
 dry cargo, 5.34–5.42
 laytime averaged, 5.75
Dock
 see also Loading and discharging; Port
 arrived ship and, 3.45–3.49, 3.75–3.79
 nomination of, 3.6
 obstructions beyond control of charterer in,
  4.320–4.322
 port area compared, 3.62
 specified destination reached and, 1.21
Dock charter
 arrived ship and, 3.70, 3.72, 3.85
 commencement of laytime and, 3.38–3.47
 defined, 3.38
 delay and, 1.21, 3.42
 destination and, 3.39–3.47
 detention and, 8.12

Dock charter—*cont.*
  documentation and, 8.47–8.51
  liability for delay and, 1.21
Documentation
  see also Legal readiness
  completion of laytime and, 5.61–5.63
  detention and, 8.47–8.51
Duty
  see also Obligation
  to act to enable vessel to become arrived ship,
    charterer's, 3.339–3.345
  to have cargo at loading place ready for shipment,
    charterer's, 4.15–4.16
  to lessen effect of strike, 4.286–4.304

Equipment
  breakdown, demurrage and, 6.115
  physical readiness and, 3.150–3.161
Estimated time of arrival (ETA), 3.238–3.241
Estoppel, 3.279–3.280, 3.284, 3.289–3.294
Exceptions to demurrage, 1.30, 6.97–6.110
Exceptions to despatch, 7.11, 7.30–7.33
Exceptions to detention, 8.64
Exceptions to laytime, 1.24
  see also Adverse weather; Holiday; Strike
  "any other cause beyond control of the
    charterers" and, 4.63–4.92
  Asbatankvoy and, 4.57
  availability of hold and, 2.163
  ballasting and, 4.36–4.40
  bill of lading and, 4.41–4.43
  congestion and, 4.97–4.100
  demurrage and, 1.30
  despatch and, 7.30–7.33
  detention and, 1.30
  Exxonvoy 84 and, 4.60
  fault and, 4.49–4.56
  general exceptions clause and, 4.57–4.92
  interruptions differentiated, 1.23
  overtime and, 4.93–4.96
Expenses, shifting, 4.438–4.451
Exxonvoy 69 charter (later *Asbatankvoy* charter)
  hoses: mooring at sea terminals clause, 5.46
  notice of readiness clause, 4.396
  notice of readiness and demurrage and, 6.127
  safe berthing—shifting clause, 4.396
Exxonvoy 84 charter
  ballasting and, 4.38
  deviation clause, 6.167
  general exceptions clause and, 4.60
  ice clause, 4.122
  lightening/discharge at sea clause, 4.464
  liquid cargo and, 5.55
  notice of readiness and, 3.224, 3.306, 6.129
  readiness and readiness and, 3.306
  shifting clause, 4.296
  storm and, 6.120

Fault
  see also Default
  charterer's, 6.61–6.69
  exclusion of, 4.49–4.56

Fault—*cont.*
  meaning of, 4.25–4.27
  shipowner's, 4.17–4.40, 6.70–6.96
Finavoy charter, 5.53
Fixed laytime
  advantage to shipowner, 2.4
  calendar days and, 2.6–2.13
  contra proferentem rule and, 4.5
  conventional days and, 2.14–2.16
  expression of, 2.5
  preferred to customary laytime, 1.20
  risk of delay lies with charterer, 1.17–1.18,
    2.1–2.3
  running days and, 2.17–2.22
  Saturdays and other incomplete days, 2.80–2.90
  weather permitting and, 2.92–2.125, 2.133–2.139
  weather working days and, 2.41–2.79, 2.91,
    2.140–2.143
  working days, 2.23–2.40
  working hours per working day, 2.126–2.132
Free pratique
  congestion and, 3.186–3.187
  Indian cases and, 3.205–3.206
  Voylayrules 1993 and, 3.180
Freight. *See* Cargo
Frost, 4.115–4.121
Frustration
  basis of doctrine, 9.9–9.14
  charterer's duty to have cargo at loading place
    ready for shipment and, 4.16
  consecutive voyages and, 9.27–9.31
  demurrage and, 1.35–1.36
  destruction of ship or cargo, 9.15–9.17
  illegality, 9.41–9.47
  inordinate delay, 9.18–9.40
  Law Reform (Frustrated Contracts) Act 1943,
    9.50
  question of law and question of fact, 9.2–9.8
  restraint of princes clause and, 9.47
  self-induced, 9.48–9.49
  war and, 9.21, 9.23, 9.25–9.26, 9.47

Gas Free certificate, 3.189–3.191
Gencon charter
  cesser clause, 6.258
  demurrage and, 6.5, 6.92, 6.92
  lien clause, 6.230, 6.258
  lost waiting time and, 5.117
  running hours, 2.36
  running working days, 2.35
  strike clause, 4.346–4.379
General average, demurrage and, 6.89–6.90
General exceptions clauses. *See* Exceptions
Geographical area, 3.4–3.6
Government interference, demurrage and, 6.107
Guarantee
  see also Warranty
  colliery, 3.495–3.496, 6.98
  discharge, 6.45, 6.56

Hatch
  see also Working hatch

Hatch—*cont.*
  Charterparty Laytime Definitions 1980 and, 2.161
  rate per, 2.164–2.171
Heating, 6.137–6.147
Hold
  availability of, 2.163
  cleaning of, 3.133–3.140
  readiness and, 3.142–3.146
Holiday, 4.173
  see also Saturday; Sunday
  BIMCO calendar, 4.198
  charterparty, 4.195–4.196
  Charterparty Laytime Definitions 1980 and, 4.175
  Christmas, demurrage and, 6.92–6.94
  custom and, 4.183–4.187, 4.220–4.225
  defined, 4.174–4.176
  demurrage and, 6.92–6.94
  excepted periods and, 4.244–4.258
  general or local, 4.189–4.190
  legal, 4.191
  local law, 4.226–4.232
  non-working, 4.197
  official and local, 4.192–4.194
  overtime and, 4.219
  part, 4.209–4.213
  Ramadan and, 4.213
  regulations and, 4.176–4.182
  Voylayrules 1993 and, 4.175
  weekend clause, 4.240–4.242
  working day and, 4.199–4.208
Hook, rate per, 2.172–2.175
Hose, completion of laytime and, 5.44–5.60,
  5.64–5.68
Hurricane hawser, 3.37

Ice, 4.122–4.129
Illegality
  charterer's duty to have cargo at loading place
    ready for shipment and, 4.15–4.16
  frustration and, 9.41–9.47
Implied term
  demurrage and, 6.17, 6.142
  frustration and, 9.9–9.12, 9.44
  illegality and, 9.41
"In regular turn/in usual turn", 3.464
Indian cases, Customs clearance and, 3.200–3.206
Indorsee, liability for demurrage, 6.197–6.211
Infestation, 3.132
Interruptions to laytime
  see also Adverse weather; Holiday
  The Altus, 4.47–4.48
  ballasting, 4.36–4.40
  bill of lading and, 4.41–4.45
  bunkering, 4.32–4.35
  communication with vessel, 4.46
  congestion, 4.97–4.100
  contra proferentem rule, 4.5–4.12
  customary laytime and, 4.4
  defined, 4.1
  exceptions differentiated, 1.23
  exclusion of fault, 4.49–4.56
  fault of shipowner and, 4.17–4.31

Interruptions to laytime—*cont.*
  fixed laytime and, 4.3
  general exception clauses, 4.57–4.62
    "any other cause beyond control of charterer",
      4.63–4.64
    principle A cases, 4.65–4.81
    principle B cases, 4.82–4.85
    principle C cases, 4.86–4.92
  general principles, 4.13–4.16
  overtime ordered by port authority to count as
    laytime, 4.93–4.96
  weather permitting and, 2.107–2.110
Intertankvoy 76 charter
  completion of laytime and, 5.51
  heating warranty and, 6.143

Labour
  alternative, 4.302–4.304
  inefficiency, 4.28
  strike or lock-out of any class essential to loading
    and discharging, 4.331–4.333
The Laura Prima
  decision, 4.396–4.400
  limits of decision, 4.401–4.422
Lay days
  calculation of, 2.12
  continuity of, 2.11
  custom and, 2.13
Laycan spread, 3.246
Laytime
  see also Averaging laytime; Commencement of
    laytime; Completion of laytime; Customary
    laytime; Exceptions to laytime; Fixed
    laytime; Interruptions to laytime; Reversing
    laytime
  defined, 1.9
  development of law, 1.1–1.6
  standardised definitions, 1.7
Laytime definitions, App A
  see also Charterparty Laytime Definitions 1980
  standardised, 1.7
Legal readiness, 3.165–3.168
  common law, 3.169–3.170
  free pratique and quarantine and, 3.171–3.184,
    3.186, 3.194
  Gas Free certificate and, 3.189–3.191
  implied requirements, 3.197–3.199
    Indian cases, 3.200–3.206
  Tank Vessel Examination Letter and, 3.192–3.193
Liability for delay, charterer's, detention and,
  8.52–8.57
Liability for demurrage, 6.184–6.191
  before and after shipment, 6.253–6.258
  cesser clauses, 6.227–6.232
    waiver of, 6.252
  construction of charter, 6.233–6.243
  incorporation of charterparty terms into bill of
    lading, 6.192–6.196
  lien for demurrage and, 1.31
    effectiveness of, 6.244–6.251
    nature of, 6.220–6.226
  of bill of lading holder *inter se*, 6.263–6.273

Liability for demurrage—*cont.*
  of charterer, 1.31, 6.212–6.219
  of reciver, 1.31
  of shipper, consignee, indorsee and receiver,
    6.197–6.211
Lien
  Asbatankvoy and, 6.190
  cesser clause and, 6.227–6.232
  Conlinebill and, 6.220
  construction of charter and, 6.233–6.243
  demurrage and, 1.31, 6.220–6.226
  detention and, 8.24–8.28, 8.65–8.67
  effectiveness of, 6.244–6.251
  Gencon charter and, 6.230, 6.258
Lightening, 4.456–4.466
  Exxonvoy 84 and, 4.464
  time used in, 4.467–4.471
Lighterage
  detention and, 8.8
  surf and, 4.130–4.133
Limitation. *See* Time bar
Lloyd's Maritime Law Newsletter, 1.5
Loaded voyage, 1.10
Loading and discharging
  see also Discharging operation; Loading
    operation; Readiness to load and discharge
  alternative methods of, 4.294–4.301
  commencement of obligation, 2.225–2.234
  demurrage and, 6.70–6.80
  despatch and
    completed within laytime allowed, 1.32–1.33
    delay after, 7.34
  nomination of berth, carriage of edible vegetable
    oils, 5.148
  not completed within laytime allowed, 1.28
  proportion of cargo for an obstructed port,
    3.462–3.463
  strike or lock-out of any class of workman
    essential to, 4.331–4.333
Loading operation, 1.10
  alternative methods of, 4.294–4.301
  as per colliery guarantee, 3.495–3.496
  ballasting and, 4.36, 4.37, 4.40
  colliery guarantee and, 3.495–3.496
  completion of laytime and, 5.20–5.33
  control of, 1.13, 1.17
  daylight in, 2.275
  delay and, 1.14
  despatch and, 7.12–7.16
  detention and, 8.33–8.40
  discharging time and, 5.97–5.99
  dry cargo, 5.20–5.33
  ice and, 4.124–4.129
  illegality and, 9.43
  laytime averaged, 5.75
  liquid cargo, 5.43–5.68
  obstructions and, 4.320–4.324
  rate per hatch and, 2.164–2.171
  reachable on arrival and, 3.403–3.404
  reversing and, 5.86–5.96
  surf and, 4.130–4.133
  ullaging and, 5.59

Loading operation—*cont.*
  working hatch and, 2.147–2.162
Loading voyage, 1.10
Lock-out. *See* Strike

Master
  refusal to sign triplicate bill of lading, demurrage
    and, 6.95
  right to claim demurrage, 6.259–6.262
Mitigation, demurrage and, 6.50–6.57
Multiple charters,
  Bimchemvoy charter and, 5.101
  carriage of edible vegetable oils, 5.145–5.147
    commencement of laytime and waiting time,
      5.149–5.150
    laytime and demurrage, 5.151–5.161
    nomination of loading and discharging berths,
      5.148
    squeegeeing and sweeping, 5.162–5.163
    transhipment, 5.164–5.167
  Centrocon completion clause and, 5.100
  commencement and running of laytime and,
    5.111–5.116
  demurrage and, 5.140–5.144
  overstowed cargo and, 5.121–5.132
  part cargo and, 5.107–5.108
  to be read together or separately, 5.103–5.110
  time lost in waiting for berth, 5.117–5.139
  Vegoilvoy charter and, 5.109

New Worldwide Tanker Nominal Freight Scale, 6.24
Nomination
  change in, 3.13–3.18
  detention and, 8.16–8.18
  express or implied right of, 3.26
  failure of, 3.22–3.23
  late, 3.24–3.25
  of berth, 3.6, 3.17–3.18, 5.135, 5.148
  of dock, 3.6
  of port, 3.6–3.11, 3.13–3.16
  Worldscale and, 3.21
Norgrain charter, 3.400–3.401
Notice of readiness
  see also Readiness to load and discharge
  acceptance of, 3.274–3.301
  additional, at subsequent loading port, 3.220
  anchorage and, 3.263–3.264
  agents and, 3.208–3.210
  Asbatankvoy clause 6 and, 3.265–3.273
  Baltic Code 2000 and, 3.207
  berth and, 3.265–3.273
  Bimchemvoy charter and, 3.301
  cancellation of charter and, 3.302–3.308
  commencement of laytime and, 3.253–3.257
  correctness of, 3.248–3.264
  defective, 3.288–3.301
  defined, 3.207
  demurrage and, 6.123–6.132
  despatch and, 7.21–7.24
  estoppel and, 3.280–3.284
  express provisions, 3.224–3.237
  Exxonvoy 84 and, 3.224, 6.129

Notice of readiness—*cont.*
  given before commencement date for laytime, 3.246–3.247
  in advance of arrival, 3.238–3.241
  in writing, 3.212
  inchoate, 3.260
  insufficient supplies of water or bunkers invalidating, 3.162–3.164
  non-provision of cargo and, 3.216–3.218
  on Saturday, 3.227–3.235
  premature, 3.258–3.264
  time lapse between readiness and commencement of laytime, 3.242–3.245
  Vegoilvoy charter and, 3.208, 5.149
  Voylayrules 1993 and, 3.207, 3.225
  when and how to be given, 3.211–3.223

Obligation
  see also Duty
  to load/discharge, commencement of, 2.225–2.234
Obstacle
  beyond control of charterer
    in dock or other loading place, 4.320–4.322
    on railways, 4.323–4.324
  created by charterer, 3.326–3.328
    congestion due to other commitments, 3.332–3.338
    duty to act to enable vessel to become arrived ship, 3.339–3.345
    failure to have cargo available or arrangements for discharge, 3.329–3.331
  nature of, 3.451–3.454
Overtime
  exceptions to laytime and, 4.93–4.96
  holiday and, 4.219
  ordered by port authority to count as laytime, 4.93–4.96
  Saturday, 4.219
  weather working day and, 2.74
  working hours per working day and, 2.126–2.129

Parker test, 3.92–3.101
Physical readiness, 3.119–3.120
  bunkering and, 3.164
  insufficient supply of water and, 3.162–3.163
  of equipment, 3.150–3.161
  of hold, 3.122–3.146
  overstowed cargo and, 3.147–3.149
Pilotage district, 3.58
Port
  see also Anchorage; Berth; Whether in port or not
  alternative, 4.289
  ambit of, 3.460–3.461
  arrived ship and, 3.102–3.103
  arrival within, 3.51–3.63
  at immediate end effective disposition of charterer and, 3.64–3.113
  authority, 3.60, 4.93–4.96
  change of berth within, 4.294–4.301
  commercial area of, 3.84, 3.87–3.88, 3.93–3.95
  custom of, 2.48–2.51, 3.66–3.68
  demurrage and, 6.178–6.183

Port—*cont.*
  dock area compared, 3.62
  intended how close vessel can get to, 3.460–3.461
  intermediate, 8.9–8.10
  limits, 3.53–3.59
  nomination of, 3.6–3.11, 3.13–3.16, 8.16–8.18
  obstructed, proportion of cargo to be loaded/ discharged at, 3.462–3.463
  Parker test and, 3.92–3.101
  permanent and temporary absence from, 6.178–6.183
  pipeline disruption at loading, frustration and, 9.36–9.38
  reachable on arrival and, 8.19–8.20
  waiting area and, 3.54, 3.61–3.63
  "whether in port or not", 3.370–3.376
Port charter
  arrived ship and, 3.48, 3.72–3.74, 3.104–3.107, 3.268
  arrival within port and, 3.51–3.63
  at immediate end effective disposition of charterer and, 3.64–3.113
  commencement of laytime and, 3.48–3.113
  destination and, 1.21, 3.73–3.74
  in regular turn/in usual turn and, 3.464
  liability for delay and, 1.21
  multiple charterers and, 5.112
  Reid test and, 3.48, 3.102
  shifting and, 4.392–4.393
  weather permitting and, 2.102
  "whether in berth or not" and, 3.347
Proof of loss, demurrage and, 6.52, 6.58–6.59
Pumping warranty, 6.141–6.142, 6.148–6.164

Quarantine, 3.171–3.184

Railways
  discharge of ship and, 8.46
  obstructions beyond control of charterer on, 4.323–4.324
Rate
  demurrage, 1.29, 6.20–6.25, 6.112–6.122
  despatch, 7.2, 7.26
  freight, 6.24
  per hatch, 2.164–2.171
  per hook, 2.172–2.175
  total daily, 2.176–2.190
  working cargo, 2.164–2.190
  working hatch, 2.145–2.162, 2.191–2.204
Reachable on arrival clause
  see also "so near thereto as she may safely get" clause
  always accessible clause and, 3.423–3.442
  arrived ship and, 3.403–3.407, 3.410–3.411
  Asbantankvoy charter and, 3.402
  Baltic Code 2000 and, 3.428
  berth and, 3.409–3.415
  commencement of laytime and, 3.402–3.427
  Conoco weather clause and, 4.170
  demurrage and, 6.131
  destination and, 3.401
  detention and, 8.19–8.20, 8.30

Reachable on arrival clause—*cont.*
loading operation and, 3.403–3.404
port and, 8.19–8.20
"reachable" and, 3.407
shifting and, 4.394–4.400
tankers and, 3.403–3.406
Voylayrules 1993 and, 3.425
"whether in berth or not" and, 3.424
Readiness to load and discharge, 3.114
see also Notice of readiness
bunkering and, 3.164
cleaning and, 3.133–3.140
free pratique and quarantine and, 3.171–3.184,
3.186, 3.194
insufficient supply of water and, 3.162–3.163
lien and, 3.115
of equipment, 3.150–3.161
of hold, 3.122–3.146
overstowed cargo and, 3.147–3.149
readiness and readiness, 3.302–3.308
work before laytime commences, 3.309–3.316
Reasonable period, demurrage and, 6.17
Reasonable time, customary laytime and,
2.206–2.215
Receiver
delay due to, 2.235–2.252
liability for demurrage, 1.31, 6.197–6.211
Reid text, 1.21, 3.48, 3.102
Repudiation, 1.35
"Restraint of princes" clause
demurrage and, 6.106, 6.108
frustration and, 9.47
Reversing, 1.26, 5.69–5.72
calculation of, 5.74–5.76
cases on, 5.86–5.96
defined, 5.73
despatch and, 7.25–7.29
laytime and, 1.26, 5.69–5.76, 7.28
loading time added or deducted from discharging
and, 5.97–5.99
Voylayrules 1993 and, 5.73
Richards Bay coal charter, 3.143
Rights, Master's, to claim demurrage, 6.259–6.262
Riot, 4.328–4.330
Risk
apportionment, 1.14
degree known to exist, 3.458–3.459
of delay, 1.14–1.18
Running days, 2.17–2.22
Running hours, 2.21
Running working days, 2.35

Saturday
as working day, 4.214–4.218
Baltimore form C and, 4.234–4.239
custom and, 4.220–4.225
fixed laytime and, 2.80–2.90
interruptions and exceptions to laytime and,
4.214–4.218
local law, 4.226–4.232
Saturdays today, 4.233
notice of readiness on, 3.227–3.235

Saturday—*cont.*
overtime and, 4.219
Vancouver strike cases and, 4.215–4.216
weather interruptions and, 2.83–2.90
weekend clause and, 4.240–4.243
Severable voyage, frustration and, 9.32–9.34
Shellvoy 3 charter, 3.37
Shifting
Asbatankvoy and, 4.425
Baltimore form C and, 4.424
berth and, 4.423–4.429
bunkering and, 4.32–4.35
custom and, 4.390–4.391
demurrage and, 6.111
enforced, 4.430–4.437
expenses, 4.438–4.451
Exxonvoy 84 charter clause, 4.296
from anchorage to berth, 4.381–4.384
from anchorage outside port, 4.392–4.393
from one berth to another, 4.423–4.429
Laura Prima decision and, 4.401–4.422
reachable on arrival and, 4.393–4.400
time not to count and, 4.385–4.389
warping, 4.452–4.455
Ship
see also Arrived ship
destruction of, frustration and, 9.15–9.17
on demurrage, strike commencing after, 1.30
Shipowner
advantage of fixed laytime to, 2.4
control of adventure by, 1.13–1.14
delay arising without default of, 2.253–2.273
demurrage and
acts preventing, 6.86–6.96
default of, 6.70–6.96
losing right to claim, 1.31
deviation and, 6.169–6.177
fault of, 4.17–4.31
ballasting and deballasting, 4.36–4.40
bunkering, 4.32–4.35
exclusion of, 4.49–4.56
risk of delay under customary laytime charter lies
with, 1.16
Shipper
delay due to, 2.235–2.252
liability for demurrage, 6.197–6.211
So near thereto as she may safely get clause,
3.443–3.450
see also Berth; Waiting time, lost
degree of risk known to exist, 3.458–3.459
how close to intended port vessel can get,
3.460–3.461
length of anticipated delay, 3.457
length of time actually spent waiting, 3.455–3.456
nature of obstacle, 3.451–3.454
proportion of cargo to be loaded/discharged at
obstructed port, 3.462–3.463
Specified destination. *See* Destination
Squeegeeing and sweeping, carriage of edible
vegetable oils and, 5.162–5.163
STB Voy charter
ballasting and, 4.39

STB Voy charter—*cont.*
  completion of laytime and, 5.64
  half rate demurrage and, 6.113
  hose and, 5.64
  nomination of port and, 3.13
  shifting and, 4.388
Stevedore, 6.54–6.57, 6.78–6.84
Stoppage
  Centrocon strike clause and, 4.327
  defined, 4.325
  partial, 4.326
  Welsh coal charter and, 4.326
Storm
  Asbatankvoy and, 6.117
  Exxonvoy 84 and, 6.120
  half rate demurrage and, 6.117–6.122
Strike, 1.23, 4.259–4.260
  see also Centrocon charter, strike clause; *Gencon*
      charter, strike clause
  causation, 4.271–4.273
  congestion and consequential delay, 4.277–4.285
  defined, 4.261–4.270
  demurrage and, 6.72, 6.104–6.105, 6.110
  duty to lessen effect, 4.286–4.311
  frustration and, 9.24, 9.29
Sugar Charterparty 1969 charter
  demurrage and, 6.107
  strikes and *force majeure* clause, 4.61
Sunday
  holiday and, 4.253–4.254
  running days and, 2.17–2.22
  weather working day and, 2.47
Surf, 4.130–4.133
Sweeping. *See* Squeegeeing and sweeping
Swell, 4.134–4.138

Tank Vessel Examination Letter, 3.192–3.193
Tanker
  Asbatankvoy and, 6.158
  crude oil washing and, 6.135
  demurrage and, 6.132, 6.161
  Exxonvoy 84 charter and, 6.149
  frustration and, 9.44–9.47
  heating and, 6.132, 6.137–6.147
  illegality and, 9.46–9.47
  Intertankvoy 76 charter and, 5.51, 6.143
  nomination of port and, 3.13–3.16
  pumping warranties and, 6.141–6.142,
      6.148–6.164
  reachable on arrival and, 3.403–3.406
  remaining on board and, 6.133
  ullaging and, 5.59, 6.136
Time
  see also Overtime; Waiting time
  loading added or deducted from discharging,
      5.97–5.99
  payment of demurrage, 6.285–6.287
  reasonable customary laytime and, 2.206–2.215
  used in lightening, 4.467–4.471
Time bar, claim for demurrage, 6.274–6.284
Time not to count, shifting and, 4.385–4.389

Time to commence on being reported at Custom
      House clause, 3.491–3.494
Transhipment, 5.164–5.168
Tug, 3.415–3.416
Turn
  in regular/usual, 3.464–3.477
  loss of, 3.481–3.482

Ullaging, 5.55, 5.59, 6.136

Vancouver Strikes case, 3.7, 4.215–4.216
Vegoilvoy charter
  demurrage clause, 5.151
  laytime clause, 5.151
  multiple charters and, 5.146
  notice of readiness and, 3.208, 5.149
Vessel. *See* Ship
Voyage
  approach, 1.10
  carrying, 1.10
  consecutive
    detention and, 8.21–8.23
    frustration and, 9.27–9.31
  loaded, 1.10
  loading, 1.10
  severable, 9.32–9.34
Voyage charterparty
  see also individually named types of charter;
      Customary laytime; Fixed laytime
  control of adventure and, 1.13–1.14
  frustration of, 9.7, 9.27–9.33
  repudiation of, 1.35
  simplest form, 1.12
  stages of, 3.2, 3.269–3.270
Voylayrules 1993, 1.7, App C
  always accessible, 3.425
  berth, 3.30
  berth or no birth, 3.363
  demurrage, 1.9, 6.1
  despatch, 7.1–7.3
  excepted, 4.258
  excluded, 4.258
  holiday, 4.175
  in writing, 3.225
  laytime, 1.9
  notice of readiness, 3.207
  part holiday and, 4.210
  per hatch per day, 2.170
  per working hatch per day, 2.147
  reachable on her arrival, 3.425
  reversible, 5.73
  running days, 2.20
  strike, 4.266
  time lost waiting for berth to count as loading/
      discharging time or as laytime, 3.380
  to average, 5.73
  unless sooner commenced, 3.316
  unless used, 4.248
  vessel being in *free pratique*, 3.180, 3.205
  vessel having been entered at the Custom House,
      3.180, 3.205
  weather working day, 2.91

Voylayrules 1993—cont.
  weather working day of 24 consecutive hours,
    2.141
  whether in berth or not, 3.363

Waiting time
  see also So near thereto as she may safely get
    clause
  carriage of edible vegetable oils and, 5.149–5.150
  lost
    demurrage in respect of, 3.484–3.490
    how it should be counted, 3.394–3.397
    multiple charters and, 5.117–5.139
    Norgrain charter and, 3.400–3.401
    to count as laytime, 3.377–3.393
    to count in full, 3.398–3.399
Waiver
  of cesser clause, 6.252
  of charter, 3.290
War
  demurrage and, 6.95
  frustration and, 9.21–9.23, 9.25–9.26, 9.47
Warping, 4.452–4.455
Warranty
  see also Guarantee
  tanker, 6.132–6.164
Weather
  see also Adverse weather
  Beaufort Scale and, 6.119–6.121
  reversing and, 5.74–5.76
Weather permitting
  24 consecutive hours, 24 running hours,
    2.132–2.139
  arrived ship and, 2.93
  running hours, running days, 2.92–2.111
  weather working days, 2.111
  working hours, working days of 24 hours,
    2.112–2.125
Weather working day
  see also Working day
  24 consecutive hours, 2.140–2.143
  arrived ship and, 2.55
  averaging and, 5.75
  calculation of weather interruptions in, 2.59–2.79
  Charterparty Laytime Definitions 1980 and, 2.44
  custom of the port and, 2.48–2.51
  defined, 2.41–2.44
  ice and, 4.129
  overtime and, 2.64
  Saturday and, 2.80–2.90
  Sunday and, 2.47
  Voylayrules 1993 and, 2.91, 2.141
  weather permitting, 2.111
Weekend clause, 4.240–4.243
Welsh coal charter
  rate per working hatch and, 2.149
  stoppage and, 4.326
"Whether in berth or not" (WIBON)
  anchorage and, 3.348
  berth and, 3.346
  berth charter and, 3.347, 3.348–3.352
  Centrocon strike clause and, 3.367

"Whether in berth or not" (WIBON)—*cont.*
  Charterparty Laytime Definitions 1980 and, 3.363
  commencement of laytime and, 3.346–3.369
  congestion and, 3.367
  dock charter and, 3.361
  port charter and, 3.347
  reachable on arrival and, 3.423–3.424
  Voylayrules 1993 and, 3.363, 3.364–3.366
"Whether in port or not" (WIPON), 3.370–3.376
WIBON. *See* "Whether in berth or not"
WIPON. *See* "Whether in port or not"
Words and phrases
  see also Definitions
  always accessible, 3.425, 3.428
  "any other cause beyond control of charterer",
    4.63–4.92
  "at immediate and effective disposition of
    charterer", 3.64–3.113
  berth, 3.30
  berth or no berth, 3.363
  demurrage, 1.9, 6.1
  despatch, 7.1–7.3
  excepted, 4.258
  excluded, 4.258
  holiday, 4.175
  in writing, 3.225
  laytime, 1.9
  laytime per working hatch per day and, 2.161
  notice of readiness, 3.207
  on demurrage, 6.6, 6.97
  once on demurrage, always on demurrage, 1.30,
    6.97, 6.100, 6.103
  part holiday and, 4.210
  per hatch per day, 2.168, 2.170
  per working hatch per day, 2.147
  reachable on her arrival, 3.425, 3.428
  reversible, 5.73
  running days, 2.20
  strike, 4.266
  time lost waiting for berth to count as loading/
    discharging time or as laytime, 3.380
  to average, 5.73
  unless sooner commenced, 3.316
  unless used, 4.247, 4.248
  vessel being in *free pratique*, 3.180, 3.205
  vessel having been entered at the Custom House,
    3.180, 3.205
  weather working day, 2.44, 2.91
  weather working day of 24 consecutive hours,
    2.140, 2.141
  whether in berth or not, 3.363
Working cargo
  see also Cargo
  availability of hold and, 2.163
  rate per hatch, 2.164–2.171
  rate per hook, 2.172–2.175
  total daily rate, 2.176–2.190
  working hatches and, 2.145–2.162, 2.191–2.204
Working day
  see also Holiday; Weather working day
  custom and, 2.25
  fixed laytime and, 2.23–2.40

Working day—*cont.*
    Saturday as, 4.214–4.218
    weather permitting, 2.112–2.125
Working hatch
    available, 2.191–2.204, 2.145–2.162
    daily rate and, 2.176–2.190
    rate per hatch and, 2.164–2.171

Working hours, 2.126–2.132
"Working time saved", 7.4
Working to rule
Worldfood charter, 3.146
Worldscale
    demurrage and, 6.24
    nomination of port and, 3.21